# THE NATIONAL UNDERWRITER COMPANY

## 2015 Social Security & Medicare Facts

## Joseph F. Stenken, J.D., CLU® ChFC®

With all the tax and policy changes affecting Social Security and Medicare, retirement and financial planning professionals, attorneys, and CPAs need a single resource that will guide decisions today—and in the future.

The greatly enhanced ***2015 Social Security & Medicare Facts*** will help you quickly settle important planning issues for your clients. The book's convenient Q&A format will help you save a significant amount of time in preparation and planning.

The new edition delivers completely up-to-date answers to over 500 Social Security and Medicare benefits questions covering:

- Retirement & disability benefits
- Filing for benefits
- Loss of Social Security benefits due to "excess" retirement earnings
- Social Security taxes
- Railroad retirement
- Benefits for federal government employees
- Medicare Part A, Hospital Insurance
- Medicare Part B, Medical Insurance
- Medicare Part C, Medicare Advantage
- Medicare Part D, Prescription Drug Insurance
- Medigap insurance
- Medicaid
- How to submit Medicare claims as well as filing appeals
- Social Security coverage
- Benefit computation
- Taxation of Social Security benefits
- Wages & self-employment income
- Benefits for service members & veterans

Highlights of the 2015 Edition:

- Case studies illustrating over three dozen real-life strategies used to ensure that your clients get the opportunity to analyze, review, and choose different strategies that work best for them for maximizing Social Security benefits
- Over 30 new Q&As and significant new content regarding
  - Retirement and benefits eligibility
  - Benefits computation and maximization
  - Annual earnings test
  - Delayed retirement credits
  - Spousal benefits
  - Survivor's benefits
  - Children's benefits
  - Public employees—Windfall Elimination Provision/Government Pension Offset
  - Disability benefits
  - Taxation of benefits/repayment of benefits
- Discussion of the "File and Suspend" and "Restricted Application" techniques
- Updated 2015 numbers regarding the Earnings Base and Cost of Living Adjustments
- Discussion of same-sex marriage and its effect on Social Security and Medicare benefits
- Additional citations to authority

Written by Joseph F. Stenken, J.D., CLU®, ChFC®, one of the foremost experts on retirement planning and estate planning, ***2015 Social Security & Medicare Facts*** is the practical reference you can rely on.

Related Titles Also Available:

- Healthcare Reform Facts
- Tax Facts on Insurance & Employee Benefits
- Tax Facts on Investments
- Tax Facts on Individuals & Small Business
- Health Savings Accounts Facts
- Retirement Plans Facts
- The Tools & Techniques of Employee Benefit & Retirement Planning
- Field Guide to Estate Planning, Business Planning & Employee Benefits

# 2015 SOCIAL SECURITY & MEDICARE FACTS

Social Security Coverage
Maximization Strategies for Social Security Benefits
Medicare/Medicaid
Social Security Taxes
Retirement & Disability
Service Members' and Veterans' Benefits
Benefits for Federal Government Employees

Joseph F. Stenken, J.D., CLU®, ChFC®

**This publication is designed to provide accurate and authoritative information in regard to the subject matter covered. It is sold with the understanding that the publisher is not engaged in rendering legal, accounting or other professional service. If legal advice or other expert assistance is required, the services of a competent professional person should be sought.**— *From a Declaration of Principles jointly adopted by a Committee of the American Bar Association and a Committee of Publishers and Associations.*

**Circular 230 Notice** – The content in this publication is not intended or written to be used, and it cannot be used, for the purposes of avoiding U.S. tax penalties.

ISBN 978-1-941627-28-0



The National Underwriter Company
4157 Olympic Blvd., Suite 225, Erlanger, KY 41018



Printed in U.S.A.

The National Underwriter Company publishes the following Social Security/Medicare publications:

Social Security & Medicare Facts
Social Security Planner
Medicare Planner

# ABOUT SUMMIT PROFESSIONAL NETWORKS

Summit Professional Networks supports the growth and vitality of the insurance, financial services and legal communities by providing professionals with the knowledge and education they need to succeed at every stage of their careers. We provide face-to-face and digital events, websites, mobile sites and apps, online information services, and magazines giving professionals multi-platform access to our critical resources, including Professional Development; Education & Certification; Prospecting & Data Tools; Industry News & Analysis; Reference Tools and Services; and Community Networking Opportunities.

Using all of our resources across each community we serve, we deliver measurable ROI for our sponsors through a range of turnkey services, including Research, Content Development, Integrated Media, Creative & Design, and Lead Generation.

For more information, go to http://www.SummitProfessionalNetworks.com.

## About The National Underwriter Company

The National Underwriter Company is a Summit Professional Network.

For over 110 years, The National Underwriter Company has been the first in line with the targeted tax, insurance, and financial planning information you need to make critical business decisions. Boasting nearly a century of expert experience, our reputable Editors are dedicated to putting accurate and relevant information right at your fingertips. With *Tax Facts*, *Tools & Techniques*, *National Underwriter Advanced Markets*, *Field Guide*, *FC&S®*, *FC&S Legal* and other resources available in print, eBook, CD, and online, you can be assured that as the industry evolves National Underwriter will be at the forefront with the thorough and easy-to-use resources you rely on for success.

## The National Underwriter Company
## Update Service Notification

This National Underwriter Company publication is regularly updated to include coverage of developments and changes that affect the content. If you did not purchase this publication directly from The National Underwriter Company and you want to receive these important updates sent on a 30-day review basis and billed separately, please contact us at (800) 543-0874. Or you can mail your request with your name, company, address, and the title of the book to:

The National Underwriter Company
4157 Olympic Boulevard
Suite 225
Erlanger, KY 41018

If you purchased this publication from The National Underwriter Company directly, you have already been registered for the update service.

## National Underwriter Company Contact Information

To order any National Underwriter Company title, please

- call 1-800-543-0874, 8-6 ET Monday – Thursday and 8 to 5 ET Friday
- online bookstore at www.nationalunderwriter.com, or
- mail to The National Underwriter Company, Orders Department, 4157 Olympic Blvd., Ste. 225, Erlanger, KY 41018

# PREFACE TO 2015 SOCIAL SECURITY AND MEDICARE FACTS

The 2015 edition of *Social Security and Medicare Facts* is designed to provide you with all the information needed to help your clients plan for retirement. Our goal is to supply you with a hands-on reference tool administering not only the basic information about Social Security and Medicare benefits, but also answers to some of the more complex and confusing aspects and issues associated with these tools. For the 2015 edition we have expanded our coverage of this topic by adding information on planning techniques to help your clients maximize their Social Security benefits. Especially important in this area is the addition of the "Maximization of Benefits" section which expand on our coverage of using the practice of "file and suspend", "restricted application". In addition, there is focus on the Windfall Elimination Provision, Delayed Retirement Credits, and the Government Pension Offset. We have also added a Case Studies component of the publication illustrating dozens of examples of how certain actions will affect the amount that your clients collect – or do not collect – from Social Security during their retirement years.

Whether your clients work in the private sector, for the government (federal, state, or local), in connection with the railroad industry, or in the military, this book has information on their retirement, disability, and survivor benefits. Using this reference tool can help you present your clients with the knowledge they need in order to know what to expect in retirement, when they die, or if they should unexpectedly become disabled.

I want to thank Deborah Miner, who many years ago entrusted me with revising and updating this publication, and William Wagner who has been a help to me over the years. My thanks also extend to the folks at National Underwriter Company/Summit Professional Networks who have worked so hard to help me with this 2015 edition, especially Michael Thomas, Emily Brunner, and Connie Jump.

Joe Stenken
November, 2014

# ACKNOWLEDGEMENTS

Special thanks to Ben Templin, J.D., Professor of Law at Thomas Jefferson School of Law, and Susan Cancelosi, J.D., LL.M, Associate Professor of Law at Wayne State University, for their thorough review, expert analysis, and contributions to this edition of the book.

# ABOUT THE AUTHOR

**Joseph Stenken, J.D., CLU®, ChFC®**, is Advanced Sales Marketing Counsel with the Ameritas Life Insurance Corporation's Advanced Sales National Design Team. In this position he assists agents with comprehensive case design and analyzes strategies that are tailored to meet individual clients' needs. He also presents webinars and teleconferences for the Ameritas sales force and writes for a quarterly company newsletter for agents and clients. His expertise includes estate planning, business continuation, executive compensation, and retirement income planning.

Before joining Ameritas, he was an Associate Editor in the Tax and Financial Planning department of The National Underwriter Company. He wrote and edited material for both *Tax Facts on Insurance & Employee Benefits* and *Tax Facts on Investments*, as well as *The Social Security Manual*. He has also been involved in the editing of all the *Tools and Techniques* series of books that are published by The National Underwriter Company.

## About the Lead Developmental Editors

**Marc Kiner** is the President of Premier Social Security Consulting, LLC, and has thirty years' experience in public accounting. Marc's primary areas of service are to privately-held businesses and to individuals. He consults with clients on a variety of complex tax and business issues. Marc obtained his Bachelors of Science degree in Accounting and Finance and a Master's degree from the University of Cincinnati. He is licensed to practice as a CPA in the State of Ohio.

**Jim Blair** is the lead Social Security consultant at Premier Social Security Consulting, LLC. A former Social Security Administrator, Operations Supervisor as well as a District Manager, Mr. Blair has over thirty-five years' experience in helping individuals manage their Social Security benefits, retirement, survivors, disability and health insurance.

## About the Publisher

**Kelly B. Maheu, J.D.**, is Managing Director of the Professional Publishing Division of The National Underwriter Company, a Division of Summit Professional Networks. Kelly has been with The National Underwriter Company since 2006, serving in editorial, content acquisition, and product development roles prior to being named Managing Director.

Prior to joining The National Underwriter Company, Kelly worked in the legal and insurance fields for LexisNexis®, Progressive Insurance, and a Cincinnati insurance defense litigation firm.

Kelly has edited and contributed to numerous books and publications including the *Personal Auto Insurance Policy Coverage Guide*, *Cyberliability and Insurance*, *The National Underwriter Sales Essentials Series*, and *The Tools and Techniques of Risk Management for Financial Planners*.

Kelly earned her law degree from The University of Cincinnati College of Law and holds a BA from Miami University, Ohio, with a double major in English/Journalism and Psychology.

## About the Managing Editor

**Richard H. Cline, J.D.**, is the Manager, Tax and Insurance Content for the Professional Publishing Division at the National Underwriter Company. He is responsible for both the print and online versions of Tax Facts as well as developing new tax products for our customers.

Richard joined the company in 2013 but has over twenty-five years of tax editing and publishing experience. Prior to joining our team, Richard worked for Lexis-Nexis, CCH, Inc., and PricewaterhouseCoopers.

He has a B.S. degree from Franklin and Marshall College in Lancaster, Pennsylvania, and earned his law degree from Tulane University in New Orleans, Louisiana.

## About the Editor

**Michael D.Thomas, J.D.**, is an Editor and Manager of Online Product Development with the Professional Publishing Division of the National Underwriter Company, Summit Professional Networks. He is responsible for the editorial process for the 2015 edition of *Social Security & Medicare Facts*. He is also responsible for the editing and development of health care publications for Summit Professional Networks.

Prior to joining Summit Professional Networks, Mike spent over twenty-five years with LexisNexis, where he was responsible for the editorial content and new product development of new online and traditional legal products, including *Health Law*, *Insurance Law*, *Social Security Law*, *Labor & Employment Law*, *Family Law*, as well as other legal research tools. In addition, he worked as a Field Agent for Knights of Columbus Insurance specializing in life, health, disability income, long-term care insurance as well as annuity sales.

Mike has a Bachelor of Arts from Tufts University and a Juris Doctorate from the University of Dayton.

## Editorial Services

**Connie L. Jump**, Manager, Editorial Operations

**Emily Brunner**, Editorial Assistant

# SUMMARY TABLE OF CONTENTS



## PART I: SOCIAL SECURITY



## PART II: MEDICARE



## APPENDICES

# LIST OF QUESTIONS

# PART I: SOCIAL SECURITY

## UNDERSTANDING AND PLANNING FOR SOCIAL SECURITY

1. What is the Social Security Act?

2. What programs are covered by the Social Security Act?

3. Who is covered by Social Security?

4. In general, who can receive Social Security benefits and what do the phrases Normal Retirement Age (NRA) and Full Retirement Age (FRA) mean?

### Normal Retirement Age and Full Retirement Age

5. When will same-sex couples be eligible to receive spousal Social Security benefits?

6. Increasingly, the government has experienced the threat of, or actual shutdowns of services. What happens to Social Security benefits during government shutdowns?

7. What federal agency administers the Social Security or OASDI program?

8. Where can I get forms related to Social Security and disability?

9. How does a person obtain a Social Security number?

10. How can a person check on his Social Security earnings record and receive an estimate of future Social Security benefits?

11. What will happen to Social Security benefit payments when the Trust Fund becomes insolvent?

12. Where and how does a person apply for Social Security benefits?

13. Which government agency issues a beneficiary's Social Security payment?

14. When does a Social Security beneficiary receive a monthly direct deposit?

15. To whom is a benefit payment made payable and how are benefits received?

16. If a husband and wife are both receiving monthly benefits, do they receive one or two monthly payments?

17. If several children are entitled to benefits, does each child receive a separate payment?

18. Can a power of attorney be granted for the purpose of collecting and managing payments?

# RETIREMENT AND DISABILITY BENEFITS



## Retirement Benefits



## Disability Benefits

## Spouse's Benefit



## Child's Benefits (Child of Retired or Disabled Worker)

64. Under what circumstances is a child considered to be dependent upon a stepparent?

65. Can a child receive benefits based on one parent's Social Security account even though the other parent is working and furnishing support?

66. When is a child a full-time elementary or secondary school student?

67. Is the disabled child of a retired or disabled worker entitled to benefits past age 22?

68. What is the amount of the benefit for a retired or disabled worker's child?

69. Can a child lose his benefits by working?

70. If the retired or disabled parent loses benefits, will the child lose benefits also?

71. Will a child lose his or her benefits if he or she marries?

72. When does a child's benefit end?

73. If a child is neither disabled nor a full-time elementary or secondary student, when does the benefit end?

74. Who files application for a child's benefits?

75. Who receives a child's benefits?

## Survivor's Benefits

76. What benefits are payable to the survivors of a deceased insured worker?

## Mother's or Father's Benefit

77. Is the surviving spouse of an insured worker entitled to a monthly Mother's or Father's benefit at any age?

78. Can a divorced spouse qualify for a survivor's benefit?

79. Must a worker be fully insured at death to qualify for the mother's or father's benefit?

80. What is the amount of a mother's or father's benefit?

81. What are the differences between a mother's or father's benefit and a widow(er)'s benefit?

82. Is a mother's or father's benefit payable regardless of the surviving spouse's need?

83. Can a surviving spouse lose some or all of the benefits by working?

84. If the only child in a surviving spouse's care loses benefits by working, will this cause the child's mother or father to lose benefits?

85. Must a surviving spouse file application for a mother's or father's benefit?

## Child's Benefit (Child of Deceased Worker)



## Widow(er)'s Benefit

106. Can the divorced spouse of a deceased worker qualify for a widow(er)'s benefit?

107. What are the requirements for a divorced spouse to be able to file for spousal benefits from the former spouse?

108. What is the earliest age at which a widow(er) can receive a widow(er)'s benefit?

109. What is the monthly rate of a widow(er)'s benefit?

110. How much will a spouse, aged sixty-four, collect when an older spouse dies at age sixty-nine before filing or receiving benefits?

111. How does remarriage affect a widow(er)'s benefits?

112. If a widow(er) is entitled to a retirement benefit and a widow(er)'s benefit, will the widow(er) receive both benefits?

113. How does the delayed retirement credit affect a widow(er)'s benefit?

114. Can a widow(er) lose benefits by working?

115. Will a widow(er)'s benefits be reduced if the widow(er) is receiving a government pension?

116. How is the effect of public employee pension income on SS benefits calculated?

117. When do widow(er)'s benefits end?

## Disabled Widow(er)'s Benefits

118. Is a disabled widow(er) entitled to benefits starting before age sixty?

## Parent's Benefits

119. Under what circumstances is a deceased worker's parent entitled to benefits?

120. Who is a parent for the purpose of receiving a parent's benefit?

121. What is the amount of a parent's monthly benefit?

122. Can a parent receive benefits, even if the worker's widow(er) and children are eligible for benefits?

123. May benefits payable to a parent reduce the benefits payable to the worker's widow(er) and children?

124. Is a parent's benefit starting at age sixty-two smaller than one starting at age sixty-five?

125. If a person is entitled to a parent's benefit and a retirement benefit, will he receive both full benefits?

126. Can a person lose a parent's benefit by working?

127. When do a parent's benefits end?

128. If a parent remarries after the worker's death, will the parent lose benefits?

### Lump-Sum Death Payment

129. What is the amount of the Social Security lump-sum death payment?

130. Is the lump-sum death benefit payable only if the worker was fully insured at death?

131. Must an application be made for the lump-sum death benefit?

## COVERAGE

132. How does someone become qualified for retirement, survivor, and disability benefits under Social Security?

133. How does someone obtain a quarter of coverage as an employee?

134. How does someone obtain a quarter of coverage as a self-employed person?

135. What calendar quarters cannot be counted as quarters of coverage even though the earnings requirement has been met?

### Fully Insured

136. How does a person become fully insured?

137. Must a person be fully insured to qualify for retirement benefits?

138. How do you determine the number of quarters of coverage needed for a person to be fully insured for retirement benefits?

139. Can a person be fully insured for retirement benefits even though not working in covered employment for many years?

140. Can a person become fully insured after retirement age?

141. How do you determine the number of quarters of coverage needed for a person to be fully insured at death?

### Currently Insured

142. What benefits are payable if a person is only currently insured at death?

143. When is a person currently insured?

### Insured Status for Disability Benefits

144. What insured status requirements must be met to qualify a person for disability benefits?

### Computing Benefits

145. In general, how are Social Security benefits determined?

## FILING FOR BENEFITS

### General Information

146. What procedure should be followed to determine if a person is eligible for Social Security benefits?

147. At what time should the survivors of a deceased worker file for survivor's benefits?

148. When should a person file an application for disability benefits?

149. When should a person file an application for the lump-sum death payment?

### Proof Required

150. What proofs are required before survivors' and retirement benefits can be paid?

151. What are acceptable proofs of death?

152. What are the best forms of proof of age and family relationship?

### Right to Appeal

153. Is there a review procedure available if a person is disappointed with the Social Security Administration's initial determination regarding benefits?

154. How can a person appeal the reconsideration determination?

155. How is a hearing request made and how long will it take from the request to the actual hearing?

156. What will a hearing cost?

157. If a person disagrees with the hearing decision, may he ask for a review?

158. May a person file a civil action in the United States District Court?

159. Are there situations where the Social Security Administration may not recover an overpayment to a beneficiary?

## BENEFIT COMPUTATION

160. How are benefits computed under the simplified old-start benefit computation method?

### Primary Insurance Amount

161. What is the Primary Insurance Amount (PIA)?

## "Wage Indexing" Benefit Computation Method



## Transitional Guarantee Benefit Method



## Minimum and Maximum Single Benefits Increase in Benefits

## Reduction in Benefits

181. When a person elects to start receiving a retirement benefit before full retirement age, how is the benefit reduced?

182. If the spouse of a retired worker starts receiving a spouse's benefit before full retirement age, how is the benefit reduced?

183. If a widow(er) elects to start receiving a widow(er)'s benefit before full retirement age, how is the benefit reduced?

184. How do the benefit reduction rules affect a high-earning spouse who dies after reaching Full Retirement Age (FRA) with a surviving spouse who is younger than Full Retirement Age?

185. How are benefits figured if a beneficiary starts receiving a reduced retirement benefit and later becomes entitled to a larger spouse's benefit?

## Recomputation of Benefits

186. Under what circumstances are benefits recomputed?

187. If a person is simultaneously entitled to two or more benefits, which benefit will be paid?

## Disability Freeze

188. How does a period of disability affect retirement and survivor's benefits?

## Calculating the Exact Benefit Amount

189. In calculating the exact amount of each monthly benefit, how must the figures be rounded?

# MAXIMIZATION OF BENEFITS

190. When is the best time to apply for Social Security retirement benefits, and what are some of the ways of maximizing Social Security Benefits over time?

191. What is the "file and suspend" strategy for applying for, but not yet receiving, Social Security benefits?

192. What is a "restricted application," strategy for planning for and maximizing Social Security benefits?

193. Are there differences in strategies for maximizing Social Security benefits for a married couple depending upon the earnings history of the couple?

194. Are there any strategies a widow or widower can use to maximize benefits?

195. Can a husband and wife both receive retirement benefits?

196. What kind of planning can be done regarding when Social Security benefits are started?

## Year of Retirement

216. What if a person dies after filing and suspending but before receiving benefits? Can the widow collect that lump sum?

217. If a husband files and suspends and the wife takes spousal benefits at age sixty-two, will the wife get a stepped-up spousal benefit if the husband dies at age seventy-two after delaying his benefit until age seventy?

218. Can a working couple both at FRA claim both file and suspend and restricted to receive two Social Security checks?

219. What is the best strategy in a situation where the husband is age sixty-six with an income of $150,000 per year and the wife is aged sixty-eight, with an income of $50,000 per year?

220. What is the best strategy in a situation where the husband is age sixty-six with an income of $150,000 per year and the wife is aged sixty-eight, with an income of $50,000 per year and the wife has already filed for benefits.

221. What option might one use if there is a significant difference in ages between spouses, for example, if the husband is twelve years older than wife?

222. What are the limitations of the "do-over" as an option? If a spouse dies can the surviving spouse still do a do-over within one year of starting benefits?

# LOSS OF BENEFITS BECAUSE OF "EXCESS" EARNINGS

## Retirement Test

223. Can a person lose some or all Social Security benefits by working?

224. What are the general rules for loss of benefits because of excess earnings?

225. How are "excess" earnings charged against benefits?

226. Can a person who is receiving dependent's or survivor's benefits lose benefits by working?

227. If a widow's benefits are withheld because of work, will this necessarily reduce the total amount of benefits payable to the family?

228. How is the loss of benefits figured for the year in which the worker reaches full retirement age?

229. What kinds of earnings will cause loss of benefits?

230. How does the Annual Earnings Test work?

231. What is meant by "substantial services" in self-employment?

232. Must a Social Security beneficiary report earnings to the Social Security Administration?

233. How are a life insurance agent's first-year and renewal commissions treated for purposes of the retirement test?

## TAXATION OF SOCIAL SECURITY BENEFITS

234. Are Social Security benefits subject to federal income taxation?

235. What are the base amounts?

236. What portion of Social Security benefits are subject to income taxes?

237. Why is nontaxable interest income included in a taxpayer's adjusted gross income?

238. Are workers' compensation benefits included in the definition of Social Security benefits for tax purposes?

239. How are overpayments and lump-sum retroactive benefits taxed?

240. What reporting requirements must be met by the Social Security Administration?

241. Are Social Security benefits subject to income tax withholding?

242. If a recipient of Social Security benefits elects Medical Insurance (Part B) under Medicare and the premiums are deducted from the individual's benefits, is the whole benefit, before the deduction, a Social Security benefit?

## SOCIAL SECURITY TAXES

243. What are the Social Security and Medicare tax rates for employers and employees?

244. If an employee works for two employers during the year and more than the maximum tax is paid on his or her wages, will the overpayment be refunded to the employee and his or her employers?

245. Does an employer receive an income tax deduction for Social Security tax payments?

246. Must Social Security taxes be paid on cash tips?

247. How does an individual report Social Security taxes on domestic help?

248. What is the rate of Social Security and Medicare tax for a self-employed person?

249. If a self-employed person also receives wages as an employee, what portion of income is subject to tax as self-employment income?

250. Must a Social Security beneficiary who works pay Social Security and Medicare taxes?

251. How does a life insurance agent pay Social Security taxes on first-year and renewal commissions?

252. Must the self-employment tax be included in a person's estimated tax return?

253. What is the federal income tax deduction for medical expense insurance premiums?

# WAGES AND SELF-EMPLOYMENT INCOME

254. What earnings are subject to Social Security tax and are counted in computing Social Security benefits?

255. For Social Security purposes, what is meant by the term "wages"?

256. Are only payments in cash counted as wages?

257. Are employer payments for group life insurance covered wages?

258. Are vacation pay and severance pay wages?

259. Are payments on account of sickness or accident disability counted as wages for Social Security purposes?

260. Are payments made under a deferred compensation plan counted as wages?

261. Are payments made to or from a qualified pension or annuity plan counted as wages?

262. If a teacher takes a reduction in salary to provide funds for a tax-sheltered annuity, how are his or her wages computed for Social Security purposes?

263. Are cash tips considered wages?

264. Do wages include the portion of an employee's Social Security taxes paid by an employer?

265. Are salesperson's commissions wages?

266. Under what circumstances are the first-year and renewal commissions of a life insurance agent treated as wages?

267. Is the value of meals and lodging furnished by an employer to an employee considered wages for Social Security taxation purposes?

## Self-Employment Income

268. What is taxable and creditable self-employment income?

269. How is the amount of self-employment income figured if a person has both wages and net earnings from self-employment in the same year?

270. In general, what constitutes net earnings from self-employment?

271. How does a self-employed life insurance agent report first-year and renewal commissions?

# RAILROAD RETIREMENT

## Employee and Spouse Annuities



## Survivor Benefits



## Railroad Retirement Taxes



# BENEFITS FOR SERVICE MEMBERS AND VETERANS

## Military Retirement



### Survivor Annuity

### Disability Retirement



### Reservists' Retirement Pay



## Veterans

### Dependency and Indemnity Compensation



### Disability Benefits – Service-Connected



### Death Benefits – Service-Connected



### Pension, Disability, and Death Benefits Not Service-Connected

## Survivor Benefits



## Disability Benefits



## Thrift Savings Plan



# Civil Service Retirement System



## Computing the CSRS Annuity

### Death Benefits

348. Is there a death benefit under the CSRS?

### Annuity Eligibility Requirements

349. Who is eligible for a survivor annuity?

### Computing the Survivor Annuity

350. How is the survivor annuity computed?

### Lump-Sum Death Benefit

351. When does the lump-sum death benefit become payable?

### Annuity Payments

352. How are annuity payments made?

### Disability Retirement

353. When is an annuity payable for disability retirement?

### Cost-of-Living Adjustments

354. Is there a cost-of-living adjustment to CSRS annuities?

### Refund of Contributions

355. Is there a refund of contributions if an employee leaves government service?

## Life Insurance Benefits

356. In general, what life insurance benefits are available to federal civil service employees?

357. How does an employee designate the beneficiary or beneficiaries?

358. When does insurance coverage cease?

359. Can an employee convert to an individual policy?

360. What is the cost of basic insurance?

361. What optional insurance coverages are available to the civil service employee?

362. May a retiring employee continue life insurance coverage?

# CASE STUDIES USED IN PLANNING FOR SOCIAL SECURITY MAXIMIZATION

CASE STUDY #1: George and Joan

CASE STUDY #2: Gary and Lynn

# PART II: MEDICARE

## INTRODUCTION

1014. What are the rules regarding self-referrals?

1015. What are Quality Improvement Organizations?

1016. When should a person use the Medicare fraud and abuse hotline?

1017. Should a person receive Medicare benefits through the original fee-for-service Medicare Parts A and B (Hospital Insurance and Medical Insurance) or through a Medicare Advantage plan?

# PART A: HOSPITAL INSURANCE

## Eligibility

1018. Who is eligible for benefits under Part A (Hospital Insurance)?

1019. What are the special eligibility rules for persons with End-Stage Renal Disease (ESRD)?

1020. What are the special eligibility rules for government employees?

1021. When is Medicare considered a secondary payer?

1022. Can a person age sixty-five or over qualify for Part A (Hospital Insurance) benefits without qualifying for Social Security or Railroad Retirement benefits?

1023. Is there any way that an individual not automatically eligible for Part A (Hospital Insurance) can be enrolled?

## Administration

1024. How do the Centers for Medicare & Medicaid Services (CMS) administer Part A (Hospital Insurance)?

1025. What is the Prospective Payment System?

1026. Is Part A (Hospital Insurance) a compulsory program?

## Financing Part A (Hospital Insurance)

1027. How is Part A (Hospital Insurance) financed?

## Benefits

1028. In general, what benefits are provided under Part A (Hospital Insurance)?

## Qualified Medicare Beneficiaries

1029. When will a state pay Medicare costs for a person who is elderly or disabled with low income?

1030. How does a person qualify for assistance under the QMB program?

1031. What if a person's income is slightly higher than the poverty level?

1032. How does a person apply for QMB or SLMB assistance?

## Inpatient Hospital Services

1033. Specifically, what inpatient hospital services are paid for under Part A (Hospital Insurance)?

1034. Are inpatient hospital benefits provided for care in a psychiatric hospital?

1035. What special provisions apply to care in Religious Nonmedical Health Care Institutions (RNHCI)?

1036. Can patients choose their own hospitals?

1037. Must a doctor certify that hospitalization is required?

1038. What must a hospital do to qualify for Medicare payments?

## Hospice Care

1039. What is hospice care?

1040. How is hospice care covered under Part A (Hospital Insurance)?

1041. What is the hospice benefit period?

1042. What does the patient pay for hospice care?

1043. How is respite care covered?

## Skilled Nursing Facility Care

1044. What is a qualified skilled nursing facility?

1045. Does Part A (Hospital Insurance) pay for custodial care in a skilled nursing facility?

1046. Do most nursing home residents qualify for Part A (Hospital Insurance) coverage?

1047. Under what circumstances does a patient qualify for skilled nursing facility benefits under Part A (Hospital Insurance)?

1048. What items and services generally are (and are not) covered under Part A (Hospital Insurance) when provided in a participating skilled nursing facility?

1049. What provisions are made under Part A (Hospital Insurance) for care in a skilled nursing facility?

1050. How much does the patient pay for skilled nursing facility care?

1051. When can payment be made for skilled nursing care under Part A (Hospital Insurance)?

## Home Health Care

1052. When are postinstitutional home health services covered under Part A (Hospital Insurance)?

1053. What conditions must be met for Part A (Hospital Insurance) to cover home health visits?

1054. What postinstitutional home health services are covered under Part A (Hospital Insurance)?

1055. How does Medicare pay the costs of home health services?

## General Information

1056. Does Part A (Hospital Insurance) pay the cost of outpatient hospital services?

1057. Does a person need to be in financial need to receive Part A (Hospital Insurance) benefits?

1058. Will the deductible and coinsurance amounts paid by patients for Part A (Hospital Insurance) remain the same in future years?

1059. What is Medicare's position regarding treatment of a patient with a living will or durable power of attorney for health care?

# PART B: MEDICAL INSURANCE

## Eligibility

1060. Who is eligible for Part B (Medical Insurance) benefits?

1061. How does a person enroll in Part B (Medical Insurance)?

1062. What if a person declines to enroll during the Part B (Medical Insurance) initial enrollment period?

1063. Is there a special enrollment period for disabled workers who lose benefits under a group health plan?

1064. How does a person terminate or cancel coverage under Part B (Medical Insurance)?

## Financing Part B (Medical Insurance)

1065. How is Part B (Medical Insurance) financed?

1066. How is Income determined for purposes of setting a person's Part B (Hospital Insurance) Premium?

1067. What is a Qualified Medicare Beneficiary?

1068. How are premiums paid under Part B (Medical Insurance)?

1069. How are "approved charges" for covered medical services determined under Part B (Medical Insurance)?

1070. How are Part B (Medical Insurance) payments made?

1071. How can a person find out if a doctor accepts assignment of all Medicare claims?

1072. What are Medicare providers and Medicare suppliers?

1073. What portion of the cost must be borne by the patient?

1074. How does a patient find out how much Medicare will pay on a claim?

## Benefits

1075. What doctors' services are covered under Part B (Medical Insurance)?

1076. What outpatient hospital services are covered under Part B (Medical Insurance)?

1077. When are outpatient physical therapy and speech-language pathology services covered under Part B (Medical Insurance)?

1078. Are partial hospitalization services connected to mental health services covered?

1079. Are certified nurse-midwife services covered under Part B (Medical Insurance)?

1080. Is dental work covered under Part B (Medical Insurance)?

1081. What medical equipment is covered under Part B (Medical Insurance)?

1082. Is ambulance service covered by Part B (Medical Insurance)?

1083. How much will Medicare Part B (Medical Insurance) pay for outpatient treatment of mental illness?

1084. When is the cost of vaccines covered?

1085. Is the cost of antigens covered under Part B (Medical Insurance)?

1086. When is a liver transplant covered under Part B (Medical Insurance)?

1087. Can Part B (Medical Insurance) help pay for outpatient services at a comprehensive outpatient rehabilitation facility?

1088. Are home health services covered under Part B (Medical Insurance)?

1089. Are independent clinical laboratory services covered under Part B (Medical Insurance)?

1090. Are screening pap smears and pelvic exams covered by Part B (Medical Insurance)?

## Medicare Coverage of Blood



## Private Contracts



# PART C: MEDICARE ADVANTAGE

## Definition

## Eligibility, Election, and Enrollment



## Benefits and Beneficiary Protections



## Premiums



## Contracts with Medicare Advantage Organizations



## Medigap Insurance Program



## Medicare Advantage Marketing Rules

# PART D: PRESCRIPTION DRUG INSURANCE



## Prescription Drug Marketing Rules



# MEDIGAP INSURANCE

# HOW TO SUBMIT CLAIMS AND APPEALS

## Claims Procedure



## Appeals Procedure



# MEDICAID

## Overview



## Medicaid Eligibility

## Medicaid Services



## Payment Under Medicaid



## Long-Term Care



## Exempt Income and Resources



## Spousal Impoverishment

## Medicaid Transfer Rules

1186. Can a person transfer property in order to meet the eligibility requirements for Medicaid?

1187. How is the penalty period determined after an improper transfer of assets?

1188. What are the rules under Medicaid regarding the purchase of annuities?

## Trusts

1189. Can a trust be used to shelter a Medicaid applicant's assets?

1190. Are there exceptions to the trust rules under Medicaid?

1191. What is a Special Needs Trust (SNT)?

1192. What are the three different types of Special Needs Trusts (SNT)?

1193. What is a family-type Special Needs Trust (SNT)?

1194. What is a pooled Special Needs Trust (SNT)?

1195. What is a court-ordered Special Needs Trust (SNT)?

1196. Should a Special Needs Trust (SNT) be set up during the grantor's life or as part of the grantor's will?

1197. What is the future of Special Needs Trusts (SNT)?

## Estate Recoveries

1198. Can a state recover nursing home and long-term care Medicaid expenses from the estate of a deceased Medicaid recipient?

## Discrimination

1199. Does federal law require that Medicaid patients be admitted to any (and all) nursing homes?

## Managed Care

1200. How has managed care changed the original Medicaid program?

## State LTC Partnership Program

1201. What is a "qualified state long-term care insurance partnership?"

# INTRODUCTION

*Social Security & Medicare Facts* provides the reader with a description of Social Security, Medicare, benefits for federal government employees, benefits for service members and veterans, and benefits for workers covered under the Railroad Retirement System.

Social Security is administered by the Social Security Administration and provides old age, survivors, and disability benefits. Medicare provides hospital and medical insurance for the aged and disabled, and is administered by the Centers for Medicare & Medicaid Services.

The original Social Security Act provided only retirement benefits for wage and salary earners. In 1939, benefits were added for family members after the worker's death or retirement. Most amendments have expanded the scope of the Social Security program – by extending coverage to more groups of persons, by increasing benefits, by creating new benefits (such as disability), by liberalizing requirements for benefits, or by increasing the wage base for taxes and benefits.

Today, the largest and most common programs under the Social Security Act and its amendments are: (i) Federal Old-Age (Retirement), Survivors, and Disability Insurance (OASDI), (ii) Temporary Assistance for Needy Families (TANF), (iii) Health Insurance for Aged and Disabled (Medicare), (iv) Grants to States for Medical Assistance Programs for low income citizens—(Medicaid), (v) State Children's Health Insurance Program for low income citizens—(SCHIP), and (vi) Supplemental Security Income (SSI).

This new 2015 edition of *Social Security & Medicare Facts* includes new discussions of planning techniques designed to maximize benefits, especially for married couples. There is also information on the ability of same-sex couples to receive benefits, a discussion of the ability to pay future benefits, as well as the impact of federal government gridlock on benefits received through the Social Security system. In addition, there is a new section detailing methods and practices for maximizing benefits, as well as Case Studies of a variety of situations and how various actions can help to maximize the benefits collected under the Social Security program.

# PART I
# SOCIAL SECURITY

# UNDERSTANDING AND PLANNING FOR SOCIAL SECURITY

## 1. What is the Social Security Act?

The Social Security Act has established numerous programs which provide supplemental income for insured individuals and their families in the event of disability, when they retire, or at death. This supplemental income acts as a safety net – especially in old age – and keeps an estimated 43 percent of elderly American out of the poverty.[1]

Congress passed the Social Security Act in 1935 and the retirement benefits program went into effect on January 1, 1937. The law has been amended many times since its original enactment.

There have been many changes in Social Security and the United States since 1935. In 1935 the life expectancy was only age sixty, while today it is seventy-nine. Therefore, in 1935 most people would not have lived long enough to collect Social Security retirement benefits. While today, many retirees are concerned they will outlive their retirement savings.

In 1935 Social Security was designed to supplement a retiree's retirement income. Today, Social Security provides about 40 percent of the average retiree's income. This statistic worries many analysts who contend that workers rely too much on Social Security and should save more.

In 1935, the worker/retiree ratio was about 160:1. Today it is about 3:1. When the program began, Social Security paid out about $35 million in benefits annually. Today it pays out over $675 billion annually.

Finally, in 1935, the poverty rate for seniors exceeded 50 percent. Today the poverty rate for seniors is less than 9.5 percent.

Nearly 90 percent of Americans over the age of sixty-five receive some Social Security income and approximately 35 percent of that same group relies almost entirely on Social Security payments alone. With longer life expectancy, and the recent issues with the economy it has become increasingly important to understand and plan for Social Security benefits. With a thorough understanding of the program and useful strategies for applying for and receiving Social Security, most recipients can increase the amount of benefits they would receive if they simply apply for Social Security at Full Retirement Age (FRA – also called Normal Retirement Age).

## 2. What programs are covered by the Social Security Act?

The original Social Security Act (1935) and the current version of the Act, as amended, encompass several social welfare and social insurance programs.

1. www.cbpp.org/cms/?fa=view&id=3851.

The following programs are covered by the Social Security Act:

- Social Security (retirement, survivors, and disability insurance).
- Medicare (hospital and medical insurance for the aged, the disabled, and those with end-stage renal disease).
- Unemployment insurance.
- Black lung benefits.
- Supplemental Security Income (SSI).
- Public assistance and welfare services, including aid to needy families with children, medical assistance, maternal and child health services, child-support enforcement, family and child welfare services, food stamps, and energy assistance.

The Federal Old-Age (Retirement), Survivors, and Disability Insurance program (OASDI) is the main program that people think of when they think of the term "Social Security". This program covers workers and their dependents.[1]

## 3. Who is covered by Social Security?

Most workers are covered by Social Security and if they work long enough will be entitled to retirement benefits and/or disability.

However, certain individuals are not covered by Social Security. Individuals who started working for the federal government before 1984 are not covered by Social Security, except those who elected to transfer into the system during a 1987 transition period (see Q 318). Those who are not covered by Social Security are instead covered under the Civil Service Retirement System (see Q 334).

Also, certain individuals who work in the railroad industry are not covered by Social Security. Instead, these workers are covered under the Railroad Retirement System, which is governed by the Railroad Retirement Act (see Q 272).

Finally, there are other special circumstances where an individual would not be covered by Social Security. These include certain farm workers, workers of a family business, or domestic workers.

## 4. In general, who can receive Social Security benefits and what do the phrases Normal Retirement Age (NRA) and Full Retirement Age (FRA) mean?

- A disabled insured worker under age sixty-five.
- A retired insured worker at age sixty-two or over.

1. 42 U.S.C. 402.

- The spouse of a retired or disabled worker entitled to benefits who: (1) is age sixty-two or over or (2) has in care a child under age sixteen (or over age sixteen and disabled), who is entitled to benefits on the worker's Social Security record.

- The divorced spouse of a retired or disabled worker entitled to benefits if age sixty-two or over and married to the worker for at least ten years.

- The divorced spouse of a fully insured worker who has not yet filed a claim for benefits if both are age sixty-two or over, were married for at least ten years, and have been finally divorced for at least two continuous years.

- The dependent, unmarried child of a retired or disabled worker entitled to benefits, or of a deceased insured worker if the child is: (1) under age eighteen, or (2) under age nineteen and a full-time elementary or secondary school student, or (3) age eighteen or over but under a disability that began before age twenty-two.

- The surviving spouse (including a surviving divorced spouse) of a deceased insured worker if the widow(er) is age sixty or over.

- The disabled surviving spouse (including a surviving divorced spouse in some cases) of a deceased insured worker, if the widow(er) is age fifty to fifty-nine and becomes disabled within a specified period.

- The surviving spouse (including a surviving divorced spouse) of a deceased insured worker, regardless of age, if caring for an entitled child of the deceased who is either under age sixteen or disabled before age twenty-two.

- The dependent parents of a deceased insured worker at age sixty-two or over.

In addition to monthly survivor benefits, a lump-sum death payment is payable upon the death of an insured worker. For explanation of these benefits and eligibility requirements, see RETIREMENT AND DISABILITY BENEFITS, Q 23 to Q 131.

## Normal Retirement Age and Full Retirement Age

For many years Normal Retirement Age (NRA) meant the age when someone was eligible for benefits that were not reduced for taking early benefits (see Q 181 and Q 204). But recently this phrase has come to mean, among planners and the general public, the age when many people "normally" apply for benefits, which is when they are generally first eligible – at age sixty-two.

As a result of this shift in language, a new phrase has developed among planners and the public to describe the age when unreduced benefits may be received – Full Retirement Age (FRA). As may seem obvious, FRA refers to the age at which a person qualifies for full Social Security benefits. This age is now determined by a person's year of birth and for those born in 1960 and later is now age sixty-seven. This shift in terms has started to affect guidance put out by the Social Security Administration (SSA), although the SSA still uses both phrases to describe when unreduced benefits may be taken.

For the 2015 edition of *Social Security & Medicare Facts* the phrase "Normal Retirement Age" has been replaced by "Full Retirement Age" to describe the age at which unreduced benefits may be taken.

## 5. When will same-sex couples be eligible to receive spousal Social Security benefits?

After the June 2013 U.S. Supreme Court ruling in *United States v. Windsor*,[1] same sex couples who were married in a jurisdiction where same sex marriages are recognized are eligible for spousal benefits, such as the spousal survivor benefit, the spousal retirement benefit, and the lump sum death benefit.

The Social Security Administration reviewed its own policies regarding same-sex marriage after the Supreme Court decision, and concluded that same-sex couples who are legally married in one state remain married for federal tax purposes even if they reside in a state that does not recognize their marriage.[2] The Social Security Administration does not currently recognize same sex civil unions or domestic partnerships as the equivalent of marriage, so couples in those relationships are not eligible for benefits.

The Social Security Administration recommends that same sex couples who think they might be eligible for benefits should apply for benefits now in order to protect themselves against loss of potential benefits.

## 6. Increasingly, the government has experienced the threat of, or actual shutdowns of services. What happens to Social Security benefits during government shutdowns?

To date, the policy during a government shutdown or the threat of a government shutdown has been to insure that benefit payments continue without interruption. Although payments continue without interruption, some services provided at regional offices are curtailed. When a government shutdown is anticipated, see the Social Security Administration website (www.ssa.gov) for announcements of curtailment of services.

## 7. What federal agency administers the Social Security or OASDI program?

The Social Security Administration. The central office is located in Baltimore, Maryland. The administrative offices and computer operations are housed at this location.

The Social Security Administration is an independent agency in the executive branch of the federal government. It is required to administer the retirement, survivors, and disability program under the Social Security and the Supplemental Security Income (SSI) programs. The commissioner of the Social Security Administration is appointed by the President and approved by the Senate and serves a term of six years.

1. 570 U.S. ___ (2013).
2. Rev. Rul. 2013-17.

In recent years, the Social Security has increasingly provided it services through its website at www.ssa.gov. Many of the services that were traditionally carried out through local Social Security offices or through the mail can now be done online at www.ssa.gov/onlineservices. These services allow a person to apply for benefits, get a Social Security Statement, appeal a decision, find out about qualifying for benefits, estimate future benefits, and do other activities related to the management of benefits.

Alternatively, the local Social Security office is the place where a person can apply for a Social Security number, check on an earnings record, apply for Social Security benefits, black lung benefits, SSI, and Hospital Insurance (Medicare Part A) protection, enroll for Medical Insurance (Medicare Part B), receive assistance in applying for food stamps, and get full information about individual and family rights and obligations under the law. Also, a person can call the Social Security Administration's toll-free telephone number, 1-800-772-1213, to receive these services. This toll-free telephone number is available from 7 a.m. to 7 p.m. any business day. From a touch-tone phone, recorded information and services are available twenty-four hours a day, including weekends and holidays. People who are deaf or hard of hearing may call 1-800-325-0778 between 7 a.m. and 7 p.m. Monday through Friday.

Regular visits to outlying areas are made by the Social Security office staff to serve people who live at a distance from the city or town in which the office is located. The visits are made to locations called contact stations. A schedule of these visits may be obtained from the nearest Social Security office.

Social Security Administration regional offices are located in Atlanta, Boston, Chicago, Dallas, Denver, Kansas City, New York, Philadelphia, San Francisco, and Seattle. Approximately 1,400 Social Security offices throughout the United States, Puerto Rico, the Virgin Islands, Guam, and American Samoa deal directly with the public. Each region also has a number of teleservice centers located primarily in metropolitan areas. These offices handle telephone inquiries and refer callers appropriately. To find a local office, visit the Social Security Administration website at www.ssa.gov/pgm/reach.htm.

The Office of Hearings and Appeals administers the nationwide hearings and appeals program for the Social Security Administration. Administrative law judges, located in or traveling to major cities throughout the United States, hold hearings and issue decisions when a claimant or organization has appealed a determination affecting rights to benefits or participation in programs under the Social Security Act. The Appeals Council, located in Falls Church, Virginia, may review hearing decisions. (See FILING FOR BENEFITS, Q 146 to Q 159.)

The Office of Central Records Operations maintains records of an individual's earnings and prepares benefit computations.

## 8. Where can I get forms related to Social Security and disability?

The Social Security Administration provides many, though not all, of its forms online at www.ssa.gov/online. Increasingly, the Social Security Administration encourages people to go online to download, fill out, and submit forms. These forms, however, can still be obtained from the local Social Security Office during regular business hours.

## 9. How does a person obtain a Social Security number?

By filling out Form SS-5 (Application for a Social Security Card) and submitting evidence of age, identity, and citizenship or alien status.

Parents applying for a Social Security number for their children under age seven will need to furnish only a birth record if no other record of age or identity has been established for the child.

Applicants eighteen and older must apply in person at a Social Security office.

A Social Security number is needed not only for Social Security purposes, but also for income tax purposes. The Internal Revenue Service uses this number as a taxpayer identification number for processing tax returns and controlling the interest and dividend reports of banks and other financial institutions. Failure to put a valid Social Security number on a tax return may mean a delay or reduction in any refund claimed.

A Social Security number is also needed by persons age one or older who are claimed as dependents on someone's federal income tax return. All income tax returns claiming dependents (whether taxpayer's children or others) one year old or older must show the dependent's Social Security number. Failure to include a dependent's Social Security number on a tax return could result in the Internal Revenue Service disallowing related items such as the personal exemption, child tax credit, child care credit, or earned income credit.

A person must have a Social Security number in order to receive Social Security benefits. Those lacking a Social Security number are required to apply for one. Beneficiaries on the Social Security rolls prior to May 10, 1989 are not required to have a Social Security number. However, as a practical matter, Social Security numbers are also commonly used by many nongovernmental entities, such as health care providers or banks, for tracking and security purposes.

If the Social Security card is lost, a person can apply for a duplicate card by filling out another Form SS-5 and showing a driver's license, voter registration card, school identification card, or other official proof of identity. The new card will have the same number as the one that was lost.

If a person wishes to correct or update the identifying information given on the original application for a Social Security number, a new Form SS-5 must be submitted. A change in name (for example, upon marriage) should always be reported.

Foreign-born applicants of any age must submit evidence of United States citizenship or alien status.

Form SS-5 can be obtained from any local Social Security office or online from the Social Security Administration's website. Forms must be either mailed to or presented to a local Social Security office.

Some businesses advertise that they can provide Social Security cards or name changes for a fee. There is no need to use such a business. Getting a Social Security number is free through the Social Security Administration.[1]

1. See www.ssa.gov/ssnumber.

## 10. How can a person check on his Social Security earnings record and receive an estimate of future Social Security benefits?

The Social Security Statement containing both an estimate of benefits and a record of earnings is available either online or by the mail. To access the statement online, a person must create a *my Social Security* account at www.ssa.gov/myaccount/. This account also allows a person to manage personal information such as changing an address or the way in which a direct deposit is received.

To receive the statement by mail, a person should fill out Form SSA-7004 (Request for Social Security Statement). The form is available at the Social Security Administrations website at www.ssa.gov, at any Social Security office, or by calling the Social Security Administration's toll-free number, 1-800-772-1213. A statement of total wages and self-employment income credited to the earnings record and an estimate of current Social Security disability and survivor benefits and future Social Security retirement benefits will be mailed to the individual.

If all earnings have not been credited, the individual should contact a Social Security office and ask how to correct the records. The time limit for correcting an earnings record is set by law. An earnings record can be corrected at any time up to three years, three months, and fifteen days after the year in which the wages were paid or the self-employment income was derived. "Year" means calendar year for wages and taxable year for self-employment income. An individual's earnings record can be corrected after this time limit for a number of reasons, including to correct an entry established through fraud; to correct a mechanical, clerical, or other obvious error; or to correct errors in crediting earnings to the wrong person or to the wrong period.

The Social Security Administration must provide individuals, age twenty-five or older, who have a Social Security number and have wages or net self-employment income, with a Social Security account statement upon request. These statements must show: (1) the individual's earnings, (2) an estimate of the individual's contributions to the Social Security program (including a separate estimate for Medicare Part A Hospital Insurance), and (3) an estimate of the individual's current disability and survivor benefits and also future benefits at retirement (including spouse and other family member benefits) and a description of Medicare benefits.

Earnings and benefit estimates statements are automatically mailed on an annual basis to all persons age twenty-five or over who are not yet receiving benefits.

This earnings and benefit estimates statements contain the following information:

(1) The individual's Social Security taxed earnings as shown by Social Security Administration records as of the date selected to receive a statement.

(2) An estimate of the Social Security and Medicare Part A Hospital Insurance taxes paid on the individual's earnings.

(3) The number of credits (i.e., quarters of coverage, not exceeding forty) that the individual has for both Social Security and Medicare Hospital Insurance purposes,

and the number the individual needs to be eligible for Social Security benefits and also for Medicare Hospital Insurance coverage.

(4) A statement as to whether the individual meets the credit (quarters of coverage) requirements for each type of Social Security benefit, and also whether the individual is eligible for Medicare Hospital Insurance coverage.

(5) Estimates of the monthly retirement, disability, dependents' and survivors' insurance benefits potentially payable on the individual's record if he meets the credits (quarters of coverage) requirements. If the individual is age fifty or older, the estimates will include the retirement insurance benefits he could receive at age sixty-two (or his current age if he is already over age sixty-two), at full retirement age (currently age sixty-six to sixty-seven, depending on year of birth) or at the individual's current age if he is already over full retirement age, and at age seventy. If the individual is under age fifty, the Social Security Administration may provide a general description, rather than estimates, of the benefits that are available upon retirement.

(6) A description of the coverage provided under the Medicare program.

(7) A reminder of the right to request a correction in an earnings record.

(8) A remark that an annually updated statement is available upon request.

## 11. What will happen to Social Security benefit payments when the Trust Fund becomes insolvent?

Social Security and disability benefits are financed through the payroll tax. In 2013, the revenue collected by this tax went to pay out benefits that were due. The payroll tax was insufficient to pay out all benefits, so the balance was made up by interest payments due on government bonds held in the Social Security trust funds.

In 2013, the trust funds that help finance both Social Security and disability benefits were projected to run out in 2033, according to the intermediate assumptions of the Office of the Chief Actuary in the Social Security Administration.

If nothing is done to reform Social Security, then it is projected that starting sometime in 2033, beneficiaries will receive only 77 percent of the benefits currently projected as being payable.[1] In other words, the projected payroll tax revenues will be sufficient to pay only 77 percent of the projected benefits.

## 12. Where and how does a person apply for Social Security benefits?

A person can apply for Social Security benefits online at www.ssa.gov, by mail, by telephone, or by visiting one of 1,300 Social Security field offices. The online application for benefits is the

1. *The 2013 Annual Report of the Board of Trustees of the Federal Old-Age and Survivors Insurance and Federal Disability Insurance Trust Funds*, pp 4, 11 (2013).

most efficient way to apply for benefits, and increasingly the Social Security Administration is encouraging people to apply using this method. The Social Security Administration estimates that completing the application online will take only ten to thirty minutes.[1]

Someone who does not live in the United States should consult the Social Security Administration's website resource on International Programs and Resources at www.ssa.gov/international for general information. The Office of International Operations provides online instructions for how to apply for benefits if living overseas at www.ssa.gov/foreign/index.html. A person may also contact a U.S. embassy or consulate for information.

## 13. Which government agency issues a beneficiary's Social Security payment?

Social Security benefit payments are issued, and electronic deposits are made by the Treasury Department – not by program service centers. However, questions about a missing direct deposit should be directed to a Social Security office or by calling 1-800-772-1213 between 7 a.m. and 7 p.m. Monday through Friday.[2]

On March 1, 2013, the government required that all beneficiaries for Social Security or Supplemental Security Income receive payments electronically. Prior to that, a person could have received a check through the mail. The electronic payment must be made either through a direct deposit to a bank account or to a Direct Express® Debit MasterCard® card. The Direct Express® Debit MasterCard® is a prepaid debit card payment option for those who do not have a bank account.

In some limited circumstances, a person can still seek a waiver and receive a check. The Treasury Department provides the following exception:[3]

- Check recipients living in remote areas without sufficient banking infrastructure may apply for a waiver, as well as check recipients for whom electronic payments would impose a hardship due to a mental impairment. Automatic waivers are granted to people born on or before May 1, 1921, and people who qualify for this waiver do not need to submit an application.
- For more information or to request a waiver, call 855-290-1545. You may also print and fill out a waiver form and return it to the address on the form.

## 14. When does a Social Security beneficiary receive a monthly direct deposit?

For persons who started receiving benefits on or before May 1, 1997, Social Security benefits are direct deposited into the specified account on the third day of the month following the month for which the payment is due. For example, payments for January are delivered on February 3rd.

1. https://secure.ssa.gov/iCLM/rib.
2. See https://faq.ssa.gov/ics/support/KBAnswer.asp?questionID=3823&hitOffset=49+48+29+27+6+4&docID=12615
3. See www.fms.treas.gov/godirect/about-faq/index.html#exceptions [0]

If the third day of the month falls on a weekend or federal holiday, deposits are made on the first day preceding the third of the month that is not a Saturday, Sunday, or federal holiday. For example, if the third is a Saturday or Sunday, deposits are made on the preceding Friday.

Persons who began receiving Social Security benefits after May 1, 1997, will be paid on a different monthly schedule than that described above. The payment day will be selected, based on the day of the month on which the insured individual was born. Insured individuals born on the 1st through the 10th of the month will be paid on the second Wednesday of each month. Insured individuals born on the 11th through the 20th of the month will be paid on the third Wednesday of each month. Insured individuals born after the 20th of the month will be paid on the fourth Wednesday of each month. New beneficiaries living in foreign countries will have deposits made on the third day of the month. Note, however, that deposits cannot be made in some countries. See the International Programs section of the Social Security Administration's website at www.socialsecurity.gov/international/payments.html for more information.

If a direct deposit is not made, then report the nonreceipt by calling 1-800-772-1213 (TTY 1-800-325-0778) between 7 a.m. and 7 p.m., Monday through Friday. The following information will be needed to report the nonreceipt: (1) the Social Security claim number on which the benefit is being paid, (2) the period of payment covered by the missing deposit, and (3) the name and account number of the bank where the deposit was to be made.

A change in the direct deposit account to which benefits are deposited should be reported promptly to the Social Security Administration through your online *my Social Security* account, by telephone, or in writing signed by the payee. Promptly reporting a change of in the bank account will avoid having the deposits going to an incorrect or old account.

## 15. To whom is a benefit payment made payable and how are benefits received?

Payment is made direct deposit to a beneficiary's account with a financial institution, or to a representative payee if the beneficiary is incapable of managing finances.

All beneficiaries with accounts in financial institutions will have their benefit checks deposited directly into these accounts instead of mailed to their homes. A financial institution may be a bank, trust company, savings and loan association, or a federal or state chartered credit union. The beneficiary continues to be responsible for notifying the Social Security Administration of any changes that affect eligibility to receive benefits. Beneficiaries without accounts in financial institutions will receive a payment to a Direct Express® Debit MasterCard®. The Direct Express® Debit MasterCard® is a prepaid debit card payment option for those who do not have a bank account.

A minor child (a child under eighteeen years of age) is ordinarily considered incapable of managing benefit payments and a representative payee (usually a parent, close relative, or legal guardian) will be selected to receive payments on the child's behalf.

However, payment will be made directly to a child over eighteen, or to a child under eighteen if there is no indication that the child is immature or unstable and it appears to be in the minor's best interest to make direct payment.

Also, if alcoholism or drug addiction is a contributing factor in determining that an individual is entitled to disability benefits, the benefits must be paid through a representative payee.

For a beneficiary outside the United States direct deposit may be available into a bank or financial institution in the country where they live.

## 16. If a husband and wife are both receiving monthly benefits, do they receive one or two monthly payments?

If a husband and wife have both have worked, they will each be paid their own Social Security benefit by direct deposit to their elected bank account.

However, monthly benefits payable to a husband and wife who are entitled on the same Social Security record and are living at the same address are usually combined in one payment.

## 17. If several children are entitled to benefits, does each child receive a separate payment?

No. Social Security benefit payments for minor children in one family unit are usually combined in one payment. Where the children customarily reside in different households, separate payments will be issued to each family group.

## 18. Can a power of attorney be granted for the purpose of collecting and managing payments?

Yes. If payments are to be deposited in an account at a United States financial institution, completion of SF-1199A (Direct Deposit Sign-Up Form) is required. This form can be obtained on the Social Security Administration's website.[1] If payments are to be directed to a foreign financial institution, Standard Form 233 (Power of Attorney by Individual to a Bank for the collection of checks drawn on the Treasury of the United States) must be completed.

## 19. Can Social Security benefits be assigned?

No. The provision in the Social Security Act (Section 207) prohibiting assignment of benefits or subjecting them to the operations of bankruptcy laws may not be superseded by another law unless the other law does so by express reference to Section 207. Some bankruptcy courts have considered Social Security benefits listed by the debtor to be income for purposes of bankruptcy proceedings and have ordered the Social Security Administration to send all or part of a debtor's benefit payment to the trustee in bankruptcy. Such orders are not appropriate.

## 20. Can Social Security benefits be attached for the beneficiary's debts?

Benefits are not subject to levy, garnishment, or attachment, except in very restricted circumstances, such as by court order for the collection of child support or alimony, or by the Internal Revenue Service for unpaid federal taxes.

1. See http://www.ssa.gov/deposit/1199a.pdf.

A U.S. district court reaffirmed the right of the Internal Revenue Service to seize Social Security benefits to collect overdue taxes. The plaintiff owed the IRS over $100,000. The IRS sent a notice of levy to the Social Security Administration, garnishing the plaintiff's entire Social Security benefit for one month and approximately half of his benefit for each month thereafter. The plaintiff sought reimbursement of the benefit garnished by the IRS and a judgment declaring future benefits exempt from collection. The court ruled that Social Security benefits are subject to levy by the IRS, and that the IRS may garnish the plaintiff's Social Security benefits until his federal income taxes and assessed penalties are paid.[1]

## 21. Are Social Security benefits subject to federal taxes?

Up to one-half of the Social Security benefits received by taxpayers whose incomes exceed certain base amounts are subject to income taxation.[2] The base amounts are $32,000 for married taxpayers filing jointly, $25,000 for unmarried taxpayers, and zero for married taxpayers filing separately who did not live apart for the entire taxable year.[3]

There is an additional tier of taxation based upon a base amount of $44,000 for married taxpayers filing jointly, $34,000 for unmarried taxpayers, and zero for married taxpayers filing separately who did not live apart for the entire taxable year.[4] The maximum percentage of Social Security benefits subject to income tax increases to 85 percent under this second tier of taxation.[5] (The rules listed in the paragraph above continue to apply to taxpayers not meeting these thresholds.)

After the end of the year, Form SSA-1099 (Social Security Benefit Statement) is sent to each beneficiary showing the amount of benefits received. A worksheet (IRS Notice 703) is enclosed for figuring whether any portion of the Social Security benefits received is subject to income tax.

For a detailed explanation of taxation of benefits, see TAXATION OF SOCIAL SECURITY BENEFITS, Q 234 to Q 242.

## 22. What happens when a Social Security overpayment is made to a Social Security beneficiary by mistake?

An overpayment made to a beneficiary is normally recovered from a beneficiary by withholding future payments until the overpayment is paid back.[6] If a beneficiary receives an overpayment, he should contact the Social Security Administration directly as soon as possible to make the SSA aware of the overpayment. If a beneficiary received a notice of overpayment and believes the notice is incorrect, then he should file Form SSA-561, Request for Reconsideration, which is available on the Social Security Administration's website.[7]

1. *Leining v. U.S.*, 97-1 USTC ¶50,254 (D. Conn. 1996).
2. IRC Sec. 86.
3. IRC Sec. 86(c)(1).
4. IRC Sec. 86(c)(2).
5. IRC Sec. 86(a)(2).
6. See http://www.ssa.gov/pubs/EN-05-10098.pdf.
7. See www.ssa.gov/online/ssa-632.html.

# RETIREMENT AND DISABILITY BENEFITS

## 23. What Social Security benefits are available for retired or disabled workers and their families?

There are different types of benefits available for workers and their dependents. The following benefits are available for workers and their families while the worker is still alive:

- A monthly Retirement benefit for a retired worker
- A monthly Disability benefit for a disabled worker
- A monthly Spouse's benefit for a retired or disabled worker's spouse if: (1) at least 62 years old, or (2) caring for at least one child (under age 16, or over age 16 and disabled (if disability began before age 22)) of the retired or disabled worker
- A monthly Child's benefit for a retired or disabled worker's child if the child is: (1) under age eighteen, (2) age eighteen and a full-time high school or elementary school student, or (3) age eighteen or over and disabled, if the disability began before age twenty-two

# RETIREMENT BENEFITS

## 24. In general, what requirements must be met to qualify a person for retirement benefits?

An individual is entitled to a retirement benefit if he or she: (1) is fully insured, (2) is at least age sixty-two throughout the first month of entitlement, and (3) has filed an application for retirement benefits.[1]

## 25. Must a person be fully insured to qualify for retirement benefits?

Yes, however, a small monthly benefit is payable to some men who reached age seventy-two before 1972 and some women who reached age seventy-two before 1970.[2]

## 26. What is the earliest age at which a person can start to receive retirement benefits?

Age sixty-two. A retired worker who is fully insured can elect to start receiving a reduced benefit at any time between ages sixty-two[3] and full retirement age (which is gradually increasing from sixty-five to sixty-seven; see Q 5 and subsequent explanation) when he would receive the full benefit rate. A person is not required to be completely retired to receive retirement benefits. A person is considered "retired" if the retirement test is met. (See LOSS OF BENEFITS BECAUSE OF "EXCESS" EARNINGS, Q 223 to Q 233.)

1. 42 U.S.C. 402(a).
2. 42 U.S.C. 428.
3. 42 U.S.C. 402(a)(2).

The retirement age when unreduced benefits are available (previously age sxty-five) increased by two months per year for workers reaching age sixty-two in 2000-2005. It is age sixty-six for workers reaching age sixty-two in 2006-2016. It will increase again by two months per year for workers reaching age sixty-two in 2017-2022. Finally, the retirement age will be age sixty-seven for workers reaching age sixty-two after 2022 (i.e., reaching age sixty-seven in 2027).[1] See Q 181 for more detailed information about the increase in the full retirement age.

The full retirement age for spouse's benefits (also previously age sixty-five) moves upward in exactly the same way as that for workers. The full retirement age for widow(er)'s benefits also rises but in a slightly different manner (beginning for widow(er)s who attain age sixty in 2000 and reaching a full retirement age of sixty-seven in 2029).

Reduced benefits will continue to be available at age sixty-two, but the reduction factors are revised so that there is a further reduction of up to a maximum of 30 percent for workers entitled at age sixty-two after the retirement age is increased to age sixty-seven (rather than only 20 percent for entitlement at age sixty-two under previous law). See Q 183.

## 27. Must a person file an application for retirement benefits?

Yes. A person can file an application within three months before the first month in which he becomes entitled to benefits. The earliest date for filing would be three months before the month of attaining age sixty-two.

As evidence of age, a claimant must ordinarily submit one or more of the following: birth certificate; church record of birth or baptism; Census Bureau notification of registration of birth; hospital birth record; physician's birth record; family Bible; naturalization record; immigration record; military record; passport; school record; vaccination record; insurance policy; labor union or fraternal record; marriage record; other evidence of probative value.

If a person is receiving Social Security disability benefits for the month before the month he reaches full retirement age, no application is required; the disability benefit ends and the retirement benefit begins automatically. For an explanation of how to file for benefits, see FILING FOR BENEFITS, Q 146 to Q 159.

## 28. What is the amount of a retirement benefit?

A retirement benefit that starts at full retirement age (see Q 26) equals the worker's Primary Insurance Amount (PIA).[2] But a worker who elects to have benefits start before full retirement age will receive a monthly benefit equal to only a percentage of the PIA. The PIA will be reduced by 5/9 of 1 percent for each of the first thirty-six months the worker is under full retirement age when payments commence and by 5/12 of 1 percent for each such month in excess of thirty-six. (See Table 10 for reduced retirement benefits.)

As a general rule, a person taking reduced retirement benefits before full retirement age will continue to receive a reduced rate after normal retirement age.

1. 42 U.S.C. 416.
2. 20 CFR §404.201.

An individual can obtain higher retirement benefits by working past full retirement age. See Q 205.

## 29. What is the first month for which a retired person receives a retirement benefit?

A monthly benefit is available to a retired worker when he reaches age sixty-two, provided he is fully insured.

Workers and their spouses (including divorced spouses) do not receive retirement benefits for a month unless they meet the requirements for entitlement throughout the month. The major effect of this provision is to postpone, in the vast majority of cases, entitlement to retirement benefits for persons who claim benefits in the month in which they reach age sixty-two to the next month. Only in the case of a person who attains age sixty-two on the first or second day of a month can benefits be paid for the month of attainment of age sixty-two. Note that a person attains his age on the day preceding the anniversary of his birth. For example, if an individual was born on May 2, 1953, he is considered sixty-two years old on May 1, 2015.

Most entitlement requirements (other than the entitlement of the worker) affecting young spouses or children of retired or disabled workers are deemed to have occurred as of the first of the month in which they occurred. However, in the case of a child who is born in or after the first month of entitlement of a retired or disabled worker, benefits are not payable for the month of birth (unless born on the first day of the month).

Retroactive benefits are usually prohibited if permanently reduced benefits (as compared with what would be payable for the month the application is filed) would occur in the initial month of eligibility. However, retroactive benefits may be applied for if: (1) with respect to widow(er)'s benefits, the application is for benefits for the month of death of the worker, if filed for in the next month, and (2) retroactive benefits for any month before attaining age sixty are applied for by a disabled widow(er) or disabled surviving divorced spouse.

## 30. Can a person receive retirement benefits regardless of the amount of his wealth or the amount of his retirement income?

Yes, a person is entitled to retirement benefits regardless of how wealthy he is. Also, the amount of retirement income a person receives (e.g. dividends, interest, rents, etc.) is immaterial. A person is subject to loss of benefits only because of excess earnings arising from his personal services (see Q 31 and LOSS OF BENEFITS BECAUSE OF "EXCESS" EARNINGS, Q 223 to Q 233).

## 31. Can a person lose retirement benefits by working?

Yes, a person can lose some or all monthly benefits if she is under the full retirement age (see Q 26) for all of 2015 and his or her earnings for the year exceed $15,720.[1] A person may lose benefits if she reaches full retirement age in 2015 and if she earns over $41,880, but only those earnings earned before the month he or she reaches full retirement age count towards the

1. See 42 U.S.C. 403.

$41,880 limit. The amount of loss depends on the amount of earnings in excess of these earnings limits. In no case will a person lose benefits for earnings earned after reaching full retirement age. For the initial year of retirement of a person who is under the full retirement age for all of 2015, the monthly earnings limit is $1,310. For purposes of this test, "earnings" include not only earnings in covered employment, but also earnings in noncovered employment in the United States. As to noncovered employment outside the United States, benefits are lost for any month before reaching full retirement age when so employed for more than forty-five hours, regardless of the amount of earnings. It should be noted that benefits are not truly "lost" as benefits at full retirement age will be increased to account for benefits withheld due to later earnings.

The dollar exempt amounts mentioned above will be increased automatically after 2014 as wage levels rise. (See LOSS OF BENEFITS BECAUSE OF "EXCESS" EARNINGS, Q 223 through Q 233.) See Q 183 for a discussion of the increase in the full retirement age.

### 32. When do retirement benefits end?

Retirement benefits end at the worker's death. No retirement benefit is paid for the month of death.

## DISABILITY BENEFITS

### 33. In general, what requirements must be met to qualify a person for disability benefits?

A worker is entitled to disability benefits if he: (1) is insured for disability benefits; (2) is under age sixty-five; (3) has been disabled for twelve months, or is expected to be disabled for at least twelve months, or has a disability that is expected to result in death; (4) has filed application for disability benefits; and (5) has completed a five-month waiting period or is exempted from this requirement.[1]

Determinations of disability are generally made by Disability Determination Services (DDS), which are agencies of each individual state. The Social Security Administration makes disability insurance determinations for persons living outside the United States (and for a few other applicants whose cases are specifically excluded from the federal-state regulations). Disability claims and supporting evidence are sent to the DDS located in the state where the claimant resides. The evaluation team makes every reasonable effort to obtain medical evidence from the claimant's treating sources. This team is composed of a medical consultant and a lay disability evaluation specialist, and is responsible for making the disability determination.

The Social Security Administration's Office of Program and Integrity Reviews may reverse a DDS finding that no disability exists, or, on the basis of evidence in the folder, reverse an allowance of disability.

The claimant may request a reconsideration of the claim and submit new evidence, if available. A reconsideration determination as to disability is generally handled by the DDS that

1. 42 U.S.C. 423.

made the original determination, and is reviewed by a special group in the Office of Disability Operations. In a further appealed case, an administrative law judge or the Appeals Council of the Office of Hearings and Appeals may issue an independent decision.

The Social Security Administration uses a multi-step process to determine whether someone is eligible for disability benefits. These steps are as follows:

**Step 1**: Is the individual engaging in substantial gainful activity? If yes, deny. If no, continue to Step 2.

**Step 2**: Does the individual have a severe medically determinable physical or mental impairment? If no, deny. If yes, continue to Step 3.

**Step 3**: Does the individual have an impairment included in the Listing of Impairments? If yes, allow. If no, continue to Step 4.

**Step 4**: Does the impairment prevent the individual from doing past relevant work? If the individual is able to do work that was done in the past, deny. If not, continue to Step 5.

**Step 5**: Does the impairment prevent the individual from doing any other work? If yes, allow. If no, deny.

See Q 326 for additional information on disability claims.

## 34. What insured status is required for disability benefits?

Generally, a person is insured for disability benefits if he: (1) is fully insured; and (2) has worked under Social Security for at least five of the ten years (twenty-out-of-forty quarters) just before becoming disabled, or if disability begins before age thirty-one but after age twenty-four, for at least one-half of the quarters after reaching age twenty-one and before becoming disabled (but not fewer than six). If a person becomes disabled before the quarter in which he attains age twenty-four, he must have six quarters of coverage in the twelve quarter period ending with the quarter in which the disability began.[1]

However, a person who had a period of disability that began before age thirty-one, who subsequently recovered and then became disabled again at age thirty-one or later, is again insured for disability benefits if he has one quarter of coverage for every two calendar quarters elapsing after age twenty-one and through the quarter in which the later period of disability began (up to a maximum of twenty quarters of coverage out of the last "countable" forty calendar quarters), but excluding from such elapsed quarters any quarters in the previous period of disability which were not quarters of coverage. Quarters acquired during the first period of disability are excluded in counting the "elapsed" quarters, however, and the quarters of coverage must be acquired during the measuring period. This provision provides relief to those workers who could otherwise not get disability benefits because they did not have time following recovery from an earlier disability to work long enough before a second disability to meet the twenty-out-of-forty quarters insured status test.

1. 42 U.S.C. 423(c).

## 35. How disabled must a person be to qualify for disability benefits?

Disability is defined as the inability to engage in any substantial gainful activity by reason of any medically determinable physical or mental impairment, which can be expected to result in death or that has lasted or can be expected to last for a continuous period of not less than twelve months.[1] A person must be not only unable to do his previous work but cannot (considering age, education, and work experience) engage in any other kind of substantial work that exists in the national economy. It is immaterial whether such work exists in the immediate area, or whether a specific job vacancy exists, or whether the worker would be hired if he applied for work.

The worker's impairment or impairments must be the primary reason for his or her inability to engage in substantial gainful activity, although age, education, and work experience are also taken into consideration in determining the worker's ability to do work other than previous work.

The term "substantial gainful activity" is used to describe a level of work activity that is both substantial and gainful. Substantial work activity involves the performance of significant physical or mental duties, or a combination of both, which are productive in nature. Gainful work activity is activity for remuneration or profit, whether or not a profit is realized. For work activity to be substantial it need not necessarily be performed on a full-time basis; work activity performed on a part-time basis may also be substantial.

Illegal activities can constitute substantial gainful activity. For example, tax fraud is an illegal activity that can be both substantial and gainful because of the possibility of significant mental activity and potential gain involved.

Impairments related to the commission of a felony for which the individual is subsequently convicted, or related to confinement in a correctional facility for conviction of a felony, may not be used to establish a disability for Social Security benefits.

## 36. Does blindness qualify a person for disability benefits?

A special definition of "disability" is provided for an individual age fifty-five or over who is blind. Such an individual is disabled for the purpose of disability benefits, if he is unable to engage in substantial gainful activity requiring skills or abilities comparable to those of any gainful activity in which he has previously engaged with some regularity and over a substantial period of time.

A person who is not statutorily blind and is earning (in 2015) more than $1,090 a month (net of impairment-related work expenses) is ordinarily considered to be engaging in substantial gainful activity.

The Social Security Act has established a higher substantial gainful activity amount for statutorily blind individuals. The monthly substantial gainful activity amount for blind individuals is $1,820 (in 2015).

1. 42 U.S.C. 423(d).

Blindness, for Social Security purposes, means either central visual acuity of 20/200 or less in the better eye with the use of a correcting lens, or a limitation in the fields of vision such that the widest diameter of the visual field subtends an angle of twenty degrees or less. However, no benefits will be payable for any month in which the individual engages in substantial gainful activity.

## 37. At what age can a person receive disability benefits?

At any age under the normal retirement age (see Q 26).[1] If a person is receiving disability benefits when he or she reaches normal retirement age, the disability benefit automatically ends and a retirement benefit begins.

## 38. Is there a waiting period for disability benefits?

Yes, there is a full five-month waiting period.[2] Generally, benefits will start with the sixth full month of disability. However, if an application is not made until later, benefits are payable retroactively for up to twelve months, beginning with the first month after the waiting period.

Ordinarily, no benefits are payable for the first five full months of disability. Under some circumstances, however, where the person has had a prior period of disability, benefits will begin with the first full month of disability. Benefits will begin with the first full month of disability if: (1) the new disability arises within five years after the previous one ended; and (2) the new disability is expected to last for at least twelve months, or to result in death.

## 39. When must an application for disability benefits be filed?

An application for disability benefits may be filed before the first month for which the person can be entitled to benefits. An application filed before the first month in which the applicant satisfies the requirements for disability benefits is valid only if the applicant satisfies the requirements at some time before a final decision on his application is made. If the applicant is found to satisfy the requirements, the application is deemed to have been filed in the first month in which he satisfied the requirements. An application for disability benefits may be made retroactively effective for as many as twelve months before the one in which the application is filed. For an explanation of how to file for benefits, see FILING FOR BENEFITS, Q 146 to Q 159.

Social Security disability benefits may be reinstated without a new disability application if, during the fifteen-month period following a trial work period, a person who has not recovered medically no longer engages in substantially gainful activity. (See Q 48.)

## 40. What is the amount of a disability benefit?

The amount of a disabled worker's benefit generally equals his Primary Insurance Amount (PIA), determined as if the worker were at full retirement age and eligible for retirement benefits in the first month of his waiting period.[3]

1. 42 U.S.C. 423(a)(1)(B).
2. 42 U.S.C. 423(c)(2).
3. 42 U.S.C. 423(a)(2).

However, the formula for determining a disabled worker's Average Indexed Monthly Earnings (AIME) and PIA differs from the formula used for a retiring worker. See Primary Insurance Amount, Q 161 to Q 172. There are also different limits on the amount of family benefits that can be paid to a disabled worker and his family. See Maximum Family Benefits, Q 173 to Q 176.

Disability benefits may be reduced before the worker attains full retirement age (see Q 26) to fully or partially offset a workers' compensation benefit or disability benefit under a federal, state, or local public law. This reduction will be made only if the total benefits payable to the worker (and dependents) under both programs exceed the higher of 80 percent of his "average current earnings" before the onset of disability, or the family's total Social Security benefit.

"Average current earnings" is defined as the highest of: (1) the "average monthly wage" used for computing primary insurance amounts for some beneficiaries, even though not used for this particular one; or (2) the average monthly earnings from covered employment during the highest five consecutive years after 1950; or (3) the average monthly earnings based on the one calendar year of highest earnings from covered employment during a period consisting of the year in which disability began and the five preceding years. Note that the "highest earnings" in items (2) and (3) are determined *without* considering the maximum taxable earnings base.

Different factors are used in determining whether there is an offset and the amount of the offset. The factors used are determined by the date the worker first became disabled and the date the worker first became entitled to benefits. For workers who first became disabled after February 1981, and who first became entitled to disability benefits after August 1981, benefits paid as workers' compensation and received under a federal, state, or local public program will be considered in determining the amount of the offset.

Specifically excluded are all VA disability benefits, needs-based benefits, federal benefits based on employment covered for Social Security purposes, and state and local benefits based on covered state and local employment. Private pension or insurance benefits will also not be considered in determining the amount of the offset. The offset of benefits will continue until the worker reaches normal retirement age.

For a worker disabled and receiving benefits prior to the above dates, only benefits paid as workers' compensation are considered in determining the amount of the offset. The offset of benefits stops when the worker reaches age sixty-two (rather than normal retirement age).

The amount of the reduction is the amount by which Social Security benefits plus workers' compensation, and, where applicable, public disability benefits exceeds 80 percent of the average current earnings. The combined payments after the reduction will never be less than the total Social Security benefits were before the reduction. However, the amount of Social Security benefits can fluctuate based on the decrease or increase in the amount of workers' compensation. In addition, the amount of the reduction is adjusted periodically to take into account increases in national earnings levels (as applied to the initially-determined average current earnings), but this adjustment will never decrease the amount of benefits payable on the worker's earnings record.

When a state workers' compensation law, and, where applicable, a federal, state, or local public disability benefit law or plan, *generally* provides for periodic payments but permits a lump-sum settlement, either in the form of a commutation or compromise agreement that discharges the liability of the insurer or the employer, such settlement is a substitute for periodic payments and is subject to the offset provisions. In this situation, the lump sum is prorated to reflect, as accurately as possible, the monthly rate that would have been paid had the lump sum award not been made. Medical and legal expenses incurred by the worker in connection with the workers' compensation/public disability benefit claim may be excluded from computing the offset.

In Oregon, when prorating a lump-sum award or settlement made under Oregon workers' compensation law for a permanent disability, the Social Security Administration will treat the lump sum as a substitute for periodic payments and will calculate the offset rate on a monthly basis by dividing the lump sum by the number of months between the date of the award and the date the worker reaches age sixty-five. However, if a workers' compensation award expressly establishes an offset rate under the Oregon statutory scheme, the Social Security Administration will prorate the lump-sum award according to that expressly stated offset rate.[1]

Workers' compensation payments for loss of bodily function, in addition to wage loss, can be used to offset Social Security disability insurance benefits. In a New Hampshire case, the claimant applied for, and was found entitled to, Social Security disability benefits. However, these benefits were offset because he also received New Hampshire workers' compensation payments, including a permanent impairment lump-sum award. After unsuccessfully appealing his case through administrative channels, the claimant appealed to the district court, claiming that the portion of his lump-sum settlement representing compensation for permanent impairment was not subject to offset. The district court held that permanent impairment payments under workers' compensation were to compensate an individual for loss of bodily function (not loss of wages), and thus could not be used to offset Social Security disability benefits.

The U.S. Court of Appeals for the First Circuit reversed the decision of the district court, holding that, although permanent impairment awards may be paid regardless of any actual loss of wages, the awards were never intended to be a departure from, or an exception to, the wage-loss principle. Permanent impairment benefits under New Hampshire workers' compensation law are for compensable disability under a state workers' compensation law and, therefore, are subject to offset against Social Security disability benefits.[2]

## 41. Is a person entitled to disability benefits regardless of wealth?

Yes, benefits are not payable on a "needs" basis. If a person meets the requirements for entitlement, disability benefits are payable regardless of wealth.

## 42. Can a disabled person receive disability benefits even though his spouse is employed?

Yes, if the person is entitled to benefits based on his own earnings record. Entitlement to benefits as a worker is entirely independent of a spouse's employment.

1. Social Security Acquiescence Ruling 95-2(9).
2. *Davidson v. Sullivan*, 942 F.2d 90 (1st Cir. 1991).

## 43. What is the trial work period?

A trial work period is provided as an incentive for personal rehabilitation efforts for disabled workers, disabled widow(er)s and childhood disability beneficiaries who are still disabled but return to work. It allows them to perform services in as many as nine months (within a sixty-consecutive-month period if nine months of services were not completed before January 1992) without affecting their right to benefits during the trial work period, if their impairment does not improve during this period. (Because benefits will continue for the month the disability is determined to have ceased and the two months after that, benefits may be paid for at least twelve months during which the individual works.)

A person is generally entitled to a trial work period if receiving disability insurance benefits, child's benefits based on disability, or widow(er)'s or surviving divorced spouse's benefits based on disability.

The trial work period begins with the month in which the person becomes entitled to disability insurance benefits, to child's benefits based on disability, or to widow(er)'s or surviving divorced spouse's benefits based on disability. It cannot begin before the month in which the person files an application for benefits. It ends with the close of whichever of the following calendar months is earlier:

1. The ninth month (whether or not the months have been consecutive) in which the person has performed services if that ninth month is prior to January 1992.

2. The ninth month (whether or not the months have been consecutive and whether or not the previous eight months of services were prior to January 1992) in which the person has performed services within a rolling 60-month period if that ninth month is after December 1991.

3. The month in which new evidence, other than evidence relating to any work the person did during the trial work period, shows that the person is not disabled, even though the person has not worked a full nine months. The Social Security Administration may find that the disability has ended at any time during the trial work period if the medical or other evidence shows that the person is no longer disabled.

A person is not entitled to a trial work period if:

1. the person is entitled to a period of disability but not to disability insurance benefits, child's benefits based on disability, or widow(er)'s or surviving divorced spouse's benefits based on disability; or

2. the person performs work demonstrating the ability to engage in substantial gainful activity during any required waiting period for benefits; or

3. the person performs work demonstrating the ability to engage in substantial gainful activity within twelve months of the onset of the impairment(s) that prevented him from performing substantial gainful activity and before the date of the decision awarding him disability benefits; or

4. the person performs work demonstrating the ability to engage in substantial gainful activity at any time after the onset of the impairment(s) that prevented him from engaging in substantial gainful activity but before the month he files his application for disability benefits.

## 44. What is the reentitlement period?

The reentitlement period is an additional period after nine months of trial work during which a person may continue to test his or her ability to work if she has a disabling impairment. A person will not be paid benefits for any month after the second month following the month disability ceased due to substantial gainful activity in this period in which he or she did substantial gainful activity. A person will be paid benefits for months in which he or she did not do substantial gainful activity.

If anyone else is receiving monthly benefits based on a disabled person's earnings record, that individual will not be paid benefits for any month for which the disabled person cannot be paid benefits during the reentitlement period. If a disabled person's benefits are stopped because he or she does substantial gainful activity, the benefits may be started again without a new application and a new determination of disability if the person discontinues doing substantial gainful activity during this period. In determining, for reentitlement benefit purposes, whether a person does substantial gainful activity in a month, the Social Security Administration considers only work in or earnings for that month. It does not consider the average amount of work or earnings over a period of months. See Q 48.

## 45. Can a person become entitled to disability benefits after becoming entitled to some other type of Social Security benefit?

Yes. For example, a person who is receiving a reduced retirement benefit before full retirement age can become entitled to disability benefits. However, the disability benefit is actuarially reduced for the months that the person has already received retirement benefits.

## 46. Will a disabled person lose benefits by refusing to accept rehabilitation services?

Yes, a person will lose the disabled worker's benefit by refusing without good cause to accept vocational rehabilitation services.

Good cause for refusing vocational rehabilitation services exists if, for example, the person is a member of any recognized church or religious sect that teaches reliance solely upon prayer or spiritual means for the treatment of any impairment, and refusal to accept vocational rehabilitation services is based solely on adherence to these teachings.

## 47. What are the special rules for disability benefits when alcoholism or drug addiction is involved?

An individual is not considered disabled if alcoholism or drug addiction is a contributing factor material to the Social Security Administration's determination that the individual is disabled.

A beneficiary who qualifies for disability benefits on a basis other than alcoholism or drug addiction, but is determined by the Social Security Administration to have an alcohol or drug addiction and to be incapable of managing the disability benefits, must have the disability benefit paid to a representative payee. The Social Security Administration must notify the beneficiary that benefits are being deposited to a representative payee because of alcoholism or drug addiction. In addition, the Social Security Administration must refer these individuals to the appropriate state agency administering the state plan for substance abuse treatment services.

The Social Security Administration determines whether drug addiction or alcoholism is a contributing factor material to the determination of disability by evaluating which physical and mental limitations would remain if the disabled person stopped using drugs or alcohol. If the Social Security Administration determines that the disabled person's remaining limitations are not disabling, the Social Security Administration will find that drug addiction or alcoholism is a contributing factor material to the determination of disability and deny disability benefits.

## 48. When do a person's disability benefits end?

The last month of entitlement to a disabled worker's benefit generally is whichever of the following occurs earliest: (1) the second month after the month in which the disability ceases, (2) the month before the month the worker attains full retirement age (at which time benefits are automatically converted to retirement benefits), or (3) the month before the month in which the worker dies.

However, there are certain conditions under which benefits may continue or reentitlement to benefits may be established after disability ceases:

1. *Benefits for persons in vocational rehabilitation programs.* Benefits for disabled and blind workers participating in a vocational rehabilitation program may continue until completion of the program, or for a specified period of time in certain situations where disability ceases prior to completion of the program. This provision applies only to disabled individuals who have medically recovered, who began the vocational rehabilitation program before disability ceased, and for whom the Social Security Administration has determined that continued participation in the vocational rehabilitation program would increase the likelihood of permanent removal from the disability benefit rolls.

2. *Extended period of eligibility for reentitlement to benefits following trial work period.* Individuals who continue to have a disabling impairment receive an extended period of eligibility immediately following the completion of a nine-month trial work period. If disability ceased because of work activity and earnings subsequently fall below the level considered substantial gainful activity within a specified period, benefits may be reinstated without the need for a new application and disability determination. This reentitlement period to disability benefits is thirty-six months. Benefits for the family of the worker are suspended during this period if the worker's benefits are suspended.

*Example 1*. A disabled person completes the trial work period in December 2011. He is then working at the substantial gainful activity level and continues to do so throughout the 36 months following completion of his trial work period and thereafter. The disabled person's termination month is January 2015, which is the 37th month–that is, the first month in which the disabled person performed substantial gainful activity after the 36th month following his trial work period.

*Example 2*. A disabled person completes the trial work period in December 2011 but she is not able to work at the substantial gainful activity level until March 2015, three months after the last month of his reentitlement period. The disabled person's termination month is June 2015 – that is, the third month after the earliest month he or she performed substantial gainful activity.

The Social Security Administration may use a "medical improvement standard" to terminate disability benefits. Benefits can be terminated only if: (1) there is substantial evidence that there has been medical improvement in the individual's impairment or combination of impairments (other than medical improvement which is not related to the person's ability to work), *and* the individual is able to engage in substantial gainful activity (see Q 35); (2) there is substantial evidence demonstrating that, although there is no medical improvement, the person has benefited from advances in medical or vocational therapy or technology related to the ability to work, *and* the person is now able to perform substantial gainful activity; (3) there is substantial evidence that, although there is no medical improvement, the person has benefited from vocational therapy, *and* the beneficiary can now perform substantial gainful activity; (4) there is substantial evidence that, based on new or improved diagnostic techniques or evaluations, the person's impairment or combination of impairments is not as disabling as it was considered to be at the time of the prior determination, and therefore the individual is able to perform substantial gainful activity; (5) there is substantial evidence, either in the file at the original determination or newly obtained, showing that the prior determination was in error; (6) there is substantial evidence that the original decision was obtained by fraud; or (7) if the individual is engaging in substantial gainful activity and fails without good cause to cooperate in the review or follow prescribed treatment or cannot be located.

### 49. Are benefits payable to the family of a disabled worker?

Yes. (See SPOUSE'S BENEFIT and CHILD'S BENEFIT, immediately following.)

## SPOUSE'S BENEFIT

### 50. Is the spouse of a retired or disabled worker entitled to benefits?

Yes, an individual is entitled to spouse's benefits on a worker's Social Security record if:[1]

- the worker is entitled to retirement or disability benefits; and
- the individual has filed an application for spouse's benefits; and
- the spouse is not entitled to a retirement or disability benefit based on a primary insurance amount equal to or larger than one-half of the worker's primary insurance amount; and

1. 42 U.S.C. 402(b), 402(c)

- the spouse is either age sixty-two or over, or has in their care a child under age sixteen, or disabled, who is entitled to benefits on the worker's Social Security record.

The spouse of a worker must also meet *one* of the following conditions: (1) the spouse must have been married to the worker for at least one year just before filing an application for benefits; (2) the spouse must be the natural mother or father of the worker's biological child; (3) the spouse was entitled or potentially entitled to spouse's, widow(er)'s, parent's, or childhood disability benefits in the month before the month of marriage to the worker; or (4) the spouse was entitled or potentially entitled to a widow(er)'s, parent's, or child's (over eighteen) annuity under the Railroad Retirement Act in the month before the month of marriage to the worker. A spouse is "potentially entitled" if he or she meets all the requirements for entitlement other than the filing of an application and attaining the required age.

## 51. In light of the Supreme Court decision regarding same-sex marriage, will Social Security benefits be available to same-sex couples?

The decision by the U.S. Supreme Court in *United States v. Windsor*[1] to invalidate Section 3 of the Defense of Marriage Act (DOMA) has led to federal agencies, including the Social Security Administration (SSA) and Health and Human Services (HHS), implementing policies to allow benefits to same-sex married couples. These benefits would include Social Security spousal benefits as well as benefits for a spouse under the Medicare program. Currently, these same benefits are not available for domestic partnerships or other arrangements that are not considered "marriage."

Both the SSA and HHS have begun taking applications for benefits from same-sex couples and also paying benefits to these couples.

## 52. What is meant by having a child "in care"?

Having a child in care is a basic requirement for spouse's benefits when the spouse is under age sixty-two and for mother's and father's benefits (see Q 77 to Q 90).[2] "In care" means that the mother or father: (1) exercises parental control and responsibility for the welfare and care of a child under age sixteen or mentally incompetent child age sixteen or over, or (2) performs personal services for a disabled mentally competent child age sixteen or over.

## 53. Is the divorced spouse of a retired or disabled worker entitled to a spouse's benefits?

The spouse is entitled to a divorced spouse's benefit on the worker's Social Security record if:[3] (1) the worker is entitled to retirement or disability benefits, (2) the spouse has filed an application for divorced spouse's benefits, (3) the spouse is not entitled to a retirement or disability benefit based on a primary insurance amount that equals or exceeds one-half the worker's primary insurance amount, (4) the spouse is age sixty-two or over, (5) the spouse is not married, and (6) the spouse was married to the worker for at least ten years before the date the divorce became final.

1. 570 U.S. ___ (2013).
2. 42 U.S.C. 402(b)(1)(B), 402(c)(1)(B).
3. 42 U.S.C. 402(b)(1), 402(c)(1).

A divorced spouse who is age sixty-two or over and who has been divorced for at least two years is able to receive benefits based on the earnings of a former spouse who is eligible for retirement benefits, regardless of whether the former spouse has retired or applied for benefits. This two-year waiting period for independent entitlement to divorced spouse's benefits is waived if the worker was entitled to benefits prior to the divorce. A spouse whose divorce took place after the couple had begun to receive retirement benefits, and whose former spouse (the worker) returned to work after the divorce (thus causing a suspension of benefits), will not lose benefits on which he or she had come to depend.

## 54. What is the amount of a spouse's benefit?

If the spouse of a retired or disabled worker is caring for the worker's child under age sixteen or disabled child, the monthly benefit equals half of the worker's PIA, regardless of his age.[1] If the spouse is not caring for a child, monthly benefits starting at full retirement age likewise equal half of the worker's PIA; but if the spouse chooses to start receiving benefits at or after age sixty-two, but before full retirement age, the benefit is reduced. (See Table 10 for spouse's reduced benefits.)

If the spouse chooses to receive, and is paid, a reduced spouse's benefit for months before full retirement age, the spouse is not entitled to the full spouse's benefit rate upon reaching full retirement age. A reduced benefit rate is payable for as long as the spouse remains entitled to spouse's benefits. (But see Q 189, Recomputation of Benefits.)

A spouse will not always receive a spouse's full benefit; under the following circumstances a spouse will receive a smaller amount:

(1) If the total amount of monthly benefits payable on the worker's Social Security account exceeds the Maximum Family Benefit, all benefits (except the worker's benefit) will be reduced proportionately to bring the total within the family maximum limit. (See BENEFIT COMPUTATION, Q 159 to Q 189.)

(2) If a spouse who is not caring for a child elects to start receiving a spouse's benefit at age sixty-two (or at any time between age sixty-two and full retirement age), the benefit will be reduced by 25/36 of 1 percent for each of the first thirty-six months that the spouse is under full retirement age when benefits commence, and by 5/12 of 1 percent for each such month in excess of thirty-six.

(3) If the spouse is entitled to a retirement or disability benefit that is smaller than the spouse's benefit rate, the spouse will receive a spouse's benefit equal to only the difference between the retirement or disability benefit and the full spouse's benefit rate.

(4) The amount of a spouse's monthly benefit is usually reduced if the spouse receives a pension based on his or her own work for a federal, state, or local government that is not covered by Social Security on the last day of such employment. However, the Social Security Protection Act of 2004 generally requires that a person work in a situation covered by Social Security for five years to be exempt from this Government Pension Offset (GPO). See Q 59 for more information on the GPO.

1. 42 U.S.C. 402(b)(2), 402(c)(2).

If a spouse is entitled to a retirement or disability benefit that is larger than the spouse's benefit rate, he or she will receive only the retirement or disability benefit.

## 55. What is the amount of a divorced spouse's benefit?

The amount of a divorced spouse's benefit is the same as a spouse's benefit amount.[1] As a general rule, it will equal half of the beneficiary's former spouse's PIA and will be reduced if he or she elects to start receiving benefits before full retirement age. However, a divorced spouse's benefit is paid independently of other family benefits. In other words, it will not be subject to reduction because of the family maximum limit, and will not be taken into account in figuring the maximum limit for the former spouse's family.

## 56. Must a spouse be dependent upon the worker for support to be eligible for a spouse's benefits?

No, a spouse is entitled to benefits if the worker is receiving benefits and the spouse is otherwise qualified. A spouse need not be dependent upon the worker, and may be independently wealthy.

## 57. May a spouse lose benefits if the worker works or if the spouse works?

Yes, a spouse can lose some or all of his or her monthly benefits if the worker is under the full retirement age for the entire year and earnings exceed $15,720 (in 2015).[2] A spouse may also lose benefits in the year the worker reaches full retirement age if the worker earns over $41,880 (in 2015), but only earnings earned before the month the worker reaches full retirement age count towards the $41,880 limit. Similarly, if the spouse is under full retirement age for the entire year and has earnings of over $15,720 (or earnings of over $41,880 in the year that full retirement age is attained), some or all benefits can be lost. (See LOSS OF BENEFITS BECAUSE OF "EXCESS" EARNINGS, Q 223 to Q 233.) See Q 183 for a discussion of the increase in the full retirement age.

When both the worker and the spouse have earnings in excess of the earnings limitation: (1) 50 percent of the worker's "excess" earnings are charged against the total monthly family benefits if the worker is under the full retirement age, and 33⅓ percent in the year the worker is to reach the full retirement age, and then (2) the spouse's "excess" earnings are charged against his or her own benefits in the same manner, depending upon the age of the spouse, but only to the extent that those benefits have not already been charged with the worker's excess earnings.

> *Example.* Mr. Smith, age sixty-two on January 1, 2015, is entitled to a monthly retirement benefit of $346, and his wife, also age sixty-two on January 1, 2015, is entitled to a monthly spouse's benefit of $162. Mr. Smith had earnings that were $4,064 in excess of the earnings limitation. His wife had earnings that were $1,620 in excess of the earnings limitation. Mr. Smith's earnings are charged against the total monthly family benefit of $508 ($346 + $162), so neither Mr. Smith nor his wife receives payments for January through April (50 percent of $4,064 = $2,032, and 4 × $508 = $2,032). The wife's excess earnings are charged only against her own benefit of $162. As her benefits for January through April were charged with the worker's excess earnings, the charging of her own earnings cannot begin until May; she thus receives no benefits for May through September (50 percent of $1,620 = $810, and 5 × $162 = $810).

1. 42 U.S.C. 402(b)(2), 402(c)(2).
2. See 42 U.S.C. 403(b)(1).

*Exception*. The excess earnings of the worker do not cause deductions from the benefits of an entitled divorced spouse who has been divorced from the worker at least two years or whose former spouse was entitled to benefits before the divorce.

## 58. When does a spouse's benefit end?

A spouse's benefits end when: (1) the spouse dies; (2) the worker dies (in this case, the spouse will be entitled to widow(er)'s, mother's, or father's benefits); (3) the worker's entitlement to disability benefits ends and he or she is not entitled to retirement benefits (unless the divorced spouse meets the requirements for an independently entitled divorced spouse); (4) the spouse is under age sixty-two and there is no longer a child of the worker under sixteen or disabled who is entitled to child's benefits; (5) the spouse becomes entitled to retirement or disability benefits and his or her PIA is equal to or larger than one-half of the worker's PIA; (6) the spouse and the worker are divorced before the spouse reaches age sixty-two and before the spouse and worker had been married for ten years; or (7) the divorced spouse marries someone other than the worker. However, the divorced spouse's benefit will not be terminated by marriage to an individual entitled to widow(er)'s, mother's, father's or parent's monthly benefits, or to an individual age eighteen or over who is entitled to childhood disability benefits.

A spouse is not entitled to a spouse's benefit for the month in which any of the above events occurs. The last payment will be the payment for the preceding month.

## 59. Will a spouse's benefit be reduced if the spouse is receiving a government pension?

Social Security benefits payable to spouses – including surviving spouses and divorced spouses – are reduced (but not below zero) by two-thirds of the amount of any governmental (federal, state, or local) retirement benefit payable to the spouse based on *his or her own earnings* in employment not covered by Social Security, if that person's last day of employment was not covered by Social Security (but see below for SSPA 2004). Thus, for the affected group, the spouse's benefit is reduced two dollars for every three dollars of the government pension.

The Social Security Protection Act of 2004 (SSPA 2004) requires a person to work in covered employment for the last sixty months (instead of one day) of employment to be exempt from the government pension offset (GPO). This change will not apply to someone whose last day of government service was before July 1, 2004. Also, the required sixty months will be reduced for each month of government service that was covered by Social Security before the enactment of SSPA 2004. These reduced months of service must be performed after enactment.

This offset against Social Security benefits did not apply prior to December 1977, or if the individual: (1) met all the requirements for entitlement to Social Security benefits that existed and were applied in January 1977, and (2) received or was eligible to receive a government pension between December 1977 and December 1982. In addition, it does not apply to those first eligible to receive a government pension prior to July 1983 if they also meet the one-half support test.

Generally, federal workers hired before 1984 are part of the Civil Service Retirement System (CSRS) and are not covered by Social Security. Most Federal workers hired after 1983 are covered by the Federal Employees' Retirement System Act of 1986 (FERS), which includes coverage by Social Security. The FERS law provided that employees covered by the CSRS could – from July 1, 1987 to December 31, 1987 – make a one-time election to join FERS (and thereby obtain Social Security coverage). Thus, a CSRS employee who switched to FERS during this period immediately became exempt from the government pension offset. Also, an employee who elected FERS on or before December 31, 1987 is exempt from the government pension offset, even if that person retired from government service before his FERS coverage became effective.

However, federal employees who elect to become covered under FERS during any election period which may occur on or after January 1, 1988, are exempt from the government pension offset only if they have five or more years of federal employment covered by Social Security after January 1, 1988. This rule also applies to certain legislative branch employees who first become covered under FERS on or after January 1, 1988.

Pensions based wholly on service performed as a member of a uniformed service, whether on active or inactive duty, are excluded from the offset.

## CHILD'S BENEFITS (Child of Retired or Disabled Worker)

### 60. Is a child of a retired or disabled parent entitled to Social Security benefits?

Yes, if: (1) the parent is entitled to retirement or disability benefits; (2) the child is (or was) dependent upon the parent (but see Q 62 to Q 65); (3) the child is under age eighteen, or between the ages of eighteen and nineteen and a full-time elementary or high school student, or eighteen or over and under a disability that began before age twenty-two; (4) the child is unmarried (but see Q 71); and (5) an application for the child's benefit has been filed.

A grandchild or step-grandchild is considered the child of the worker in the following certain circumstances:

1. The grandchild's natural or adoptive parents are deceased or disabled: (1) at the time the worker became entitled to retirement or disability benefits or died, or (2) at the beginning of the worker's period of disability, which continued until the worker became entitled to disability or retirement benefits; or

2. The grandchild was legally adopted by the worker's surviving spouse in an adoption decreed by a court, and the grandchild's natural or adopting parent or stepparent was not living in the same household and making regular contributions to the child's support at the time the insured worker died.

The grandchild or step-grandchild also must be dependent on the insured. (See Q 62.)

An illegitimate child is eligible for child's benefits if the worker: (1) has acknowledged in writing that the child is his or her son or daughter, (2) has been decreed by a court to be the father or mother of the child, (3) has been ordered by a court to contribute to the support of the child because the child is his or her son or daughter, or (4) has been shown to be the child's father or mother by other satisfactory evidence and was living with the child or contributing to the child's support when the child's application is filed (in life cases) or when the worker died (in survivor cases).

## 61. Who is considered a "child" of a retired or disabled worker for benefit purposes?

The term "child" includes the worker's: (1) legitimate child, or any child who would have the right under applicable state law to inherit intestate personal property from the worker as a child; (2) stepchild, under certain circumstances; (3) legally adopted child; (4) illegitimate child, under certain circumstances (see Q 60); and (5) grandchild or step-grandchild, under certain circumstances (see Q 60).

A stepchild-stepparent relationship arises when the worker marries the child's natural parent or marries the child's adopting parent after the adoption. Death of the stepparent does not end the relationship. If the stepparent and the child's natural parent are divorced, the stepparent-stepchild relationship ends. However, in either case, there is no termination of a stepchild's existing established entitlement to child's benefits as a child of a stepparent. A stepchild must have been a stepchild of the parent on whose Social Security record the claim for benefits is filed for at least one year before the day the child's application is filed (if the parent is alive).

## 62. Must a child be dependent upon the worker to qualify for child's benefits?

Yes, a child must be dependent upon the worker to qualify for benefits on the worker's Social Security record. The factors that determine whether a child is dependent upon a worker vary, depending upon whether the worker is the natural parent (see Q 63), the legally adopting parent, the stepparent (see Q 64), or the grandparent (see below).

To be dependent on the worker, a grandchild or step-grandchild must have: (1) begun living with the worker before the grandchild became eighteen years old, and (2) lived with the worker in the United States and received at least one-half support for the worker. The support test is met if the worker provides one-half of the support: (1) for the year before the month the worker became entitled to retirement or disability benefits or died; or (2) if the worker had a period of disability that lasted until he or she became entitled to benefits or died, for the year immediately before the month in which the period of disability began.

## 63. Is a child considered to be dependent upon his father or mother regardless of actual dependency?

A child is deemed to be dependent upon his parent (father or mother). The fact that the parent and child are not living together, or the parent is not contributing to the child's support, is not a factor unless the child has been adopted by another person.

## 64. Under what circumstances is a child considered to be dependent upon a stepparent?

The child is considered dependent upon a stepparent if the stepparent is contributing at least one-half of the child's support, or if the child is living with the stepparent.

## 65. Can a child receive benefits based on one parent's Social Security account even though the other parent is working and furnishing support?

Yes. A good example would be where the child is entitled to benefits due to the death of his or her mother who was a covered worker. The fact that the child's father was supporting him or her would not matter.

## 66. When is a child a full-time elementary or secondary school student?

A child may be eligible for child's benefits if she is a full-time elementary or secondary school student.

A child is a full-time elementary or secondary school student if she attends a school that provides elementary or secondary education as determined under the law of the state or other jurisdiction in which it is located. Participation in the following programs also meets the requirements:

(1) The child is instructed in elementary or secondary education at home in accordance with a home-schooling law of the state or other jurisdiction in which the child resides. Students in these types of situations include a wide range of individuals. For example, home-schooling students may be in that situation for religious reasons or because the parents do not agree with the local school curriculum.

(2) The child is in an independent study elementary or secondary education program in accordance with state law or other jurisdiction in which she resides, which is administered by the local school or school district jurisdiction. Students in independent study programs may include those individuals who cannot take advantage of the traditional school setting, such as hard-to-keep-in-school students (unable to adjust or delinquents), single mothers, or expectant mothers.

A child must be in full-time attendance in a day or evening course of at least thirteen weeks duration and must be carrying a subject load which is considered full-time for day students under the institution's standards and practices. If a child is in a home-schooling program, the child must be carrying a subject load that is considered full-time for day students under standards and practices set by the state or other jurisdiction in which the child resides.

To be considered in full-time attendance, a child's scheduled attendance must be at the rate of at least twenty hours per week. If a child is in an independent study program, the number of hours spent in school attendance are determined by combining the number of hours of attendance at a school facility with the agreed-upon number of hours spent in independent study.

A child may still be considered in full-time attendance if the scheduled rate of attendance is below twenty hours per week if the Social Security Administration finds that:

(1) the school attended does not schedule at least twenty hours per week and going to that particular school is the child's only reasonable alternative; or

(2) the child's medical condition prevents him or her from having scheduled attendance of at least twenty hours per week. To prove that a child's medical condition prevents scheduling twenty hours per week, the Social Security Administration may request that the child provide appropriate medical evidence or a statement from the school.

A child enrolled solely in correspondence courses is not a full-time elementary or secondary school student.

Benefits paid to students age eighteen who attend elementary or secondary schools on a full-time basis end with the last month they are full-time students or, if earlier, the month before the month they become age nineteen.

## 67. Is the disabled child of a retired or disabled worker entitled to benefits past age 22?

Yes, if the disability began before the child reached age twenty-two and continued until the filing date of the application. The definition of "disability" is the same as for a worker applying for disability benefits (see Q 35).

## 68. What is the amount of the benefit for a retired or disabled worker's child?

The child of a retired or disabled worker is entitled to a monthly benefit equal to 50 percent of his parent's PIA. Usually this is an amount equal to one-half of the worker's benefit, but if the worker has elected to receive a reduced retirement benefit before full retirement age (see Q 26), the child's benefit will be based on one-half of his parent's PIA, not on one-half of the reduced benefit. If the worker receives a larger benefit than the PIA due to delayed retirement beyond full retirement age, the child's benefit is still only 50 percent of the PIA.

Although a child's full benefit is equal to one-half his parent's PIA, in many cases the benefit actually paid to a child will be smaller because of the "family maximum" limit. Thus, if the total amount of benefits based on the parent's Social Security account exceeds the family maximum, all benefits (except the worker's benefit) will be reduced to bring the total within the family maximum. (See Q 173, Maximum Family Benefits and Table 11.)

Notice that the benefit for a retired or disabled worker's child is less than the benefit for a deceased worker's child. The child of a deceased worker is entitled to a benefit equal to 75 percent of his deceased parent's PIA (see Q 91, Child's Benefit, Child of Deceased Worker).

## 69. Can a child lose his benefits by working?

Yes, a child can lose some or all of his benefits if he or she works and earns over $15,720 in 2015. (See LOSS OF BENEFITS BECAUSE OF "EXCESS" EARNINGS, Q 223 to Q 233.)

## 70. If the retired or disabled parent loses benefits, will the child lose benefits also?

Yes. For example, if a disabled worker loses his benefits because he refuses to accept rehabilitation services, his child's benefits will be stopped also. Or, if the disabled worker recovers and is no longer entitled to benefits, the child's benefits will end.

## 71. Will a child lose his or her benefits if he or she marries?

Yes, with one exception: a disabled child age eighteen or over will not lose his or her benefits because of marriage to another disabled child age eighteen or over who is receiving child's benefits, or because of marriage to a person entitled to retirement, widow(er)'s, mother's, father's, parent's, disability, or spouse's benefits.

## 72. When does a child's benefit end?

Child's benefits end when: (1) the child dies; (2) the child marries (but not if the child is a disabled child over eighteen and the child marries another Social Security beneficiary); (3) the child's parent is no longer entitled to disability benefits, unless entitlement ended because the insured parent became entitled to retirement benefits or died; or (4) the child reaches age eighteen and is neither under a disability nor a full-time student. Benefits for full-time elementary or secondary school students end when the child reaches age nineteen. Entitlement to childhood disability benefits ends when the child over age eighteen ceases to be under a disability, which began before age twenty-two, unless the child is age eighteen to nineteen and a full-time elementary or secondary school student.

The beneficiary is not entitled to child's insurance benefits for the month in which any of the above events occur, except that a disabled child's benefits will end with the second month following the month in which the child ceases to be under a disability.

Also, if the benefits of a stepchild are based on the wages or self-employment income of a stepparent who is subsequently divorced from the child's natural parent, the stepchild's benefit ends the month after the month in which the divorce becomes final.

A child's benefit may also end if the child is missing. In 1993, the Social Security Administration suspended benefits for a child who disappeared mysteriously and was missing for five years. Further payment of benefits was suspended until the beneficiary's whereabouts and continuing eligibility for benefits were determined.[1]

## 73. If a child is neither disabled nor a full-time elementary or secondary student, when does the benefit end?

When the child reaches age eighteen, unless the child marries before then. The last benefit is the benefit for the month preceding the month when the child reaches age eighteen.

1. Social Security Ruling SSR 93-3.

### 74. Who files application for a child's benefits?

If the child is at least age eighteen and physically and mentally competent, the child must file the application form. Otherwise, an application may be filed on the child's behalf by a legal guardian or by the person (e.g., parent or relative) who is caring for the child. (See FILING FOR BENEFITS, Q 146 to Q 159.)

### 75. Who receives a child's benefits?

A representative payee, such as a parent or relative, will be appointed to receive the child's benefits. However, if the child is over age eighteen and competent, payment will be made directly to the child. Also, if the child is under eighteen, away from home (e.g., in the Army), and is deemed mature enough to handle the benefit, payment may be made directly to the child.

## SURVIVOR'S BENEFITS

### 76. What benefits are payable to the survivors of a deceased insured worker?

- Mother's or Father's benefit (monthly benefit for widow(er), regardless of age, who is caring for at least one child, under sixteen or disabled before age twenty-two, of the deceased worker) – see Q 77 to Q 90.
- Child's benefit (monthly benefit for each child who is: (1) under age eighteen, (2) over age eighteen and disabled before age twenty-two, or (3) under age nineteen and attending a full-time elementary or high school) – see Q 981to Q 103.
- Widow(er)'s benefit (monthly benefit for widow(er), or surviving divorced widow(er), age sixty or older) – see Q 104 to Q 117.
- Disabled Widow(er)'s benefit (monthly benefit for a disabled widow(er), age fifty to sixty) – see Q 118.
- Parent's benefit (monthly benefit for parent age sixty-two or older who was dependent upon deceased worker for support) – see Q 119 to Q 128.
- Lump sum death payment – see Q 129 to Q 131.

## MOTHER'S OR FATHER'S BENEFIT

### 77. Is the surviving spouse of an insured worker entitled to a monthly mother's or father's benefit at any age?

Yes, if caring for a child of the deceased worker under age sixteen or disabled before age twenty-two. Otherwise, a surviving spouse is not eligible for benefits until age sixty (age fifty if disabled).

The surviving spouse of a fully or currently insured worker is entitled to a mother's or father's benefit at any age if: (1) he or she is caring for a child of the deceased worker under age sixteen or disabled before age twenty-two who is entitled to a child's benefit on the deceased worker's account; (2) he or she is not married; (3) he or she is not entitled to widow(er)'s benefits; (4) he or she is not entitled to a retirement benefit based on his or her own work record that is equal to or larger than the amount of the unadjusted mother's or father's benefit; and (5) he or she has filed an application for benefits.

One of the following requirements must also be met: (1) the surviving spouse was married to the deceased worker for at least nine months before the worker died (see exception below); (2) the surviving spouse is the biological parent of the worker's child; (3) the surviving spouse legally adopted the worker's child during their marriage and before the child reached age eighteen; (4) the surviving spouse was married to the worker when they both legally adopted a child under age eighteen; (5) the worker legally adopted the surviving spouse's child during their marriage and before the child reached age eighteen; or (6) the surviving spouse was entitled or potentially entitled to spouse's, widow(er)'s, father's, mother's, parent's, or childhood disability benefits in the month before the month the surviving spouse married the deceased worker.

A surviving spouse is "potentially entitled" if he or she meets all requirements for entitlement, other than the filing of an application and attainment of the required age.

There is an exception to the requirement that the surviving spouse be married to the deceased worker for at least nine months before the worker died. The rule is waived if the worker's death was accidental, or if it occurred in the line of duty while a member of a uniformed service serving on active duty, or if the surviving spouse who was married to the worker at the time of death, was previously married to and divorced from the worker and the previous marriage had lasted nine months. The worker's death is defined as accidental only if the worker received bodily injuries solely through violent, external, and accidental means and, as a direct result of the bodily injuries and independently of all other causes, died within three months after the day the injuries were received. The exception does not apply if, at the time of the marriage, the worker could not reasonably have been expected to live for nine months.

## 78. Can a divorced spouse qualify for a survivor's benefit?

Yes, a person is entitled to mother's or father's benefits as a surviving divorced spouse of a worker who died fully or currently insured if he or she: (1) is the parent of the worker's child, or was married to the worker when either of them adopted the other's child or when both of them adopted a child and the child was then under eighteen; (2) filed an application for these benefits; (3) is not married; (4) is not entitled to a widow(er)'s benefits, or to a retirement benefit that is equal to or larger than the mother's or father's full benefit; and (5) has in care the worker's child who is entitled to child's benefits based on the worker's earnings record. The child must be under age sixteen or disabled.

## 79. Must a worker be fully insured at death to qualify for the mother's or father's benefit?

No; the mother's or father's benefit is payable if the worker was *either* fully or currently insured (See Q 141 to Q 143).

## 80. What is the amount of a mother's or father's benefit?

The amount of a mother's or father's benefit is equal to 75 percent of the deceased spouse's Primary Insurance Amount (PIA). However, because of the "family maximum" limit, the monthly benefit actually received by the surviving spouse may be less. If the total benefits payable on one worker's Social Security account exceed the family maximum, all benefits are reduced proportionately to bring the total within the family maximum. (See Maximum Family Benefits, Q 173.) A surviving divorced mother's or father's benefit is the same amount. However, benefits paid to a divorced mother or father will not be reduced because of the limit on total family benefits, and such benefits are not counted in figuring the total benefits payable to others on the basis of the deceased worker's account.

If the surviving spouse is entitled to a smaller retirement or disability benefit based on his own earnings record, he will receive the benefit based on his own account, and will receive as a mother's or father's benefit only the difference between the mother's or father's benefit rate and the other benefit rate.

## 81. What are the differences between a mother's or father's benefit and a widow(er)'s benefit?

A *mother's or father's* benefit is payable to a surviving spouse at any age, but he or she must be caring for at least one child under age sixteen or a disabled child of the deceased spouse. A *widow(er)'s* benefit is not payable until the surviving spouse reaches age sixty unless the surviving spouse is disabled, in which case benefits may begin at age fifty.

A surviving spouse will qualify for a *mother's or father's* benefit if the deceased spouse was either fully or currently insured at death. However, a surviving spouse will not qualify for a *widow(er)'s* benefit unless the deceased spouse was fully insured at death.

A full *mother's or father's* benefit is equal to only 75 percent of the deceased spouse's PIA. A full *widow(er)'s* benefit (at the full retirement age, see Q 26) is equal to 100 percent of the deceased spouse's PIA.

## 82. Is a mother's or father's benefit payable regardless of the surviving spouse's need?

Yes, if the surviving spouse qualifies (see Q 77), he or she will receive benefits regardless of wealth.

## 83. Can a surviving spouse lose some or all of the benefits by working?

Yes, in 2015, by earning over $15,720 a year if under the full retirement age (see Q 26) for the entire year. In the year the surviving spouse reaches full retirement age, benefits may be lost by earning over $41,880. However, only earnings earned before the month the surviving spouse reaches full retirement age count toward the $41,880 limit. (See LOSS OF BENEFITS BECAUSE OF "EXCESS" EARNINGS, Q 223 to Q 233.) The loss of benefits by a surviving spouse will not cause the children to lose their benefits.

## 84. If the only child in a surviving spouse's care loses benefits by working, will this cause the child's mother or father to lose benefits?

No. (See LOSS OF BENEFITS BECAUSE OF "EXCESS" EARNINGS, Q 223 to Q 233.)

## 85. Must a surviving spouse file application for a mother's or father's benefit?

Yes, unless receiving a spouse's benefit before the worker's death. The application should be filed within six months after the worker's death, because no more than six month's benefit will be paid retroactively.

## 86. When do a mother's or father's benefits begin?

If a surviving spouse qualifies, benefits will begin with a payment for the month in which his or her spouse died (but see Q 85).

## 87. When do a mother's or father's benefits end?

Mother's or father's benefits end when: (1) there is no longer a child of the deceased under age sixteen or disabled in the parent's care; (2) in the case of a surviving divorced father or mother, no natural or legally adopted child of the surviving spouse under age sixteen or disabled is entitled to a child's benefit on the deceased worker's earnings record; (3) the surviving spouse becomes entitled to a widow(er)'s benefit; (4) the surviving spouse dies; (5) the surviving spouse becomes entitled to retirement benefits in an amount equal to or greater than three-fourths of the deceased spouse's PIA; or (6) the surviving spouse marries. However, if the surviving spouse marries a person entitled to retirement, disability, divorced spouse's, widow(er)'s, father's, mother's, parent's, or childhood disability benefits, the marriage has no effect on entitlement (unless marriage is to a child under age eighteen or a full-time student under the age nineteen, in which case both benefits terminate).

If the subsequent marriage ends, the surviving spouse may be reentitled to mother's or father's benefits on the prior deceased spouse's (or former spouse's) earnings record, beginning with the month the subsequent marriage ends.

The surviving spouse can receive no further benefits until he or she becomes entitled to a widow(er)'s benefit at age sixty (or a disabled widow's or widower's benefits at age fifty). The period during which the surviving spouse is entitled to no benefits is known as the *black-out period*. The fact that a child's benefits will continue after age sixteen does not entitle the child's mother or father to a continuation of benefits.

## 88. Will a mother's or father's benefit be reduced if he or she is receiving a government pension?

Social Security benefits payable to spouses – including surviving spouses and divorced spouses – are reduced (but not below zero) by two-thirds of the amount of any governmental (federal, state, or local) retirement benefit payable to the spouse based on *his or her own earnings* in employment not covered by Social Security if that person's last day of employment is not covered by Social Security. Thus, for the affected group, the spouse's benefit is reduced two dollars for every three dollars of the government pension. However, the Social Security Protection Act of 2004 generally requires that a person work in covered employment for five years (instead of one day) to be exempt from this Government Pension Offset (GPO). See Q 59 for more information on the GPO.

This offset against Social Security benefits does not apply if the individual: (1) met all the requirements for entitlement to Social Security benefits that existed and were applied in January 1977, and (2) received or was eligible to receive a government pension between December 1977 and December 1982.

Pensions based wholly on service performed as a member of a uniformed service, whether on active or inactive duty, are excluded from the offset.

### 89. Will a mother's or father's benefits stop when the youngest child (or only child) reaches age sixteen?

Yes (unless the child is disabled and was disabled before age twenty-two), and he or she will not become eligible for widow(er)'s benefits until age sixty. The time when a surviving spouse is not entitled to any Social Security benefits is commonly called the *black-out period*. But if the surviving spouse is caring for a disabled child whose disability began before age twenty-two, mother's or father's benefits will not stop so long as the child continues to be disabled and entitled to a child's benefits. If the surviving spouse is disabled, he or she may qualify for a disabled widow(er)'s benefit at age fifty. (See Q 117.)

### 90. Does a mother or father continue to receive benefits until the youngest child (or only child) is age twenty-two if the child is attending school?

No. A mother's or father's benefits are payable only so long as the child in his or her care is under age sixteen or disabled. See Q 66.

## CHILD'S BENEFIT (Child of Deceased Worker)

### 91. Is a child of a deceased worker entitled to Social Security benefits?

If a worker dies either fully *or* currently insured, each child who meets the relationship requirements is entitled to a child's benefit if: (1) under age eighteen, or over age eighteen and disabled by a disability that began before age twenty-two, or under age nineteen and a full-time elementary or secondary school student; (2) not married; (3) dependent upon the deceased parent; and (4) an application has been filed for benefits.

The Social Security Administration agreed to pay a survivor's benefit to a child who was conceived through artificial insemination after her father's death. An administrative law judge ruled in 1995 that the child was entitled to $700 a month in Social Security child's benefits.

### 92. Must a parent be fully insured at death to qualify the child for a child's benefits?

No, the child is eligible for benefits on the parent's Social Security account, if the parent was either fully or currently insured at death. (See Q 141 to Q 143.)

## 93. Must a child have been dependent upon the deceased parent to be eligible for a child's benefit?

Yes, the child must have been dependent upon the deceased worker.

The factors that determine whether a child is dependent upon a worker vary, depending upon whether the worker is the natural parent, the legally adopting parent, the stepparent, or the grandparent.

A child is "deemed" dependent upon the worker if the child has not been legally adopted by someone other than the worker and: (1) is the legitimate child of the worker, (2) an illegitimate child who would have the right under applicable state law to inherit intestate property from the worker as a child, (3) the child of a void or voidable marriage, (4) the child of an invalid ceremonial marriage, or (5) the legally adopted child of the worker adopted prior to the worker's death.

## 94. Under what circumstances is a child considered dependent upon a grandparent, step-grandparent, great-grandparent, or step great-grandparent?

A child is dependent upon a grandparent, step-grandparent, great-grandparent, or step great-grandparent if the child: (1) began living with the worker before he or she reached age eighteen, and (2) lived with the worker in the United States and received at least one-half support from the worker. The support test is met if the worker provides one-half of the support: (1) for the year before the month the worker died; or (2) if the worker had a period of disability that lasted until he or she became entitled to benefits, for the year immediately before the month in which the period of disability began.

## 95. Under what circumstances is a child considered dependent upon a stepfather or stepmother?

The child is considered dependent upon a stepfather or stepmother if the stepfather or stepmother is contributing at least one-half of the child's support. The child is not required to live with the stepfather or stepmother.

A stepchild must have been the stepchild of the insured worker for at least nine months immediately preceding the day the worker died, unless the worker and the child's natural or adopting parent were previously married, divorced, and then remarried at the time of the worker's death, and the nine-month-duration-of-relationship requirement was met at the time of the divorce. If the death of the worker was accidental or occurred in the line of duty while a member of a uniformed service serving on active duty, the nine-month requirement may be considered satisfied, unless at the time of the marriage, the worker could not have been expected to live for nine months. A child who was not legally adopted by the worker will nevertheless be treated as a legally adopted child if the child was living in the worker's home or receiving at least one-half of his support from the worker at the time of the worker's death, and the child is adopted by the worker's surviving spouse after the worker's death (but only if adoption proceedings were instituted by the worker before his death or adoption by the surviving spouse occurs within two years after the worker's death). However, such a child will not be treated as the worker's legally adopted child if at the time of the worker's death he was receiving regular contributions toward his support from someone other than the worker or the worker's spouse or a public or private welfare organization.

A child is eligible for benefits based on his parent's Social Security earnings record, even if the child was supported by a stepparent when the parent died.

## 96. Can a child receive benefits based on a deceased parent's Social Security account, even though the other parent is still living and supporting the child?

Yes.

## 97. Is a child age eighteen or over entitled to benefits if attending school?

A child may be eligible for child's benefits if she is under age nineteen and a full-time elementary or secondary school student.

Benefits paid to a student age eighteen who attends elementary or secondary schools on a full-time basis end with the last month that the student is a full-time student or, if earlier, the month before the month the student becomes age nineteen.

A child is a full-time elementary or secondary school student if she attends a school that provides elementary or secondary education, as determined under the law of the state or other jurisdiction in which it is located. Participation in one of the following programs also meets the following requirements:

(1) The child is instructed in elementary or secondary education at home in accordance with a home-schooling law of the state or other jurisdiction in which the child resides. Students in these types of situations include a wide range of individuals. For example, home-schooling students may be in that situation for religious reasons or because the parents do not agree with the local school curriculum.

(2) The child is in an independent study elementary or secondary education program in accordance with state law or other jurisdiction in which she resides, which is administered by the local school or school district jurisdiction. Students in independent study programs may include those individuals who cannot take advantage of the traditional school setting, such as hard-to-keep-in-school students (unable to adjust or delinquents), single mothers, or expectant mothers.

A child must be in full-time attendance in a day or evening course of at least thirteen weeks duration and must be carrying a subject load that is considered full-time for day students under the institution's standards and practices. If a child is in a home-schooling program, the child must be carrying a subject load that is considered full-time for day students under standards and practices set by the state or other jurisdiction in which the child resides.

To be considered in full-time attendance, a child's scheduled attendance must be at the rate of at least twenty hours per week. If a child is in an independent study program, the number of hours spent in school attendance are determined by combining the number of hours of attendance at a school facility with the agreed-upon number of hours spent in independent study.

A child may still be considered in full-time attendance if the scheduled rate of attendance is below twenty hours per week if the Social Security Administration finds that:

(1) the school attended does not schedule at least twenty hours per week, and going to that particular school is the child's only reasonable alternative; or

(2) the child's medical condition prevents him or her from having scheduled attendance of at least twenty hours per week. To prove that a child's medical condition prevents scheduling twenty hours per week, the Social Security Administration may request that the child provide appropriate medical evidence or a statement from the school.

A child enrolled solely in correspondence courses is not a full-time elementary or secondary school student.

## 98. What is the amount of the monthly benefit for a child of a deceased worker?

The surviving child's benefit is equal to 75 percent of the deceased parent's primary insurance amount. However, because of the "family maximum" limit, the monthly benefit actually received by the child may be less. If the total amount payable in benefits based on one worker's Social Security account exceeds the "family maximum," all benefits are reduced proportionately to bring the total within the "family maximum." (See Maximum Family Benefits, Q 173 to Q 176.)

A child entitled to benefits based on more than one worker's record will receive the benefit based on the record that provides the highest amount, if the payment does not reduce the benefits of any other individual who is entitled to benefits based on the same earnings record.

## 99. Will a child lose benefits if the child works or the child's parent works?

The child can lose part or all of his benefits if he earns over $15,720 in 2015. However, none of the child's benefits will be lost because his surviving parent works. Also, the child's work will not affect the parent's benefits. (See LOSS OF BENEFITS BECAUSE OF "EXCESS" EARNINGS, Q 223 to Q 233.)

## 100. If a child is entitled to benefits on more than one person's Social Security account, will the child receive both benefits?

No, the child will receive only the higher benefit. (But see Q 187.)

## 101. When does a child's benefit begin?

Ordinarily, the first benefit is payable for the month in which the parent died. However, unless the child was receiving benefits before the parent's death, an application should be filed within six months after death. Benefits will be paid retroactively for not more than six months.

### 102. When does a child's benefit end?

A child's benefit ends: (1) at death, (2) at age eighteen (age nineteen if a full-time elementary or secondary school student), (3) when disability ceases if benefits are received only because the child was disabled before age twenty-two (but further benefits may be available if disability occurs again within seven years after childhood disability benefits terminate), or (4) when married. However, marriage of a disabled child age eighteen or over to another Social Security beneficiary over age eighteen (other than to a person receiving child's benefits under age eighteen or age eighteen as a full-time elementary or secondary school student) will ordinarily not terminate the child's benefits.

The benefits of a childhood disability beneficiary, regardless of sex, continue after the child's spouse is no longer eligible for benefits as a childhood disability beneficiary or disabled worker beneficiary.

The child is not entitled to a payment for the month in which any of the foregoing events occur, but benefits will be continued through the second month after the month that a disabled child's disability ceases.

A child's benefit may end if the child is missing. In 1993, the Social Security Administration suspended benefits for a child who disappeared mysteriously and was missing for five years. Further payment of benefits was suspended until the beneficiary's whereabouts and continuing eligibility for benefits could be determined.[1]

### 103. Will a child's benefits end if the child marries?

Yes, as a general rule. However, marriage of a disabled child over age eighteen to another Social Security beneficiary over age eighteen will ordinarily not terminate the child's benefits (see Q 102).

## WIDOW(ER)'S BENEFIT

### 104. Is the widow(er) of an insured worker entitled to benefits if there are no children in his or her care?

A widow(er) is entitled to a widow(er)'s benefit based on the deceased spouse's earnings if: (1) the widow(er) is age sixty or over, or is at least age fifty but not age sixty and is disabled; (2) the worker died fully insured; (3) the widow(er) is not entitled to a retirement benefit that is equal to or larger than the worker's primary insurance amount; (4) the widow(er) has filed an application for widow(er)'s benefits; and (5) the widow(er) is not married except under special circumstances discussed below.

In addition, *one* of the following conditions must be met: (1) the widow(er) was married to the deceased worker for at least nine months immediately prior to the worker's death (see exceptions below); (2) the widow(er) is the biological mother or father of the worker's child (this requirement is met if a live child was born to the worker and the widow(er), although the child need not still survive); (3) the widow(er) legally adopted the worker's child during

1. Social Security Ruling SSR 93-3.

their marriage and before the child reached age eighteen; (4) the widow(er) was married to the worker when they both legally adopted a child under age eighteen; (5) the worker legally adopted the widow(er)'s child during their marriage and before the child reached age eighteen; or (6) the widow(er) was entitled (or potentially entitled) to spouse's, widow(er)'s, father's (based on the record of a fully insured individual), mother's (based on the record of a fully insured individual), parent's, or childhood disability benefits, or to a widow(er)'s, child's (age eighteen or over) or parent's annuity under the Railroad Retirement Act, in the month before the month the widow(er) married the deceased worker.

A widow(er) is "potentially entitled" if he or she meets all requirements for entitlement, other than filing of an application and attainment of the required age.

The nine-month duration of marriage requirement is waived if the worker's death was accidental or it occurred in the line of duty while a member of a uniformed service serving on active duty, or if the widow(er) who was married to the worker at the time of death, was previously married to and divorced from the worker and the previous marriage had lasted nine months.

The worker's death is "accidental" if he or she received bodily injuries solely through violent, external, and accidental means and, as a direct result, died within three months after the day the injuries were received. The exception to the nine-month duration of marriage requirement does not apply if, at the time of marriage, the worker could not reasonably have been expected to live for nine months.

An application for widow(er)'s benefits is not required if the person was age sixty-five or over and entitled to spouse's benefits for the month immediately preceding the month in which the worker died, or if the person was entitled to mother's or father's benefits for the month immediately preceding the month in which age sixty-five was attained. If an entitled spouse is between ages sixty-two and sixty-five when the worker dies and the spouse is not also entitled to a disability or retirement benefit, the spouse's benefits will automatically be converted to widow(er)'s benefits.

## 105. Must the worker be fully insured at death to qualify the widow(er) for a widow(er)'s benefit?

Yes, the widow(er) will not be entitled to a widow(er)'s benefit at age sixty or over if the worker was only currently insured at death (see Q 81, Q 142, and Q 143).

## 106. Can the divorced spouse of a deceased worker qualify for a widow(er)'s benefit?

A widow(er) is entitled to surviving divorced spouse's benefits on the worker's Social Security record if: (1) the surviving divorced spouse was married to the worker for at least ten years prior to the date the divorce became final; (2) the surviving divorced spouse is age sixty or over, or is at least age fifty but not age sixty and is disabled; (3) the deceased spouse died fully insured; (4) the surviving divorced spouse is not married (but see Q 109 below); (5) the surviving divorced spouse is not entitled to a retirement benefit that is equal to or greater than the deceased worker's primary insurance amount (PIA); and (6) the surviving divorced spouse has filed an application for widow(er)'s benefits.

A surviving divorced spouse meets the ten-year marriage requirement, even if, within the ten-year period, they were divorced, provided they remarried each other no later than the calendar year after the year of the divorce.

## 107. What are the requirements for a divorced spouse to be able to file for spousal benefits from the former spouse?

These requirements include:

1) an application must actually be filed;

2) the marriage must have lasted ten years or longer;

3) if the divorce was less than two years ago, the ex-spouse upon whose record the benefits are being paid must have also filed an application;

4) each party must be at least sixty-two years of age.

## 108. What is the earliest age at which a widow(er) can receive a widow(er)'s benefit?

A widow(er) can elect to start receiving a reduced widow(er)'s benefit at age sixty (see Q 109). A disabled widow(er) can start receiving benefits at age fifty.

## 109. What is the monthly rate of a widow(er)'s benefit?

A widow(er) who is eligible for a widow(er)'s benefit may apply for a reduced benefit at any time between sixty and full retirement age, or may wait until full retirement age to receive a full widow(er)'s benefit. If the widow(er) is full retirement age or older when benefits commence, the monthly benefit is equal to 100 percent of the deceased worker's PIA (the amount the worker would have been entitled to receive upon retirement at full retirement age), plus any additional amount the deceased worker was entitled to because of delayed retirement credits (the delayed retirement credit is discussed at Q 113 and Q 183). If the worker was actually receiving benefits that began before full retirement age, the widow(er) would be entitled to an amount equal to the reduced benefit the worker would have been receiving had he lived (but not less than 82.5 percent of the PIA).

If the widow(er) chooses to receive, and is paid, a reduced widow(er)'s benefit for months before full retirement age, he or she is not entitled to the widow(er)'s full benefit rate upon reaching full retirement age. A reduced benefit is payable for as long as he or she remains entitled to widow(er)'s benefits.

If the widow(er)'s full retirement age is sixty-five, the widow(er)'s benefit is reduced by 19/40 of 1 percent for each month that the widow(er) is under age sixty-five when the benefits commence. A benefit beginning at age sixty will equal 71.5 percent of the deceased worker's PIA. If the widow(er)'s full retirement age is more than sixty-five, the 71.5 percent at age sixty will remain unchanged, but the reduction factor will be different (based on 71.5 percent at age sixty and 100 percent at full retirement age).

The monthly payment amount of a widow(er) who remarries after attaining age sixty is not reduced.

If there are other survivors entitled to benefits based on the deceased worker's earnings record, the widow(er) could receive a smaller benefit because of the family maximum limit. (See Maximum Family Benefits, Q 173 to Q 176, and Table 11.)

If the widow(er) has in care the deceased spouse's child, under sixteen or disabled, who is entitled to child's benefits, for some months while he or she is under sixty-five, his or her widow(er)'s benefits are not reduced for those months below 75 percent of the deceased spouse's PIA.

The surviving divorced spouse's benefit is the same amount as a widow(er)'s benefit. However, it is paid independently of benefits for the former spouse's family. In other words, it is not subject to reduction because of the family maximum limit, and does not affect the family maximum for the former spouse's family.

A widow(er) who files an application for actuarially reduced widow(er)'s benefits in the calendar month following the month his or her spouse died is entitled to one month of retroactive benefit payments.

## 110. How much will a spouse, aged sixty-four, collect when an older spouse dies at age sixty-nine before filing or receiving benefits?

The spouse is eligible for 100 percent of what the deceased was eligible for in the month of death. If the full retirement age benefit was $2,000 and the spouse died at age sixty-eight, the deceased spouse would have earned twenty-four percent delayed retirement credits, then the surviving spouse's benefit is based on $2,000 plus 16 percent. However, if the surviving spouse takes the benefit at age sixty-four, it will be reduced because of age.

## 111. How does remarriage affect a widow(er)'s benefits?

The remarriage of a widow(er) or surviving divorced spouse after age sixty, or the remarriage of a disabled widow(er) or disabled surviving divorced spouse after age fifty and after the date he or she became disabled, will not prevent that individual from becoming entitled to benefits on his or her prior deceased spouse's Social Security record.

A widow(er) or a surviving divorced spouse's remarriage before age sixty will prevent entitlement unless the subsequent marriage ends, whether by death, divorce, or annulment. If the subsequent marriage ends, the widow(er) or surviving divorced spouse may become entitled or reentitled to benefits on the prior deceased spouse's earnings record beginning with the month the subsequent marriage ends.

A widower is entitled to benefits even when remarriage takes place prior to the death of the former spouse.

There is a distinct advantage in being able to receive the widow(er)'s benefit instead of the spouse's benefit. Part or all of a spouse's benefit could be lost if the new spouse is under full retirement age and loses benefits by working and earning more than the Social Security earnings limit. The widow(er)'s benefit, on the other hand, will be unaffected by the new spouse's work.

## 112. If a widow(er) is entitled to a retirement benefit and a widow(er)'s benefit, will the widow(er) receive both benefits?

No, the widow(er) will receive the retirement benefit plus the difference if the widow(er)'s benefit is greater. In other words, the widow(er) will receive only the larger benefit. (See also Reduction in Benefits, Q 181 to Q 185.)

However, it is possible to take a widow(er)'s benefit for a period of time (such as starting at age sixty), and then later apply for a full retirement benefit at full retirement age. It is also possible to take a retirement benefit for a period of time (such as starting at age sixty-two), and then later apply for a full widow(er)'s benefit at the full retirement age.

## 113. How does the delayed retirement credit affect a widow(er)'s benefit?

A widow(er) whose spouse reaches age sixty-five after 2007 receives an increase in benefits equal to 8 percent, for each year (2/3 of 1 percent per month) in which the spouse deferred retirement benefits between age sixty-five and age seventy. For spouses' reaching age sixty-five prior to 2008, the increases per year of deferring retirement were as follows: age sixty-five in 2006-2007, 7.5 percent; age sixty-five in 2004-2005, 7 percent; age sixty-five in 2002-2003, 6.5 percent; age sixty-five in 2000-2001, 6 percent; age sixty-five in 1998-99, 5.5 percent; age sixty-five in 1996-97, 5 percent; age sixty-five in 1994-95, 4.5 percent; age sixty-five in 1992-93, 4.0 percent; age sixty-five in 1990-91, 3.5 percent; age sixty-five in 1982-89, 3 percent; and age sixty-five before 1982, 1 percent.

The delayed retirement credit is based on the year of attainment of age sixty-two (not the year of work), and it can be earned only after full retirement age. (See Q 183 for further information.)

A surviving divorced spouse is entitled to the same increase that had been applied to the benefit of the deceased worker or for which the deceased worker was eligible at the time of death.

## 114. Can a widow(er) lose benefits by working?

Yes. Although benefits are payable regardless of how wealthy the widow(er) is, the widow(er) will lose some or all benefits if she is under the normal retirement age (see Q 26) for the entire year and her earnings exceed $15,720 in 2015. In the year the widow(er) reaches normal retirement age, the widow(er) will lose some or all benefits if her earnings exceed $41,880 in 2015. However, only earnings earned before the month that normal retirement age is reached count towards the $41,880 limit. See LOSS OF BENEFITS BECAUSE OF "EXCESS" EARNINGS, Q 225 to Q 233.

## 115. Will a widow(er)'s benefits be reduced if the widow(er) is receiving a government pension?

Social Security benefits payable to spouses – including surviving spouses and divorced spouses – are reduced (but not below zero) by two-thirds of the amount of any governmental (federal, state, or local) retirement benefit payable to the spouse based on *his or her own earnings* in employment not covered by Social Security if that person's last day of employment was not covered by Social Security. Thus, for the affected group, the spouse's benefit is reduced two dollars for every three dollars of the government pension. However, the Social Security Protection Act of 2004 generally requires that a person work in covered employment for five years to be exempt from this Government Pension Offset (GPO). See Q 59 for more information on the GPO.

This offset against Social Security benefits does not apply if the individual: (1) met all the requirements for entitlement to Social Security benefits that existed and applied in January 1977, and (2) received or was eligible to receive a government pension between December 1977 and December 1982.

Generally, federal workers hired before 1984 are part of the Civil Service Retirement System (CSRS) and are not covered by Social Security. Federal workers hired after 1983 are covered by the Federal Employees' Retirement System Act of 1986 (FERS), which includes Social Security coverage. Legislation provided an opportunity for federal employees covered by CSRS to join FERS in 1987 (and thereby obtain Social Security coverage). Thus, a CSRS employee who switched to FERS during this period immediately became exempt from the government-pension offset.

Federal employees who switch from CSRS to FERS during any election period on or after January 1, 1988, are exempt from the government-pension offset only if they have five or more years of federal employment covered by Social Security beginning January 1, 1988. This rule also applies to certain legislative branch employees who first become covered under FERS on or after January 1, 1988.

Pensions based wholly on service performed as a member of a uniformed service, whether on active or inactive duty, are excluded from the offset.

## 116. How is the effect of public employee pension income on SS benefits calculated?

There are TWO factors that come into play – firstly, the Windfall Elimination Provision – which affects Social Security benefits based upon what you can receive on your own work record because of pensions from a job which did NOT contribute to Social Security. Under the WEP, the Social Security benefit reduction is capped at one-half of the amount of the pension from noncovered employment, which substantially reduces the WEP penalty and prevents the WEP adjustment from falling disproportionately on households in the lowest earnings category. Social Security benefits are based on the worker's average monthly earnings adjusted for inflation. This average is separated into three brackets: The first is 90 percent of the first $816 of a person's average wage. With WEP, the 90 percent can be as low at 40 percent. The fact sheets on WEP and GPO from Social Security provide further reference– Publication Numbers 05-10045 (WEP) and 05-10007 (GPO)

Secondly, the Government Pension Offset (GPO), reduces Social Security benefits paid to spouses or survivors when the spouse or survivor earned a pension from a government job that was not covered by Social Security. The GPO reduction equals two-thirds of the amount of the pension payment from noncovered government work.

## 117. When do widow(er)'s benefits end?

Widow(er)'s benefits end when: (1) the widow(er) dies, or (2) the widow(er) becomes entitled to a retirement benefit which is as large as or larger than the deceased worker's primary insurance amount, or (3) the widow(er)'s disability ceases.

If a widow(er)'s disability ceases, the last month of entitlement is the second month after the month in which the disability ceased, except that entitlement continues if the widow(er) becomes age sixty-five on or before the last day of the third month after the disability ends.

# DISABLED WIDOW(ER)'S BENEFIT

## 118. Is a disabled widow(er) entitled to benefits starting before age sixty?

A disabled widow(er) (or surviving divorced widow(er)) who otherwise qualifies for a widow(er)'s benefit can start receiving a disabled widow(er)'s benefit at any time after attaining age fifty and before attaining age sixty. The monthly benefit will be based on 100 percent of the deceased spouse's PIA, but will be reduced by 28.5 percent so that the benefit equals 71.5 percent of the deceased spouse's PIA at age sixty. The monthly benefit remains at 71.5 percent of the deceased spouse's PIA for disabled widow(er)'s between ages fifty and fifty-nine. Once established, the benefit rate remains the same; it will not be increased when the widow(er) reaches age sixty or full retirement age.

Disabled widow(er)'s benefits are payable to a disabled widow(er) or surviving divorced spouse age fifty to fifty-nine if the individual: (1) meets the definition of disability for disabled workers, (2) became disabled no later than seven years after the month the worker died or seven years after the last month the widow(er) was previously entitled to benefits on the worker's earnings record, (3) has been disabled throughout a waiting period of five consecutive full calendar months, except that no waiting period is required if the widow(er) was previously entitled to disabled widow(er)'s benefits, and (4) meets the nondisability requirements for a surviving spouse or a surviving divorced spouse.

The first month of entitlement to disabled widow(er)'s benefits is the *latest* of the following months: (1) either the sixth consecutive calendar month of disability, where a waiting period is required, or the first full calendar month of disability, if a waiting period is not required; (2) the month the insured spouse died; (3) the twelfth month before the month the widow(er) applied for benefits; or (4) the month the widow(er) attains age fifty.

Widow(er)s must meet the definition of disability used to determine if workers are entitled to disability benefits. In other words, the widow(er) must be unable to engage in any substantial gainful activity by reason of physical or mental impairment. The impairment must be medically determinable and expected to last for at least twelve months or result in death.

If benefits to a widow(er) who is disabled based on drug addiction or alcoholism are terminated after thirty-six months of benefits, that person cannot become entitled again to widow(er)'s benefits if drug addiction or alcoholism is a contributing factor material to the later determination of disability. See Q 47.

# PARENT'S BENEFITS

## 119. Under what circumstances is a deceased worker's parent entitled to benefits?

The parent of a deceased insured person is entitled to a parent's benefit if: (1) the insured person was fully insured at the time of death, (2) the parent files an application for parent's benefits, (3) the parent has reached age sixty-two, (4) the parent is not entitled to a retirement benefit that is equal to or larger than the amount of the unadjusted parent's benefit after any increase to the minimum benefit, (5) the parent was receiving at least one-half support from the insured person, (6) evidence that the support requirement was met has been filed with the Social Security Administration within the appropriate time limit, and (7) the parent has not remarried since the insured person's death.

The support requirement must be met at: (1) the time that the insured person died, or (2) the beginning of a period of disability that was established for the deceased if it continued up until the month in which he or she died. Evidence of support must be filed within the two-year period: (1) after the date of the death of the insured person, if that point is being used; or (2) after the month in which the insured person had filed an application to establish a period of disability, if that point is being used. Evidence of support must be filed within the appropriate period, even though the parent may not be eligible for benefits at that time (e.g., has not reached retirement age). The time limit may be extended for good cause.

The insured provided one-half of a parent's support if: (1) the insured made regular contributions for the parent's ordinary living costs, (2) the amount of these contributions equaled or exceeded one-half of the parent's ordinary living costs, and (3) any income (from sources other than the insured person) for support purposes was one-half or less of the parent's ordinary living costs.

The insured was not providing at least one-half of the parent's support unless the insured had done so for a reasonable period of time. Ordinarily, the Social Security Administration will consider a reasonable period to be the twelve-month period immediately preceding the time when the one-half support requirement must be met.

## 120. Who is a parent for the purpose of receiving a parent's benefit?

One of the following conditions must be met: (1) the parent is a natural parent and would be eligible under the law of the state of the worker's domicile to share in the intestate property of the worker as the worker's father or mother; (2) the parent has legally adopted the insured person before the insured person attained age sixteen; or (3) the person claiming benefits became the deceased's stepparent by a marriage entered into before the deceased had attained age sixteen.

## 121. What is the amount of a parent's monthly benefit?

A parent's benefit is equal to 82.5 percent of the deceased worker's Primary Insurance Amount (PIA), if there is only one eligible parent. If two parents are entitled to benefits, the benefit for each is 75 percent of the worker's PIA. The full benefit is payable at age sixty-two. However, because of the maximum family limit, the monthly benefit actually received by a parent may be less. If total monthly benefits payable on the basis of one worker's earnings record exceeds the family maximum, all benefits are reduced proportionately, to bring the total within the family maximum (see Maximum Family Benefits, Q 173 to Q 176).

### 122. Can a parent receive benefits, even if the worker's widow(er) and children are eligible for benefits?

Yes. (But see Q 123.)

### 123. May benefits payable to a parent reduce the benefits payable to the worker's widow(er) and children?

Yes, because the total amount of monthly benefits based on one worker's Social Security account is limited by a maximum family benefit ceiling. If total benefits computed separately exceed this limit, all benefits are reduced proportionately to bring the total within the family maximum. (See Maximum Family Benefits, Q 173 to Q 176.)

### 124. Is a parent's benefit starting at age sixty-two smaller than one starting at age sixty-five?

No, the full parent's benefit is payable (to a father or mother) at age sixty-two.

### 125. If a person is entitled to a parent's benefit and a retirement benefit, will he receive both full benefits?

If the parent is also eligible for a retired worker's benefit based on his own earnings record, he will receive the retired worker's benefit if it equals or exceeds the parent's benefit. However, he is not compelled to take a reduced retired worker's benefit before full retirement age (see Q 26). He can receive the parent's benefit and then switch to a full retired worker's benefit at full retirement age.

### 126. Can a person lose a parent's benefit by working?

Yes, a person will lose some or all benefits if the person is under normal retirement age for the entire year and his earnings exceed $15,720 in 2015. In the year the person reaches normal retirement age (see Q 31), he will lose some or all benefits if his earnings exceed $41,880 in 2015. However, only earnings earned before the month that he or she reaches normal retirement age count toward the $41,400 limit. (See LOSS OF BENEFITS BECAUSE OF "EXCESS" EARNINGS, Q 223 to Q 233.)

### 127. When do a parent's benefits end?

When the parent dies, marries (but see Q 128), or when the parent becomes entitled to a retirement benefit or disability benefit equal to or larger than the amount of the unadjusted parent's benefit.

### 128. If a parent remarries after the worker's death, will the parent lose benefits?

Yes, unless the marriage is to a person entitled to monthly Social Security benefits as a divorced spouse, widow(er), mother, father, parent, or a disabled child age eighteen or over.

# LUMP-SUM DEATH PAYMENT

## 129. What is the amount of the Social Security lump-sum death payment?

A lump-sum death benefit of $255 is paid upon the death of an insured worker, provided he is survived by a spouse who was living in the same household as the deceased at the time of death, or a spouse or dependent child eligible to receive Social Security benefits for the month of death based on his earnings record.

Also, the lump-sum death benefit is paid to a spouse when the widow(er) and the deceased customarily lived together as husband and wife in the same residence. While temporary separations do not necessarily preclude the Social Security Administration from considering a couple to be living in the same household, extended separations (including most that last six months or more) generally indicate the couple was not living in the same household.

"Living in the same household" requires a male and female living together as husband and wife in the same residence. The couple may be considered to be living in the same household although one of them is temporarily absent from the residence. An absence is considered temporary if:

(1) it was due to service in the United States Armed Forces;

(2) it was six months or less and neither spouse was outside of the United States during this time, and the absence was due to business, employment, or confinement in a hospital, nursing home, other medical institution, or a penal institution;

(3) it was for an extended separation, regardless of the duration, due to the confinement of either spouse in a hospital, nursing home, or other medical institution, if the evidence indicates that the spouses were separated solely for medical reasons and the spouses otherwise would have resided together;

(4) it was based on other circumstances, and it is shown that the spouses could have expected to live together in the near future.

The lump-sum death payment is paid in the following order of priority:

(1) The widow(er) of the deceased wage earner who was living in the same household as the deceased wage earner (or customarily lived together as husband and wife in the same residence) at the time of death

(2) The widow(er) (excluding a divorced spouse) who is eligible for or entitled to benefits based on the deceased wage earner's record for the month of death

(3) Children who are eligible for, or entitled to, benefits based on the deceased wage earner's record for the month of death

If no surviving widow(er) or child as defined above survives, no lump sum is payable.

However, if an otherwise eligible widow(er) dies before making application for the lump-sum death payment or before negotiating the benefit check, the legal representative of the estate of the deceased widow(er) may claim the lump-sum payment. Where the legal representative of the estate is a state or political subdivision of a state, the lump-sum death benefit is not payable.

The lump-sum death benefit is not payable to an otherwise ineligible child of the wage earner after the wage earner's widow, who applied for the benefit, died before it could be paid.[1]

## 130. Is the lump-sum death benefit payable only if the worker was fully insured at death?

No, it is payable if the worker was either fully or currently insured.

## 131. Must an application be made for the lump-sum death benefit?

An application need not be made by the widow(er) if he or she was receiving a spouse's benefit when the insured person died. Otherwise, an application must be filed within two years after the insured person's death unless good cause can be shown why the application was not filed within the two-year period.

1. Social Security Ruling 85-24a, October 1985.

# COVERAGE

## 132. How does someone become qualified for retirement, survivor, and disability benefits under Social Security?

By becoming "insured". Most types of benefits are payable if the person is *fully* insured. Some types of benefits are payable if the person is either *fully* or *currently* insured. A special insured status is required for disability benefits (see Q 144).

A person becomes insured by acquiring a certain number of *quarters of coverage*.

## 133. How does someone obtain a quarter of coverage as an employee?

For 2015, an employee receives one quarter of coverage for each $1,220 of earnings up to a maximum of four quarters.[1]

> *Example*. Mrs. Hall works for two months in 2015 and earns $2,500. She is credited with two quarters of coverage for the year because she receives one quarter of coverage for each $1,220 of earnings, up to a maximum of four. In order to receive four quarters of coverage in 2015, Mrs. Hall would have needed earnings totaling $4,880 ($1,220 x 4 = $4,880).

This method of determining quarters of coverage will also be used for years after 2014, but the measure of earnings ($1,220 in 2015) will automatically increase each year, to take into account increases in average wages.

However, see Q 135 for quarters that cannot be counted as quarters of coverage, regardless of whether the earnings requirement has been met.

## 134. How does someone obtain a quarter of coverage as a self-employed person?

For 2015, a person who is self-employed receives one quarter of coverage for each $1,220 of earnings from self-employment, up to a maximum of four quarters.[2]

Note that earnings from self-employment are gross receipts minus expenses in the business. So if the business suffers a loss or if profits are low for a particular year, the self-employed person could earn less than four quarters of coverage.

> *Example*. Mr. Smith is self-employed. His gross receipts for the year are $50,000, but his expenses for the year are $48,000. Because his earnings from self-employment are only $2,000 he earns only one quarter of coverage. If Mr. Smith had incurred expenses in excess of $48,780 he would not have earned any quarters of coverage ($50,000 – $48,780 = $1,220).

1. See Generally 20 CFR 404.
2. See Generally 20 CFR 404.

## 135. What calendar quarters cannot be counted as quarters of coverage even though the earnings requirement has been met?

A calendar quarter cannot be counted as a quarter of coverage if:

- it begins after the calendar quarter in which the person died;
- it has not started yet;
- it is within a period of disability that is excluded in figuring benefit rights (see BENEFIT COMPUTATION, Q 160 to Q 189). (However, the beginning and ending quarters of a prior disability period may be counted as quarters of coverage if the earnings requirement is met in these quarters.)

*Example*. Mr. Smith dies on June 24, 2015, after having earned $118, 500 (the maximum earnings base for 2015). Normally he would be credited with four quarters of coverage for that year (see Q 133). However, he is credited with only two because the quarters after his death cannot be counted.

# FULLY INSURED

## 136. How does a person become fully insured?

By acquiring a sufficient number of quarters of coverage to meet either of these two tests:[1]

1. A person is fully insured if she has forty quarters of coverage (a total of ten years in covered work). Once a person has acquired forty quarters of coverage, she is fully insured for life, even if he or she spends no further time in covered employment or covered self-employment.

2. A person is fully insured if: (a) she has at least six quarters of coverage; and (b) she has acquired at least as many quarters of coverage as there are years elapsing *after* 1950 (or, if later, after the year in which he or she reaches age twenty-one) and *before* the year in which he or she dies, becomes disabled, or reaches (or will reach) age sixty-two, whichever occurs first. (However, if a year, or any part of a year, fell within an established period of disability, that year need not be counted.) Note that prior to 1975, there is a transition period in effect for men. See Q 138 and Q 141.

The two tests above serve only to determine the *number* of quarters of coverage needed to be fully insured. It is immaterial when these quarters of coverage were acquired (but they can be acquired only after 1936). Also, in applying test No. 2, it is not necessary that the quarters of coverage be acquired during the elapsed period. All quarters of coverage, whether within or outside the elapsed period, are counted to determine whether the person has the required number.

(For method of determining fully insured status for retirement benefits, see Q 137 to Q 140. For method of determining fully insured status for survivors' benefits, see Q 141. For method of determining fully insured status for disability benefits, see Q 144.)

1. 42 U.S.C. 414.

## 137. Must a person be fully insured to qualify for retirement benefits?

Yes, in addition to other requirements (see RETIREMENT AND DISABILITY BENEFITS, Q 23 to Q 131), a person must be fully insured.

## 138. How do you determine the number of quarters of coverage needed for a person to be fully insured for retirement benefits?

Count the number of years *after* 1950 (or, if later, after the year in which the person attained age twenty-one), and *before* attaining age sixty-two. Do not count a year any part of which was in an established period of disability. Generally, this is the minimum number of quarters of coverage a person will need to be fully insured. However, the person must have at least six quarters of coverage to be fully insured, and a person is fully insured in any event if the person has forty or more quarters of coverage.[1]

See APPENDIX A, TABLE 2, for minimum numbers of quarters of coverage needed to be fully insured for retirement benefits.

> *Example 1*. Mr. Jones applies for retirement benefits in 2015; he attained age 62 in 2013. He needs 40 quarters of coverage to be fully insured (there are 40 years between 1972 and 2013, the year he attained age 62).

> *Example 2*. Miss Johnson applies for retirement benefits in 2015, the year she attains age 65. She needs 40 quarters of coverage to be fully insured (there are 40 years between 1971 and 2012, the year she attained age 62).

> *Example 3*. Mr. Jackson was born in 1953 and will be 62 in 2015. Normally, he would need 40 quarters of coverage to be fully insured for retirement benefits. However, Mr. Jackson had a period of disability lasting from August 1989 to February 1991. Therefore, he would need only 37 quarters of coverage to be fully insured for retirement benefits (the three years, 1989-1991, would not be counted in determining the number of quarters of coverage required.)

## 139. Can a person be fully insured for retirement benefits even though not working in covered employment for many years?

Yes. To be fully insured for retirement benefits, a person needs at least as many quarters of coverage as there are years after 1950 (or, if later, the year of the person's twenty-first birthday) and before the year when the person reaches age sixty-two. However, it is immaterial when these quarters of coverage were acquired.

> *Example*. Mrs. Luck was born in 1950. In 2015 (at age 65), she applied for retirement benefits. She needs 40 quarters of coverage to be fully insured (1 quarter of coverage for each year between 1971 and 2012). Mrs. Luck worked in covered employment for 10 years (acquiring 40 quarters of coverage) prior to her 35th birthday in 1985. Mrs. Luck is fully insured – she has the required 40 quarters of coverage.

## 140. Can a person become fully insured after retirement age?

Yes. A person can acquire quarters of coverage after age sixty-two.

1. 42 U.S.C. 414.

## 141. How do you determine the number of quarters of coverage needed for a person to be fully insured at death?

Count the number of years *after* 1950 or, if later, after the year in which the person reached age twenty-one and *before* the year the person dies. (But do not count a year any part of which was in an established period of disability.) A person needs at least this many quarters of coverage to be fully insured at death. However, no person can be fully insured with fewer than six quarters of coverage; and a person is fully insured in any event with forty quarters of coverage.

NOTE: A person born in 1929 reached age twenty-one in 1950. Consequently, for persons born in 1929 or before, count the years after 1950 and before the year of death. For persons born after 1929, see APPENDIX A, TABLE 4 for year of 21st birthday.

*Example 1.* Mr. Smith, who was born in 1953, dies in 2015. He is fully insured if he has 40 quarters of coverage (there are 40 years between 1974, the year he reached age 21, and 2015, the year in which he died, so that the maximum of 40 quarters of coverage applies).

*Example 2.* Mr. Jones, who was born in 1973, dies in 2015. He is fully insured if he has 20 quarters of coverage (there are 20 years between 1994, the year in which he reached age 21, and 2015, the year in which he died).

The above rule applies to persons who die before age sixty-two. If a person dies after reaching age sixty-two, count only the years between 1950 (or the year of attainment of age twenty-one, if later) and age sixty-two.

# CURRENTLY INSURED

## 142. What benefits are payable if a person is only currently insured at death?

Child's benefits, mother's or father's benefits, and the lump-sum death payment. Benefits for a widow(er) age sixty or over, and benefits for a dependent parent, are payable only if the worker was *fully insured* at death.

## 143. When is a person currently insured?

A person is currently insured if he has at least six quarters of coverage during the full thirteen-quarter period ending with the calendar quarter in which he: (1) died, or (2) most recently became entitled to disability benefits, or (3) became entitled to retirement benefits.[1]

The six quarters of coverage need not be consecutive, but they must be acquired *during* the thirteen-quarter period. As insured status is based on quarters of coverage, one can work for as little as two months in two different years and be currently insured. (Calendar quarters, any part of which are in an established prior period of disability, are not counted in figuring the thirteen-quarter period, except that the first and last quarters of the disability period are counted if they are quarters of coverage.)

*Example.* Mrs. Smith, who reached age 21 in 2010, dies in February, 2015. Mrs. Smith had started to work in covered employment on October 1, 2013 and worked until her death. During that period, she acquired nine quarters of coverage (four in 2013, because her earnings in October-December were at least

$4,640; four in 2014, because her earnings in the year were at least $4,800; and one in 2015, because her earnings in January and February were at least $1,220). Mrs. Smith was currently insured at death because she had more than the required six quarters of coverage in the 13-calendar-quarter period.

## INSURED STATUS FOR DISABILITY BENEFITS

### 144. What insured status requirements must be met to qualify a person for disability benefits?

A person is insured for disability benefits if he or she is fully insured (see Q 141) and has at least twenty quarters of coverage during a forty-quarter period ending with the quarter in which the person is determined to be disabled.[1]

In order to meet the twenty-out-of-forty-quarters requirement, the twenty quarters of coverage need not be consecutive, but they must all be acquired during the forty-quarter period. (A quarter any part of which was included in a prior period of disability is not counted as one of the forty quarters, unless it was a quarter of coverage and was either the first or last quarter of the period.) Generally speaking, this requirement is met if the person has worked five years in covered employment or covered self-employment out of the last ten years before disability.

Special insured status is needed by individuals who are disabled before age thirty-one to qualify for disability benefits or to establish a period of disability. The special insured-status requirements are met if, in the quarter that disability is determined to have begun or in a later quarter, a person:

1. Is disabled before the quarter in which age thirty-one is attained, and
2. Has credits in one-half of the quarters, during the period beginning with the quarter after the quarter in which the person attained age twenty-one and ending with the quarter in which the person became disabled.

The credits must be earned in this period. If the number of elapsing quarters is an odd number, the next lower even number is used, and a minimum of six credits is required. If a person became disabled before the quarter in which age twenty-four is attained, the person must have six quarters of coverage in the twelve-quarter period ending with the quarter in which the disability began.

A special insured status can apply to disabled individuals over age thirty-one who had a previous period of disability established prior to the attainment of age thirty-one; had then met, and currently meet, the special insured requirements (as set out above); and who do not currently meet the 20/40 rule or fully insured status requirements.

To qualify for entitlement to disability benefits, fully insured status is required for a person who meets the statutory definition of blindness.

1. 42 U.S.C. 423(c).

If a disability period is established for a person, his or her earnings record is frozen, and the period of disability may be excluded in determining his or her insured status when she becomes eligible for retirement benefits or dies. The disability period may also be excluded in figuring his or her Primary Insurance Amount for benefit purposes (see Computing Benefits). The same insured status is required to qualify a person for a disability "freeze" as is required for disability benefits.

# COMPUTING BENEFITS

## 145. In general, how are Social Security benefits determined?

Benefits payable under the retirement, survivors, and disability benefits program are almost always based on the insured's Social Security earnings since 1950. (Under some circumstances – where an individual has little or no earnings since 1950 – benefits may be computed based on earnings since 1937.)

The wage indexing formula is used to compute benefits if disability, death, or age sixty-two occurs after 1978. (See Q 162).

If disability, death, or age sixty-two occurred before 1979, benefits are determined using the simplified old-start benefit computation method. (See Q 160.)

A transition period took place from 1979 through 1983. A worker who became sixty-two, or a worker who died after reaching age sixty-two during this period, is guaranteed that the method producing the larger benefit will be used.

To be eligible for the guarantee, the worker must: (1) have had income credited for one year prior to 1979, and (2) must not have been disabled prior to 1979.

The transitional guarantee does not apply to disability computations – even if disability occurs after reaching age sixty-two. It does, however, apply to benefits for survivors if the insured becomes sixty-two – then dies – during the transition period. (See Q 177.)

# FILING FOR BENEFITS

## GENERAL INFORMATION

### 146. What procedure should be followed to determine if a person is eligible for Social Security benefits?

An application must be filed for a person to become entitled to benefits, including Medicare, or to establish a period of disability under the retirement, survivors, and disability programs. The easiest and quickest way for most people to apply for benefits is by filling out an application on the Social Security Administration's website, www.ssa.gov. The process normally takes between ten and thirty minutes.

Alternatively, a person can apply by phone, the mail, or by visiting one of the Social Security Administration's 1,400 field offices.[1]

Since a person age sixty-five or older who is entitled to monthly benefits under Social Security or railroad retirement is automatically entitled to Medicare Part A Hospital Insurance and Part B Medical Insurance, no separate application for these is required. However, a person who is *eligible* for monthly Social Security benefits and is at least age sixty-five may apply for Hospital Insurance and Medical Insurance without applying for Social Security benefits. Also, an application is necessary for persons age sixty-five or older who have no Social Security coverage or other entitlement, but who wish to file for Hospital Insurance and Medical Insurance, and who are willing to pay the monthly premiums involved.

Prompt filing of an application is generally advantageous, even if the person is still working. Delay may result in fewer payments, since monthly benefits cannot be paid retroactively in some instances and not for more than twelve months (depending on the situation) before the month in which the application is filed.

A person may be entitled to monthly benefits retroactively for months before the month in which he filed an application for benefits. Retirement and survivor claims may be paid for up to six months retroactively and benefits may be paid in certain cases involving disability up to twelve months retroactively. The claimant is entitled to benefits beginning with the first month in the retroactive period in which all the requirements for entitlement to benefits are met (except for the filing of an application). For example, if a man reaches age sixty-six in March 2015 and is then fully insured but does not file an application for retirement benefits until March 2016, he may be entitled retroactively beginning with the month of September 2015.

Retroactive benefits for months prior to attainment of full retirement age are not payable to a retired worker, a spouse, or a widow(er), if this would result in a permanent reduction of the monthly benefit amount. However, there are exceptions to this rule, which permit payment of retroactive benefits even though it causes an actuarial reduction in benefits. This limitation does not apply if the applicant is a surviving spouse or surviving divorced spouse who is under a disability and could be entitled to retroactive benefits for any month before attaining age sixty.

1. See www.ssa.gov/careers/locations.html#a0=0

A widow(er) or surviving divorced spouse who files an application in the month after the month of the worker's death may be entitled to benefits in the month of his or her death if otherwise eligible in that month.

Regulations issued by the Social Security Administration establish deemed filing dates for applications filed by persons who have received misinformation about eligibility from the Social Security Administration. The Social Security Administration may establish an earlier filing date when there is evidence that the Social Security Administration gave the claimant misinformation, which caused the claimant not to file an application at the appropriate time.

> *Example.* Mr. Smith contacts a Social Security office at age sixty-two to inquire about applying for retirement benefits. He is told by an employee of the Social Security Administration that he must be age sixty-five to be eligible for retirement benefits. This information is incorrect and causes Mr. Smith to delay filing an application for retirement benefits for three years. When he reaches age sixty-five, he contacts the Social Security Administration and is told that he could have received reduced retirement benefits at age sixty-two. After filing an application for retirement benefits, Mr. Smith provides information to show that a Social Security Administration employee provided misinformation, and requests a deemed filing date based on the misinformation he received when he was age sixty-two.

If the Social Security Administration determines that a person failed to apply for monthly benefits because it gave the person incorrect information about eligibility for such benefits, the Social Security Administration will deem an application for such benefits to have been filed with the Social Security Administration on the later of: (1) the date on which the misinformation was provided to the person; or (2) the date on which the person met all of the requirements for entitlement to the benefits, other than the requirement for filing an application for benefits.

Preferred evidence that misinformation was given by the Social Security Administration includes a notice, letter, or other document issued by the Social Security Administration and addressed to the claimant, or the Social Security Administration's record of the claimant's letter, phone call, or visit to an office of the Social Security Administration. In the absence of preferred evidence, the Social Security Administration will consider statements by the claimant about possible misinformation and other evidence. The claimant's statements, however, must be supported by other evidence in order for the Social Security Administration to find that the claimant was given misinformation.

A person may make a claim for benefits based on misinformation at any time. The claim must be in writing and must contain the information that was provided by the Social Security Administration and why this information resulted in the person not filing an application for Social Security benefits.

A person cannot receive more than one full monthly benefit. If eligible for more than one monthly benefit, the amount payable will be equal to the largest one for which the person is eligible.

Each application form is clearly worded to show its scope as an application for one or more types of benefits. For example, the present applications for entitlement to Medicare Part A Hospital Insurance protection, or for monthly Social Security benefits, may be applications for all benefits that a claimant may be entitled to on any Social Security earnings record. The scope of any application may, however, be expanded or restricted, as the claimant desires, if appropriate remarks are added in writing prior to adjudication. The Social Security Administration will use the application to make an *initial determination* regarding the amount of benefits, if any.

## 147. At what time should the survivors of a deceased worker file for survivor's benefits?

An application should be filed immediately in the month of death by or for *each* person who is entitled to a benefit as a survivor of a deceased worker.

An application for the lump-sum death payment must be filed within the two-year period after the worker's death by the person eligible for the lump sum, unless the eligible person is the widow(er) of the deceased worker and was entitled to spouse's benefits for the month before the month in which the worker died. In the latter case, no application for the lump sum is required.

## 148. When should a person file an application for disability benefits?

An application for the establishment of a period of disability may be filed before the first day this period can begin. In these circumstances, the application will be effective if the person actually becomes eligible for the benefit, or for the period of disability, at some time before a final decision on the application is made.

When a person applies for monthly disability benefits, he simultaneously applies for a "disability freeze" (see Q 188).

## 149. When should a person file an application for the lump-sum death payment?

An application for the lump-sum death payment must be filed within a two-year period by the person eligible for the lump sum, unless the eligible person is the widow(er) of the deceased worker and was entitled to spouse's benefits for the month before the month in which the worker died. In the later case, no application for the lump sum is required.

An application filed after the two-year period will be deemed to have been filed within the two-year period if there is good cause for a failure to file the application in time. Good cause means that the claimant did not file the lump-sum death payment application within the time limit because of: (1) circumstances beyond the claimant's control, such as extended illness, communication difficulties, etc.; (2) incorrect or incomplete information given the claimant by the Social Security Administration; (3) efforts to get the evidence to support the claim, not realizing she could file the application within the time limit and submit the supporting evidence later; or (4) unusual or unavoidable circumstances that show that the claimant could not reasonably be expected to have been aware of the need to file the application within a specified period.

# PROOF REQUIRED

## 150. What proofs are required before survivors' and retirement benefits can be paid?

Social Security survivors' and retirement benefits cannot be paid until satisfactory proofs have been furnished. Claimants must prove their identity and that they have met all the requirements to be entitled to the benefits which are being claimed. Evidence usually required to be submitted to the Social Security Administration in claims for monthly benefits is summarized below:

- *Insured person*: evidence of age. If disability is involved, evidence to establish disability.
- *Spouse (sixty-two or over)*: evidence of age and marriage.
- *Spouse under sixty-two (child in care)*: evidence of marriage and child in care.
- *Divorced spouse (sixty-two or over)*: evidence of age, marriage and divorce.
- *Child*: evidence of age, parent-child relationship, dependency or support, school attendance (if eighteen to nineteen years old and not disabled), and death of the worker in survivor claims. If disability is involved, evidence to establish disability.
- *Widow(er) (sixty or over, fifty or over if disabled)*: evidence of age, marriage, and death of worker. If disability is involved, evidence to establish disability.
- *Surviving divorced spouse*: evidence of age, marriage, divorce, and death of worker. If disability is involved, evidence to establish disability.
- *Widow(er) under sixty-two or surviving divorced mother or father (child in care)*: evidence of marriage, divorce (surviving divorced mother or father only), parent-child relationship, child in care, and death of worker.
- *Parent*: evidence of age, parent-child relationship, dependency or support, and death of worker.

## 151. What are acceptable proofs of death?

Evidence of death may consist of:

(1) a certified copy of a public record of death;

(2) a statement of death by the funeral director;

(3) a statement of death by the attending physician or the superintendent, physician, or intern of the institution where the person died;

(4) a certified copy of the coroner's report of death or the verdict of the coroner's jury;

(5) a certified copy of an official report of death or finding of death, made by an agency or department of the United States government that is authorized or required to make such report or finding in the administration of any law of the United States.

Recent court cases have held that a claimant had to show only that the missing person had been absent for seven years, and that the Social Security Administration had the burden of proving that the individual was still alive, or an explanation to account for the individual's absence in a manner consistent with continued life.

Social Security Administration regulations conform with these court cases, by providing that the presumption of death arises when a claimant establishes that an individual has been absent from his residence and not heard from for seven years. Once the presumption arises, the burden then shifts to the Social Security Administration to rebut the presumption, either by presenting evidence that the missing individual is still alive or by providing an explanation to account for the individual's absence in a manner consistent with continued life rather than death.

The regulations also state that the presumption of death can be rebutted by evidence that establishes that the person is still alive or explains the individual's absence in a manner consistent with continued life. Two examples are provided. In one, evidence in a claim for surviving child's benefits showed that the worker had wages posted in his earnings record in the year following his disappearance. It was established that the wages belonged to the worker and were for work done after he was supposed to have disappeared. The presumption of death is rebutted by evidence (wages belonging to the worker) that the worker is still alive. In a second example, evidence showed that the worker left the family home shortly after a woman, whom he had been seeing, also disappeared. The worker phoned his wife a few days after he left home to tell her he was starting a new life in California. The presumption of death is rebutted in this case, because the evidence explains the worker's absence in a manner consistent with continued life.

No one *convicted* of the felonious and intentional homicide of the worker can be entitled to benefits on the worker's earnings record. Further, the convicted person is considered not to exist in deciding the rights of other persons to benefits on the worker's record.

## 152. What are the best forms of proof of age and family relationship?

Proof of age is required when age is a factor in determining benefit rights. A public record of birth or a religious record of birth or baptism established or recorded before the individual's fifth birthday must be submitted as proof of age, if available. Where such a document is unavailable, the individual must submit another document or documents that may serve as the basis for a determination of date or birth, provided the evidence is corroborated by other evidence or by information in the records of the Social Security Administration.

Some records that may be submitted are listed below; these records must show the individual's date of birth or age:

(1) School record

(2) Census record

(3) Bible or other family record

(4) Religious record of confirmation or baptism in youth or early adult life

(5) Insurance policy

(6) Marriage record

(7) Employment record

(8) Labor union record

(9) Fraternal organization record

(10) Military record

(11) Voting record

(12) Vaccination record

(13) Delayed birth certificate

(14) Birth certificate of child, showing age of parent

(15) Physician's or midwife's record of birth

(16) Passport

(17) Immigration record

(18) Naturalization record

A person should obtain, and file among his or her valuable papers, the most acceptable form of proof of the ages and relationships of all members of his or her family. This will save time, effort, and money later, when Social Security benefits become payable.

A natural legitimate parent-child relationship may be shown by the child's birth or baptismal certificate if it shows the worker to be the child's parent. If the child is illegitimate, he or she may be considered the worker's child for Social Security purposes if he or she is legitimated, or can inherit the worker's intestate personal property under applicable state law. The evidence required would depend on state law requirements for legitimation or inheritance rights.

The legal adoption of a child may be provided by an amended birth certificate issued as the result of an adoption.

A step-relationship is proved by: (1) first proving the relationship between the child and the natural (or adopting) parent, and (2) then proving the marriage between the natural (or adopting) parent and the stepparent.

Evidence of full-time school attendance is required if a child age eighteen to nineteen is not under a disability. Necessary information is obtained from the child and verified by the school or schools involved.

A ceremonial marriage may be proved by: (1) a certified copy of the public record of the marriage, (2) a certified copy of the religious record of the marriage, or (3) the original marriage certificate.

Evidence to prove a common-law marriage in those states that recognize such marriages must, where obtainable, include: (1) If the husband and wife are living, a statement from each and a statement from a blood relative of each; (2) If either the husband or wife is dead, a statement from the surviving widow or widower and statements from two blood relatives of the decedent; and (3) If both a husband and wife are dead, a statement from a blood relative of the husband and from a blood relative of the wife.

Evidence of termination of a marriage may be required if the claimant's right to benefits depends upon the validity of a subsequent marriage or the termination of a prior marriage. The termination of a marriage may be established by: (1) a certified copy of the divorce decree; (2) a certified copy of the annulment decree; (3) a certified copy of the death certificate; or (4) if none of the above is available, any other evidence of probative value.

Evidence that a child is in a claimant's care usually consists of: (1) statements by the claimant; (2) where the claimant and the child are living apart, statements by the person with whom the child is living or by an official of the school which the child is attending, or both; and (3) statements of other people who know the facts, if necessary.

Evidence of support includes a statement from the claimant, and whatever other evidence may be necessary to substantiate the claimant's statements concerning support.

Evidence of United States citizenship may be required in certain cases (for instance, to determine coverage status of people working in foreign countries or the applicability of the alien nonpayment provision). The most acceptable evidence is a birth certificate showing birth within the United States. Other acceptable evidence includes: (1) Certificate of Naturalization; (2) Citizenship Certificate issued by the Immigration and Naturalization Service to United States citizens who derived their citizenship through another person; (3) a United States passport issued by the Department of State; (4) Consular report of birth issued by the Department of State; (5) proof of marriage to a male United States citizen before September 22, 1922; (6) a card of identity and registration as a United States citizen, or an official communication from an American Foreign Service post indicating the individual is registered there as a United States citizen; or (7) Form I-197 (United States Citizen Identification Card).

## RIGHT TO APPEAL

### 153. Is there a review procedure available if a person is disappointed with the Social Security Administration's initial determination regarding benefits?

There is an administrative review process for a person who is dissatisfied with the Social Security Administration's action concerning a claim for benefits. After the Social Security Administration makes an initial determination, further review may be requested by the person or his representative. The administrative review process consists of several steps that must be requested in writing, usually within specified time periods, and in the following order:

(1) The person or representative may request that the initial determination be reconsidered. A reconsideration is a reexamination of the administrative records that results in another determination.

(2) If there is still disagreement with the reconsidered determination, the person or representative may request a hearing before an administrative law judge of the Office of Hearings and Appeals.

(3) If the person disagrees with the administrative law judge's decision or dismissal, he may request a review by the Appeals Council of the Office of Hearings and Appeals, which has the authority to deny or grant review or dismiss the request for any reason for which the administrative law judge could have dismissed. Also, the Appeals Council may, on its own motion, review an administrative law judge's decision.

(4) After Appeals Council review (or denial of review), a person who is still dissatisfied may file a civil action in a federal district court.

An initial determination becomes final unless reconsideration is requested within sixty days from the date notice of the initial determination is received by the person or the person's representative.

Reconsideration is the first step in the administrative review process that is provided if there is dissatisfaction with the initial determination. The request for reconsideration may be made by the claimant, by another person whose benefit rights are affected by the determination, or by the appointed representative of either. The reconsideration must be requested in writing by the person (or the person's representative).

The reconsideration process is an independent reexamination of all evidence on record related to the case by the Social Security Administration. It is based on evidence submitted for the initial determination, plus any additional information that the claimant or representative may submit in connection with the reconsideration. The reconsideration is not limited to the issues raised by the claimant. A reconsideration is made by a member of a different staff from the one that made the initial determination and who is specially trained in the handling of reconsiderations. The claimant receives a personalized notice detailing the basis for the determination in his case.

When a person can demonstrate that he failed to appeal an adverse decision because of reliance on incorrect, incomplete, or misleading information provided by the Social Security Administration, his failure to appeal may not serve as the basis for denial of a second application for any Social Security benefit. This protection applies to both initial denials and reconsiderations. The Social Security Administration is required to include, in all notices of denial, a clear, simple description on the effect of reapplying for benefits rather than filing an appeal.

The Social Security Administration issued a ruling in 1995 on establishing good cause for late filing of a request for administrative review, for a claimant who received an initial or reconsideration determination notice that did not state that filing a new application instead of a request for administrative review could result in the loss of benefits. The Social Security Administration will make a finding of good cause for late filing of a request for administrative review for a claim, if the claimant received an initial or reconsideration determination notice and demonstrates that, as a result of the notice, he did not timely request such review. Notices covered by this ruling include only those dated prior to July 1, 1991, that did not state that filing a new application for benefits instead of a request for review could result in the loss of benefits. If the adjudicator determines that good cause exists, the Social Security Administration will extend the time for requesting administrative review and take the action that would have been appropriate had the claimant filed a timely request for administrative review.[1]

## 154. How can a person appeal the reconsideration determination?

A hearing before an administrative law judge may be requested by the person or appointed representative who disagrees with the reconsidered determination, or by a person who can show that the reconsidered determination will harm the person's rights under the Social Security Act.

The person and/or person's representative may appear in person, submit new evidence, examine the evidence used in making the determination under review, give testimony, and present and question witnesses. If a person properly waives the right to an oral hearing, the administrative law judge will ordinarily make a decision on the basis of the evidence already submitted or otherwise obtained by the person or any other party to the hearing.

If the claim is about the amount of Part A Hospital Insurance benefits under Medicare, the amount in question must be $100 or more. Carriers review complaints about the amount of Medical Insurance benefits under Medicare.

A person may also be able to use an expedited appeals procedure, if he or she has no dispute with the findings of fact of the reconsideration determination beyond a contention that a section of the applicable statute is unconstitutional. (For further details, see Q 157.)

Notice of time and place of the hearing is sent by the administrative law judge to the parties to the hearing at least twenty days before the date set for the hearing. The hearing is usually held in the area where the person requesting the hearing resides, although the person may be required to travel up to seventy-five miles. (Travel expenses are paid by the government, if travel over seventy-five miles is required.)

At times, the administrative law judge will examine the evidence and certify a case to the Appeals Council with a recommended decision. (See Q 157.)

## 155. How is a hearing request made and how long will it take from the request to the actual hearing?

A request for a hearing is made by filling out Form HA-501, "Request for Hearing," or by writing a letter to the nearest Social Security office, a presiding officer, or with the Appeals Council. If the hearing request is for disability benefits, then the appeal may be made online.

The request for a hearing must be made within sixty days after the date that the notice of the reconsidered decision is received and must include: (1) the name and Social Security number of the individual; (2) the reason for disagreeing with the reconsidered or revised determination; (3) a statement of additional evidence that will be submitted; and (4) the name and address of the individual's representative, if any. The sixty-day time limit can be extended if there is a good reason.

1. Social Security Ruling SSR 95-1p.

A beneficiary of disability benefits has the option of having his benefits continued through the hearing stage of appeal if there was a determination of medical improvement (also called medical cessation). But where benefits are adversely affected because of the performance of substantial gainful activity (also called work cessation) benefits may not be continued. If the earlier unfavorable determinations are upheld by the administrative law judge, the benefits that were received during the appeal process are subject to recovery by the Social Security Administration. (If an appeal is made in good faith, recovery may be waived.) Medicare eligibility is also continued, but Medicare benefits are not subject to recovery.

In recent years, the Social Security Administration has come under criticism for its backlog of hearings. In the 2008 fiscal year, the average processing time was 514 days. Since that time, the Social Security Administration has devoted efforts to steadily decrease the processing time 31 percent so that it was 353 days at the end of the 2012 fiscal year. However, by late June in the 2013 fiscal year, the processing time had increased to an average of 378 days.[1]

## 156. What will a hearing cost?

There is no charge for a hearing. Of course, if a person is represented by a lawyer, he or she must pay that fee. A person must also pay for all travel expenses, unless the hearing is held more than seventy-five miles from home. If this happens, a person is reimbursed for reasonable travel expenses.

## 157. If a person disagrees with the hearing decision, may he ask for a review?

Yes. A review of the hearing by the Appeals Council of the Office of Hearings and Appeals must be in writing and must be filed within sixty days from the date the person or the person's representative receives notice of the administrative law judge's action.

Within sixty days from the date of the administrative law judge's decision or dismissal, the Appeals Council may on its own initiative decide to review the action that was taken. Notice of this review is mailed to all parties at the last known address.

The Appeals Council will review a hearing decision or dismissal where: (1) there appears to be an abuse of discretion by the administrative law judge; (2) there is an error of law; (3) the presiding officer's action, findings, or conclusions are not supported by substantial evidence; or (4) there is a broad policy or procedural issue that may affect the general public interest.

The Appeals Council will notify the person whether it will review the case. If the Appeals Council decides to review the case, the claimant or representative may request an appearance before the Appeals Council for the presentation of oral arguments. If the Appeals Council determines that a significant question of law or policy is presented, or that oral arguments would be beneficial in rendering a proper decision, the appearance will be granted. The claimant may also

1. See http://oig.ssa.gov/audits-and-investigations/top-ssa-management-issues/social-security-disability-hearings-backlog. See also www.ssa.gov/appeals

file written statements in support of his claim. The Appeals Council will notify the claimant of its action in the case.

The Appeals Council may deny or dismiss a party's request for review, or it may grant the request and either issue a decision or remand the case to an administrative law judge. If the Appeals Council denies a request for review of a decision by an administrative law judge, the administrative law judge's decision becomes a final decision of the Social Security Administration, subject to judicial review (except when judicial review is precluded in certain Medicare cases). If the Appeals Council grants a request for review and issues a decision, that decision also becomes a final decision of the Social Security Administration, subject to judicial review except in certain Medicare cases.

If an administrative law judge makes a decision in favor of a person in a disability case and the Appeals Council does not render a final decision within 110 days, interim disability benefits are provided to the person. (Delays in excess of twenty days caused by or on behalf of the claimant do not count in determining the 110-day period.) These benefits begin with the month before the month in which the 110-day period expires, and are not considered overpayments if the final decision is adverse, unless the benefits are fraudulently obtained.

## 158. May a person file a civil action in the United States District Court?

Yes, a person dissatisfied with the decision of the Appeals Council or denial of the request for review of the administrative law judge's decision by the Appeals Council may bring suit in a federal district court. To file a civil action regarding the amount of Part A Hospital Insurance benefits under Medicare, however, the amount in question must be $1,000 or more. The Social Security Act does not provide for court review of a determination concerning the amount of benefits payable under Medicare Part B Medical Insurance.

The civil action in the court must be filed within sixty days from the date notice of the Appeals Council decision or denial of the request for review is received by the person or appointed representative. This time limit may be extended by the Appeals Council for good reason.

The court may issue a decision on the record or remand for further development. There is no right to court action where the Appeals Council has dismissed a request for review, or denied a request for review of an administrative law judge's dismissal.

A person may be able to advance directly from a reconsideration determination to a federal district court by filing a claim contending that the applicable statute of the Social Security Act is unconstitutional. This procedure, known as expedited appeals process, is allowable when: (1) the individual has presented a claim at the reconsideration level, (2) the only issue is the constitutionality of the statutory requirement, (3) the claim is neither invalid or cognizable under a different section of the Social Security Act, and (4) the amount in controversy is $1,000 or more.

In order to reach a federal district court after a reconsideration determination, the Social Security Administration must determine that the claim raises a constitutional question and is appropriate for treatment under the expedited appeals procedure. After this is done, the Social Security Administration and the person must sign an agreement that identifies the constitutional issue involved and explains the final reconsideration determination.

A person must file for expedited judicial review within sixty days after the date of receipt of notice of the reconsideration determination. An extension of time is available if good cause is established for not filing on time.

Should the Social Security Administration determine that a claim is not appropriate for expedited judicial review before a federal district court, its decision is final and not subject to administrative or judicial review. It is required, however, to notify the person filing the claim of its decision, and to treat the person's request as a request for a reconsideration, a hearing, or an Appeals Council review (whichever is appropriate).

The Supreme Court has held that the Social Security Act does not permit a person to have subject-matter jurisdiction to the federal district courts to review a decision of the Social Security Administration not to reopen a previously adjudicated claim for Social Security benefits. The Court found that, unless the claim was based on a constitutional challenge, the Act did not authorize judicial review to reopen a final decision on disability benefits after the sixty-day limit for a review by civil action had terminated.[1]

## 159. Are there situations where the Social Security Administration may not recover an overpayment to a beneficiary?

Yes, the Social Security Administration is barred from recovering an overpayment if recovery is "against equity and good conscience." According to the Social Security regulations, recovery of an overpayment is "against equity and good conscience" under three conditions: (1) if the beneficiary has changed his or her position for the worse, (2) if the beneficiary relinquished a valuable right because of reliance upon a notice that a payment would be made or because of the overpayment itself, or (3) if the beneficiary was living in a separate household from the overpaid person or the eligible spouse, and did not receive the overpayment.

The Ninth Circuit Court of Appeals has broadened the definition of "against equity and good conscience."[2] The case involved a former inmate who had been in prison from 1963 to 1985 on a felony conviction, and who had been receiving Social Security disability benefits while in prison. Although the Social Security Act was amended in 1980 to prohibit payment of disability benefits to certain incarcerated felons, he continued to receive benefits until 1982 and was unaware of the change in the law. After learning about the change in the law, the inmate informed the Social Security Administration of his situation. The Social Security Administration requested repayment. The inmate requested a waiver of recovery for the overpayment; a personal conference with a government representative was held in 1984, but no decision was issued at that time. The inmate was released from prison in 1985 and spent his overpayment.

1. *Califano v. Sanders*, 430 U.S. 99 (1977).
2. *Quinlivan v. Sullivan*, 916 F.2nd 524 (9th Cir. 1990).

The Ninth Circuit held that requiring the former inmate to repay the overpayment was against equity and good conscience because Congress intended a broad concept of fairness to apply to waiver requests, one that takes into account the facts and circumstances of each case. The court noted that the former inmate had no material goods, no means of transportation, no income, and had only worked in a few temporary jobs. Also, the court pointed to the presence of a psychological impairment as a factor in favor of waiver of recovery of the overpayment.

Social Security regulations address the rights of individuals regarding overpayment and waiver determinations. The rules follow policy established as a result of a series of court decisions. Whenever an initial determination is made that more than the correct amount of payment has been made, and the Social Security Administration seeks adjustment or recovery of the overpayment, the individual involved must be immediately notified.

The notice must include: (1) the overpayment amount, and how and when it occurred; (2) a request for full, immediate refund, unless the overpayment can be withheld from the next month's benefit; (3) the proposed adjustment of benefits if refund is not received within thirty days after the date of the notice and adjustment of benefits is available; (4) an explanation of the availability of a different rate of withholding; (5) an explanation of the right to request waiver of adjustment or recovery, and the automatic scheduling of a file review and prerecoupment hearing if a request for waiver cannot be approved after initial paper review; (6) an explanation of the right to request reconsideration of the fact and/or amount of the overpayment determination; (7) instructions about the availability of forms for requesting reconsideration and waiver; (8) an explanation that, if the individual does not request waiver or reconsideration within thirty days of the date of the overpayment notice, adjustment or recovery of the overpayment will begin; (9) a statement that a Social Security Administration office will help the individual complete and submit forms for appeal or waiver requests; and (10) a statement that the individual receiving the notice should notify the Social Security Administration promptly if reconsideration, waiver, a lesser rate of withholding, repayment by installments, or cross-program adjustment is wanted.

There can be no adjustment or recovery in any case where an overpayment has been made to an individual who is without fault, if adjustment or recovery would either defeat the purpose of the Social Security Act or be against equity and good conscience.

If an individual requests waiver of adjustment or recovery within thirty days after receiving a notice of overpayment, no action will be taken until after the initial waiver determination is made. If an individual requests waiver of adjustment or recovery more than thirty days after receiving a notice of overpayment, the Social Security Administration will stop any adjustment or recovery actions until after the initial waiver determination is made.

When waiver is requested, the individual should provide the Social Security Administration with information to support the contention that the individual is without fault in causing the overpayment, and that adjustment or recovery would either defeat the purpose of the Social Security Act or be against equity and good conscience. That information, along with supporting documentation, is reviewed to determine if waiver can be approved. If waiver cannot be approved after this review, the individual is notified in writing and given the dates, times, and place of the file review and personal conference. The file review is always scheduled at least five days before the personal conference.

At the file review, the individual and the individual's representative have the right to review the claims file and applicable law and regulations with the decision maker or another Social Security Administration representative who is prepared to answer questions.

At the personal conference, the individual is given the opportunity to: (1) appear personally, testify, cross-examine any witnesses, and make arguments; (2) be represented by an attorney or other representative, although the individual must be present at the conference; and (3) submit documents for consideration by the decision maker.

The decision maker: (1) explains the provisions of law and regulations applicable to the issue, (2) briefly summarizes the evidence already on file, (3) ascertains from the individual whether the information presented is correct and understandable, (4) allows the individual and the individual's representative to present the individual's case, (5) allows each witness to present information and allows the individual and the individual's representative to question each witness, (6) ascertains whether there is any further evidence, (7) reminds the individual of any evidence promised by the individual that has not been presented, (8) allows the individual and the individual's representative to present a proposed summary or closing statement, (9) explains that a decision will be made and the individual will be notified in writing, and (10) explains repayment options and further appeal rights in the event the decision is adverse to the individual.

The Social Security Administration will issue a written decision, specifying the findings of fact and conclusions in support of the decision to approve or deny waiver and advising of the individual's right to appeal the decision. If waiver is denied, adjustment or recovery of the overpayment begins, even if the individual appeals.

If the individual is dissatisfied with the initial determination, reconsideration is the first step in the administrative review process. If dissatisfied with the reconsidered determination, the individual may request a hearing before an administrative law judge.

# BENEFIT COMPUTATION

## 160. How are benefits computed under the simplified old-start benefit computation method?

The simplified old-start benefit computation method must be used if disability, death, or age sixty-two occurred before 1979.

**Step I.** Count the number of years elapsed after 1950 (or after year the insured reached age twenty-one, if later) and before (not including) the year of death, disability, or year of attaining age sixty-two (sixty-five for a worker born before 1911, sixty-four if born in 1911, sixty-three if born in 1912).

**Step II.** Subtract five. (Also subtract any years that fell wholly or partly in a period of disability.) The result is the number of years of earnings (but not less than two) to be used in computing Average Monthly Earnings (AME).

**Step III.** List earnings for each year starting with 1951 and including the year in which the worker died – or the year *prior* to disability or application for old-age benefits. Earnings listed cannot exceed the maximum earnings base for that particular year (see Q 164).

**Step IV.** From this list, select years of highest earnings (same number found in step I).

**Step V.** Total the earnings in the selected years – divide by the number of months in those years (drop cents). This is the worker's AME.

A worker's AME are subject to recalculation, if earnings in his year of retirement or year of disability are higher than the lowest year of earnings used in the original calculation. Earnings in the last year are substituted for earnings in the lowest year if this results in higher AIME.

**Step VI.** Determine the insured's Primary Insurance Amount (PIA).

# PRIMARY INSURANCE AMOUNT

## 161. What is the Primary Insurance Amount (PIA)?

The Primary Insurance Amount (PIA) is the basic unit used to determine the amount of each monthly benefit payable under Social Security. It applies to both the old and new method of computing benefits.

A disabled worker – or a retired worker whose retirement benefits start at normal retirement age – receives monthly benefits equal to the PIA.[1] Retired workers who are fully insured and whose retirement benefits start *after* full retirement age also receive an additional delayed retirement credit. (See Q 183.)

1. 42 U.S.C. 402(a); 20 CFR §404.201.

Monthly benefits for members of an insured worker's family (dependent's and survivor's benefits) are all figured as percentages of the worker's PIA. (See Appendix A, Table 1.)

The total amount of monthly benefits payable on a worker's Social Security account is limited by a "maximum family benefit," which is also related to the worker's PIA.

In some instances, monthly benefits will be reduced if the insured elects to receive benefits before a specified age. (See Q 205.)

The retirement benefit is reduced if the retired worker elects to start receiving a benefit at or after age sixty-two but before full retirement age. The benefit for the spouse of a retired worker is also reduced if received before full retirement age. (See Q 185, Q 205, and Appendix A, Table 10.)

The benefit for a widow(er) is reduced if he or she elects to start receiving benefits at or after age sixty but before full retirement age. (See Q 186 and Appendix A, Table 11.)

Disabled widow(er)'s benefits are payable beginning at age fifty for disability occurring before age sixty, and are always reduced from what would have been payable at full retirement age. (See Q 118.)

The law provides a minimum benefit for insured workers and for survivors of insured workers when the worker had many years of coverage. (See Q 178 and Q 179.)

## "WAGE INDEXING" BENEFIT COMPUTATION METHOD

### 162. In general, how is the PIA computed under the "wage indexing" method?

It is based on "indexed" earnings over a fixed number of years after 1950. (Indexing is a mechanism for expressing prior years' earnings in terms of their current dollar value.) Previous computations used actual earnings and a PIA Table. The "wage indexing" method uses a formula to determine the PIA.

**Step I.** Index the earnings record

**Step II.** Determine the Average Indexed Monthly Earnings (AIME)

**Step III.** Apply the PIA formula to the AIME

### 163. Who should use the "wage indexing" benefit computation method?

The "wage indexing" method applies where first eligibility is after 1978. First eligibility is the earliest of: (1) the year of death, (2) the year disability begins, or (3) the year the insured becomes sixty-two.

However, if the worker was entitled to a disability benefit before 1979, and that benefit terminated more than twelve months before death, another disability, or age sixty-two, the new method will be used in determining the PIA for the subsequent entitlement. (See Q 172.)

## 164. What earnings are used in computing a person's Average Indexed Monthly Earnings (AIME)?

The AIME is based on Social Security earnings for years after 1950. This includes wages earned as an employee and/or self-employment income. (For an explanation of the terms wages and self-employment income, see WAGES AND SELF-EMPLOYMENT INCOME, Q 254 to Q 271.)

Only earnings credited to the person's Social Security account can be used and the maximum earnings creditable for specific years are as follows:

$118,500 for 2015
$117,000 for 2014
$113,700 for 2013
$110,100 for 2012
$106,800 for 2009-2011
$102,000 for 2008
$97,500 for 2007
$94,200 for 2006
$90,000 for 2005
$87,900 for 2004
$87,000 for 2003
$84,900 for 2002
$80,400 for 2001
$76,200 for 2000
$72,600 for 1999
$68,400 for 1998
$65,400 for 1997
$62,700 for 1996
$61,200 for 1995
$60,600 for 1994
$57,600 for 1993
$55,500 for 1992
$53,400 for 1991
$51,300 for 1990
$48,000 for 1989
$45,000 for 1988
$43,800 for 1987
$42,000 for 1986
$39,600 for 1985
$37,800 for 1984
$35,700 for 1983
$32,400 for 1982
$29,700 for 1981
$25,900 for 1980
$22,900 for 1979
$17,700 for 1978
$16,500 for 1977
$15,300 for 1976
$14,100 for 1975
$13,200 for 1974
$10,800 for 1973
$9,000 for 1972
$7,800 for years 1968-1971
$6,600 for years 1966-1967
$4,800 for years 1959-1965
$4,200 for years 1955-1958
$3,600 for years 1951-1954

## 165. How is the earnings record indexed for the AIME computation?

The AIME is based on the earnings record after wages have been indexed.[1] Indexing creates an earnings history that more accurately reflects the value of the individual's actual earnings

1. 20 CFR 404.210.

in comparison to the national average wage level at the time of eligibility. Earnings for each year are indexed up to the "indexing year"," – the second year before the worker reaches age sixty-two – or dies or becomes disabled before age sixty-two.

Wages are indexed by applying a ratio to the worker's earnings for each year beginning with 1951. The ratio is the "indexing average wage" for the second year before the year of the worker's eligibility for benefits or death, divided by the "indexing average wage" for the year being indexed. Thus, indexed earnings for each year are computed as follows:

$$\text{Worker's Actual Earnings (Up to the Social Security Maximum) for Year to be Indexed} \times \frac{\text{Average Earnings of All Workers in Indexing Year (Second year before Eligibility or Death)}}{\text{Average Earnings of All Workers for Year being Indexed}}$$

*Example.* Mr. Martin earned $15,000 in 1989 and reached age sixty-two in 2015. The indexing average wage for 2013 (his "indexing year") was $44,888.16 and the indexing average wage for 1989 was $20,099.55. Indexed earnings for 1988 are computed as follows:

$$\$15{,}000 \times \frac{\$44{,}888.16}{\$20{,}099.55} = \$33{,}499.38$$

Indexed earnings of $33,499.38 are used in place of actual earnings for 1989 in Mr. Martin's AIME computation.

The indexing formula must be applied to earnings in each year after 1950 – up to, but not including, the "indexing year." Actual earnings are used for the indexing year and all later years.

The list below shows the indexing average wages for each year beginning with 1951. These amounts must be used in 2014 to index earnings from 1951 through the "indexing year."

| | | | | | | | |
|---|---|---|---|---|---|---|---|
| 1964 | $4,576.32 | 1977 | $9,779.44 | 1989 | $20,099.55 | 2001 | $32,921.92 |
| 1965 | $4,658.72 | 1978 | $10,556.03 | 1990 | $21,027.98 | 2002 | $33,252.09 |
| 1966 | $4,938.36 | 1979 | $11,479.46 | 1991 | $21,811.60 | 2003 | $34,064.95 |
| 1967 | $5,213.44 | 1980 | $12,513.46 | 1992 | $22,935.42 | 2004 | $35,648.55 |
| 1968 | $5,571.76 | 1981 | $13,773.10 | 1993 | $23,132.67 | 2005 | $36,952.94 |
| 1969 | $5,893.76 | 1982 | $14,531.34 | 1994 | $23,753.53 | 2006 | $38,651.41 |
| 1970 | $6,186.24 | 1983 | $15,239.24 | 1995 | $24,705.66 | 2007 | $40,405.48 |
| 1971 | $6,497.08 | 1984 | $16,135.07 | 1996 | $25,913.90 | 2008 | $41,334.97 |
| 1972 | $7,133.80 | 1985 | $16,822.51 | 1997 | $27,426.00 | 2009 | $40,711.61 |
| 1973 | $7,580.16 | 1986 | $17,321.82 | 1998 | $28,861.44 | 2010 | $41,673.83 |
| 1974 | $8,030.76 | 1987 | $18,426.51 | 1999 | $30,469.84 | 2011 | $42,971.61 |
| 1975 | $8,630.92 | 1988 | $19,334.04 | 2000 | $32,154.82 | 2012 | $44,321.67 |
| 1976 | $9,226.48 | | | | | 2013 | $44,888.16 |

Each year, before November 1, the Social Security Administration publishes the indexing average wage for the next indexing year. The indexing average wage for 2014 – the "indexing year" for those reaching age sixty-two, or dying or becoming disabled before age sixty-two in 2016 – will be published by November 2015.

It is important to remember that the "indexing year" is related to the year of first *eligibility* and not necessarily to the year of *entitlement*. A person filing for a retirement benefit in 2015 at age sixty-four is first *eligible* in 2013 (at age sixty-two) and the earnings record will be indexed based on the indexing year 2011 (two years prior to first eligibility).

## 166. How is a person's Average Indexed Monthly Earnings (AIME) determined?

Earnings listed in the records of the Social Security Administration – up to the annual wage limitation – are the basis for computing the AIME.

**Step I**. Count the *number* of years *after* 1950 (or after year person reached age twenty-one, if later) and *up to* (not including) the year of attaining age sixty-two (or the year of disability or death, if before age sixty-two). The number of years counted is the number of *computation elapsed years*.

**Step II**. Subtract five from the number of computation elapsed years when computing the AIME for *retirement* or *death benefits*. The number remaining (if less than two, use two) is the *number of computation base years* to be used in computing the AIME.

*Example 1*. An insured worker attained age sixty-two on December 2, 2014, and filed his application for retirement benefits on January 3, 2015. There are forty elapsed years, counting the years from age twenty-two (1974) through 2013. The number of computation years is thirty-five (forty minus five).

*Example 2*. An insured worker died on November 3, 2015, at the age of fifty-nine. The widow filed a claim for mother's benefits on November 10, 2015. There are thirty-seven elapsed years beginning with 1978 (age twenty-two) through 2014. There are thirty-two computation years (thirty-seven minus five).

The number of years to be subtracted for *disability benefits* is scaled accordingly to the worker's age, under the following schedule:

| Worker's Age in year of disability | Number of dropout years |
|---|---|
| Under 27 | 0 |
| 27 through 31 | 1 |
| 32 through 36 | 2 |
| 37 through 41 | 3 |
| 42 through 46 | 4 |
| 47 and over | 5 |

*Example 3*. An insured woman attained age forty in January 2015 and is found entitled to disability benefits. It is determined that her waiting period began on March 1, 2015. The elapsed years run from 1997 (age twenty-two) through 2014 and total eighteen. Because the woman is forty years old, there are fifteen computation years (eighteen minus three).

**Step III**. List Social Security earnings in the *computation base years*. (See Q 164 for Social Security earnings limits.) Computation base years are years *after* 1950, up to and *including* the year of death, or the year *before* entitlement to retirement or disability benefits. (A person is not entitled to benefits until an application for benefits is filed.)

Notice that the year of death is included as a computation base year, but the year in which an application is made for retirement or disability benefits is not included. However, for benefits payable for the next year after an application is made for retirement or disability benefits, the AIME for retirement or disability benefits will be recomputed, and earnings for this final year substituted for the lowest year if the result is a higher AIME.

Where benefits are estimated for entitlement at some future time, use anticipated earnings (but not over the Social Security maximum) for future computation base years.

**Step IV**. Index earnings in each computation base year up to, but not including, the "indexing year." (See Q 165 for instructions on how to index earnings.)

**Step V**. From the list of indexed earnings (and nonindexed earnings for and after the "indexing year"), select years of highest earnings (same number as found in Step II). Selected years need not be in consecutive order.

**Step VI**. Total indexed and nonindexed earnings for the selected years are divided by the number of months in the number of years found in Step II, dropping cents. This is the person's AIME.

If a person does not have earnings covered by Social Security in as many years as are required to be used as benefit computation years, total earnings must nevertheless be divided by the number of months in the required number of years. In other words, one or more years of zero earnings must be used. (See Q 167.)

**AIME for Widow(er)'s Benefits**. In computing aged widow(er)'s benefits for the spouse of a worker who died before age sixty-two, the deceased worker's earnings are indexed to wages up to the earliest of: (1) two years before the worker would have reached age sixty-two; (2) two years before the survivor becomes eligible for aged widow(er)'s benefits; or (3) two years before the survivor becomes eligible for disabled widow(er)'s benefits. This computation applies only if it results in a higher benefit than the standard computation above (including applicable cost-of-living adjustments for the deferred period before benefits start). It will provide higher benefits for many widow(er)s whose spouses died before age sixty-two and will assure that the widow(er)'s initial benefit reflects wage levels prevailing nearer the time that he or she comes on the rolls.

## EXAMPLES

In each of the three examples provided below, the worker earned at least the Social Security maximum each year. See Q 164 for the Social Security maximum for a particular year.

**Example I. Computation of AIME for person entitled to retirement benefits.**

Mr. Smith, born in 1953, reaches age sixty-two on November 1, 2015. On November 1st he retires and applies for retirement benefits. Earnings and months in thirty-five years must be used in computing his AIME (forty computation elapsed years, 1975-2014, minus five). Mr. Smith has worked in covered employment and earned at least the Social Security maximum in every year after 1974. Earnings are indexed from 1975-2012. Mr. Smith's earnings in 2013, his "indexing year" and the next two years are not indexed.

Indexed earnings that apply to each example in-whole or in-part are as follows:

| | | | | | |
|---|---|---|---|---|---|
| 1964 | $47,082.19 | 1982 | $100,085.50 | 2000 | $106,375.27 |
| 1965 | $46,249.44 | 1983 | $105,156.64 | 2001 | $109,623.26 |
| 1966 | $59,991.95 | 1984 | $105,160.53 | 2002 | $114,609.48 |
| 1967 | $56,826.56 | 1985 | $105,666.23 | 2003 | $114,641.88 |
| 1968 | $62,839.69 | 1986 | $108,839.76 | 2004 | $110,682.46 |
| 1969 | $59,406.50 | 1987 | $106,699.61 | 2005 | $109,326.47 |
| 1970 | $56,597.81 | 1988 | $104,477.24 | 2006 | $109,400.01 |
| 1971 | $53,890.00 | 1989 | $107,198.01 | 2007 | $108,316.88 |
| 1972 | $56,630.89 | 1990 | $109,509.45 | 2008 | $110,768.01 |
| 1973 | $63,955.40 | 1991 | $109,896.92 | 2009 | $117,756.47 |
| 1974 | $73,781.77 | 1992 | $108,622.07 | 2010 | $115,037.55 |
| 1975 | $73,332.05 | 1993 | $111,770.84 | 2011 | $111,542.55 |
| 1976 | $74,436.71 | 1994 | $114,518.66 | 2012 | $111,507.22 |
| 1977 | $75,735.89 | 1995 | $111,195.39 | 2013 | $113,700.00 |
| 1978 | $75,266.97 | 1996 | $108,609.19 | 2014 | $117,000.00 |
| 1979 | $89,545.92 | 1997 | $107,040.24 | 2015 | $118,500.00 |
| 1980 | $92,908.22 | 1998 | $106,382.43 | | |
| 1981 | $96,795.81 | 1999 | $106,954.30 | | |

Mr. Smith's highest AIME is obtained by selecting the highest thirty-five years of the forty years from 1975 to 2014. His AIME is $9,066 ($3,807,774.57 ÷ 420).

His AIME will later be recomputed to include earnings in 2015 and, if this results in a higher AIME, the higher benefit will be paid beginning the following year. Thus, if Mr. Smith earned at least $118,500 in 2015, the recomputation will be based on the highest thirty-five years of the forty-one years from 1975 to 2015, giving him an AIME of $9,127 ($3,833,366.35 ÷ 420).

### Example II. Computation of AIME for disability benefits.

Mr. Jones, born in February 1969, is disabled as a result of an accident on October 15, 2015. He applies for disability benefits on December 1, 2015. In computing his AIME for disability benefits, twenty benefit computation years must be used (twenty-four years in 1991-2014, less four). Mr. Jones has worked in covered employment every year since 1990 and in each year (including the year in which he became disabled) was paid at least the maximum Social Security earnings base for that year.

Earnings in 1991-2012 are indexed. Earnings in 2013-2015 are not adjusted because they were paid in and after his "indexing year" (2013).

Mr. Jones' highest AIME is obtained by selecting the highest twenty years of the twenty-four years from 1991 to 2014. His AIME is $9,327 ($2,238,525.33 ÷ 240).

The AIME will be recomputed to include earnings in 2015 and, if this results in a higher AIME, the higher benefit will be paid beginning the following year. If Mr. Jones earned at least $118,500 in 2015, the recomputation will be based on the highest twenty years of the twenty-five years from 1991 to 2015, giving him an AIME of $9,369 ($2,248,708.45 ÷ 240).

**Example III. Computation of AIME for person who dies before retirement age.**

Mr. Martin dies in November, 2015, at age sixty (he was born in February 1955). In computing his AIME, thirty-three benefit computation years must be used (thirty-eight years in 1977-2014, less five). Mr. Martin has worked in covered employment every year since 1976 and in each year (including the year of death) was paid at least the maximum Social Security earnings base for that year. Earnings in Mr. Martin's computation base years through 2012 are indexed. Actual earnings in 2013-2015 are not adjusted because 2013 is his "indexing year."

Mr. Martin's highest AIME is obtained by selecting the highest thirty-three years of the thirty-eight years from 1977 to 2015. Mr. Martin's AIME is $9,435 ($3,736,570.54 ÷ 396).

## 167. How are Average Indexed Monthly Earnings (AIME) computed for a self-employed individual whose self-employment came under Social Security after 1951?

The same formula and starting date (1951) are used as in the computation for employees. In many cases, this will mean that years of zero earnings must be used in the AIME contribution.

*Example*. Dr. Smith, a physician, came under Social Security in 1965. He applies for retirement benefits in 1995 when he reaches age sixty-two. Earnings and months in thirty-five years must be used in computing his AIME (forty elapsed years, 1955-1994, less five). Social Security earnings in his elapsed years are at the-maximum creditable amount in 1965-1994.

Although Dr. Smith has covered earnings in only thirty years before 1995, the total earnings for these thirty years must be divided by the number of months in thirty-five years (420). His AIME is computed by indexing his earnings from 1965-1992, adding actual earnings in 1993 and 1994 to total indexed earnings, and dividing by 420. Thus, his AIME is $3,127 ($1,313,559 ÷ 420).

Recomputation to include Dr. Smith's earnings in 1995 (assuming they are at least $61,200) will give him an AIME of $3,273.

## 168. An individual is considering early retirement at age fifty-five. If she retires at fifty-five with NO earned income for the next seven years, how will this affect her benefits at age sixty-two?

Benefits are based on the highest thirty-five years of indexed earnings. The effect in this case is generally that the highest earning years are often the last years of employment, therefore benefits may not be as high as estimated by the Social Security Administration.

## 169. Do social security benefits increase by continuing to work and contributing to social security?

It depends. When benefits are computed, Social Security uses the highest thirty-five years of indexed earnings. If the current earnings exceed the lowest year used in the computation, the benefits will increase. If the current earnings are less, then there will be no change.

## 170. How is the Primary Insurance Amount (PIA) for a person who first becomes eligible in 2015 determined?

The Primary Insurance Amount (PIA) is determined by applying a formula to the person's Average Indexed Monthly Earnings (AIME). Where first eligibility is in calendar year 2015, the PIA is the sum of three separate percentages of portions of the AIME. It is found by taking 90 percent of the first $826 or less of the AIME, 32 percent of the AIME in excess of $826 through $4,980, and 15 percent of the AIME in excess of $4,980.

If the resulting PIA is not an even multiple of ten cents, it is rounded to the next lower multiple of ten cents.

The percentage figures and the dollar figures in the PIA formula will remain constant for computations and recomputations where first eligibility is in 2015, no matter when entitlement is established.

The PIA is subject to cost-of-living increases beginning with the year of first eligibility. (See Q 202.)

*Example 1*. Mr. Bell, born May 10, 1953, filed an application for retirement benefits on May 1, 2015. His AIME is $5,000. His PIA is calculated as follows:

90% of $826 = $743.40

32% of $4,154 = $1,329.28

15% of $20 = $3.00

$743.40 + $1,329.28 + $3.00 = PIA of $2,075.60

*Example 2*. Mr. Jones, born February 13, 1953, filed an application for retirement benefits on February 10, 2015. His AIME is $600. His PIA is $540 (90 percent of $600 = $540).

Note, however, that the PIA is calculated differently if eligibility begins before 2015. The percentages in the PIA formula remain constant but the dollar amounts differ each year. The dollar amounts in the formula since 1979 are as follows:

| Eligibility Begins | AIME Dollar Amounts |
|---|---|
| 1979 | $180 and $1,085 |
| 1980 | $194 and $1,171 |
| 1981 | $211 and $1,274 |
| 1982 | $230 and $1,388 |

| Eligibility Begins | AIME Dollar Amounts |
|---|---|
| 1983 | $254 and $1,528 |
| 1984 | $267 and $1,612 |
| 1985 | $280 and $1,691 |
| 1986 | $297 and $1,790 |
| 1987 | $310 and $1,866 |
| 1988 | $319 and $1,922 |
| 1989 | $339 and $2,044 |
| 1990 | $356 and $2,145 |
| 1991 | $370 and $2,230 |
| 1992 | $387 and $2,333 |
| 1993 | $401 and $2,420 |
| 1994 | $422 and $2,545 |
| 1995 | $426 and $2,567 |
| 1996 | $437 and $2,635 |
| 1997 | $455 and $2,741 |
| 1998 | $477 and $2,875 |
| 1999 | $505 and $3,043 |
| 2000 | $531 and $3,202 |
| 2001 | $561 and $3,381 |
| 2002 | $592 and $3,567 |
| 2003 | $606 and $3,653 |
| 2004 | $612 and $3,689 |
| 2005 | $627 and $3,779 |
| 2006 | $656 and $3,955 |
| 2007 | $680 and $4,100 |
| 2008 | $711 and $4,288 |
| 2009 | $744 and $4,483 |
| 2010 | $761 and $4,586 |
| 2011 | $749 and $4,517 |
| 2012 | $767 and $4,624 |
| 2013 | $791 and $4,768 |
| 2014 | $816 and $4,917 |
| 2015 | $826 and $4,980 |

*Example 3*. Mr. Smith, born March 12, 1943, filed an application for retirement benefits on August 19, 2008. His AIME was $4,200. As he became eligible for retirement benefits in 2005 (the year he reached age 62), his PIA is calculated as follows:

90 percent of \$627 = \$564.30

32 percent of \$3,152 = \$1,008.64

15 percent of \$421 = \$63.15

\$564.30 + \$1,008.64 + \$63.15 = \$1,636.09 = PIA of \$1,636

This amount is subject to a 4.1 percent increase in December 2005, a 3.3 percent increase in December 2006, a 2.3 percent increase in December 2007, a 5.8 percent increase in December 2008, no increases in December 2009 or 2010, a 3.6 percent increase in December 2011, a 1.7 percent increase in December 2012, a 1.5 percent increase in December 2013, and a 1.7 percent increase in December 2014. Thus, his PIA is \$1,703 for December 2005, \$1,759.10 for December 2006, \$1,799.50 for December 2007, \$1,903.80 for December 2008, 2009, and 2010, \$1,972.30 for December 2011, \$2,005.80 for December 2012, \$2,035.80 for December 2013, and \$2,070.40 for December 2014.

## Formula for Workers Receiving a Pension from Work Not Covered by Social Security

If a worker receives a pension from a job not covered by Social Security, and the worker also has enough Social Security credits to be eligible for retirement or disability benefits, a different formula may be used to figure the Social Security benefit. This formula results in a lower benefit. But the worker's pension from the job not covered by Social Security is not affected by this change.

The reason a different formula is used is that Social Security benefits are weighted in favor of low earners (i.e., low earners' benefits represent a higher percentage of their prior earnings than do the benefits of workers with higher earnings). If the benefits of people who work for only a portion of their careers in jobs covered by Social Security were computed as if they had been long-term, low-wage workers, these individuals would receive the advantage of the weighted benefit formula. Instead, a modified formula eliminates this unintended windfall.

The modified formula does not affect survivor benefits. It affects only workers who reach age sixty-two or become disabled after 1985 and first become eligible after 1985 for a monthly pension based in whole or in part on work not covered by Social Security. A worker is considered eligible to receive a pension if he meets the requirements of the pension, even if he continues to work.

The modified formula does not apply if:

- the worker is a federal worker hired after December 31, 1983;
- the worker was employed on January 1, 1984, by a nonprofit organization that was mandatorily covered under Social Security on that date;
- the worker has thirty or more years of substantial earnings under Social Security;
- the worker's only pension from work not covered by Social Security is based solely on railroad employment;
- the worker's only work not under Social Security was before 1957.

The modified formula is used in figuring the Social Security benefit beginning with the first month for which the worker receives both a Social Security benefit and a pension from work not covered under Social Security.

Social Security benefits are normally based on the worker's AIME. In figuring benefits, the first part of the average earnings is multiplied by 90 percent; the second part is multiplied by 32 percent; and any part of the AIME remaining is multiplied by 15 percent. In the modified benefit formula, the 90 percent used in the first factor is reduced.

Benefits for workers first eligible in 2015 who use the modified formula are determined by taking 40 percent of the first $826 of Average Indexed Monthly Earnings; 32 percent of AIME from $826 to $4,980; and 15 percent of AIME above $4,980.

The reduction was phased in gradually for workers who reached sixty-two or became disabled in 1986 through 1989. The phase-in applies as follows:

| Year Person Became 62 or Disabled | First Factor |
|---|---|
| 1986 | 80 percent |
| 1987 | 70 percent |
| 1988 | 60 percent |
| 1989 | 50 percent |
| 1990 or later | 40 percent |

Workers with thirty or more years of substantial Social Security coverage are not affected by the modified benefit formula. Workers with twenty-one to twenty-nine years of Social Security coverage (as defined in Q 178) will have the first factor reduced as follows:

| Years of Coverage | First Factor |
|---|---|
| 30 or more | 90 percent |
| 29 | 85 percent |
| 28 | 80 percent |
| 27 | 75 percent |
| 26 | 70 percent |
| 25 | 65 percent |
| 24 | 60 percent |
| 23 | 55 percent |
| 22 | 50 percent |
| 21 | 45 percent |
| 20 or less | 40 percent |

In this formula, a worker is credited with a year of coverage if earnings equal or exceed the figures shown for each year in the following chart.

| Year | Earnings | Year | Earnings |
|---|---|---|---|
| 1937-50 | $900 | 1991 | $9,900 |
| 1951-54 | 900 | 1992 | 10,350 |
| 1955-58 | 1,050 | 1993 | 10,725 |
| 1959-65 | 1,200 | 1994 | 11,250 |
| 1966-67 | 1,650 | 1995 | 11,325 |
| 1968-71 | 1,950 | 1996 | 11,625 |
| 1972 | 2,250 | 1997 | 12,150 |
| 1973 | 2,700 | 1998 | 12,675 |
| 1974 | 3,300 | 1999 | 13,425 |
| 1975 | 3,525 | 2000 | 14,175 |
| 1976 | 3,825 | 2001 | 14,925 |
| 1977 | 4,125 | 2002 | 15,750 |
| 1978 | 4,425 | 2003 | 16,125 |
| 1979 | 4,725 | 2004 | 16,275 |
| 1980 | 5,100 | 2005 | 16,725 |
| 1981 | 5,550 | 2006 | 17,475 |
| 1982 | 6,075 | 2007 | 18,150 |
| 1983 | 6,675 | 2008 | 18,975 |
| 1984 | 7,050 | 2009 | 19,800 |
| 1985 | 7,425 | 2010 | 19,800 |
| 1986 | 7,875 | 2011 | 19,800 |
| 1987 | 8,175 | 2012 | 20,475 |
| 1988 | 8,400 | 2013 | 21,075 |
| 1989 | 8,925 | 2014 | 21,750 |
| 1990 | 9,525 | 2015 | 22,050 |

A guarantee is provided to protect workers with relatively low "noncovered" pensions. It provides that the reduction in the Social Security benefit under the modified formula cannot be more than one-half of that part of the pension attributable to earnings after 1956 not covered by Social Security. Effective for benefits based on applications filed in or after November 1989, the amount of the pension considered when determining the windfall guarantee is the amount payable in the first month of concurrent entitlement to both Social Security and the pension from noncovered employment.

## 171. How is the Primary Insurance Amount (PIA) determined after 2015?

For individuals who attain age sixty-two, or become disabled or die before age sixty-two in any calendar year after 2015, the PIA will be determined by formulas using the same percentage amounts listed in Q 170 above. However, the bend points (dollar amounts) will be adjusted yearly as average wages rise or fall.

On or before November 1 of each year, the Social Security Administration must publish in the Federal Register the bend points (dollar amounts) that will be used in computing the PIA for those eligible in the year after publication. The bend points for 2015 are $826 and $4,980.

Remember that the bend points used in calculating an individual's PIA are determined from the year the individual first became *eligible* for the benefits and not necessarily the year first *entitled* to benefits.

## 172. How is the PIA computed for an individual who was previously entitled to a disability benefit?

The PIA is not always computed under the "wage indexing" benefit computation method when a worker reaches age sixty-two or becomes disabled. Other benefit computations may be required if the worker was previously entitled to a disability benefit.

The PIA will be computed or recomputed under the simplified old-start benefit computation method if the individual was entitled to a disability benefit before 1979 and fewer than twelve months have passed between the prior entitlement to the disability benefit and current entitlement to benefits.

If an individual has been entitled to a disability benefit either before or after 1979 – but within twelve months of current entitlement to retirement, disability, or death benefits – the PIA is the largest of the following:

(1) The PIA (including one computed under the simplified old-start benefit computation method) that was used in figuring the individual's previous disability benefit – increased by any cost-of-living or general benefit increases that occurred since the individual was last entitled

(2) The special minimum PIA

(3) A recomputation of the former PIA, to take into account earnings after the disability entitlement ended

If an individual's entitlement to a disability benefit ended more than twelve months before his current entitlement to benefits, a new PIA must be computed under the "wage indexing" method. The PIA will be the higher of the recalculated PIA or the individual's PIA during the last month of his former entitlement to disability benefits (without regard to any interim cost-of-living increases).

## 173. How is the Maximum Family Benefit determined under the wage indexing method in 2015?

The following formula determines the Maximum Family Benefit for those reaching age sixty-two or dying before age sixty-two in 2015:

(1) 150 percent of the first $1,056 of PIA, plus

(2) 272 percent of PIA over $1,056 through $1,524, plus

(3) 134 percent of PIA over $1,524 through $1,987 plus

(4) 175 percent of PIA over $1,987.

The result is the family maximum. (The final figure should be rounded to the next lower multiple of $.10 if not an even multiple of $.10.) The Maximum Family Benefit is subject to cost-of-living increases beginning with the year of first eligibility. (See Q 202.)

The Maximum Family Benefit is calculated differently if eligibility begins before 2015. The percentages in the Maximum Family Benefit formula remain constant, but the dollar amounts differ each year. The dollar amounts in the formula since 1979 are as follows:

| Eligibility Begins | PIA Dollar Amounts |
|---|---|
| 1979 | $230, $332, and $433 |
| 1980 | $248, $358, and $467 |
| 1981 | $270, $390, and $508 |
| 1982 | $294, $425, and $554 |
| 1983 | $324, $468, and $610 |
| 1984 | $342, $493, and $643 |
| 1985 | $358, $517, and $675 |
| 1986 | $379, $548, and $714 |
| 1987 | $396, $571, and $745 |
| 1988 | $407, $588, and $767 |
| 1989 | $433, $626, and $816 |
| 1990 | $455, $656, and $856 |
| 1991 | $473, $682, and $890 |
| 1992 | $495, $714, and $931 |
| 1993 | $513, $740, and $966 |
| 1994 | $539, $779, and $1,016 |
| 1995 | $544, $785, and $1,024 |
| 1996 | $559, $806, and $1,052 |
| 1997 | $581, $839, and $1,094 |
| 1998 | $609, $880, and $1,147 |
| 1999 | $645, $931, and $1,214 |
| 2000 | $679, $980, and $1,278 |
| 2001 | $717, $1,034, and $1,349 |
| 2002 | $756, $1,092, and $1,424 |
| 2003 | $774, $1,118, and $1,458 |
| 2004 | $782, $1,129, and $1,472 |
| 2005 | $801, $1,156, and $1,508 |

| Eligibility Begins | PIA Dollar Amounts |
|---|---|
| 2006 | $838, $1,210, and $1,578 |
| 2007 | $869, $1,255, and $1,636 |
| 2008 | $909, $1,312, and $1,711 |
| 2009 | $950, $1,372, and $1,789 |
| 2010 | $972, $1,403, and $1,830 |
| 2011 | $957, $1,382, and $1,803 |
| 2012 | $980, $1,415, and $1,845 |
| 2013 | $1,011, $1,459, and $1,903 |
| 2014 | $1,042, $1,505, and $1,962 |
| 2015 | $1,056, $1,524, and $1,987 |

## Disability

For a disabled worker and family, benefits may not exceed the lesser of 85 percent of the Average Indexed Monthly Earnings (AIME) on which the worker's disability benefit is based, or 150 percent of the disability benefit payable to the worker alone. However, in no case will a family's benefit be reduced below 100 percent of the benefit that would be payable to the worker alone.

This limit on family disability benefits applies to workers who first become entitled to disability benefits after June 30, 1980. A worker who first becomes entitled to disability benefits in the first six months of 1980 will compute the maximum family benefit in the same manner as those who reach age sixty-two or die in 1980.

> *Example.* Mr. Smith becomes entitled to disability benefits on October 1, 2015. His AIME is $2,000 and he would be eligible to receive $1,119 a month in disability payments on his own. However, Mr. Smith also has a wife and a 10 year-old child. His maximum family benefit is the lesser of 85 percent of his AIME (85 percent × $2,000 = $1,700), or 150 percent of his disability benefit (150 percent × $1,119 = $1,678.50). As 150 percent of his disability benefit is less than 85 percent of his AIME, his maximum family benefit is $1,678.50.

## 174. How is the Maximum Family Benefit determined under the simplified old-start benefit computation method?

Maximum Family Benefits applicable under the law in December 1978 remain in effect for those individuals who attained age sixty-two, became disabled, or died before January 1979. Maximum Family Benefits – based on the worker's Average Monthly Earnings (AME) – are listed in the June 1978 benefit table of the Social Security Administration. (See Table 13. Consumer Price Index increases after June 1978 must be applied to Maximum Family Benefits listed in Table 13.)

## 175. How are individual benefit rates reduced to bring the total amount payable within the family maximum limit?

Adjustment of individual benefit rates because of the family maximum limit is required, whenever the total monthly benefits of all the beneficiaries payable on *one* Social Security account exceed the family maximum that can be paid on that record for the month. All the benefit rates, except the retirement or disability benefit and benefits payable to a divorced spouse or surviving divorced spouse, must be reduced to bring the total monthly benefits payable within the family maximum. This means that, even though a beneficiary's benefit rate is originally set by law as a percentage of the insured person's PIA, the actual benefit paid may be less when the total monthly benefits payable on one earnings record exceed the family maximum prescribed by law.

The entitlement of a divorced spouse to a spouse's benefit or a surviving divorced spouse's benefit does not result in reducing the benefits of other categories of beneficiaries. Likewise, the entitlement of a legal spouse where a deemed spouse is also entitled will not affect the benefit of other beneficiaries entitled in the month. The other dependents or survivors benefits are reduced for the maximum, not taking into account the existence of the divorced spouse, surviving divorced spouse, or the legal spouse. Nor are the benefits of the divorced spouse, surviving divorced spouse, or the legal spouse ever reduced because of the family maximum. (See Q 55 and Q 111.)

Adjustment for the family maximum is made by proportionately reducing all the monthly benefits subject to the family maximum on the Social Security earnings record (except for retired worker's or disabled worker's benefits) to bring the total monthly benefits payable within the limit applicable in the particular case.

The individual reduced benefit rates are figured as follows:

(1) If the insured person is alive, the insured person's benefit is subtracted from the applicable family maximum amount. Any remainder is divided among the other persons entitled to benefits on the insured person's Social Security earnings record.

(2) If the insured worker is dead and all monthly benefits are based on the same percentage (e.g., all are based on 100 percent of the PIA, or all are based on 75 percent), the applicable family maximum is divided equally among all those who are entitled to benefits on the Social Security earnings record.

(3) If the insured person is deceased and some benefits are based on 100 percent, some on 82.5 percent, and some on 75 percent of the PIA, each beneficiary is paid a proportionate share of the applicable family maximum based on that beneficiary's original benefit rate.

This adjustment is made after any deductions that may be applicable. Thus, where: (1) reduction for the family maximum is required, and (2) a benefit payable to someone other than the worker must be withheld, the reapportionment for the maximum is made as if the beneficiary whose benefit must be withheld were not entitled to the amounts withheld.

*Example 1*. Mr. Edwards dies before age 62 in 2015, leaving a widow age 35 and two small children. His AIME is $2,500, and his PIA is $1,279. The full benefit for the widow and each child is $959.25 (75 percent of $1,273.20). However, the sum of the full benefits is $2,877.75 (3 × $959.25), which exceeds $2,190 – the maximum family benefit for a PIA of $1,279. Thus, the benefit actually payable to each beneficiary is $730 (1/3 of $2,190).

When a person is entitled to benefits based on two different earnings records, only the amount of benefits actually paid on a record is considered in determining how much to reduce monthly benefits because of the family maximum. Any amount not paid because of a person's entitlement on another earnings record is not included. The effect of this provision is to permit payment of up to the full maximum benefits to other beneficiaries who are not subject to a deduction or reduction.

*Example 2*. Mr. Smith, his wife, and two children are entitled to benefits. Mr. Smith's PIA is $1,250 and his family maximum is $2,111. Due to the maximum limit, the monthly benefits for his wife and children must be reduced to $287 each ($861 ÷ 3). Their original rates (50 percent of Mr. Smith's benefit) are $625 each. Mr. Smith's children are also entitled to benefits on their own records. One child is entitled to $390 per month and the other child is entitled to $280 per month. This causes a reduction in the benefit to the first child to $103, and the benefit to the second child to $0.

In computing the total benefits payable on Mr. Smith's record, only the benefits actually paid to the children, or $103, are considered. This allows payment of an additional amount to Mrs. Smith, increasing her benefit to $625.00 (50 percent of her husband's benefit). This is how the calculation works: (1) The amount available under the family maximum for the wife and children is $861 ($2,111 – $1,250 = 861); (2) Subtract the amount that is due the children after a reduction due to entitlement to their own benefits ($103); (3) The amount available for Mrs. Smith is $758 ($861 – $103 = $758); and (4) The amount payable to Mrs. Smith is $625, which is the lesser of $625 and $758.

### 176. If one or more members of a family cease to be entitled to benefits, will the benefits of the remaining beneficiaries be increased?

Yes, if their benefits have been reduced because of the family maximum limit.

*Example*. Mr. Jones dies in 2015, leaving a widow and two children, aged 6 and 12, entitled to survivor's benefits. His AIME is $1,800; his PIA, $1,055; and the maximum family benefit is $1,582. As the full benefit for each family member is $791.25 (75 percent of $1,055), the total of all three benefits exceeds the family maximum of $1,582 (3 × $791.25 = $2,373.75). Initially then, each beneficiary receives only $527 (1/3 of $1,582, rounded to the next lowest dollar). Eventually, the older child reaches age 18, and his benefits end. The widow and younger child then receive their full benefits (the widow until the child attains age 16, and the child until attaining age 18 or, if enrolled in a full-time elementary or secondary school program, upon attaining age 19) because the sum of these two benefits does not exceed the maximum family benefit.

## TRANSITIONAL GUARANTEE BENEFIT METHOD

### 177. What is the transitional guarantee benefit method?

To provide a degree of protection for workers nearing retirement when decoupling was implemented, those who reach age sixty-two after 1978 and before 1984 are guaranteed a retirement benefit no lower than they would have received under the simplified old-start benefit computation method as of December 1978. The benefit computed under this method is known as the transitional guarantee PIA.

Those eligible for retirement benefits in the transition period are eligible for the larger of the PIA under the "wage indexing" benefit computation method or the transitional guarantee method.

The PIA under the transitional guarantee method is based on the June 1978 benefit table. (See Table 13.) The benefit table will not be subject to future automatic benefit increases, but an individual's retirement benefits will automatically increase beginning with age sixty-two for cost-of-living adjustments.

To be eligible for the guarantee, an individual must: (1) have had income credited for one year prior to 1979, and (2) must not have been disabled prior to 1979.

The transitional guarantee does not apply to disability computations, even when the disability begins after age sixty-two. It does apply to survivors of individuals who attain age sixty-two in the transition period and who die in or after the month they reach age sixty-two.

The transitional guarantee method is basically the same as the simplified old-start benefit computation method, but earnings in the year in which the worker reached age sixty-two and any year thereafter may not be included in the benefit computation.

> *Example*. Mr. White, born 1917, reaches age 62 on October 7, 1979. He retires one day later and applies for retirement benefits. Earnings and months in 23 years must be used in computing his AME (28 computation elapsed years, 1951-1978, less 5). Mr. White has worked in covered employment and earned at least the Social Security maximum in every year after 1950. Social Security earnings in his computation base years are therefore as follows: $3,600 (1951-1954); $4,200 (1955-1958); $4,800 (1959-1965); $6,600 (1966-1967); $7,800 (1968-1971); $9,900 (1972); $10,800 (1973); $13,200 (1974); $14,100 (1975); $15,300 (1976); $16,500 (1977); $17,700 (1978). Mr. White's highest AME is obtained by selecting the 23 years 1956-1978. His AME is $678 ($187,200 ÷ 276), and his PIA is $486.10.

The PIA computed above under the transitional guarantee method will be used if it is higher than Mr. White's PIA computed under the "wage indexing" method.

The PIA under the transitional guarantee method is subject to cost-of-living increases beginning with the month applicable for the year of first eligibility. A worker who attains age sixty-two in 1982 is entitled to a transitional guarantee PIA determined from the PIA Table printed in 1978. The PIA was not affected by cost-of-living benefit increases in 1979, 1980, or 1981, but the June 1982 cost-of-living increase and subsequent increases apply.

## MINIMUM AND MAXIMUM SINGLE BENEFITS INCREASE IN BENEFITS

### 178. Do benefits increase when the cost-of-living increases?

The Social Security Act provides for automatic increases in benefits and in the maximum earnings base (earnings subject to Social Security taxes) due to changing economic conditions.

The automatic increases in benefits are determined by increases in the Consumer Price Index for All Urban Wage Earners and Clerical Workers prepared by the Department of Labor. (But see Q 204.) The increases in the maximum earnings base are determined from increases in average nationwide wages, if there has been a cost-of-living increase in benefits for the preceding December. (See Q 255.)

Benefits have been raised by the following percentages since 1977:

| Month/Year | Increase in Benefits |
|---|---|
| July 1977 | 5.9% |
| July 1978 | 6.5% |
| July 1979 | 9.9% |
| July 1980 | 14.3% |
| July 1981 | 11.2% |
| July 1982 | 7.4% |
| January 1984 | 3.5% |
| January 1985 | 3.5% |
| January 1986 | 3.1% |
| January 1987 | 1.3% |
| January 1988 | 4.2% |
| January 1989 | 4.0% |
| January 1990 | 4.7% |
| January 1991 | 5.4% |
| January 1992 | 3.7% |
| January 1993 | 3.0% |
| January 1994 | 2.6% |
| January 1995 | 2.8% |
| January 1996 | 2.6% |
| January 1997 | 2.9% |
| January 1998 | 2.1% |
| January 1999 | 1.3% |
| January 2000 | 2.5% |
| January 2001 | 3.5% |
| January 2002 | 2.6% |
| January 2003 | 1.4% |
| January 2004 | 2.1% |
| January 2005 | 2.7% |
| January 2006 | 4.1% |
| January 2007 | 3.3% |
| January 2008 | 2.3% |
| January 2009 | 5.8% |
| January 2010 | 0.0% |
| January 2011 | 0.0% |
| January 2012 | 3.6% |
| January 2013 | 1.7% |
| January 2014 | 1.5% |
| January 2015 | 1.7% |

There can be no cost-of-living computation quarter in any calendar year if, in the year prior to that year, a general benefit increase has been enacted or become effective.

The amount of excess earnings that results in loss of benefits will be increased whenever there is an automatic cost-of-living benefit increase and nationwide average wages have risen (the increase is based on the rise in average wages). (See Q 224.)

## 179. Who is entitled to a cost-of-living benefit increase?

Individuals using the "wage indexing" benefit computation method are entitled to cost-of-living increases, beginning with the year of first eligibility (the year of attaining age sixty-two, or disability or death before age sixty-two). The PIA is calculated for the year of first eligibility and the cost-of-living increases in that year and subsequent years will be added. As long as eligibility exists in any month of the year, the PIA will be increased by the automatic-benefit increase percentage applicable to the check sent in January of the following year.

> *Example.* Mr. Johnson attains age 62 in November 2013, and waits until January 2015 to apply for benefits. The PIA is calculated and will be increased by the automatic cost-of-living benefit increases applicable to December 2013 and December 2014. The resultant PIA will be payable in the benefit paid for January 2015.

The automatic cost-of-living increase provisions in effect in December 1978 continue to apply for those who reached age sixty-two, became disabled, or died before January 1979. A revised benefit table is published each year by the Social Security Administration. See Table 13. These revised tables are *not* applicable to individuals who become eligible for benefits *after 1978*, except those using the transitional guarantee.

Beneficiaries using the transitional guarantee will also receive cost-of-living increases beginning with the year of first eligibility. (See Q 177.)

## 180. How will the cost-of-living stabilizer affect future cost-of-living benefit increases?

The Social Security Amendments of 1983 include a provision designed to protect the system from the kinds of trust-fund depletions that occur when price increases outpace wage gains. This stabilizer provision goes into effect if reserves in the trust fund providing retirement, disability, and survivor benefits fall below 20 percent of what is needed to provide benefits for a year. When the stabilizer takes effect, automatic cost-of-living benefit increases are based on the lower of the percentage increase in the Consumer Price Index or the percentage rise in the nationwide average wage.

Later, if the fund reserves exceed 32 percent of what is estimated to be needed for a year, recipients will be entitled to extra cost-of-living increases, to compensate for losses in inflation protection resulting from having benefit increases tied to wage levels in the past (if this occurred).

## REDUCTION IN BENEFITS

### 181. When a person elects to start receiving a retirement benefit before full retirement age, how is the benefit reduced?

A fully insured worker can start receiving retirement benefits the month after she reaches age sixty-two (or the month she reaches age sixty-two if his or her birthday is on the first or second of the month), or for any month thereafter. (See Q 29.) However, if the worker elects to start receiving benefits before full retirement age, the benefit is reduced.

In making the reduction, the worker's PIA must first be determined. The PIA is then reduced by 5/9 of 1 percent (1/180) for each of the first thirty-six months that the worker is under full retirement age when the benefits commence and by 5/12 of 1 percent (1/240) for each such month in excess of thirty-six. (The amount of the reduction, if not an even multiple of ten cents, is increased to the next higher multiple of ten cents.) For example, if the worker's PIA is $1,000, and he elects to retire and start receiving benefits twenty-four months before his full retirement age, his benefit will be reduced by $133.40 (24 × 1/180 × $1,000), giving him a monthly benefit of $866.60. Ordinarily, he will continue to receive the reduced benefit even after full retirement age (but see Recomputation of Benefits, Q 189).

### 182. If the spouse of a retired worker starts receiving a spouse's benefit before full retirement age, how is the benefit reduced?

First, the spouse's full benefit is determined. This is one-half of the retired worker's PIA. (Where the retired worker is receiving a reduced retirement benefit starting before full retirement age, the spouse's full benefit is computed as 50 percent of the retired worker's PIA, not 50 percent of the reduced benefit.) The spouse's full benefit is then reduced by 25/36 of 1 percent (1/144) for each of the first thirty-six months that the spouse is under full retirement age when benefits commence and by 5/12 of 1 percent (1/240) for each month in excess of thirty-six. (The amount of the reduction, if not an even multiple of ten cents, is increased to the next higher multiple of ten cents.)

For example, suppose that the retired worker's PIA is $1,000, and the spouse's full benefit is $500 (1/2 of $1,000). If the spouse takes the benefit exactly twenty-four months before his full retirement age, the full benefit will be reduced by $83.40 (24 × 1/144 × $500), giving the spouse a monthly benefit of $416.60 ($500 – $83.40). If a spouse starts receiving benefits for the month thirty-six months before full retirement age, the benefit under this formula will be 75 percent of the full benefit, or 37.5 percent of the retired worker's PIA. Ordinarily, the spouse will continue to receive the reduced benefit even after normal retirement age (but see Recomputation of Benefits, Q 189). (See also Table 10.)

### 183. If a widow(er) elects to start receiving a widow(er)'s benefit before full retirement age, how is the benefit reduced?

The widow(er)'s full benefit must first be determined. The full benefit (to which he would be entitled by waiting until full retirement age) is 100 percent of the deceased spouse's PIA. When the full retirement age was sixty-five, this benefit was reduced by 19/40 of 1 percent (19/4000) for each month that the widow(er) was under full retirement age when benefits began.

For example, suppose that the deceased spouse's PIA was $1,000. The widow(er)'s full benefit would have been $1,000. However, if the widow(er) elected to receive benefits starting with the month of his sixtieth birthday (sixty months before age sixty-five), the full widow(er)'s benefit would have been reduced by $285 (60 × 19/4000 × $1,000), resulting in a benefit of $715 ($1,000 - $285). The amount of the reduction, if not an even multiple of ten cents, is increased to the next higher multiple of ten cents. A benefit beginning with the month of a widow(er)'s sixtieth birthday accordingly will equal 71.5 percent of the spouse's PIA.

When the full retirement age is more than sixty-five, the 71.5 percent reduction at age sixty remains unchanged, but the reduction factor will be different (based on 71.5 percent at age sixty and 100 percent at full retirement age). Ordinarily, the widow(er) will continue to receive the reduced benefit, even after full retirement age (but see Recomputation of Benefits, Q 189). (See Table 11 for widow(er)'s reduced benefits.)

If the widow(er)'s deceased spouse started receiving benefits before full retirement age, the widow(er)'s benefit cannot exceed the deceased spouse's reduced benefit or, if larger, 82.5 percent of his PIA.

The benefit of a disabled widow(er) who starts receiving benefits before age sixty is equal to 71.5 percent of his spouse's PIA. (See Q 118.)

### 184. How do the benefit reduction rules affect a high-earning spouse who dies after reaching Full Retirement Age (FRA) with a surviving spouse who is younger than Full Retirement Age?

The "Reduction Factor" depends upon the year that the widow attains full retirement age (FRA). If the FRA is age sixty-six, the reduction factor is the original benefit multiplied by the number of months that benefits are taken before FRA multiplied by 19 multiplied by .01 divided by 48.

For example: if the original benefit is $2,000 and the widow takes benefits at age sixty

- $2,000 x the Reduction Factor (RF) times 19 multiplied by .01 /48 = $570;
- the spouse will receive $1340 as a result of the Reduction Factor. ($2,000 – $570 = $1340).

### 185. How are benefits figured if a beneficiary starts receiving a reduced retirement benefit and later becomes entitled to a larger spouse's benefit?

The beneficiary will continue to receive the retirement benefit reduced in the regular manner. (See Q 181.) When he becomes entitled to the larger spouse's benefit, he will receive, in addition, a partial spouse's benefit. This benefit will be based on the difference between a spouse's full benefit (1/2 of his spouse's PIA) and the beneficiary's PIA. If he becomes entitled to the spouse's benefits at or after full retirement age, the spouse's benefit will equal this difference. If he becomes entitled to the spouse's benefit before full retirement age, this difference must be reduced by 25/36 of 1 percent (1/144) for each of the first thirty-six months that he is under full retirement age when the spouse's benefits commence, and 5/12 of 1 percent (1/240) for each month in excess of thirty-six.

## RECOMPUTATION OF BENEFITS

### 186. Under what circumstances are benefits recomputed?

Automatic recomputation of benefits is provided each year to take account of any earnings a beneficiary might have that would increase his benefit amount. Also, the recomputation takes into account the final year's earnings in the case of retirement and disability benefits. The recomputation for a living beneficiary is effective with January of the year following the one in which the earnings were received. A recomputation affecting survivor's benefits is effective with the month of death.

The "wage indexing" computation method must be used to recompute the PIA for an individual who has earnings after 1978, if the PIA was originally computed (or could have been computed) under this method.

The actual dollar amounts in the records of the Social Security Administration for the year of entitlement and each later year will annually be compared with the earnings in the base years that were used in the last computation. Higher earnings in any year that was not used in the last computation will be substituted for one or more years of lower earnings that were used, and the PIA will be recomputed.

The PIA will be recomputed using the same "bend points" and "indexing year" that applied when current eligibility was established. (See Q 170.) Recomputation must result in a PIA increase of at least one dollar to be effective.

A PIA computed using the transitional guarantee benefit computation method or the simplified old-start benefit computation method – based on eligibility after 1978 – cannot be recomputed to include earnings in or after the year of current eligibility.

### 187. If a person is simultaneously entitled to two or more benefits, which benefit will be paid?

A person may be entitled to more than one Social Security benefit at the same time. For example, a woman may be entitled to a parent's benefit on her deceased child's account and to a spouse's benefit on her husband's account. However, only the highest benefit will be paid, except when one of the benefits is a retirement or disability benefit. The lower benefit cannot be paid, even though the higher benefit is not payable for one or more months. But if the higher benefit is terminated, the lower benefit will be reinstalled automatically.

If a person is entitled to retirement or disability benefits and to a higher benefit, he or she will receive the retirement or disability benefit plus the difference between this benefit and the higher one. Payment, however, may be made in a single check. If one benefit is not payable for one or more months, the other benefit may be payable. For example, if a spouse's benefit is not payable for some months because of the worker's excess earnings, he or she will nevertheless receive a retirement benefit.

A child may be entitled to child's benefits on more than one earnings record, for example, his father's record and his mother's record. A child can receive the benefit based on the PIA that will result in the highest original benefit. However, if the highest original benefit is payable on the lowest PIA, he is paid on this account only if it would not reduce (after the reduction for the family maximum) the benefit of any beneficiary because of his entitlement.

## DISABILITY FREEZE

### 188. How does a period of disability affect retirement and survivor's benefits?

A person who has an established period of disability will have his or her earnings record "frozen" during the period of disability. This means that the years of disability need not be included in computing his or her AIME. Otherwise, if the worker died or recovered and returned to work before he or she reached retirement age, the years of zero earnings in his or her period of disability might reduce his or her PIA for retirement or survivors' benefits. In figuring the number of years that must be used in computing the worker's AIME, a year which fell wholly or partly within a period of disability is not counted. However, a year that is partly within a period of disability will be used as a computation base year, if inclusion of earnings for that year will produce a higher AIME.

## CALCULATING THE EXACT BENEFIT AMOUNT

### 189. In calculating the exact amount of each monthly benefit, how must the figures be rounded?

Benefits for members of a worker's family, if not an even multiple of one dollar, are rounded (after deducting the premium for Medical Insurance under Medicare, if any) to the next lower multiple of one dollar. For example, if the PIA of a deceased worker is $444.30, a child's survivor benefit is figured as $333.20 (75 percent of $444.30). However, this amount will be rounded to $333.00 (the next lower multiple of one dollar).

# MAXIMIZATION OF BENEFITS

## 190. When is the best time to apply for Social Security retirement benefits, and what are some of the ways of maximizing Social Security Benefits over time?

Many individuals treat deciding which benefits to collect and when as a one-time choice. However, there are a few cases that offer opportunities to switch between different types of benefits over time.

An individual who qualifies for both individual and spousal benefits and who is at least Full Retirement Age (FRA – also called Normal Retirement Age (NRA)) when filing for benefits can choose which benefits to collect. This option enables him or her to collect spousal benefits (which are highest at FRA) while allowing his or her own benefits to receive Delayed Retirement Credits (DRCs). The individual can then file for his or her own benefits at a later date, potentially as late as age seventy, and claim increased individual benefits. As a reminder, in order to collect "spouse only" benefits, the individual cannot have filed for his or her own individual benefits. Therefore, at any given time, only one spouse may be collecting spousal benefits.

In addition, an individual who qualifies for both individual and survivor benefits can choose which benefits to collect. This option enables him or her to collect survivor benefits, potentially as early as age sixty, while allowing his or her own benefits to increase and potentially receive DRCs. The individual can then switch to his or her own benefits at a later date, potentially as late as age seventy, and claim higher individual benefits. On the other hand, the individual could also elect to collect his or her individual benefits early and switch to the survivor benefits at a later date.

## 191. What is the "file and suspend" strategy for applying for, but not yet receiving, Social Security benefits?

File and suspend is a strategy that allows the primary earner to delay and grow benefits at a guaranteed 8 percent per year while the lower-earning spouse collects every month. The primary earner can file for benefits, making the spouse eligible for the spousal benefit, and then immediately request that the retirement benefit be suspended. The person requests to receive no checks, and that triggers the 8 percent growth per year. Then years later he or she can draw Social Security benefits.

Filing and suspending also allows an individual to retroactively change his or her mind about suspending and start collecting as if he or she had not suspended. For example, if an individual files and suspends at age sixty-six and then decides at age sixty-nine that he or she should have begun collecting at age sixty-six, he or she can retroactively reverse the decision. The SSA will send the individual a lump-sum payment of the benefits he or she would have collected without the suspension and, going forward, will pay monthly benefits based on beginning collection at age sixty-six.

## 192. What is a "restricted application," strategy for planning for and maximizing Social Security benefits?

Another concept in Social Security planning strategy is the restricted application. This strategy can be used when there is a disparity in the earnings history of the spouses. The lower earner will file an application for retirement benefits. Then the higher earner will file a "restricted application" for spousal benefits on the spouse's earnings record. The higher earner then delays retirement to age seventy to get the 8 percent growth. This will allow the higher earner to collect half of the spouses retirement benefit until turning seventy without adversely affecting delayed earnings.

## 193. Are there differences in strategies for maximizing Social Security benefits for a married couple depending upon the earnings history of the couple?

Yes. Depending on whether the members of the couple had a large difference in earnings or similar earnings, there will generally be different considerations.

### Married Couple—Large Difference in Benefits

This collection strategy, often referred to as the Hybrid Approach, tends to work best for couples who are around the same age with one individual entitled to benefits that are more than double those of the other spouse.

This approach entails the lower earner claiming individual benefits early to start the flow of income and adding adjusted spousal benefits later, with the higher earner deferring, which maximizes benefits as well as potential survivor benefits. The lower earner would file at age sixty-two and collect individual benefits. When the lower earner reaches full retirement age, assuming the higher earner is also at least FRA, the higher earner would file for benefits to allow spousal benefits to be paid but suspend collecting until reaching age seventy.

By filing for benefits when the lower earner reaches FRA, the higher earner enables the spouse to collect unreduced adjusted spousal benefits in addition to the lower earner's reduced individual benefits. The higher earner deferring collection to age seventy allows for the highest possible benefits to be paid not only during the higher earner's lifetime, but also as survivor benefits when the higher earner passes.

### Married Couple—Small Difference in Benefits

This collection strategy, sometimes referred to as a Two High Earners strategy, tends to work best for couples who are entitled to similar benefits.

This approach entails the lower earner claiming spousal benefits at FRA and switching to individual benefits at age seventy, while the higher earner defers until age seventy, maximizing potential survivor benefits. When the lower earner reaches FRA, assuming the higher earner is also at least FRA, the higher earner would file for benefits to allow spousal benefits to be paid, but suspend collecting until reaching age seventy.

By filing for benefits when the lower earner reaches FRA, the higher earner enables the spouse to collect unreduced spousal benefits. Since the lower earner has attained FRA, the lower earner can choose to collect "spouse only" benefits (which are their highest at FRA) and defer collecting individual benefits until later when benefits have accumulated delayed retirement credits. The higher earner deferring collection to age seventy allows for the highest possible benefits to be paid not only during the higher earner's lifetime, but also as survivor benefits when the higher earner passes.

## 194. Are there any strategies a widow or widower can use to maximize benefits?

Yes. A potential for strategic collection occurs when a widow or widower is entitled to survivor benefits as well as his or her own individual benefits. Since survivor benefits can be collected earlier than other benefits (as young as age sixty) and are usually highest at FRA, the usual best strategy involves the widow or widower collecting survivor benefits beginning at age sixty while deferring collecting individual benefits until age seventy when they are at their highest.

Collecting survivor benefits early starts the flow of income while allowing the individual to defer collecting his or her own benefits until they are higher.

## 195. Can a husband and wife both receive retirement benefits?

Yes. If each is entitled to receive benefits based on his or her own earnings record, each can receive retirement benefits independently of the other's benefits. However, a woman or man who is entitled to a retirement benefit and a spouse's benefit cannot receive both in full. (For details of how a spouse's benefit is determined, see Q 54.)

## 196. What kind of planning can be done regarding when Social Security benefits are started?

People today are much more interested in how they can maximize benefits. In dealing with clients now, it is more than just a question of "When should I take benefits?" Married couples can engage in planning, especially if both have worked and paid into Social Security for most of their careers. These planning techniques include taking a spousal benefit for a certain period of time and then switching to a benefit on the worker's own record. Or, a worker filing for benefits, but then electing not to take the benefits so that a spouse can take benefits.

Among the strategies available for married couples are:

- Both Husband and Wife file for retirement benefits at age sixty-two.
- Wife files for retirement benefits at age sixty-two. Husband files for spousal benefits at age sixty-two. Husband files for retirement benefits on his own at age seventy.
- Wife takes retirement benefits at age sixty-two. Husband files for retirement benefits at his full retirement age and suspends his benefits. Wife files for spousal benefits at this time. Husband reinstates his benefits at age seventy. This is often called, "File & Suspend" (see Q 191).

- Wife takes retirement benefits at her full retirement age Husband takes spousal benefits at his full retirement age. Husband files for retirement benefits at age seventy. This is often referred to as "Restricted Application" (see Q 192).

- Wife files for retirement benefits at her full retirement age. Husband files for retirement benefits at his full retirement age and suspends his benefits. Wife files for spousal benefits when husband files at his full retirement age. Husband reinstates his retirement benefits at age seventy.

- Husband files for retirement benefits at his full retirement age and suspends his benefits. Wife files for spousal benefits at her full retirement age. Husband reinstates his retirement benefits at age seventy and Wife files for her own retirement benefits at age seventy.

- Wife files for retirement at her full retirement age and suspends benefits. Husband files for spousal benefits at his full retirement age. Wife reinstates her retirement benefits at age seventy and Husband files for his own retirement benefits at age seventy.

- Husband takes retirement benefits at age sixty-two. Wife files for spousal benefits at her full retirement age; Wife files for her own retirement benefits at age seventy.

Among strategies available for widows or widowers are:

- Widow/Widower takes the higher benefit at the earliest time, thus she would take Widows/Widowers benefits at age sixty or retirement benefits at age sixty-two.

- Widow/Widower takes benefits at age sixty, then begins benefits on own retirement at full retirement age.

- Widow/Widower takes benefits at age sixty, then begins benefits on own retirement at age seventy.

- Widow/Widower takes her own retirement at age sixty-two, and then begins Widows/Widowers benefits at full retirement age.

## 197. In a situation where there is a lower earning spouse aged sixty-two and a higher earning spouse aged sixty-six – can the lower earning spouse claim her benefit at age sixty-two and then switch to a spousal benefit when higher earning spouse applies at age seventy?

This depends on the lower earning spouse's full retirement age benefit. If the FRA is less than 50 percent of the higher earning spouse's FRA benefit, then they can take their own at age sixty-two and the additional spousal benefit when their spouse files. However, their part is still reduced. They would never reach one-half of their spouse's FRA benefit. Once someone takes a reduced benefit on their own work record, it remains reduced.

## 198. Can you file for spousal benefits only at FRA if your spouse is only sixty-two and has not filed?

No. You can only file the restricted application at full retirement age if your spouse is sixty-two and has not filed for benefits.

## 199. If a person files for a spousal benefit before age seventy and then begins receiving monthly benefits at age seventy, do they get BOTH the spousal amount plus the age seventy monthly benefit?

No, they get the higher benefit of the two.

## 200. What is the best time to file for Social Security retirement benefits?

The decision on when to apply for Social Security retirement benefits depends on a number of factors. Taking benefits early (before full retirement age) will result in a permanent reduction of benefits. Taking retirement benefits later will result in a high benefit amount, but a shorter life may result in lower total benefits. The Social Security Administration provides a Retirement Planner on its website which includes a number of calculators to help a person determine the right time to file for benefits and the effect on benefits of filing early or late.

However, the federal government does allow an individual a "re-do" if he or she decides that the application for retirement benefits was made too early. By filing Form 521, an individual can request that the original application for retirement benefits be withdrawn and a new application date be substituted. The catch is that the individual must pay back all retirements benefits received up to the date of the withdrawal. However the federal government does not charge a penalty or interest for filing a Form 521, but the individual must have the cash to repay the federal government. Note that a "re-do" can only be done within one year of first filing for benefits.

Another consideration on for when to take retirement benefits is how much income will be earned in the year for which benefits are applied. Too much earned income will result in a loss of benefits (see Q 223).

Additionally, since Social Security benefits may be subject to income taxation (see Q 234), the individual's income and tax situation should be considered.

A person should access the Social Security Administration's website or get in touch with a Social Security office two or three months before reaching age sixty-two. The website and/or the Social Security office will furnish the information needed to decide whether or not to file an application for retirement benefits at that time. Because of the rules regarding retroactive benefits, a person should consider filing for benefits on January 1 of the year that he attains full retirement age, which may actually be older than age sixty-five (see Q 26).

If a worker does not file an application, he should contact the Social Security office again: (1) two or three months before retirement; (2) as soon as the worker knows that he will neither earn more than the monthly exempt amount in wages nor render substantial services in self-employment in one or more months of the year, regardless of expected total annual earnings; or (3) two or three months before the worker reaches FRA, even if still working.

It may be advantageous to delay filing an application for benefits where: (1) the person is under the FRA and wishes to wait and receive an unreduced benefit at FRA but benefits are not payable because of earnings (application at or near retirement may provide higher benefits in the year of retirement), or (3) the person would lose benefits payable under some other program.

## 201. When should a person file for retirement benefits?

A person should get in touch with a Social Security office two or three months before reaching age sixty-two. The Social Security office will furnish the information needed to decide whether or not to file an application for retirement benefits at that time. Because of the rules regarding retroactive benefits, a person should consider filing for benefits on January 1 of the year that he or she attains full retirement age (see Q 26).

If a worker does not file an application, he should contact the Social Security office again: (1) two or three months before retirement; (2) as soon as the worker knows that he will neither earn more than the monthly exempt amount in wages nor render substantial services in self-employment in one or more months of the year, regardless of expected total annual earnings; or (3) two or three months before the worker reaches FRA, even if still working.

It may be advantageous to delay filing an application for benefits where: (1) the person is under the FRA and wishes to wait and receive an unreduced benefit at FRA, (2) the person is at the FRA but benefits are not payable because of earnings (application at or near retirement may provide higher benefits in the year of retirement), or (3) the person would lose benefits payable under some other program.

# YEAR OF RETIREMENT

## 202. If age 62 is the computation age, is there any advantage to waiting until full retirement age to collect benefits?

Yes, the full PIA is payable at full retirement age, (see Q 181), with a reduced amount paid in case of an earlier retirement age. Age sixty-two is used to determine elapsed years but earnings are counted to full retirement age. Thus, early retirement usually affects the benefit in two ways. The PIA usually will be smaller (because fewer years of possibly higher earnings will be used in computing the AIME), and the lower PIA will be subject to reduction (5/9 of 1 percent per month for the first thirty-six months under the full retirement age and 5/12 of 1 percent per month for any additional months under the full retirement age).

## 203. Can a person obtain higher retirement benefits by working past retirement age?

Yes, in two ways.

First, workers who continue on the job receive an increase in retirement benefits for each year they work between full retirement age and seventy. Note that this is *not* an increase in the worker's PIA. Other benefits based on the PIA, such as those payable to a spouse, are not affected.

This delayed retirement credit is also payable to a worker's surviving spouse receiving a widow(er)'s benefit.

Beginning in 1990, the delayed retirement credit payable to workers who attain age sixty-two after 1986 and who delay retirement past the full retirement age, the full-benefit age (gradually rising from age sixty-five to age sixty-seven) is gradually increased. The delayed retirement credit is increased by one-half of 1 percent every other year until reaching 8 percent per year in 2009 or later. The higher delayed retirement credits are based on the year of attaining age sixty-two and are payable only at and after full retirement age.

**Delayed Retirement Credit Rates**

| Attain Age 62 | Monthly Percentage | Yearly Percentage |
|---|---|---|
| 1979-1986 | 1/4 of 1% | 3% |
| 1987-1988 | 7/24 of 1% | 3.50% |
| 1989-1990 | 1/3 of 1% | 4% |
| 1991-1992 | 3/8 of 1% | 4.50% |
| 1993-1994 | 5/12 of 1% | 5% |
| 1995-1996 | 11/24 of 1% | 5.50% |
| 1997-1998 | 1/2 of 1% | 6% |
| 1999-2000 | 13/24 of 1% | 6.50% |
| 2001-2002 | 7/12 of 1% | 7% |
| 2003-2004 | 5/8 of 1% | 7.50% |
| 2005 or after | 2/3 of 1% | 8% |

Workers, who became age sixty-five before 1990 (and after 1981) and continued on the job, received an increase in retirement benefits usually equal to 3 percent for each year (1/12 of 3 percent for each month) they worked between age sixty-five and seventy. (The factor was only 1 percent for workers who became age sixty-five before 1982.)

Second, working past the full retirement age frequently results in a higher AIME. The reason: In figuring the *number* of years to be used in the computation, the year in which the person reaches age sixty-two and succeeding years are not counted. (See Q 166). But those years can be selected as years of highest earnings.

## 204. Will the retirement age at which unreduced benefits are available ever be increased?

Yes, the Social Security Amendments of 1983 increased the full retirement age (the age at which unreduced benefits are available), by two months per year for workers reaching age sixty-two in 2000-2005 – to age sixty-six; maintained age sixty-six for workers reaching age sixty-two in 2006-2016; increased by two months a year the retirement age for workers reaching age sixty-two in 2017-2022; and maintained age sixty-seven for workers reaching age sixty-two after 2022. It does not change the age of eligibility for Medicare.

The 1983 amendments do not change the availability of reduced benefits at sixty-two (sixty for widow(er)s), but revise the reduction factors so that there is a further reduction (up to a maximum of 30 percent for workers entitled at age sixty-two after the full retirement age is increased to age sixty-seven, rather than only up to 20 percent for entitlement at age sixty-two under prior rules). There is no increase in the maximum reduction in the case of widow(er) s, but some increases in the reduction occur at ages over sixty and under full retirement age.

**Effects of Retirement-Age Provision in Social Security Amendments of 1983***

| Year of Birth | Attainment of Age 62 | Full retirement age (Year/ Months) | Date of Attainment of Full retirement age[1] | Age-62 Benefit as Percent of PIA[2] |
|---|---|---|---|---|
| 1938 | 2000 | 65/2 | March 1, 2003 | 79.2 |
| 1939 | 2001 | 65/4 | May 1, 2004 | 78.3 |
| 1940 | 2002 | 65/6 | July 1, 2005 | 77.5 |
| 1941 | 2003 | 65/8 | September 1, 2006 | 76.7 |
| 1942 | 2004 | 65/10 | November 1, 2007 | 75.8 |
| 1943-1954 | 2005-2016 | 66/0 | January 1, 2009-2020 | 75.0 |
| 1955 | 2017 | 66/2 | March 1, 2021 | 74.2 |
| 1956 | 2018 | 66/4 | May 1, 2022 | 73.3 |
| 1957 | 2019 | 66/6 | July 1, 2023 | 72.5 |
| 1958 | 2020 | 66/8 | September 1, 2024 | 71.7 |
| 1959 | 2021 | 66/10 | November 1, 2025 | 70.8 |
| 1960 and after | 2022 and after | 67/0 | January 1, 2027 and after | 70.0 |

* Full retirement age is for worker and spouse benefits only. Full retirement age for widow(er)s is based on attainment of age 60 in 2000 or later, so that Full retirement age is age 67 beginning 2029.

1. Birth date assumed to be January 2 of year (for benefit-entitlement purposes, the Social Security Administration considers a person to reach a given age on the day before the anniversary of his birth, thus, someone born on the 1st of the month is considered to reach a given age on the last day of the previous month). For later months of birth, add number of months elapsing after January up to birth month.

2. Applies present-law reduction factor (5/9 of 1 percent per month) for the first 36 months' receipt of early retirement benefits and new reduction factor of 5/12 of 1 percent per month for additional months.

## 205. How are a beneficiary's benefits figured when he is entitled to a reduced retirement benefit and a larger spouse's benefit simultaneously?

The beneficiary will receive the retirement benefit, reduced in the regular manner. (See Q 181.) That is, the PIA is reduced by 5/9 of 1 percent (1/180) for each of the first thirty-six months that he is under full retirement age when benefits commence, and 5/12 of 1 percent (1/240) for each month in excess of thirty-six. The beneficiary will also receive a spouse's benefit based on the difference between the full spouse's benefit (1/2 of his or her spouse's PIA) and his or her PIA. This spouse's benefit is reduced by 25/36 of 1 percent (1/144) for each of the first thirty-six months that he is under full retirement age when benefits commence, and 5/12 of 1 percent (1/240) for each month in excess of thirty-six. (See Q 185.)

## 206. What are the advantages and disadvantages of using file and suspend?

There are two advantages and one disadvantage.

The advantages include: 1) If you file and suspend, you allow anyone else eligible on your work record (i.e., spouse or child) to draw their benefits. 2) You also create a safety net so if at some point before you reach age seventy, you can request your benefits all the way back to when you filed (i.e., age sixty-six).

The disadvantage to file and suspend is that there are limitations on having a Health Savings Account (HSA) – if you file and suspend, you will at least have Part A of Medicare. Participating in Medicare precludes you from contributing to a Health Savings Account.

## 207. How does a "restricted application" differ from file and suspend?

"File and Suspend" is the action of filing for benefits on your own work record but suspending payment. You will earn delayed retirement credits and create the "safety net".

A "Restricted application" is filing for spousal credits for someone else's work record. You can still earn delayed retirement credits on your own work record but draw benefits as a spouse at the same time.

## 208. Can both spouses "file and suspend" at the same time?

Yes.

## 209. Is it possible to file and suspend and also file a restricted application?

No. You can only do one at a time.

## 210. Can both husband and wife file a restricted application for the other's spousal benefit?

No. To file a restricted application, the other spouse must have already filed for benefits or filed and suspended on their own work record.

## 211. Can you file and suspend at sixty-two to allow a nonworking spouse who is in ill health to collect one-half of benefit?

You cannot file and suspend until full retirement age.

## 212. In a situation where a husband is aged sixty-six and working, can he file and suspend if his wife is age sixty-two? Assuming the wife has her own earning credits, can she then wait until she is seventy to begin benefits or should she file a restricted application at her own FRA?

Yes, the husband can file and suspend at his full retirement age. The wife can wait until age seventy but should consider the restricted application at her own full retirement age.

**213. After filing a restricted application, does one have to wait until reaching age seventy to begin their own benefit?**

No. A person is not locked in until age seventy but can begin benefits at any time.

**214. Can we assume that a single person can only use the File and Suspend strategy and not the Restricted application?**

Yes, unless they have an ex-spouse and were married to them for over ten years.

**215. When a spouse files and suspends and delays collecting until age seventy, will the other spouse get an amount equal to half of the income based on the delayed retirement credits or based on the full retirement age benefit?**

No. The spousal benefit is based on the full retirement age benefit amount. A current spouse does not receive any advantage of the delayed retirement credits.

**216. What if a person dies after filing and suspending but before receiving benefits? Can the widow collect that lump sum?**

No, only the person filing the application can request the lump sum. The widow would still get the delayed retirement credits, which results in a higher monthly benefit.

**217. If a husband files and suspends and the wife takes spousal benefits at age sixty-two, will the wife get a stepped-up spousal benefit if the husband dies at age seventy-two after delaying his benefit until age seventy?**

Yes. The spouse taking a reduced benefit either on their own or as a spouse does not affect the survivor's benefit. If the surviving spouse is full retirement age when their spouse dies, they will get 100 percent of what the deceased was receiving or was eligible to receive.

**218. Can a working couple both at FRA claim both file and suspend and restricted to receive two Social Security checks?**

Both can file and suspend but only one can do the restricted application. You cannot do both and you cannot file on another's record unless they have also filed.

**219. What is the best strategy in a situation where the husband is age sixty-six with an income of $150,000 per year and the wife is age sixty-eight, with an income of $50,000 per year?**

This depends on the PIA of each but assuming that the husband has the higher PIA, he needs to file and suspend while the wife should file a restricted application. This will ensure the maximization of benefits.

## 220. What is the best strategy in a situation where the husband is age sixty-six with an income of $150,000 per year and the wife is age sixty-eight, with an income of $50,000 per year and the wife has already filed for benefits.

If the wife filed over a year ago, she cannot withdraw her application, which means the husband should consider filing the restricted application.

## 221. What option might one use if there is a significant difference in ages between spouses, for example, if the husband is twelve years older than wife?

Normally in this case, the older individual (in this case, the husband) is looking at the same options as a single person – however – unlike the single person, they DO want to maximize survivor benefits. For example, the older spouse takes benefits at age seventy and the younger spouse takes benefits at age sixty. This works because based on life expectancies, the younger spouse will collect survivor benefits for many years.

## 222. What are the limitations of the "do-over" as an option?

The "do-over" still exists, with limitations. It must be done within the first year and can only be done once.

# LOSS OF BENEFITS BECAUSE OF "EXCESS" EARNINGS

## RETIREMENT TEST

### 223. Can a person lose some or all Social Security benefits by working?

Yes, if the person is under full retirement age (see Q 26) for all of 2015 and earns over $15,720; or in the year the person reaches full retirement age he or she earns over $41,880, except that only earnings earned before the month he or she reaches full retirement age count towards the $41,880 limit.[1] An alternative test applies in the initial year of retirement if it produces a more favorable result (see the last "bullet" of Q 224). See Q 185 for a discussion of the full retirement age.

The annual exempt amounts will be increased each year as wage levels rise.

A beneficiary who is older than the full retirement age can earn any amount without losing benefits. Regardless of how much earnings are in the year of attaining full retirement age, no benefits are withheld for the month in which full retirement age is reached, or for any subsequent month. Also, earnings in and after the month in which a person attains full retirement age will not be included in determining total earnings for the year.

The retirement test does not apply to individuals entitled to benefits because of their disability or to beneficiaries outside the United States whose work is not covered by Social Security.

| Annual Exempt Amounts | | |
|---|---|---|
| **Year** | **Year Retirement Age Reached** | **Under Retirement Age** |
| 1985 | $7,320 | $5,400 |
| 1986 | 7,800 | 5,760 |
| 1987 | 8,160 | 6,000 |
| 1988 | 8,400 | 6,120 |
| 1989 | 8,880 | 6,480 |
| 1990 | 9,360 | 6,840 |
| 1991 | 9,720 | 7,080 |
| 1992 | 10,200 | 7,440 |
| 1993 | 10,560 | 7,680 |
| 1994 | 11,160 | 8,040 |
| 1995 | 11,280 | 8,160 |
| 1996 | 11,520 | 8,280 |
| 1997 | 13,500 | 8,640 |
| 1998 | 14,500 | 9,120 |

1. 42 U.S.C. § 403(f).

| Year | Year Retirement Age Reached | Under Retirement Age |
|---|---|---|
| 1999 | 15,500 | 9,600 |
| 2000 | 17,000 | 10,080 |
| 2001 | 25,000 | 10,680 |
| 2002 | 30,000 | 11,280 |
| 2003 | 30,720 | 11,520 |
| 2004 | 31,080 | 11,640 |
| 2005 | 31,800 | 12,000 |
| 2006 | 33,240 | 12,480 |
| 2007 | 34,440 | 12,960 |
| 2008 | 36,120 | 13,560 |
| 2009-2011 | 37,680 | 14,160 |
| 2012 | 38,880 | 14,640 |
| 2013 | 40,080 | 15,120 |
| 2014 | 41,400 | 15,480 |
| 2015 | 41,880 | 15,720 |

## 224. What are the general rules for loss of benefits because of excess earnings?

When the beneficiary is older than the full retirement age (see Q 26), no benefits are lost because of his earnings. If he is under the full retirement age, the following rules apply:[1]

- If no more than $41,880 is earned in 2015 by a beneficiary who reaches the full retirement age in 2015, no benefits will be lost for that year.
- If more than $41,880 is earned in 2015 before the month the beneficiary reaches full retirement age, one dollar of benefits will ordinarily be lost for each three dollars of earnings over $41,880.
- If not more than $15,720 is earned in 2015 by a beneficiary who is under the full retirement age for the entire year, no benefits will be lost for that year.
- If more than $15,720 is earned in 2015 by a beneficiary who is under the full retirement age for the entire year, one dollar of benefits will ordinarily be lost for each two dollars of earnings over $15,720.
- No matter how much is earned during 2015, no *retirement* benefits in the *initial year of retirement* will be lost for any month in which the beneficiary neither: (1) earns over $1,310 as an employee if retiring in a year prior to the year he reaches full retirement age, nor (2) renders any substantial services in self-employment.

1. 42 U.S.C. 403(f).

The initial year of retirement is the first year in which he is both entitled to benefits and has a month in which he does not earn over the monthly exempt wage amount (as listed previously) and does not render substantial services in self-employment.

When the monthly earnings test applies, regardless of the amount of annual earnings, the beneficiary gets full benefits for any month in which earnings do not exceed the monthly exempt amount, and the beneficiary does not perform substantial services in self-employment.

The attainment of full retirement age in a year determines which test applies. The full retirement age test applies if the beneficiary attains full retirement age on or before the last day of the taxable year involved. The "under full retirement age" test applies if the beneficiary does not attain full retirement age on or before the last day of the taxable year. See Q 185 for a discussion of the increase in the full retirement age.

*Example*. Dr. James, who reports his earnings on a calendar year basis, reaches full retirement age (sixty-six years old) on June 18, 2015. The under full retirement age test ($15,480 for 2014) applies for calendar year 2014, and the full retirement age test ($41,880) applies for calendar year 2015. However, none of Dr. James earnings earned in June through December, 2015, count towards the $41,880 limit.

*Example*. Miss Norton, who reports her earnings on the basis of a fiscal year ending June 30, attains full retirement age (sixty-six years old) on September 15, 2015. The under full retirement age test ($15,720) applies for her fiscal year July 1, 2014 through June 30, 2015. The full retirement age test ($41,880) applies for her next fiscal year; however, only earnings earned in July and August, 2015 count towards the $41,880 limit.

## 225. How are "excess" earnings charged against benefits?

In determining the amount of benefits for a given year that will be lost, two factors must be taken into consideration: (1) the amount of the person's "excess" earnings for the year, and (2) the months in the year that can actually be charged with all or a portion of the excess earnings potentially chargeable in the initial year of retirement.[1]

Both wages earned as an employee and net earnings from self-employment are combined for purposes of determining the individual's total earnings for the year. Only "excess earnings" are potentially chargeable against benefits. If a person is under the full retirement age for the entire year and earns $15,720 or less (in 2015) for the year, there are no "excess earnings." If earnings for the year are more than $15,720, one-half of the amount over $15,720 is "excess earnings." In the year a person reaches the full retirement age, he or she can earn up to $41,880 (in 2015) before losing benefits. However, only earnings earned before the month the person reaches full retirement age count toward the $41,880 limit. See Q 183 for a discussion of the full retirement age.

Excess earnings are charged against retirement benefits in the following manner. They are charged first against all benefits payable on the worker's account for the first month of the year. If any excess earnings remain, they are charged against all benefits payable for the second month of the year, and so on until all the excess earnings have been charged, or no benefits remain for the year. However, a month cannot be charged with any excess earnings and must be skipped if

1. 20 CFR Part 404, Subpart E.

the individual: (1) was not entitled to benefits for that month, (2) was over full retirement age in that month, or (3) in the initial year of retirement he or she did not earn over $1,310 (using 2015 figures) if he or she retires in a year before the year he or she reaches full retirement age, or (4) he or she did not render substantial services as a self-employed person in that month.

If the excess earnings chargeable to a month are less than the benefits payable to the worker and to other persons on his account, the excess is chargeable to each beneficiary in the proportion that the original entitlement rate of each bears to the sum of all their original entitlement rates.

> *Example 1*. Dr. Brown partially retires in January 2015 at the age of sixty-two. Based on his earnings history and the age he starts receiving benefits, his Social Security benefit is $1,200 per month. He practices for three months in 2015 and earns $30,000. The remainder of his initial year of retirement is spent in Florida playing golf. Despite the fact that Dr. Brown has excess earnings in 2015 that would, under the annual test, cause a benefit loss of $7,140, he will lose only the $3,600 in benefits for the three months during which he performed substantial services in self-employment, because 2015 is his initial year of retirement.

> *Example 2*. Dr. Smith, who partially retired in 2014 at age sixty-two, practices for four months in 2015 and earns $32,000. As 2015 is his second year of retirement, the monthly-earnings test does not apply. His benefit will be reduced by $1 for each $2 of earnings over $15,720. This means that Dr. Smith's benefits in 2015 will be reduced by $8,140 (½ of the amount in excess of $15,720).

> *Example 3*. Mr. Martin is sixty-six years old and has not retired. He earns $45,000 a year. Mr. Martin receives Social Security retirement benefits of $700 a month. Because he is over the full retirement age, he loses none of his benefits by working.

The annual exempt amount is not prorated in the year of death. In addition, the higher exempt amount applies to persons who die before their date of birth in the year that they otherwise would have attained full retirement age.

## 226. Can a person who is receiving dependent's or survivor's benefits lose benefits by working?

Yes, if the person is under the full retirement age for the entire year and earns over $15,720 (in 2015), or in the year the person reaches full retirement age he earns over $41,880. Only earnings earned before the month the person reaches full retirement age count toward the $41,880 limit.[1] The same "retirement test" applies as applies to retirement beneficiaries (see Q 224). However, the excess earnings of a person receiving dependent's or survivor's benefits are not charged against the benefits payable to other dependents or survivors. For example, a child's excess earnings are not chargeable against a mother's benefits. A retirement beneficiary's excess earnings, on the other hand, *are* chargeable against a dependent's benefits, as those benefits are based on the retirement beneficiary's Social Security account. See Q 183 for a discussion of the full retirement age.

## 227. If a widow's benefits are withheld because of work, will this necessarily reduce the total amount of benefits payable to the family?

No. Where there are several children, all survivor benefits may have to be reduced to come within the maximum family benefit. Even though the mother works and loses her benefits, the

1. 42 U.S.C. § 403(f).

maximum may still be payable to the children. In many cases, however, loss of the mother's benefits will reduce the total amount of benefits payable to the family.[1]

*Example 1*. Mr. Smith dies in 2015, leaving a widow and four small children. His PIA is $700. If it were not for the maximum family limit, the widow and each child would be entitled to a survivor's benefit of $525 (75 percent% of $700). However, because the maximum family benefit for a PIA of $700 is $1,050, each beneficiary receives only $210 (1/5 of $1,050, rounded to the next lower even dollar). Mrs. Smith goes to work and earns an amount sufficient to eliminate her mother's benefits ($1 is withheld for every $2 of excess earnings). Nevertheless, the family still receives $1,050 in benefits, because each child's benefit is raised to $262 (1/4 of $1,050, rounded to the next lower even dollar).

*Example 2*. Mr. Jones dies in 2015, leaving a widow and two small children. His PIA is $800 and the maximum family benefit is $1,200. If it were not for the maximum family limit, the widow and each child would be entitled to a monthly benefit of $600 (75 percent of $800). Because of the family maximum limit, however, each receives only $400 (1/3 of $1,200, rounded to the next lower even dollar). Mrs. Jones goes to work and earns an amount sufficient to eliminate her widow's benefits. Each child then receives a full benefit of $600.

## 228. How is the loss of benefits figured for the year in which the worker reaches full retirement age?

In the year in which a person reaches full retirement age, his earnings in and after the month in which he reaches full retirement age will not be included in determining his total earnings for the year.[2]

## 229. What kinds of earnings will cause loss of benefits?

*Wages* received as an employee and net *earnings* from self-employment. Bonuses, commissions, fees, and earnings from all types of work, whether or not covered by Social Security, count for the retirement test. For example, earnings from family employment are counted – even though such employment is not covered by Social Security. Earnings above the Social Security "earnings base" are counted. Income as an absentee owner counts as "earnings" for the retirement test.[3] If the person renders substantial services as a self-employed person (even in another business), such income also will count as "earnings" for the taxable year in the initial year of retirement.

The following types of income are *not* counted as "earnings" for purposes of the retirement test:[4]

- Any income from employment earned in or after the month the individual reaches full retirement age. (Self-employment income earned in the year is not examined as to when earned, but rather is prorated by months, even though actually earned after full retirement age.) See Q 183 for a discussion of full retirement age.

- Any income from self-employment received in a taxable year after the year the individual becomes entitled to benefits, but not attributable to significant services

1. See 20 CFR Part 404, Subpart E.
2. 42 U.S.C. 403(f).
3. 42 U.S.C. 403(f).
4. 20 CFR Part 404, Subpart E.

performed after the first month of entitlement to benefits. This income is excluded from gross income only for purposes of the earnings test.

- Damages, attorneys' fees, interest, or penalties paid under court judgment or by compromise settlement with an employer based on a wage claim. However, back pay recovered in such proceedings counts for the earnings test.
- Payments to secure release of an unexpired contract of employment.
- Certain payments made under a plan or system established for making payments because of the employee's sickness or accident disability, medical or hospitalization expenses, or death.
- Payments from certain trust funds that are exempt from income tax.
- Payments from certain annuity plans that are exempt from income tax.
- Pensions and retirement pay.
- Sick pay, if paid more than six months after the month the employee last worked.
- Payments-in-kind for domestic service in the employer's private home, for agricultural labor, for work not in the course of the employer's trade or business, or the value of meals and lodging furnished under certain conditions.
- Rentals from real estate that cannot be counted in earnings from self-employment because, for instance, the beneficiary did not materially participate in production work on the farm, the beneficiary was not a real estate dealer, etc.
- Interest and dividends from stocks and bonds (unless they are received by a dealer in securities in the course of business).
- Gain or loss from the sale of capital assets, or sale, exchange, or conversion of other property that is not stock in trade or includable in inventory.
- Net operating loss carryovers resulting from self-employment activities.
- Loans received by employees, unless the employees repay the loans by their work.
- Workers' compensation and unemployment compensation benefits.
- Veterans' training pay.
- Pay for jury duty.
- Prize winnings from contests, unless the person enters contests as a trade or business.
- Tips paid to an employee that are less than twenty dollars a month or are not paid in cash.

- Payments by an employer that are reimbursements specifically for travel expenses of the employee and that are so identified by the employer at the time of payment.
- Payments to an employee as a reimbursement or allowance for moving expenses, if they are not counted as wages for Social Security purposes.
- Royalties received in or after the year in which a person reaches full retirement age, to the extent that they flow from property created by the person's own personal efforts that she copyrighted or patented before the taxable year in which she reached full retirement age. These royalties are excluded from gross income from self-employment only for purposes of the earnings test.
- Retirement payments received by a retired partner from a partnership, provided certain conditions are met.
- Certain payments or series of payments paid by an employer to an employee or any of his or her dependents on or after the employment relationship has terminated because of death, retirement for disability, or retirement for age and paid under a plan established by the employer.
- Payments *from* Individual Retirement Accounts (IRAs) and Keogh Plans.

In other words, a person can receive almost any amount of investment or passive income without loss of benefits.

## 230. How does the Annual Earnings Test work?

If you take Social Security benefits before reaching full retirement age, and you earn income in excess of the annual earnings limit, your Social Security benefit will be reduced. Only "earned income" applies – NOT investment income. The annual earnings test limits (in 2015) earnings to $15,720. If your earnings exceed $15,720, Social Security will withhold one dollar of benefits for each two dollars that exceeds the earnings test limit.

During the year you reach full retirement age, and up until the month you reach full retirement age, Social Security will deduct one dollar for every three dollars you earn over the annual earnings limit, however you can earn up to (in 2015) $41,880 during the year you reach full retirement age.

Once you reach full retirement age, you are no longer subject to the annual earnings limit; you can earn as much as you like without incurring a reduction in your Social Security benefits. Your social benefits may however still be subject to income taxes.

## 231. What is meant by "substantial services" in self-employment?

Whether a self-employed beneficiary is rendering "substantial services" in the initial year of retirement is determined by the actual services rendered in the month. The test is whether the person can reasonably be considered retired in the month. In applying the test, consideration is given to such factors as: (1) the amount of time devoted to the business (including all time spent at the place of business or elsewhere) in any activity related to the business (including the time spent in planning and managing, as well as doing physical work); (2) the nature of the services; (3) the relationship of the activities performed before retirement to those performed after retirement; and (4) other circumstances, such as the amount of capital the beneficiary has invested in the business, the type of business establishment, the presence of a paid manager, partner, or family member who manages the business, and the seasonal nature of the business.[1]

Generally, services of forty-five hours or less in a month are not considered substantial. However, as few as fifteen hours of service a month could be substantial if, for instance, they involved management of a sizeable business or were spent in a highly skilled occupation. Services of fewer than fifteen hours a month are never considered substantial.

The amount of earnings is not controlling. High earnings do not necessarily mean that substantial services were rendered, nor do low or no earnings mean that they were not rendered.

NOTE: The "substantial services" test is used only for the initial year of retirement. After that, the amount of earnings alone determines whether benefits will be lost.

## 232. Must a Social Security beneficiary report earnings to the Social Security Administration?

The Social Security Administration uses earnings information for workers that has been reported by employers on W-2 income tax forms – or income reported by the self-employed on their tax forms. For most beneficiaries, the process is totally automated, with the Social Security Administration receiving and processing earnings information reported for tax purposes and using that information to adjust the Social Security benefits payable accordingly.

Benefits will be stopped for the number of months necessary to offset excess earnings. If too much has been withheld, the beneficiary will receive a check for the underpayment. If too little, the overpayment will be withheld from future benefits or must be refunded.

## 233. How are a life insurance agent's first-year and renewal commissions treated for purposes of the retirement test?

Whether original (first year) and renewal commissions from the sale of life insurance policies are wages or earnings from self-employment depends upon the status of the agent when the sale of the policy was completed. If the agent was an employee when the sale of the policy was consummated, both original and renewal commissions from that policy are wages. If the agent was self-employed when the sale of the policy was completed, both the original and renewal commissions from the policy are earnings from self-employment.[2]

Each insurance company normally furnishes its agents with sufficient information identifying policies on which commission payments are made, amounts of payments that are regular commissions, the commuted value of the renewals, service fees, efficiency income, etc., to enable a beneficiary to figure how much the earnings are for Social Security purposes.

1. 20 CFR Part 404, Subpart E.
2. 20 CFR Part 404, Subpart E.

A life insurance agent will receive retirement benefits for the month in which full retirement age is reached, and for every month thereafter, regardless of whether still working and regardless of how much is earned.

Moreover in the *initial year of retirement*, and regardless of the amount of earnings for the taxable year, benefits will not be lost for any month in which the individual neither: (1) earns more than $1,310 (if under full retirement age) as an employee, nor (2) renders substantial services in self-employment. See Q 183 for a discussion of the full retirement age.

It is necessary to determine whether the agent was an employee or a self-employed person when the policy was sold. (For status of a life insurance agent as an employee or as a self-employed person under Social Security, see Q 271.)The reason is that, for retirement test purposes,"wages" of an employee are treated as earnings in the year in which they are earned. But net earnings for self-employment are treated as earnings in the year in which they are received.

Original (first-policy-year) commissions are earnings for purposes of the retirement test for the month and year in which an employee-agent completed the sale of the policy. As a rule, an employee-agent is paid the original commission on a policy according to the way the insured person pays the premium. The entire original commission is earnings for the month in which the agent completed the sale of the policy, regardless of whether the commission is received on a monthly, quarterly, semi-annual, or annual basis.

Renewal commissions of an employee-agent are earnings for purposes of the retirement test for the month in which the employee completed the sale of the life insurance policy and are includable in total earnings for the taxable year. They are deferred compensation for services rendered in completing the sale.

All of the renewal commissions that an employee-agent anticipates receiving from a life insurance policy sold while an employee must be reported as earnings for purposes of the retirement test for the month and year in which the original sale of the policy was completed. If the anticipated renewal commissions fail to materialize (thus making incorrect the total annual or monthly earnings), any benefit previously withheld but now due the beneficiary will be paid.

An employee-agent beneficiary must include the following in figuring total earnings for purposes of the retirement test for a taxable year:

- All original commissions on life insurance policies sold during the year.
- All anticipated renewal commissions on life insurance policies sold in the year. If the agent-beneficiary cannot determine the exact amount of anticipated renewals from such policies, as a last resort it should be assumed that they equal the amount of the original commission.
- Insurance service fees, persistency fees, and the like earned during the year.
- All renewal commissions received in the taxable year from policies sold in prior years while self-employed.
- All remuneration classified as earnings from other jobs, trades, or business.

Thus, renewal commissions on business in past years are not "earnings" for retirement test purposes when received by the agent-beneficiary if he was an employee when the policies were sold.

An employee-agent earns commission on a life insurance policy in the month in which the last act required for entitlement to the commission is performed. The acts to be performed before entitlement to commissions are usually set out in the agent's contract with the company, or can be determined from the company's regulations, rules, or practices. The agent should submit a copy of the contract or other evidence if there is any doubt about the last act required.

The month in which the company approves the policy is not the month in which the commission was earned, unless it happens to coincide with the last act required of the agent (for instance, if later in that month the agent forwarded the first premium due on the approved policy and this qualified for the commission). Similarly, the month in which the agent delivered the policy and collected the initial premium is not the month in which the commission was earned if the agent qualified for the commission when the customer signed the policy application.

This same rule applies to converted policies. If the conversion of the life insurance policy resulted in new commissions, the commissions are earned in the month in which the agent performed the last act that qualified for those new commissions. In the latter case, it is immaterial that the conversion was accomplished with the help of another agent through the insistence of the purchaser of the policy; some action (even if it is only the signature) was required of the selling agent in order to be entitled to the new rate of commissions.

If the life insurance agent is a self-employed person when the policy is sold, first-year and renewal commissions are treated as earnings for purposes of Social Security taxes for the taxable year in which they are received. When a policy is sold, there should be reported in the year of sale only the first-year commission received on the policy in that year. Renewal commissions on such a policy will be treated as earnings for purposes of Social Security taxes in the year when received. Renewal commissions received in a year after the year of entitlement to Social Security benefits are not included as earnings for purposes of the retirement test, if they were the result of services rendered in or prior to the initial month of entitlement.

A self-employed agent includes the following in figuring total earnings for a particular taxable year for purposes of the retirement test:

- Original commissions received during the year.
- Renewal commissions received during the year from policies sold while a self-employed agent, if the policies were sold after the initial month of entitlement to Social Security benefits, but not for such policies sold in or before such initial month. Further, there will be excluded all renewal commissions received from policies sold in prior years while an employee. Also excluded will be anticipated renewal commissions on policies sold during the current year while self-employed.
- All net earnings from self-employment derived during the year in the form of insurance service fees, persistency fees, etc.

- All remuneration classified as earnings from other jobs, trades, or businesses.
- Any net loss from other self-employment during the year.

| Are Self-Employed Earnings Subject to Social Security Retirement Test? | | |
|---|---|---|
| | **Commissions Received In** | |
| **Time of Sale** | **Year of First Entitlement*** | **Year After Year of First Entitlement*** |
| Prior to Year of First Entitlement | Yes | No |
| | | |
| In Year of First Entitlement | | |
| (1) Sold in months through month of First Entitlement | Yes | No |
| (2) Sold in months after month of First Entitlement | Yes | Yes |
| | | |
| After Year of First Entitlement | Yes | Yes |

* Entitlement means (a) being eligible by virtue of age and insured status (i.e., having the required number of quarters of coverage), and (b) having filed a claim for benefits.

The receipt of renewal commissions in the initial year of retirement on policies sold by a self-employed agent will not necessarily result in a loss of benefits, even though they exceed the earnings limit for the taxable year. The reason is that such "self-employment" earnings cannot be charged against benefits for any month in the initial year of retirement in which the agent-beneficiary does not render any substantial services in self-employment. Even large amounts of renewal commissions will not cause loss of any benefits if the agent-beneficiary renders no substantial services in self-employment during the taxable year in which the commissions are received.

Generally, repeat commissions paid on casualty insurance policies (e.g., accident and health) differ from renewal commissions in the life insurance field. This is true even though the repeat commissions are sometimes called "renewal" commissions. Each repeat commission is, in fact, for a policy written for a new and different term.

Ordinarily, the rate of commission on these repeats is the same regardless of how many times the insurance is extended for a new term. In life insurance renewals, on the other hand, there is a limit on the number of years for which renewal commissions are paid on the same life insurance policy. Regardless of the amount of work done by an agent when a casualty insurance policy is extended, the commission paid is for the new term only. It is not additional compensation for the original term of the policy. For these reasons, repeat commissions from accident and health policies are normally earned in the month in which the policy is extended. Thus, they are wages for the month and year if the agent then was an employee. If the agent then was self-employed, they may be included as earnings from self-employment for the year in which they are received.

# TAXATION OF SOCIAL SECURITY BENEFITS

## 234. Are Social Security benefits subject to federal income taxation?

Social Security retirement, survivor, and disability benefits may be subject to federal income taxes in some cases. The person who has the legal right to receive the benefits must determine if the benefits are taxable. For example, if a parent and child both receive benefits, but the payment for the child is made to the parent's account, the parent must use only the parent's portion of the benefits in figuring if benefits are taxable. The portion of the benefits that belongs to the child must be added to the child's other income to see if any of those benefits are taxable.

If the only income a person receives is Social Security benefits, the benefits generally are not taxable and he probably does not need to file a tax return. However, if a person has other income in addition to benefits, he may have to file a return (even if none of the benefits are taxable).

If the total of a person's income plus half of his or her benefits is more than the *base amount*, some of the benefits are taxable. Included in the person's total income is any tax-exempt interest income, excludable interest from United States savings bonds, and excludable income earned in a foreign country, United States possession, or Puerto Rico.[1]

Voluntary federal income tax withholding is allowed on Social Security benefits. Recipients may submit a Form W-4V if they want federal income tax withheld from their benefits. Beneficiaries are able to choose withholding at 7 percent, 10 percent, 15 percent, or 25 percent of their total benefit payment.

## 235. What are the base amounts?

The base amount is as follows, depending upon a person's filing status:[2]

- $32,000 for married couples filing jointly
- $0 for married couples filing separately and who lived together at any time during the year
- $25,000 for other taxpayers

If a person is married and files a joint return, the person and his spouse must combine their incomes and their Social Security benefits when figuring if any of their combined benefits are taxable. Even if the spouse did not receive any benefits, the person must add the spouse's income to his when figuring if any of his benefits are taxable.

*Example.* Jim and Julie Smith are filing a joint return for 2014 and both received Social Security benefits during the year. Jim received net benefits of $6,600, while Julie received net benefits of $2,400. Jim also received a taxable pension of $10,000 and interest income of $500. Jim did not have any tax-exempt interest

1. IRC Sec. 86.
2. IRC Sec. 86(c)(1).

income. Jim and Julie's Social Security benefits are not taxable for 2014 because the sum of their income ($10,500) and one-half of their benefits ($9,000 ÷ 2 = $4,500) is not more than their base amount ($32,000).

Any repayment of Social Security benefits a person made during the year must be subtracted from the gross benefits received. It does not matter whether the repayment was for a benefit the person received in that year or in an earlier year.

## 236. What portion of Social Security benefits are subject to income taxes?

The amount of benefits to be included in taxable income depends on the person's total income plus half his or her Social Security benefits. The higher the total, the more benefits a person must include in taxable income. Depending upon a person's income, he or she may be required to include either up to 50 percent or up to 85 percent of benefits in income.

### 50 Percent Taxable

If a person's income plus half of his Social Security benefits is more than the following *base amount* for his filing status, up to 50 percent of his or her benefits will be included in his or her gross income:[1]

- $32,000 for married couples filing jointly
- $0 for married couples filing separately and who lived together at any time during the year
- $25,000 for all other taxpayers

### 85 Percent Taxable

If a person's income plus half of his or her Social Security benefits is more than the following *adjusted base amount* for his or her filing status, up to 85 percent of his or her benefits will be included in his or her gross income:[2]

- $44,000 for married couples filing jointly
- $0 for married couples filing separately and who lived together at any time during the year
- $34,000 for other taxpayers

If a person is married filing separately and *lived with* his or her spouse at any time during the year, up to 85 percent of his or her benefits will be included in his or her gross income.

## 237. Why is nontaxable interest income included in a taxpayer's adjusted gross income?

Nontaxable interest income is included in income to limit opportunities for manipulation of tax liability on benefits. Individuals whose incomes consist of different mixes of taxable and

1. IRC Sec. 86(c)(1).
2. IRC Sec. 86(c)(2).

nontaxable income are treated the same as individuals whose total income is taxable for federal income tax purposes.

## 238. Are workers' compensation benefits included in the definition of Social Security benefits for tax purposes?

Yes, also included in the definition of Social Security benefits for tax purposes are workers' compensation benefits, to the extent they cause a reduction in Social Security and Railroad Retirement tier I disability benefits.[1] This is intended to assure that these social insurance benefits, which are paid in lieu of Social Security payments, are treated similarly for purposes of taxation.

## 239. How are overpayments and lump-sum retroactive benefits taxed?

Special rules are provided for dealing with overpayments and lump-sum retroactive benefit payments.[2] Benefits paid to an individual in any taxable year are reduced by any overpayments repaid during the year. Taxpayers who received a lump-sum payment of retroactive benefits may treat the benefits as wholly payable for the year in which they receive them, or may elect to attribute the benefits to the tax years in which they would have fallen had they been paid timely. No benefits for months before 1984 are taxable, regardless of when they are paid.

> *Example 1*. Ms. Jones is single. In 2013, she applied for Social Security disability benefits but was told she was ineligible to receive them. She appealed the decision and won her appeal. In 2014, she received a lump-sum payment of $6,000, which included $2,000 for 2013. She has two choices. She can use her 2014 income to figure the taxable part of the entire $6,000 payment, or she can use her 2013 income to figure the taxable part of the $2,000 received for 2013. In the latter case, for 2013 she would include only the $4,000 attributable to 2014.

> *Example 2*. Assume that Mr. Jackson receives a $1,000 Social Security benefit in 2014, $400 of which is attributable to 2013. Assume also that the $1,000 benefit would increase Mr. Jackson's 2014 gross income by $500 (i.e., by the full 50 percent), but that the $400 would have increased his 2013 gross income by only $150, and the remaining $600 would have increased his 2013 gross income by $300. He may limit the increase in 2014 gross income to only $450, the sum of the increases in gross income that would have occurred had the $400 been paid in 2013.

## 240. What reporting requirements must be met by the Social Security Administration?

The Commissioner of Social Security must file annual returns with the Secretary of the Treasury setting forth the amounts of benefits paid to each individual in each calendar year, together with the name and address of the individual. The Commissioner of Social Security must also furnish similar information to each beneficiary by January 31 of the year following the benefit payments. The statement will show the total amount of Social Security benefits paid to the beneficiary, the total amount of Social Security benefits repaid by the beneficiary to the Social Security Administration during the calendar year, and the total reductions in benefits to offset workers' compensation benefits received by the beneficiary.

1. IRC Sec. 86(d)(3).
2. IRC Secs. 86(d)(2), 86(e).

## 241. Are Social Security benefits subject to income tax withholding?

Voluntary federal income tax withholding on Social Security benefits is allowed. Recipients may submit a Form W-4V if they want federal income tax withheld from their benefits. Recipients may choose withholding at 7 percent, 10 percent, 15 percent, or 25 percent of their total benefit payment.

## 242. If a recipient of Social Security benefits elects Medical Insurance (Part B) under Medicare and the premiums are deducted from the individual's benefits, is the whole benefit, before the deduction, a Social Security benefit?

Yes, the individual is treated as if he received the whole benefit and later paid separately for the Medical Insurance (Part B) coverage. Both the Commissioner of Social Security and the Railroad Retirement Board will include the entire amount as paid to the individual in the statements they furnish.

# SOCIAL SECURITY TAXES

## 243. What are the Social Security and Medicare tax rates for employers and employees?

The tax rate is the same for both the employer and the employee. Every employer who employs one or more persons and every employee in covered employment is subject to the tax imposed under the Federal Insurance Contributions Act (FICA).[1]

The tax consists of two taxes: the OASDI tax (the tax for old-age, survivors, and disability insurance) and the Hospital Insurance (HI) tax (for Medicare Part A).

For 2015, the maximum earnings base (the maximum amount of annual earnings subject to the tax) for the OASDI tax is $118,500. There is no maximum earnings base for the HI tax. All wages and self-employment income are subject to the HI tax.

For employees and employers, the rate of the OASDI tax is 6.20 percent, and the rate of the HI tax is 1.45 percent. Thus, the maximum OASDI tax for an employee in 2015 (with maximum earnings of $118,500) is $7,347. The maximum HI tax is unlimited because all wages are subject to the tax.

**OASDI TAX ON EMPLOYEES AND EMPLOYERS**

| Year | % Rate (OASDI) | Max. Wage Base | Max. Tax (each) | Max. Tax (both) |
|---|---|---|---|---|
| 1986 | 5.70 | $42,000 | $2,394.00 | $4,788.00 |
| 1987 | 5.70 | 43,800 | 2,496.60 | 4,993.20 |
| 1988 | 6.06 | 45,000 | 2,727.00 | 5,454.00 |
| 1989 | 6.06 | 48,000 | 2,908.80 | 5,817.60 |
| 1990 | 6.20 | 51,300 | 3,180.60 | 6,361.20 |
| 1991 | 6.20 | 53,400 | 3,310.80 | 6,621.60 |
| 1992 | 6.20 | 55,500 | 3,441.00 | 6,882.00 |
| 1993 | 6.20 | 57,600 | 3,571.20 | 7,142.40 |
| 1994 | 6.20 | 60,600 | 3,757.20 | 7,514.40 |
| 1995 | 6.20 | 61,200 | 3,794.40 | 7,588.80 |
| 1996 | 6.20 | 62,700 | 3,887.40 | 7,774.80 |
| 1997 | 6.20 | 65,400 | 4,054.80 | 8,109.60 |
| 1998 | 6.20 | 68,400 | 4,240.80 | 8,481.60 |
| 1999 | 6.20 | 72,600 | 4,501.20 | 9,002.40 |
| 2000 | 6.20 | 76,200 | 4,724.40 | 9,448.80 |
| 2001 | 6.20 | 80,400 | 4,984.80 | 9,969.60 |
| 2002 | 6.20 | 84,900 | 5,263.80 | 10,527.60 |

1. IRC Secs. 3101, 3111.

| Year | % Rate (OASDI) | Max. Wage Base | Max. Tax (each) | Max. Tax (both) |
|---|---|---|---|---|
| 2003 | 6.20 | 87,000 | 5,394.00 | 10,788.00 |
| 2004 | 6.20 | 87,900 | 5,449.80 | 10,899.60 |
| 2005 | 6.20 | 90,000 | 5,580.00 | 11,160.00 |
| 2006 | 6.20 | 94,200 | 5,840.40 | 11,680.80 |
| 2007 | 6.20 | 97,500 | 6,045.00 | 12,090.00 |
| 2008 | 6.20 | 102,000 | 6,324.00 | 12,648.00 |
| 2009-2011 | 6.20 | 106,800 | 6,621.60 | 13,243.20 |
| 2012 | 6.20 | 110,100 | 6,826.20 | 13,652.40 |
| 2013 | 6.20 | 113,700 | 7,049.40 | 14,098.80 |
| 2014 | 6.20 | 117,000 | 7,254.00 | 14,508.00 |
| 2015 | 6.20 | 118,500 | 7,347.00 | 14,694.00 |

Note: The 1.45 percent Medicare tax applies to all wages.

The OASDI maximum earnings base and maximum tax are subject to automatic adjustment in 2016, and after based on changes in wage levels.

Under the Patient Protection and Affordable Care Act of 2010, new Medicare taxes are imposed starting in 2013. Under the provisions of the new law most taxpayers will continue to pay the 1.45 percent Medicare tax, but single people earning more than $200,000 and married couples earning more than $250,000 will be taxed at an additional 0.9 percent (2.35 percent in total) on the excess over those base amounts. Self-employed persons will pay 3.8 percent on earnings over those thresholds.

Employers will collect the extra 0.9 percent on wages exceeding $200,000 just as they would withhold Medicare taxes and remit them to the IRS. However, companies won't be responsible for determining whether a worker's combined income with his or her spouse made them subject to the tax.

Instead, some employees will have to remit additional Medicare taxes when they file income tax returns, and some will get a tax credit for amounts overpaid. Married couples with combined incomes approaching $250,000 will have to keep tabs on both spouses' pay to avoid an unexpected tax bill.

Beginning in 2013, a Medicare tax will, for the first time, be applied to investment income. A new 3.8 percent tax will be imposed on net investment income of single taxpayers with Adjusted Gross Income (AGI) above $200,000 and joint filers with AGI over $250,000.

Net investment income is interest, dividends, royalties, rents, gross income from a trade or business involving passive activities, and net gain from disposition of property (other than property held in a trade or business). Net investment income is reduced by the deductions that are allocable to that income. However, the new tax won't apply to income in tax-deferred retirement accounts such as 401(k) plans.

Not all earnings are subject to Social Security taxes. A person can be an employee but be exempt from the Social Security tax. An example is an individual hired by a federal agency on a temporary basis as an emergency firefighter to help fight forest fires. The individual performed the service for three months, twelve hours a day, and the federal agency supplied the necessary equipment and gave him directions on a daily basis. The Internal Revenue Service ruled that, although the individual was an employee under common-law rules, he was exempt from Social Security taxes, as the Internal Revenue Code exempts from the definition of employment those services performed for the United States by an individual serving on a temporary basis in case of fire or other emergencies.

## 244. If an employee works for two employers during the year and more than the maximum tax is paid on his or her wages, will the overpayment be refunded to the employee and his or her employers?

Each employer is required to withhold the employee's tax, and to pay the employer's tax, on wages up to the maximum earnings base for the year. Consequently, if an employee works for more than one employer during the year, the taxes paid may exceed the maximum payable for the year. In this case, the employee is entitled to a refund of his or her overpayment, or the overpayment will be credited to his or her income tax for the year. His or her employers, however, are not entitled to any refund or credit. Each employer is liable for tax on his or her wages, up to the maximum earnings base.

However, a group of corporations concurrently employing an individual will be considered a single employer if one of the group serves as a common paymaster for the entire group. This will result in such corporations having to pay no more in Social Security taxes than a single employer pays.

## 245. Does an employer receive an income tax deduction for Social Security tax payments?

Yes, the employer's Social Security tax is deductible as a business expense, but only if wages upon which taxes are paid are also deductible.[1]

## 246. Must Social Security taxes be paid on cash tips?

Yes, an employee must pay Social Security taxes on cash tips of twenty dollars or more a month from one employer. These tips are treated as wages for Social Security and income tax withholding purposes, and must be reported. Cash tips of less than twenty dollars a month are not reported.

The employee is required to report tips to an employer within ten days following the month in which the tips equal or exceed twenty dollars.

The employer must pay the usual employer tax on tips.

The employer must withhold income tax and deduct the employee Social Security and Hospital Insurance (HI) tax on tips reported to him. The withholding is to be made from any

1. See IRC Sec. 162.

wages (other than tips) that are under the employer's control. Employers may deduct the tax due on tips during a calendar quarter on an estimated basis, and adjust the amount deducted from wages paid to the employee either during the calendar quarter or within thirty days thereafter. If these wages are not sufficient to cover the employee tax due, the employee may (but is not required to) furnish the employer with additional funds to cover the tax.

The employee is directly responsible for paying any portion of the employee tax that the employer cannot collect from wages or from funds furnished by the employee. The employer is required to give statements to both the employee and the Internal Revenue Service, showing the difference between the amount of the employee tax due and the amount collected by the employer.

Food or beverage establishments are provided with a business tax credit, equal to the amount of the employer's Social Security tax obligation (7.65 percent) attributable to reported tips in excess of those treated as wages for purposes of satisfying the minimum wage provisions of the Fair Labor Standards Act (FLSA). An employer must pay a Social Security tax on the tip income of employees, and tips can be counted as satisfying one-half of the minimum wage requirement.

The credit also applies to tips received from customers in connection with the delivery or serving of food or beverages, regardless of whether the food or beverages are for consumption on an establishment's premises. The credit is available, even if the employee failed to report the tips.[1]

## 247. How does an individual report Social Security taxes on domestic help?

The threshold amount for Social Security coverage of a domestic worker is $1,900 in 2015.[2] This threshold amount is indexed in future years for increases in average wages in the economy. Indexing occurs in $100 increments, rounded down to the nearest $100.

Exempt from Social Security taxes are any wages paid to a worker for domestic services performed in any year during which the worker is under age eighteen, except for workers under age eighteen whose principal occupation is household employment. Being a student is considered to be an occupation for purposes of this test. Thus, for example, the wages of a student who is sixteen years old and also babysits will be exempt from the reporting and payment requirements, regardless of whether the amount of wages paid is above or below the threshold. On the other hand, the wages of a seventeen-year-old single mother, who leaves school and goes to work as a domestic to support her family, will be subject to the reporting and payment requirements.

Employers may satisfy their tax obligations through regular estimated tax payments or increased tax withholding from their own wages. Estimated tax penalties will apply in appropriate circumstances.

*Example 1*. Assume an employer pays a domestic employee $1,000 in wages for calendar year 2015. Because the amount of these taxes is below the $1,900 threshold, the employer is not subject to reporting.

1. For further information regarding income and employment taxes on tips, see *IRS Publication 531 (Reporting Tip Income)*.
2. See IRC Sec. 3121(x).

*Example 2*. Assume an employer pays a domestic employee $2,000 in wages for calendar year 2015. Because the amount of these wages is above the $1,900 threshold, the employer is subject to reporting.

## 248. What is the rate of Social Security and Medicare tax for a self-employed person?

The tax on self-employed persons is imposed under the Self-Employment Contributions Act.[1]

The self-employment tax consists of two taxes: the OASDI tax (the tax for old-age, survivors, and disability insurance) and the Hospital Insurance (HI) tax (for Medicare Part A).

For 2015, the maximum earnings base (the maximum amount of net earnings subject to the tax) for the OASDI tax is $118,500. There is no maximum earnings base for the HI tax. In other words, all earnings from self-employment are subject to the HI tax.

The rate of the OASDI tax is 12.40 percent, and the rate of the HI tax is 2.90 percent. Thus, the maximum OASDI tax for a self-employed person in 2015 (with maximum earnings of $118,500) is $14,694. The maximum HI tax for a self-employed person is unlimited, because all self-employment earnings are subject to the tax.

For self-employed taxpayers with income above $200,000 ($250,000 for married filing jointly) the HI tax will be 3.8 percent in tax years 2013 and after.

There is a special federal (and generally following through to state) income tax deduction of 50 percent of the Social Security and Medicare self-employment tax.[2] This income tax deduction is designed to treat the self-employed in much the same manner as employees and employers are treated for Social Security, Medicare, and income tax purposes under present law.

**OASDI TAX ON SELF-EMPLOYED PERSONS***

| Year | % Rates (OASDI) | Max. Earnings Base | Max. Tax |
|---|---|---|---|
| 1986 | 11.40 | $42,000 | $4,788.00 |
| 1987 | 11.40 | 43,800 | 4,993.20 |
| 1988 | 12.12 | 45,000 | 5,454.00 |
| 1989 | 12.12 | 48,000 | 5,817.60 |
| 1990 | 12.40 | 51,300 | 6,361.20 |
| 1991 | 12.40 | 53,400 | 6,621.60 |
| 1992 | 12.40 | 55,500 | 6,882.00 |
| 1993 | 12.40 | 57,600 | 7,142.40 |
| 1994 | 12.40 | 60,600 | 7,514.40 |
| 1995 | 12.40 | 61,200 | 7,588.80 |
| 1996 | 12.40 | 62,700 | 7,774.80 |

1. IRC Sec. 1401.
2. IRC Sec. 164.

| Year | % Rates (OASDI) | Max. Earnings Base | Max. Tax |
|---|---|---|---|
| 1997 | 12.40 | 65,400 | 8,109.60 |
| 1998 | 12.40 | 68,400 | 8,481.60 |
| 1999 | 12.40 | 72,600 | 9,002.40 |
| 2000 | 12.40 | 76,200 | 9,448.80 |
| 2001 | 12.40 | 80,400 | 9,969.60 |
| 2002 | 12.40 | 84,900 | 10,527.60 |
| 2003 | 12.40 | 87,000 | 10,788.00 |
| 2004 | 12.40 | 87,900 | 10,899.60 |
| 2005 | 12.40 | 90,000 | 11,160.00 |
| 2006 | 12.40 | 94,200 | 11,680.80 |
| 2007 | 12.40 | 97,500 | 12,090.00 |
| 2008 | 12.40 | 102,000 | 12,648.00 |
| 2009-2011 | 12.40 | 106,800 | 13,243.20 |
| 2012 | 12.40 | 110,100 | 13,652.40 |
| 2013 | 12.40 | 113,700 | 14,098.80 |
| 2014 | 12.40 | 117,000 | 14,508.00 |
| 2015 | 12.40 | 118,500 | 14,694.00 |

* There is a special income tax deduction of 50 percent of the self-employment tax.
Note: The 2.90 percent Medicare tax applies to all self-employment earnings.

The OASDI maximum earnings base and maximum tax are subject to automatic adjustment in 2016, and after based on changes in wage levels.

If a self-employed person reports earnings on a fiscal-year basis, the tax rate to be used is the one that applies to the calendar year in which the fiscal year began.

## 249. If a self-employed person also receives wages as an employee, what portion of income is subject to tax as self-employment income?

Only the difference between the maximum earnings base for the year and the wages received as an employee is subject to tax as self-employment income.[1]

*Example 1.* Mr. Smith, an attorney, is employed as a part-time instructor for a law school, and his salary is $30,000 a year. During 2015, Mr. Smith earned an additional $100,000 from his private practice, which counts as $92,350 for Social Security purposes (i.e., 92.35 percent of $100,000). Only $88,500 of his net earnings from self-employment is subject to the OASDI self-employment tax ($118,500 - $30,000). Note, however, that all of Mr. Smith's wages and $92,350 of his self-employment income are subject to the HI self-employment tax, because all wages and self-employment income are subject to the HI tax.

1. IRC Sec. 1402(b)(2).

No self-employment tax is due unless net earnings from self-employment are at least $434 for the taxable year ($400/92.35 percent). Nevertheless, in some cases, the amount of income subject to OASDI self-employment tax may be less than $400.

*Example 2.* Assume the same facts as in Example 1, except that Mr. Smith's salary as a law instructor is $118,300. Mr. Smith's net earnings from self-employment after application of the 92.35 percent factor ($92,350) exceed $400, and therefore must be reported. However, only $200 is subject to the OASDI self-employment tax ($118,500 - $118,300), but the entire $118,300 is subject to the HI tax.

## 250. Must a Social Security beneficiary who works pay Social Security and Medicare taxes?

Yes, even though receiving Social Security benefits, the beneficiary must pay taxes at the same rate as other individuals. Social Security and Medicare taxes must be paid even if the earnings are too small to increase the Social Security benefits the beneficiary will receive in the future.

*Example.* Ms. Anderson, age seventy-three, receives $800 a month in Social Security retirement benefits. She also works part-time and earns $4,000 for the year. Ms. Anderson must pay $306 in Social Security and Medicare HI taxes.

## 251. How does a life insurance agent pay Social Security taxes on first-year and renewal commissions?

If the agent is an *employee* when the policy is sold, both first-year and renewal commissions are *wages* at the time they are paid. Consequently, they are subject to the employer-employee tax in the year they are received by him. It does not matter whether, at the time of payment, the agent is an employee or a self-employed person. If the agent is a self-employed individual when the policy is sold, first-year and renewal commissions are treated as net earnings from self-employment in the year they are received.[1] (See Social Security Taxes, Q 243 to Q 253).

Renewal commissions paid to the estate (or other beneficiary) of a deceased life insurance agent in a year after death are not subject to the employer-employee tax. Renewal commissions paid to a disabled life insurance agent are not subject to the Social Security tax, if he or she became entitled to disability insurance benefits before the year in which the renewal commission is paid and did not work for the employer during the period for which the payment is made. The renewal commissions of a self-employed agent do not constitute net earnings from self-employment to a widow(er) (they were not derived from a trade or business carried on by the widow(er)).

## 252. Must the self-employment tax be included in a person's estimated tax return?

Yes.

1. 20 CFR Part 404, Subpart K.

## 253. What is the federal income tax deduction for medical expense insurance premiums?

No premiums other than those for medical expense insurance will qualify for the deduction. If the taxpayer itemizes deductions, he or she may deduct the full amount of the medical expense insurance premiums subject to the 7.5 percent adjusted gross income floor. A self-employed individual may be able to deduct up to 100 percent of medical expense insurance premiums.[1] The monthly premium for Medicare Part B is treated as a medical expense insurance premium for this purpose.

1. IRC Sec. 162(l).

## WAGES AND SELF-EMPLOYMENT INCOME

### 254. What earnings are subject to Social Security tax and are counted in computing Social Security benefits?

Earnings that are the *wages* of an employee or the *self-employment income* of a self-employed person. However, earnings are counted as "wages" or as "self-employment income" only if they are earned in employment or self-employment covered by the Social Security Act.

### 255. For Social Security purposes, what is meant by the term "wages"?

"Wages" mean pay received by an employee for employment covered by the Social Security Act. The maximum amount of wages subject to the Old-Age, Survivors and Disability Insurance tax (OASDI) and credited to a worker's Social Security record for any calendar year cannot exceed:

$4,800 paid in any of the years .......... 1959-1965
$6,600 paid in any of the years .............. 1966-1967
$7,800 paid in any of the years .............. 1968-1971
$9,000 paid in the year ........................ 1972
$10,800 paid in the year....................... 1973
$13,200 paid in the year....................... 1974
$14,100 paid in the year....................... 1975
$15,300 paid in the year....................... 1976
$16,500 paid in the year....................... 1977
$17,700 paid in the year....................... 1978
$22,900 paid in the year....................... 1979
$25,900 paid in the year....................... 1980
$29,700 paid in the year....................... 1981
$32,400 paid in the year....................... 1982
$35,700 paid in the year....................... 1983
$37,800 paid in the year....................... 1984
$39,600 paid in the year....................... 1985
$42,000 paid in the year....................... 1986
$43,800 paid in the year....................... 1987
$45,000 paid in the year....................... 1988
$48,000 paid in the year....................... 1989
$51,300 paid in the year....................... 1990
$53,400 paid in the year....................... 1991
$55,500 paid in the year....................... 1992
$57,600 paid in the year....................... 1993
$60,600 paid in the year....................... 1994
$61,200 paid in the year....................... 1995
$62,700 paid in the year....................... 1996
$65,400 paid in the year....................... 1997
$68,400 paid in the year....................... 1998
$72,600 paid in the year....................... 1999

$76,200 paid in the year....................... 2000
$80,400 paid in the year....................... 2001
$84,900 paid in the year....................... 2002
$87,000 paid in the year....................... 2003
$87,900 paid in the year....................... 2004
$90,000 paid in the year....................... 2005
$94,200 paid in the year....................... 2006
$97,500 paid in the year....................... 2007
$102,000 paid in the year ..................... 2008
$106,800 paid in any of the years........... 2009-2011
$110,100 paid in the year ..................... 2012
$113,700 paid in the year ..................... 2013
$117,000 paid in the year ..................... 2014
$118,500 paid in the year ..................... 2015

Employees pay the tax on wages up to the base amount from each employer, but receive a refund on their income tax returns for the excess of total taxes paid over the tax on the base amount. Each employer pays the tax on wages up to the base amount for all of its employees. In addition to the regular Social Security tax on wages, all wages are subject to the Part A Medicare Hospital Insurance tax (HI).

The maximum earnings base is automatically adjusted each year by the Social Security Administration, if average nationwide (covered and noncovered) total wages have increased.

Note that the maximum amount of wages subject to the OASDI tax is also the maximum amount credited to a worker's record. For example, if an employee is paid $118,500 or less in 2015, the full amount of wages will be subject to OASDI tax and will be credited to the Social Security record for benefit purposes. But if an employee is paid $120,000 in 2015, only $118,500 will be subject to OASDI tax and credited to the Social Security record (but HI taxes will be paid on the entire $120,000). In other words, earnings in excess of the maximum amount for a particular calendar year are not considered wages for Social Security coverage purposes.

A stabilizer provision protects the system from trust-fund depletions that could occur when price increases outpace wage gains. This stabilizer provision goes into effect if reserves in the trust funds providing retirement, disability, and survivor benefits fall below 20 percent of what is needed to meet outgo for a year. When the stabilizer takes effect, automatic cost-of-living benefit increases will be based on the lower of the annual percentage increase in the Consumer Price Index or the annual percentage rise in the nation's average wage.[1]

Later, if the fund reserves exceed 32 percent of what is estimated to be needed for a year, recipients will be entitled to extra cost-of-living increases, to compensate for losses in inflation protection resulting from having benefit increases tied to wage levels.[2]

1. 42 USC 415(i)(1)(C).
2. 42 USC 415(i)(5)(A).

## 256. Are only payments in cash counted as wages?

No, amounts paid by check, promissory note, or in other media (such as goods, clothing, board or lodging) usually count as wages. In a few cases, however, only cash pay is counted (see Q 267; Domestic and Household Workers, Q 247).

Any fringe benefit that is not specifically excluded from Social Security taxes is wages for Social Security purposes. The amount of wages is the difference between the discount price paid by the employee for the benefit and its fair market value.

The following five categories of fringe benefits are *not* wages:

(1) De minimis fringe (a property or service furnished by the employer that is so small in value that accounting for it would be administratively impractical)

(2) Gyms and other athletic facilities (the value of an employer-provided on-premises athletic facility)

(3) No-additional-cost service (any service provided by an employer to the employee for the employee's use)

(4) Qualified employee discount (employee discount with respect to property or services)

(5) Working-condition fringe (any employer-provided service or property to the employee, such as a parking space)

Ordinarily, only pay actually received by the employee in a calendar year is counted as wages for that year. However, pay that is "constructively received" during the year is also counted. Wages are constructively received when they have been credited or set apart for the employee without any substantial limitation or restriction on the time or manner of payment and are available to him so that he can get them at any time. A special provision applies to pay under a nonqualified deferred compensation plan that is generally based on payments made after 1983.

## 257. Are employer payments for group life insurance covered wages?

The cost of group-term life insurance that is includable in the gross income of the employee is considered "wages" subject to Social Security tax.[1] This provision does not apply to coverage of former employees who separated from service before January 1, 1989, to the extent the cost is not for any period the employee was employed by the employer after separation.

The general rule is that the employee may exclude the cost of the first $50,000 of employer-provided group-term life insurance from income. Therefore, generally, only the cost of coverage in excess of $50,000 will be subject to the Social Security tax.

1. IRC Sec. 3121(a)(2).

The employer is required to report amounts includable in the wages of current employees for purposes of the Social Security tax on the employees' W-2. Generally, the employer may treat the wages as though paid on any basis, so long as they are treated as paid at least once each year.

The Social Security tax must be paid by the employee if the payment for the group-term life insurance is considered wages, and is for periods during which there is no longer an employment relationship between the employer and the employee. The employer is required to state the portion of an employee's wages that consist of payments for group-term life insurance and the amount of the Social Security tax separately.

## 258. Are vacation pay and severance pay wages?

Yes, but the Internal Revenue Service ruled in 1996 that contributions of an employee's forfeitable vacation pay benefit, to a qualified stock purchase plan with a cash or deferred arrangement, are excludable from gross wages for Social Security purposes.

The company involved in the ruling had established a qualified stock-purchase plan with profit-sharing features and cash or deferred arrangements. Company employees were entitled to annual leave based on years of service, and had to use it during the same year or forfeit it. Employees who did not use all of their paid vacation in excess of two weeks could elect to have the equivalent in pay contributed to the qualified plan. The employees could take the vacation time, forfeit the time, or contribute its value to the plan. They did not have the option to receive cash or any other taxable benefit in lieu of the contribution to the plan. Thus, the Internal Revenue Service considered the contribution of vacation pay to be a nonelective employer contribution and excluded from wages for Social Security purposes under IRC Sec. 3121(a)(5)(A).[1]

## 259. Are payments on account of sickness or accident disability counted as wages for Social Security purposes?

Yes, generally payments made to, or on behalf of, an employee or an employee's dependents for sickness or disability are considered wages. The following payments, however, are specifically excluded from the definition of wages:

(1) Any payment that an employer makes to an employee, or on the employee's behalf, on account of the employee's sickness or accident disability, or related medical or hospitalization expenses, if the payment is made more than six consecutive months following the last calendar month in which the employee worked for the employer. Payments made during the six consecutive months are included as wages.

(2) The exclusion listed in (1) above also applies to any payment made by a third party (such as an insurance company). In addition, if the employee contributed to the employer's sick pay plan, that portion of the third-party payments attributable to the employee's contribution is not wages.

1. TAM 9635002.

(3) Payments of medical or hospitalization expenses connected with sickness or accident disability are excluded from wages beginning with the first payment, only if made under a plan or system of the employer for medical or hospitalization expenses connected with sickness or accident disability.

(4) Payments under workers' compensation law are not wages.

For payments to be excluded under a plan or system, the plan must provide for all employees generally or for a class or classes of employees. Some or all of the following features may also be a part of the plan:

- Set a definite basis for determining who is eligible, such as length of service, or occupation, or salary classification
- Set definite standards for determining the minimum duration of payments
- Provide a formula for determining the minimum amount to be paid an eligible employee

Sick pay that is not paid under a plan or system by the employer is counted as wages for Social Security purposes, if paid before the end of six calendar months after the last month in which the employee worked.

## 260. Are payments made under a deferred compensation plan counted as wages?

Yes, generally, under a special timing rule, the "amount deferred" by an employee under a traditional nonqualified deferred compensation plan – whether a salary reduction or supplemental plan, whether a funded or unfunded plan, or whether a private or (eligible or ineligible) Section 457 plan – of an employer covered by the Social Security tax is considered "wages" for Social Security tax purposes at the *later of*: (1) when the services are performed, or (2) when the employee's rights to such amount are no longer subject to a substantial risk of forfeiture.[1] Once an amount is treated as wages, it (and any income attributable to it) will not be treated as wages for Social Security tax purposes in any later year.[2]

In general, many employees would prefer to have amounts deferred treated as wages for Social Security purposes at the time the services are performed. At such time, their salaries, in all likelihood, already exceed the Social Security taxable wage base (in 2015, $118,500 for OASDI), and the amounts deferred would thus escape Social Security taxes. (Remember, however, that the HI tax applies to all wages.)

Regulations expressly identify certain plans and benefits that do not provide for the deferral of compensation for Social Security tax purposes: stock options, stock appreciation rights, and other stock value rights; some restricted property received in connection with the performance of services; compensatory time, disability pay, severance pay, and death

1. IRC Sec. 3121(v)(2)(A).
2. IRC Sec. 3121(v)(2)(B).

benefits; certain benefits provided in connection with impending termination (including window benefits); excess (golden) parachute payments; benefits established twelve months before an employee's termination, if indication that benefits were provided in contemplation of termination; benefits established after termination of employment; and compensation paid for current services.[1]

Under the regulations, the manner in which the amount deferred for a period is determined depends upon whether the nonqualified deferred compensation plan is an *account balance plan* or a *nonaccount balance plan*. If the plan is an *account balance plan*, the amount deferred for a period equals the principal amount credited to the employee's account for the period, increased or decreased by any income or loss attributable to the principal amount through the date the principal amount is required to be taken into account as wages for Social Security tax purposes. A plan is an *account balance plan* only if, under the terms of the plan, a principal amount is credited to an individual account for an employee, the income attributable to each principal account is credited or debited to the individual account, and the benefits payable to the employee are based solely on the balance credited to the individual account.[2]

If the plan is a *nonaccount balance plan*, the amount deferred for a period equals the present value of the additional future payment or payments to which the employee has obtained a legally binding right under the plan during that period.

## 261. Are payments made to or from a qualified pension or annuity plan counted as wages?

No, neither the employer's contribution to the plan nor payments to the employee from the plan are treated as wages. They are not subject to Social Security tax and are not creditable for benefit purposes.

The following payments made to or under a deferred compensation plan are *excludable* from the definition of wages:

(1) Payments made from or to qualified pension, profit-sharing, or stock bonus plans if, at the time of payment, the trust is exempt from tax under IRC Sec. 501(a), unless the payment is made to an employee of the trust as remuneration for services rendered as an employee and not as a beneficiary of the trust[3]

(2) Payments made under or to an IRC Sec. 403(a) annuity plan[4]

(3) Payments made under a simplified employee pension (SEP), other than any contributions made pursuant to a salary reduction agreement described in IRC Sec. 408(k)(6)[5]

1. Treas. Regs. §§31.3121(v)(2)-1(b)(4), 31.3306(r)(2)-1(a).
2. Treas. Regs. §§31.3121(v)(2)-1(c)(1), 31.3306(r)(2)-1(a); see also Let. Rul. 9417013 (amounts deferred in defined-contribution-type plan with delayed vesting are amounts attributable to employer contributions when such amounts vest).
3. IRC Sec. 3121(a)(5)(A).
4. IRC Sec. 3121(a)(5)(B).
5. IRC Sec. 3121(a)(5)(C).

(4) Payments under an annuity contract described in IRC Sec. 403(b), other than a payment for the purchase of the contract that is made by reason of a salary reduction agreement (whether evidenced by a written instrument or otherwise)[1]

(5) Payments under or to an exempt governmental deferred compensation plan[2]

(6) Payments to supplement pension benefits under a plan or trust described above to take into account some or all of the increase in the cost of living since retirement[3]

(7) Payments under a cafeteria plan (IRC Sec. 125), if the payment is not treated as wages without regard to the plan and it is reasonable to believe that IRC Sec. 125 would not treat any wages as constructively received[4]

(8) Payments under a SIMPLE IRA plan arrangement, other than elective contributions under IRC Sec. 408(p)(2)(A)(i)[5]

(9) Amounts exempted from Section 457 requirements under Section 457(e)(11)(A)(ii) (plans paying solely length of service awards to bona fide volunteers (or their beneficiaries) on account of qualified services performed by such volunteers) and maintained by an eligible employer[6]

However, the definition of wages *does* include certain employer contributions under qualified cash or deferred arrangements that are not included in gross income.[7]

## 262. If a teacher takes a reduction in salary to provide funds for a tax-sheltered annuity, how are his or her wages computed for Social Security purposes?

The salary before the reduction will be treated as wages.[8] In other words, the amount of reduction, although paid to the insurer by the employer, is nevertheless not considered an employer contribution to a retirement fund. For example, suppose that a teacher, whose salary is $45,000, takes a $2,000 salary cut for 2015 so that this amount can be used to purchase a tax-sheltered annuity for his or her benefit. Social Security taxes will still be payable on the full $45,000, and this is the amount that will be credited to the teacher's Social Security account for benefit purposes.

Employer payments from employer funds into such plans are excluded from wages.

1. IRC Sec. 3121(a)(5)(D).
2. IRC Sec. 3121(a)(5)(E).
3. IRC Sec. 3121(a)(5)(F).
4. IRC Sec. 3121(a)(5)(G).
5. IRC Sec. 3121(a)(5)(H).
6. IRC Sec. 3121(a)(5)(I).
7. IRC Sec. 3121(v)(1)(A).
8. See IRC Sec. 3121(a)(5)(D); Rev. Rul. 65-208, 1965-2 CB 383.

## 263. Are cash tips considered wages?

Tips received by an employee in the course of employment by any one employer are wages for Social Security purposes, if the tips total twenty dollars or more in a calendar month. This includes all tips received directly from customers, tips from charge customers that are paid by the employer to the employee, and any tips received under a tip-splitting arrangement. Noncash tips, such as passes, tickets, or services, are not counted as wages. Tips are considered received when the employee reports the tips to the employer. If the employee fails to report the tips to the employer, the tips are treated as received when the employee actually received them.

For each calendar month during which an employee receives twenty dollars or more in tips, the employee must give the employer a written statement of cash and charge tips by the tenth day of the month after the month in which the tips are received. IRS Form 4070 (Employee's Report of Tips to Employer), which is in IRS Publication 1244 (Employee's Daily Record of Tips and Report to Employer), is available for this purpose.

A club, hotel, or restaurant may require customers to pay a service charge, which is given to the employees. The employee's share of this service charge is not a tip, but is part of wages paid to the employee by the employer.

(For method of reporting tips, see SOCIAL SECURITY TAXES, Q 243 to Q 253.)

## 264. Do wages include the portion of an employee's Social Security taxes paid by an employer?

Yes, except for domestic service in the private home of the employer and agricultural labor. However, payments by a state or local employer are wages for Social Security tax purposes, only if the payment is pursuant to a salary reduction agreement (whether evidenced by a written instrument or otherwise). The term "salary reduction agreement" includes any salary reduction arrangement, regardless of whether there is approval or choice of participation by individual employees or whether such approval or choice is mandated by state statute.

## 265. Are salesperson's commissions wages?

Yes, they are wages if the salesperson is an employee. (See Social Security Taxes, Q 243 to Q 253.) When the commissions are the sole pay and no advances are given, the commissions are wages in the calendar year in which they are paid. However, when advances are made against future commissions, the year in which the advances are paid is the year to which the amount advanced is credited.

## 266. Under what circumstances are the first-year and renewal commissions of a life insurance agent treated as wages?

If the agent is an *employee* when the policy is sold, both first-year and renewal commissions are treated as wages when they are *paid* to him. Thus, the commissions are subject to the employer-employee tax in each year as he receives them (see SOCIAL SECURITY TAXES, Q 243 to Q 253). For retirement-test purposes, however, if the agent is an employee when the policy is sold, both first-year and renewal commissions are treated as "earned" in the month and year in which the policy was sold (see LOSS OF BENEFITS BECAUSE OF "EXCESS" EARNINGS, Q 223 to Q 233).

### 267. Is the value of meals and lodging furnished by an employer to an employee considered wages for Social Security taxation purposes?

The Supreme Court has held that the value of meals and lodging furnished to an employee for the convenience of the employer is not wages for Social Security coverage and tax purposes.[1]

Such meals must be provided at the employer's place of business. The employee must accept lodging at the employer's place of business in order for the value of the lodging to be excluded from wages.

The Social Security Amendments of 1983 state, however, that the exclusion of income from income tax withholding by the employer does not necessarily affect the treatment of the income for Social Security coverage and taxation purposes in other cases.

## SELF-EMPLOYMENT INCOME

### 268. What is taxable and creditable self-employment income?

It is that part of an individual's net earnings from self-employment that is subject to Social Security tax and counted for Social Security benefits. In determining what part of a person's net earnings from self-employment is creditable for Social Security purposes, the following rules apply:

- 92.35 percent of all net earnings from self-employment is taxable and creditable self-employment income unless the trade, business, or profession is not covered by the Social Security Act. The 92.35 percent factor has been used only in 1990 and after (when the self-employed first began paying the full employer-employee tax rate).
- If such amount for the taxable year is less than $400, the net earnings are not treated as self-employment income. That is, no Social Security tax is paid on the net earnings, and they are not credited to the person's Social Security account.
- The maximum amount of self-employment income for a taxable year that is subject to the Old-Age, Survivors, and Disability Insurance tax (OASDI) and used to determine benefits cannot exceed:

  $118,500............................ 2015
  $117,000............................ 2014
  $113,700............................ 2013
  $110,100............................ 2012
  $106,800.........................2009-2011

1. *Rowan Companies, Inc. v. U.S.*, 452 U.S. 247 (1981).

| | |
|---|---|
| $102,000 | 2008 |
| $97,500 | 2007 |
| $94,200 | 2006 |
| $90,000 | 2005 |
| $87,900 | 2004 |
| $87,000 | 2003 |
| $84,900 | 2002 |
| $80,400 | 2001 |
| $76,200 | 2000 |
| $72,600 | 1999 |
| $68,400 | 1998 |
| $65,400 | 1997 |
| $62,700 | 1996 |
| $61,200 | 1995 |
| $60,600 | 1994 |
| $57,600 | 1993 |
| $55,500 | 1992 |
| $53,400 | 1991 |
| $51,300 | 1990 |
| $48,000 | 1989 |
| $45,000 | 1988 |
| $43,800 | 1987 |
| $42,000 | 1986 |
| $39,600 | 1985 |
| $37,800 | 1984 |
| $35,700 | 1983 |
| $32,400 | 1982 |
| $29,700 | 1981 |
| $25,900 | 1980 |
| $22,900 | 1979 |
| $17,700 | 1978 |
| $16,500 | 1977 |
| $15,300 | 1976 |
| $14,100 | 1975 |
| $13,200 | 1974 |
| $10,800 | 1973 |
| $9,000 | 1972 |
| $7,800 | 1968-1971 |
| $6,600 | 1966-1967 |
| $4,800 | 1959-1965 |

There is no limit to the amount of self-employment income subject to the (Part A) Medicare Hospital Insurance tax (HI). The HI tax applies to all self-employment income.

Net earnings in excess of the maximum amount for a particular taxable year are not considered self-employment income for Social Security purposes.

## 269. How is the amount of self-employment income figured if a person has both wages and net earnings from self-employment in the same year?

If a person has both wages (as an employee) and net earnings from self-employment in a taxable year, *self-employment income* is the difference, if any, between wages and the maximum Social Security earnings base for that year (see Q 268).

> *Example*. Mr. Smith, an attorney, is also employed part-time as an instructor in a law school. In 2015, he draws a salary of $30,000 from the school and also earns $100,000 in private practice, which counts as $92,350 for Social Security purposes (i.e., 92.35 percent of $100,000). His self-employment income for OASDI purposes for 2015 is $88,500 ($118,500 maximum less $30,000 wages). Only $88,500 is subject to self-employment Social Security tax. $30,000 is subject to the employer-employee tax. Note, however, that $92,350 of the $100,000 earned in private practice is subject to the Part A Medicare Hospital Insurance tax for self-employed individuals. In addition, Mr. Smith must pay the Medicare Hospital Insurance tax for employees on the $30,000 he earned as a law school instructor.

## 270. In general, what constitutes net earnings from self-employment?

Net earnings from self-employment may be the net income from a trade, business, or profession carried on by the individual alone, or it may be his or her distributive share of the ordinary net income of a partnership. In computing net earnings from self-employment, gross income and deductions are, for the most part, the same as for income tax purposes. However, the following differences must be taken into account:

- Rentals from real estate are excluded in determining net earnings from self-employment unless: (1) the rentals are received in the course of a trade or business by a real estate dealer; or (2) services are rendered primarily for the convenience of the occupants of the premises, as in the case of hotels, motels, etc. (but income from renting property for business or commercial use (such as a store, factory, office space, etc.) is excluded, regardless of the amount of services rendered to the tenant); or (3) in the case of farm rentals, the farm landlord materially participates in the management or in the production of farm commodities on land rented to someone else.

- Dividends on stock and interest on bonds do not count for Social Security, unless they are received in the course of business by a dealer in stocks or securities. The term "bond" includes debentures, notes, certificates, and other evidence of indebtedness issued with interest coupons or in registered form by a corporation. Bonds also include government bonds. Other interest received in the course of a trade or business *does* count for Social Security. For example, interest received by a merchant on accounts or notes receivable are included in computing net earnings from self-employment.

- Partnerships are treated as individuals when it comes to the dividend and interest exclusion. Dividends and interest on securities held for investment are excluded from net earnings of the partners. However, if a partnership is in business as a securities dealer, income on the securities held for resale by the partnership is included as net earnings of the partners.

- Capital gains and losses, and gains and losses from the sale or exchange of property which is not inventory or stock in trade, are excluded in computing net earnings from self-employment.
- Retirement payments received by a retired partner from a partnership, of which the individual is a member or a former member, are excluded from net earnings from self-employment if the following conditions are met:
  (1) The payments are made under a written plan of the partnership that provides for periodic payments because of retirement, to partners generally or to a class or classes of partners, to continue at least until the partner's death
  (2) The partner rendered no services in any business conducted by the partnership (or its successors) during the taxable year of the partnership ending within or with the taxable year in which such payments were received
  (3) At the end of the partnership's taxable year, there is no obligation from the other partners to the retired partner other than for the retirement payments under the plan
  (4) The partner's share in the capital of the partnership has been paid in full by the end of the partnership's taxable year
- No deductions for net operating losses of other years are permitted in determining net earnings from self-employment.
- The following retirement benefits for ministers are not considered earnings from self-employment:
  (1) Retirement benefits received from a church plan after retirement
  (2) The rental value or allowance of a parsonage, including utilities, furnished to the minister after retirement
- Income taxable as "dividends" to shareholders of a Subchapter S corporation (a corporation electing not to be taxed as a corporation) is not considered "net earnings from self-employment."

## 271. How does a self-employed life insurance agent report first-year and renewal commissions?

If the agent is self-employed *when the policy is sold*, commissions are treated as earnings from self-employment in the year they are paid to the agent. It is immaterial whether the agent is an employee or self-employed when the commissions are received. For retirement-test purposes, renewal commissions paid to a self-employed agent after retirement are not included as earnings after the initial month of retirement if they were the result of services rendered prior to retirement (See Social Security Taxes, Q 243 to Q 253). (For treatment of commissions as "earnings" for "retirement test" purposes, see LOSS OF BENEFITS BECAUSE OF "EXCESS" EARNINGS, Q 223 to Q 233.)

# RAILROAD RETIREMENT

## EMPLOYEE AND SPOUSE ANNUITIES

### 272. Who is eligible for an employee annuity?

The Railroad Retirement Act[1] provides annuities for employees who have reached a specific age and have been credited with a specified number of years of service. The Act also provides annuities for employees who become disabled. The basic requirement for a regular employee retirement annuity is 120 months (ten years) of creditable railroad service (or five years, if the five years are performed after 1995). Service months need not be consecutive and, in some cases, military service may be counted as railroad service.

Benefits are based on months of service and earnings credits. Earnings are creditable up to certain annual maximums on the amount of compensation subject to railroad retirement taxes.

(1) *Annuities based on ten years of service (or five years in certain cases).* An employee with ten years of railroad service (or five years, if the five years were performed after 1995), but less than thirty years of service, is eligible for an annuity if he: (1) has attained retirement age, or (2) has attained age sixty-two (the annuity cannot begin prior to the first full month during which the employee is age sixty-two) but is less than retirement age. Early retirement annuity reductions are applied to annuities awarded before retirement age.

(2) *Annuities based on thirty years of service.* An employee who has been credited with thirty years of railroad service is eligible for a regular annuity based on age and service the first full month he or she is age sixty. Early retirement reductions are applied to annuities awarded before age sixty-two.

Starting in the year 2000, the age at which full benefits are payable increases in gradual steps until it reaches age sixty-seven. This affects people born in 1938 and later. Reduced annuities will still be payable at age sixty-two, but the maximum reduction will be 30 percent, rather than 20 percent, by the year 2022. Part of an annuity is not reduced beyond 20 percent if the employee had any creditable railroad service before August 12, 1983. These reductions do not affect those who retire at age sixty-two with thirty years of service.

There are two types of disability annuities for employees who have been credited with at least ten years of railroad service. An employee may receive an *occupational disability* at age sixty, if he or she has at least ten years of railroad service, or at any age, if the employee has at least twenty years (240 months) of service, when the employee is permanently disabled for his or her *regular railroad occupation*. An employee who cannot be considered for a disability annuity based on ability to work in his or her regular railroad occupation may receive a *total disability* annuity at any age, if he or she is permanently disabled for *all regular work* and has at least ten years (120 months) of creditable railroad service.

1. 45 U.S.C. 231 et. seq.

A five-month waiting period beginning with the month after the month of the onset of disability is required before disability annuity payments can begin.

While an annuity based on disability is not paid until the employee has stopped working for a railroad, employment rights need not be relinquished until the employee attains age sixty-five.

## 273. Who is entitled to a supplemental annuity?

An employee with a current connection with the railroad industry at the time of retirement may qualify for a supplemental annuity, in addition to the regular employee annuity. Supplemental annuities are paid from a separate account funded by employer taxes in addition to those assessed for regular annuities. The supplemental annuity is reduced if the employee receives a private pension based on contributions from a railroad employer.

An employee is entitled to a supplemental annuity if he or she: (1) has been credited with railroad service in at least one month before October 1981, (2) is entitled to the payment of an employee annuity awarded after June 30, 1966, (3) has a current connection with the railroad industry when the employee annuity begins, (4) has given up the right to return to work, and either (5) is age sixty-five or older and has completed twenty-five years of service, or (6) is age sixty or older and under age sixty-five, has completed thirty years of service, and is awarded an annuity on or after July 1, 1974.

A supplemental annuity that begins after December 21, 1974 does not affect the payment of the regular employee annuity. The payment of a supplemental annuity does not affect the amount of a spouse or survivor annuity.

## 274. What is a current connection with the railroad industry?

An employee who worked for a railroad in at least twelve of the thirty consecutive months immediately preceding the month his annuity begins will meet the current-connection requirement. If the employee has twelve months' service in an earlier thirty-consecutive-month period, he may still meet the current-connection requirement. This alternative generally applies if the employee did not have any regular employment outside the railroad industry after the end of the thirty-consecutive-month period that included twelve months of railroad service.

If an employee died before retirement, railroad service in at least twelve of the thirty consecutive months before death will meet the current-connection requirement for the purpose of paying survivor benefits.

## 275. When is a spouse eligible for spouse annuities?

The Railroad Retirement Act provides annuities for the spouse (and divorced spouse) of an employee who is entitled to an employee annuity. A spouse may receive an annuity based on age, or on having a child of the employee in his or her care. A divorced spouse may only receive an annuity based on age. No spouse or divorced spouse annuity may be paid based upon disability.

To be eligible for an annuity, a spouse must: (1) be the husband or wife of an employee who is entitled to an annuity, and (2) stop working for any railroad employer.

Where the employee has completed ten years but less than thirty years of railroad service, and has attained age sixty-two, the spouse must be: (1) retirement age or older, (2) less than retirement age and have in his or her care a disabled child or a minor child (a child under eighteen years old if the spouse claimant is a wife or under sixteen years old if the spouse claimant is a husband) of the employee, or (3) age sixty-two or older but under retirement age. (In such case, all annuity components are reduced for each month the spouse is under retirement age at the time the annuity begins.)

Where the employee has completed thirty years of railroad service and is age sixty or older, the spouse must be: (1) age sixty or older, (2) less than age sixty and have in his or her care a disabled or minor child of the employee, or (3) age sixty but less than retirement age.

To be eligible for a *divorced spouse annuity*, the employee annuitant must be at least age sixty-two, must have been married for at least ten years, and the divorced spouse must: (1) be the divorced wife or husband of an employee, (2) stop working for a railroad employer, (3) not be entitled to a retirement or disability benefit under the Social Security Act, based on a Primary Insurance Amount (PIA) that is equal to or greater than one-half of the employee's Tier I PIA, and either (4) have attained retirement age, or (5) have attained age sixty-two but be under retirement age. (The annuity is reduced for each month the spouse is under retirement age at the time the annuity begins.)

The amount of the divorced spouse's annuity is, in effect, equal to what Social Security would pay in the same situation, and therefore less than the amount of the spouse annuity otherwise payable.

## SURVIVOR BENEFITS

### 276. What survivor benefits are payable under the Railroad Retirement Act?

The Railroad Retirement Act provides annuities for the widow(er), surviving divorced spouse, or remarried widow(er) of an employee. The deceased employee must have completed ten years of railroad service (or five years of service after 1995) and have had a current connection with the railroad industry at the time of his or her death. A widow(er), surviving divorced spouse, or remarried widow(er) may receive an annuity based on age, on disability, or on having a child of the employee in his or her care.

A *widow(er)* of an employee who has completed ten years of railroad service (or five years of service after 1995) and had a current connection with the railroad industry at death is eligible for an annuity if he or she has not remarried, and (1) has attained retirement age, (2) is at least fifty but less than sixty years of age and becomes disabled (this results in a reduced annuity), (3) is less than retirement age but has in his or her care a child who either is under age eighteen (sixteen with respect to the tier I component) or is disabled and who is entitled to a child's annuity, or (4) is at least sixty years of age but has not attained retirement age. If eligibility is based on (4), all components of the annuity are reduced for each month the widow(er) is age sixty-two or over but under retirement age when the annuity begins. For each month the widow(er) is at least sixty but under age sixty-two, all components of the annuity are reduced as if the widow(er) were age sixty-two.

A *surviving divorced spouse* of an employee who completed ten years of railroad service (or five years of service after 1995) and had a current connection with the railroad industry at death is eligible for an annuity, if he or she: (1) is unmarried, (2) was married to the employee for at least ten years, and (3) is not entitled to a Social Security retirement benefit that is equal to or higher than the surviving divorced spouse's annuity before any reduction for age. In addition, the divorced spouse must meet one of the following requirements: (1) have attained retirement age, (2) be at least fifty years old but less than retirement age and disabled (this results in a reduced annuity), (3) be less than retirement age but have in his or her care a child who either is under age sixteen or is disabled and who is entitled to a child's benefit, or (4) is at least sixty years of age but has not attained retirement age. In this case, the annuity is reduced for each month the surviving spouse is under retirement age when the annuity begins.

If a surviving divorced spouse marries after attaining age sixty (or age fifty if he or she is a disabled surviving divorced spouse), the marriage is deemed not to have occurred.

A widow(er) of an employee who completed ten years of railroad service (or five years of service after 1995) and had a current connection with the railroad industry at death is eligible for an annuity as a *remarried widow(er)*, if he or she: (1) remarried either after having attained age sixty (after age fifty if disabled) or before age sixty but the marriage terminated, and (2) is not entitled to a Social Security retirement benefit that is equal to or higher than the full amount of the remarried widow(er) annuity before any reduction for age. In addition, the remarried widow(er) must meet one of the following requirements: (1) have attained retirement age, (2) be at least fifty but less than sixty years of age and disabled (this results in a reduced annuity), (3) have not attained retirement age but have in his or her care a child who either is under age sixteen or is disabled, and who is entitled to a child's annuity, or (4) be at least age sixty but have not attained retirement age. (In this case, the annuity is reduced for each month the remarried widow(er) is under retirement age when the annuity begins.)

## 277. Are children and other dependents eligible for survivor benefits?

Other survivor annuities are payable to:

- A child under age eighteen.
- A child age eighteen in full-time attendance at an elementary or secondary school, until the student attains age nineteen or the end of the school term after the student attains age nineteen.
- A disabled child over age eighteen, if the child became totally and permanently disabled before age twenty-two.
- A dependent grandchild meeting any of the requirements described previously for a child, if both the grandchild's parents are deceased or disabled.

- A parent at age sixty who was dependent on the employee for at least half of the parent's support. If the employee was also survived by a widow(er) or child who can qualify for an annuity, the parent's annuity is limited to the amount that Social Security would pay.

In order to be eligible for a child's annuity, the child must be: (1) a child of an employee who has completed ten years of railroad service (or five years of service after 1995) and had a current connection with the railroad industry when he died, (2) unmarried at the time the application was filed, and (3) dependent upon the employee.

## 278. What happens to survivors with dual benefits?

Survivor annuities, like retirement annuities, consist of Tier I and Tier II components. Tier I is based on the deceased employee's combined railroad retirement and Social Security credits, and is generally equivalent to the amount that would have been payable under Social Security. Tier II amounts are percentages of the deceased employee's Tier I amount.

The Tier I portion is reduced by the amount of any Social Security benefits received by a survivor annuitant, even if the Social Security benefits are based on the survivor's own earnings. This reduction follows the principles of Social Security law under which only the higher of a retirement or survivor benefit is, in effect, payable to a beneficiary. When both railroad retirement annuities and Social Security benefits are payable, the payments are generally combined into a single payment, issued through the Railroad Retirement Board.

The Tier I annuity portion of a widow's or widower's annuity may be reduced for receipt of any federal, state, or local government pension based on the widow(er)'s own earnings. The reduction does not apply if the employment on which the public pension is based was covered under Social Security as of the last day of the individual's employment.

Military service pensions based entirely on active duty before 1957 will cause a reduction. However, payments from the Department of Veterans Affairs will not cause a reduction. For those subject to the government-pension reduction, the Tier I reduction is equal to two-thirds of the amount of the government pension.

If a widow or widower is qualified for a railroad retirement employee annuity as well as a survivor annuity, a special guarantee applies in some cases. If both the widow (or widower) and the deceased employee started railroad employment after 1974, only the railroad retirement employee annuity or the survivor annuity chosen by the annuitant is payable. If either the deceased employee or the survivor annuitant had some service before 1975 but had not completed 120 months of railroad service before 1975, the employee annuity and the Tier II portion of the survivor annuity would be payable to the widow or widower. The Tier I portion of the survivor annuity would be payable, only to the extent that it exceeds the Tier I portion of the employee annuity. If either the deceased employee or the survivor annuitant completed 120 months of railroad service before 1975, the widow or dependent widower would receive both an employee annuity and a survivor annuity, without a full dual-benefit reduction.

## 279. Are there work and earnings limitations for those receiving survivor annuities?

A survivor annuity is not payable for any month in which the survivor works for a railroad or railroad union.

Survivors who are receiving Social Security benefits have their railroad retirement annuity and Social Security benefit combined for earnings-limitation purposes. The combined annuity and benefits are reduced by one dollar for every two dollars of earnings over $15,720 (in 2015) if the survivor is under the full retirement age. Benefits are reduced by one dollar for every three dollars of earnings over $41,880 (for 2015) in the year an annuitant reaches full retirement age; however, only earnings earned prior to the month the full retirement age is reached count toward the $41,880 limit. The earnings limitation does not apply to annuitants who are older than the full retirement age, starting with the month they reach full retirement age. See Q 183 for a discussion of the full retirement age.

If the annuitant is under the full retirement age in the first year benefits are payable, if the individual earns more than the annual exempt amount, work deductions apply only if monthly earnings are greater than 1/12 of the annual exempt amount ($1,310 in 2015).

These earnings restrictions do not apply to disabled widows or widowers under age sixty or to disabled children. However, any work or earnings by a disability annuitant is reviewed to determine whether it indicates recovery from the disability.

## 280. When do survivor benefits end?

Payment stops upon death, and no annuity is payable for the month of death.

A *widow(er)'s annuity* or *surviving divorced spouse's* benefit stops if: (1) the annuity was based on caring for a child under age eighteen (sixteen, for a surviving divorced spouse) or a disabled child and the child is no longer under age eighteen (sixteen, for a surviving divorced spouse) or disabled, or (2) the annuity was based on disability and the beneficiary recovers from the disability before age sixty. A disability annuity can be reinstated if the disability recurs within seven years. Remarriage will reduce a widow(er)'s annuity rate, and, in some cases, prevent payment.

A *child's* or *grandchild's annuity* will stop if the child: (1) marries, (2) reaches age eighteen, or (3) recovers from the disability on which the annuity was based. If the child is eighteen and a full-time elementary or high school student, the annuity stops upon graduation from high school, attainment of age nineteen, or the end of the first school term after attainment of age nineteen.

A *parent's survivor annuity* may stop upon remarriage; in certain cases, a remarried parent is entitled to a tier I benefit.

# RAILROAD RETIREMENT TAXES

## 281. What are the railroad retirement tax rates for employees and employers?

Railroad retirement Tier I taxes are coordinated with Social Security taxes, and increase automatically when Social Security taxes rise. Employees and employers pay Tier I taxes that are the same as Social Security taxes. In addition, both employees and employers pay Tier II taxes, to finance railroad retirement benefit payments over and above Social Security levels.

Tier I is the first level of the regular annuity for employees. It is calculated in generally the same way as a Social Security benefit.

Tier II is the second tier of a regular annuity, and is computed under a separate formula. Tier II is based on railroad service alone. Tier II benefits are equal to 7/10 of 1 percent of the employee's average monthly earnings, using the Tier II tax base in the 60 months of highest earnings multiplied by the employee's years of service in the rail industry.

The Tier I tax rate for employees and employers is 7.65 percent. In 2014, the Tier II tax rate for employers is 12.6 percent and the Tier II tax rate for employees is 4.4 percent. Tier II taxes are imposed on a maximum of $87,000 of earnings (in 2014). The Tier II tax rates are adjusted each year based on the amount of assets and expenses of the railroad retirement system. Note that 2015 Tier II numbers were not available as of this 2015 edition went to press.

**Tax Rate For Employees And Employers**

| Employers and Employees each | | Tier II tax rate | |
|---|---|---|---|
| Hospital insurance (HI) tax rate | Tier I tax rate including HI tax | Employers | Employees |
| 1.45 | 7.65 | 12.6% (2014) | 4.4% (2014) |

* Medicare Hospital Insurance (HI) tax applies to all annual earnings.

**Regular Railroad Retirement Taxes**

| *Tier I* | *Tax rate* | *Taxable earnings* |
|---|---|---|
| Employees | 7.65% | $117,000* (2014) |
| Employers | 7.65% | 117,000* (2014) |
| *Tier II* | | |
| Employees | 4.4% (2014) | $87,000 (2014) |
| Employers | 12.6% (2014) | 87,000 (2014) |

*Taxes on Someone Earning $117,000* (2014)

| | *Tier I* | *Tier II* | *Total* |
|---|---|---|---|
| Employees | $8,950.50 | $3,828.00 | $12,778.50 |
| Employers | 8,950.50 | 10,962.00 | 19,912.50 |

* Medicare Hospital Insurance (HI) tax applies to all annual earnings.

Railroad employees who also worked for a Social Security-covered employer in the same year may, under certain circumstances, receive a tax credit or refund equivalent to any excess Social Security taxes withheld.

Employees who worked for two or more railroads in a year, or who had Tier I taxes withheld from their Railroad Retirement Board sickness insurance benefits in addition to their railroad earnings, may be eligible for a tax credit or refund of any excess Tier I or Tier II railroad retirement taxes withheld. Such tax credits or refunds may be claimed on an employee's federal income tax return.

# BENEFITS FOR SERVICE MEMBERS AND VETERANS

## MILITARY RETIREMENT

### 282. In general, who is entitled to military retirement benefits?

Members of the armed forces may retire after a certain amount of active service. Monthly retirement pay is based on a percentage of base pay of the highest rank held, as well as number of years of service.

Service members who become disabled while in service may be placed on either temporary or permanent disability retirement, depending on the degree and length of disability, and also on whether they satisfy certain other conditions of eligibility.

Reservists are entitled to receive retirement benefits if they meet certain eligibility requirements.

Members of the uniformed services may also participate in the federal Thrift Savings Plan (see Q 286, Q 332).

### 283. What retirement benefits are available for those who first became members before August 1, 1986?

An immediate annuity is available to a servicemember who completes twenty years of service. No benefit is available to a servicemember who does not complete twenty years of service.

The retirement annuity is based in part on the servicemember's retirement "pay base," as well as the date on which the individual became a member of the uniformed service.

For those becoming members of a uniformed service for the first time *on or before September 7, 1980*, the retired pay base equals the servicemember's final monthly basic pay to which he was entitled the day before retirement.

For persons becoming members of a uniformed service for the first time *after September 7, 1980*, the monthly retired pay base is one thirty-sixth of the total amount of the monthly basic pay that the servicemember received for the highest thirty-six months (whether or not consecutive) of active duty.

In order to compute the monthly retirement benefit, the monthly retired pay base is multiplied by an amount equaling 2.5 percent for each year of service, up to a maximum of thirty years. The benefits range from 50 percent at twenty years of service to 75 percent at thirty or more years of service.

Retired pay is adjusted annually by the increase in the cost of living, as measured by the Consumer Price Index for All Urban Wage Earners and Clerical Workers (CPI).

The uniformed services retirement system is noncontributory. However, the servicemember contributes, while on active duty, to the Social Security system and, thereby, earns eligibility for a Social Security retirement benefit. Members may also contribute to the federal Thrift Savings Plan (see Q 286).

## 284. What is the retirement system for those who first become members on or after August 1, 1986?

Under the Military Retirement Reform Act of 1986, anyone who becomes a member of a uniformed service on or after August 1, 1986 is subject to a new retirement system.

The average monthly basic pay for the highest three years of pay during service becomes the pay base for servicemembers. This is known as "high-3." The multiplier, or percentage, for each year of service that is multiplied by the pay base remains unchanged at 2.5 percent for each year of service. The maximum number of years creditable toward retirement is thirty – or 75 percent of pay base.

Under this system, where the servicemember has retired and has completed fewer than thirty years of service, the percent reached above is reduced by one percentage point for each year between thirty years and the number of years completed.

This means that a twenty-year retiree will receive 40 percent of the pay base (as opposed to 50 percent under the system for those who became servicemembers before August 1, 1986). A thirty-year retiree, however, will receive the full 75 percent of the pay base, the same as under the old system.

| | Multiplier | |
|---|---|---|
| **Years of Service** | **Before 62** | **After 62** |
| 20 | 40.0 | 50.0 |
| 21 | 43.5 | 52.5 |
| 22 | 47.0 | 55.0 |
| 23 | 50.5 | 57.5 |
| 24 | 54.0 | 60.0 |
| 25 | 57.5 | 62.5 |
| 26 | 61.0 | 65.0 |
| 27 | 64.5 | 67.5 |
| 28 | 68.0 | 70.0 |
| 29 | 71.5 | 72.5 |
| 30 | 75.0 | 75.0 |

Cost-of-living adjustments to retirement benefits are guaranteed in years of inflation. Annual benefit increases will equal the increase in the Consumer Price Index (CPI), less one percentage point. This formula is known as "CPI Minus 1."

There is a one-time recomputation of retirement pay at age sixty-two, in recognition of the fact that at about age sixty-two military retirement pay becomes the primary source of retirement income for career military personnel. At the point when a retiree reaches age sixty-two, retirement pay is recomputed as if the one percentage point penalty for retirement at less than thirty years of service had not been applied. Additionally, at the same time, the retirement pay is increased to the level it would have reached if cost-of-living adjustments had been made under the full CPI rather than the "CPI Minus 1" formula.

In short, at age sixty-two, the level of military retirement pay is restored to the level at which it would have been under the law for military members who entered the service prior to August 1, 1986. Note, however, that all cost-of-living adjustments after age sixty-two are under the "CPI Minus 1" formula. Thus, military retirees will lose 1 percent to inflation each year after age sixty-two.

A servicemember retiring after thirty years of service will receive 75 percent of basic pay both before and after age sixty-two. His retirement pay will be affected only by the change in the cost-of-living adjustment formula.

### 285. May servicemembers contribute to the Thrift Savings Plan?

Yes. All active duty and Ready Reserve members of the uniformed services can participate in the Thrift Savings Plan (TSP) (see Q 332). The uniformed services include the Army, Navy, Air Force, Marine Corps, Coast Guard, Public Health Service, and the National Oceanic and Atmospheric Administration.

Uniformed service members can contribute up to 100 percent of their base pay. If a member contributes from base pay, he or she can elect to contribute up to 100 percent of any incentive pay, special pay, or bonus pay. Contributions to the TSP generally cannot exceed $18,000 (in 2015). Catch-up contributions for members over age fifty are also available (see Q 332).

The individual service secretaries may designate certain critical specialties as eligible for matching contributions in the same way that contributions are matched for FERS participants. There is no automatic 1 percent contribution for uniformed service members.

## Survivor Annuity

### 286. What is the Survivor Benefit Plan?

The Survivor Benefit Plan provides survivor benefits for eligible widows, widowers, and dependent children of eligible military personnel. Benefits are essentially the same as those provided federal government employees.

Those eligible to participate in the Survivor Benefit Plan (SBP) must be: (1) entitled to retired or retainer pay, or (2) eligible for retired pay but for the fact that they are under sixty years of age. The standard annuity is paid to those entitled to retired or retainer pay. The reserve-component annuity is paid to those who are eligible but under age sixty. If a person entitled to retired or retainer pay is married or has a dependent child, he is automatically covered by the SBP *with maximum coverage*, unless he elects lesser coverage or declines participation before the first day he becomes eligible for the retired or retainer pay. Unmarried service personnel who have no dependent children can elect a survivor annuity in favor of someone who has an insurable interest in their life. Retired pay is, of course, reduced for Plan participants.

A retiree who has a spouse and a child (or children) at retirement can elect survivor benefits for the *spouse only* or for the *child (or children) only*. Absent some election, coverage for both the spouse and child (or children) is automatic. The spouse must concur in: (1) an election not to participate in the plan, (2) an election to provide the spouse with an annuity at less than the maximum level, and (3) an election to provide an annuity for a dependent child but not the spouse.

An election not to participate in the Plan by a person eligible for retired pay is irrevocable unless revoked before the date on which the person first becomes entitled to that pay. An election by a person under age sixty not to participate in the Plan becomes irrevocable if not revoked by the end of the ninety-day period beginning on the date he receives notification that he has completed the required years of service.

## 287. Who is eligible to receive Survivor Benefit Plan benefits?

The Survivor Benefit Plan provides a monthly annuity payment effective the first day after the death of the retiree. The annuity is paid to one of the following:

- The eligible surviving widow or widower
- The surviving dependent children in equal shares, if the eligible widow or widower or eligible former spouse is dead, dies, or otherwise becomes ineligible
- The dependent children in equal shares, if the retiree elected to provide an annuity for dependent children but not for the spouse or former spouse
- The former spouse under certain conditions

The following criteria apply for the purposes of determining eligible beneficiaries:

- A *widow* is the surviving wife of a person who, if not married to the retiree at the time he became eligible for retired pay, was married to him for at least one year immediately before his death, or is the mother of issue by that marriage.
- A *widower* is the surviving husband of a retiree who, if not married to the person at the time she became eligible for retired pay, was married to her for at least one year immediately before her death, or is the father of issue by that marriage.
- A *former spouse* is the surviving former husband or wife of a person who is eligible to participate in the Plan.
- A *dependent child* is a person who is: (1) unmarried, (2) under eighteen years of age; or at least eighteen, but under twenty-two years of age, and pursuing a full-time course of study or training in a high school, vocational school or college; or incapable of self-support because of a mental or physical incapability existing before age eighteen or incurred on or after that birthday, but before age twenty-two, while

pursuing such a full-time course of study or training, (3) the child of a retiring participant, including an adopted child, a stepchild, foster child, or recognized natural child who lived with the retiree in a regular parent-child relationship.

- A *person with an insurable interest* is any person who has a bona fide financial interest in the continued life of the retiree. The relationship of the person to the retiree normally does not extend beyond the mother, father, brother, sister, or single child of the retiree.

The annuity payable to a surviving spouse of the retiree is paid for life, except that if the annuitant remarries before age fifty-five, the remarriage terminates the annuity. If the remarriage is terminated by death, annulment, or divorce, payment of the annuity is resumed upon the termination of the remarriage.

## 288. What is the amount of the Survivor Benefit Plan annuity?

The amount of a Survivor Benefit Plan annuity payable to a widow, widower, former eligible spouse, or dependent children is based on a figure known as the *base amount*. The base amount is: (1) the amount of monthly retired pay to which a retiree became entitled when first eligible, or later became entitled to by being advanced on the retired list, performing active duty, or being transferred from the temporary disability retired list to the permanent disability retired list; or (2) any lesser amount designated by the retiree on or before the first day of eligibility for retired pay, but not less than $300.

A retiree who wants maximum survivor benefits for a spouse and children (at the cost of maximum reduction in retirement pay), will designate as the base amount on which survivor benefits are figured the full amount of retired pay. For a lower level of survivor benefits (in exchange for a smaller reduction in retirement pay), a base amount less than full retirement pay will be designated.

The following are categories of dependents and the rules for determining the amount of annuity payable:

(1) In the case of a standard annuity for a widow, widower or child, the monthly annuity is an amount equal to 55 percent of the base amount, if the beneficiary is under sixty-two years of age or is a dependent child when becoming entitled to the annuity. If the beneficiary (other than a dependent child) is sixty-two years of age or older when becoming entitled to the annuity, the monthly annuity is an amount equal to 35 percent of the base amount.

(2) In the case of a standard annuity for an ex-spouse or person with an insurable interest in the annuitant (other than a widow, widower, or dependent child), the monthly annuity payable to the beneficiary is an amount equal to 55 percent of the retired pay of the person who elected to provide the annuity.

(3) An annuity is also payable to a surviving spouse of a member who dies on active duty after: (a) becoming eligible to receive retired pay, (b) qualifying for retired pay, except that he or she has not applied for or been granted that pay, or (c)

completing twenty years of active service but before he or she is eligible to retire as a commissioned officer because he or she has not completed ten years of active commissioned service. An annuity is payable to the dependent child of the servicemember if there is no surviving spouse or if the servicemember's surviving spouse subsequently dies.

If a person receiving an annuity in (3) in preceding list is under sixty-two or is a dependent child when the servicemember or former servicemember dies, the monthly annuity is an amount equal to 55 percent of the retired pay to which the servicemember or former servicemember would have been entitled if the servicemember or former servicemember had been entitled to that pay based upon his or her years of active service when he or she died.

If a person receiving an annuity in (3) in the preceding list (other than a dependent child) is sixty-two or older when the servicemember or former servicemember dies, the monthly annuity is an amount equal to 35 percent of the retired pay to which the servicemember or former servicemember would have been entitled if the servicemember or former servicemember had been entitled to that pay based upon his or her years of active service when he or she died.

## 289. Are Survivor Benefit Plan annuities subject to cost-of-living increases?

Whenever retirees receive a cost-of-living increase in their retired pay, Survivor Benefit Plan annuities are increased at the same time by the same total percent. The percentage is applied to the monthly annuity payable before any reduction is made, in consideration of the annuitant's eligibility for Dependency and Indemnity Compensation or Social Security survivor benefits.

## 290. How does the Survivor Benefit Plan reduce the regular retirement annuity?

The Survivor Benefit Plan reduces the regular retirement annuity according to the following formulas:

Where the individual first becomes a member of the uniformed service before March 1, 1990, the reduction is the lesser of:

(1) an amount equal to 2.5 percent of the first $364 of the base amount of the annuity subject to the survivor benefit, plus 10 percent of the remainder; or

(2) an amount equal to 6.5 percent of the base amount of the annuity subject to the survivor benefit.

Where the individual first becomes a member of the uniformed service on or after March 1, 1990, the reduction for the Survivor Benefit Plan is a flat 6.5 percent of the base amount of the annuity.

"Base amount" does not include cost-of-living increases.

## Disability Retirement

### 291. When is a servicemember entitled to retire on permanent disability?

When he has been called or ordered to active duty for a period of more than thirty days (excluding Ready Reserve training duty), and:

(1) he is unfit to perform his duties because he has incurred a physical disability while entitled to basic pay;

(2) the disability is of a permanent and stable nature based on commonly accepted medical principles;

(3) the disability is not due to intentional or willful neglect, and not incurred during a period of unauthorized absence; and

(4) one of the following applies: (a) the disability is rated at least 30 percent under the Department of Veterans Affairs disability rating schedule, or (b) the service member has completed at least twenty years of service.

Where the service member has not completed twenty years of service but has a disability of at least 30 percent, as explained in (a) in preceding list, one of the following tests must additionally be satisfied:

(1) The disability must be incurred in the line of duty.

(2) The disability must be the proximate result of performing active duty.

(3) The servicemember must have completed at least eight years of service.

Where the active-duty or inactive training period is thirty days or less, a regular servicemember or reservist is entitled to permanent disability based on *injury* where the following conditions are met:

(1) He is unfit to perform his duties because he has incurred a physical disability while entitled to basic pay

(2) The disability is of a permanent and stable nature based on commonly accepted medical principles

(3) The disability is the proximate result of performing active duty or inactive training

(4) The disability is not due to intentional misconduct or willful neglect, and not incurred during a period of unauthorized absence

(5) One of the following applies: (a) the disability is rated at least 30 percent under the Department ofVeterans Affairs disability rating schedule, or (b) the servicemember has completed at least twenty years of service

## 292. How is disability retirement pay determined?

Disability retirement pay is figured by either of two methods, at the retiree's option, up to a maximum of 75 percent of basic pay: (1) 2.5 percent of monthly basic pay multiplied by the number of years of active service, or (2) the percentage rating of disability.

A servicemember who meets the requirements of temporary disability may be placed on temporary disability retirement for up to five years. Retired pay for temporary disability is no less than 50 percent of basic pay. A servicemember will be permanently retired for physical disability if still disabled after five years.

# Reservists' Retirement Pay

## 293. Are Reservists entitled to retired pay?

To qualify for retired pay in the Reserves, a person must complete at least twenty years of "satisfactory Federal service" as a member of the armed forces. He meets this requirement for a year by earning at least fifty points each year. Points are earned for both inactive duty and active duty. The branch of service will advise the reservist of point totals and the number of years of satisfactory federal service he has completed. The last eight qualifying years must have been spent in a Reserve unit. Entitlement to Reserve retired pay begins at age sixty.

The Reserve point system is an element used in computing retirement pay. In totaling points, there is no limit to the number of active points that may be earned in a year, but no more than sixty inactive-duty points may be counted for any one year.

## 294. How is Reserve retired pay computed?

Generally, reserve retired pay is computed by:

(1) dividing the reservist's cumulative active- and inactive-point total by 360, to convert the points into years of service;

(2) taking the monthly basic pay rate for the member's grade and length of service at the time he or she becomes entitled to retired pay at age sixty;

(3) multiplying that rate by 2.5 percent × the years of service that are credited to him or her through the point conversion process (but not in excess of thirty years).

Where the reservist first became a member after September 7, 1980, instead of using his or her actual pay rate as described in (2) above, he or she uses an average of the basic monthly pay to which he or she would have been entitled had he or she been on active duty for the three years in which he or she was a member of an armed force.

## 295. How does the Survivor Benefit Plan work for Reservists?

Generally, the Survivor Benefit Plan for Reservists follows the rules for the regular service member's Survivor Benefit Plan. With respect to the amount of reduction in retired pay of the reserve component annuity, the reduction is the lesser of:

(1) an amount equal to 2.5 percent of the first $364 of the base amount of the annuity subject to the survivor benefit, plus 10 percent of the remainder; or

(2) an amount equal to 6.5 percent of the base amount of the annuity subject to the survivor benefit.

# VETERANS

## Dependency and Indemnity Compensation

### 296. What is Dependency and Indemnity Compensation?

Dependency and Indemnity Compensation (DIC) is the benefit program providing monthly payments to a surviving spouse, child, or parent of the veteran due to a *service-connected* death that occurs after 1956. (Where the death occurred prior to 1957, certain survivors could have elected to take benefits under DIC.)

Generally, DIC is payable to survivors of servicemembers or reservists who died from: (1) disease or injury incurred or aggravated in the line of duty while on active or inactive duty training, or (2) disability compensable under laws administered by the Department of Veterans Affairs.

Veterans and dependents may obtain information on benefits by calling the toll-free number 1-800-827-1000. Callers are automatically connected to the Department of Veterans Affairs regional office serving the area from which their call originates.

### 297. Who is eligible for DIC benefits?

DIC benefits are payable to an eligible *surviving spouse*, regardless of the survivor's income or employment status. The survivor's death or remarriage terminates the benefit. Benefit eligibility is not reestablished if the survivor's remarriage is terminated by death or divorce. A surviving spouse may receive DIC payments, as well as Social Security survivor benefits.

The surviving spouse must have been married: (1) before expiration of fifteen years after the end of the period of active duty, active duty for training, or inactive training duty, in which the injury or disease causing death was incurred or aggravated; (2) for one or more years; or (3) for any period of time if a child was born of or before the marriage.

The surviving spouse's benefit is increased when the spouse has children under age eighteen. Where there is no surviving spouse eligible to receive DIC, children under eighteen are eligible to receive DIC benefits.

The definition of "*child*" includes the veteran's legitimate child, legally adopted child, stepchild who is a member of the veteran's household or was a member at the time of the veteran's death, and illegitimate child (provided a number of requirements are met).

DIC payments are made to children who are unmarried and who: (1) are under age eighteen; or (2) before attaining age eighteen, become permanently incapable of self-support; or (3) after attaining age eighteen and until completion of education or training (but not after attaining age twenty-three), are pursuing a course of instruction at an approved educational institution.

Eligibility of *parents* to receive DIC is measured by an annual income test, rather than by dependency. A remarriage of a parent does not terminate the benefits. Parent's DIC benefits continue until death.

### 298. How is the amount of the DIC benefit determined?

DIC payments to surviving spouses of veterans whose service-connected deaths occur on or after January 1, 1993, are standardized; there had been a schedule of benefits based on the military rank of the deceased veteran. In 2014, a monthly base rate of $1,233.23 will be payable to the surviving spouses of all such veterans. That rate is increased by $261.87 a month, if the veteran was totally disabled due to service-connected disabilities continuously for at least eight years prior to death. Note that 2015 numbers were not available as this 2015 edition went to press.

If there is a surviving spouse with one or more children below the age of eighteen of a deceased veteran, the DIC paid monthly to the surviving spouse is increased by $305.52 for each child.

In addition to an annual limitation, the amount of DIC payable monthly to a *parent* depends upon whether there is only one parent, whether two surviving parents are or are not living together, and whether a parent has remarried and is living with a spouse.

The maximum monthly benefit payable to *one parent only* is $611. No DIC is payable if the parent's annual income exceeds $14,391. *Two parents not living together* are entitled to a maximum monthly benefit of $442 each. Again, no DIC is paid to a parent whose annual income exceeds $14,391. *Two parents living together* (or remarried parents living with spouses, when both parents are alive) are entitled to a maximum monthly benefit of $415 each. No DIC is paid to a parent if total combined annual income exceeds $19,344. The monthly rate of DIC payable to a parent is increased by $331 if such parent is: (1) a patient in a nursing home, or (2) helpless or blind, or so nearly helpless and blind as to need or require the regular aid and attendance of another person.

## Death Prior to January 1, 1993

For surviving spouses of veterans who died prior to January 1, 1993, monthly payments are made according to the veteran's pay grade at the time of death or under the new formula, whichever provides the highest benefit. (See Appendix C, Table 4, Servicemembers and Veterans Tables, for benefits based on pay grade.)

If the veteran did not die in active service, the pay grade will be determined as of: (1) the time of last discharge or release from active duty, or (2) the time of discharge or release from any period of active duty for training or inactive duty training, if death results from service-connected disability incurred during such period. The discharge must have been other than dishonorable.

The monthly rate of DIC is increased by $305.52 if the surviving spouse is: (1) a patient in a nursing home, or (2) helpless and blind, or so nearly helpless and blind as to need the regular aid and attendance of another person.

The monthly rate of DIC will be increased by $143.12, if the surviving spouse is permanently housebound by reason of disability and does not qualify for the aid and attendance allowance described above.

## DIC Benefits for Children

If a *child* is under age eighteen, and there is no surviving spouse entitled to DIC, DIC is paid in equal shares to the children of the deceased veteran at the following monthly rates: one child, $520.70; two children, $749.07; three children, $977.45; more than three children, $977.45 plus $185.75 for each child in excess of three.

If a child is eighteen or over, and the child became permanently incapable of self-support while under eighteen and eligible for DIC, the child's DIC is continued past age eighteen and increased by $305.52 per month. If DIC is payable to a surviving spouse with a child, age eighteen or older, who became permanently incapable of support while under eighteen, the Department of Veterans Affairs will pay an additional sum of $520.70 for such child.

If DIC is payable to a spouse with a child, age eighteen or over and under age twenty-three, who is attending an approved educational institution, DIC is paid to the child, concurrently with the payment of DIC to the spouse, in the amount of $258.83 per month.

## Disability Benefits – Service-Connected

### 299. What benefits are available for service-connected disability?

There are three kinds of benefits for a service-connected disability: (1) compensation paid by Department of Veterans Affairs, (2) severance pay, and (3) disability retirement pay. Disability retirement is discussed in BENEFITS FOR FEDERAL GOVERNMENT EMPLOYEES, Q 317 to Q 362.

Monthly compensation is paid by the Department of Veterans Affairs without regard to other income, on the basis of average impairments of earning capacity in civilian employment. A person eligible for both disability retirement pay and this compensation may elect which to receive, but cannot receive full benefits from both sources.

The veteran must be disabled by injury or disease incurred in, or aggravated by, active service in the line of duty. Discharge or separation must be other than dishonorable, and the injury cannot have resulted from willful misconduct. Reservists disabled while on active training duty may qualify for compensation.

The monthly compensation amount depends on the veteran's degree of disability. The rates in the subsequent table are for 2014. Note that 2015 numbers were not available as this 2015 edition went to press.

| Degree of Disability | Rate |
|---|---|
| 10% | $131 |
| 20 | 259 |
| 30 | 401 |
| 40 | 578 |
| 50 | 822 |
| 60 | 1,041 |
| 70 | 1,312 |
| 80 | 1,526 |
| 90 | 1,714 |
| 100 | 2,858 |

A service-connected disability rating may be increased or decreased in accordance with medical findings of changes in the affected condition. However, once a condition has been rated at or above a particular evaluation for twenty continuous years, the rating is protected by law and may not be changed (unless the rating was established by fraud).

Any veteran entitled to monthly compensation whose disability is rated not less than 30 percent is entitled to additional compensation for dependents. The current rates listed below are based upon 100 percent disability. If the disability rating is at least 30 percent, but less than 100 percent, the amount of dependent benefits will be approximately the same percent of these rates as the percent-of-disability rating.

The monthly compensation rates for dependents are as follows:

| **Spouse and —** | **Amount** |
|---|---|
| no children | $159 |
| 1 child | 276 |
| 2 children | 355 |
| 3 children | 434 |
| additional children, each | 79 |
| **If no surviving spouse —** | |
| 1 child | 107 |
| 2 children | 186 |
| 3 children | 264 |
| additional children, each | 79 |
| **Dependent parent(s)** | |
| each parent | 128 |

A child's benefit usually ends at age eighteen. However, each dependent child between ages eighteen and twenty-three who is attending an approved school is eligible for $256 monthly if the veteran is totally disabled, and a proportionate amount if the veteran is partially disabled.

The spouse of a totally disabled veteran is entitled to $305 a month if: (1) a patient in a nursing home; or (2) helpless and blind, or so nearly helpless and blind as to need or require the regular aid and attendance of another person. The spouse of a veteran who is not totally disabled, but at least 30 percent disabled, is entitled to a proportionate monthly benefit.

These dependency allowances are not payable if the serviceman receives any other allowance for dependents under any other law (with the exception of Social Security benefits). The higher of the two amounts may be elected, but not both. Social Security benefits for total and permanent disability will not be reduced by the amount of any service-connected disability compensation received from the Department of Veterans Affairs.

Service personnel are entitled to *disability severance pay* when separated from service for physical disability, but are not eligible for disability retirement pay where: (1) the rated disability is less than 30 percent, or (2) length-of-service credits are insufficient.

Disability severance pay is a lump sum equal to twice the monthly base and longevity pay multiplied by years of service, but not exceeding the amount of two years' basic pay, and is payable by the member's branch of service.

Veterans with a 10 percent disability rating may be entitled to a program of vocational rehabilitation, if the Department of Veterans Affairs finds that the veteran has a "serious employment handicap" and needs rehabilitative services to prepare for, obtain, or retain suitable employment.

Any veteran receiving a pension awarded between January 30, 1985, and December 31, 1995 can apply for a vocational rehabilitation evaluation. If an evaluation shows the veteran can achieve a vocational goal if provided the appropriate rehabilitative services, the Department of Veterans Affairs will help develop a plan of services which can lead to employment. There is no requirement that a pensioner participate in an evaluation or training and, if the veteran elects to enter a rehabilitative program, the pension benefit is protected until the veteran is employed.

The Department of Veterans Affairs makes disability payments based on a presumption that veterans who served in Vietnam were exposed to Agent Orange and other herbicides. The conditions the Department of Veterans Affairs recognizes on this basis are soft-tissue sarcoma, non-Hodgkin's lymphoma, chloracne, Hodgkin's disease, Porphyria Cutanea Tarda (PCT), multiple myeloma (a cancer involving the bone marrow), and respiratory cancers (lung, bronchus, larynx, and trachea). All Department of Veterans Affairs medical centers provide a special examination to assist Vietnam veterans who were exposed to Agent Orange in determining their current health status.

## Death Benefits – Service-Connected

### 300. What other service-connected death benefits are available?

The Department of Veterans Affairs reimburses survivors up to $2,000 (or more, in the case of a federal employee who dies in the performance of duty) for the burial expenses of a veteran who dies as a result of service-connected disability or disabilities.

When a member of the armed forces dies while on active duty, active or inactive training duty, or while receiving hospital treatment for a service-connected ailment, his or her branch of service will provide for the disposition of his or her remains. Additional costs of transportation of the remains of the deceased may be allowed if the veteran died while hospitalized or residing in a Department of Veterans Affairs facility, or while in transit, at Department of Veterans Affairs' expense, to or from a hospital, domiciliary, or a Department of Veterans Affairs regional office.

Other allowances include burial in a national cemetery, American flag, and transportation from place of death to place of burial. The next of kin is also entitled to a headstone, or a headstone monetary allowance (in the event the veteran purchased a headstone prior to death).

A lump sum of $100,000 is paid to the survivors of a servicemember who dies on active duty or active or inactive training duty. An amount of $12,420 is paid to a former servicemember who dies within 120 days after separation from active duty. This death gratuity is paid by the branch of service of the deceased to the spouse, if living; otherwise to any children in equal shares; otherwise to parents, brothers or sisters, as designated by the deceased.

Dependents of a servicemember may remain in government housing for ninety days without charge after the servicemember's death.

Survivors and dependents may also be eligible for the survivors' and dependents' educational assistance program. The purpose of this program is: (1) to enable children to obtain an education they might not otherwise have had an opportunity to obtain; and (2) to enable surviving spouses to prepare to support themselves and their families at a standard of living that the veteran, but for death or disability, could have expected to provide.

## Pension, Disability, and Death Benefits Not Service-Connected

### 301. When is a veteran eligible for nonservice-connected pension, disability, and death benefits?

Veterans with limited income who are discharged under conditions other than dishonorable may be eligible for: (1) an Improved Pension, (2) Section 306 pension, or (3) old law pension. The old law pension is for veterans who died before July 1, 1960.

The pension-eligible veteran must have:

(1) had ninety days active service during the Mexican border period, World War I, World War II, the Korean Conflict, or Vietnam Era;

(2) been discharged because of service-connected disability; or

(3) at the time of death been receiving (or entitled to receive) compensation or retirement pay based on a service-connected disability incurred during wartime.

### 302. When is a surviving spouse and dependents eligible for nonservice-connected pension, disability, and death benefits?

A surviving spouse must have lived continuously with the veteran from the time of marriage until the veteran's death, except where there was a separation due to the misconduct of, or caused by, the veteran, without fault on the surviving spouse's part. The surviving spouse's valid remarriage or death permanently terminates the benefit. However, if the remarriage is annulled, or is terminated by death or divorce (unless the divorce was secured by fraud or collusion), the surviving spouse is not barred from receiving benefits.

The surviving spouse must have been married to the veteran: (1) for at least one year; or (2) for any period, if a child was born either before or after the marriage. For Vietnam Era veterans, the marriage must have taken place before May 8, 1985.

## 303. Are children entitled to benefits?

Unmarried children and surviving spouses under eighteen of a deceased veteran may be eligible for a pension. The pension is based on need. Regardless of the income limit, however, benefits will be denied a child or surviving spouse who owns capital which, in the Department of Veterans Affairs' judgment, should be consumed for his or her support.

Unmarried children and surviving spouses over eighteen may qualify for pensions in their own right, if they are: (1) permanently incapable of self-support since prior to age eighteen, or (2) under twenty-three and attending a Department of Veterans Affairs approved educational institution.

## 304. What is the amount of the Improved Pension?

Under the "Improved Pension Program," which went into effect on January 1, 1979, the maximum annual rates payable (effective December 1, 2013) are presented in the subsequent tables. Note that 2015 numbers were not available as this 2015 edition went to press.

| **Veterans and Dependents** | |
|---|---|
| Veteran without dependent spouse or child | $12,652 |
| Veteran with one dependent (spouse or child) | $16,569 |
| Veteran in need of regular aid and attendance without dependents | $21,107 |
| Veteran in need of regular aid and attendance with one dependent | $25,022 |
| Veteran permanently housebound without dependents | $15,462 |
| Veteran permanently housebound with one dependent | $19,380 |
| Mexican border period and World War I veteran | add $2,874 to the applicable annual rate |
| Increase for each additional dependent child | $2,161 |

| **Spouse and Dependents** | |
|---|---|
| Surviving spouse without dependent children | $8,485 |
| Surviving spouse with one dependent child | $11,107 |
| Surviving spouse in need of regular aid and attendance without dependent child | $13,563 |
| Surviving spouse in need of regular aid and attendance with one dependent child | $16,180 |
| Surviving spouse permanently housebound without dependent child | $10,371 |
| Surviving spouse permanently housebound with one dependent child | $12,988 |
| Increase for each additional dependent child | $2,161 |
| Child not in custody of veteran's surviving spouse, or child if no living surviving spouse of the veteran | $2,161 |

Benefits are generally paid monthly and are reduced by the annual countable income of the claimant and any dependent of the claimant. Generally, all nonpension income is included for this purpose, but income paid for certain educational or medical expenses are excluded from the computation.

In addition, the pension may be denied or discontinued if the claimant's net worth is such that it is reasonable that some portion of the estate be used for his support. Additional pension for a child may be denied if the child's net worth is excessive.

Pensioners must provide income and net worth reports to the Department of Veterans Affairs on an annual basis.

## 305. What is the Section 306 Pension?

The veteran, surviving spouse, and children who came on the pension rolls on or after July 1, 1960 but prior to January 1, 1979 may continue to receive a pension at the monthly rate in effect as of December 31, 1978. The pension will be paid so long as the veteran remains permanently and totally disabled, there is no charge in dependency, and income does not exceed the adjusted income limitation. The income limitation is Consumer Price Index (CPI)-sensitive.

Pensions range from $5 to $197 monthly for veterans with no dependents, and up to $222 per month for veterans with dependents. If the annual income of a veteran with no children exceeds $13,941, no pension is paid. Where there is one child and annual income exceeds $18,739, no pension is paid.

A surviving spouse with no minor children may receive up to $139 a month but, if annual income exceeds $13,941, no pension is paid. Where there is one child and annual income exceeds $18,739, no pension is paid.

Where there is no eligible surviving spouse, a child may receive sixty-one dollars a month with twenty-six dollars added for each additional child and the total divided among them. A child is not entitled if the income, not counting his or her own earnings, exceeds $11,398.

## 306. What is the Old Law Pension?

Eligible veterans, their surviving spouses and children of certain deceased veterans who died before July 1, 1960, may be entitled to an Old Law pension or death benefit. Where the veteran's surviving spouse or children are claiming Old Law death benefits, it must be shown that the veteran died of causes not due to service. The veteran must have served during World War I, World War II or the Korean conflict.

These pensions are not payable to a veteran or surviving spouse without children, or to an entitled child, if the claimant receives other income over $12,205 annually, or to a veteran or surviving spouse with child if his or her other income is in excess of $17,594.

# GOVERNMENT LIFE INSURANCE

## Servicemembers' Group Life Insurance

### 307. Who is eligible to be insured automatically under Servicemembers' Group Life Insurance (SGLI)?

Any member of the uniformed services (Army, Navy, Air Force, Marine Corps, Coast Guard, Commissioned Corps of the United States Public Health Service, and the National Oceanic and Atmospheric Administration) on active duty, active duty for training, or inactive duty training in a commissioned, warrant, or enlisted rank or grade, or as a cadet or midshipman of one of the service academies. Also, any member of the Ready Reserve in a unit or position that may require active duty or active duty for training, and each year performs at least twelve periods of inactive-duty training that is creditable for retirement purposes.

### 308. What is the amount and nature of the coverage?

The maximum amount of SGLI is $400,000. Members on active duty in the Uniformed Services of the Army, Navy, Air Force, Marine Corps, Coast Guard, Commissioned Corps of the United States Public Health Service, and the National Oceanic and Atmospheric Administration are automatically insured for $400,000.

Automatic insurance coverage is $400,000, unless the member elects in writing: (1) not to be insured, or (2) to be insured for less than $400,000. Members may elect coverage in increments of $50,000, between $50,000 and $400,000. Any person who elects not to be insured or to be insured in an amount less than $400,000 may thereafter be insured for $400,000 upon written application, proof of good health, and compliance with such other terms and conditions as may be prescribed by the Administrator.

The coverage under SGLI is group-term life insurance evidenced by a certificate issued to the insured and is entirely separate from and in addition to any other government life insurance the insured may have or later acquire. The insurance is underwritten by a pool of commercial insurers, with one acting as the primary insurer and the others participating as reinsurers.

The program is administered by the Office of Servicemembers' Group Life Insurance, 290 West Mt. Pleasant Ave., Livingston, New Jersey, 07039, and is supervised by the Department of Veterans Affairs. The phone number of the Office of Servicemembers' Group Life Insurance is 1-800-419-1473.

### 309. When is coverage terminated and can the policy be converted?

A servicemember may convert SGLI coverage to Veterans' Group Life Insurance (VGLI) upon separation from service. A servicemember has 120 days following separation to apply for VGLI. The member will be sent a computer printout application, usually within forty-five to sixty days following release from duty. The completed application and the first premium must be sent within 120 days after separation from service. If an application for VGLI is filed after this 120-day period, proof of insurability must be provided, and the application must be submitted within one year after the SGLI terminates. A servicemember is not eligible to apply for VGLI more than one year and 120 days after separation from service.

SGLI may be converted to an individual policy of life insurance with a commercial company that participates in SGLI within 120 days following release from active duty. The policies are issued at a standard premium rate regardless of health. A policy cannot be issued for an amount greater than the prior SGLI coverage.

## 310. Who pays the cost of SGLI?

The government pays, from a revolving fund in the U.S. Treasury, the administrative expenses of the SGLI program and costs traceable to the extra hazard of duty in the uniformed services. The balance is paid by the insured members. A serviceman pays, by deduction, seven cents a month per $1,000, or twenty-eight dollars a month for $400,000 of insurance. A Ready Reservist (one who is assigned to a unit or position that requires at least twelve periods of inactive-duty training that is creditable for retirement purposes) pays the same rates as those servicemen on active duty. Reservists with part-time coverage pay a premium at an annual rate of twenty-eight dollars a year for $400,000 of coverage.

## 311. How does a person designate a beneficiary?

Death proceeds are paid to the beneficiary or beneficiaries designated by the insured in writing. If no named beneficiary survives, payment is made in the following order of preference: (1) surviving spouse, (2) child or children of the insured and descendants of deceased children by representation, (3) insured parents or their survivors, (4) executor or administrator of insured's estate, or (5) insured's other next of kin entitled under laws of the insured's domicile at time of his or her death.

An adopted child may qualify for SGLI based on the death of both his or her natural and adopted parents. But no person who consents to the adoption of a child may be recognized as a parent for SGLI purposes. A child, in other words, cannot claim from more than one father or one mother in an adoption case. An illegitimate child is considered the child of his or her natural mother.

If a person otherwise entitled to payment does not make claim within one year after the insured's death, or if payment to that person is prohibited by federal law, payment may be made in the order of precedence as if the person had not survived the insured, and any such payment is a bar to recovery by any other person.

If a person entitled to benefits does not file a claim for benefits within two years after the insured's death and there is no notice that a claim will be made, the Department of Veterans Affairs may pay the benefit to someone it deems is appropriate. Such payment is a bar to recovery by any other person.

The insured may elect settlement of the proceeds either in a lump sum or in thirty-six equal monthly installments. If no election is made by the insured, the payment will be made in a lump sum.

## Veterans' Group Life Insurance

### 312. Who is eligible for Veterans' Group Life Insurance (VGLI)?

Servicemembers leaving active duty can convert their SGLI to Veterans' Group Life Insurance (VGLI) without medical examination. The day after SGLI coverage ceases for any member on active duty for training, or inactive duty training, the policy is automatically converted to VGLI, subject to timely payment of the initial premium. Reservists performing active duty or inactive duty for training under a call or orders specifying a period of less than thirty-one days, who are injured or disabled, and become uninsurable at standard rates, are eligible for VGLI. Also, members of the Individual Ready Reserve and Inactive National Guard are eligible for SGLI. An application for coverage must be filed by a member of these groups.

All Retired Reserve SGLI policyholders will have their policies automatically exchanged for policies under the VGLI program. Retired reservists may retain lifetime coverage under VGLI, instead of being cut off from coverage at age sixty-one or when receiving retired pay (as is the case with Retired Reserve SGLI).

In addition, VGLI is extended generally to reservists and National Guard members who decide to separate prior to reaching twenty-year retirement.

Veterans, who were granted a service-connected disability but are otherwise in good health, may apply to the Department of Veterans Affairs for up to $10,000 life insurance coverage at standard insurance rates, within two years from the date the Department of Veterans Affairs notifies the veteran that the disability has been rated as service-connected. This applies even if the disability rating is 0 percent.

### 313. What is the amount of Veterans' Group Life Insurance?

The maximum amount of VGLI is $400,000. No one may carry a combined amount of SGLI and VGLI in excess of $400,000 at any one time. Also, the amount is limited to an amount equal to or less than the amount of the veteran's terminating SGLI. VGLI is available only in increments of $10,000.

VGLI is *renewable* five-year term insurance. It has no cash, loan, paid-up, or extended values, and lapses for nonpayment of premiums (except in the case of a mental incompetent who dies within one year after becoming insured).

VGLI has a reinstatement period of five years after a policy has lapsed.

### 314. How is the beneficiary designated under Veterans' Group Life Insurance?

VGLI proceeds are paid to the designated beneficiary or beneficiaries when a valid claim is established. If no beneficiary survives, or the insured fails to designate a beneficiary, payment is made in the following order of preference: (1) surviving spouse, (2) child or children of the insured and descendants of deceased children by representation, (3) insured's parents or survivor of them, (4) executor or administrator of insured's estate, or (5) insured's other next of kin entitled under laws of the insured's domicile at the time of death.

There are no restrictions on beneficiary designations, and the insured may change the designation without the knowledge or consent of the beneficiary. This right cannot be waived or restricted. The Department of Veterans Affairs does not recognize state court divorce decrees that require veterans to keep their ex-spouses as beneficiaries on their Department of Veterans Affairs life insurance policies. The forms required for a change of beneficiary may be obtained from the Office of Servicemembers' Group Life Insurance, any Department of Veterans Affairs office, or by calling the Department of Veterans Affairs Insurance Center at 1-800-669-8477.

Any designation of beneficiary or beneficiaries for SGLI filed with a uniformed service is considered a designation for VGLI, but only for sixty days after the VGLI becomes effective. Where the insured is incompetent at the end of the sixty-day period, the designation made for SGLI may continue in force until the disability is removed, but not for more than five years after the effective date of the insured's VGLI.

The designation of beneficiary or beneficiaries, except for a designation by an incompetent, must be in writing signed by the insured and received by the administrative office to be effective.

No claim for VGLI will be denied because of a failure to file a claim within four years of the insured's death.

If the insured, in the application for VGLI, does not limit the beneficiary's payments, the beneficiary can elect to receive the insurance in a single payment or in thirty-six equal monthly installments.

Payment of benefits under VGLI, made to or on account of a beneficiary, are exempt from taxation and the claims of creditors. The benefits are not liable to attachment, levy, or seizure by or under any legal or equitable process.

## 315. What are the premium rates for Veterans' Group Life Insurance?

Premium rates depend on age. Premium payment options include the use of automatic payments by deductions from Department of Veterans Affairs benefits or retirement checks, and an option to take a one-month discount for annual payments.

**VETERANS' GROUP LIFE INSURANCE**

**Monthly Premium Rate**

| Amount of Insurance | Age 29 & Below | Age 30-34 | Age 35-39 | Age 40-44 | Age 45-49 | Age 50-54 |
|---|---|---|---|---|---|---|
| $400,000 | $32.00 | $40.00 | $52.00 | $68.00 | $88.00 | $144.00 |
| 390,000 | 31.20 | 39.00 | 50.70 | 66.30 | 85.80 | 140.40 |
| 380,000 | 30.40 | 38.00 | 49.40 | 64.60 | 83.60 | 136.80 |
| 370,000 | 29.60 | 37.00 | 48.10 | 62.90 | 81.40 | 133.20 |
| 360,000 | 28.80 | 36.00 | 46.80 | 61.20 | 79.20 | 129.60 |
| 350,000 | 28.00 | 35.00 | 45.50 | 59.50 | 77.00 | 126.00 |
| 340,000 | 27.20 | 34.00 | 44.20 | 57.80 | 74.80 | 122.40 |

| Amount of Insurance | Monthly Premium Rate Age 29 & Below | Age 30-34 | Age 35-39 | Age 40-44 | Age 45-49 | Age 50-54 |
|---|---|---|---|---|---|---|
| 330,000 | 26.40 | 33.00 | 42.90 | 56.10 | 72.60 | 118.80 |
| 320,000 | 25.60 | 32.00 | 41.60 | 54.40 | 70.40 | 115.20 |
| 310,000 | 24.80 | 31.00 | 40.30 | 52.70 | 68.20 | 111.60 |
| 300,000 | 24.00 | 30.00 | 39.00 | 51.00 | 66.00 | 108.00 |
| 290,000 | 23.20 | 29.00 | 37.70 | 49.30 | 63.80 | 104.40 |
| 280,000 | 22.40 | 28.00 | 36.40 | 47.60 | 61.60 | 100.80 |
| 270,000 | 21.60 | 27.00 | 35.10 | 45.90 | 59.40 | 97.20 |
| 260,000 | 20.80 | 26.00 | 33.80 | 44.20 | 57.20 | 93.60 |
| 250,000 | 20.00 | 25.00 | 32.50 | 42.50 | 55.00 | 90.00 |
| 240,000 | 19.20 | 24.00 | 31.20 | 40.80 | 52.80 | 86.40 |
| 230,000 | 18.40 | 23.00 | 29.90 | 39.10 | 50.60 | 82.80 |
| 220,000 | 17.60 | 22.00 | 28.60 | 37.40 | 48.40 | 79.20 |
| 210,000 | 16.80 | 21.00 | 27.30 | 35.70 | 46.20 | 75.60 |
| 200,000 | 16.00 | 20.00 | 26.00 | 34.00 | 44.00 | 72.00 |
| 190,000 | 15.20 | 19.00 | 24.70 | 32.30 | 41.80 | 68.40 |
| 180,000 | 14.40 | 18.00 | 23.40 | 30.60 | 39.60 | 64.80 |
| 170,000 | 13.60 | 17.00 | 22.10 | 28.90 | 37.40 | 61.20 |
| 160,000 | 12.80 | 16.00 | 20.80 | 27.20 | 35.20 | 57.60 |
| 150,000 | 12.00 | 15.00 | 19.50 | 25.50 | 33.00 | 54.00 |
| 140,000 | 11.20 | 14.00 | 18.20 | 23.80 | 30.80 | 50.40 |
| 130,000 | 10.40 | 13.00 | 16.90 | 22.10 | 28.60 | 46.80 |
| 120,000 | 9.60 | 12.00 | 15.60 | 20.40 | 26.40 | 43.20 |
| 110,000 | 8.80 | 11.00 | 14.30 | 18.70 | 24.20 | 39.60 |
| 100,000 | 8.00 | 10.00 | 13.00 | 17.00 | 22.00 | 36.00 |
| 90,000 | 7.20 | 9.00 | 11.70 | 15.30 | 19.80 | 32.40 |
| 80,000 | 6.40 | 8.00 | 10.40 | 13.60 | 17.60 | 28.80 |
| 70,000 | 5.60 | 7.00 | 9.10 | 11.90 | 15.40 | 25.20 |
| 60,000 | 4.80 | 6.00 | 7.80 | 10.20 | 13.20 | 21.60 |
| 50,000 | 4.00 | 5.00 | 6.50 | 8.50 | 11.00 | 18.00 |
| 40,000 | 3.20 | 4.00 | 5.20 | 6.80 | 8.80 | 14.40 |
| 30,000 | 2.40 | 3.00 | 3.90 | 5.10 | 6.60 | 10.80 |
| 20,000 | 1.60 | 2.00 | 2.60 | 3.40 | 4.40 | 7.20 |
| 10,000 | 0.80 | 1.00 | 1.30 | 1.70 | 2.20 | 3.60 |

## VETERANS' GROUP LIFE INSURANCE (CONTINUED)

| Amount of Insurance | Monthly Premium Rate Age 55-59 | Age 60-64 | Age 65-69 | Age 70-74 | Age 75 & Over |
|---|---|---|---|---|---|
| $400,000 | $268.00 | $432.00 | $600.00 | $920.00 | $1,840.00 |
| 390,000 | 261.30 | 421.20 | 585.00 | 897.00 | 1,794.00 |
| 380,000 | 254.60 | 410.40 | 570.00 | 874.00 | 1,748.00 |

| Amount of Insurance | Monthly Premium Rate Age 55-59 | Age 60-64 | Age 65-69 | Age 70-74 | Age 75 & Over |
|---|---|---|---|---|---|
| 370,000 | 247.90 | 399.60 | 555.00 | 851.00 | 1,702.00 |
| 360,000 | 241.20 | 388.80 | 540.00 | 828.00 | 1,656.00 |
| 350,000 | 234.50 | 378.00 | 525.00 | 805.00 | 1,610.00 |
| 340,000 | 227.80 | 367.20 | 510.00 | 782.00 | 1,564.00 |
| 330,000 | 221.10 | 356.40 | 495.00 | 759.00 | 1,518.00 |
| 320,000 | 214.40 | 345.60 | 480.00 | 736.00 | 1,472.00 |
| 310,000 | 207.70 | 334.80 | 465.00 | 713.00 | 1,426.00 |
| 300,000 | 201.00 | 324.00 | 450.00 | 690.00 | 1,380.00 |
| 290,000 | 194.30 | 313.20 | 435.00 | 667.00 | 1,334.00 |
| 280,000 | 187.60 | 302.40 | 420.00 | 644.00 | 1,288.00 |
| 270,000 | 180.90 | 291.60 | 405.00 | 621.00 | 1,242.00 |
| 260,000 | 174.20 | 280.80 | 390.00 | 598.00 | 1,196.00 |
| 250,000 | 167.50 | 270.00 | 375.00 | 575.00 | 1,150.00 |
| 240,000 | 160.80 | 259.20 | 360.00 | 552.00 | 1,104.00 |
| 230,000 | 154.10 | 248.40 | 345.00 | 529.00 | 1,058.00 |
| 220,000 | 147.40 | 237.60 | 330.00 | 506.00 | 1,012.00 |
| 210,000 | 140.70 | 226.80 | 315.00 | 483.00 | 966.00 |
| 200,000 | 134.00 | 216.00 | 300.00 | 460.00 | 920.00 |
| 190,000 | 127.30 | 205.20 | 285.00 | 437.00 | 874.00 |
| 180,000 | 120.60 | 194.40 | 270.00 | 414.00 | 828.00 |
| 170,000 | 113.90 | 183.60 | 255.00 | 391.00 | 782.00 |
| 160,000 | 107.20 | 172.80 | 240.00 | 368.00 | 736.00 |
| 150,000 | 100.50 | 162.00 | 225.00 | 345.00 | 690.00 |
| 140,000 | 93.80 | 151.20 | 210.00 | 322.00 | 644.00 |
| 130,000 | 87.10 | 140.40 | 195.00 | 299.00 | 598.00 |
| 120,000 | 80.40 | 129.60 | 180.00 | 276.00 | 552.00 |
| 110,000 | 73.70 | 118.80 | 165.00 | 253.00 | 506.00 |
| 100,000 | 67.00 | 108.00 | 150.00 | 230.00 | 460.00 |
| 90,000 | 60.30 | 97.20 | 135.00 | 207.00 | 414.00 |
| 80,000 | 53.60 | 86.40 | 120.00 | 184.00 | 368.00 |
| 70,000 | 46.90 | 75.60 | 105.00 | 161.00 | 322.00 |
| 60,000 | 40.20 | 64.80 | 90.00 | 138.00 | 276.00 |
| 50,000 | 33.50 | 54.00 | 75.00 | 115.00 | 230.00 |
| 40,000 | 26.80 | 43.20 | 60.00 | 92.00 | 184.00 |
| 30,000 | 20.10 | 32.40 | 45.00 | 69.00 | 138.00 |
| 20,000 | 13.40 | 21.60 | 30.00 | 46.00 | 92.00 |
| 10,000 | 6.70 | 10.80 | 15.00 | 23.00 | 46.00 |

These premium rates (listed on the previous three pages) are subject to change, depending on emerging experience.

## 316. How is Veterans' Group Life Insurance converted to an individual policy?

VGLI may be converted to an individual policy at any time, upon written application for conversion to the participating company selected and payment of the required premiums. The individual policy will be issued without medical examination on a plan currently written by the company.

On request, the administrative office will furnish a list of life insurance companies participating in the program and companies (not participating in the program) that meet qualifying criteria, terms, and conditions established by the administrator, and that agree to sell insurance to former members in accordance with the rules described.

# BENEFITS FOR FEDERAL GOVERNMENT EMPLOYEES

## INTRODUCTION

### 317. What are the two retirement systems for federal employees?

There are two retirement systems for federal employees: the Civil Service Retirement System (CSRS) and the Federal Employees' Retirement System (FERS).

The CSRS, created in 1920, was the only retirement system for federal employees until the FERS became public law in 1986. FERS created a new federal retirement program coordinated with Social Security retirement benefits for federal employees hired after 1983. Federal employees in FERS are automatically covered by Social Security and must pay Social Security taxes, while federal employees who remain in CSRS are exempt from Social Security taxes. FERS also provides a guaranteed basic annuity and a tax-deferred savings plan similar to a Section 401(k) retirement plan.

## FEDERAL EMPLOYEES' RETIREMENT SYSTEM

### 318. Who is covered under the Federal Employees' Retirement System?

The Federal Employees' Retirement System (FERS) is a three-tier retirement system for federal workers who began work with the government after 1983. In addition, a number of federal employees hired before 1984 elected to transfer from the Civil Service Retirement System (CSRS) to FERS during a 1987 transfer period.

The following are excluded from FERS coverage:

- A person not covered by Social Security, including a person covered by full CSRS
- A person who has served without a break in service of more than 365 days since December 31, 1983, in the position of: (a) Vice President, (b) member of Congress, (c) a senior executive Service or Senior Foreign Service noncareer appointee, or (d) persons appointed by the President or Vice President to positions where the maximum rate of basic pay is at or above the rate for Level V of the Executive Schedule
- An employee who is rehired after December 31, 1986, who has had a break in service and who, at the time of the last separation from the service, had at least five years of civilian service creditable under CSRS rules, any part of which was covered by CSRS or the Foreign Service Retirement system
- An employee who has not had a break in service of more than three days ending after December 31, 1986, and who, as of December 31, 1986, had at least five years of creditable civilian service under CSRS rules (even if none of this service was covered by CSRS)

## 319. Who is eligible for FERS benefits?

Unreduced retirement benefits are provided at age sixty with twenty or more years of service, at age sixty-two with five or more years of service, and at "minimum retirement age" with thirty years of service. The minimum retirement age is currently fifty-six.

The "minimum retirement age" for employees with thirty or more years of service is gradually increasing. Until the year 2003, an employee with thirty years of service could have retired at age fifty-five. Beginning in the year 2003, the minimum retirement age increased by two months every year until year 2009. Thus, as of 2009 the employee had to be age fifty-six to retire with thirty or more years of service. Age fifty-six continues to be the minimum retirement age until 2020. Beginning in the year 2021, the minimum retirement age again increases by two-month increments until the year 2027. The minimum retirement age for employees with thirty or more years of service is fifty-seven in the year 2027 and after. The minimum retirement age for reduced benefits is also being gradually increased from fifty-five to fifty-seven. An employee must have at least ten years of service to be eligible for reduced retirement benefits. For an employee retiring with less than thirty years of service, a reduction of 5 percent per year for each year under age sixty-two is imposed. Thus, benefits for an employee retiring at age fifty-five are reduced 35 percent.

An employee can leave government employment prior to the date that he is eligible for a retirement benefit and still be eligible for a Basic Annuity at a later date. If the employee has five years of creditable service and does not withdraw contributions when he terminates government service, he may receive a deferred, unreduced annuity when he attains age sixty-two with at least five years of civil service employment; age sixty with at least twenty years of service; or at minimum retirement age (currently age fifty-five) with at least thirty years of service.

An employee is entitled to a Basic Annuity at age fifty with twenty years of service, or at any age after completing twenty-five years of service, if: (1) his retirement is involuntary (except by removal by cause for misconduct or delinquency) and he did not decline a reasonable offer for a position which is not lower than two grades below his present position; or (2) his retirement is voluntary because his agency is undergoing a major reduction in employees, reorganization, or a transfer of function in which a number of employees are separated or downgraded.

### Basic Annuity

## 320. What is the Basic Annuity?

The Basic Annuity is the second tier of benefits under FERS. Social Security is the first tier of benefits. Social Security includes retirement, disability, and survivor benefits, and health insurance benefits under Medicare. The Basic Annuity provides retirement, disability, and survivor benefits in addition to those provided by Social Security. The Basic Annuity guarantees a specific monthly retirement payment, based on the employee's age, length of creditable service, and "high-3" years' average salary. An employee must have five years of creditable service and be subject to FERS at separation in order to be eligible for a Basic Annuity.

## 321. How much must an employee contribute to the Basic Annuity?

An employee contributes 0.8 percent of his or her basic pay to the Basic Annuity. Certain FERS members pay an additional 0.5 percent to the Basic Annuity. These members include firefighters, law enforcement personnel, air traffic controllers, members of Congress, and Congressional employees. Basic pay does not include bonuses, overtime pay, military pay, holiday pay, cash awards, or special allowances given in addition to basic pay. The federal government makes a contribution to the Basic Annuity plan pursuant to a formula.

## 322. What annuities are available to a retiring employee?

The following annuities are available to a retiring federal employee:

- An annuity, with no survivor benefit
- A lump-sum credit of the employee's contributions (excluding interest), with a reduced annuity
- An annuity to the employee for life, with a survivor annuity payable for the life of the surviving spouse
- A lump-sum credit of the employee's contributions (excluding interest), with a reduced annuity that is further reduced to provide a survivor benefit
- A reduced annuity with a survivor benefit to a person with an insurable interest, provided the employee is in good health

Note, however, that an employee cannot elect against providing survivor benefits to his spouse, unless his spouse consents to the election in writing.

## 323. What is the amount of the Basic Annuity?

The amount of the Basic Annuity depends on the employee's years of service and highest three-year (high-3) average salary. It also depends on whether an annuity supplement is added into the Basic Annuity formula.

For employees under age sixty-two (or age sixty-two or older with less than twenty years of FERS service), the formula, not including the supplement where applicable, is:

- 1.0 percent × high-3 average salary x length of service

For employees age sixty-two or older with at least twenty years of FERS service, the formula is:

- 1.1 percent × high-3 average salary x length of service

(No annuity supplement is payable if the employee is age sixty-two or older.)

For certain employees, including law enforcement officers, firefighters, air traffic controllers, and employees of Congress, the formula is:

(1) 1.7 percent × high-3 average salary × years of service up to twenty years, plus

(2) 1.0 percent × high-3 average salary × years of service over twenty years, plus

(3) the annuity supplement, where applicable.

All periods of creditable service are totaled to determine length of service. Years and months of creditable service (extra days are dropped) are then used in the annuity computation formula.

High-3 average salary is the highest pay obtainable by averaging an employee's rates of basic pay in effect over any three consecutive years of service. The three years need not be continuous, but they must consist of consecutive periods of service. In other words, two or more separate periods of employment that follow each other can be joined to make up the three consecutive years.

*Example.* Steve James retires at age 65 after 30 years of civil service employment. His high-3 average salary is $31,000 ($30,000 + $31,000 + $32,000 ÷ 3 = $31,000). His FERS benefit is computed as follows:

(1) 1.1 percent × $31,000 = $341

(2) $341 × 30 years of service = $10,230 Basic Annuity.

## 324. How is the Basic Annuity adjusted for cost-of-living increases?

The Basic Annuity for employees age sixty-two or older is adjusted for cost-of-living increases pursuant to the following schedule:

(1) Where the change in the Consumer Price Index for All Urban Wage Earners and Clerical Workers (CPI) for the year is less than 2.0 percent, the annuity is increased by the full amount of the CPI increase.

(2) Where the change in the CPI for the year is at least 2.0 percent, but is not more than 3.0 percent, the annuity is increased by 2.0 percent.

(3) Where the change in the CPI for the year is more than 3.0 percent, the annuity is increased by the CPI less 1 percent. For example, if the CPI increases 4.5 percent, the Basic Annuity will increase 3.5 percent.

The cost-of-living increase for 2015 is 1.7 percent.

## 325. What is the Annuity Supplement?

An Annuity Supplement is added to the Basic Annuity as a substitute for Social Security, when the employee is receiving the Basic Annuity and is under age sixty-two. It is equal to the estimated amount of Social Security benefits that the employee would be eligible to receive at age sixty-two based on civil service employment earnings. The supplement ends when the employee first becomes eligible for a Social Security retirement benefit (age sixty-two).

The supplement is payable to: (1) employees who retire after the minimum retirement age (currently age fifty-six) with thirty years of service; (2) employees who retire at age sixty with twenty years of service; and (3) employees who retire involuntarily and have reached minimum retirement age (currently age fifty-six).

The supplement is not subject to cost-of-living increases, and is reduced for excess earnings after retirement in much the same way that Social Security benefits are reduced for excess earnings. In 2014, the supplement is reduced by one dollar for every two dollars that the beneficiary earns over $15,720.

## Survivor Benefits

### 326. What survivor benefits are payable under FERS?

Survivor benefits are paid upon the death of an employee or retired civil service employee. Benefits are paid on a monthly basis or in a lump sum to eligible survivors. The spouse, former spouse, and dependent children of a deceased employee may be entitled to a survivor annuity.

A spouse may be entitled to a "post-retirement survivor benefit." The annuity of a married employee who retires is generally reduced by 10 percent to provide a survivor annuity for the spouse, unless the employee and his or her spouse both waive the survivor annuity. A surviving spouse is entitled to 50 percent of the employee's unreduced annuity increased by cost-of-living benefit adjustments. There is also a 5 percent reduction in the annuity of a married employee who retires and selects a 25 percent survivor annuity.

There is a permanent actuarial reduction in the retiree's annuity in the case of a retiree who marries after retirement and elects a survivor benefit. The reduction may not be more than 25 percent of the retiree's annuity. The reduction is permanent and unaffected by any future termination of the marriage.

The surviving spouse must have been married to the employee for at least nine months or must be the parent of a child of the marriage at the time of death, or the death of the retired employee must have been accidental.

If the survivor is under age sixty and Social Security survivor benefits are *not* payable, benefits are the lesser of: (1) current CSRS survivor benefits; or (2) 50 percent (25 percent if elected) of accrued annuity plus a Social Security "equivalent." When Social Security survivor benefits are payable, FERS pays 50 percent (25 percent if elected) of the deceased retiree's annuity.

If the employee was unmarried at the time of retirement and then married after retirement, he or she may elect a reduced annuity with a survivor benefit for his or her spouse. Such an election must take place within two years after the marriage.

If the spouse dies before the retired employee, and the retired employee remarries, the new spouse is eligible to receive the same survivor benefits as the former spouse. The retired employee must elect to take a reduced annuity with a survivor benefit for his or her new spouse.

A retired employee and spouse who have elected against a survivor benefit can change their election within eighteen months. The retired employee must pay the full cost of providing the survivor annuity if an election is made during this second election period.

There is also a survivor benefit for the spouse of an employee who dies prior to retirement. The surviving spouse is entitled to the basic employee death benefit, which is a guaranteed amount of $31,786.21 (in 2014), plus 50 percent of the employee's final salary or, if higher, his or her "high-3" average. In addition, if the deceased employee completed ten or more years of service, the surviving spouse is entitled to an annuity equal to 50 percent of the unreduced annuity the employee would have been entitled to had he or she reached retirement age. Survivor benefits are subject to cost-of-living adjustments. Note that 2015 numbers were not available as this 2015 edition went to press.

The $31,786.21 payment, which is indexed to the Consumer Price Index, can be paid in a lump sum or in monthly installments over a three-year period.

The surviving spouse must have been married to the employee for at least nine months or must be the parent of a child of the marriage, or the death of the employee must have been accidental. The deceased employee must also have at least eighteen months of creditable service while subject to FERS.

## 327. Is the former spouse of a deceased employee entitled to a survivor benefit?

Yes, the former spouse of a deceased employee may be entitled to a survivor benefit if he or she: (1) was married to the deceased employee for at least nine months; (2) has not remarried prior to age fifty-five; and (3) a court order or court-approved property settlement agreement provides for payment of a survivor annuity to the former spouse.

The survivor annuity is payable to a former spouse when: (1) the deceased employee has at least eighteen months of creditable service under FERS; or (2) the deceased former employee has title to a deferred annuity and has ten years of service.

A former spouse who does not meet the requirements listed above may still be entitled to an annuity if the retiree, at the time of retirement, elected to provide the former spouse with a survivor annuity.

The amount of the survivor annuity for a former spouse is the same as that for a spouse, except that the Guaranteed Amount ($31,786.21, see Q 326) is not payable unless payment is required under a court order or agreement. Note that 2015 numbers were not available as this 2015 edition went to press.

## 328. Is there a survivor benefit for the children of a deceased employee?

If a retiree or an employee has eighteen months of creditable service under FERS before he or she dies, his or her dependent children are entitled to monthly annuities reduced by the amount of any Social Security survivor benefits they receive. The annuity begins on the day after the death, and ends on the last day of the month before the one in which the child: (1) dies; (2) marries; (3) reaches age eighteen; or (4) if over eighteen, becomes capable of self-support. The annuity of a child who is a student ends on the last day of the month before the child: (1) marries; (2) dies; (3) ceases to be a student; or (4) attains the age of twenty-two. If a student drops out of school or his annuity is terminated, it can be restored if he later returns to school and is still under age twenty-two and unmarried.

Annuity payments restart again if the child's marriage has ended and he or she is still eligible for benefits because of disability or enrollment as a full-time student while under age twenty-two. If a child's marriage ends because of divorce or death, the child's annuity and health benefits coverage is restored, beginning the first day of the month in which dissolution of the marriage occurs.

The amount of the benefit depends on whether the child is eligible to receive Social Security benefits and whether the deceased worker's spouse is still living.

If the retiree or employee is survived by a spouse or the child has a living parent, each eligible child is entitled to receive an annuity in 2014 equal to the lesser of:

(1) $1,506 per month, divided by the number of qualified children;

(2) $502 per month.

Note that 2015 numbers were not available as this 2015 edition went to press.

If the retiree or employee is *not* survived by a spouse or the child has *no* living parent, each eligible child is entitled to receive an annuity in 2014 equal to the lesser of:

(1) $1,807 per month, divided by the number of qualified children;

(2) $602 per month.

## 329. Is a person with an insurable interest in a retiree or employee eligible for a survivor benefit?

A retiree or employee can designate that a survivor annuity be paid to a person with an insurable interest in the life of the retiree or employee. The benefit is equal to 50 percent of the retiree's benefit, but is reduced, depending on the difference in the age of the person with the insurable interest and the age of the retiring employee.

If the age difference is thirty years or more, the annuity is reduced 40 percent; if the age difference is twenty-five to twenty-nine years, the reduction is 35 percent; if the age difference is twenty to twenty-four years, the reduction is 30 percent; if the age difference is fifteen to nineteen years, the reduction is 25 percent; if the age difference is ten to fourteen years, the reduction is 20 percent; if the age difference is five to nine years, the reduction is 15 percent; if the age difference is less than five years, the reduction is 10 percent.

## 330. When is a lump-sum survivor benefit paid?

A lump-sum survivor benefit is payable immediately after the death of an employee if the employee: (1) has *less* than eighteen months of creditable service; or (2) leaves *no* widow(er), former spouse, or children who are eligible for a survivor annuity.

The lump-sum survivor benefit is the amount paid into the Civil Service Retirement and Disability Fund by the employee. It also includes accrued interest.

The employee, former employee, or annuitant has the right to name the lump-sum survivor benefit beneficiary. If no beneficiary is named, the lump sum is payable to the widow(er); if there is no widow(er), it is paid to his living children in equal shares; if no children, it is paid to his parents; if no parents, it is paid to the executor or administrator of his estate; if none of the above, it is paid to the next of kin under the laws of the state where the deceased was domiciled.

# Disability Benefits

## 331. What disability benefits are paid under FERS?

Disability benefits are payable to an employee with eighteen months of creditable service who, because of injury or disease, can no longer perform his job in a useful and efficient manner. The beneficiary is entitled to a benefit equal to 60 percent of his high-3 average pay during the first year of disability, reduced dollar for dollar by any Social Security disability benefit. After the first year, the beneficiary is entitled to 40 percent of his high-3 average pay, reduced by 60 percent of the Social Security disability benefit. The benefit is further adjusted at age sixty-two to equal the *lesser* of: (1) a retirement benefit computed as if he had worked during his years of disability; or (2) the disability benefit he would receive after the benefit is offset by any Social Security disability benefit. Disability benefits are adjusted after the first year of disability by the increase in the Consumer Price Index for All Urban Wage Earners and Clerical Workers (CPI). Where the change in the CPI for the year is less than 2.0 percent, the benefit is increased by the full amount of the CPI increase. Where the change in the CPI for the year is at least 2.0 percent but is not more than 3.0 percent, the benefit is increased by 2 percent. Where the change in the CPI for the year is more than 3.0 percent, the benefit is increased by the CPI less 1 percent. Periodic medical examinations are required until the beneficiary reaches age sixty.

# Thrift Savings Plan

## 332. What is the Thrift Savings Plan for FERS employees?

The Thrift Plan creates a third tier of benefits under FERS. A thrift plan account is set up automatically for every employee covered under FERS. Members of the uniformed services may also participate in the Plan (see Q 286).

The government contributes 1 percent of pay to an account for each employee, even if the employee declines to contribute to the plan. In addition, the government matches employee contributions as follows:

(1) Contributions up to the first 3 percent of pay, dollar for dollar

(2) Contributions that are more than 3 percent but not more than 5 percent of pay, fifty cents per dollar

A FERS employee may contribute up to 100 percent of his or her salary towards the Thrift Plan. However, the maximum amount that a FERS employee can contribute is $18,000 in 2015.

Federal employees who are fifty or older are allowed to make additional "catch-up" contributions of $6,000 in 2015.

Contributions, and earnings on contributions, are not subject to federal income taxation until distributed to the employee at retirement. In addition, contributions reduce the employee's gross income for federal income tax purposes. (Contributions are subject to Social Security taxes, however.)

Contributions can be directed by employees to five investment funds:

(1) Government Securities Investment (G) Fund

(2) Fixed Income Index Investment (F) Fund

(3) Common Stock Index Investment (C) Fund

(4) Small Capitalization Stock Index Investment (S) Fund

(5) International Stock Index Investment (I) Fund

FERS employees may elect to invest any portion of their current account balances and/or future contributions in the G Fund, F Fund, C Fund, S Fund, or I Fund.

The Thrift Savings Plan also allows participants to invest in five Lifecycle funds. These Lifecycle funds are L 2050, L 2040, L 2030, L 2020, and L Income. These L funds invest their assets in the G, F, C, S, and I funds in different proportions. It is recommended that, if a participant chooses a lifecycle fund, that he or she choose the one closest to when the money will be needed.

Thrift Plan payments may be made in the following manner:

(1) At retirement or disability, if eligible for a Basic Annuity, the payment may be made as an immediate or deferred annuity, a lump-sum payment, a fixed-term payment, or by transfer to an IRA or other qualified pension plan

(2) At death, funds in the Thrift Plan are paid to eligible survivors or to beneficiaries as specified by FERS

(3) At termination of employment, if eligible for a deferred Basic Annuity, the payment may be made as an immediate or deferred annuity, a transfer to an IRA or other

qualified pension plan, or over a fixed term after the employee retires with a Basic Annuity

(4) At termination of employment, if not eligible for a deferred Basic Annuity, the payment must be transferred to an IRA or qualified pension plan

(5) At age fifty-nine-and-a-half or during a period of financial hardship (See next.)

A participant must withdraw his or her account balance in a single payment or begin receiving his or her Thrift Savings Plan account balance in monthly payments (or in the form of a Thrift Savings Plan annuity) by April 1 of the later of: (1) the year following the year in which the participant reaches age seventy-and-a-half, or (2) the year following the year in which the participant separates from federal service. If the participant does not make an election so that payment can be made by this deadline, the Federal Retirement Thrift Investment Board must use the Thrift Savings Plan to purchase an annuity for the participant.

A participant who has turned age fifty-nine-and-a-half can withdraw an amount up to his or her vested Thrift Savings Plan account balance before separating from government employment. A participant is allowed only one withdrawal under this provision. In addition, a participant can obtain a withdrawal before separating from government employment on the basis of financial hardship. A financial hardship withdrawal is limited to the amount the participant contributed to the Thrift Savings Plan (plus the earnings attributed to those contributions). There is no limit on the number of such withdrawals. The participant may ask the Thrift Savings Plan to transfer all or a portion of the withdrawal to an IRA or other eligible retirement plan.

A participant can continue to contribute to the Thrift Savings Plan after obtaining an aged-based withdrawal, but is not eligible to contribute to the Thrift Savings Plan for a period of six months after obtaining a financial hardship withdrawal. After six months of ineligibility to contribute, the participant can resume Thrift Savings Plan contributions only by making a new Thrift Savings Plan election on Form TSP-1.

The spouse of a FERS participant must consent to an in-service withdrawal and the spouse of a CSRS participant is entitled to notice when the participant applies for an in-service withdrawal.

Federal employees who separate or enter leave-without-pay status to serve in the military may make up contributions to the Thrift Plan missed because of military service. A federal employee would be permitted to contribute an amount equal to what an employee would have been eligible to contribute. The federal government must give such an employee two to four times the length of his military service to make up the Thrift Plan contributions. The government would match employee contributions in the same manner as regular matching contributions under the Thrift Plan.

### 333. Can members of the Civil Service Retirement System take advantage of the Thrift Plan?

Yes, but the government does not contribute to the employee's plan, no matter how much the employee contributes. The Federal employee may contribute up to 100 percent of annual pay, but the contribution is limited to $18,000 in 2015. Additional catch-up contributions of $6,000 are allowed for those who are age fifty or older in 2015.

## CIVIL SERVICE RETIREMENT SYSTEM

### 334. Which federal employees are covered under the Civil Service Retirement System?

The Civil Service Retirement System (CSRS) covers employees of the U.S. government and the District of Columbia who were hired before January 1, 1984, unless coverage is specifically excluded by law. Among the exclusions from CSRS coverage are employees who are subject to another federal retirement system. Employees subject to the Federal Employees' Retirement System (FERS) are excluded from participation in CSRS.

CSRS coverage for pre1984 employees is automatic for all federal employees except those who are employed by Congress. Congressional employees had to elect coverage.

### 335. Who is eligible for a CSRS retirement annuity?

An employee must meet two requirements in order to be eligible for a CSRS retirement annuity. First, the employee must complete at least five years of civilian service with the government. Second, the employee, unless retiring on account of total disability, must have been employed under the CSRS for at least one year out of the last two years before separation from service.

The total service of an employee or member of Congress is measured in full years and months. Anything less than a full month is not counted. An employee's service is credited from the date of original employment to the date of separation. No credit is allowed for a period of separation from service in excess of three calendar days.

An employee is allowed credit for periods of military service, if performed prior to the date of separation from a civilian position.

### 336. How are CSRS benefits paid for?

CSRS benefits are funded by deductions from the basic pay of covered employees, matching contributions from their employing agencies, and by payments from the General Treasury for the balance of the cost of the system. Under the current law, the employee and the employing agency *each* contribute:

- 8.0 percent of basic pay for Members of Congress
- 7.5 percent of basic pay for Congressional employees, law enforcement officers, and firefighters
- 7.0 percent of basic pay for other employees

The portion of compensation withheld and contributed to the retirement and disability fund is includable in the employee's gross income, in the same taxable year in which it would have been included if it had been paid to the employee directly. No refund is allowed for taxes attributable to mandatory contributions from the employee's salary to the Civil Service Retirement Fund.

## 337. Who is entitled to an immediate annuity?

An immediate annuity begins no later than one month after separation from service. This includes an annuity for an employee who retires optionally – for age, for disability, or due to involuntary separation from service. It does not include an annuity for a separated employee who is entitled to a deferred retirement annuity at a future date.

An employee who is separated from service is entitled to an annuity:

(1) at age fifty-five with thirty years of service;

(2) at age sixty with twenty years of service;

(3) at age sixty-two with five years of service;

(4) at age fifty with twenty years of service as a law enforcement officer or firefighter, or a combination of such service totaling at least twenty years.

An employee whose separation is involuntary, except for removal for cause on charges of misconduct or delinquency, is entitled to a reduced annuity after twenty-five years of service or after age fifty and twenty years of service. However, no annuity is payable if the employee has declined a reasonable offer of another position in the employee's agency for which the employee is qualified, which is not lower than two grades (pay levels) below the employee's grade and which is within the employee's commuting area.

Also entitled to this reduced annuity is an employee who, while serving in a geographic area designated by the Office of Personnel Management, is voluntarily separated during a period in which: (1) the agency in which the employee is serving is undergoing a major reorganization, a major reduction in force, or a major transfer of function; and (2) a significant percentage of employees serving in this agency will be separated or subject to an immediate reduction in the rate of basic pay.

Such early retirements must be approved by the Office of Personnel Management. The annuities are reduced by 2 percent for each year the employee is under age fifty-five.

## 338. Are there alternative forms of CSRS retirement annuities?

Yes, an employee may, at the time of retirement, elect the following alternative forms of annuities:

(1) Payment of an annuity to the employee for life

(2) Payment of an annuity to the employee for life, with a survivor annuity payable for the life of a surviving spouse

(3) Payment of an annuity to the employee for life, with benefit to a named person having an insurable interest

(4) Election of lump-sum credit option and reduced monthly annuity

## 339. What is an annuity for life?

The annuitant has a right to receive monthly payments during his or her lifetime unless she is convicted of certain offenses against the United States. Upon the annuitant's death, any accrued annuity that remains unpaid will be paid to: (1) the deceased annuitant's executor or administrator; or (2) if there is no executor or administrator, to the decedent's next of kin under state law, after thirty days have passed from the date of death.

## 340. What are the features of an annuity with a survivor benefit?

An annuity with survivor benefit entitles the survivor to an annuity equal to 55 percent of the annuity amount prior to reduction for the election of the survivor benefit. An annuity for a married employee will automatically include an annuity for a surviving spouse, unless the employee and spouse waive the spouse's annuity in writing. The written-waiver requirement can be overcome only in instances where the employee's spouse cannot be located or where other exceptional circumstances are present.

Generally, the survivor benefit is paid until the survivor dies or remarries. However, remarriage of a widow or widower who is at least age fifty-five does not terminate the survivor annuity. Where the survivor annuity is terminated because the survivor had remarried prior to reaching age fifty-five, the annuity may be restored if the remarriage is dissolved by death, annulment, or divorce.

Where the spouse properly consents, an employee may elect to reduce that portion of the annuity that is to be treated as a survivor annuity.

The portion of the employee's annuity treated as a survivor annuity will be reduced according to a formula. The reduction is 2.5 percent of the first $3,600 chosen as a base, plus 10 percent of any amount over $3,600. For example, if the employee chooses $4,800 as a base, the reduction in the annual annuity would be 2.5 percent of the first $3,600 ($90 a year), plus 10 percent of the $1,200 balance ($120 a year), making a total reduction of $210 ($90 + $120) a year.

If marriage is terminated after retirement by the divorce, annulment, or death of the spouse named as beneficiary, the retiree may elect to have the annuity recomputed, and payment at the single-life unreduced rate will be made for each full month the employee is not married. Should the employee remarry, he has two years from the date of remarriage to notify the Office of Personnel Management in writing that he wants the annuity reduced again to provide a survivor annuity for the new spouse.

If a retired employee dies, absent a waiver of benefits by the survivor, the surviving spouse will receive 55 percent of the yearly annuity that the deceased employee had earned at the time of death. This earned annuity is computed in the same manner as if the deceased employee had retired, but with no reduction for being under age fifty-five, and no increase for voluntary contributions.

The surviving spouse's annuity begins on the day after the employee's death and terminates on the last day of the month before the surviving spouse dies or remarries before age fifty-five.

## 341. How does an annuity with benefit to a named person having an insurable interest work?

If the employee is in good health at retirement, she may elect an Annuity with Benefit to Named Person Having an Insurable Interest. A disabled dependent relative or former spouse is considered as having an insurable interest. An employee electing this annuity will have her annuity reduced by a percentage amount as follows:

| Age of Named Person In Relation to Retiring Employee's Age | Reduction in Annuity of Retiring Employee |
|---|---|
| Older, same age, or less than 5 years younger | 10% |
| 5 but less than 10 years younger | 15% |
| 10 but less than 15 years younger | 20% |
| 15 but less than 20 years younger | 25% |
| 20 but less than 25 years younger | 30% |
| 25 but less than 30 years younger | 35% |
| 30 or more years younger | 40% |

Upon the employee's death after retirement, the named beneficiary will receive an annuity equal to 55 percent of the employee's reduced annuity rate. The survivor's annuity begins on the day after the retired employee's death and terminates on the last day of the month before the survivor dies. However, if the person named as having an insurable interest dies before the employee, the employee's annuity will be restored to life rate upon written request.

## 342. Is there a lump-sum credit option upon retirement under CSRS?

Employees are allowed to receive a payment equal to the value of the contributions they made to the retirement program over their working years. The lump-sum payments option is paid in one payment at first and then in two installments of equal amounts. Workers eligible to voluntarily retire who have a critical or life-threatening illness can receive the lump sum in one payment.

## 343. How is the reduced annuity computed?

First, determine the amount of the member's contributions into the plan. The member's regular annuity is then calculated. To determine the amount of monthly reduction of the annuity, the computation is as follows:

- LS/PV = monthly reduction in annuity, where LS equals the lump-sum credit and PV equals the present value factor of the annuity

The present value factors of CSRS and FERS appear in the Reduced Annuity Tables, below.

To obtain the amount of the reduced monthly annuity, subtract the monthly reduction figure obtained above from the amount of the regular (unreduced) monthly annuity.

*Example*. Mr. Edwards, a member of the CSRS, is 64 at the time he retires from government service. His contributions to CSRS total $25,000. His present value factor (from the table) is 168.2. Using the formula above, $25,000 ÷ 168.2 = $148.63. Mr. Edwards' monthly annuity would therefore be reduced by $148.63.

## REDUCED ANNUITY TABLES

### CSRS

*Present Value Factors*

| *Age at Retirement* | *Factor* | *Age at Retirement* | *Factor* |
|---|---|---|---|
| 40 | 277.6 | 66 | 157.9 |
| 41 | 274.7 | 67 | 153.1 |
| 42 | 272.1 | 68 | 148.0 |
| 43 | 269.1 | 69 | 142.8 |
| 44 | 265.0 | 70 | 138.0 |
| 45 | 260.0 | 71 | 133.1 |
| 46 | 255.1 | 72 | 128.0 |
| 47 | 250.8 | 73 | 123.1 |
| 48 | 245.9 | 74 | 118.4 |
| 49 | 240.3 | 75 | 113.5 |
| 50 | 234.8 | 76 | 108.2 |
| 51 | 230.2 | 77 | 103.2 |
| 52 | 225.9 | 78 | 98.2 |
| 53 | 221.4 | 79 | 93.1 |
| 54 | 216.8 | 80 | 88.4 |
| 55 | 211.9 | 81 | 83.6 |
| 56 | 207.2 | 82 | 78.4 |
| 57 | 202.3 | 83 | 73.7 |
| 58 | 197.6 | 84 | 69.5 |
| 59 | 193.1 | 85 | 65.8 |
| 60 | 188.7 | 86 | 62.0 |
| 61 | 183.7 | 87 | 57.9 |
| 62 | 178.3 | 88 | 54.0 |
| 63 | 173.2 | 89 | 50.7 |
| 64 | 168.2 | 90 | 47.2 |
| 65 | 163.0 | | |

**FERS**

*Present Value Factors for Most Employees*

| *Age at Retirement* | *Factor* | *Age at Retirement* | *Factor* |
|---|---|---|---|
| 40 | 185.6 | 66 | 149.4 |
| 41 | 185.3 | 67 | 145.1 |
| 42 | 185.2 | 68 | 140.5 |
| 43 | 184.9 | 69 | 135.9 |
| 44 | 184.1 | 70 | 131.5 |
| 45 | 182.8 | 71 | 127.0 |
| 46 | 181.6 | 72 | 122.4 |
| 47 | 180.7 | 73 | 118.0 |
| 48 | 179.5 | 74 | 113.6 |
| 49 | 177.9 | 75 | 109.0 |
| 50 | 176.4 | 76 | 104.1 |
| 51 | 175.4 | 77 | 99.5 |
| 52 | 174.7 | 78 | 94.9 |
| 53 | 174.1 | 79 | 90.1 |
| 54 | 173.3 | 80 | 85.7 |
| 55 | 172.5 | 81 | 81.1 |
| 56 | 171.8 | 82 | 76.2 |
| 57 | 171.2 | 83 | 71.8 |
| 58 | 170.7 | 84 | 67.8 |
| 59 | 170.5 | 85 | 64.2 |
| 60 | 170.5 | 86 | 60.6 |
| 61 | 170.1 | 87 | 56.7 |
| 62 | 167.5 | 88 | 52.9 |
| 63 | 163.0 | 89 | 49.7 |
| 64 | 158.5 | 90 | 46.4 |
| 65 | 154.0 | | |

## Computing the CSRS Annuity

### 344. How is the amount of the CSRS annuity determined?

The amount of an annuity depends primarily on the employee's length of service and high-3 average pay. These two factors are used in a formula to determine the basic annuity, which may then be reduced or increased for various reasons.

The high-3 average pay is the highest pay obtainable by averaging the rates of basic pay in effect during any three consecutive years of service, with each rate weighted by the time it was in effect. The three years need not be continuous, but they must consist of consecutive periods of service. Thus, two or more separate periods of employment that follow each other may be joined to make up the three consecutive years of service on which the high-3 average pay is based. The pay rates for each period of employment are weighted on an annual basis.

*Example*. Mr. Smith's final three years of government service included pay rates of:

| | | | | | | |
|---|---|---|---|---|---|---|
| 6 months at $14,500 | — | ½ year | × | $14,500 | = | $7,250 |
| 18 months at $15,000 | — | 1½ years | × | $15,000 | = | 22,500 |
| 12 months at $15,000 | — | 1 year | × | $15,000 | = | 15,000 |
| | | | | | | $44,750 |

Mr. Smith's average pay is computed as:

$$\frac{\$44{,}750}{3} = \$14{,}917$$

A three-step formula is used to determine the basic annuity.

- *Step I*. 1.5 percent × Average Pay × number of years of service up to five years, plus
- *Step II*. 1.75 percent × Average Pay × number of years of service over five and up to ten years, plus
- *Step III*. 2 percent × Average Pay × number of years of service over ten.

Note that for employees with over ten years of service, all three steps apply. For those with fewer than ten years of service, only steps I and II apply. For those with fewer than five years of service, only Step I applies.

*Example*. Mr. Martin retires from civil service employment with 30 years of service. The three consecutive years of service with the highest rates of basic pay were his last three years before retirement.

| | |
|---|---|
| Rate of pay during 28th year of service | $14,500 |
| Rate of pay during 29th year of service | 15,000 |
| Rate of pay during 30th year of service | 15,500 |
| | $45,000 (total) |

$$\frac{\$45{,}000}{3} = \$15{,}000$$

The general formula, using Mr. Martin's $15,000 average pay and 30 years of service, is applied as follows:

| | | | | | | | |
|---|---|---|---|---|---|---|---|
| 1. | 1.5% | × | $15,000 | × | 5 years | = | $1,125.00 |
| 2. | 1.75% | × | $15,000 | × | 5 years | = | 1,312.50 |
| 3. | 2% | × | $15,000 | × | 20 years | = | 6,000.00 |
| | | | | | Basic Annuity | = | $8,437.50 |

The employee's basic annuity may not exceed 80 percent of his average pay. If the formula produces an amount exceeding the 80 percent maximum, it must be reduced to an amount that equals 80 percent of the average pay.

## 345. What is the substitute computation method?

A substitute computation method is provided as an alternative for employees with a high-3 of under $5,000. Instead of taking the 1.5 percent, 1.75 percent, and 2 percent of the high-3 average pay, the employee may substitute 1 percent of the high-3 average pay plus $25 for all parts of the general formula. If the high-3 average pay is between $2,500 and $3,333, substitute the 1 percent plus $25 for the 1.5 percent and 1.75 percent in the first and second parts of the general formula. If the high-3 average pay is between $3,334 and $4,999, substitute the 1 percent plus $25 for the 1.5 percent in the first part of the general formula.

## 346. How is the benefit determined for disability retirement?

An employee under age sixty who retires on account of total disability will receive no less than the guaranteed minimum annuity, which is the *lesser* of:

(1) 40 percent of the employee's high-3 average pay; or

(2) the amount obtained under the general formula, after adding to years of actual service the number of years the employee is under age sixty on the date of separation.

An employee must have completed at least five years of government service in order to be eligible for disability benefits. The provision for a minimum disability annuity does not apply to employees over age sixty. The disability annuity rate for an employee over age sixty is always computed by using actual service in the general formula.

## 347. Can an employee obtain a larger retirement annuity by making voluntary contributions?

Yes, an employee can obtain a larger retirement annuity by making voluntary contributions, in multiples of twenty-five dollars, to purchase an additional annuity. Total voluntary contributions may not exceed 10 percent of the employee's total basic pay.

Voluntary contributions are interest-bearing. The interest rate is determined at the end of each year by the Treasury Department. Each $100 in the account provides an additional annuity in the amount of seven dollars, plus twenty cents for each full year the employee is over age fifty-five at retirement.

# Death Benefits

## 348. Is there a death benefit under the CSRS?

Death benefits are of two kinds: survivor annuities and lump-sum payments. Survivor annuities are payable to an employee's surviving spouse and children upon the death of the employee. A lump-sum benefit is payable upon the death of the employee if there is no spouse or dependent children entitled to an annuity, or, if one is payable, after the right of the last person entitled thereto has been terminated.

While not formally called a "death benefit," where the employee has retired, annuities are payable to the surviving spouse (unless the spouse had waived survivor benefit entitlement) and, where applicable, payable to a named person with an insurable interest.

## Annuity Eligibility Requirements

### 349. Who is eligible for a survivor annuity?

*Employee's Spouse*. In order for the surviving spouse to qualify for a survivor annuity:

(1) the spouse must have been married to the employee for at least nine months before death; or

(2) the spouse must be the parent of the deceased's child born of the marriage.

These requirements are waived where: (1) the employee dies as a result of an accident; or (2) the employee had previously married and subsequently divorced the surviving spouse, and the aggregate time married is at least nine months.

*Employee's Child*. Generally, for a deceased employee's child to qualify for the survivor annuity, the child must be unmarried, under eighteen years of age, and a dependent of the employee. The following rules also apply:

(1) An adopted child is considered to be the employee's child.

(2) A stepchild is considered to be the employee's child, even if the child did not live with the deceased employee. An illegitimate child, however, must prove he or she was dependent upon the deceased employee.

(3) An illegitimate child is considered to be the employee's child, even if the child did not live with the deceased employee. An illegitimate child, however, must prove he or she was dependent upon the deceased employee.

(4) A child who lived with the employee and for whom the employee had filed an adoption petition is considered to be the employee's child, but only where the surviving spouse did in fact adopt the child following the employee's death.

Notwithstanding the age requirement above, each of the following persons is considered to be a child for purposes of the survivorship annuity:

(1) An unmarried dependent child, regardless of age, who is incapable of self-support because of a mental or physical disability incurred before age eighteen

(2) An unmarried dependent child between eighteen and twenty-two, who is a student (pursuing a full-time course of study or training in residence in a high school, trade school, college, university, or comparable recognized educational institution)

Benefits for a child end upon marriage. However, annuity payments restart again if the child's marriage has ended and he or she is still eligible for benefits because of disability or enrollment as a full-time student while under age twenty-two. If a child's marriage ends because of divorce or death, the child's annuity and health benefits coverage is restored beginning the first day of the month in which dissolution of the marriage occurs.

## Computing the Survivor Annuity

### 350. How is the survivor annuity computed?

If an employee dies after completing at least eighteen months of civilian service, there is a guaranteed minimum survivor annuity based upon the employee's average pay over the total civilian service. The annuity, however, is at least 55 percent of the smaller of: (1) 40 percent of the deceased employee's high-3 average pay, or (2) the regular computation obtained after increasing service by the period of time between the date of death and the date the employee would have become age sixty.

This guaranteed minimum does not apply if 55 percent of the employee's earned annuity produces a higher benefit than the guaranteed minimum. Also, since active service cannot be projected beyond age sixty in any case, the guaranteed minimum does not apply where the employee dies after reaching age sixty.

For 2014, where an employee is survived by a spouse and is survived by children who qualify for survivor benefits, each surviving child is entitled to a benefit equal to whichever of the following amounts is the least: (1) 60 percent of the employee's high-3 average pay, divided by the number of qualified children, (2) $1,506 per month, divided by the number of qualified children, or (3) $502 per month. Note that 2015 numbers were not available as this 2015 edition went to press.

When an employee leaves no surviving spouse but leaves children who qualify for survivor benefits, each child will be paid the least of: (1) 75 percent of the employee's high-3 average pay, divided by the number of qualified children; (2) $1,807 per month, divided by the number of qualified children; or (3) $602 per month.

A child's annuity begins on the day after the employee or annuitant dies and continues until the last day of the month before the child marries, dies, or reaches age eighteen, except in the following cases:

(1) For a child age eighteen or over who is incapable of self-support because of a disability that began before age eighteen, payments stop at the end of the month before the child becomes capable of self-support, marries, or dies.

(2) The annuity of a student age eighteen or over stops at the end of the month before the child ceases to be a student, reaches age twenty-two, marries, or dies, whichever occurs first.

## Lump-Sum Death Benefit

### 351. When does the lump-sum death benefit become payable?

The lump-sum death benefit becomes payable to the estate of the proper party where the employee dies:

(1) without a survivor; or

(2) with a survivor, but the survivor's right to an annuity terminates before a claim for a survivor annuity has been filed.

The lump-sum benefit consists of the amount paid into the Civil Service Retirement and Disability Fund by the employee, plus any accrued interest.

If all rights to a CSRS annuity cease before the total annuity paid equals the lump-sum credit, the difference between the lump-sum credit and the total annuity paid becomes payable to the estate of the proper party. Thus, if an employee leaves a spouse or children who are eligible for a survivor annuity, a lump-sum death benefit may be payable after all survivors' annuities have been paid. The lump-sum benefit would consist of that portion of the employee's lump-sum credit that has not been exhausted by the annuity payments to survivors.

## Annuity Payments

### 352. How are annuity payments made?

Annuities are paid by monthly check. The Office of Personnel Management authorizes the payment, and the Treasury Department issues the check. After the initial check, each regular check is dated the first workday of the month after the month for which the annuity is due. For example, the annuity payment for the month of April will be made by a check dated May 1.

An employee annuity begins on the first day of the month after: (1) separation from service, or (2) pay ceases and the service and age requirements for entitlement to an annuity are met. Any other annuity payable begins on the first day of the month after the occurrence of the event on which payment is based.

## Disability Retirement

### 353. When is an annuity payable for disability retirement?

An immediate annuity is payable to an employee for disability retirement when each of the following conditions is met:

(1) The employee has completed five years of civilian service.

(2) The employee has become totally disabled for useful and efficient service in the position occupied, or the duties of a similar position at the same grade or level.

A claim for disability retirement must be filed with the Office of Personnel Management before separation from service or within one year thereafter. The one-year requirement may be waived in cases of incompetency.

The annuity payable will be the earned annuity based on the high-3 average salary, the years of actual service, and the three-part formula (see Q 344), but not less than:

(1) 40 percent of the high-3 average salary, or (2) the amount computed under the general formula after adding to years of actual service the number of years he is under age sixty on the date of separation.

Unless the disability is permanent in nature, an employee receiving a disability retirement annuity must be medically examined annually until age sixty. The Government pays for the examination.

Upon recovery before reaching age sixty, the annuity is continued temporarily (not to exceed one year) to give the individual an opportunity to find a position. If re-employed in Government service within the year, the annuity stops on re-employment. If the individual is not re-employed, the annuity stops at the expiration of the 180-day period.

## Cost-of-Living Adjustments

### 354. Is there a cost-of-living adjustment to CSRS annuities?

Annuities for retirees and survivors are subject to a cost-of-living adjustment in December of each year. The increases are reflected in the annuity payment received the following month. The percentage of the cost-of-living increase each year is determined by the average price index for the third quarter of each year over the third quarter average of the Consumer Price Index for Urban Wage Earners and Clerical Workers of the previous year.

Annuitants receive a 1.7 percent cost-of-living adjustment in 2015.

## Refund of Contributions

### 355. Is there a refund of contributions if an employee leaves government service?

Yes, an employee who leaves government service or transfers to government work under another retirement system may withdraw his retirement lump-sum credit (contributions plus any interest payable), so long as the employee: (1) is separated from the job for at least thirty-one consecutive days, (2) is transferred to a position that is not subject to CSRS or FERS and remains in that position for at least thirty-one consecutive days, (3) files an application for a refund of retirement deductions, (4) is not reemployed in a position subject to CSRS or FERS at the time the application is filed, *and* (5) will not become eligible to receive an annuity within thirty-one days after filing the application.

# LIFE INSURANCE BENEFITS

### 356. In general, what life insurance benefits are available to federal civil service employees?

All federal civil service employees – whether CSRS or FERS members – and employees of the District of Columbia are automatically insured under the provisions of a group policy purchased by the U.S. Office of Personnel Management.

Basic insurance coverage may be declined by written notice only. If coverage has been declined, the employee cannot obtain coverage for at least one year and, then, only if the applicant is in good health. Special rules apply if the employee has experienced a break in service of at least 180 days. Under this exception, all previous waivers of life insurance coverage are canceled, but any of the optional coverages must be affirmatively elected within thirty-one days after the employee's return. Each insured receives a certificate setting forth the group insurance benefits, to whom benefits are payable, to whom claims are submitted, and summarizing the provisions of the policy. The group insurance is underwritten by a large number of private insurance companies and claims are settled by the Office of Federal Employees' Group Life Insurance, P.O. Box 2627, Jersey City, N.J. 07303-2627.

Group insurance includes: (1) group-term life coverage without a medical examination, and (2) accidental death and dismemberment insurance protection. The amount of each type of insurance is based on the employee's "basic insurance amount," which is determined by rounding the employee's annual salary to the next higher multiple of $1,000, and adding $2,000. However, in no case may the basic insurance amount be less than $10,000.

The group accidental death and dismemberment insurance provides payment for: (1) loss of life or loss of two or more members, and (2) loss of one hand or one foot, or for permanent and total loss of sight in one eye. The accidental death benefit equals the employee's basic insurance amount and is paid in addition to the group life insurance.

An insured individual who is certified by a doctor as terminally ill may elect to receive a lump-sum payment of Basic Insurance. Optional insurance is not available for payment as a Living Benefit. The effective date of a Living Benefit election is the date on which the Living Benefit payment is cashed or deposited. Once an election becomes effective, it cannot be revoked. No further election of Living Benefits can be made. If the insured individual has assigned his or her insurance, he or she cannot elect a Living Benefit; nor can an assignee elect a Living Benefit on behalf of an insured individual. If an individual has elected a Living Benefit, he or she may assign his or her remaining insurance. An individual may elect to receive either a full Living Benefit (all of the Basic Insurance) or a partial Living Benefit (a portion of the Basic Insurance, in a multiple of $1,000). The amount of Basic Insurance elected as a Living Benefit will be reduced by an actuarial amount representing the amount of interest lost to the fund because of the early payment of benefits.

An individual may assign ownership of all life insurance, except Option C (which covers family members). If an individual wishing to make an assignment owns more than one type of coverage, he or she must assign all the insurance; an individual cannot assign only a portion of the coverage. Option C cannot be assigned. If the insurance is assigned to two or more individuals, corporations, or trustees, the insured individual must specify percentage shares (rather than dollar amounts or types of insurance) to go to each assignee.

## 357. How does an employee designate the beneficiary or beneficiaries?

An employee's designation of beneficiary or beneficiaries is made in a signed and witnessed writing that is received before the employee's death by his employing office. If no beneficiary is designated when the employee dies, payment is made in the following order: to the employee's widow or widower; or, if none, to the child or children of the employee in equal shares and descendants of deceased children by representation; or, if none, to the parents of the employee in equal shares or the entire amount to the surviving parent; or, if none, to the duly appointed executor or administrator of the employee; or, if none, to the next of kin of the employee, under the law of the employee's domicile at the time of death.

Beneficiaries receiving insurance proceeds in excess of $7,500 receive a money market account instead of a check from the government. Beneficiaries entitled to less than $7,500 receive a single check from the government for the full amount of insurance coverage. Insurance proceeds earn interest in the money market account. Beneficiaries receive special checkbooks and can write checks on the money market account for $250, up to the full amount of the insurance payment.

## 358. When does insurance coverage cease?

Subject to the exceptions below, an employee's group insurance coverage ceases on the earliest of: (1) the date of separation from the service, (2) the date on which a period of twelve months of continuous nonpay status ends, or (3) the date of any other change in employment that results in the employee's ineligibility for insurance coverage. In addition, coverage may be terminated at the end of the pay period in which it is determined that periodic pay, after all other deductions, is insufficient to cover the required withholdings (such as court-ordered child support) to a point at which deductions for federal employee group life insurance cannot be made.

An exception to the termination rule occurs where: (1) the employee retires on an immediate annuity, or (2) the employee becomes entitled to workers' compensation.

An employee who does not want insurance may waive group insurance coverage. In such a case, coverage ceases on the last day of the pay period in which the agency receives the employee's waiver of coverage.

## 359. Can an employee convert to an individual policy?

Yes, if coverage ceases as a result of one of the occurrences described in Q 358 above, the employee may apply for an individual life insurance policy. The employee's coverage cannot exceed the amount for which he was insured at the time of the terminating event. The conversion excludes the Option C coverage. (See Q 361.)

The employee's request for conversion information must be submitted to the Office of Federal Employee's Group Life Insurance and postmarked within thirty-one days following the date of the terminating event, or within thirty-one days of the date the employee received notice of loss of the group coverage and right to convert, whichever is later. Detailed information concerning how to apply for the policy may be obtained from the Office of Federal Employees' Group Life Insurance, P.O. Box 2627, Jersey City, N.J. 07303-2627.

## 360. What is the cost of basic insurance?

The employee pays two-thirds, by means of salary withholding, of the cost of that amount of group-term life and accidental death and dismemberment that equals his or her basic insurance amount. The cost of the additional group-term life (i.e., that amount in excess of his or her basic insurance amount) is paid entirely by the government. The amount withheld from the bi-weekly pay of an employee is fifteen cents for each $1,000 of his or her basic insurance amount; the amount withheld from the monthly pay of an employee is 32.5 cents for each $1,000 of coverage. The following table shows the amount withheld from pay to meet the employee's share of the cost.

**INSURANCE WITHHOLDINGS**

**Amount of Withholdings Per Pay Period**

| Basic Insurance Amount | Biweekly | Monthly | Basic Insurance Amount | Biweekly | Monthly |
|---|---|---|---|---|---|
| $18,000 | $2.70 | $5.85 | $80,000 | $12.00 | $26.00 |
| 19,000 | 2.85 | 6.18 | 81,000 | 12.15 | 26.33 |
| 20,000 | 3.00 | 6.50 | 82,000 | 12.30 | 26.65 |
| 21,000 | 3.15 | 6.83 | 83,000 | 12.45 | 26.98 |
| 22,000 | 3.30 | 7.15 | 84,000 | 12.60 | 27.30 |
| 23,000 | 3.45 | 7.48 | 85,000 | 12.75 | 27.63 |
| 24,000 | 3.60 | 7.80 | 86,000 | 12.90 | 27.95 |
| 25,000 | 3.75 | 8.13 | 87,000 | 13.05 | 28.28 |
| 26,000 | 3.90 | 8.45 | 88,000 | 13.20 | 28.60 |
| 27,000 | 4.05 | 8.78 | 89,000 | 13.35 | 28.93 |
| 28,000 | 4.20 | 9.10 | 90,000 | 13.50 | 29.25 |
| 29,000 | 4.35 | 9.43 | 91,000 | 13.65 | 29.58 |
| 30,000 | 4.50 | 9.75 | 92,000 | 13.80 | 29.90 |
| 31,000 | 4.65 | 10.08 | 93,000 | 13.95 | 30.23 |
| 32,000 | 4.80 | 10.40 | 94,000 | 14.10 | 30.55 |
| 33,000 | 4.95 | 10.73 | 95,000 | 14.25 | 30.88 |
| 34,000 | 5.10 | 11.05 | 96,000 | 14.40 | 31.20 |
| 35,000 | 5.25 | 11.38 | 97,000 | 14.55 | 31.53 |
| 36,000 | 5.40 | 11.70 | 98,000 | 14.70 | 31.85 |
| 37,000 | 5.55 | 12.03 | 99,000 | 14.85 | 32.18 |
| 38,000 | 5.70 | 12.35 | 100,000 | 15.00 | 32.50 |
| 39,000 | 5.85 | 12.68 | 101,000 | 15.15 | 32.83 |
| 40,000 | 6.00 | 13.00 | 102,000 | 15.30 | 33.15 |
| 41,000 | 6.15 | 13.33 | 103,000 | 15.45 | 33.48 |
| 42,000 | 6.30 | 13.65 | 104,000 | 15.60 | 33.80 |
| 43,000 | 6.45 | 13.98 | 105,000 | 15.75 | 34.13 |
| 44,000 | 6.60 | 14.30 | 106,000 | 15.90 | 34.45 |
| 45,000 | 6.75 | 14.63 | 107,000 | 16.05 | 34.78 |
| 46,000 | 6.90 | 14.95 | 108,000 | 16.20 | 35.10 |
| 47,000 | 7.05 | 15.28 | 109,000 | 16.35 | 35.43 |
| 48,000 | 7.20 | 15.60 | 110,000 | 16.50 | 35.75 |
| 49,000 | 7.35 | 15.93 | 111,000 | 16.65 | 36.08 |
| 50,000 | 7.50 | 16.25 | 112,000 | 16.80 | 36.40 |
| 51,000 | 7.65 | 16.58 | 113,000 | 16.95 | 36.73 |

**INSURANCE WITHHOLDINGS (cont'd)**
**Amount of Withholdings Per Pay Period**

| Basic Insurance Amount | Biweekly | Monthly | Basic Insurance Amount | Biweekly | Monthly |
|---|---|---|---|---|---|
| 52,000 | 7.80 | 16.90 | 114,000 | 17.10 | 37.05 |
| 53,000 | 7.95 | 17.23 | 115,000 | 17.25 | 37.38 |
| 54,000 | 8.10 | 17.55 | 116,000 | 17.40 | 37.70 |
| 55,000 | 8.25 | 17.88 | 117,000 | 17.55 | 38.03 |
| 56,000 | 8.40 | 18.20 | 118,000 | 17.70 | 38.35 |
| 57,000 | 8.55 | 18.53 | 119,000 | 17.85 | 38.68 |
| 58,000 | 8.70 | 18.85 | 120,000 | 18.00 | 39.00 |
| 59,000 | 8.85 | 19.18 | 121,000 | 18.15 | 39.33 |
| 60,000 | 9.00 | 19.50 | 122,000 | 18.30 | 39.65 |
| 61,000 | 9.15 | 19.83 | 123,000 | 18.45 | 39.98 |
| 62,000 | 9.30 | 20.15 | 124,000 | 18.60 | 40.30 |
| 63,000 | 9.45 | 20.48 | 125,000 | 18.75 | 40.63 |
| 64,000 | 9.60 | 20.80 | 126,000 | 18.90 | 40.95 |
| 65,000 | 9.75 | 21.13 | 127,000 | 19.05 | 41.28 |
| 66,000 | 9.90 | 21.45 | 128,000 | 19.20 | 41.60 |
| 67,000 | 10.05 | 21.78 | 129,000 | 19.35 | 41.93 |
| 68,000 | 10.20 | 22.10 | 130,000 | 19.50 | 42.25 |
| 69,000 | 10.35 | 22.43 | 131,000 | 19.65 | 42.58 |
| 70,000 | 10.50 | 22.75 | 132,000 | 19.80 | 42.90 |
| 71,000 | 10.65 | 23.08 | 133,000 | 19.95 | 43.23 |
| 72,000 | 10.80 | 23.40 | 134,000 | 20.10 | 43.55 |
| 73,000 | 10.95 | 23.73 | 135,000 | 20.25 | 43.88 |
| 74,000 | 11.10 | 24.05 | 136,000 | 20.40 | 44.20 |
| 75,000 | 11.25 | 24.38 | 137,000 | 20.55 | 44.53 |
| 76,000 | 11.40 | 24.70 | 138,000 | 20.70 | 44.85 |
| 77,000 | 11.55 | 25.03 | 139,000 | 20.85 | 45.18 |
| 78,000 | 11.70 | 25.35 | 140,000 | 21.00 | 45.50 |
| 79,000 | 11.85 | 25.68 | | | |

## 361. What optional insurance coverages are available to the civil service employee?

Optional insurance coverages currently available include: (1) optional life insurance (termed Option A – Standard Insurance); (2) additional optional life insurance (Option B – Additional Insurance); and (3) optional life insurance on family members (Option C – Family Coverage). Beneficiary provisions for optional insurances on the life of the employee are the same as for basic (regular) insurance.

### Option A – Standard Insurance

Employees covered under the basic life insurance program can purchase $10,000 of optional group-term life insurance. This coverage includes accidental death and dismemberment.

The premium is paid entirely by the employee through withholding, and the cost is as follows:

| Age Group | Withholding for $10,000 Insurance Biweekly | Monthly |
|---|---|---|
| Under age 35 | $0.30 | $0.65 |
| 35 through 39 | 0.40 | 0.87 |
| 40 through 44 | 0.60 | 1.30 |
| 45 through 49 | 0.90 | 1.95 |
| 50 through 54 | 1.40 | 3.03 |
| 55 through 59 | 2.70 | 5.85 |
| 60 and over | 6.00 | 13.00 |

Where Option A insurance has been declined, the employee is eligible to enroll for this coverage only by meeting the two requirements for canceling a waiver of basic life insurance. Neither a retiree nor an employee receiving basic life insurance while receiving workers' compensation can cancel a previous declination of Option A – Standard.

## Option B – Additional Optional Insurance

An employee with basic life insurance can purchase Option B – additional optional life insurance on himself – without regard to whether he has purchased Option A insurance. Option B coverage comes in one, two, three, four, or five multiples of an employee's annual pay (after the pay has been rounded to the next higher thousand).

The cost of Option B insurance, like Option A, is paid entirely by the employee through withholdings. The rates per $1,000 of coverage are as follows:

| Age Group | Withholding for $1,000 Insurance Biweekly | Monthly |
|---|---|---|
| Under age 35 | $0.02 | $0.043 |
| 35 through 39 | 0.03 | 0.065 |
| 40 through 44 | 0.05 | 0.108 |
| 45 through 49 | 0.08 | 0.173 |
| 50 through 54 | 0.13 | 0.282 |
| 55 through 59 | 0.23 | 0.498 |
| 60 through 64 | 0.52 | 1.127 |
| 65 through 69 | 0.62 | 1.343 |
| 70 through 74 | 1.14 | 2.470 |
| 75 through 79 | 1.80 | 3.900 |
| 80 and over | 2.40 | 5.200 |

Retiring employees or compensationers can elect to continue Option B coverage on an unreduced basis by continuing to pay premiums after age sixty-five. Annuitants and compensationers who elect unreduced Option B can later cancel that election and have the full reduction.

## Option C – Family Coverage

Option C – life insurance coverage on the life of spouse and dependents – is available in either one, two, three, four, or five multiples of coverage. One multiple is equal to $5,000 for a spouse and $2,500 for each dependent child. The cost of this insurance is paid entirely by the employee through withholding. The rates for coverage of the spouse and child (or children) are as follows:

| | Withholding per Multiple | |
|---|---|---|
| **Age of Person** | **Biweekly** | **Monthly** |
| Under age 35 | $0.22 | $0.48 |
| 35 through 39 | 0.29 | 0.63 |
| 40 through 44 | 0.42 | 0.90 |
| 45 through 49 | 0.63 | 1.37 |
| 50 through 54 | 0.94 | 2.04 |
| 55 through 59 | 1.52 | 3.29 |
| 60 through 64 | 2.70 | 5.85 |
| 65 through 69 | 3.14 | 6.80 |
| 70 through 74 | 3.60 | 7.80 |
| 75 through 79 | 4.80 | 10.40 |
| 80 and over | 6.60 | 14.30 |

Retiring employees can choose to elect unreduced Option C coverage by continuing to pay premiums after age sixty-five. Annuitants and compensationers who elect unreduced Option C can later cancel that election and have the full reduction.

Foster children are covered under Option C. Dependency of the foster child must be established before the child is approved for coverage under Option C.

### 362. May a retiring employee continue life insurance coverage?

With respect to basic (regular) life insurance, an employee who retires on an immediate annuity can continue his basic life insurance (excluding accidental death and dismemberment), so long as he satisfies the "five or less than five" rule. This requires that the retiree be insured either: (1) through the five years of service immediately preceding his retirement; or (2) if less than five years, then throughout the period or periods of service during which he was entitled to coverage. An additional requirement for continuing basic insurance is that the employee cannot have converted the policy to an individual life policy.

The retiring employee's basic life options are as follows:

| | Election | Monthly Cost Before 65 | Monthly Cost After 65 |
|---|---|---|---|
| 1. | 75% REDUCTION — Amount of insurance reduces 2% per month after age 65 to a minimum of 25% of Basic Insurance Amount at retirement. | $.325 per $1,000* | No Cost |
| 2. | 50% REDUCTION — Amount of insurance reduces 1% per month after age 65 to a minimum of 50% of Basic Insurance Amount at retirement. | $.965 per $1,000* | $.64 per $1,000* |
| 3. | NO REDUCTION — 100% of Basic Insurance Amount at retirement is retained after age 65. | $2.265 per $1,000* | $1.94 per $1,000* |

*of Basic Insurance Amount at retirement

Where the employee chooses the 75 percent Reduction and retired before December 31, 1989, there is no cost to the individual after retirement, regardless of age. If the employee retires after December 31, 1989 and elects the 75 percent Reduction, the life insurance withholdings will be at the same rate to age sixty-five as for active employees, and withholdings will be deducted from his annuity. After the individual reaches age sixty-five, withholding will stop.

Where the employee chooses the 50 percent Reduction or No Reduction, the full cost of the additional protection is deducted from the retiree's monthly annuity payment. The withholdings begin at retirement and continue for life or until the election is canceled or coverage is otherwise discontinued.

Where the employee elected Option A – Standard Insurance, the retiree may continue the insurance so long as it was in force during the "five or less than five" period explained earlier. The cost of the Option A life insurance will be withheld from the annuity until the end of the calendar month in which he attains age sixty-five. After that time, the Option A life insurance will be continued without cost to the retiree.

Option A life insurance, in all cases, is subject to a reduction of 2 percent at the end of each full calendar month following the date on which the employee attains age sixty-five or retires, whichever occurs later. These reductions continue until a minimum (but in no event, less than 25 percent of the amount of Option A life in force before the first reduction) is reached.

An employee who retires on an immediate annuity can continue the amount of Option B – Additional Life Insurance so long as it was in force for the required "five or less than five" period explained above. The full cost of the Option B life that is continued will be withheld from the retiree's annuity until the calendar month in which the retiree attains age sixty-five. Beginning with the end of that calendar month, Option B life insurance will be continued without cost to the retiree. The amount of Option B life insurance is subject to a reduction of 2 percent each month beginning with the second calendar month after the date on which the employee attains age sixty-five or retires, whichever occurs later. These reductions continue for fifty months, at which time the Option B life coverage ends.

Retiring employees or compensationers can elect to continue Option B coverage on an unreduced basis by continuing to pay premiums after age sixty-five. Annuitants and compensationers who elect unreduced Option B can later cancel that election and have the full reduction. Annuitants and compensationers who have Option B coverage on a reduction schedule will be offered the opportunity to elect an unreduced schedule on a prospective basis.

An employee who retires on an immediate annuity may continue his Option C – Family Coverage that was in force during the "five or less than five" period. The full cost of the optional family coverage that is continued will be withheld from the retiree's annuity until the calendar month in which the retiree attains age sixty-five. Beginning with the end of that calendar month, the optional family life coverage will be continued without cost to the retiree. Optional family life coverage that is continued after retirement is subject to the same method of reduction as is the additional optional life insurance (see previous). Thus, coverage of optional family life will end following the expiration of the same fifty months.

Retiring employees can choose to elect unreduced Option C coverage by continuing to pay premiums after age sixty-five. Annuitants and compensationers who elect unreduced Option C can later cancel that election and have the full reduction.

A recipient of federal workers' compensation avoids a termination of federal employee group life insurance so long as he has met the "five or less than five" rule. This rule applies to basic life insurance, as well as any of the optional coverages. No accidental death and dismemberment insurance is available to the workers' compensation recipient.

# CASE STUDIES USED IN PLANNING FOR SOCIAL SECURITY MAXIMIZATION

As people approach retirement age, a common concern which arises is that they won't have enough money to maintain the lifestyle to which they became accustomed to during their working years. Interest in understanding how Social Security benefits are calculated and established – and how to MAXIMIZE those benefits – is becoming more of an interest to individuals now that postretirement income has been shifted largely from the employer to the individual. The traditional "Defined Benefit" pension plan established by the employer as a fringe benefit has shifted to the "Defined Contribution" plan, such as 401(k) plans, managed by the individual.

Even with concerns over the future, Social Security represents a source of retirement income that most individuals consider a critical and expected component of one's retirement plan. Social Security provides workers (who have reached the defined eligibility) – as well as spouses, widows/widowers, and dependent children with an identified and steady monthly income that will increase over time – and in many cases, continue for as long as the individual lives. Although it doesn't fully replace an individual's earnings, in many cases it serves as a significant portion (or all) of the income of retirees. With this in mind, it is obvious that it is important to think about and analyze when advising an individual on when they should claim benefits under Social Security.

There are a myriad of strategies that can help maximize Social Security benefits for an individual or a couple. These strategies will vary based on the individual situation, the individuals involved, and the goals and desires of the parties. There is no "cookie-cutter" or "one-size-fits-all" situation; for each individual or couple involved, there can literally be a dozen or more strategies that can be formulated. Which strategy is "best" or correct will vary. One party may wish to maximize monthly income, while another may wish to establish a program to maximize lifetime benefits (the total amount collected from start of benefits to end-of-life).

Strategies will be affected by a number of factors:

- Income level over last thirty-five years (determination of Primary Insurance Amount [PIA])
- Income levels of spouse and eligibility for benefits
- Income needs during retirement
- Desire to maximize monthly income versus total benefits collected
- Life expectancy
- Age and Life expectancy of spouse
- Widow/Widower benefits
- Other sources of income: pensions, 401(k), investments

- Application of Earnings Test
- Marital status (Single, Married, Divorced)
- Filing date including
    - Reduction Factor for early filing
    - Use of Delayed Retirement Credit by waiting to file after Full Retirement Age (FRA)
    - Use of "File and Suspend", Spousal Benefit, "Restricted Application" strategies
- Effect of other provisions such as Public Employee Pensions, Windfall Elimination Provision (WEP) and Government Pension Offset (GPO)

The Case Studies included in this section, developed by Premier Social Security Consulting, LLC and their principals, Marc Kiner and Jim Blair are not designed to be all-inclusive. As stated above, each situation is unique and will require both investigation and analysis. These Case Studies are designed to show you selected situations and some of the various outcomes that will result based on the different choices made. As you will see, the outcomes will vary based on the variance of the different factors detailed above. Please keep in mind that the figures used in the Case Studies are based upon cash flow not Present Value. Often different choices will cause one spouse's benefits to increase while the other spouse's is lessened – but coordination of choices can lead to a higher combined benefit. Depending upon the choices made, the dollar amounts of the money collected over the life of the beneficiary can vary greatly – literally by hundreds of thousands of dollars and often 15, 20 or even close to 30 percent. Winding the confusing and complicated road of Social Security benefits requires both skill and focus. It is necessary to consider all factors – to review all options – to ensure the most favorable and lucrative outcome.

# CASE STUDY #1

## George and Joan

Overview of Couple: Case Study 1 involves George and Joan, a married couple four years apart in age. Both will reach Full Retirement Age (FRA) at age sixty-six. The husband, George had significantly more income than the wife, Joan. Joan is expected to survive George by approximately six years.

**George**

- **Date of Birth: November 14, 1946**
- **Full Retirement Age: 66**
- **Projected Death Age: 82.09**
- **Full Retirement Age Benefit: $2,647**

**Joan**

- **Date of Birth: September 7, 1950**
- **Full Retirement Age: 66**
- **Projected Death Age: 84.06**
- **Full Retirement Age Benefit: $724**

| | George | Joan | Combined | Widow's benefit |
|---|---|---|---|---|
| Strategy 1 | $547,110 | $439,091 | $986,201 | $3,512 |
| Strategy 2 | $537,336 | $440,369 | $977,705 | $3,512 |
| Strategy 3 | $538,060 | $439,171 | $977,231 | $3,512 |
| Strategy 4 | $541,446 | $396,277 | $937,723 | $2,911 |

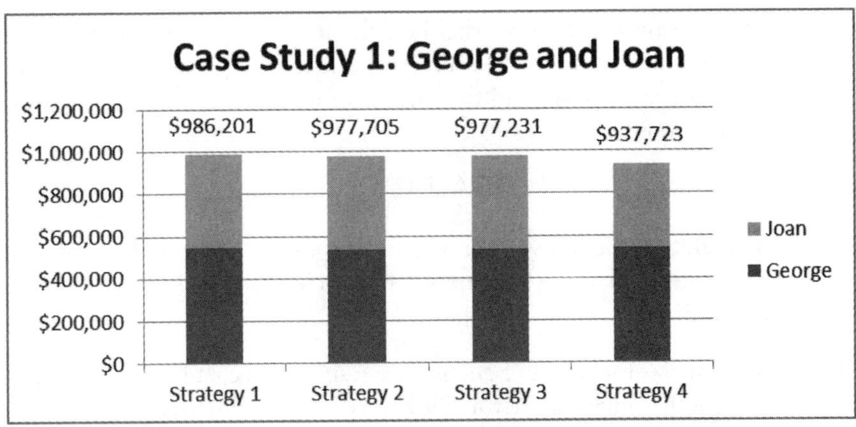


### STRATEGY #1

- **August 2014**: Joan files for worker benefits at age sixty-three and eleven months, resulting in the application of a twenty-five month Reduction Factor. She receives $623 which constitutes 86.11 precent of PIA. George files a "restricted application" at age sixty-seven and nine months for 100.00 percent of Spousal Benefit, receiving $362 per month.

- **November 2016**: George files for worker benefits at age seventy, resulting in a forty-eight month Delayed Retirement Credit. He receives $3,512 which constitutes 132.00 percent of PIA. Joan files at age sisty-six and two months for 100.00 percent of Spousal Benefit, collecting $599 per month.

### STRATEGY #2

- **February 2014**: George initiates "file and suspend" of benefits at age sixty-seven and six months.
- **September 2016**: Joan files for worker benefits at Full Retirement Age at age sixty-six, resulting in 100 percent of PIA. She receives $724 per month. Joan also files at age sixty-six for 100.00 percent of Spousal Benefit, collecting $599 per month.
- **November 2016**: George files for worker benefits at age seventy, resulting in a forty-eight month Delayed Retirement Credit. He receives $3,512 which constitutes 132.00 percent of PIA.

### STRATEGY #3

- **September 2016**: Joan files for worker benefits at Full Retirement Age at age sixty-six, resulting in 100.00 percent of PIA. She receives $724 per month. George files a "restricted application" at age sixty-nine and ten months for 100.00 percent of Spousal Benefit and collects $362 per month.
- **November 2016**: George files for worker benefits at age seventy, resulting in a forty-eight month Delayed Retirement Credit. He receives $3,512 which constitutes 132.00 percent of PIA. Joan files at age sixty-six and two months for 100.00 percent of Spousal Benefit, collecting $599 per month.

### STRATEGY #4

- **February 2014**: George files for worker benefits at age sixty-seven and three months resulting in a fifteen months Delayed Retirement Credit. He receives $2,911 which constitutes 110.00 percent of PIA.
- **August 2014**: Joan files for worker benefits at age sixty-three and eleven months, resulting in a twenty-five month Reduction Factor. She receives $623 which constitutes 86.11 percent of PIA. Joan files for Spousal Benefits at the same time, resulting in a twenty-five month Reduction Factor of 82.64 percent allowing her to collect $495 per month.

# CASE STUDY #2

## Gary and Lynn

Overview of Couple: Case Study 2 involves Gary and Lynn, a married couple approximately seven years apart in age. Gary will reach FRA at 66 years of age, while Lynn reaching FRA at sixty-six years and ten months. Their earnings have been fairly similar, with Gary's PIA being slightly higher than his wife's. Lynn is expected to survive Gary by approximately nine years.

**Gary**

- **Date of Birth: September 1, 1952**
- **Full Retirement Age: 66**
- **Projected Death Age: 81.02**
- **Full Retirement Age Benefit: $2,283**

**Lynn**

- **Date of Birth: August 6, 1959**
- **Full Retirement Age: 66 and 10 months**
- **Projected Death Age: 83.02**
- **Full Retirement Age Benefit: $2,139**

| | Gary | Lynn | Combined | Widow's benefit |
|---|---|---|---|---|
| Strategy 1 | $416,765 | $511,753 | $928,518 | $3,013 |
| Strategy 2 | $406,755 | $512,762 | $919,517 | $3,013 |
| Strategy 3 | $417,789 | $422,643 | $840,432 | $2,283 |
| Strategy 4 | $374,900 | $356,720 | $731,620 | $1,630 |

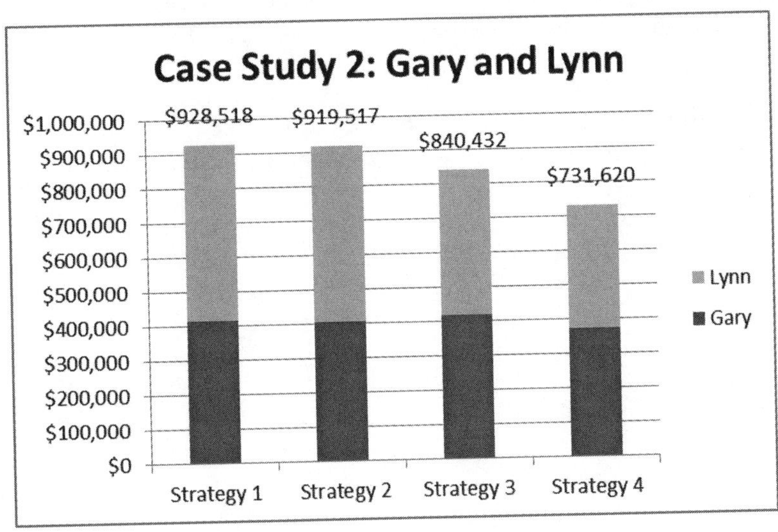


### STRATEGY #1

- **September 2021**: Lynn files for worker benefits at age sixty-two and one month, resulting in a fifty-seven month Reduction Factor. Lynn collects $1,297 constituting 71.25 percent of

PIA. Gary files a "restricted application" at age sixty-nine and one month for 100.00 percent of Spousal Benefits and collects $1,089.

- **August 2022**: Gary files for worker benefits at age seventy, resulting in a forty-eight month Delayed Retirement Credit. Gary collects $3,013 constituting 132.00 percent of PIA.

## STRATEGY #2

- **August 2022**: Gary files for worker benefits at age seventy, resulting in a forty-eight month Delayed Retirement Credit. Gary collects $3,013 constituting 132.00 percent of PIA.
- **June 2026**: Lynn files for worker benefits at age sixty-six and ten months, at Full Retirement Age. Lynn collects $2,139, constituting 100.00 of PIA.

## STRATEGY #3

- **August 2022**: Gary files for worker benefits at age seventy, resulting in a forty-eight month Delayed Retirement Credit. Gary collects $3,013 constituting 132.00 percent of PIA.
- **June 2026**: Lynn files for worker benefits at age sixty-six and ten months, at Full Retirement Age. Lynn collects $2,139, constituting 100.00 of PIA.

## STRATEGY #4

- **September 2014**: Gary files for worker benefits at age sixty-two and one month, resulting in a forty-seven month Reduction Factor. Gary collects $1,630, constituting 75.42 percent of PIA.
- **September 2021**: Lynn files for worker benefits at age sixty-two and one month, resulting in s fifty-seven month Reduction Factor. Lynn collects $1,297, constituting 71.25 percent of PIA.

# CASE STUDY #3

## Gary and Lynn

Overview of Couple: Case Study 3 involves Gary and Lynn, the same married couple illustrated in Case Study 2. They are approximately seven years apart in age. Gary will reach FRA at sixty-six years of age, while Lynn reaching FRA at sixty-six years and ten months. Their earnings have been fairly similar, with Gary's PIA being slightly higher than his wife's. In this example, however, both are expected to live longer than the national average, with Joan expected to survive George by approximately thirteen years, living to the age of ninety.

**Gary**

- **Date of Birth: September 1, 1952**
- **Full Retirement Age: 66**
- **Projected Death Age: 84.00**
- **Full Retirement Age Benefit: $2,283**

**Lynn**

- **Date of Birth: August 6, 1959**
- **Full Retirement Age: 66 and 10 months**
- **Projected Death Age: 90.00**
- **Full Retirement Age Benefit: $2,139**

| Case Study 3: Gary and Lynn | | | | |
|---|---|---|---|---|
| | **Gary** | **Lynn** | **Combined** | **Widow's benefit** |
| Strategy 1 | $509,197 | $738,173 | $1,247,370 | $3,013 |
| Strategy 2 | $519,207 | $700,475 | $1,219,682 | $3,013 |
| Strategy 3 | $430,320 | $594,642 | $1,024,962 | |
| Strategy 4 | $430,320 | $486,110 | $916,430 | $1,630 |

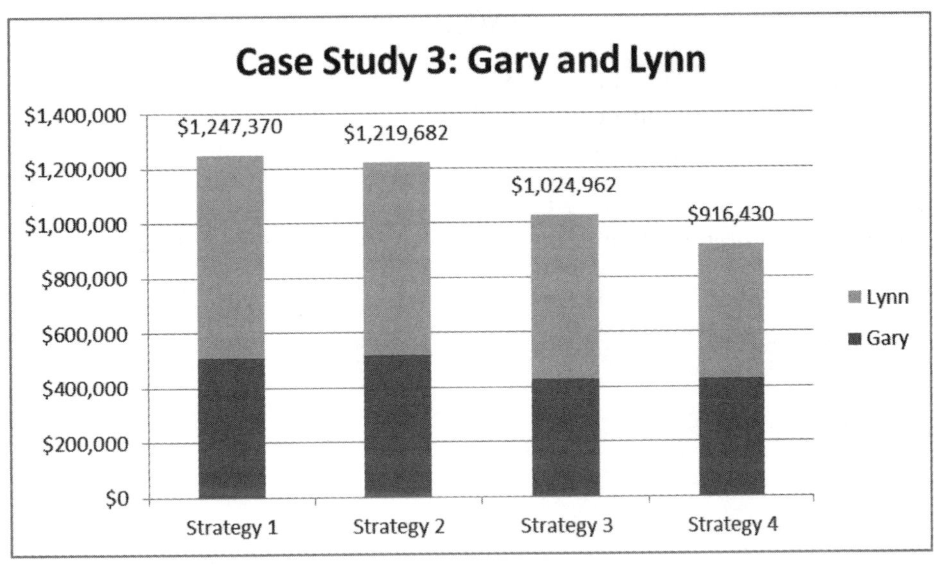

## STRATEGY #1

- **August 2022**: Gary files for worker benefits at age seventy, resulting in a forty-eight month Delayed Retirement Credit. Gary collects $3,013, constituting 132.00 percent of PIA.
- **June 2026**: Lynn files a "restricted application" at age sixty-six and ten months (Full Retirement Age) for 100.00 percent of Spousal Benefit. Lynn collects $1,141.
- **August 2029**: Lynn files for worker benefits at age seventy, resulting in a thirty-eight month Delayed Retirement Credit. Lynn collects $2,680, constituting 125.33 percent of PIA.

## STRATEGY #2

- **September 2021**: Lynn files for worker benefits at age sixty-two and one month, resulting in a fifty-seven month Reduction Factor. Lynn collects $1,297, constituting 71.25 percent of PIA. Gary files a "restricted application" at age sixty-nine and one month for 100.00 percent of Spousal Benefit. Gary collects $910.
- **August 2022**: Gary files for worker benefits at age seventy, resulting in a forty-eight month Delayed Retirement Credit. Gary collects $3,013, constituting 132.00 percent of PIA.

## STRATEGY #3

- **September 2014**: Gary files for worker benefits at age sixty-two and one month, resulting in a forty-seven month Reduction Factor. Gary collects $1,630, constituting 75.42 percent of PIA.
- **June 2026**: Lynn files for worker benefits at age sixty-six and ten months (Full Retirement Age) for 100.00 percent of PIA. Lynn collects $2,139.

## STRATEGY #4

- **September 2014**: Gary files for worker benefits at age sixty-two and one month, resulting in a forty-seven month Reduction Factor. Gary collects $1,630, constituting 75.42 percent of PIA.
- **June 2026**: Lynn files for worker benefits at age sixty-two and one month, resulting in a fifty-seven month Reduction Factor. Lynn collects $1,297, constituting 71.25 percent of PIA.

# CASE STUDY #4

## Mike and Rita

Overview of Couple: Case Study 4 involves Mike and Rita, a married couple where the wife is almost three years older than the husband. Both Mike and Rita reach FRA at sixty-six years of age. The husband, Mike, had moderately more income than the wife, Rita. Despite being a few years older, Rita is expected to survive Mike by approximately two years.

**Mike**

- **Date of Birth: March 10, 1952**
- **Full Retirement Age: 66**
- **Projected Death Age: 81.05**
- **Full Retirement Age Benefit: $2,482**

**Rita**

- **Date of Birth: December 25, 1950**
- **Full Retirement Age: 66**
- **Projected Death Age: 84.06**
- **Full Retirement Age Benefit: $1,788**

| | Mike | Rita | Combined | Widow's benefit |
|---|---|---|---|---|
| Strategy 1 | $491,724 | $428,960 | $920,684 | $3,276 |
| Strategy 2 | $448,812 | $467,431 | $916,243 | $3,276 |
| Strategy 3 | $434,742 | $470,208 | $904,950 | |
| Strategy 4 | $434,742 | $369,828 | $804,570 | $1,882 |

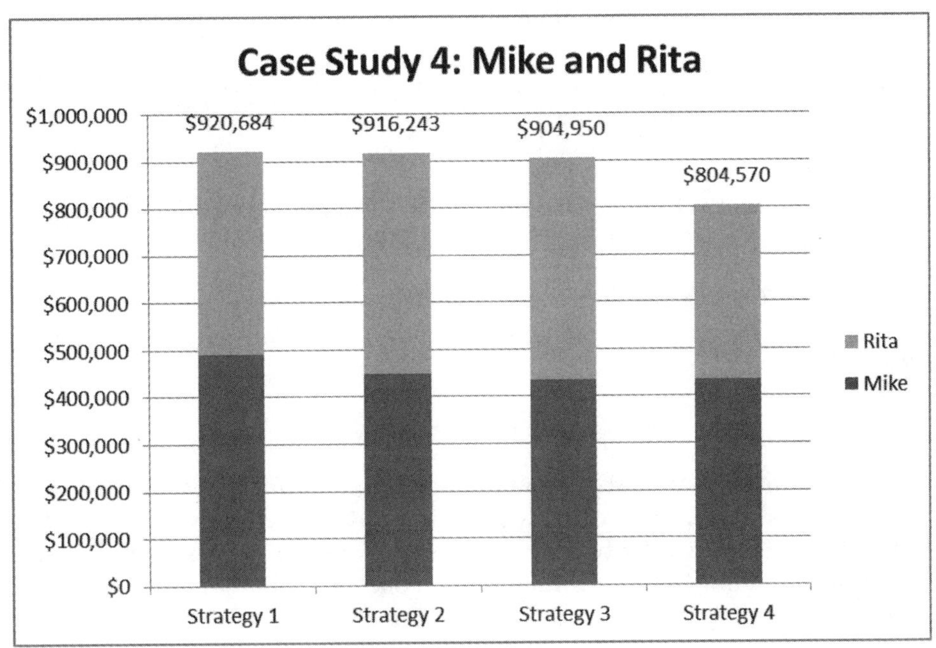

## STRATEGY #1

- **December 2016**: Rita initiates "file and suspend" of benefits at age sixty-six.
- **May 2018**: Mike files a "restricted application" at age sixty-six for 100.00 percent of Spousal Benefit, collecting $894.
- **December 2020**: Rita files for worker benefits at age seventy, resulting in a forty-eight month Delayed Retirement Credit. She receives $2,360 constituting 132.00 percent of PIA.
- **May 2022**: Mike files for worker benefits at age seventy, resulting in a forty-eight month Delayed Retirement Credit. He receives $3,276 constituting 132.00 percent of PIA.

## STRATEGY #2

- **May 2018**: Mike initiates "file and suspend" of benefits at age sixty-six. Rita files a "restricted application" at age sixty-seven and five months for 100.00 percent of Spousal Benefit, collecting $1,241.
- **December 2020**: Rita files for worker benefits at age seventy, resulting in a forty-eight month Delayed Retirement Credit. Rita collects $2,360 constituting 132.00 percent of PIA.
- **May 2022**: Mike files for worker benefits at age seventy, resulting in a forty-eight month Delayed Retirement Credit. Mike collects $3,276 constituting 132.00 percent of PIA.

## STRATEGY #3

- **July 2014**: Mike files for worker benefits at age sixty-two and two months, resulting in a forty-six month Reduction Factor. He collects $1,882 which constitutes 75.83 percent of PIA.
- **December 2016**: Rita files a "restricted application" at age sixty-six for 100.00 percent of Spousal Benefit and collects $1,241.
- **December 2020**: Rita files for worker benefits at age seventy, resulting in a forty-eight month Delayed Retirement Credit. Rita collects $2,360 constituting 132.00 percent of PIA.

## STRATEGY #4

- **July 2014**: Mike files for worker benefits at age sixty-two and two months, resulting in a forty-six month Reduction Factor. He collects $1,882 which constitutes 75.83 percent of PIA. Rita files for worker benefits at age sixty-three and seven months, resulting in a twenty-nine month Reduction Factor. She collects $1,438 which constitutes 83.89 percent of PIA.

# CASE STUDY #5

## Paul and Kirsten

Overview of Couple: Case Study 5 involves Paul and Kirsten, a married couple five years apart in age. Both Paul and Kirsten will reach Full Retirement Age at age sixty-six. The husband, Paul had significantly more income than the wife, Kirsten. Kirsten is expected to survive Paul by approximately six years.

**Paul**

- **Date of Birth: September 6, 1949**
- **Full Retirement Age: 66**
- **Projected Death Age: 81.11**
- **Full Retirement Age Benefit: $2,418**

**Kirsten**

- **Date of Birth: October 9, 1953**
- **Full Retirement Age: 66**
- **Projected Death Age: 83.0**
- **Full Retirement Age Benefit: $1,482**

| | **Paul** | **Kirsten** | **Combined** | **Widow's benefit** |
|---|---|---|---|---|
| Strategy 1 | $490,399.00 | $408,955.00 | $899,354.00 | $3,191.00 |
| Strategy 2 | $456,313.00 | $439,738.00 | $896,051.00 | $3,191.00 |
| Strategy 3 | $456,945.00 | $348,642.00 | $805,587.00 | $2,229.00 |

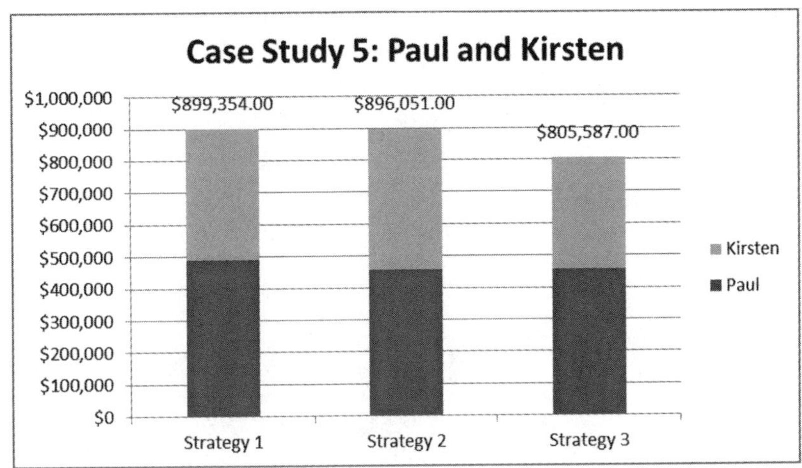


### STRATEGY #1

- **November 2015**: Kirsten files for worker benefits at age sixty-two and one month, resulting in the application of a forty-seven month Reduction Factor. She collects $1,117 constituting 75.42 percent of PIA. Paul files a "restricted application" at age sixty-six and two months for 100.00 percent of Spousal Benefit and collects $741.

- **September 2019**: Paul files for worker benefits at age seventy, resulting in a forty-eight month Delayed Retirement Credit. He collects $3,191 constituting 132.00 percent of PIA.

### STRATEGY #2

- **September 2015**: Paul initiates "file and suspend" of benefits at age sixty-six.
- **September 2019**: Paul files for worker benefits at age seventy, resulting in a forty-eight month Retirement Credit. Paul collects $3,191 resulting in 132.00 percent of PIA.
- **October 2019**: Kirsten files a "restricted application" at age sixty-six for 100.00 percent of Spousal Benefit and collects $1,209.
- **October 2023**: Kirsten files for worker benefits at age seventy, resulting in a forty-eight month Delayed Retirement Credit. She collects $1,956 constituting 132.00 percent of PIA.

### STRATEGY #3

- **July 2014**: Paul files for worker benefits at age sixty-four and ten months resulting in a fourteen-month Reduction Factor. He collects $2,229 constituting 92.22 percent of PIA.
- **Oct, 2019**: Kirsten files for worker benefits at age sixty-six collects $1,482 constituting 100 percent of PIA.

# CASE STUDY #6

## Mark and Cindy

Overview of Couple: Case Study 6 involves Mark and Cindy, a married couple less than a year apart in age. This couple, both born at the latter end of the Baby Boom, will reach FRA later than those born a decade earlier. Mark will achieve FRA at sixty-six years and eight months, while Cindy will reach FRA at sixty-six years and ten months. The husband, Mark had significantly more income than the wife, Cindy. Cindy is expected to survive Mark by approximately three years.

**Mark**

- **Date of Birth: September 4, 1958**
- **Full Retirement Age: 66 and 8 months**
- **Projected Death Age: 82**
- **Full Retirement Age Benefit: $2,543**

**Cindy**

- **Date of Birth: July 18, 1959**
- **Full Retirement Age: 66 and 10 months**
- **Projected Death Age: 84.10**
- **Full Retirement Age Benefit: $1,292**

| | **Mark** | **Cindy** | **Combined** | **Widow's benefit** |
|---|---|---|---|---|
| Strategy 1 | $466,848 | $419,014 | $885,862 | $3,242 |
| Strategy 2 | $484,936 | $364,872 | $849,808 | $3,242 |
| Strategy 3 | $428,527 | $355,258 | $783,785 | $1,793 |
| Strategy 4 | $428,527 | $280,870 | $709,397 | $1,793 |

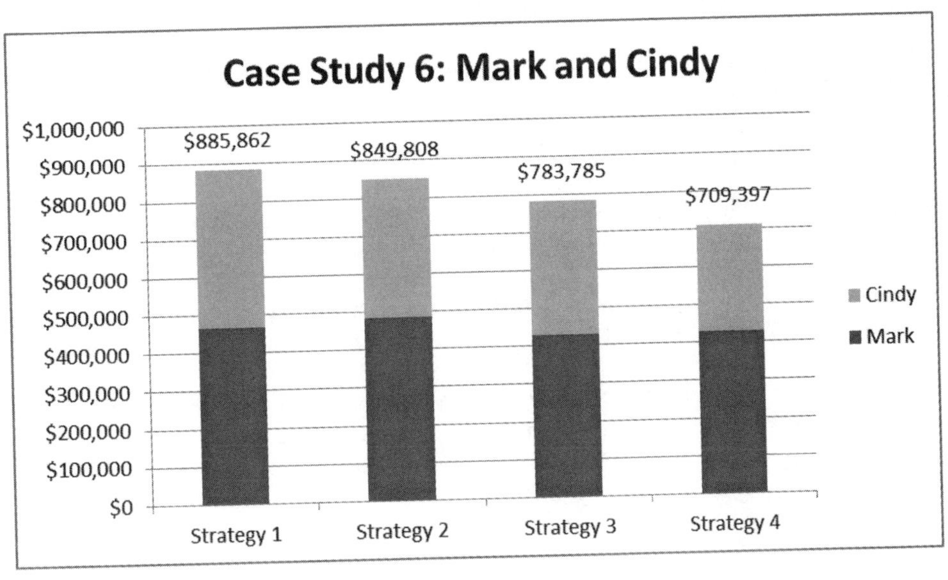

## STRATEGY #1

- **May 2025**: Mark initiates "file and suspend" of benefits at age sixty-six and eight months.
- **May 2026**: Cindy files a "restricted application" at age sixty-six and ten months for 100.00 percent of Spousal Benefit. She collects $1,271.
- **September 2028**: Mark files for worker benefits at age seventy, resulting in a forty-month Delayed Retirement Credit. He collects $3,242 constituting 126.67 percent of PIA.
- **July 2029**: Cindy files for worker benefits at age seventy, resulting in a thirty-eight month Delayed Retirement Credit. She collects $1,702 constituting 125.33 percent of PIA.

## STRATEGY #2

- **May 2026**: Cindy files for worker benefits at age sixty-six and ten months for 100.00 percent of PIA. She collects $1,292. Mark files a "restricted application" at age sixty-seven and eight months for 100.00 percent of Spousal Benefit, collecting $646.
- **September 2028**: Mark files for worker benefits at age seventy, resulting in a forty-month Delayed Retirement Credit. He collects $3,242 constituting 126.67 percent of PIA.

## STRATEGY #3

- **October 2020**: Mark files for worker benefits at age sixty-two and one month, resulting in a fifty-five month Reduction Factor. He collects $1,793 constituting 72.08 percent of PIA.
- **May 2026**: Cindy files a "restricted application" at age sixty-six and ten months for 100.00 percent of Spousal Benefit. She collects $1,271.
- **July 2029**: Cindy files for worker benefits at age seventy, resulting in a thirty-eight month Delayed Retirement Credit. She collects $1,702 constituting 125.33 percent of PIA.

## STRATEGY #4

- **October 2020**: Mark files for worker benefits at age sixty-two and one month, resulting in a fifty-five month Reduction Factor. He collects $1,793 constituting 72.08 percent of PIA.
- **August 2021**: Cindy files for worker benefits at age sixty-two and one month, resulting in a fifty-seven month Reduction Factor. She collects $833 constituting 71.25 percent of PIA.
- **August 2021**: Cindy files for Spousal Benefits at age sixty-two and one month, resulting in a fifty-seven month Reduction Factor. She collects $49 constituting 66.25 percent of Spousal Benefit.

# CASE STUDY #7

## Gordon and Cynthia

Overview of Couple: Case Study 7 involves Gordon and Cynthia, a married couple three years apart in age. The husband, Gordon, was the sole breadwinner. Cynthia has no retirement benefits of her own. Gordon will reach FRA at age sixty-six and two months, while Cynthia's FRA is sixty-six years and sixmonths. Cynthia is expected to survive Gordon by approximately six years.

**Gordon**

- **Date of Birth: January 13, 1955**
- **Full Retirement Age: 66 and 2 months**
- **Projected Death Age: 80.08**
- **Full Retirement Age Benefit: $2,338**

**Cynthia**

- **Date of Birth: December 5, 1957**
- **Full Retirement Age: 66 and 6 months**
- **Projected Death Age: 83.05**
- **Full Retirement Age Benefit: $0**

| | Gordon | Cynthia | Combined | Widow's benefit |
|---|---|---|---|---|
| Strategy 1 | $392,960 | $367,250 | $760,210 | $3,070 |
| Strategy 2 | $406,812 | $308,792 | $715,604 | $2,338 |
| Strategy 3 | $384,898 | $264,948 | $649,846 | $1,727 |

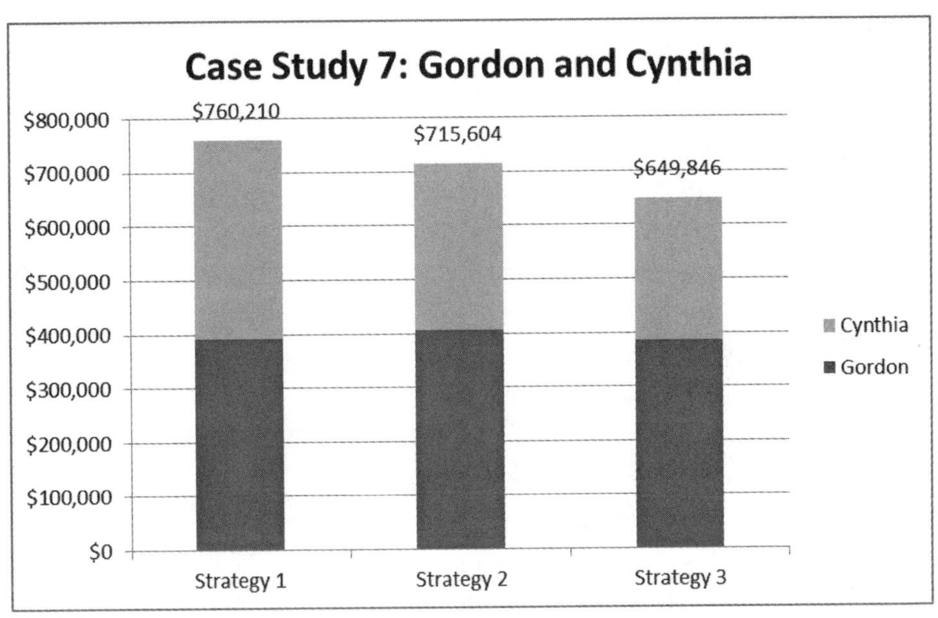

## STRATEGY #1

- **March 2021**: Gordon initiates "file and suspend" of benefits at age sixty-six and two months.
- **June 2024**: Cynthia files at age sixty-six and six months for 100.00 percent of Spousal Benefit. She collects $1,174.
- **January 2025**: Gordon files for worker benefits at age seventy, resulting in a forty-six months Delayed Retirement Credit. He collects $3,070 constituting 130.67 percent of PIA.

## STRATEGY #2

- **March 2021**: Gordon files for worker benefits at age sixty-six and two months for 100.00 percent of PIA. He collects $2,338.
- **March 2021**: Cynthia files at age sixty-three and three months for Spousal Benefits, resulting in a thirty-nine month Reduction Factor. She collects $862, constituting 73.75 percent of Spousal Benefit.

## STRATEGY #3

- **February 2017**: Gordon files for worker benefits at age sixty-two and one month, resulting in forty-nine month Reduction Factor. He collects $1,727 constituting for 74.58 percent of PIA.
- **January 2020**: Cynthia files at age sixty-two and one month for Spousal Benefits, resulting in fifty-three month Reduction Factor. She collects $ 785, constituting 67.92 percent of Spousal Benefit.

# CASE STUDY #8

## Ron and Candi

Overview of Couple: Case Study 8 involves Ron and Candi, a married couple approximately five years apart in age. The husband, Ron, earned significantly more than his wife Candi. Both Ron and Candi will reach Full Retirement Age at age sixty-six. Candi is expected to survive Ron by approximately seven years.

**Ron**

- **Date of Birth: July 23, 1947**
- **Full Retirement Age: 66**
- **Projected Death Age: 82.06**
- **Full Retirement Age Benefit: $2,498**

**Candi**

- **Date of Birth: May 17, 1952**
- **Full Retirement Age: 66**
- **Projected Death Age: 84.04**
- **Full Retirement Age Benefit: $903**

| Case Study 8: Ron and Candi | | | | |
|---|---|---|---|---|
| | **Ron** | **Candi** | **Combined** | **Widow's benefit** |
| Strategy 1 | **$510,719** | **$439,380** | **$950,099** | $3,297 |
| Strategy 2 | $501,347 | $389,340 | $890,687 | $2,681 |
| Strategy 3 | **$494,950** | **$378,668** | **$873,618** | $3,297 |

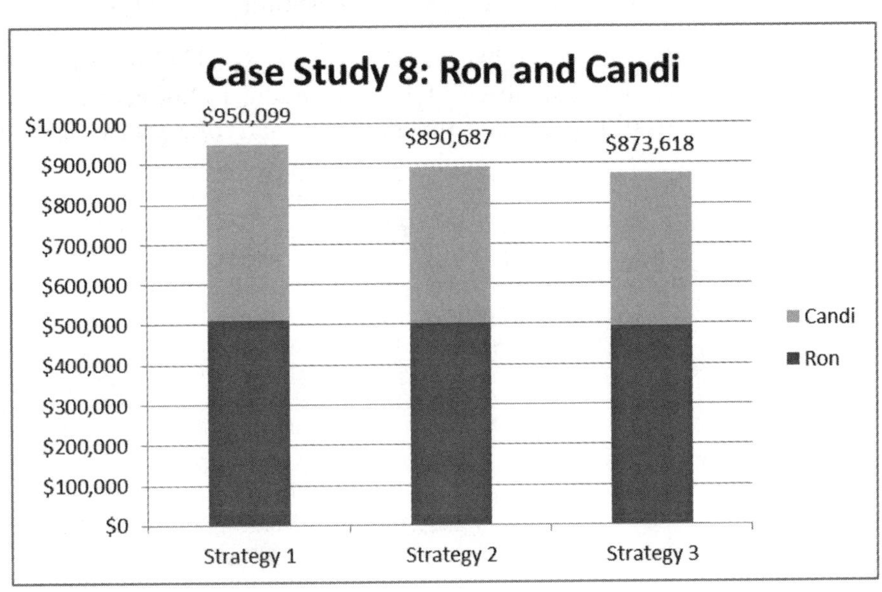

## STRATEGY #1

- **June 2014**: Candi files for worker benefits at age sixty-two and one month, resulting in a forty-seven month Reduction Factor. Candi collects $660 constituting 75.42 percent of PIA. Ron files a "restricted application" at age sixty-six and eleven months for 100.00 percent of Spousal Benefit and collects $437.

- **July 2017**: Ron files for worker benefits at age seventy, resulting in a forty-eight month Delayed Retirement Credit. Ron collects $3,297 constituting 132.00 percent of PIA. Candi files at age sixty-five and two months for Spousal Benefit, resulting in a ten month Reduction Factor. Candi collects $348.

## STRATEGY #2

- **June 2014**: Ron files for worker benefits at age sixty-six and eleven months, resulting in eleven months Delayed Retirement Credit. Ron collects $2,681 constituting 107.33 percent of PIA.

- **May 2018**: Candi files for worker benefits at age sixty-six for 100.00 percent of PIA and collects $903. Candi files at age sixty-six for 100.00 percent of Spousal Benefit and collects $346.

## STRATEGY #3

- **July 2017**: Ron files for worker benefits at age seventy, resulting in forty-eight months Delayed Retirement Credit. Ron collects $3,297, constituting 132.00 percent of PIA.

- **January 2020**: Candi files for worker benefits at age seventy, resulting in forty-eight months Delayed Retirement Credit. Candi collects $1,191 constituting 132.00 percent of PIA. Candi files at age seventy for 100.00 percent of Spousal Benefit and collects fifty-eight dollars.

# CASE STUDY #9

## Mike and Leslie

Overview of Couple: Case Study 9 involves Mike and Leslie, a married couple almost eleven years apart in age. This age difference results in their Full Retirement Ages being a year apart – Mike reaches FRA at sixty-six, while Leslie reaches FRA at age sixty-seven. The husband, Mike, made slightly less than his wife, Leslie. Leslie is expected to survive Mike by approximately twelve years.

**Mike**

- **Date of Birth: March 16, 1951**
- **Full Retirement Age: 66**
- **Projected Death Age: 81.08**
- **Full Retirement Age Benefit: $2,023**

**Leslie**

- **Date of Birth: November 12, 1961**
- **Full Retirement Age: 67**
- **Projected Death Age: 82.11**
- **Full Retirement Age Benefit: $2,198**

| | Mike | Leslie | Combined | Widow's benefit |
|---|---|---|---|---|
| Strategy 1 | $380,324 | $458,771 | $839,095 | |
| Strategy 2 | $373,800 | $422,375 | $796,175 | |
| Strategy 3 | $365,092 | $422,375 | $787,467 | |
| Strategy 4 | $365,092 | $401,765 | $766,857 | $1,652 |

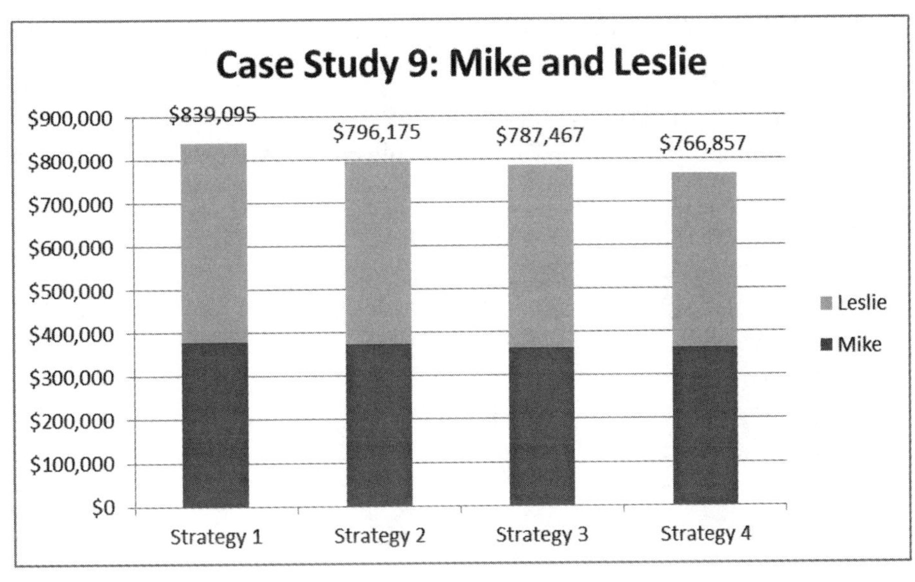

## STRATEGY #1

- **March 2017**: Mike files for worker benefits at age sixty-six for 100.00 percent of PIA. He collects $2,023.
- **November 2028**: Leslie files a "restricted application" at age sixty-seven for 100.00 percent of Spousal Benefit. She collects $1,011.
- **November 2031**: Leslie files for worker benefits at age seventy, resulting in a thirty-six month Delayed Retirement Credit. She collects $2,725 constituting 124.00 percent of PIA.

## STRATEGY #2

- **March 2021**: Mike files for worker benefits at age seventy, resulting in forty-eight months Delayed Retirement Credit. He collects $2,670 constituting 132.00 percent of PIA.
- **November 2031**: Leslie files for worker benefits at age seventy, resulting in a thirty-six month Delayed Retirement Credit. She collects $2,725 constituting 124.00 percent of PIA.

## STRATEGY #3

- **June 2014**: Mike files for worker benefits at age sixty-three and three months, resulting in a thirty-three month Reduction Factor. Mike collects $1,652 constituting 81.67 percent of PIA.
- **November 2031**: Leslie files for worker benefits at age seventy, resulting in a thirty-six month Delayed Retirement Credit. She collects $2,725 constituting 124.00 percent of PIA.

## STRATEGY #4

- **June 2014**: Mike files for worker benefits at age sixty-three and three months, resulting in a thirty-three month Reduction Factor. Mike collects $1,652 constituting 81.67 percent of PIA.
- **December 2023**: Leslie files for worker benefits at age sixty-two, and one month, resulting in a fifty-nine month Reduction Factor. She collects $1,547 constituting 70.42 percent.

# CASE STUDY #10

## Paul and Anne

Overview of Couple: Case Study 10 involves Paul and Anne, a married couple five years apart in age. Paul will reach FRA at age sixty-six, while Anne will achieve FRA at age sixty-six and four months. The husband, Paul, made slightly less than his wife, Anne. Anne is expected to survive Paul by approximately seven years.

**Paul**

- **Date of Birth: May 20, 1951**
- **Full Retirement Age: 66**
- **Projected Death Age: 81.08**
- **Full Retirement Age Benefit: $2,142**

**Anne**

- **Date of Birth: May 29, 1956**
- **Full Retirement Age: 66 and 4 months**
- **Projected Death Age: 83.03**
- **Full Retirement Age Benefit: $2,343**

| | Paul | Anne | Combined | Widow's benefit |
|---|---|---|---|---|
| Strategy 1 | $402,696 | $544,044 | $946,740 | |
| Strategy 2 | $384,675 | $544,044 | $928,719 | |
| Strategy 3 | $402,696 | $481,323 | $884,019 | $2,142 |
| Strategy 4 | $384,675 | $447,243 | $831,918 | |

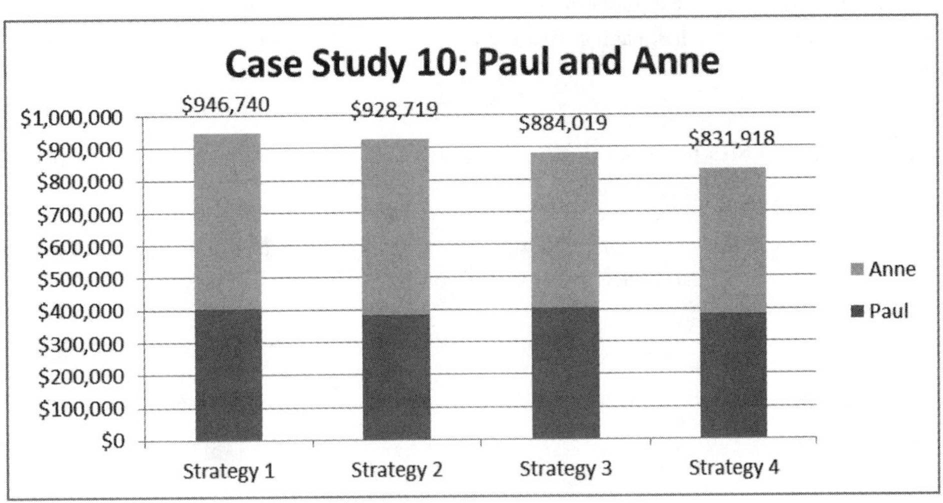

## STRATEGY #1

- **May 2017**: Paul files for worker benefits at age sixty-six for 100.00 percent of PIA. He collects $2,142.
- **July 2022**: Anne files a "restricted application" at age sixty-six and four months for 100.00 percent of Spousal Benefit. She collects $1,071.
- **March 2026**: Anne files for worker benefits at age seventy, resulting in a forty-four month Delayed Retirement Credit. She collects $3,030 constituting 129.33 percent of PIA.

## STRATEGY #2

- **June 2014**: Paul files for worker benefits at age sixty-three and one month, resulting in a twenty-five month Reduction Factor. Paul collects $1,725 constituting 80.56 percent of PIA.
- **July 2022**: Anne files a "restricted application" at age sixty-six and four months for 100.00 percent of Spousal Benefit. She collects $1,071.
- **March 2026**: Anne files for worker benefits at age seventy, resulting in a forty-four month Delayed Retirement Credit. She collects $3,030 constituting 129.33 percent of PIA.

## STRATEGY #3

- **May 2017**: Paul files for worker benefits at age sixty-six for 100.00 percent of PIA. He collects $2,142.
- **April 2018**: Anne files for worker benefits at age sixty-two and one month, resulting in a fifty-one month Reduction Factor. Anne collects $1,727 constituting 73.75 percent of PIA.

## STRATEGY #4

- **June 2014**: Paul files for worker benefits at age sixty-three and one month, resulting in a twenty-five month Reduction Factor. Paul collects $1,725 constituting 80.56 percent of PIA.
- **April 2018**: Anne files for worker benefits at age sixty-two and one month, resulting in a fifty-one month Reduction Factor. Anne collects $1,727 constituting 73.75 percent of PIA.

# CASE STUDY #11

## Harold and Belinda

Overview of Couple: Case Study 11 involves Harold and Belinda, a married couple four years apart in age. Harold and Belinda, were both born in the early 1950s. Harold will reach Full Retirement Age at sixty-six years and two months while Belinda will reach FRA at age sixty-six. The husband, Harold, made moderately more than his wife, Belinda. Although Belinda is expected to live to age eighty-four, she is expected to die approximately the same year as Harold.

**Harold**

- **Date of Birth: June 10, 1955**
- **Full Retirement Age: 66 and 2 months**
- **Projected Death Age: 80.06**
- **Full Retirement Age Benefit: $2,331**

**Belinda**

- **Date of Birth: April 1, 1951**
- **Full Retirement Age: 66**
- **Projected Death Age: 84.06**
- **Full Retirement Age Benefit: $1,738**

| | Harold | Belinda | Combined | Widow's benefit |
|---|---|---|---|---|
| Strategy 1 | **$423,644** | **$401,450** | **$825,094** | $3,045 |
| Strategy 2 | $423,644 | **$362,113** | $785,757 | $3,045 |
| Strategy 3 | **$383,670** | $401,450 | $785,120 | $3,045 |
| Strategy 4 | **$383,670** | **$362,113** | **$745,783** | $3,045 |

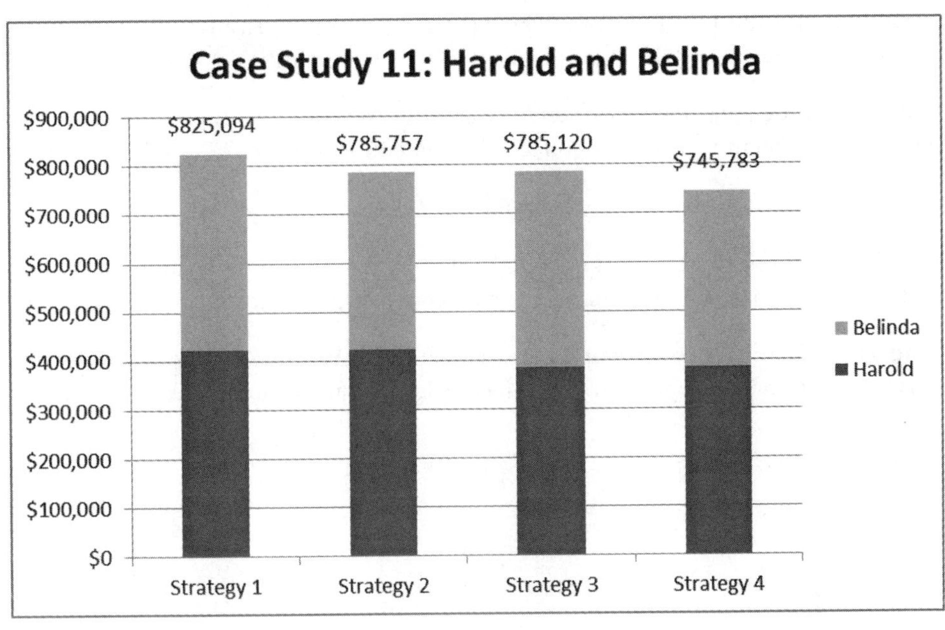

## STRATEGY #1

- **March 2017**: Belinda initiates "file and suspend" of benefits at age sixty-six.
- **August 2021**: Harold files a "restricted application" at age sixty-six and two months for 100.00 percent of Spousal Benefit. He collects $869.
- **June 2025**: Harold files for worker benefits at age seventy, resulting in forty-six month Delayed Retirement Credit. Harold collects $3,045 constituting 130.67 percent of PIA.
- **March 2021**: Belinda files for worker benefits at age seventy, resulting in forty-eight months Delayed Retirement Credit. She collects $2,294 constituting 132.00 percent of PIA.

## STRATEGY #2

- **May 2014**: Belinda files for worker benefits at age sixty-three and two months, resulting in a thirty-four month Reduction Factor. She collects $1,409 constituting 81.11 percent of PIA.
- **August 2021**: Harold files a "restricted application" at age sixty-six and two months for 100.00 percent of Spousal Benefit. He collects$869.
- **June 2025**: Harold files for worker benefits at age seventy, resulting in forty-six month Delayed Retirement Credit. Harold collects $3,045 constituting 130.67 percent of PIA.

## STRATEGY #3

- **June 2025**: Harold files for worker benefits at age seventy, resulting in forty-six month Delayed Retirement Credit. Harold collects $3,045 constituting 130.67 percent of PIA.
- **March 2021**: Belinda files for worker benefits at age seventy, resulting in forty-eight months Delayed Retirement Credit. She collects $2,294 constituting 132.00 percent of PIA.

## STRATEGY #4

- **May 2014**: Belinda files for worker benefits at age sixty-three and two months, resulting in a thirty-four month Reduction Factor. She collects $1,409 constituting 81.11 percent of PIA.
- **June 2025**: Harold files for worker benefits at age seventy, resulting in forty-six month Delayed Retirement Credit. Harold collects $3,045 constituting 130.67 percent of PIA.

# CASE STUDY #12

## Deke and Ex-Spouse Joanie

Overview of Case Study: Case Study 12 involves a divorced couple, Deke and his ex-wife Joanie. Deke will reach Full Retirement Age at age sixty-six. This illustration provides illustrations of the different strategies that Deke can take when filing.

**Deke**

- **Date of Birth: August 23, 1949**
- **Full Retirement Age: 66**
- **Projected Death Age: 82.02**
- **Full Retirement Age Benefit: $2,069**

**Joanie**

- **Date of Birth: n/a**
- **Full Retirement Age: n/a**
- **Projected Death Age: n/a**
- **Full Retirement Age Benefit: $792**

| | Deke | Joanie | Combined | Widow's benefit |
|---|---|---|---|---|
| Strategy 1 | $436,742 | | $436,742 | n/a |
| Strategy 2 | $401,386 | | $401,386 | n/a |
| Strategy 3 | $398,726 | | $398,726 | n/a |
| Strategy 4 | $398,110 | | $398,110 | n/a |

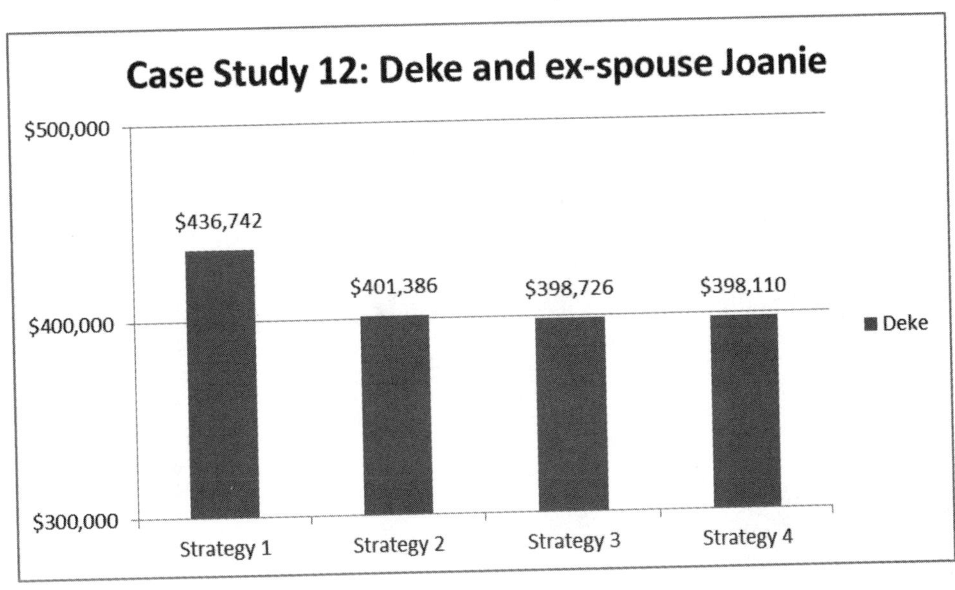

## STRATEGY #1

- **August 2015**: Deke files a "restricted application" at age sixty-six for 100.00 percent of ex-Spousal Benefits and collects $396, which is one-half of Joanie's Full Retirement benefit.

- **August 2019**: : Deke files for worker benefits at age seventy, resulting in forty-eight months Delayed Retirement Credit. Deke collects $2,731, constituting 132.00 percent of PIA.

## STRATEGY #2

- **August 2015**: : Deke files for worker benefits at age sixty-six (Full Retirement Age) and collects $2,069 at 100.00 percent of PIA.

## STRATEGY #3

- **August 2019**: Deke files for worker benefits at age seventy, resulting in forty-eight months Delayed Retirement Credit. Deke collects $2,731, constituting 132.00 percent of PIA.

## STRATEGY #4

- **September 2014**: : Deke files for worker benefits at age sixty-five and one month, resulting in eleven months Reduction Factor. Deke collects $1,942, constituting 93.89 percent of PIA.

# PART II
# MEDICARE

# INTRODUCTION

## 1001. What is Medicare?

Medicare is a federal health insurance program for persons sixty-five or older and for certain younger persons who either have permanent kidney failure or are disabled.

Medicare is administered by the Centers for Medicare & Medicaid Services (CMS), a federal agency in the Department of Health and Human Services. The Social Security Administration processes applications for Medicare and provides general information about the program. Although Medicare is a federal government program, much of the program is handled through the private sector. For example, various private insurance companies – called Medicare Administrative Contractors (MACs) – process and pay Medicare claims under contracts with CMS. Medicare beneficiaries receive health care through private service providers, including: hospitals and outpatient centers, nursing homes, and home health agencies; physicians; suppliers of medical equipment; and clinical laboratories. CMS also contracts with groups of doctors and other health care professionals to monitor the quality of care delivered to Medicare beneficiaries. CMS is located at 7500 Security Boulevard, Baltimore, Maryland 21244. The website for CMS is cms.hhs.gov.

Medicare consists of Part A (Hospital Insurance), Part B (Medical Insurance), Part C (Medicare Advantage, formerly known as Medicare+Choice), and Part D (Prescription Drug Insurance). Medicare Parts A and B are often referred to collectively as "original" or "traditional" or "fee-for-service" Medicare.

Part A (Hospital Insurance) provides insurance for institutional care, primarily inpatient hospital care, as well as skilled nursing home care, post-hospital home health care, and hospice care. Part A is financed for the most part by Social Security payroll tax deductions, which are deposited in the Federal Hospital Insurance Trust Fund. Medicare beneficiaries share some Part A costs through payment of deductibles and coinsurance and, occasionally, premiums.

Part B (Medical Insurance) provides insurance for physician's services, outpatient hospital care, physical therapy, ambulance trips, durable medical equipment, and a number of other services not covered under Part A. Part B is financed through monthly premiums and coinsurance paid by those who enroll and contributions from the federal government, both of which are deposited into the Federal Supplementary Medical Insurance Trust Fund. The government's share of the cost of Medicare Part B usually is about 75 percent of program costs.

Part C (Medicare Advantage) provides insurance through contracts between CMS and a variety of different private managed care and fee-for-service organizations. Most Medicare beneficiaries can choose to receive benefits through the original Medicare fee-for-service program (Parts A and B) or through a Medicare Advantage plan. Medicare beneficiaries who enroll in a Medicare Advantage plan pay both the Part B premium and any additional premium and cost-sharing required by the plan itself. Types of Medicare Advantage plans include the following:

- Coordinated care plans, including Health Maintenance Organizations (HMOs) and Preferred Provider Organizations (PPOs). In an HMO, a Medicare beneficiary must obtain health care through affiliated health care providers except in an emergency.

In a PPO, a Medicare beneficiary may obtain health care through providers outside the PPO's network, but may be charged more for using such providers.

- Private fee-for-service (PFFS) plans that reimburse providers on a fee-for-service basis. Private plans establish their own rate schedules for payments to providers and for charges to Medicare beneficiaries. Although Medicare limits how much may be charged to beneficiaries, the payment schedules may be different than what traditional Medicare pays.

Part D (Prescription Drug Insurance) provides insurance for outpatient prescription drugs through private insurance companies. In exchange for a monthly premium, Medicare Part D participants receive limited coverage for prescription drug benefits up to a catastrophic coverage threshold, above which Part D will cover roughly 95 percent of prescription drug costs.

## 1002. What federal agency administers Medicare?

The Centers for Medicare & Medicaid Services (CMS), whose central office is in Baltimore, Maryland, directs the Medicare program as well as the federal portion of the Medicaid program, the State Children's Health Insurance Program (SCHIP), and the new Health Insurance Marketplace under the Patient Protection and Affordable Care Act (PPACA). Before 2001 CMS was called the Health Care Financing Administration (HCFA). The Social Security Administration processes Medicare applications and claims, but it does not set Medicare policy. CMS sets the standards that health care providers such as hospitals, skilled nursing facilities, home health agencies, and hospices must meet in order to be certified as qualified providers of services. It also establishes the reimbursement rates for all Medicare-covered services.

## 1003. In light of the Supreme Court decision regarding same-sex marriage, will Social Security benefits be available to same-sex couples?

The decision by the U.S. Supreme Court in *United States v. Windsor*[1] to invalidate Section 3 of the Defense of Marriage Act (DOMA) has led to federal agencies, including the Social Security Administration (SSA) and Health and Human Services (HHS), implementing policies to allow benefits to same-sex married couples. These benefits would include Social Security spousal benefits as well as benefits for a spouse under the Medicare program. The situation is still in a state of change. Currently, if married in a state that recognizes same-sex marriages and also living in a state that also recognizes same-sex marriage, then benefits can be paid. If the couple lives in a state that does NOT recognize same-sex marriage, then benefits will not currently be paid.

Social Security is recommending that even if in a state that does not recognize same-sex marriage, that the couple file anyway because if the law changes, they will be protected. It is possible, under the Full Faith and Credit Clause of the U.S. Constitution, that eventually if married in a state that recognizes same-sex marriage, it will not matter as to the state of domicile.

1. 570 U.S. ___ (2013).

## 1004. Who can provide services or supplies under Medicare?

A wide array of health care organizations and medical professionals can offer services or supplies to Medicare beneficiaries. All such providers must meet any licensing requirements applicable under state or local law. Certain types of institutional providers must meet additional Medicare certification requirements and sign participation agreements with CMS before payments will be made for their services. Such providers include:

- Hospitals
- Skilled nursing facilities
- Home health agencies
- Hospice programs
- Certain outpatient rehabilitation facilities
- Certain diagnostic laboratories
- Certain organizations providing outpatient physical therapy and speech pathology services
- Certain facilities providing kidney dialysis or transplant services
- Rural health clinics

Medicare provider participation agreements include numerous rules that participating providers must agree to follow, many of which relate to how much such providers can charge Medicare beneficiaries. Other rules, however, mandate cooperation with quality improvement organizations and state health agency and accrediting organizations. Different rules apply to different types of Medicare providers. For example, hospitals are subject to additional requirements, such as compliance with the Emergency Medical Treatment and Active Labor Act (EMTALA), which prohibits refusing to treat certain indigent patients who need emergency care. Despite these rules, a nonparticipating hospital may still be paid by Medicare in case of emergency treatment provided to a Medicare beneficiary, assuming the nonparticipating hospital is the closest one available to handle the emergency.

In addition to the specified types of providers who must satisfy certification requirements and sign participation agreements to receive payment, other types of providers – such as physicians and certain suppliers – are encouraged to sign participation agreements primarily governing how they are paid. For physicians and suppliers, whether they are participating or nonparticipating does not affect their eligibility to be paid by Medicare; only the mechanisms for payment vary.

## 1005. In general, what benefits are provided under the Part A (Hospital Insurance) program?

The program, which automatically covers eligible persons, generally provides the following benefits:

- The cost of inpatient hospital care for up to ninety days in each benefit period (also known as a "spell of illness") (for 2015, the patient pays a deductible amount of $1,260 for the first sixty days plus $315 a day for each day in excess of sixty). There are also sixty nonrenewable lifetime reserve days with coinsurance of $630 a day in 2015.
- The cost of post-hospital skilled nursing facility care for up to 100 days in each benefit period (the patient pays $157.50 a day in 2015 after the first twenty days).
- The cost of home health service visits (subject to a limit of 100 post-institutional home health service visits in a spell of illness for Medicare beneficiaries enrolled in Parts A and B) made under a plan of treatment established by a physician. Additional coverage for home health care services that do not meet the Part A coverage criteria may be available under Part B (Medical Insurance). (See Q 1009.)
- The cost of hospice care for terminally ill patients.

For a detailed explanation of these benefits, see Q 1018 through Q 1059.

## 1006. In general, what benefits are provided under Part B (Medical Insurance)?

Part B (Hospital Insurance), which is a voluntary program that must be elected by an eligible Medicare beneficiary, generally provides coverage of the following benefit costs (subject in most cases to a 20 percent copayment requirement in addition to an annual deductible):

- Physicians' services, whether furnished in a hospital, clinic, office, home, or elsewhere.
- A one-time initial wellness physical within twelve months of enrolling in Part B (Medical Insurance), plus a yearly wellness visit to develop or update a personalized plan based on individual health profile.
- Various screening tests (including tests for breast cancer, cardiovascular disease, colorectal cancer, diabetes, glaucoma, HIV, obesity, prostate cancer, and sexually transmitted infections, as well as annual pap smears and pelvic exams), plus in some cases self-management training, counseling, and supplies. Most screening tests do not require cost-sharing.
- Certain preventive measures (including annual flu shot, pneumococcal vaccine, and Hepatitis B vaccine for certain beneficiaries; generally no cost-sharing).
- Pulmonary rehabilitation services for individuals with certain levels of chronic obstructive pulmonary disease.

- Home health care visits, if not covered under Part A (Hospital Insurance) (subject to special rules, including in most cases no cost-sharing other than for durable medical equipment).
- Outpatient medical and surgical services, supplies, and outpatient hospital services for the diagnosis or treatment of an illness or injury.
- Laboratory services (generally no cost-sharing), and X-rays, MRIs, CT scans, EKGs and certain other diagnostic tests.
- Outpatient physical therapy, speech language pathology, and occupational therapy services (subject to specific rules and limits; some services to inpatients may be covered depending on the circumstances).
- Rural health clinic services and federally qualified health center services.
- Prosthetic and orthotic devices (subject to various limits), including replacement of such devices; and surgical dressings and casts.
- Home dialysis supplies and equipment, self-care home dialysis support services, institutional dialysis and supplies, and kidney disease education services (subject to various limits).
- Certain chiropractic and podiatric services (subject to various restrictions).
- Rental or purchase of durable medical equipment, such as walkers.
- Ambulance services, under certain circumstances.
- Eyeglasses (or contact lenses) following cataract surgery (subject to various limits).
- Lung, heart, kidney, pancreas, intestine, and liver transplants, under certain circumstances, and immunosuppressive drugs after a transplant.
- Outpatient mental health services (subject in some cases to additional copayment requirements).

For a detailed explanation of these benefits, see Q 1065 through Q 1108.

## 1007. In general, what benefits are provided under Part C (Medicare Advantage)?

Part C (Medicare Advantage), is a voluntary program that must be elected by an eligible Medicare beneficiary. A Medicare Advantage Plan is offered by a private company that contracts with Medicare to provide a person with all his Part A and Part B benefits. Medicare Advantage Plans include Health Maintenance Organizations (HMOs), Preferred Provider Organizations (PPOs), Private Fee-for-Service Plans (PFFS), Special Needs Plans (SNPs), and Medicare Medical Savings Account Plans (MSAs). Most Medicare Advantage Plans offer prescription drug coverage.

Part C (Medicare Advantage), generally provides coverage of the following benefit costs:

- Choice of primary care physician based on the type of plan selected. For example, In HMO Plans, a primary care physician, hospital choice, and services generally must be chosen from those in the plan's network (except emergency care, out-of-area urgent care, or out-of-area dialysis).

- Prescription drug costs are covered in most plans. For some PFFS plans a person may need to join a Medicare Prescription Drug Plan to get coverage.

- In order to see a specialist a person with a Medicare Advantage HMO or SNP plan will generally need to get a referral. Those who have Part C PPO or PFFS plans will generally not need a referral in order to see a specialist.

- Pulmonary rehabilitation services for individuals with certain levels of chronic obstructive pulmonary disease.

For a detailed explanation of these benefits, see Q 1114 through Q 1131.

## 1008. In general, what benefits are provided under Part D (Prescription Drug Insurance)?

Prescription drug coverage is available to everyone covered by Medicare. A person must join a plan, run by an insurance company or other private company approved by Medicare, in order to receive Medicare drug coverage. Each plan can vary in cost and in the drugs that may be covered.

- Part D (Prescription Drug Plan) plans are sometimes called "PDPs" and add drug coverage to Original Medicare, some Medicare Cost Plans, some Medicare Private Fee-for-Service (PFFS) Plans, and Medicare Medical Savings Account (MSA) Plans.

- There are rules to understand in enrolling in a specific Part D (Prescription Drug Plan), as enrolling in this type of plan may preclude the use of Part C (Medicare Advantage) prescription drug coverage.

For a detailed explanation of these rules and benefits, see Q 1132 through Q 1138.

## 1009. What is the difference between home health care coverage under Part A (Hospital Insurance) and Part B (Medical Insurance)?

Medicare coverage of home health services unassociated with a hospital or skilled nursing facility stay has been gradually transferred from Part A to Part B. For most beneficiaries, Medicare Part A continues to cover the first 100 visits in a spell of illness following a three-day hospital stay or a skilled nursing facility stay. For persons with Part A coverage only, the post-institutional and 100-visit limitations do not apply.

Under Part B (Medical Insurance), home health care coverage does not require a preceding institutional stay nor does it have a 100-visit limit, but coverage is nonetheless subject to various restrictions. If a patient exhausts Part A coverage for home health care, Medicare benefits may still be available for the care under Part B. Other than the Part B coinsurance required for durable medical equipment, if applicable, there is no copayment requirement for home health care coverage.

## 1010. Is there any overall limit to the benefits a person can receive under Medicare?

While Medicare contains many limits on individual benefits, including financial cost-sharing obligations for beneficiaries, and provides no coverage in certain circumstances, the program imposes no single overall limit on the amount of benefits any individual person may receive. Under Part A (Hospital Insurance), benefits begin anew in each benefit period (although lifetime reserve days for inpatient hospital care are limited to sixty total), but inpatient care in a psychiatric hospital is subject to a lifetime limit of 190 days. Part B (Medical Insurance) generally does not impose dollar limits.

Medicare may limit benefit payments for services for which other third-party insurance programs (e.g., workers' compensation, automobile or liability insurance, and employer health plans) may ultimately be liable. Such limits arise under Medicare's Coordination of Benefits and Secondary Payer programs.

## 1011. When do Medicare benefits become available?

Medicare benefits generally become available at the beginning of the month in which an individual reaches age sixty-five. An individual whose birthday falls on the first day of a month is treated as having reached age sixty-five on the last day of the month immediately preceding his or her birthday, Assuming an individual is otherwise eligible for Medicare, benefits become available at age sixty-five even if the individual is still working. Individuals who qualify for Medicare on the basis of disability – other than those who are disabled due to Lou Gehrig's disease (amyotrophic lateral sclerosis) – must be continuously disabled for tweny-four months before they will be able to receive Medicare benefits. There is no waiting period for Medicare benefits when eligibility is based on disability due to Lou Gehrig's disease or on end-stage renal disease.

## 1012. What is a Medicare card?

A Medicare card is issued after a person becomes eligible for Medicare benefits. The card shows the person's coverage (Part A - Hospital Insurance, Part B - Medical Insurance, or both) and the effective date of each type of coverage. The card also shows the person's Medicare claim number. The claim number usually has nine digits (similar to a Social Security number, but not the same number) and one or two letters. On some cards, there will be another number after the letter. When a husband and wife both have Medicare, each receives a separate card and claim number. Each spouse must use the exact name and claim number shown on his or her card.

Important points to remember include:

- A covered person should always show his Medicare card when receiving services that Medicare covers in whole or in part.
- A covered person should always write his entire Medicare claim number (including any letters) on all checks for Medicare premium payments, all claims, and any correspondence about Medicare. Also, the covered person should have his Medicare card available when making a telephone inquiry relating to Medicare.
- A covered person should carry his Medicare card whenever away from home.
- If a Medicare card is lost, a replacement card should be requested immediately through the Medicare Replacement Card section of the Social Security Administration's website (mymedicare.gov). A replacement card may also be requested by going to a Social Security office or calling Social Security at 1-800-772-1213. Social Security can provide temporary proof of Medicare coverage until a replacement card arrives (in approximately four weeks from the date of a request).
- A covered person should use his Medicare card only after the effective date(s) shown on the card.
- Medicare cards made of metal or plastic, which are sold by some manufacturers, are not a substitute for the officially issued Medicare card.
- No one should ever permit another individual to use his Medicare card.

## 1013. What care is not covered under Part A (Hospital Insurance) and Part B (Medical Insurance)?

Medicare Parts A (Hospital Insurance) and B (Medical Insurance) contain a number of specific exclusions. These include the following:

Medicare does not pay for services that are not reasonable and necessary for the diagnosis or treatment of an illness or injury. These services include drugs or devices that have not been approved by the Food and Drug Administration (FDA); medical procedures and services performed using drugs or devices not approved by FDA; and services, including drugs or devices, not considered safe and effective because they are experimental or investigational. In addition, Medicare does not pay for most outpatient prescription drugs (except under Medicare Part D), routine or annual physical exams (other than the Welcome to Medicare initial visit and annual wellness visits introduced by the Affordable Care Act (PPACA), most dental care and dentures, routine foot care, routine eye care, hearing aids, personal comfort items, or cosmetic surgery.

Medicare also does not cover custodial care when that is the only kind of care the patient needs. Care is considered custodial when it is primarily for the purpose of helping with daily living or meeting personal needs and could be provided safely and reasonably by persons without professional skills or training. Much of the care provided in nursing homes to people with chronic long-term illnesses or disabilities is considered custodial care. For example, custodial care includes help in walking, getting in and out of bed, bathing, dressing, eating, and taking medicine. Even if an individual is in a participating hospital or skilled nursing facility or the individual is receiving care from a participating home health agency, Medicare does not cover the stay if the patient needs only custodial care. There are exceptions to the custodial care restrictions in the case of hospice care.

If a doctor places an individual in a hospital or skilled nursing facility when the kind of care the individual needs could be provided elsewhere, the individual's stay will not be considered reasonable and necessary, and Medicare will not pay for it. If an individual stays in a hospital or skilled nursing facility longer than necessary, Medicare payments will end when inpatient care is no longer reasonable or necessary.

If a doctor (or other practitioner) comes to treat a person or that person visits the doctor for treatment more often than is medically necessary, Medicare will not pay for the "extra" visits.

Medicare will not pay for services performed by immediate relatives or members of a patient's household. Nor will Medicare pay for services paid for by another government program. Medicare will not pay for any item or service with regard to which there is no legal obligation to pay (for the beneficiary or anyone else), such as free health-related services (e.g., vaccinations) provided at community events. In certain cases, such as health care covered by workers' compensation or an employer-based health plan for an active employee, Medicare acts as secondary payer, paying to the extent of Medicare's coverage limits but only after another source of insurance pays and then only to the extent the primary payer did not cover the item or service.

Medicare generally does not pay for any health services provided outside the United States, but there are exceptions for emergencies and for inpatient hospital care where the foreign hospital is closer to an individual's residence than a comparable U.S. hospital and is equipped to handle the needed care.

Under Medicare law a person will not be held responsible for payment of the cost of certain health care services for which the person was denied Medicare payment if the person did not know or could not reasonably be expected to know that the services were not covered by Medicare. This provision is often referred to as a "Waiver of Liability." The waiver provision applies only when the care was denied because it was one of the following: (1) custodial care, (2) not reasonable or necessary under Medicare program standards for diagnosis or treatment, (3) for home health services, the patient was not homebound or not receiving skilled nursing care on an intermittent basis, or (4) the only reason for the denial is that, in error, the patient was placed in a skilled nursing facility bed that was not approved by Medicare.

The limitation of liability provision also does not apply to Part B (Medical Insurance) services provided by a nonparticipating physician or supplier who did not accept assignment of the claim. However, in certain situations Medicare will protect the patient from paying for services provided by a nonparticipating physician on a nonassigned basis that are denied as "not reasonable and necessary." If a physician knows or should know that Medicare will not pay for a particular service as "not reasonable and necessary," the physician must give the patient written notice—before performing the service—of the reasons why the physician believes Medicare will not pay. The physician must get the patient's written agreement to pay for the services. If the patient does not receive this notice, the patient is not required to pay for the service. If the patient pays for the service, but did not receive a notice, the patient may be entitled to a refund.

## 1014. What are the rules regarding self-referrals?

Doctors cannot make self-referrals for certain designated health services. Designated health services include (1) clinical laboratory services, (2) physical therapy services, (3) occupational therapy services, (4) radiology services, including MRI, CAT scans, and ultrasound services, (5) radiation therapy services and supplies, (6) durable medical equipment and supplies, (7) parenteral and enteral nutrients, equipment, and supplies, (8) prosthetics, orthotics, and prosthetic devices and supplies, (9) home health services, (10) outpatient prescription drugs, and (11) inpatient and outpatient hospital services.

The law prohibits a doctor who has a financial relationship with an entity from referring Medicare patients to that entity to receive a designated health service. The prohibition also applies if a doctor's immediate family member has a financial relationship with the entity. A financial relationship can exist as an ownership or investment interest in *or* a compensation arrangement with an entity. The law is triggered by the mere fact that a financial relationship exists; it does not matter what the doctor intends when making a referral.

An entity cannot bill Medicare, Medicaid, the beneficiary, or anyone else for a designated health service furnished to a Medicare patient under a prohibited referral. If a person collects any amount for services billed in violation of the law, a refund must be made. A person can be subject to a civil money penalty or exclusion from Medicare if that person: (1) presents or causes to be presented a claim to Medicare or bill to any individual, third-party payer, or other entity for any designated health service the person knows or should know was furnished as the result of a prohibited referral, or (2) fails to make a timely refund.

## 1015. What are Quality Improvement Organizations?

Quality Improvement Organizations (QIOs), previously known as peer review organizations, are groups of practicing doctors and other health care professionals who are paid by the federal government to review the care given to Medicare patients. Generally, QIOs are private, not-for-profit organizations. Each state has a QIO that decides, for Medicare payment purposes, whether care is reasonable, necessary, and provided in the most appropriate setting. QIOs also decide whether care meets the standards of quality generally accepted by the medical profession. QIOs have the authority to deny payments if care is not medically necessary or not delivered in the most appropriate setting.

QIOs investigate individual patient complaints about the quality of care and respond to (1) requests for review of notices of noncoverage issued by hospitals to beneficiaries, and (2) requests for reconsideration of QIO decisions by beneficiaries, physicians, and hospitals.

The QIO will tell the patient in writing if the service received was not covered by Medicare.

If a patient is admitted to a Medicare-participating hospital, the patient will receive *An Important Message from Medicare*, which explains the patient's rights as a hospital patient and provides the name, address and phone number of the QIO in the patient's state.

If a patient believes he has been improperly refused admission to a hospital, forced to leave a hospital too soon, or denied coverage of a medical procedure or treatment, the patient should ask for a written explanation of the decision. This written notice must fully explain how the patient can appeal the decision, and it must give the patient the name, address and phone number of the QIO where an appeal or request for review can be submitted.

If a patient disagrees with the decision of a QIO, the patient can appeal by requesting reconsideration. Then, if the patient disagrees with the QIO's reconsideration decision and the amount in question is $200 or more, the patient can request a hearing by an Administrative Law Judge. Cases involving $2,000 or more can eventually be appealed to a federal court. QIOs also provide alternate dispute resolution options.

Different appeal procedures apply to issues involving other types of Part A (Hospital Insurance) coverage such as skilled nursing facility, home health, or hospice care.

For a detailed explanation of the appeals process, see Q 1139 through Q 1149.

## 1016. When should a person use the Medicare fraud and abuse hotline?

If a person has reason to believe that a doctor, hospital, or other provider of health care services is performing unnecessary or inappropriate services, or is billing Medicare for services not received, the person should report this information to Medicare at 1-800-MEDICARE. The person reporting alleged fraud and abuse should be prepared to communicate details of the transactions raising questions, including (1) the exact nature of the suspected wrongdoing, (2) the date it occurred, and (3) the name and address of the party involved.

If an individual reports information that serves as the basis for the collection of $100 or more, CMS may pay a portion of the amount collected to the individual (up to a maximum of $1,000).

## 1017. Should a person receive Medicare benefits through the original fee-for-service Medicare Parts A and B (Hospital Insurance and Medical Insurance) or through a Medicare Advantage plan?

A person living in an area serviced by a Medicare Advantage plan has a choice between traditional Medicare Parts A and B or a Medicare Advantage plan. If a person chooses Parts A and B, that beneficiary can go to almost any doctor, hospital, or other health care provider the beneficiary prefers. Generally, a fee is charged each time a service is used, Medicare pays its share of the bill, and the patient is responsible for paying the balance. Beneficiaries may purchase a private Medicare Supplemental Insurance (Medigap) policy to cover or help defray the patient's share of charges not covered by Medicare. See Q 1139 through Q 1149 on Medigap insurance.

Medicare Advantage plans in general cover the same core benefits as original Medicare Parts A and B, but may also include other coverage, including prescription drug coverage.

Because Medicare Advantage plans are structured to be more inclusive, beneficiaries covered by Medicare Advantage do not need to purchase a separate Medigap plan (and are usually prohibited from doing so). Medicare Advantage plans are provided through private insurers, and the exact terms of the plans – including beneficiary cost-sharing obligations – are established by the private insurers, subject to approval by CMS. Medicare Advantage plans may also charge additional premiums (in addition to the Medicare Part B premium) to reflect the additional benefits offered. Most types of Medicare Advantage plans contain managed care features that attempt to control costs by limiting the providers to which a beneficiary may go for care (or imposing higher cost-sharing requirements if a beneficiary obtains services from an out-of-network provider).

An individual who elects a Medicare Advantage plan one year can always return to traditional Medicare Parts A and B (Hospital and Medical Insurance) in a different year. Also, regardless of whether a person chooses Parts A and B (Hospital and Medical Insurance) Medicare or a Medicare Advantage plan, the individual retains all Medicare protections and appeal rights. See Q 1109 through Q 1131 for a detailed description of Medicare Advantage.

# PART A: HOSPITAL INSURANCE

## ELIGIBILITY

### 1018. Who is eligible for benefits under Part A (Hospital Insurance)?

All persons age sixty-five and over who are entitled to monthly Social Security cash benefits (or would be entitled except that an application for cash benefits has not been filed), or monthly cash benefits under Railroad Retirement programs (whether retired or not), are eligible for Medicare Part A benefits. An individual may be eligible for Social Security or Railroad Retirement program benefits based on the individual's own work record or as the current or surviving spouse of someone eligible for such benefits. Such individuals are eligible for Part A (Hospital Insurance) benefits if they are at least sixty-five years old. For example, a woman age sixty-five or over who is entitled to a spouse's or widow's Social Security benefit is eligible for benefits under Part A.

Persons age sixty-five and over can receive Medicare benefits even if they continue to work. Enrollment in the program while working will not affect the amount of future Social Security benefits.

Certain Social Security or Railroad Retirement disability beneficiaries are eligible for Medicare Parts A and B after entitlement to disability benefits for twenty-four months or more. Eligible categories of disability beneficiaries include disabled workers at any age, disabled widows and widowers at least age fifty but not yet age sixty-five, beneficiaries age eighteen or older who receive benefits because of disability beginning before age twenty-two, and disabled qualified Railroad Retirement annuitants. Medicare coverage is automatic. No application is required.

A person who becomes reentitled to disability benefits within five years after the end of a previous period of entitlement (within seven years in the case of disabled widows or widowers and disabled children) is automatically eligible for Medicare coverage without the need to wait another twenty-four months. In addition, in most cases, an individual covered by Medicare on the basis of disability, but who loses disability benefits for some reason, will again be eligible for Medicare coverage without needing to meet the twenty-four month waiting period requirement, if the current impairment is the same as (or directly related to) that in the previous period of disability.

Medicare coverage will continue if an individual returns to work during a nine-month trial period and for up to fifteen additional months (a total of twenty-four months).

Individuals with ALS (Amyotrophic Lateral Sclerosis, also known as Lou Gehrig's disease) are eligible for Medicare Part A (Hospital Insurance) the first month they are eligible for Social Security or Railroad Retirement disability benefits. The normal twenty-four month waiting period does not apply.

Medicare Part A also covers individuals with End-Stage Renal Disease (ESRD) who are not yet age sixty-five but who are either currently or fully insured for, or are entitled to, Social Security or Railroad Retirement benefits. Spouses or dependent children of eligible individuals may also be covered if the spouse or dependent child has ESRD.

## 1019. What are the special eligibility rules for persons with End-Stage Renal Disease (ESRD)?

Insured workers (and their spouses and dependents) with ESRD who require renal dialysis or a kidney transplant are deemed disabled for Medicare coverage purposes even if they are working. Coverage can begin with the first day of the third month after the month dialysis treatments begin. This three-month waiting period is waived if the individual participates in a self-care dialysis training course during the waiting period.

Medicare coverage for an ESRD patient who is a candidate for a kidney transplant begins with the month in which the patient is hospitalized for the transplant, if the transplant occurs during the three-month period beginning with that month. If a transplant is delayed more than two months following the initial month of hospitalization for a transplant, coverage is effective on the first day of the second month before the month of transplant.

Coverage is also provided under Medicare for the self-administration of erythropoietin for home renal dialysis patients.

For some individuals who have Medicare solely on the basis of their end-stage renal disease, Medicare is the secondary payer if the person with ESRD has large-employer group health plan coverage either directly or through a family member. During this period, if an employer plan pays less than the provider's charges, Medicare may supplement the plan's payments. (See Q 1021.)

## 1020. What are the special eligibility rules for government employees?

In general, federal employees began paying the Hospital Insurance (HI) portion of Social Security taxes in 1983 and thus became eligible for Medicare. A transitional provision provides credit for retroactive hospital quarters of coverage for federal employees who were employed before 1983 and also on January 1, 1983. Certain categories of federal employees are not covered, however, including inmates in federal penal institutions, certain interns, and certain temporary employees.

State and local government employees hired after March 31, 1986, generally also pay HI taxes and are covered under Medicare. A person who was performing substantial and regular service for a state or local government before April 1, 1986, is not covered, provided he was a bona fide employee on March 31, 1986, and the employment relationship was not entered into in order to meet the requirements for exemptions from coverage.

State or local government employees who were employed before April 1, 1986, but whose employment terminated after March 31, 1986, are covered under Medicare if they are later rehired. Certain individuals are not automatically covered under Medicare even if employed by a state or local government, including those employed:

(1) to relieve them of unemployment;

(2) in a hospital, home, or institution where they are inmates or patients;

(3) on a temporary basis because of an emergency such as a storm, earthquake, flood, fire or snow;

(4) as interns, student nurses or other student employees of District of Columbia government hospitals, unless the individuals are medical or dental interns or medical or dental residents in training.

State governments may voluntarily enter into agreements to extend Medicare coverage to employees not covered under the rules above.

## 1021. When is Medicare considered a secondary payer?

There are limitations on Medicare payments for services covered under group health plans. Medicare is secondary payer, under specified conditions, for services covered under any of the following:

- Group health plans of employers that employ at least twenty employees and that cover Medicare beneficiaries age sixty-five or older who are covered under the plan by virtue of an individual's current employment status with an employer or the current employment status of a spouse of any age.
- Group health plans (without regard to the number of individuals employed and irrespective of current employment status) that cover individuals who have end-stage renal disease. Generally, group health plans are always primary payers throughout the first thirty months of end-stage renal disease based on Medicare eligibility or entitlement.
- Large group health plans (that is, plans of employers that employ at least 100 employees) that cover Medicare beneficiaries who are under age sixty-five, entitled to Medicare on the basis of disability, and covered under the employer plan by virtue of the individual's or a family member's current employment status with an employer.

A "group health plan" means any arrangement made by one or more employers or employee organizations to provide health care directly or through other methods such as insurance or reimbursement, to current or former employees, the employer, others associated or formerly associated with the employer in a business relationship, or their families, that:

(1) is of, or contributed to by, one or more employers or employee organizations;

(2) involves more than one employer or employee organization and provides for common administration; and

(3) provides substantially the same benefits or the same benefit options to all those enrolled under the arrangement.

Group health plans include self-insured plans, plans of governmental entities (federal, state, and local), and employee organization plans (union plans, employee health and welfare funds, or other employee organization plans). Group health plans also include employee-pay-all plans, which are plans under the auspices of one or more employers or employee organizations but which receive no financial contributions from them. Not included in the definition of group health plans are plans that are unavailable to employees, for example, a plan only for self-employed persons.

A large group health plan means a group health plan that covers employees of either:

- a single employer or employee organization that employed at least 100 full-time or part-time employees on 50 percent or more of its regular business days during the previous calendar year; or
- two or more employers, or employee organizations, at least one of which employed at least 100 full-time or part-time employees on 50 percent or more of its regular business days during the previous calendar year.

An employer or insurer is prohibited from offering Medicare beneficiaries financial or other benefits as incentives not to enroll in, or to terminate enrollment in, a group health plan that is, or would be, primary to Medicare. The prohibition precludes offering to Medicare beneficiaries an alternative to the employer primary plan (for example, coverage of prescription drugs) unless the beneficiary has primary coverage other than Medicare. An example would be primary coverage through an employee's own or a spouse's employer.

Other prohibited actions by group health plans or large group health plans include, but are not limited to, the following:

- Failure to pay primary benefits as required
- Offering coverage that is secondary to Medicare to individuals entitled to Medicare
- Terminating coverage because the individual has become entitled to Medicare, except as permitted under certain COBRA continuation coverage provisions
- In the case of a large group health plan, denying or terminating coverage because an individual is entitled to Medicare on the basis of disability without denying or terminating coverage for similarly situated individuals who are not entitled to Medicare on the basis of disability
- Imposing limitations on benefits for a Medicare-entitled individual that do not apply to others enrolled in the plan, such as providing less comprehensive health care coverage, excluding benefits, reducing benefits, charging higher deductibles or coinsurance, providing for lower annual or lifetime benefit limits, or more restrictive pre-existing illness limitations
- Charging a Medicare-entitled individual higher premiums

- Requiring a Medicare-entitled individual to wait longer for coverage to begin
- Paying providers and suppliers no more than the Medicare payment rate for services furnished to a Medicare beneficiary but making payments at a higher rate for the same services to an enrollee who is not entitled to Medicare
- Providing misleading or incomplete information that would have the effect of inducing a Medicare entitled individual to reject the employer plan, thereby making Medicare the primary payer. An example of this would be informing the beneficiary of the right to accept or reject the employer plan but failing to inform the individual that, if he rejects the plan, the plan will not be permitted to provide or pay for secondary benefits
- Including in its health insurance cards, claims forms, or brochures distributed to beneficiaries, providers, and suppliers, instructions to bill Medicare first for services furnished to Medicare beneficiaries without stipulating that such action may be taken only when Medicare is the primary payer
- Refusing to enroll an individual for whom Medicare would be secondary payer, when enrollment is available to similarly situated individuals for whom Medicare would not be secondary payer

If a group health plan or large group health plan makes benefit distinctions among various categories of individuals (distinctions unrelated to the fact that the individual is disabled), the group health plan or large group health plan may make the same distinctions among the same categories of individuals entitled to Medicare whose plan coverage is based on current employment status. For example, if a group health plan or large group health plan does not offer coverage to employees who have worked less than one year and who are *not* entitled to Medicare on the basis of disability or age, the group health plan or large group health plan is not required to offer coverage to employees who have worked less than one year and who *are* entitled to Medicare on the basis of disability or age.

A group health plan or large group health plan may pay benefits secondary to Medicare for an aged or disabled beneficiary who has current employment status if the plan coverage is COBRA continuation coverage because of reduced hours of work. Medicare is primary payer for this beneficiary because, although he has current employment status, the group health plan coverage is by virtue of the COBRA law rather than by virtue of the current employment status.

## Aged Beneficiaries and Spouses

Medicare benefits are secondary to benefits payable by a group health plan for services furnished during any month in which the individual is age sixty-five or older, eligible for Medicare Part A, and meets one of the following conditions:

(1) The individual is covered under a group health plan of an employer that has at least twenty employees (including a multiemployer plan in which at least one of the

participating employers meets that condition), and coverage under the plan is by virtue of the individual's current employment status.

(2) The individual is the aged spouse (including a divorced or common-law spouse) of an individual (of any age) who is covered under a group health plan by virtue of the individual's current employment status.

## Disabled Beneficiaries

Medicare benefits are secondary to benefits payable by a large group health plan for services furnished during any month in which the individual (1) is entitled to Medicare Part A benefits on the basis of disability, (2) is covered under a large group health plan, and (3) has large group health plan coverage by virtue of her own or a family member's current employment status.

Medicare becomes primary if the services are (1) furnished to Medicare beneficiaries who have declined to enroll in the group health plan, (2) not covered under the plan for the disabled individual or similarly situated individuals, (3) covered under the plan but not available to particular disabled individuals because they have exhausted their benefits under the plan, (4) furnished to individuals whose COBRA continuation coverage has been terminated because of the individual's Medicare entitlement, or (5) covered under COBRA continuation coverage notwithstanding the individual's Medicare entitlement.

## End-stage Renal Disease

A group health plan may not take into account that an individual is eligible for or entitled to Medicare benefits on the basis of end-stage renal disease. An individual who has end-stage renal disease but who has not filed an application for entitlement to Medicare on that basis is eligible for Medicare based on end-stage renal disease. A group health plan may not differentiate in the benefits it provides between individuals who have end-stage renal disease and others enrolled in the plan, on the basis of the existence of end-stage renal disease, or in any other manner.

Generally, Medicare is secondary payer during the first thirty months of end-stage renal disease-based eligibility or entitlement. Medicare becomes primary after the thirtieth month of end-stage renal disease-based eligibility or entitlement.

Examples of group health plan actions that constitute differentiation in plan benefits (and that may constitute "taking into account" Medicare eligibility or entitlement) include:

- terminating coverage of the individuals with end-stage renal disease, when there is no basis for such termination unrelated to end-stage renal disease that would result in termination for individuals who do not have end-stage renal disease;
- imposing on persons who have end-stage renal disease, but not on others enrolled in the plan, benefit limitations such as less comprehensive health plan coverage, reductions in benefits, exclusions of benefits, a higher deductible or coinsurance, a

longer waiting period, a lower annual or lifetime benefit limit, or more restrictive pre-existing illness limitations;

- charging individuals with end-stage renal disease higher premiums;
- paying providers and suppliers less for services furnished to individuals who have end-stage renal disease, such as paying 80 percent of the Medicare rate for renal dialysis;
- failure to cover routine maintenance dialysis or kidney transplants, when a plan covers other dialysis services or other organ transplants.

## Other Secondary Payer Rules

An employee may reject the employer's plan and retain Medicare as the primary payer, but regulations prevent employers from offering a health plan or option designed to induce the employee to reject the employer's plan and retain Medicare as primary payer.

For persons who are not eligible for Social Security or Railroad Retirement benefits, see Q 1022.

Medicare is also the secondary payer:

(1) when medical care can be paid for under no-fault insurance or liability insurance (including automobile insurance);

(2) if the individual is entitled to veterans benefits;

(3) if the individual is entitled to black lung benefits; or

(4) if the individual is covered by workers' compensation.

Although Medicare is sometimes the secondary payer when liability insurance is available, Medicare may make a conditional payment if it receives a claim for services covered by liability insurance. In these cases, Medicare recovers its conditional payment from the settlement amount when the liability settlement is reached.

A third-party payer must give notice to Medicare if it learns that Medicare has made a primary payment in a situation where the third party payer made or should have made the primary payment. A third-party payer is considered to learn that Medicare has made a primary payment when the third-party payer receives information that Medicare had made a primary payment, or when it receives information sufficient to draw the conclusion that Medicare has made a primary payment.

*Example 1.* The third-party payer has received a copy of an Explanation of Medicare Benefits form, and the form shows that Medicare has made a primary payment for services for which the third party has made, or ought to have made, primary payment.

*Example 2.* A beneficiary for whom Medicare should be secondary payer states in correspondence provided to the third party payer that Medicare has made primary payment for a given item or service for which the beneficiary has primary coverage under the third party payer's plan.

*Example 3.* A beneficiary who is eligible for Medicare files a claim for primary payment with a third party payer, the claim is denied, the beneficiary appeals, and the denial is reversed. (The third party payer should assume that Medicare made a conditional primary payment in the interim.)

The Centers for Medicare & Medicaid Services must mail questionnaires to individuals, before they become entitled to benefits under Part A (Hospital Insurance) or enroll in Part B (Medical Insurance), to determine whether they are covered under a primary plan. Payments will not be denied for covered services solely on the grounds that a beneficiary's questionnaire fails to note the existence of other health plan coverage.

Providers and suppliers are required to complete information on claim forms regarding potential coverage under other plans. Civil monetary penalties are established for an entity that knowingly, willfully, and repeatedly fails to complete a claim form with accurate information.

Contractors are required to submit annually a report to the Centers for Medicare & Medicaid Services regarding steps taken to recover mistaken payments.

## 1022. Can a person age sixty-five or over qualify for Part A (Hospital Insurance) benefits without qualifying for Social Security or Railroad Retirement benefits?

Certain individuals age sixty-five or over and otherwise ineligible for Part A (Hospital Insurance) may enroll voluntarily and pay a monthly premium if they also enroll in Part B (Medical Insurance). (See Q 1060.) Any such person must also be a resident of the United States and also either a U.S. citizen or an alien lawfully admitted for permanent residence status (who has continuously resided in the United States for at least five years immediately before applying for Medicare benefits).

## 1023. Is there any way that an individual not automatically eligible for Part A (Hospital Insurance) can be enrolled?

Yes, provided the individual (1) has attained age sixty-five, (2) is enrolled in Part B (Medical Insurance) (see Q 1060 through Q 1108), (3) is a resident of the United States and is either (a) a citizen, or (b) an alien lawfully admitted for permanent residence who has resided in the United States continuously during the five years immediately preceding the month in which he applies for enrollment, and (4) is not otherwise entitled to Part A (Hospital Insurance) benefits.

Certain disabled individuals under age sixty-five may also be able to obtain Part A (Hospital Insurance) coverage by paying monthly premiums. This category of eligibility applies to someone who previously qualified for Medicare coverage on the basis of disability and continues to be disabled, but whose income exceeds the level allowed under Social Security for payment of disability income benefits to disabled persons and thus loses eligibility for Medicare benefits under the normal disability provisions.

Certain government employees who otherwise do not qualify for automatic Part A (Hospital Insurance) may also be able to enroll for Part A coverage by paying a premium.

For individuals who voluntarily enroll in Part A (Hospital Insurance) by paying a premium, the premium is $407 a month in 2015 (but see paragraph below for premium reduction exception). This premium amount increases by up to 10 percent for those who must pay a premium surcharge for late enrollment. (See Q 1061 and Q 1062.)

The Part A (Hospital Insurance) premium is reduced – by 45 percent (to $224 a month in 2015) – for individuals with credits for thirty or more quarters paid into the Social Security system (and certain current, surviving and divorced spouses of such individuals). The reduced premium amount increases by up to 10 percent for those who must pay a premium surcharge for late enrollment. (See Q 1061 and Q 1062.)

An individual who qualifies for the reduction is an individual who (1) has thirty or more quarters of coverage, (2) has been married for at least the previous one year period to a worker who has thirty or more quarters of coverage, (3) had been married to a worker who had thirty or more quarters of coverage for a period of at least one year before the death of the worker, (4) is divorced from, after at least ten years of marriage to, a worker who had thirty or more quarters of coverage at the time the divorce became final, or (5) is divorced from, after at least ten years of marriage to, a worker who subsequently died and who had thirty or more quarters of coverage at the time the divorce became final.

## ADMINISTRATION

### 1024. How do the Centers for Medicare & Medicaid Services (CMS) administer Part A (Hospital Insurance)?

The Centers for Medicare & Medicaid Services (CMS) enters into agreements with state agencies and with private insurance companies (such as Blue Cross and other health insurance organizations) to administer Part A (Hospital Insurance).

State agencies survey institutions to determine whether they meet the conditions for participation as a hospital, skilled nursing facility, home health agency, or hospice. They also help the institutions meet the conditions for participation.

Private insurance organizations contracting with CMS determine the amount of Part A (Hospital Insurance) benefits payable to hospitals, skilled nursing facilities, hospices, and home health agencies; pay Part A benefits to such providers out of funds advanced by the federal government; help the providers establish and maintain necessary financial records; serve as a channel of communication of information relating to Part A (Hospital Insurance); and audit records of hospitals, skilled nursing facilities, hospices, and home health agencies, as necessary, to insure that payment of Part A benefits is proper.

The private insurance organizations that contract with CMS to administer Part A are now called Medicare Administrative Contractors (MACs), but previously were referred to as fiscal intermediaries. Each provider of services can nominate a MAC to work with or can deal directly with the CMS. MACs are reimbursed for their reasonable costs of administration.

Most skilled nursing facilities and home health agencies must submit cost reports to MACs in a standardized electronic format. Hospitals have been required to submit cost reports in electronic format for a number of years. No payments are made to a provider unless it has furnished the information needed to determine the amount of payments due the provider. In general, providers submit this information through cost reports that cover a twelve-month period. A provider may request a delay or waiver of the electronic submission requirement by submitting a written request with supporting documentation to its MAC no later than thirty days after the end of its cost reporting period.

## 1025. What is the Prospective Payment System?

Medicare pays for most inpatient hospital care under the Prospective Payment System (PPS), called more precisely the Inpatient Prospective Payment System (IPPS). Under Medicare's PPS, hospitals are paid a predetermined rate per discharge for inpatient services furnished to Medicare beneficiaries. The predetermined rates are based on payment categories called Diagnosis-Related Groups (DRGs). In some cases, Medicare payment will be more than the hospital's cost; in other cases, the payment will be less than the hospital's costs. In special cases, where costs for necessary care are unusually high or the length of stay is unusually long, the hospital receives additional payment.

Reimbursement for inpatient hospital services is based on uniform sums for hundreds of DRGs (varying between rural and urban facilities). All other services are reimbursed on a reasonable cost basis.

Health Maintenance Organizations (HMOs) are covered by special reimbursement provisions to reward them financially because of what is believed to be their more favorable operating experience.

The PPS does not change the coverage available to a beneficiary under Part A (Hospital Insurance). For example, the PPS does not determine the length of a stay in the hospital or the extent of care a patient should receive, but is likely a factor that providers consider when providing covered care. The law requires participating hospitals to accept Medicare payments as payment in full, and those hospitals are prohibited from billing a Medicare patient for anything other than the applicable deductible and coinsurance amounts, plus any amounts due for noncovered items or services such as television, telephone or private duty nurses. Providers are limited by these Medicare payment rules even when the cost of a patient's care greatly exceeds the payment the hospital will receive from Medicare.

Despite the requirement to provide care for as long as it is medically necessary, the PPS provides hospitals with a possible incentive to refuse to admit patients for medical procedures that might not be reimbursed by Medicare. Hospitals also have an incentive to treat and discharge patients within or in less than the time frame established by the reimbursement rate for a particular DRG.

The CMS contracts with Quality Improvement Organizations (QIOs) in each state to conduct preadmission, continued stay, and retrospective reviews of the services delivered by a hospital. The reviews determine whether such services are reasonable and necessary. The QIO is also responsible for ensuring that the cost control incentives of the PPS do not adversely affect patients' access to hospitals or the quality of hospital care.

If the hospital, without consulting the QIO, recommends against admitting a patient, review of this decision may be obtained by the patient by writing the QIO in the patient's state. If the QIO participated in the preadmission denial of the patient, then a reconsideration of that denial may be requested by the patient.

For a detailed explanation of the appeal process, see Q 1139 through Q 1149.

### 1026. Is Part A (Hospital Insurance) a compulsory program?

Yes, in the sense that every person who works in employment or self-employment covered by the Social Security Act, or in employment covered by the Railroad Retirement Act, must pay the Part A (Hospital Insurance) tax, the system is compulsory. An employee working in covered employment does not have the ability to choose not to pay the Hospital Insurance (HI) tax that funds Part A. Coverage under Part A (Hospital Insurance) for eligible individuals is automatic, but an individual could choose to pay his medical expenses out-of-pocket and not take advantage of the benefits available under Part A. See Q 1018 for eligibility.

## FINANCING PART A (HOSPITAL INSURANCE)

### 1027. How is Part A (Hospital Insurance) financed?

Part A (Hospital Insurance) is financed by a separate Hospital Insurance (HI) tax imposed upon employers, employees, and the self-employed.[1] The tax must be paid by every individual, regardless of age, who is subject to the regular Social Security tax or to the Railroad Retirement tax. It must also be paid by all federal employees and by all state and local government employees (1) hired after March 1986, or (2) not covered by a state retirement system in conjunction with their employment (beginning July 2, 1991). The tax is imposed on all earnings. The rates of the HI tax are 1.45 percent each for employees and employers, and 2.90 percent for self-employed persons. There is an additional HI tax of 0.9 percent on earned income exceeding $200,000 for individuals and $250,000 for married couples filing jointly was introduced. Also there is a Medicare tax applied to investment income. A 3.8 percent tax is imposed on net investment income of single taxpayers with adjusted gross income above $200,000 and joint filers with AGI over $250,000.[2]

There is a special federal (and generally following through to state) income tax deduction of 50 percent of the OASDI/Hospital Insurance self-employment tax. This income tax deduction, which is available regardless of whether or not the taxpayer itemizes deductions, is designed to treat the self-employed in much the same manner as employees and employers are treated for Social Security and income tax purposes.

1. See 26 U.S.C. 1401(b), 3101(b).
2. 26 U.S.C. 1411.

# BENEFITS

## 1028. In general, what benefits are provided under Part A (Hospital Insurance)?

Part A (Hospital Insurance) provides the following main types of benefits:

(1) *Inpatient hospital care* for up to ninety days in each "benefit period" (also known as a "spell of illness"). The patient pays a deductible of $1,260 in 2015 for the first sixty days and coinsurance of $315 a day for each additional day up to a maximum of thirty days. In addition, each person has a nonrenewable lifetime "reserve" of sixty additional hospital days with coinsurance of $630 a day.

(2) *Posthospital extended care in a skilled nursing facility* for up to 100 days in each "benefit period." The patient pays nothing for the first twenty days in 2015. After twenty days the patient pays coinsurance of $157.20 a day for each additional day up to the maximum of 100 days (including the twenty days at no charge).

(3) The first 100 *posthospital home health service* visits following a hospital or skilled nursing facility stay. The services must be made under a plan of treatment established by a physician. There is no charge for home health care visits under Part A, except that there is 20 percent cost-sharing payable by the patient for durable medical equipment (other than the purchase of certain used items). The 100-visit and post-institutional care limits apply only to Medicare beneficiaries enrolled in both Parts A and B.

(4) *Hospice care* for terminally ill patients.

# QUALIFIED MEDICARE BENEFICIARIES

## 1029. When will a state pay Medicare costs for a person who is elderly or disabled with low income?

Federal law requires state Medicaid programs to pay Medicare costs for certain elderly and disabled persons with low incomes and very limited resources.

There are two programs to help people pay their Medicare expenses. One is called the Qualified Medicare Beneficiary (QMB) program. The other is called the Specified Low-Income Medicare Beneficiary (SLMB) program.

The QMB program is for persons with limited resources (assets) whose incomes are at or below the national poverty level. If an individual is a QMB, the program covers the cost of Medicare premiums, coinsurance, and deductibles that Medicare beneficiaries normally pay out of their own pockets. QMBs do not pay:

- Medicare's Part A hospital deductible
- the Part A daily coinsurance charges for extended hospital and skilled nursing facility stays;

- the Part B (Medical Insurance) premium, which is $104.90 per month for most individuals in 2015 (see Q 1065);
- the annual Part B deductible of $147 for 2015;
- the 20 percent coinsurance for services covered by Medicare Part B, depending on which doctor the patient goes to.

QMBs remain responsible for paying for medical supplies and services not covered by Medicare, such as routine physicals, dental care, hearing aids, and eyeglasses.

While the QMB programs helps those whose income is at or below the national poverty level, the SLMB program is for persons whose incomes are slightly higher than the poverty level, but not more than 20 percent higher (in other words, up to 120 percent of the federal poverty level). Individuals attempting to qualify for assistance under the SLMB program must satisfy the same asset limits as under the QMB program. SLMBs do not pay the monthly Part B premium, but otherwise remain responsible for Medicare's deductibles and coinsurance, as well as for charges for health care services and medical supplies not covered by Medicare.

## 1030. How does a person qualify for assistance under the QMB program?

The rules vary from state to state but **generally**, to qualify for assistance under the QMB program, a person must meet the following requirements:

(1) The person must be entitled to Part A (Hospital Insurance). If the person does not have Part A or does not know whether he or she is entitled to Part A, the individual should check with any Social Security Administration office or call 1-800-772-1213.

(2) The person's financial resources, such as bank accounts, stocks, and bonds, cannot exceed specified limits ($7,160 for an individual; $10,750 for a couple through 2015). Some things—the home you live in, one automobile, burial plots, home furnishings, personal jewelry, and life insurance—usually do not count as resources.

(3) The person's income must be at or below specified monthly limits ($993 per month for an individual, $1,331 per month for a couple, through 2015). The income limits are higher in Alaska and Hawaii. Income includes, but is not limited to, Social Security benefits, pensions, and wages. Interest payments and dividends can also count as income.

## 1031. What if a person's income is slightly higher than the poverty level?

If a person does not qualify for QMB assistance because his income is too high, he may be able to get help under the Specified Low-Income Beneficiary (SLMB) program. To qualify for SLMB assistance, a person must meet the following requirements:

(1) The person must be entitled to Hospital Insurance (Part A). If the person does not have Part A or does not know whether he is entitled to Part A, check with any Social Security Administration office or call 1-800-772-1213.

(2) A person's financial resources, such as bank accounts, stocks, and bonds, cannot exceed $7,160 for one person or $10,750 for a couple through early 2015. The following usually do not count as resources: the home you live in, one automobile, burial plots, home furnishings, personal jewelry, and life insurance.

(3) A person's income cannot exceed the national poverty level by more than 20 percent (in other words, up to 120 percent of the federal poverty level). This means the SLMB income limits through early 2015 are $1,187 monthly for an individual and $1,593 monthly for a couple.

### 1032. How does a person apply for QMB or SLMB assistance?

A person with Part A (Hospital Insurance) must file an application for Medicare assistance programs at a state, county, or local Medicaid office.

## INPATIENT HOSPITAL SERVICES

### 1033. Specifically, what inpatient hospital services are paid for under Part A (Hospital Insurance)?

Subject to a deductible and coinsurance, Medicare Part A (Hospital Insurance) pays for inpatient hospital service for up to ninety days in each "benefit period" (also called a "spell of illness"). Medicare will also pay (except for a coinsurance amount) for sixty additional hospital days over each person's lifetime (called the "lifetime reserve" days).

Medicare pays for hospital care if the patient meets the following four conditions: (1) a physician prescribes inpatient hospital care for treatment of an illness or injury, (2) the patient requires the kind of care that can be provided only as an inpatient in a hospital, (3) the hospital is participating in Medicare (except in certain emergency situations), and (4) the utilization review committee of the hospital, a Quality Improvement Organization (QIO), or the applicable Medicare Administrative Contractor (MAC) does not disapprove of the stay.

The patient must pay a deductible of $1,260 in 2015 for the first sixty days in each benefit period. If the stay is longer than sixty days during a benefit period, coinsurance of $315 a day must be paid for each additional day up to a maximum of thirty days.

Thus, a ninety-day stay in 2015 would cost the patient $10,710. After ninety days, the patient pays the full bill unless the lifetime reserve of sixty days is drawn upon. The patient must pay coinsurance of $630 a day for each of the sixty additional lifetime reserve days.

The coinsurance amounts are based on those in effect when services are furnished, rather than on those in effect at the beginning of the beneficiary's benefit period.

A "benefit period" is a way of measuring the patient's use of services under Part A (Hospital Insurance). A new ninety-day benefit period starts with each new spell of illness, beginning with the day a patient begins receiving inpatient hospital care. A benefit period ends when the patient has been out of a hospital or other facility primarily providing skilled nursing or rehabilitative services for sixty days in a row (including the day of discharge). After one benefit period has ended, another one will start whenever the patient again receives inpatient hospital care.

There is no limit to the number of ninety-day benefit periods a person can have in a lifetime (except in the case of hospitalization in a psychiatric hospital for mental illness), but the lifetime reserve of sixty days is not renewable. Also, special limited benefit periods apply to hospice care. (See Q 1041.)

*Example 1*. Mr. Smith enters the hospital on February 5. He is discharged on February 15. He has used 10 days of his first benefit period. Mr. Smith is not hospitalized again until August 20. Since more than 60 days have elapsed between his hospital stays, he begins a new benefit period in August. Part A (Hospital Insurance) will again pay for up to 60 days of inpatient hospital coverage, subject to Mr. Smith's payment of the deductible, and another 30 days subject to Mr. Smith's payment of coinsurance.

*Example 2*. Mr. Jones enters the hospital on September 14. He is discharged on September 24. He also has used 10 days of his first benefit period. He is then readmitted to the hospital on October 20. Because fewer than 60 days have elapsed between hospital stays, Mr. Jones remains in the same benefit period and will not be required to pay another hospital deductible when he re-enters the hospital on October 20. This means that the first day of his second admission is counted as the eleventh day of hospital care in that benefit period. Mr. Jones will not begin a new benefit period until he has been out of the hospital (and has not received any skilled care in a skilled nursing facility) for 60 consecutive days.

"Lifetime reserve" days include an extra sixty hospital days a patient can use if the patient has a long illness and needs to stay in the hospital for more than ninety days. A patient has only sixty reserve days in a lifetime. For example, if a patient uses eight reserve days in that individual's first hospital stay covered under Medicare Part A, he or she will have only fifty-two reserve days left to use during subsequent hospital stays, whether or not such stays fall within new benefit periods. A patient can decide when and whether to use lifetime reserve days.

If a patient does not want to use lifetime reserve days, the patient must tell the hospital in writing, either at the time of admission or at any time up to ninety days after discharge. If a patient uses reserve days and then decides that he or she did not want to use them, the patient must request approval from the hospital to have the lifetime reserve days restored. A patient must pay the full hospital costs for any day after the first ninety days in a benefit period if the patient is not using lifetime reserve days to offset the costs after the ninety days. During 2015, Part A (Hospital Insurance) pays for all covered services except $630 a day for each reserve day the patient uses.

Medicare beneficiaries have the right to receive all the hospital care that is necessary for the proper diagnosis and treatment of their illness or injury. Under federal law, a beneficiary's discharge date must be determined solely by medical needs, not by the diagnosis-related group (DRG) or Medicare payments. Beneficiaries have the right to be fully informed about decisions affecting their Medicare coverage and payment for their hospital stay and for any post-hospital services. They also have the right to request a review by a quality improvement organization (QIO) of any written notice of noncoverage they receive from the hospital stating that Medicare will no longer pay for their hospital care. QIOs are usually groups of physicians who are paid by the federal government to review medical necessity, appropriateness and quality of hospital treatment furnished to Medicare patients. (See Q 1025.)

The following inpatient services are covered by Part A (Hospital Insurance):

- *Bed and board in a semiprivate room* (two to four beds) or a ward (five or more beds). Part A (Hospital Insurance) will pay the cost of a private room only if it is required for medical reasons (e.g., the patient needs isolation for medical reasons or needs immediate hospitalization and no other accommodations are available). If the patient requests a private room, Part A will pay the cost of semiprivate accommodations; the patient must pay the extra charge for the private room. The patient or family must be told the amount of this extra charge when a private room is requested. Normally, Medicare patients are assigned to semiprivate rooms. Ward assignments are made only under extraordinary circumstances.

- *All meals*, including special diets.

- *Nursing services* provided by or under the supervision of licensed nursing personnel (other than the services of a private duty nurse or attendant).

- Services of the hospital's *medical social workers*.

- Use of regular hospital *equipment*, *supplies, and appliances*, such as oxygen tents, wheel chairs, crutches, casts, surgical dressings, splints, and hospital "admission packs" (toilet articles) when routinely furnished by the hospital to all patients. Certain equipment, supplies and appliances used by the patient in the hospital continue to be covered after the patient has been discharged. Examples include a cardiac pacemaker and an artificial limb.

- *Drugs and biologicals* ordinarily furnished by the hospital. A limited supply of drugs needed for use outside the hospital is also covered, but only if medically necessary in order to facilitate the patient's departure from the hospital and the supply is necessary until the patient can obtain a continuing supply. Drugs and biologicals that the hospital obtains for the patient from a private source (community pharmacy) are covered when the hospital is responsible for making payment to the supplier.

- *Diagnostic or therapeutic items and services* ordinarily furnished by the hospital or by others (including clinical psychologists, as defined by the Centers for Medicare & Medicaid Services), under arrangements made with the hospital.

- *Operating and recovery room costs*, including hospital costs for anesthesia services.

- Services of *interns and residents in training* under an approved teaching program.

- *Blood transfusions*, after the first three pints. Part A (Hospital Insurance) helps pay for blood (whole blood or units of packed red blood cells), blood components, and the cost of blood processing and administration. If the patient receives blood as an inpatient of a hospital or skilled nursing facility, Part A will pay for these blood costs, except for any nonreplacement fees charged for the first three pints of whole blood or units of packed red cells per calendar year. The nonreplacement fee is the amount that some hospitals and skilled nursing facilities charge for blood that is not replaced. The patient is responsible for the nonreplacement fees for the first three pints or units of blood furnished by a hospital or skilled nursing facility. If the patient is charged nonreplacement fees, the patient has the option of either paying the fees or having the blood replaced. If the patient chooses to have the blood replaced, the patient can either replace the blood personally or arrange to have another person or an organization replace it. A hospital or skilled nursing facility cannot charge a patient for any of the first three pints of blood that the patient replaces or arranges to replace. If the patient has already paid for or replaced blood under Part B (Medical Insurance) of Medicare during the calendar year, the patient does not have to meet those costs again under Part A.

- *X-rays* and other radiology services, including radiation therapy, billed by the hospital.
- *Lab tests.*
- *Respiratory or inhalation therapy.*
- *Independent clinical laboratory services* under arrangement with the hospital.
- *Alcohol detoxification and rehabilitation services* when furnished as inpatient hospital services. Alcohol detoxification and rehabilitation services may also be covered under Part B (Medical Insurance) when furnished as physician services.
- *Dental services* when the patient requires hospitalization because of the severity of the dental procedure or because of the patient's underlying medical condition and clinical status.
- Cost of *special care units*, such as an intensive care unit, coronary care unit, etc.
- *Rehabilitation services*, such as physical therapy, occupational therapy, and speech pathology services.
- *Appliances* (such as pacemakers, colostomy fittings, and artificial limbs) that are permanently installed while the patient is in the hospital.
- *Lung and heart-lung transplants*. (See Q 1099 for additional information on this coverage and what benefits are covered Part A and Part B.)

Part A (Hospital Insurance) does not pay for:

- Services of physicians and surgeons, including the services of pathologists, radiologists, anesthesiologists, and physiatrists. (Part A [Hospital Insurance] also does not pay for the services of a resident physician or intern other than those provided by an intern or resident in training under an approved teaching program.)

- Services of a private duty nurse or attendant, unless the patient's condition requires such services and the nurse or attendant is a bona fide employee of the hospital.
- Personal convenience (comfort) items supplied at the patient's request, such as television rental, radio rental, or telephone.
- The first three pints of whole blood (or packed red blood cells) received in a calendar year.
- Supplies, appliances and equipment for use outside the hospital, unless continued use is required (e.g., a pacemaker).

## 1034. Are inpatient hospital benefits provided for care in a psychiatric hospital?

Yes, but benefits for psychiatric hospital care are subject to a lifetime limit of 190 days. Furthermore, if the patient is already in a mental hospital when he becomes eligible for Medicare, the time spent there in the 150-day period before becoming eligible will be counted against the maximum of 150 days available in such cases (including any later period of such hospitalization when he has not been out of a mental hospital for at least sixty consecutive days between hospitalizations). This latter limitation does not apply to inpatient service in a general hospital for care other than psychiatric care.

## 1035. What special provisions apply to care in Religious Nonmedical Health Care Institutions (RNHCI)?

A Religious Nonmedical Health Care Institution (RNHCI) is an institution that provides nonmedical nursing items and services to Medicare beneficiaries who choose to rely solely upon a religious method of healing and who feel that acceptance of medical services would be inconsistent with their religious beliefs. In general, these institutions can participate in Medicare as hospitals, and the regular coverages and exclusions relating to inpatient hospital care will apply. Thus, the patient pays a $1,260 deductible in 2015 for the first sixty days, and coinsurance of $315 a day in 2015 for the next thirty days (plus $615 a day in 2015 for the sixty lifetime reserve days). A RNHCI may also be paid as a skilled nursing facility, but extended care benefits will be paid for only thirty days in a calendar year (instead of the usual 100 days), and the patient must pay the coinsurance amount ($157.20 a day in 2015) for each day of service (instead of only for each day after the twentieth day).

A federal district court ruled in 1996 that certain Christian Science facilities were not eligible for Medicare and Medicaid payments. In response to the ruling, Congress deleted any references to Christian Science sanatoriums in the Social Security Act and replaced them with the term "religious nonmedical health care institutions." RNHCI are subject to detailed eligibility criteria to protect the health and safety of patients and to special limits on the total amount of reimbursement available through Medicare.

## 1036. Can patients choose their own hospitals?

Except for certain emergency cases, Medicare will make payments only to "qualified" hospitals, skilled nursing facilities, home health agencies, and hospices.

Medicare generally does not pay for hospital or medical services outside the United States. (Puerto Rico, the U.S. Virgin Islands, Guam, American Samoa, and the Northern Mariana Islands are considered part of the United States.)

Medicare will pay for both emergency and nonemergency inpatient hospital care in a foreign hospital if the foreign hospital is closer to, or substantially more accessible than the nearest U.S. hospital (that is adequately equipped and available to handle the patient's care) to the patient's U.S. residence. Medicare also authorizes payment for emergency care in a Canadian hospital when the emergency occurred in transit between Alaska and another U.S. state without unreasonable delay and by the most direct route. Necessary physicians' services in connection with Mexican or Canadian hospitalization that qualifies for Medicare coverage are also authorized under Medicare. If a person receives emergency treatment in a Canadian or Mexican hospital or lives near a Canadian or Mexican hospital, he should have the hospital help him contact a Medicare administrative contractor.

## 1037. How is it certified that hospitalization is required?

CMS requires that all inpatient hospital admissions have an initial "certification" that states, among other details, that the hospitalization is reasonable and necessary and expected to last at least two "midnights." CMS provided a transition period for compliance through 2013.

## 1038. What must a hospital do to qualify for Medicare payments?

Generally, a hospital must meet certain standards and enter into a Medicare participation agreement in order to be paid by Medicare. However, Medicare may pay nonparticipating hospitals in certain emergency cases.

# HOSPICE CARE

## 1039. What is hospice care?

Hospice care is an approach to treatment that recognizes that the impending death of an individual warrants a change in focus from curative care to palliative care (relief of pain and other uncomfortable symptoms). The goal of hospice care is to help terminally ill individuals continue life with minimal disruption to normal activities. A hospice uses an interdisciplinary approach to deliver medical, social, psychological, emotional, and spiritual services through the use of a broad spectrum of professional and other caregivers, with the goal of making the individual as physically and emotionally comfortable as possible. Counseling and respite services are available to the family of the hospice patient. Hospice programs consider both the patient and the family as a unit of care.

Medicare Part A (Hospital Insurance) provides coverage for hospice care for terminally ill Medicare beneficiaries who elect to receive care from a participating hospice.

A hospice is an organization that is primarily engaged in providing pain relief, symptom management, and supportive services to terminally ill people.

## 1040. How is hospice care covered under Part A (Hospital Insurance)?

Under the Part A (Hospital Insurance) hospice benefit, Medicare pays for hospice services every day and also permits a hospice to provide appropriate custodial care, including homemaker services and counseling. Hospice care under Medicare includes both home care and inpatient care, when needed, and a variety of services not otherwise covered under Medicare (such as custodial care).

Medicare payments to a hospice are based on one of four prospectively determined rates for each day in which a qualified Medicare beneficiary is under the care of the hospice. The four rate categories are routine home care, continuous home care, inpatient respite care, and general inpatient care. Payment rates are adjusted to reflect local differences in area wage levels.

Hospice care is covered under Part A (Hospital Insurance) when the beneficiary (1) is eligible for Part A benefits, (2) is certified by a physician as terminally ill (i.e., have a life expectancy of six months or less), and (3) files a statement electing to waive all other Medicare coverage for hospice care from hospice programs other than the one chosen, and elects not to receive other services related to treatment of the terminal condition. (The beneficiary can later revoke the election.)

The following are covered hospice services:

- Nursing care provided by or under the supervision of a registered professional nurse.
- Medical social services provided by a social worker under a physician's direction.
- Counseling (including dietary counseling) with respect to care of the terminally ill patient and adjustment to the patient's approaching death.
- Short-term inpatient care (including both respite care and procedures necessary for pain control and acute and chronic symptom management) provided in a participating hospice, hospital, or skilled nursing facility. The respite care may be provided only on an intermittent, nonroutine, and occasional basis and may not be provided consecutively over longer than five days.
- Medical appliances and supplies.
- Services of a home health aide and homemaker services.
- Drugs, including outpatient drugs for pain relief and symptom management.

- Physical therapy, occupational therapy, and speech-language pathology services to control symptoms or to enable the patient to maintain activities of daily living and basic functional skills.

Services of a home health aide, homemaker services, and nursing care provided by or under the supervision of a registered professional nurse, may be provided on a twenty-four-hour, continuous basis only during periods of crisis and only as necessary to maintain the terminally ill patient at home.

The definition of hospice care also includes any other item or service which is specified in the patient's plan of care and for which Medicare may pay.

A "hospice program" for Medicare purposes is a public agency or private organization that is primarily engaged in providing the care and services listed above and makes the services available (as needed) on a twenty-four-hour basis. A hospice program also provides bereavement counseling for the immediate family of the terminally ill patient. The care and services must be provided in the patient's home, on an outpatient basis, and on a short-term inpatient basis. The nursing, physician, counseling, and medical social service benefits must be provided directly on a routine basis. The remaining hospice benefits may be provided through arrangements with other hospice programs (provided the agency or organization maintains professional management responsibility for all services).

The Centers for Medicare & Medicaid Services (CMS) may waive certain service requirements for hospices not located in urbanized areas that can demonstrate that they have been unable, despite diligent efforts, to recruit appropriate personnel. For these hospices, CMS may waive the provision requiring physical or occupational therapy or speech-language pathology services and dietary counseling.

A hospice program must have an interdisciplinary group of personnel (at least one physician, one registered nurse, one social worker, and one pastoral or other counselor) to establish the policies of the program and provide the required care and services. The group must maintain central clinical records on all patients, utilize volunteers, and is required to continue hospice care for any patient who is unable to pay for such care.

## 1041. What is the hospice benefit period?

The benefit period consists of two ninety-day periods followed by an unlimited number of sixty-day periods. At the beginning of the first ninety-day hospice benefit period, both the beneficiary's attending physician (if any) and the medical director or physician member of the hospice interdisciplinary team must certify in writing that the beneficiary is terminally ill. The medical director or physician member of the hospice interdisciplinary team must re-certify that the beneficiary is terminally ill at the beginning of all successive benefit periods.

## 1042. What does the patient pay for hospice care?

There are no deductibles under the hospice benefit. The beneficiary does not pay for Medicare-covered services for the terminal illness, except for small coinsurance amounts for outpatient drugs and inpatient respite care. For outpatient prescription drugs, the patient is responsible for about 5 percent of the cost of drugs or five dollars, whichever is less. For inpatient respite care, the patient pays 5 percent of the amount paid by Medicare for a respite care day, but the total of all coinsurance for respite care may not exceed the Medicare Part A inpatient hospital deductible for the year in which the hospice period began.

### 1043. How is respite care covered?

Respite care as an inpatient in a hospice (to give a period of relief to the family providing home care for the patient) is limited to no more than five days in a row. Respite care requires coinsurance in the amount of 5 percent of the amount that Medicare pays for the respite care. The total respite care coinsurance amount may not exceed the inpatient hospital deductible for the year in which the hospice period began.

## SKILLED NURSING FACILITY CARE

### 1044. What is a qualified skilled nursing facility?

For purposes of Medicare Part A (Hospital Insurance), a skilled nursing facility is a specially qualified facility that specializes in skilled care. It has the staff and equipment to provide skilled nursing care or skilled rehabilitative services and other related health services.

A skilled nursing facility may be a skilled nursing home, or a distinct part of an institution, such as a ward or wing of a hospital, or a section of a facility another part of which is an old-age home. Not all nursing homes will qualify; those which offer only custodial care are excluded. The facility must be primarily engaged in providing skilled nursing care or rehabilitation services for injured, disabled or sick persons. Skilled nursing care means care that can be performed only by, or under the supervision of, licensed nursing personnel. Skilled rehabilitation services may include such services as physical therapy performed by, or under the supervision of, a professional therapist. Skilled nursing care and skilled rehabilitation services must be needed and received on a daily basis (at least five days a week) or the patient is not eligible for Medicare coverage.

At least one registered nurse must be employed full-time, and adequate nursing service (which may include services by practical nurses) must be provided at all times. Every patient must be under the supervision of a physician, and a physician must always be available for emergency care. Generally, the facility must be certified by the state and meet all state licensing requirements. The facility also must have a written agreement with a hospital that is participating in the Medicare program for the transfer of patients.

Medicare also requires that qualified skilled nursing facilities provide patients with the following rights: (1) equal access and admission, (2) notice of rights and services, (3) transfer and discharge rights, (4) the right to pretransfer and predischarge notice, (5) access and visitation rights, (6) rights relating to the protection of resident funds, and (7) certain other specified rights.

An institution which is primarily for the care and treatment of mental diseases or tuberculosis is not a skilled nursing facility.

Many nursing homes in the United States do not qualify as "skilled nursing facilities" for purposes of Medicare and are not certified to provide services reimbursed by Medicare. In some facilities, only certain portions participate in Medicare.

## 1045. Does Part A (Hospital Insurance) pay for custodial care in a skilled nursing facility?

No. Medicare does not pay for custodial care when that is the only kind of care needed. Care is considered custodial when it is primarily for the purpose of helping the patient with daily living or meeting personal needs, and could be provided safely and reasonably by people without professional skills or training. For example, custodial care includes help in walking, getting in and out of bed, bathing, dressing, eating, and taking medicine.

## 1046. Do most nursing home residents qualify for Part A (Hospital Insurance) coverage?

Many residents of nursing homes will not qualify for Medicare coverage, because coverage is restricted to patients in need of skilled nursing and rehabilitative services on a daily basis. Many nursing home residents are in need primarily of custodial care, which is not covered by Medicare. The initial determination of Medicare coverage is made by the nursing home, but the nursing home cannot charge the patient for care provided before it notifies the patient in writing that it believes Medicare will not pay for the care. The patient may not challenge the nursing home's noncoverage determination until a claim has been submitted to and denied by the Medicare intermediary. The patient does have the right to require a nursing home to submit its claim to the Medicare intermediary so that the intermediary can determine if the nursing home was correct in denying coverage.

## 1047. Under what circumstances does a patient qualify for skilled nursing facility benefits under Part A (Hospital Insurance)?

In order to qualify for skilled nursing facility benefits under Part A (Hospital Insurance), the patient generally must meet all of these five conditions:

(1) The patient's condition requires daily skilled nursing or skilled rehabilitative services which, as a practical matter, can only be provided in a skilled nursing facility.

(2) The patient has been in a hospital at least three days in a row (not counting the day of discharge) before being admitted to a participating skilled nursing facility.

(3) The patient is admitted to the skilled nursing facility within a short time (generally within thirty days) after leaving the hospital.

(4) The patient's care in the skilled nursing facility is for a condition that was treated in the hospital, or for a condition that arose while receiving care in the skilled nursing facility for a condition which was treated in the hospital.

(5) A medical professional certifies that the patient needs, and receives, skilled nursing or skilled rehabilitation services (posthospital extended care) on a daily basis.

If a patient leaves a skilled nursing facility and is readmitted within thirty days, the patient does not need to have a new three-day stay in a hospital for care to be covered.

Except for a coinsurance amount payable by the patient after the first twenty days, Part A (Hospital Insurance) will pay the reasonable cost of post-hospital care in a skilled nursing facility for up to 100 days in a benefit period.

## 1048. What items and services generally are (and are not) covered under Part A (Hospital Insurance) when provided in a participating skilled nursing facility?

The following items and services are covered when provided in a participating skilled nursing facility:

- Bed and board in a semiprivate room (two to four beds in a room), unless the patient's condition requires isolation or no semiprivate rooms are available.
- Nursing care provided by, or under the supervision of, a registered nurse (but not private-duty nursing).
- Drugs, biologicals, supplies (such as splints and casts), appliances (such as wheelchairs) and equipment for use in the facility.
- Medical social services, including the assessment of the patient's medical and nursing requirements, the patient's financial resources, home situation, and the community services available to him. Such services may also include the assessment of the social and emotional factors related to the patient's illness, and the patient's need for care, response to treatment, and adjustment to care in the skilled nursing facility. Appropriate action to obtain case work services to assist in resolving problems in these areas is covered by Medicare.
- Medical services of interns and residents in training under an approved teaching program of a hospital.
- Other diagnostic or therapeutic services provided by a hospital with which the facility has a transfer agreement.
- Rehabilitation services, such as physical, occupational, and speech therapy, furnished by the skilled nursing facility, or by others under arrangements made by the skilled nursing facility.
- All meals, including special diets furnished by the facility.
- Blood transfusions, other than the first three pints of blood.
- Such other health services as are generally provided by a skilled nursing facility.

The following services are not covered even if provided by the skilled nursing facility:

- Personal convenience (comfort) items that the patient requests, such as a television, radio, or telephone
- Private duty nurses or attendants
- Any extra charges for a private room, unless it is determined to be medically necessary
- Custodial care, including assistance with the activities of daily living (i.e., walking, getting in and out of bed, bathing, dressing, and feeding), special diets, and supervision of medication that can usually be self-administered, when that is the only care required by the patient
- Physician's services provided to a patient while the patient is in a skilled nursing facility are covered by Part B (Medical Insurance), not Part A (Hospital Insurance)

## 1049. What provisions are made under Part A (Hospital Insurance) for care in a skilled nursing facility?

Federal regulations include the following services for skilled rehabilitation and nursing care: (1) insertion and sterile irrigation and replacement of catheters, (2) application of dressing involving prescription medications and aseptic techniques, (3) treatment of extensive bed sores or other widespread skin disorders, (4) therapeutic exercises or activities supervised or performed by a qualified occupational or physical therapist, (5) training to restore a patient's ability to walk, and (6) range of motion exercises that are part of a physical therapist's active treatment to restore a patient's mobility.

A number of services involving the development, management and evaluation of a patient care plan may qualify as skilled services. These services are "skilled" if the patient's condition requires the services to be provided or supervised by a professional to meet the patient's needs, promote recovery, and ensure the patient's medical safety. For example, a patient with a history of diabetes and heart problems, who is recovering from a broken arm, may require skin care, medication, a special diet, an exercise program to preserve muscle tone, and observation to detect signs of deterioration or complications. Although none of these required services necessarily falls within the definition of "skilled" on its own, the combination, provided by a professional, may be considered "skilled."

To qualify for skilled nursing facility reimbursement, skilled physical therapy must be (1) specifically related to a physician's active treatment plan, (2) of a complexity, or involving a condition, that requires a physical therapist, (3) necessary to establish a safe maintenance program or provided where the patient's condition will improve within a predictable time, and (4) of the necessary frequency and duration.

## 1050. How much does the patient pay for skilled nursing facility care?

The patient pays nothing for the first twenty days of covered services in each spell of illness; after twenty days, coinsurance is payable for each additional day, up to a maximum of eighty days. For a patient in a skilled nursing facility in 2015, the coinsurance is $157.50 a day.

Thus, a 100-day stay in a skilled nursing facility during 2015 will cost the patient $12,600.

There is no lifetime limit on the amount of skilled nursing facility care provided under Part A (Hospital Insurance). Except for the coinsurance (which must be paid after the first twenty days in each spell of illness), Medicare will cover the cost of 100 days' posthospital care in each benefit period, regardless of how many benefit periods the person may have. After 100 days of coverage, the patient must pay the full cost of skilled nursing facility care.

Skilled nursing facilities cannot require a patient to pay a deposit or other payment as a condition of admission to the facility unless it is clear that services are not covered under Medicare.

### 1051. When can payment be made for skilled nursing care under Part A (Hospital Insurance)?

Subject to the patient's coinsurance obligation after the first twenty days, Medicare Part A (Hospital Insurance) will be made for skilled nursing care only if the following conditions are met:

(1) The beneficiary files a written request for payment (another person may sign the request if it is impracticable for the patient to sign).

(2) A physician certifies that the patient needs skilled nursing care on an inpatient basis. Recertification is required for extended stays. Part A (Hospital Insurance) will not pay for a person's stay if the individual needs skilled nursing or rehabilitation services only occasionally, such as once or twice a week, or if a person does not need to be in a skilled nursing facility to obtain skilled rehabilitation services. Part A (Hospital Insurance) also generally will not pay for a person's continued stay in a skilled nursing facility if the rehabilitation services are no longer improving his or her condition and could be carried out by someone other than a physical therapist or physical therapist assistant.

(3) The facility is "participating" under Medicare law.

See Q 1047 for more information on skilled nursing care.

## HOME HEALTH CARE

### 1052. When are postinstitutional home health services covered under Part A (Hospital Insurance)?

If a person needs postinstitutional skilled health care in his or her home for the treatment of an illness or injury, Medicare pays for covered home health services furnished by a participating home health agency. In general, Part A (Hospital Insurance) covers the cost of 100 home health visits made on an "intermittent" basis during a home health spell of illness under a plan of treatment established by a physician. However, patients may be eligible for additional home health benefits under Part B (see Q 1088).

A "home health agency" is a public agency or private organization that:

(1) is primarily engaged in providing skilled nursing services and other therapeutic services;

(2) has policies, established by a group of professional personnel, including one or more physicians and one or more registered professional nurses, to govern the services which it provides, and provides for supervision of its services by a physician or registered professional nurse;

(3) maintains clinical records on all patients;

(4) is licensed pursuant to applicable state and local law;

(5) has in effect an overall plan and budget;

(6) meets additional requirements and conditions of participation as the Centers for Medicare & Medicaid Services (CMS) finds necessary in the interest of the health and safety of individuals who are furnished services by the home health agency;

(7) meets additional requirements as specified by CMS for the effective and efficient operation of the program.

A "home health agency" does not include any agency or organization that is primarily for the care and treatment of mental diseases.

A number of rules and procedures have been established to stop fraud and abuse, including regulations requiring all home health agencies serving Medicare to obtain surety bonds. Agencies must be bonded and must provide quality care to at least ten patients before applying to provide care to Medicare patients. At least seven of the ten patients must be receiving active care at the time the agency applies to participate in Medicare.

## 1053. What conditions must be met for Part A (Hospital Insurance) to cover home health visits?

In general, Part A (Hospital Insurance) pays for the first 100 home health visits in a "home health spell of illness" only if all six of the following conditions are met:

(1) The care is postinstitutional home health services

(2) The care includes intermittent skilled nursing care, physical therapy, or speech therapy

(3) The person is confined at home

(4) The person is under the care of a physician who determines the need for home health care and sets up a home health plan for the person

(5) The home health agency providing services participates in Medicare

(6) The services are provided on a visiting basis in the person's home or, if it is necessary to use equipment that cannot be readily made available in the home, on an outpatient basis in a hospital, skilled nursing facility, or licensed rehabilitation center

The term "postinstitutional home health services" means home health services furnished to an individual:

(1) After discharge from a hospital or rural primary care hospital in which the individual was an inpatient for at least three consecutive days before discharge. Home health services must be initiated within fourteen days after the date of discharge.

(2) After discharge from a skilled nursing facility in which the individual was provided posthospital extended care services covered by Medicare. Home health services must be initiated within fourteen days after the date of discharge.

The term "home health spell of illness" means a period of consecutive days (1) beginning with the first day a person is furnished postinstitutional home health services (in a month in which the person is entitled to benefits under Part A) and (2) ending with the close of the first period of sixty consecutive days thereafter for which the person is neither an inpatient in a hospital or skilled nursing facility nor provided home health services.

"Part-time or intermittent services" is defined as skilled nursing and home health services (combined) furnished any number of days per week, for less than eight hours per day and twenty-eight or fewer hours per week (or, subject to review on a case-by-case basis as to the need for care, less than eight hours each day and tthirty-five or fewer hours per week).

"Intermittent" is defined as skilled nursing care provided on fewer than seven days each week, or less than eight hours each day (combined) for twenty-one days or less (with extensions in exceptional circumstances when the need for additional care is finite and predictable).

A physician must certify that the patient is under a physician's care, under a plan of care established and periodically reviewed no less frequently than every two months by a doctor, confined to the home, and in need of skilled nursing care on an intermittent basis or physical or speech therapy, or has a continued need for occupational therapy when eligibility for home health services has been established (because of a prior need for intermittent skilled nursing care, speech therapy, or physical therapy in the current or prior certification period).

Home health aides, whether employed directly by a home health agency or made available through contract with another entity, must successfully complete a training and competency evaluation program or competency evaluation program approved by CMS.

Generally, a physician may not set up a home health care plan for a patient with any agency in which the physician has a significant ownership interest or a significant financial or contractual relationship. However, a physician who has a financial interest in an agency which is a sole community health agency may carry out certification and plan of care functions for patients served by that agency.

## 1054. What postinstitutional home health services are covered under Part A (Hospital Insurance)?

In general, the following postinstitutional home health services are covered under Part A (Hospital Insurance):

- Part-time or intermittent skilled nursing care (See Q 1053)
- Physical therapy
- Speech therapy

If a person needs part-time or intermittent skilled nursing care, physical therapy, or speech therapy, Medicare also pays for:

- Part-time or intermittent services of home health aides. Covered services include, but are not limited to (1) personal care, (2) simple dressing changes that do not require the skills of a licensed nurse, (3) assistance with medications that are ordinarily self-administered and that do not require a licensed nurse, (4) assistance with activities supportive of skilled therapy services, and (5) routine care of prosthetic devices.
- Medical social services.
- Medical supplies, including catheters, catheter supplies, ostomy bags, and ostomy care supplies.
- Durable medical equipment, including iron lungs, oxygen tents, hospital beds, and wheelchairs (subject to a 20 percent coinsurance as described below).
- Occupational therapy.

The patient generally pays nothing under Part A (Hospital Insurance) for the first 100 home health visits; Medicare pays the full approved cost of all covered home health visits. The patient may be charged, however, for any services or costs that Medicare does not cover. Also, if a patient needs durable medical equipment, the patient is responsible for a 20 percent coinsurance payment for the equipment. The home health agency will submit claims for payment. The patient does not submit bills to Medicare.

Both Part A (Hospital Insurance) and Part B (Medical Insurance) cover home health visits, but for beneficiaries covered by both Parts A and B, Part A pays for the first 100 visits following a hospital or skilled nursing facility stay while Part B pays for home health services without regard to a preceding hospital or skilled nursing facility stay.

Medicare does not cover home care services furnished primarily to assist people in meeting personal, family, and domestic needs. These noncovered services include general household services such as laundry, meal preparation, shopping, or assisting in bathing, dressing, or other personal needs.

Home health services generally not covered by Medicare also include:

- twenty-four-hour-a-day nursing care at home;
- drugs and biologicals;
- blood transfusions;
- meals delivered to the home;
- homemaker services; and
- venipuncture (drawing of blood for the purpose of obtaining a blood sample), if venipuncture is the only skilled service needed by the beneficiary.

Although a patient in general must be "confined" to home to be eligible for home health care benefits, payment will be made for services furnished at a hospital, skilled nursing facility, or rehabilitation center, if the patient's condition requires the use of equipment that ordinarily cannot be taken to the patient's home. Medicare usually will not pay the patient's transportation costs.

A patient is considered "confined to the home" if he or she has a condition, due to illness or injury, that restricts the ability to leave home except with the assistance of another person or the aid of a supportive device (such as crutches, a cane, a wheelchair, or a walker), or if the patient has a condition such that leaving home is medically unsafe. Although a patient does not have to be bedridden to be considered "confined to the home," the condition should be such that there exists a normal inability to leave home, that leaving home requires a considerable and taxing effort, and that absences from home are infrequent or of relatively short duration, or are attributable to the need to receive medical treatment.

For these purposes "infrequent" means an average of five or fewer absences per calendar month, excluding absences to receive medical treatment that cannot be furnished in the home. "Short duration" means an average of three or fewer hours per absence from the home within a calendar month, excluding absences to receive medical treatment that cannot be furnished in the home. Absences for medical treatment must be (1) based on and in conformance with a physician's order, (2) by or under the supervision of a licensed health professional, and (3) for the purpose of diagnosis or treatment of an illness or injury.

Examples of patients qualifying as homebound include (1) a person paralyzed from a stroke who is confined to a wheelchair and who requires crutches in order to walk, (2) a person who is blind or senile and requires the assistance of another person in leaving his or her residence, (3) a person who has lost the use of upper extremities and is unable to open doors, use stairways, etc., and, therefore, requires the assistance of another person to leave his or her residence, and (4) a person with a psychiatric problem if the person's illness is manifested in part by a refusal to leave his or her home environment, or is of such a nature that it would not be considered safe for the patient to leave home unattended, even if the patient has no physical limitations.

## 1055. How does Medicare pay the costs of home health services?

The Centers for Medicare & Medicaid Services (CMS) have established a prospective payment system for all costs of home health services. In defining a payment amount under a prospective payment system, CMS considers an appropriate unit of service and the number, type, and duration of visits provided within that unit of service. CMS also considers potential changes in the mix of services provided within a unit and their cost. The general design of a unit of service is to provide for continued access to quality services. All bills for service must be submitted by the home health agency for payment and not by any other person or entity.

Prospective payment amounts are intended to be standardized in a manner that eliminates the effect of variations in relative case mix and wage levels among different home health agencies in a budget-neutral manner. Under the system, CMS may recognize regional differences or differences based upon whether the services or agencies are in an urbanized area. The standard prospective payment amount (or amounts) is adjusted for each fiscal year.

# GENERAL INFORMATION

## 1056. Does Part A (Hospital Insurance) pay the cost of outpatient hospital services?

No. Outpatient diagnostic and treatment services are covered under Part B (Medical Insurance), not Part A (Hospital Insurance). (See Q 1060 through Q 1108.)

## 1057. Does a person need to be in financial need to receive Part A (Hospital Insurance) benefits?

No. Medicare benefits are not subject to any means testing.

## 1058. Will the deductible and coinsurance amounts paid by patients for Part A (Hospital Insurance) remain the same in future years?

No. The $1,260 initial deductible for Part A inpatient hospital care for 2015 is based on the 1966-68 figure of forty dollars and on increases in average per diem inpatient hospital cost since 1966 (with some legislative adjustments). Further adjustments have been made since 1987 based on increases in average national hospital costs. The daily coinsurance amounts for inpatient hospital care are based on a percentage of the deductible. Thus, the daily coinsurance for inpatient hospital care for the sixty-first through ninetieth days in a benefit period is one-fourth of the initial deductible ($315 in 2015). The coinsurance for each lifetime reserve day (a total of sixty in a lifetime), used after the ninetieth inpatient hospital stay day is half of the inpatient care deductible ($630 in 2015). The daily coinsurance for posthospital extended care in a skilled nursing facility after the first twenty days of such care (up to the maximum of 100 days, including the first twenty) is one-eighth of the inpatient hospital stay deductible (thus, $157.20 in 2015).

## 1059. What is Medicare's position regarding treatment of a patient with a living will or durable power of attorney for health care?

Medicare requires that all hospitals, skilled nursing facilities, nursing facilities, providers of home health care or personal care services, hospices, and prepaid health plans to provide a Medicare patient with written information concerning rights under state law to make decisions concerning medical care, including the right to accept or refuse medical or surgical treatment and the right to formulate – at the patient's option – advance directives. The regulations do not apply to providers of outpatient hospital services.

The term "advance directive" is defined as a written instrument, such as a living will or durable power of attorney for health care, recognized under state law, relating to the provision of health care when the individual is incapacitated. No individual is required to execute an advance directive.

The provider must (1) inform the individual, in writing, of state laws regarding advance directives, (2) inform the individual, in writing, of the policies of the provider regarding the implementation of advance directives, including (if permitted under state law) a clear and precise explanation of any objection a provider may have, on the basis of conscience, to honoring an individual's directive, (3) document in the individual's medical record whether or not the individual has executed an advance directive, (4) educate staff on issues concerning advance directives, and (5) provide for community education on issues concerning advance directives.

Written information on advance directives must be provided to an individual upon each admission to a medical facility and each time an individual comes under the care of a home health agency, personal care provider, or hospice. For example: if a person is admitted as an inpatient to a hospital and then to a nursing home, both the hospital and the nursing home are required to provide information on advance directives to the individual. If the patient is incapacitated at the time of admission and is unable to receive information or articulate whether or not an advance directive has been executed, the facility may give advance directive information to the patient's family or surrogate.

All patients are generally entitled to the medically necessary care ordered by a physician and that a provider, under normal procedures, would be required to furnish; providers cannot delay or withhold such care because the individual has not executed an advance directive or the provider is waiting for an advance directive to be executed. However, once a provider receives documentation that an advance directive has been executed, the directive takes precedence over the facility's normal procedures, to the extent required by state law.

A health care provider is not required to implement an advance directive if, as a matter of conscience, the provider cannot implement an advance directive and state law allows any health care provider to conscientiously object. The provider must inform individuals that complaints concerning noncompliance with the advance directive requirements may be filed with the state survey and certification agency.

# PART B: MEDICAL INSURANCE

## ELIGIBILITY

### 1060. Who is eligible for Part B (Medical Insurance) benefits?

Anyone who is eligible for Part A (Hospital Insurance), whether automatically or through payment of Part A premiums (including disabled individuals who lose entitlement to automatic Part A benefits but may still enroll by paying premiums), may enroll in Part B (Medical Insurance). Even if a person does not qualify for Part A benefits, that person may enroll in Part B (Medical Insurance) as long as he is at least age sixty-five, a U.S. resident and either (1) a U.S. citizen or (2) an alien lawfully admitted for permanent residence who has resided in the United States continuously during the five years immediately prior to the month in which he applies for enrollment in Part B.

See Q 1018 for eligibility rules for Part A (Hospital Insurance).

### 1061. How does a person enroll in Part B (Medical Insurance)?

Individuals who are receiving Social Security and Railroad Retirement benefits are enrolled automatically in Part B (Medical Insurance) when they become entitled to Part A (Hospital Insurance). They may, however, elect not to be covered by Part B (Medical Insurance) by signing a form sent to them by the Social Security Administration. Others may enroll online through the Social Security Administration's website (www.ssa.gov) or at the nearest Social Security office. An individual who already has Part A coverage and wants to add Part B coverage may also call 1-800-772-1213.

The initial enrollment period for Part B (Medical Insurance) is a period of seven full calendar months, the beginning and end of which is determined for each person by the day on which he is first eligible to enroll. The initial enrollment period begins on the first day of the third month before the month a person first becomes eligible to enroll and ends with the close of the last day of the third month following the month a person first becomes eligible to enroll. For example, if the person's sixty-fifth birthday is April 10, 2015, that person's initial enrollment period begins January 1, 2015 and ends July 31, 2015.

If a person decides not to enroll in the initial enrollment period, that individual may enroll later during a general enrollment period. There is a general enrollment period from January 1 through March 31 of each year, with such enrollment effective the following July 1. Under certain circumstances, a person who does not enroll during his initial enrollment period may be able to enroll during a special enrollment period. (See Q 1062.) The special enrollment period is a period provided by statute to enable certain individuals to enroll in Medicare without waiting for the general enrollment period.

In order to obtain coverage at the earliest possible date, a person must enroll before the beginning of the month in which he reaches age sixty-five. For a person who enrolls during the initial enrollment period, the effective date of coverage is as follows:

(1) If the person enrolls before the month in which age sixty-five is reached, coverage will commence the first day of the month in which age sixty-five is reached.

(2) If the person enrolls during the month in which age sixty-five is reached, coverage will commence the first day of the following month.

(3) If the person enrolls in the month after the month in which age sixty-five is reached, coverage will commence the first day of the second month after the month of enrollment.

(4) If the person enrolls more than one month (but at least within three months) after the month in which age sixty-five is reached, coverage will commence the first day of the third month following the month of enrollment.

An eight-month special enrollment period is provided if Medicare has been the secondary payer of benefits for individuals age sixty-five and older who are covered under an employer group health plan because of current employment. The special enrollment period generally begins with the month after the month in which coverage under the private plan ends. Coverage under Part B (Medical Insurance) will begin with the first day of the month after the month in which coverage under the private plan ends if the individual enrolls in that month or with the first day of the month after the month of enrollment if the individual enrolls during the balance of the special enrollment period. (See Q 1062.)

## 1062. What if a person declines to enroll during the Part B (Medical Insurance) initial enrollment period?

Anyone who is eligible but fails to enroll in Part B (Medical Insurance) during the initial enrollment period may enroll during a general enrollment period. There are general enrollment periods each year from January 1st through March 31st. Coverage begins the following July 1st.

The Part B premium will be higher for a person who fails to enroll within twelve months, or who drops out of the plan and later re-enrolls. The monthly premium will be increased by 10 percent for each full twelve months during which such an individual could have been, but was not, enrolled.

If a person declines to enroll (or terminates enrollment) at a time when Medicare is secondary payer to an employer group health plan covering that person, the months in which the individual is covered under the employer group health plan (based on current employment) will not be counted as months during which the individual could have been but was not enrolled in Part B (Medical Insurance) for the purpose of determining if the premium amount should be increased above the basic rate. Individuals to whom this applies may later enroll during a "special enrollment period." The special enrollment period lasts for eight months after the earlier of the termination of the individual's group health plan coverage or termination of employment.

In general, individuals must meet the following conditions to enroll during a special enrollment period:

(1) They must be eligible for Part B (Medical Insurance) on the basis of age or disability, but not on the basis of end-stage renal disease.

(2) When first eligible for Part B (Medical Insurance coverage), they must be covered under a group health plan on the basis of current employment status of the individual or the individual's spouse.

(3) For all months thereafter, they must maintain coverage under a group health plan. (Generally, if an individual fails to enroll in Part B (Medical Insurance) during any available special enrollment period, that individual is not entitled to any additional special enrollment periods. But if an individual fails to enroll during a special enrollment period because coverage under the same or a different group health plan was restored before the end of that particular special enrollment period, that failure to enroll does not preclude additional special enrollment periods.)

## 1063. Is there a special enrollment period for disabled workers who lose benefits under a group health plan?

Yes. Certain disabled beneficiaries are eligible for a special enrollment period and waiver of the Part B premium surcharge. These individuals are disabled beneficiaries (1) who were enrolled in an employment-based group health plan (by reason of current or former employment or the current or former employment of a family member) at the time of initially becoming eligible for Medicare, (2) who elected not to enroll in Part B during their initial enrollment period, and (3) whose continuous enrollment under the group health plan is involuntarily terminated at a time when the enrollment is by reason of the individual's former employment (or the former employment of a family member).

The special enrollment period begins on the first day of the month that includes the date of the involuntary termination and continues for six months.

## 1064. How does a person terminate or cancel coverage under Part B (Medical Insurance)?

A person's Part B (Medical Insurance) coverage continues until the individual's enrollment is terminated. A beneficiary may terminate coverage by filing a notice that he no longer wishes to participate in the program or by not paying the monthly premium.

The termination of coverage takes effect at the close of the month following the month in which a notice is filed. A grace period, however, is provided before coverage is terminated for not paying premiums. The grace period in which overdue premiums can be paid and coverage continued generally runs for three months from the month for which the unpaid premium was due, but may be extended an additional three months in certain cases where the Centers for Medicare & Medicaid Services (CMS) determines that there was good cause for failure to pay the overdue premiums within the initial three-month grace period).

A termination notice filed by a person enrolled in Part B (Medical Insurance) before the first day of the month in which Part B coverage is scheduled to begin will terminate coverage on the first day of the month in which coverage would otherwise have been effective. If a termination notice is filed in or after the month in which Part B coverage is effective, the coverage is terminated at the close of the month following the month in which the notice is filed.

In the case of a person entitled to Part A (Hospital Insurance) based on twenty-four or more months of disability, rather than on having attained age sixty-five, Part B (Medical Insurance) generally ends at the close of the last month for which the individual is entitled to Part A benefits.

## FINANCING PART B (MEDICAL INSURANCE)

### 1065. How is Part B (Medical Insurance) financed?

Medical Insurance is voluntary and is financed through premiums paid by people who enroll and through funds from the federal government. Monthly premiums are in addition to the deductible and coinsurance amounts that must be paid by beneficiaries.

Most persons enrolled pay a standard monthly premium of $104.90 per month in 2015. The basic Part B (Medical Insurance) premium is set to cover approximately 25 percent of program costs each year. The federal government pays the remaining cost from general revenues. In September-October of each year, the CMS announce the premium rate for the twelve-month period starting the following January.

Single persons with annual incomes over $85,000 (as indexed in 2015) and married couples with incomes over $170,000 (as indexed in 2015) pay a higher percentage of the cost of Part B (Medical Insurance). These higher-income beneficiaries will pay a monthly premium equal to 35 percent, 50 percent, 65 percent, or 80 percent of the total cost, depending on their income level.

The premium rate for a person who enrolls after his initial enrollment period (when he is first eligible for Part B coverage), or who re-enrolls after terminating Part B coverage, will be increased by up to 10 percent for each full twelve months the person stayed out of the program. Special enrollment periods apply to certain individuals with employer group health plan coverage, and they are not subject to the late enrollment penalty as long as they enroll during such a special enrollment period. See Q 1062 for more detail on the special enrollment period.

**Basic Monthly Premium Part B (Medical Insurance)**

| Year | Monthly Premium |
|---|---|
| 1994 | 41.10 |
| 1995 | 46.10 |
| 1996 | 42.50 |
| 1997 | 43.80 |
| 1998 | 43.80 |
| 1999 | 45.50 |
| 2000 | 45.50 |
| 2001 | 50.00 |
| 2002 | 54.00 |
| 2003 | 58.70 |
| 2004 | 66.60 |
| 2005 | 78.20 |
| 2006 | 88.50 |
| 2007 | 93.50 |
| 2008 | 96.40 |
| 2009 | 96.40 |
| 2010 | 110.50 |
| 2011 | 115.40 |
| 2012 | 99.90 |
| 2013-2015 | 104.90 |

**Income-Adjusted Monthly Premium Part B (Medical Insurance)**

| Single Taxpayer | Married Taxpayers Filing Jointly | Total Premium |
|---|---|---|
| Not greater than $85,000 | Not greater than $170,000 | $104.90 |
| $85,000 – $107,000 | $170,000 – $214,000 | 146.90 |
| $107,000 – $160,000 | $214,000 – $320,000 | 209.90 |
| $160,000 – $214,000 | $320,000 – $428,000 | 272.70 |
| More than $214,000 | More than $428,000 | 335.70 |

| Married Taxpayers Separately | Total Premium |
|---|---|
| Not greater than $85,000 | $104.90 |
| $85,000 – $129,000 | 272.70 |
| $129,000 and up | 335.70 |

## 1066. How is Income determined for purposes of setting a person's Part B (Hospital Insurance) Premium?

If the person's modified adjusted gross income is above the thresholds discussed in Q 1065, then additional Part B premiums are required. Modified adjusted gross income is adjusted gross income plus tax exempt interest income.

To determine the 2015 income-related monthly adjustment amounts, Medicare uses the most recent Federal tax return that the IRS provides. Generally, this information is from a tax return filed in 2014 for tax year 2013. Sometimes, the IRS only provides information from a return filed in 2013 for tax year 2012. If Medicare uses the 2012 tax year data and the taxpayer filed a return for tax year 2013 or did not need to file a tax return for tax year 2013, the taxpayer can contact Medicare and records will be updated.

If a person's income has gone down due to any of the following situations and the change makes a difference in the income level Medicare considers, the taxpayer should contact Medicare to explain the new information and Medicare may need a new decision about your income-related monthly adjustment amount:

- The taxpayer married, divorced, or became widowed
- The taxpayer or spouse stopped working or reduced work hours
- The taxpayer or spouse lost income-producing property due to a disaster or other event beyond the taxpayer's control
- The taxpayer or spouse experienced a scheduled cessation, termination, or reorganization of an employer's pension plan
- The taxpayer or spouse received a settlement from an employer or former employer because of the employer's closure, bankruptcy, or reorganization

If any of these apply, Medicare needs to see documentation verifying the event and the reduction in income. The documentation provided should relate to the event and may include a death certificate, a letter from an employer about retirement, or something similar. If a taxpayer filed a Federal income tax return for the year in question, a signed copy needs to be shown to Medicare.

If the taxpayer disagrees with the decision regarding the income-related monthly adjustment amounts, there is a right to appeal. The taxpayer may request an appeal in writing by completing a *Request for Reconsideration* (Form SSA-561-U2) or by contacting the local Social Security office. Appeal forms can be found on the Social Security website (www.socialsecurity.gov/online). Forms can also be requested by calling 1-800-772-1213. Taxpayers do not need to file an appeal if they are requesting a new decision because one of the events listed took place which caused income to decrease or if it can be shown that information used was wrong.

## 1067. What is a Qualified Medicare Beneficiary?

An elderly or disabled person with a low income who is eligible for Medicare may be able to have some or all Medicare expenses paid by their state. Federal law requires state Medicaid programs to pay Medicare costs for certain elderly and disabled persons with low incomes and very limited assets.

There are three programs to help people pay their Medicare expenses; (1) the Qualified Medicare Beneficiary (QMB) program, (2) the Specified Low-Income Medicare Beneficiary (SLMB) program, and (3) the Qualifying Individual (QI) program.

The QMB program is for a person with limited resources whose income is at or below the national poverty level. It covers the cost of Medicare Part A (Hospital Insurance) premiums, coinsurance and deductibles that a Medicare beneficiary normally pays out of his own pocket. The QMB program also pays the basic Part B (Medical Insurance) premium, which is $104.90 a month in 2015 for most individuals (see Q 1065).

While the QMB program helps those whose income is at or below the national poverty level, the SLMB program is for a person whose income is slightly higher than the poverty level, but not more than 20 percent higher. The program pays the Part B (Medical Insurance) premiums ($104.90 in 2015; see Q 1065) for a person qualifying under the SLMB program, but not any of the Part A or Part B deductibles and coinsurance. SLMBs also remain responsible for charges for health care services and medical supplies not covered by Medicare.

The QI program assists individuals and married couples whose income is more than 20 percent greater than the Federal poverty level, but not more than 38 percent greater, by paying the full monthly Part B (Medical Insurance) premium each month. As with SLMBs, persons covered under the QI program remain responsible for Medicare's deductibles and coinsurance and for charges for health care services and medical supplies not covered by Medicare.

See Q 1030 and Q 1031 for more details on eligibility for the QMB and SLMB programs.

The income limits for the QI Program through 2015 are $15,996 annually for an individual or $21,480 for a couple. If a person already has Medicare Part A and thinks he may qualify for QMB, SLMB, or QI assistance, he should file an application for assistance with a nearby Medicaid office.

## 1068. How are premiums paid under Part B (Medical Insurance)?

Most persons covered by Part B (Medical Insurance) have the premiums deducted from their Social Security, Railroad Retirement, or federal civil service retirement benefit payments. Persons who are not receiving any of these government benefits pay the premiums directly to the government.

Direct payment of premiums is usually made on a quarterly basis with a grace period, determined by the Centers for Medicare & Medicaid Services (CMS), of up to ninety days.

Public assistance agencies may enroll, and pay premiums for, certain public assistance recipients (usually recipients of public assistance under the Supplemental Security Income program). States must pay premiums for specified low-income persons. (See Q 1067.)

If a person's Social Security or Railroad Retirement benefits are suspended because of excess earnings, and benefits will not be resumed until the next taxable year, the person will be billed directly for overdue Medicare premiums. If Social Security or Railroad Retirement benefits will be resumed before the close of the taxable year, overdue premiums are deducted from the Social Security or Railroad Retirement cash benefits when they resume.

Premiums must be paid for the entire month of death even though coverage ends on the day of death.

## 1069. How are "approved charges" for covered medical services determined under Part B (Medical Insurance)?

There are three major elements that determine how much Medicare Part B pays for physician services: (1) a fee schedule for the payment of physician services, (2) a method to control the rates of increase in Medicare expenditures for physicians' services, and (3) limits on the amounts that nonparticipating physicians can charge beneficiaries. Payments under the fee schedule must be based on national uniform Relative Value Units (RVUs) based on the resources used in furnishing a service. National RVUs must be established for physician work, practice expense, and malpractice expense.

Adjustments in RVUs because of changes resulting from a review of those RVUs may not cause total physician fee schedule payments to differ by more than $20 million from what they would have been had the adjustments not been made. If this amount is exceeded, the Centers for Medicare & Medicaid Services (CMS) must make an adjustment to the conversion factor to preserve budget neutrality. Congress also has the power to override the statutory formula and often does so.

CMS is required to review and, if necessary, adjust the Geographic Practice Cost Indices (GPCIs) at least every three years. CMS also must phase in the adjustment over two years and implement only one-half of any adjustment if more than one year has elapsed since the last GPCI revision.

Payments may vary among fee schedule areas according to geographic indices.

## 1070. How are Part B (Medical Insurance) payments made?

Part B (Medical Insurance) payments are made in two ways. Payment can be made directly to the doctor, supplier, or other health care provider. This is the assignment method of payment. Payment can also be made directly to the patient, who then pays the provider.

Under the assignment method, the health care provider agrees to accept the amount approved by the Medicare Administrative Contractor (MAC) as total payment for Medicare-covered services.

The assignment method can save the patient time and money. The health care provider sends the claim to Medicare. Medicare pays the health care provider 80 percent of the Medicare-approved charge, after subtracting any part of the annual deductible the patient has not paid. The health care provider can charge the patient *only* for the part of the annual deductible the patient has not met and for the Part B coinsurance, which is generally the remaining 20 percent of the approved amount. Of course, a provider also can charge the patient for any services that Medicare does not cover.

If a health care provider does not accept assignment, the provider is considered "nonparticipating," and Medicare pays the patient 80 percent of the approved charge, after subtracting any part of the annual deductible the patient has not paid. The health care provider can bill the patient for the provider's actual charge, even if it is more than the charge approved by the MAC.

Doctors, suppliers, and other providers of Part B (Medical Insurance) services are in most cases required to submit Medicare claims for a patient, even if the providers do not take assignment. Claims are submitted on a form called a CMS-1500, requesting that Part B (Medical Insurance) payment be made for a patient's covered services. The provider completes the form and the patient signs it before it is sent to the proper MAC. Generally, the provider must submit a claim within one year of providing the service or may be subject to certain penalties. A patient should notify the MAC in the patient's area if a Medicare provider refuses to submit a claim to Medicare and the patient believes the services may be covered by Medicare.

If a patient is enrolled in a health care organization such as an HMO, a claim will seldom need to be submitted. Medicare generally pays an HMO a set amount, and the HMO provides medical care for its members. Doctors, suppliers, and other providers of Part B (Medical Insurance) services bill the HMO directly for reimbursement at contractually-agreed rates.

Utilizing a doctor who accepts assignment under Medicare may make a substantial difference in a patient's out-of-pocket costs.

*Example*. Jane Smith has surgery after meeting the annual deductible for Part B (Medical Insurance). Dr. Ralph Jones, who is not a participating physician and does not limit his charges to the Medicare fee schedule, bills Ms. Smith $1,200 for the surgery. The Medicare fee schedule sets the charge for this surgery at $1,100. Medicare will pay $880 (80 percent of the Medicare fee), and Ms. Smith must pay the remaining $320 of the $1,200 fee.

If Dr. Jones had been a participating physician under Medicare, Ms. Smith would have had to pay only $220 (20 percent of the approved charge of $1,100 that Medicare does not pay).

If a physician does not accept the assignment method, the physician must refund all amounts collected from Medicare beneficiaries on claims for services that are deemed not medically necessary. The MAC will send a notice to the beneficiary and physician advising them of the basis for denial, the right of appeal, and the requirement of a refund.

Even though a doctor does not accept assignment, for most covered services there are limits on the amount a nonparticipating provider can actually charge a Medicare beneficiary. In general, the most a doctor can charge is 115 percent of what Medicare approves. The 115 percent limit also applies to fees for physical and occupational therapy services, suppliers, injections, and other services billable under the physician fee schedule.

Physicians must give written notice prior to elective surgery for which the fee is $500 or more. The notice must state the physician's estimated actual charge, the estimated Medicare-approved charge, the excess of the actual charge over the approved charge, and the applicable coinsurance amount. This requirement applies to nonemergency surgical procedures only. (Emergency surgery is surgery performed under conditions and circumstances which afford no alternatives to the physician or the patient and, if delayed, could result in death or permanent impairment of health.) If the physician fails to make this fee disclosure, and the surgery was nonemergency surgery, the physician must refund amounts collected in excess of the Medicare-approved Part B (Medical Insurance) charge. The physician is subject to sanctions if the physician knowingly and willfully fails to comply with this refund requirement.

## 1071. How can a person find out if a doctor accepts assignment of all Medicare claims?

Doctors and suppliers sign agreements in advance to accept assignment on all Medicare claims. They are given the opportunity to sign participation agreements each year.

Medicare beneficiaries may use the Physician Compare tool available on the CMS website (www.medicare.gov) to find participating physicians. A listing of all Medicare approved suppliers can also be found on the CMS website (www.medicare.gov). The names and addresses of Medicare-participating doctors and suppliers are also listed by geographic area in the *Medicare-Participating Physician Directory* and the *Medicare-Participating Supplier Directory*. Both directories are available in Social Security offices, from Medicare Administrative Contractors, in state and area offices of the Administration on Aging, at most hospitals, and at www.medicare.gov. Medicare beneficiaries may also call 1-800-MEDICARE (1-800-633-4227) to locate physicians and suppliers.

Medicare-participating doctors and suppliers may display emblems or certificates that show they accept assignment on all Medicare claims.

## 1072. What are Medicare providers and Medicare suppliers?

The term "provider" generally means a hospital, a rural primary care hospital, a skilled nursing facility, a comprehensive outpatient rehabilitative facility, a home health agency, or a hospice that has in effect an agreement to participate in Medicare. A clinic, rehabilitation agency, or a public health agency that has a similar agreement to furnish outpatient physical therapy or speech pathology services, or a community mental health center with a similar agreement to furnish partial hospitalization services, is also considered a provider.

In general, "suppliers" are individuals or entities—other than doctors or health care facilities—that furnish equipment or services covered by Part B (Medical Insurance). For example, ambulance firms, independent laboratories, and entities that rent or sell medical equipment are considered suppliers.

There are different definitions of the term supplier and specific regulations governing different types of suppliers. Durable Medical Equipment, Prosthetics, Orthotics, and Supplies (DMEPOS) encompass the types of items included in the definition of "medical equipment and supplies." A "DMEPOS supplier" refers to all individuals or organizations that furnish these items. This can include a physician or Medicare Part A (Hospital Insurance) provider. A DMEPOS supplier must meet Medicare DMEPOS standards in order to obtain a supplier number. Those individuals or entities that do not furnish DMEPOS items but only furnish other types of health care services, such as physician's services or nurse practitioner services, are not subject to these standards. A supplier number is also not necessary before Medicare payment can be made with respect to medical equipment and supplies furnished incident to a physician's service.

For Medicare purposes, DMEPOS suppliers either accept or do not accept assignment. If a DMEPOS supplier accepts assignment, it agrees to accept the Medicare-approved amount as payment in full for the covered item. Such suppliers are referred to as "participating suppliers." Participating DMEPOS suppliers are listed in directories available to Medicare beneficiaries and receive Medicare Part B payment directly from the Medicare program. Nonparticipating DMEPOS suppliers may accept assignment on a case-by-case basis; for claims on which they accept assignment, they receive payment directly from Medicare. If a beneficiary receives a service from a nonparticipating DMEPOS supplier on a nonassigned basis, however, payment is made to the beneficiary (who in turn pays the DMEPOS supplier).

Medicare suppliers are required to meet a number of standards, including the following: (1) complying with all applicable state and federal license and regulatory requirements, (2) maintaining a physical facility on an appropriate site, (3) having proof of appropriate liability insurance, (4) delivering Medicare-covered items to Medicare beneficiaries, (5) honoring all warranties, (6) maintaining and repairing items rented to beneficiaries, and (7) accepting returns of substandard or unsuitable items from beneficiaries.

## 1073. What portion of the cost must be borne by the patient?

The patient pays an annual deductible each year under Part B (Medical Insurance). For 2015, the deductible is $147, which means that the patient pays for the first $147 of covered expenses incurred during the calendar year. After the deductible is met, the patient pays 20 percent of approved charges, and Medicare pays 80 percent. There is no cost-sharing for certain Part B services and supplies, including most home health services, pneumococcal vaccine, flu shots, the costs of second opinions for certain surgical procedures when Medicare requires these opinions, and certain outpatient clinical diagnostic laboratory tests.

## 1074. How does a patient find out how much Medicare will pay on a claim?

After the doctor, provider, or supplier sends in a Part B (Medical Insurance) claim, Medicare sends the patient a notice called *Explanation ofYour Medicare Part B Benefits* to explain the decision on the claim.

This notice shows what charges were made and what Medicare approved. It shows what the coinsurance is and what Medicare is paying. If the annual deductible has not been met, that is also shown. The notice also gives the address and telephone number of the Medicare Administrative Contractor.

## BENEFITS

### 1075. What doctors' services are covered under Part B (Medical Insurance)?

Under Part B (Medical Insurance), Medicare usually pays 80 percent of the approved charges for doctors' services and other services that are covered under Part B after the patient pays an annual deductible. Part B helps pay for covered services received from the doctor in the doctor's office, in a hospital, in a skilled nursing facility, in the patient's home, or any other location. Doctors' fees and services covered by Part B include:

- *Doctors' services* are covered wherever furnished in the United States. This includes the cost of house calls, office visits, and doctors' services in a hospital or other institution. Such services include the fees of physicians, surgeons, pathologists, radiologists, anesthesiologists, physiatrists, and osteopaths.

- Services from certain *specially qualified practitioners* who are not physicians but are approved by Medicare, including certified registered nurse anesthetists, certified nurse midwifes, clinical psychologists, clinical social workers (other than in a hospital), physician assistants, and nurse practitioners and clinical nurse specialists in collaboration with a physician.

- Services of *clinical psychologists* are covered if they would otherwise be covered when furnished by a physician (or as an incident to a physician's services).

- Services by *licensed chiropractors* for manual manipulation of the spine to correct a subluxation. Part B does not otherwise pay for any other diagnostic or therapeutic services, including X-rays, furnished by a chiropractor. Medicare pays for manual manipulation of the spine to correct a subluxation without requiring an X-ray (which previously was required) to prove that the subluxation exists.

- Fees of *podiatrists* are covered, including fees for the treatment of plantar warts, but not for routine foot care. Examples of common problems covered by Part B include ingrown toenails, hammer toe deformities, bunion deformities, and heel spurs. Routine foot care not covered by Part B includes cutting or removal of corns and calluses, trimming of nails, and other hygienic care. Part B does help pay for some routine foot care if the patient is being treated by a medical doctor for a medical condition affecting the patient's legs or feet (such as diabetes or peripheral vascular disease) which requires that a podiatrist or doctor of medicine or osteopathy perform the routine care.

- Medicare helps pay for therapeutic shoes and shoe inserts for people who have severe diabetic foot disease. The doctor who treats the diabetes must certify the patient's need for therapeutic shoes. The shoes and inserts must be prescribed by a podiatrist and furnished by a podiatrist, orthotist, prosthetist, or pedorthist. Medicare helps pay for one pair of therapeutic shoes per calendar year and for inserts. Shoe modifications may be substituted for inserts. The fitting of shoes or inserts is included in the Medicare payment for the shoes.

- The cost of diagnosis and treatment of *eye and ear ailments* is covered. Also covered is an *optometrist's treatment of aphakia*.
- *Plastic surgery* for purely cosmetic reasons is excluded; but plastic surgery for repair of an accidental injury, an impaired limb or a malformed part of the body is covered.
- *Radiological or pathological services* furnished by a physician to a hospital inpatient are covered.

Part B also covers (1) medical and surgical services, including anesthesia, (2) diagnostic tests and procedures that are part of the patient's treatment, (3) radiology and pathology services by doctors while the patient is a hospital inpatient or outpatient, (4) treatment of mental illness, (Medicare payments are limited), (5) X-rays, (6) services of the doctor's office nurse, (7) drugs and biologicals that cannot be self-administered, (8) transfusions of blood and blood components, (9) medical supplies, and (10) physical/occupational therapy and speech-language pathology services.

Part B does *not* cover (1) most routine physical examinations (the "Welcome to Medicare" initial screening and subsequent annual updates are generally not considered the same as a routine physical), and tests directly related to such examinations (except some Pap smears and mammograms), (2) most routine foot care and dental care, (3) examinations for prescribing or fitting eyeglasses or hearing aids and most eyeglasses and hearing aids, (4) immunizations (except annual flu shots, pneumococcal pneumonia vaccinations or immunizations required because of an injury or immediate risk of infection, and hepatitis B for certain persons at risk), (5) cosmetic surgery, unless it is needed because of accidental injury or to improve the function of a malformed part of the body, (6) most prescription drugs, (7) custodial care at home or in a nursing home, and (8) orthopedic shoes.

Charges imposed by an immediate relative (e.g., a doctor who is the son/daughter or brother/sister of the patient) are *not* covered.

Doctors cannot make self-referrals for certain designated health services. Designated health services include any of the following items or services: (1) clinical laboratory services, (2) physical therapy services, (3) occupational therapy services, (4) radiology services, including MRI, CAT scans, and ultrasound services, (5) radiation therapy services and supplies, (6) durable medical equipment and supplies, (7) parenteral and enteral nutrients, equipment, and supplies, (8) prosthetics, orthotics, and prosthetic devices and supplies, (9) home health services, (10) outpatient prescription drugs, and (11) inpatient and outpatient hospital services.

The law prohibits a doctor who has a financial relationship with an entity from referring Medicare patients to that entity to receive a designated health service. The prohibition also applies if a doctor's immediate family member has a financial relationship with an entity. A financial relationship can exist as an ownership or investment interest in, or a compensation arrangement with, an entity. The law is triggered by the mere fact that a financial relationship exists; it does not matter what the doctor intends when making a referral. An entity cannot bill Medicare, Medicaid, the beneficiary, or anyone else for a designated health service furnished to a Medicare patient under a prohibited referral.

The law prohibits Medicare payments for designated health services in violation of the law. If a person collects any amount for services billed in violation of the law, a refund must be made. A person can be subject to a civil money penalty or exclusion from Medicare if that person (1) presents or causes to be presented a claim to Medicare or bill to any individual, third-party payer, or other entity for any designated health service the person knows or should know was furnished as a result of a prohibited referral, or (2) fails to make a timely refund.

## 1076. What outpatient hospital services are covered under Part B (Medical Insurance)?

Part B (Medical Insurance) helps pay for covered services a patient receives as an outpatient from a participating hospital for diagnosis or treatment of an illness or injury. Under certain conditions, Part B helps pay for emergency outpatient care the patient receives from a non-participating hospital. The patient must meet the annual Part B (Medical Insurance) deductible before Medicare will begin paying for outpatient hospital charges and then pay a 20 percent copayment.

Major outpatient hospital services covered by Part B include (1) services in an emergency room or outpatient clinic, including same-day surgery, (2) laboratory tests billed by the hospital, (3) mental health care in a partial hospitalization psychiatric program, if a physician certifies that inpatient treatment would be required without it, (4) X-rays and other radiology services billed by the hospital, (5) medical supplies such as splints and casts, (6) drugs and biologicals that cannot be self-administered, and (7) blood transfusions furnished to the patient as an outpatient (after the first three pints).

Outpatient hospital services not covered by Part B (Medical Insurance) include (1) most routine physical examinations and tests directly related to the examinations, (2) eye or ear examinations to prescribe or fit eyeglasses or hearing aids, (3) most immunizations, (4) most prescription drugs, (5) most routine foot care, and (6) most dental care.

## 1077. When are outpatient physical therapy and speech-language pathology services covered under Part B (Medical Insurance)?

Outpatient physical therapy and speech-language pathology services are covered if received as part of a patient's treatment in a doctor's office or as an outpatient of a participating hospital, skilled nursing facility, or home health agency; or approved clinic, rehabilitative agency, or public health agency. Services must be furnished under a plan established by a physician or therapist providing the services. A physician is required to review periodically all plans of care.

A podiatrist (when acting within the scope of her practice) is a physician for purposes of establishing a plan for outpatient physical therapy. A dentist and podiatrist are also within the definition of a physician for purposes of outpatient ambulatory surgery in a physician's office.

## 1078. Are partial hospitalization services connected to mental health services covered?

Yes. Partial hospitalization services (sometimes called day treatments) related to treatment of mental illness are items and services prescribed by a physician and provided in a program under the supervision of a physician pursuant to an individualized written plan of treatment.

The program must be furnished by a hospital to its outpatients or by a community mental health center and must be in a distinct and organized intensive ambulatory treatment service offering less than twenty-four hour daily care.

Covered items and services include the following:

- individual and group therapy with physicians or psychologists (or other mental health professionals to the extent authorized by state law);
- occupational therapy requiring the skills of a qualified occupational therapist;
- services of social workers, trained psychiatric nurses, and other staff trained to work with psychiatric patients;
- drugs and biologicals furnished for therapeutic purposes (which cannot be self-administered);
- individualized activity therapies that are not primarily recreational or diversionary;
- family counseling, the primary purpose of which is treatment of the individual's condition;
- patient training and education, to the extent the training and educational activities are closely and clearly related to the individual's care and treatment;
- diagnostic services; and
- other necessary items and services (but not including meals and transportation).

## 1079. Are certified nurse-midwife services covered under Part B (Medical Insurance)?

Yes. A certified nurse-midwife is a registered professional nurse who meets the following requirements:

(1) Is currently licensed to practice in the state as a nurse-midwife in the state where services are performed (assuming the state requires such licensure)

(2) Has completed a program of study and clinical experience for nurse-midwives that is accredited by an accrediting body approved by the U.S. Department of Education

(3) Is certified as a nurse-midwife by the American College of Nurse-Midwives or the American College of Nurse-Midwives Certification Council

Certified nurse-midwife services are services furnished by a certified nurse-midwife and such services and supplies as are incident to nurse-midwife service. The service must be authorized under state law.

The definition of nurse-midwife services includes coverage of services outside the maternity cycle.

The amount paid by Part B (Medical Insurance) for such services is based upon a fee schedule and generally is covered to the same extent such services would be covered if performed by a physician. (Medicare will pay 80 percent of the lesser of the actual charge or 100 percent of the physician fee schedule charge for the service.) Payment is made by assignment only, however.

## 1080. Is dental work covered under Part B (Medical Insurance)?

Part B (Medical Insurance) helps pay for services of a dentist in certain cases when the medical problem is more extensive than the teeth or structures directly supporting the teeth. Dental work for jaw or facial bone surgery, whether required because of accident or disease, is covered. If a patient needs to be hospitalized because of the severity of a dental procedure, Part A (Hospital Insurance) may pay for the patient's inpatient hospital stay even if the dental care itself is not covered by Medicare.

Part B (Medical Insurance) generally does not pay for routine dental care, such as the treatment, filling, removal, or replacement of teeth; root canal therapy; surgery for impacted teeth; or other surgical procedures involving the teeth or structures directly supporting the teeth.

## 1081. What medical equipment is covered under Part B (Medical Insurance)?

Part B (Medical Insurance) covers a wide array of medical equipment, including: surgical dressings, splints, casts, and other devices for reduction of fractures and dislocations; rental or purchase of durable medical equipment, such as iron lungs, oxygen tents, hospital beds, and wheelchairs, for use in the patient's home; prosthetic devices, such as artificial heart valves or synthetic arteries, designed to replace part or all of an internal organ (but not false teeth, hearing aids, or eyeglasses); colostomy or ileostomy bags and certain related supplies; breast prostheses (including a surgical brassiere) after a mastectomy; braces for arm, leg, back, or neck; and artificial limbs and eyes. Orthopedic shoes are not covered unless they are part of leg braces and the cost is included in the orthopedist's charge. Adhesive tape, antiseptics, and other common first-aid supplies are also not included.

Durable medical equipment is equipment that can be used again by other patients, must primarily serve a medical purpose, must not be useful to people who are not sick or injured, and must be appropriate for use in the patient's home. Part B (Medical Insurance) pays for different kinds of durable medical equipment in different ways: some equipment must be rented, other equipment must be purchased, and for some equipment the patient may choose rental or purchase. A doctor should prescribe medical equipment for the patient.

Suppliers of medical equipment and supplies (durable medical equipment, prosthetic devices, orthotics and prosthetics, surgical dressings, home dialysis supplies and equipment, immunosuppressive drugs, therapeutic shoes for diabetics, oral cancer drugs, and self-administered erythropoietin) are not reimbursed by Medicare for these items unless they have a Medicare supplier number. A supplier cannot obtain a supplier number unless the supplier meets uniform national standards.

The standards require suppliers to (1) comply with all applicable state and federal licensure and regulatory requirements, (2) maintain a physical facility, (3) have proof of appropriate liability insurance, and (4) meet other requirements established by the Centers for Medicare & Medicaid Services. The requirement for suppliers to obtain a supplier number does not apply to medical equipment and supplies furnished as incident to a physician's service.

## 1082. Is ambulance service covered by Part B (Medical Insurance)?

Yes. Part B (Medical Insurance) helps pay for the "reasonable costs" of medically necessary ambulance transportation, including air ambulances, but only if the patient's condition does not permit the use of other methods of transportation and the ambulance, equipment and personnel meet Medicare requirements. Part B (Medical Insurance) can help pay for ambulance transportation from the scene of an accident to a hospital, from a patient's home to a hospital or skilled nursing facility, between hospitals and skilled nursing facilities, or from a hospital or skilled nursing facility to the patient's home. Also, if the patient is an inpatient in a hospital or skilled nursing facility that cannot provide a medically necessary service, Part B can help pay for round-trip ambulance transportation to the nearest appropriate facility. Medicare does not pay for ambulance use from a patient's home to a doctor's office.

Medicare also does not pay for ambulance use from the patient's home to a dialysis facility that is not in or next to a hospital.

Part B (Medical Insurance) usually helps pay for ambulance transportation only in the patient's local area. However, if there are no local facilities equipped to provide the care the patient needs, Part B will help pay for necessary ambulance transportation to the closest facility outside the patient's local area that can provide the necessary care. If the patient chooses to go to another institution that is farther away, Medicare payment will be based on the reasonable charge for transportation to the closest facility.

Necessary ambulance services in connection with a covered inpatient stay in a Canadian or Mexican hospital may also be covered by Part B.

Medicare pays for use of an air ambulance only in extremely urgent emergency situations. If a patient could have been moved by land ambulance without serious danger to life or health,

Medicare pays only the land ambulance rate. The patient is responsible for the difference between the air ambulance rate and the land ambulance rate.

## 1083. How much will Medicare Part B (Medical Insurance) pay for outpatient treatment of mental illness?

Part B (Medical Insurance) helps pay the cost of outpatient mental health services a patient receives from physicians, clinical psychologists, clinical social workers and other nonphysician practitioners. Before 2014, when treatment was furnished on an outpatient basis, mental health treatment services were subject to a payment limitation called the "outpatient mental health limitation." Under this limitation, Part B paid a lower percentage for mental health services than for other services. Beginning in 2014, however, Part B (Medical Insurance) will pay 80 percent of approved charges for outpatient mental health services just as for most other Part B services.

Partial hospitalization (sometimes called day treatment) is a program of outpatient mental health care. Partial hospitalization services mean a distinct and organized intensive ambulatory treatment program that offers less than twenty-four hour daily care and furnishes mental health care services. Under certain conditions, Part B (Medical Insurance) helps pay for these programs when provided by hospital outpatient departments or by community mental health centers.

The Centers for Medicare & Medicaid Services (CMS) define community mental health centers as any entity that (1) provides outpatient services, including specialized outpatient services for children, the elderly, individuals who are chronically mentally ill, and residents of its mental health service area who have been discharged from inpatient treatment at a mental health facility; (2) provides twenty-four-hour-a-day emergency care services; (3) provides day treatment or other partial hospitalization services, or psychosocial rehabilitation services; (4) provides screening for patients being considered for admission to state mental health facilities; (5) provides consultation and education services; and (6) meets applicable licensing or certification requirements for community mental health centers in the state in which it is located.

## 1084. When is the cost of vaccines covered?

The cost of pneumococcal pneumonia vaccine is covered, and the cost of hepatitis B vaccine for high and intermediate risk individuals is covered when it is administered in a hospital or renal dialysis facility. Also covered is the cost of flu vaccine and its administration. Neither the annual deductible nor the Part B (Medical Insurance) 20 percent coinsurance applies to flu and pneumonia vaccines. If the provider giving the patient the shot accepts assignment (i.e., accepts the Medicare payment as payment in full), there will be no cost to the patient. If the provider does not accept assignment, the patient may have to pay charges in addition to the Medicare-approved amount. Any health care professional complying with the Medicare rules can give a patient a flu shot or the pneumonia vaccine.

## 1085. Is the cost of antigens covered under Part B (Medical Insurance)?

Under certain circumstances, Part B (Medical Insurance) helps pay for antigens prepared for a patient by a physician, but only if the physician preparing the antigens also has examined the patient and developed the plan of treatment and dosage.

## 1086. When is a liver transplant covered under Part B (Medical Insurance)?

Part B (Medical Insurance) provides coverage for liver transplants for adult Medicare beneficiaries depending on the medical reason for the transplant. Generally, Part B covers transplants for end-stage liver disease unrelated to malignancies. Effective in 2012, Medicare Administrative Contractors also became authorized to cover liver transplants in cases involving specified types of malignancies.

## 1087. Can Part B (Medical Insurance) help pay for outpatient services at a comprehensive outpatient rehabilitation facility?

Under certain circumstances, Part B (Medical Insurance) helps pay for outpatient services received from a Medicare-participating Comprehensive Outpatient Rehabilitation Facility (CORF). Outpatient services must be performed by a doctor or other qualified professional. Covered services include physicians' services; physical, speech, occupation and respiratory therapies; counseling; and other related services. A CORF patient must be referred by a physician who certifies that there is a need for skilled rehabilitation services and creates (and periodically reviews) a plan of treatment for the patient. CORF services are generally subject to a special prospective payment system and to an annual limit applicable to all kinds of outpatient rehabilitation services (often referred to as the "therapy cap").

## 1088. Are home health services covered under Part B (Medical Insurance)?

For Medicare beneficiaries who have both Part A (Hospital Insurance) and Part B (Medical Insurance) coverage, home health services not directly related to hospital or skilled nursing facility stays are now covered and paid for by Part B (Medical Insurance). Part A (Hospital Insurance) covers up to 100 post-institutional home health care visits for beneficiaries with both Parts A and B. Home health services covered by Part B (Medical Insurance) tend to be for chronic conditions, and are different from home care services needed for convalescence and rehabilitation following a hospital stay. If a Medicare beneficiary continues to need home health care following exhaustion of Part A coverage, however, Part B also covers such care. Medicare pays for the costs of part-time skilled care with no coinsurance requirement and for 80 percent of the cost of durable medical equipment when supplied by a certified home health agency.

## 1089. Are independent clinical laboratory services covered under Part B (Medical Insurance)?

Part B (Medical Insurance) pays the full approved fee for covered clinical diagnostic tests provided by certain independent laboratories (or laboratories in physicians' offices) that are participating in Medicare. Such laboratories must be licensed in accordance with applicable state and local law (or otherwise approved for such licensure) and must also meet certain requirements specified in the Clinical Laboratory Improvement Amendments of 1988. In order to be paid by Medicare for approved charges, such laboratories must accept assignment for the tests and not bill the patient for the tests.

## 1090. Are screening pap smears and pelvic exams covered by Part B (Medical Insurance)?

Generally, a screening pap smear and pelvic exam (including a clinical breast exam) are covered every two years. Annual coverage is provided for women (1) at high risk for cervical or vaginal cancer or (2) of childbearing age who have had a pap smear during the preceding three years indicating the presence of cervical or vaginal cancer or other abnormality. The Part B deductible is waived for screening pap smears and pelvic exams. Pelvic exams are paid under the physician fee schedule.

## 1091. Are breast cancer screening and diagnostic mammography covered by Part B (Medical Insurance)?

Screening and diagnostic mammography are covered. "Screening mammography" is defined as a radiologic procedure furnished to a woman without signs or symptoms of breast disease, for the purpose of early detection of breast cancer, and includes a physician's interpretation of the results of the procedure. "Diagnostic mammography" means a radiologic procedure furnished to a man or woman with signs or symptoms of breast disease, or a personal history of breast cancer or a personal history of biopsy-proven benign breast disease, and includes a physician's interpretation of the results of the procedure. Medicare covers an annual screening mammogram for all women age forty and over. The Part B deductible for screening mammography is waived.

## 1092. Are prostate screening tests covered under Part B (Medical Insurance)?

Annual prostate cancer screening for men age fifty and older is covered. Covered procedures include (1) digital rectal exam and (2) Prostate-Specific Antigen (PSA) blood test. No Part B deductible or coinsurance is required for the screening PSA blood test, but Part B deductible and coinsurance is required with regard to the rectal exam. Payment to providers for the PSA blood test will be made under the clinical laboratory fee schedule, and other services will be paid under the physician fee schedule.

## 1093. How is colorectal screening covered under Part B (Medical Insurance)?

Covered colorectal screening procedures include (1) an annual fecal occult blood test for persons age fifty and over, (2) flexible sigmoidoscopy for persons age fifty and over, to be done once every four years, (3) a colonoscopy for persons at high risk for colorectal cancer, to be done once every two years (every ten years for all others), and (4) a screening barium enema for persons age fifty and over, to be done every four years for those deemed not at high risk and every two years for others. The Part B deductible is waived for these exams, but Part B coinsurance is increased to 25 percent for a patient for both flexible sigmoidoscopies and colonoscopies. Payment for screening colonoscopies is made only when the procedures are performed in a hospital.

## 1094. Are diabetes self-management services covered under Part B (Medical Insurance)?

Services furnished in non-hospital-based programs for diabetes outpatient self-management training are covered under Part B (Medical Insurance). Services must be provided by a certified provider, and the physician (or other qualified health care professional) managing the patient's condition must certify that the services are needed under a comprehensive plan of care. Certified providers for these services include physicians as well as hospital outpatient facilities and dialysis facilities.

Coverage includes certain types of home blood glucose monitors, testing strips, lancets and self-management training. Medicare also covers certain medical nutrition therapy services for individuals with diabetes or renal disease, but only if they have not separately received diabetes outpatient self-management training within a specified period and are not receiving maintenance dialysis.

## 1095. When does Medicare Part B (Medical Insurance) cover bone mass measurements?

Part B (Medical Insurance) covers procedures to identify bone mass, detect bone loss, or determine bone quality, including a physician's interpretation of the results. Persons qualifying for these procedures include estrogen-deficient women at risk for osteoporosis, individuals with vertebral abnormalities or with primary hyperparathyroidism, persons receiving long-term glucocorticoid steroid therapy, and individuals being monitored to assess the response to, or efficacy of, an approved osteoporosis drug. The Part B deductible is waived for these tests.

## 1096. Under what conditions is an injectable drug for postmenopausal osteoporosis covered by Part B (Medical Insurance)?

The cost of an injectable drug provided by a home health agency to a patient for the treatment of a bone fracture related to postmenopausal osteoporosis is covered under the following conditions: (1) the patient's attending physician certifies that the patient has suffered a bone fracture related to postmenopausal osteoporosis and is unable to learn the skills needed to self-administer (or is physically or mentally incapable of administering) the drug and (2) the patient is confined to the patient's home (in such a way as meets the requirements for Medicare coverage of home health services).

## 1097. When are eyeglasses covered under Part B (Medical Insurance)?

Part B (Medical Insurance) will pay for one pair of conventional eyeglasses or conventional contact lenses if necessary after cataract surgery with insertion of an intraocular lens.

Part B (Medical Insurance) will also pay for cataract spectacles, cataract contact lenses, or intraocular lenses that replace the natural lens of the eye after cataract surgery. Otherwise, however, Part B does not pay for routine eye exams or eyeglasses.

## 1098. Under what circumstances are the services of nurse practitioners and clinical nurse specialists covered under Part B (Medical Insurance)?

The services of nurse practitioners and clinical nurse specialists are covered when the services performed are those authorized under state law and regulations, provided there is no facility or other provider charges paid in connection with the service. Also, a clinical nurse specialist must be a registered nurse licensed to practice in the state who holds a master's degree in a defined clinical area of nursing and from an accredited educational institution.

## 1099. When are lung and heart-lung transplants covered under Part B (Medical Insurance)?

Medicare covers lung transplants for beneficiaries with progressive end-stage pulmonary disease when performed by facilities that (1) make an application to the Centers for Medicare & Medicaid Services (CMS) for approval as a lung transplant facility, (2) supply documentation showing their satisfaction of compliance with federal regulations on lung transplants, and (3) are approved by CMS under criteria based on federal regulations. Medicare also covers lung transplantation for end-stage cardiopulmonary disease when it is expected that transplant of the lung will result in improved cardiac function.

In addition, Medicare covers heart-lung transplants for beneficiaries with progressive end-stage cardiopulmonary disease when such transplants are performed in a facility that has been approved by Medicare for both heart and lung transplantation.

Facilities must meet specific criteria in areas such as patient selection, patient management, commitment, plans, experience and survival rates, maintenance of data, organ procurement, laboratory services, and billing. Facilities must have patient selection criteria for determining suitable candidates for lung transplants.

For facilities that are approved to perform lung transplants, Medicare Part A (Hospital Insurance) covers all medically reasonable and necessary inpatient services. (See Q 1018 through Q 1059 for discussion of Hospital Insurance.) Physician services, as well as other nonhospital services related to the transplant, and pre and posttransplant care, may be covered under Part B (Medical Insurance) and paid under the physician fee schedule or on a reasonable cost basis or other applicable basis. Under certain circumstances, kidney and liver transplants also may be covered.

## 1100. Are prescription drugs used in immunosuppressive therapy covered under Part B (Medical Insurance)?

Payment may be made for prescription drugs used in immunosuppressive therapy that have been approved for marketing by the Food and Drug Administration and that meet one of the following conditions:

(1) The approved labeling includes the indication for preventing or treating the rejection of a transplanted organ or tissue.

(2) The approved labeling includes the indication for use in conjunction with immunosuppressive drugs to prevent or treat rejection of a transplanted organ or tissue.

(3) The drugs have been determined by a Medicare Administrative Contractor to be reasonable and necessary for the specific purpose of preventing or treating the rejection of a patient's transplanted organ or tissue, or for use in conjunction with immunosuppressive drugs for the purpose of preventing or treating the rejection of a patient's transplanted organ or tissue.

Coverage under Part B (Medical Insurance) is generally available only for prescription drugs used in immunosuppressive therapy, furnished to an individual who receives an organ or tissue transplant for which Medicare payment is made, for up to thirty-six months after the date of discharge from the hospital during which the covered transplant was performed.

Such drugs are covered regardless of whether they can be self-administered.

## 1101. Are ambulatory surgical services covered under Part B (Medical Insurance)?

An ambulatory surgical center is a facility that provides surgical services that do not require a hospital stay. Part B (Medical Insurance) will pay for the use of an ambulatory surgical center for certain approved surgical procedures, generally those that do not pose a significant risk to the patient's health if performed in an outpatient setting (and that do not typically require an overnight hospital stay). The center must have an agreement to participate in the Medicare program. Medicare also helps pay for physician and anesthesia services that are provided in connection with the procedure.

## 1102. When are rural health clinic services covered by Part B (Medical Insurance)?

Part B (Medical Insurance) helps pay for services of physicians, nurse practitioners, physician assistants, nurse midwives, visiting nurses (under certain circumstances), clinical psychologists, and clinical social workers furnished by a rural health clinic. Part B (Medical Insurance) also helps pay for certain laboratory tests in these clinics. The patient is responsible for the annual Part B (Medical Insurance) deductible plus 20 percent of the Medicare-approved charge for the clinic services.

Rural health clinics must meet requirements concerning where they are located. They must be in areas where there are insufficient numbers of needed health care practitioners (not just primary care physicians). Clinics that no longer meet the shortage area requirements will be permitted to retain their designation only if the Centers for Medicare & Medicaid Services (CMS) determines that such clinics are essential to the delivery of primary care services that would otherwise be unavailable in the area.

## 1103. Does Medicare Part B (Medical Insurance) reimburse for telehealth services in rural areas?

Part B (Medical Insurance) payments are made for professional consultation via telecommunications systems with a health care provider furnishing a service for which Medicare payment would be made for a beneficiary residing in a rural county that was designated as a health professional shortage area (and in certain other nonurban areas).Payments for telehealth services are generally equal to what Medicare would have paid for the services if delivered other than through telecommunications. Telehealth services must be provided through certain specified types of telecommunication systems, and only certain type of sites are approved as originating sites (including physicians' offices located in certain rural areas and rural health centers).

## 1104. Does Part B (Medical Insurance) help pay for federally qualified health center services?

Federally qualified health centers are located in both rural and urban areas, and any Medicare beneficiary may seek services at them. As part of the "federally qualified health center benefit," Part B (Medical Insurance) helps pay for the following outpatient services:

(1) Physician services

(2) Services and supplies furnished as incident to a physician's professional services

(3) Nurse practitioner or physician assistant services

(4) Services and supplies furnished as incident to a nurse practitioner or physician assistant services

(5) Clinical psychologist and clinical social worker services

(6) Services and supplies furnished as incident to a clinical psychologist or clinical social worker services

(7) Visiting nurse services

(8) Nurse-midwife services

(9) Preventive primary services

Preventive primary services include medical social services, nutritional assessment and referral, preventive health education, children's eye and ear examinations, prenatal and postpartum screening, immunizations, voluntary family planning services, and other services outlined in the recommendations of the U.S. Preventive Services Task Force for patients age sixty-five and older. Preventive services do not include eyeglasses, hearing aids, group or mass information programs or health education classes, or preventive dental services. Preventive services covered under special provisions of Medicare, such as screening mammographies, may be provided by a federally qualified health center only if the center meets the special provisions that govern those benefits.

A Medicare beneficiary does not have to pay the Part B (Medical Insurance) annual deductible for services provided under the federally qualified health center benefit. A beneficiary remains responsible for 20 percent of the Medicare-approved charge for the clinic. Federally qualified health centers often provide services in addition to those specified under the Medicare federally qualified health center benefit. Examples of these services are X-rays and equipment like crutches and canes. As long as the center meets Medicare requirements to provide these services, Part B (Medical Insurance) can help pay for them. The patient is responsible for any unmet part of the patient's annual Part B (Medical Insurance) deductible plus 20 percent of the Medicare-approved charge for the service.

## 1105. What other benefits are provided under Part B (Medical Insurance)?

Additional benefits include the following:

- The cost of *blood clotting factors and supplies* related to their administration for hemophilia patients who are able to use them to control bleeding without medical or other supervision. The amount of clotting factors necessary to have on hand for a specific period is determined for each patient individually.

- *Outpatient radiation therapy* given under the supervision of a doctor.

- *Oral antinausea drugs used as part of an anticancer chemotherapeutic regimen*. The drug must be administered by a physician (or prescribed by a physician) for use immediately before, at, or within forty-eight hours after, the time of administration of the chemotherapeutic agent and used as a full replacement for the antiemetic therapy which would otherwise be administered intravenously.

- *Portable diagnostic Xray services* received by a patient at home or at other locations if they are ordered by a doctor and if they are provided by a Medicare-approved supplier.

- Under certain circumstances, *liver and kidney transplants* in a Medicare-approved facility.

- *Prosthetic devices* needed to replace an internal body organ. These include Medicare-approved corrective lenses needed after a cataract operation, ostomy bags and certain related supplies, and breast prostheses (including a surgical brassiere) after a mastectomy. Part B (Medical Insurance) also helps pay for artificial limbs and eyes, and for arm, leg, back, and neck braces. Part B does not pay for orthopedic shoes unless they are an integral part of leg braces and the cost is included in the charge for the braces. Part B also does not pay for dental plates or other dental devices.

- The drug *Epoetin alfa* when used to treat Medicare beneficiaries with anemia related to chronic kidney failure, or related to use of AZT in HIV-positive beneficiaries or for other uses that a Medicare Administrative Contractor finds medically appropriate. The Epoetin alfa must be administered incident to the services of a doctor in the office or in a hospital outpatient department. Part B (Medical Insurance) also helps pay for Epoetin alfa that is self-administered by home dialysis patients or administered by their caregivers.

- *Oral cancer drugs* if they are the same chemical entity as those administered intravenously and covered prior to 1994. In addition, off-label anticancer drugs are covered in some cases.

- *Cardiac rehabilitation* is covered if it is a comprehensive program that includes exercise, education, and counseling. Patients must meet certain conditions and have a doctor's referral. Also covered are intensive cardiac rehabilitation programs that are typically more rigorous or more intense than cardiac rehabilitation programs.

- A comprehensive program of pulmonary rehabilitation is covered if the patient has moderate to very severe Chronic Obstructive Pulmonary Disease (COPD) and has a referral for pulmonary rehabilitation from the doctor treating the chronic respiratory disease.

### 1106. What services are covered under Part B (Medical Insurance) with no cost-sharing obligation?

The number of services covered by Part B (Medical Insurance) without any cost-sharing obligations for patients – in other words, subject to neither the Part B deductible nor coinsurance – has expanded in recent years. Such services include: (1) the cost of second opinions for certain surgical procedures when Medicare requires a second opinion, (2) the cost of home health services (but a 20 percent coinsurance charge applies for durable medical equipment, except for the purchase of certain used items), (3) the cost of a flu shot and pneumococcal vaccine, (4) certain outpatient clinical diagnostic laboratory tests, and (5) a screening PSA test for prostate cancer.

## MEDICARE COVERAGE OF BLOOD

### 1107. Does Medicare help pay for blood?

Both Part A (Hospital Insurance) and Part B (Medical Insurance) can help pay for blood (whole blood or units of packed red blood cells), blood components, and the cost of blood processing and administration.

If a patient receives blood as an inpatient of a hospital or skilled nursing facility, Part A (Hospital Insurance) will pay all of the blood costs, except for a deductible charged for the first three pints of whole blood or units of packed red cells in each benefit period. The deductible is the charge that some hospitals and skilled nursing facilities make for blood which is not replaced.

The patient is responsible for the deductible for the first three pints or units of blood furnished by a hospital or skilled nursing facility in a calendar year. If the patient is charged a deductible, the patient has the option of either paying the deductible or having the blood replaced. A hospital or skilled nursing facility cannot charge a patient for any of the first three pints of blood the patient replaces. Any blood deductible satisfied under Part B (Medical Insurance) will reduce the blood deductible requirements under Part A (Hospital Insurance).

Part B (Medical Insurance) can help pay for blood and blood components received as an outpatient or as part of other covered services, except for a deductible charged for the first three pints or units received in each calendar year. After the patient has met the annual deductible, Part B (Medical Insurance) pays 80 percent of the approved charge for blood starting with the fourth pint in a calendar year.

## PRIVATE CONTRACTS

### 1108. Can physicians enter into private contracts with Medicare beneficiaries?

Yes, physicians or practitioners can sign private contracts with Medicare beneficiaries for whom no claim is to be submitted to Medicare and for which the physician or practitioner receives no reimbursement from Medicare, on a per person basis, or from an organization that receives reimbursement under Medicare for the item or service. Services provided under private contracts are not covered under Medicare.

A private contract is not valid unless it (1) is written and signed by the beneficiary before any item or service is provided pursuant to the contract, (2) is entered into when the beneficiary is not facing an emergency or urgent health care situation, and (3) contains specific items listed below.

Among other provisions, the contract must clearly indicate to the beneficiary that by signing the contract the beneficiary (1) agrees not to submit a claim to Medicare even if the items or services would otherwise by covered, (2) agrees to be responsible, through insurance or otherwise, for payment of the items and services and understands that no reimbursement will be provided under Medicare, (3) acknowledges that no limits will apply to amounts that could be charged for the items and services, (4) acknowledges that Medigap plans do not make payments for these items and services because Medicare does not make payment, and (5) acknowledges that the beneficiary has a right to have the items and services provided by other physicians or practitioners for whom payment would be made under Medicare.

Private contracts are not valid unless the physician files an affidavit with the Medicare Administrative Contractor (MAC) for the area in which the physician practices not later than ten days after the first contract to which the affidavit applies is entered into. The affidavit must identify the physician or practitioner, be signed by the physician or practitioner, and provide that – except for emergency services – the physician or practitioner will not submit any claim to Medicare for any item or service provided to any beneficiary for two years beginning on the date the affidavit is signed.

If the physician or practitioner knowingly and willfully submits a claim to Medicare for any item or service furnished to a beneficiary (except emergency services) during the two-year period, (1) the physician or practitioner will no longer be allowed to furnish services under private contracts for the remainder of the two-year period, and (2) no Medicare payment will be made for any item or service furnished by the physician or practitioner during the remainder of the two-year period.

# PART C: MEDICARE ADVANTAGE

## DEFINITION

### 1109. What is Medicare Advantage?

Medicare Advantage (formerly known as Medicare+Choice) permits contracts between the Centers for Medicare & Medicaid Services (CMS) and a variety of different private managed care and fee-for-service entities. Most Medicare beneficiaries may choose to receive benefits either through the original Medicare fee-for-service program [Medicare Part A (Hospital Insurance) and Medicare Part B (Medical Insurance)]. Main types of Medicare Advantage plans include:

- coordinated care plans, including Health Maintenance Organizations (HMOs), Preferred Provider Organizations (PPOs), and Provider-Sponsored Organizations (PSOs), and

- private fee-for-service plans which reimburse providers on a fee-for-service basis.

### 1110. What is a Health Maintenance Organization (HMO)?

A Medicare HMO is a type of managed care plan that provides to its enrolled Medicare beneficiary members, either directly or through arrangement with others, at least all the Medicare-covered services that are available to Medicare beneficiaries who are not enrolled in the HMO and who reside in the geographic area serviced by the HMO. Some HMOs also provide services not covered by Medicare, either free to the Medicare enrollee (that is, funded out of the payment Medicare makes to the HMO) or for an additional charge to the enrollee. HMOs typically charge a set monthly premium and nominal copayments for services instead of Medicare's coinsurance and deductibles.

Each HMO has its own network of hospitals, skilled nursing facilities, home health agencies, doctors, and other professionals. Depending on how the plan is organized, services are usually provided either at one or more centrally located health facilities or in the private practice offices of the doctors and other health care professionals who are part of the HMO. A beneficiary generally must receive all covered care through the HMO or from health care professionals referred to by the plan.

Most HMOs allow an enrollee to select a primary care doctor from those who are part of the HMO. If the beneficiary does not make a selection, a primary care physician will be assigned. The primary care doctor is responsible for managing the beneficiary's medical care, including admitting the beneficiary to a hospital or referring the beneficiary to specialists. The beneficiary is allowed to change his or her primary care doctor as long as another primary care doctor affiliated with the HMO is selected.

Before enrolling in an HMO, the beneficiary should find out whether the plan has a "risk" or a "cost" contract with Medicare. There is an important difference:

**Risk Plans**. These plans have "lock-in" requirements. This means that the beneficiary generally is locked into receiving all covered care through the HMO or through referrals by the plan.

In most cases, if the beneficiary receives services that are not authorized by the HMO, neither the plan nor Medicare will pay. The only exceptions recognized by all Medicare-contracting plans are for emergency services, which the beneficiary may receive anywhere in the United States, and for services the beneficiary urgently needs when temporarily out of the HMO's service area.

**Cost Plans.** These plans do not have lock-in requirements. If a beneficiary enrolls in a cost plan, the beneficiary can either go to health care providers affiliated with the HMO or go outside the plan. If a beneficiary goes outside the plan, the plan probably will not pay, but Medicare will. Medicare will pay its share of charges it approves. The beneficiary will be responsible for Medicare's coinsurance, deductibles, and other charges, just as if receiving care under the regular Medicare program.

## 1111. What is a Medicare Advantage Private Fee-For-Service (PFFS) plan?

A Medicare Advantage Private Fee-For-Service (PFFS) plan is defined as a plan that reimburses doctors, hospitals, and other providers on a fee-for-service basis, does not place them at risk, does not vary payment rates based on utilization, and does not restrict which doctor or hospital the member can use. Subject to some limits and review by the Centers for Medicare & Medicaid Services (CMS), the private insurance company, not CMS, decides how much to reimburse for services received by the beneficiary. The beneficiary pays the Part B premium ($104.90 in 2015 for most beneficiaries—see Q 1065), any additional monthly premium the private fee-for-service plan charges, and any deductible or coinsurance required by the plan, including any copayment required per visit or service.

## 1112. What is a Medicare Advantage Provider-Sponsored Organization (PSO)?

For purposes of Medicare Advantage, PSOs are public or private entities established by or organized by a health care provider (such as a hospital) or a group of affiliated health care providers (such as a geriatric unit of a hospital) that provide a substantial proportion of health care items and services directly through that provider or group. Affiliated providers share, directly or indirectly, substantial financial risk and have at least a majority financial interest in the PSO.

## 1113. What is a Medicare Advantage Religious Fraternal Benefit (RFB) plan?

An RFB plan may restrict enrollment to members of the church, convention, or group with which the society is affiliated. They must meet Medicare financial solvency requirements, and Medicare may adjust payment amounts to these plans to take into account the actuarial characteristics and experience of plan enrollees. In addition to meeting Medicare requirements, any RFB plan must also satisfy certain provisions of the Internal Revenue Code and qualify as a tax-exempt organization in accordance with the Code.

# ELIGIBILITY, ELECTION, AND ENROLLMENT

## 1114. What is the enrollment/disenrollment process for Medicare Advantage?

Beneficiaries entitled to Part A (Hospital Insurance) and enrolled in Part B (Medical Insurance) are eligible to enroll in any Medicare Advantage plan that serves the geographic area in which they reside, except beneficiaries with end-stage renal disease (although beneficiaries who develop end-stage renal disease may remain in the plan if already enrolled) and beneficiaries receiving inpatient hospice care. Part B only enrollees are ineligible.

The Centers for Medicare & Medicaid Services (CMS) have established procedures for enrollment and disenrollment in Medicare Advantage options. Newly eligible enrollees who do not choose a Medicare Advantage plan are deemed to have chosen the original Medicare fee-for-service option (in other words, Medicare Parts A and B). Individuals generally remain enrolled in the Medicare option of their choice unless and until they choose another plan. CMS retains the power to implement "passive enrollment" in cases where a Medicare Advantage plan terminates or CMS determines that remaining in the Medicare Advantage plan poses a risk to the members. Under passive enrollment, CMS treats beneficiaries as enrolled in whatever plan CMS chooses unless the beneficiaries affirmatively elect otherwise.

## 1115. What are the enrollment periods for Medicare Advantage plans?

Beneficiaries can choose a Medicare Advantage plan at initial Medicare eligibility or during one of the enrollment periods described in the subsequent list:

- The annual coordinated enrollment period runs from October 15 through December 7 of each year. Enrollments at this time are effective the following January 1. Beneficiaries may switch from one Medicare Advantage plan to another during this period.
- From January 1 through February 14 of each year, a person enrolled in a Medicare Advantage Plan can leave that plan and switch to the original Medicare fee-for-service program (Medicare Part A (Hospital Insurance) and Part B (Medical Insurance)). If a person switches to Medicare Parts A and B during this period, he or she will have until February 14 to also join a Medicare Part D (Prescription Drug Insurance) plan to add drug coverage.
- Special election periods are available in which a beneficiary can disenroll if the Medicare Advantage plan in which that beneficiary was enrolled terminates, the beneficiary moves out of the plan's service area, the beneficiary demonstrates that the plan has violated its contract or misrepresented the plan in marketing, or any other conditions specified by the Centers for Medicare & Medicaid Services (CMS).
- Newly eligible beneficiaries who elect a Medicare Advantage option may also disenroll into original Medicare fee-for-service program [Part A (Hospital Insurance) and Part B (Medical Insurance)] any time during the first twelve months of their enrollment.

Medicare Advantage plans must accept all beneficiaries on a first-come, first-served basis, subject to capacity limits.

Plans may disenroll beneficiaries only for cause (i.e., failure to pay premiums or disruptive behavior) or plan termination in a beneficiary's geographic area. Beneficiaries terminated for cause are enrolled in the original Medicare fee-for-service program. Others may have a special election period.

### 1116. How is enrollment information provided to Medicare beneficiaries?

At least fifteen days before the required November coordinated election period (see Q 1115), the Centers for Medicare & Medicaid Services (CMS) must mail to each beneficiary general information on Medicare and comparative information on Medicare Advantage plans available in their area. General information includes information on covered benefits, cost sharing, and balance billing liability under the original fee-for-service program [Medicare Part A (Hospital Insurance) and Part B (Medical Insurance)]; election procedures; grievance and appeals rights; and information on Medigap insurance and Medicare SELECT. Comparative information includes extensive information on benefits and beneficiary liability; premiums; service areas; quality and performance; and supplemental benefits. A sophisticated search engine is available at www.medicare.gov to assist beneficiaries in making a decision between Medicare Advantage and traditional Medicare Parts A and B. and in locating a Medicare Advantage plan in a beneficiary's area. Beneficiaries may also call CMS at 1-800-772-1213.

## BENEFITS AND BENEFICIARY PROTECTIONS

### 1117. What basic benefits are provided by Medicare Advantage plans?

All Medicare Advantage plans are required to provide at least the same benefits available under traditional Medicare Part A (Hospital Insurance) and Part B (Medical Insurance), with the exception of the Part A hospice benefit. If a beneficiary requires hospice services, those benefits are provided through Part A (Hospital Insurance).

Medicare Advantage plans may also offer mandatory and optional supplemental benefits, subject to approval by the Centers for Medicare & Medicaid Services (CMS). Mandatory supplemental benefits must be approved unless CMS determines that offering such benefits would substantially discourage enrollment in the Medicare Advantage plan. Medicare Advantage plans may also offer optional supplemental benefits. Optional supplemental benefits are benefits – such as vision, dental and wellness care – that a beneficiary chooses to add to his or her Medicare Advantage plan coverage. Beneficiaries who enroll in Medicare Advantage plans offering either mandatory or optional supplemental benefits (or both) pay the cost of such benefits through additional premiums or cost-sharing obligations such as copayments or coinsurance.

### 1118. What standards must Medicare Advantage plans meet for protection of beneficiaries?

In general, Medicare Advantage plans must offer similar protections to Medicare beneficiaries enrolled in traditional Medicare Part A (Hospital Insurance) and Part B (Medical Insurance), including disclosure, access, quality of care, grievance and appeals procedures, confidentiality, and information on advance directives.

### 1119. What are the rules regarding nondiscrimination for Medicare Advantage plans?

Medicare Advantage plans cannot screen potential enrollees based on their health status, nor can a Medicare Advantage plan discriminate with respect to participation, payment, or indemnification against any provider acting within the scope of the provider's license or certification.

Medicare Advantage plans may, however, selectively contract with providers based on a provider's willingness to accept the provisions of the Medicare Advantage plan's contract.

## 1120. What are the rules regarding disclosure to enrollees?

A Medicare Advantage plan must provide in a clear, accurate, and standardized form, certain plan information to each enrollee, including the plan's: service area; benefits; number, mix and distribution of providers; out-of-area coverage; emergency coverage; supplemental benefits; prior authorization rules; appeals and grievance procedures; quality assurance program; and disenrollment procedures. Upon request, enrollees must be provided comparative information, information on the plan's utilization control mechanisms, information on the number of grievances and appeals, and compensation arrangements.

## 1121. What are the access-to-services requirements for Medicare Advantage plans?

Medicare Advantage plans are permitted to select the providers who may furnish benefits to enrollees, as long as benefits are available and accessible to all enrollees with reasonable promptness and assured continuity, twenty-four hours a day, seven days a week. The plan must also cover services provided other than through the organization for (1) nonemergency services needed immediately because of an unforeseen illness or injury, if it was not reasonable to obtain the services through the plan, (2) renal dialysis services for enrollees who are temporarily out of the plan's service area, and (3) maintenance or poststabilization care after an emergency condition has been stabilized, subject to guidelines established by the Centers for Medicare & Medicaid Services (CMS).

Medicare Advantage plans are required to pay for emergency services without regard to prior authorization or whether the provider has a contractual relationship with the plan. An emergency medical condition is defined using a "prudent layperson" standard (including conditions that may be manifested by "severe pain").

Private fee-for-service plans must demonstrate that the plan includes a sufficient number and range of providers willing to furnish services. This requirement is presumed to have been met if the plan has established payment rates that are not less than payment rates under Medicare, and/or has contracts or agreements with a sufficient number and range of providers.

## 1122. Is there a quality assurance program for Medicare Advantage plans?

Medicare Advantage plans must have an internal quality assurance program. There are numerous requirements for internal quality assurance programs, including that such programs include chronic care improvement plans, conduct certain types of quality improvement projects, and encourage contracted providers to participate in various government quality improvement initiatives. Medicare Advantage plans are deemed to have satisfied certain of the Medicare quality assurance requirements by receiving accreditation (and having periodic review and re-accreditation) from a private organization approved by the Centers for Medicare & Medicaid Services (CMS). CMS may also deem Medicare Advantage plans – generally, organizations with good track records – to have satisfied certain of the quality assurance program requirements.

## 1123. How are grievances handled by Medicare Advantage plans?

Medicare Advantage plans must maintain meaningful procedures for hearing and resolving grievances. Medicare Advantage plans also must have a procedure for making determinations regarding whether an enrollee is entitled to receive services and the amount the individual is required to pay for such services. Determinations must be made on a timely basis. The explanation of a plan's determination must be in writing and must explain the reasons for the denial in understandable language and describe the reconsideration and appeals processes. The time period for reconsiderations will be specified by the Centers for Medicare & Medicaid Services (CMS) but must not be greater than sixty days after the request by the enrollee. Reconsiderations of coverage determinations to deny coverage based on lack of medical necessity must be made by a physician with expertise in the field of medicine that relates to the condition necessitating treatment.

Plans are required to have an expedited review process in cases where the normal time frame for making a determination or reconsideration could seriously jeopardize the life or health of the enrollee or the enrollee's ability to regain maximum function. Either the beneficiary or the physician can request an expedited review. Requests for expedited reviews made by physicians (even those not affiliated with the organization) must be granted by the plan. Expedited determinations and reconsiderations must be made within time periods specified by CMS, but not later than seventy-two hours after the request for expedited review, or such longer period as CMS may permit in specified cases.

CMS is required to contract with an independent, outside entity to review and resolve plan reconsiderations not favorable to the beneficiary. If the independent review is unfavorable to the beneficiary, the beneficiary has the right to the same appeals process (e.g., Administrative Law Judge, judicial review) as under existing HMO procedures.

## 1124. Are there special rules covering provider participation?

Yes, a Medicare Advantage plan must establish procedures relating to participation of physicians in the plan, such as notice of rules of participation, written notice of adverse participation decisions, and an appeals process. Medicare Advantage plans must consult with participating physicians regarding medical policy, quality, and medical management procedures.

Plans are prohibited from restricting health care professionals from advising their patients about the patient's health status or treatment options.

A provider, health professional, or other entity is treated as having a contract with a private fee-for-service plan if the provider, health professional, or other entity provides services that are covered under a private fee-for-service plan, and before providing those services, was informed of the individual's enrollment, and either was informed of the terms and conditions of payment for the services under the private fee-for-service plan or was given a reasonable opportunity to obtain information concerning the terms and conditions.

## 1125. Are there billing limits under Medicare Advantage?

Noncontracting physicians and other entities must accept as payment in full the amount that would have been paid under Medicare Advantage or a Medicare fee-for-service plan. Noncontracting providers must also accept, as payment in full, the amount that would have been paid under traditional Medicare.

Contracting physicians, providers, and other entities of private fee-for-service plans must accept as payment in full an amount not to exceed (including any deductibles, coinsurance, copayments or balance billing permitted under the plan) an amount equal to 115 percent of the plan's payment rate. Plans must establish procedures to carry out this requirement. If a plan does not establish and enforce its procedures, the plan is subject to sanctions.

Private fee-for-service plans must provide enrollees with an explanation of benefits that includes a clear statement regarding enrollee liability, including any balance billing. The plan must also provide that the hospital give enrollees prior notice before they receive inpatient services and certain other services, when the amount of balance billing could be substantial. The notice must include a good faith estimate of the likely amount of balance billing based upon the presenting conditions of the enrollee.

## PREMIUMS

### 1126. How do Medicare Advantage plans submit proposed premiums?

All Medicare Advantage plans must submit to the Centers for Medicare & Medicaid Services (CMS) information on enrollment capacity. *Managed care plans* must submit Adjusted Community Rate (ACR) proposals for basic and supplemental benefits, the plan's premium for the basic and supplemental benefits, a description of the plan's proposed cost-sharing requirements, the actuarial value of cost sharing for basic and supplemental benefits, and a description of any additional benefits and the value of these benefits. *Private fee-for-service plans* must submit ACRs for basic and additional benefits, the premium for the basic and additional benefits, a description of the plan's proposed cost-sharing requirements and the actuarial value of the cost sharing, a description of additional benefits and the actuarial value of these benefits, and the supplemental premium.

In general, the CMS must review ACRs, premiums, and the actuarial values and approve or disapprove these rates, amounts, and values. CMS does not review premiums of private fee-for-service plans.

Organizations cannot contract to enroll Medicare beneficiaries under the Medicare Advantage program until they have met standards published by the CMS.

### 1127. What other Medicare Advantage premium rules should a beneficiary know about?

- A Medicare Advantage plan can terminate an enrollee for failure to pay premiums, but only under specified conditions.
- A Medicare Advantage organization cannot offer cash or other monetary rebates as an inducement for enrollment or otherwise.
- Premiums cannot vary among plan enrollees in the same Medicare Advantage plan.

- No state can impose a premium tax or similar tax on premiums of Medicare Advantage plans or the offering of these plans.

## CONTRACTS WITH MEDICARE ADVANTAGE ORGANIZATIONS

### 1128. How does a plan become part of the Medicare Advantage program?

A Medicare Advantage plan must generally be organized and licensed under state law as a risk-bearing entity to offer health insurance or health benefits coverage.

New regional Preferred Provider Organizations (PPOs) are also eligible for temporary waiver-of-state-licensure requirements. This is intended to facilitate the introduction of these multi-state plans. The Centers for Medicare & Medicaid Services (CMS) has indicated that it will grant these waivers only in cases where the organization is licensed in one state and has submitted applications in the other states. The length of the waiver will typically be for less than one year, but will depend on how long states take to process applications.

A plan cannot receive payment from Medicare unless it has a contract with CMS. The contract period is for one year and may be automatically renewed in the absence of notice by either party of intention to terminate.

CMS can terminate a contract if (1) the organization has failed to substantially carry out the contract, (2) the organization was carrying out the contract in a manner substantially inconsistent with the efficient and effective administration of the Medicare Advantage program, or (3) the organization no longer substantially meets Medicare Advantage conditions. CMS generally may not contract with a plan that has been terminated within the last five years.

Medicare Advantage plans must meet minimum enrollment requirements: 5,000 for plans in urban areas, 1,500 for plans in rural areas. These requirements can be waived in the first three contract years.

Medicare Advantage plans must provide prompt payment to noncontracting providers and to enrollees in the case of private fee-for-service plans. If CMS determines (after notice of an opportunity for a hearing) that a plan has failed to pay providers or enrollees promptly, CMS can provide for direct payment. In these cases, CMS will reduce Medicare Advantage payments accordingly.

CMS may impose sanctions if a plan (1) fails to provide medically necessary services required under law or the contract, and the failure adversely affects or has the substantial likelihood of adversely affecting the enrollee, (2) imposes premiums in excess of the premium permitted, (3) acts to expel or refuses to reenroll an individual in violation of the Medicare Advantage requirements, (4) engages in practices that effectively deny or discourage enrollment, (5) misrepresents or falsifies information to CMS or to others, (6) violates rules regarding physician participation, (7) employs or contracts with individuals who are excluded from participation in Medicare, or (8) performs any other actions that are grounds for termination and, in the case of private fee-for-service plans, does not enforce balance billing limits. The remedies may include civil money penalties, suspension of enrollment, or suspension of payment.

Medicare Advantage plans must assume full financial risk for the provision of Medicare services, except that plans can (1) obtain insurance or make other arrangements for costs in excess of amounts periodically determined by CMS, (2) obtain insurance or make arrangements for services needing to be provided other than through the plan, (3) obtain insurance or make other arrangements for not more than 90 percent of the amount by which its fiscal year costs exceeded 115 percent of its income for the year, or (4) make arrangements with providers or health institutions to assume all or part of the risk on a prospective basis for the provision of basic services.

## MEDIGAP INSURANCE PROGRAM

### 1129. What rules apply regarding Medigap insurance and Medicare Advantage plans?

As a general matter, a Medigap insurance policy cannot be sold or issued to a Medicare beneficiary or an individual with the knowledge that the policy duplicates health benefits to which the individual is already entitled under Medicare, including under a Medicare Advantage plan.

A Medicare Advantage plan is not considered a Medigap insurance policy. Medigap insurance policies supplement original fee-for-service Medicare coverage (Medicare Part A (Hospital Insurance) and Part B (Medical Insurance)). As an alternative to original Medicare Parts A and B, Medicare Advantage plans offer at a minimum the same basic coverage as traditional fee-for-service Medicare. Medicare Advantage plans may also offer additional benefits, subject to payment of additional premiums by enrollees (if the Medicare Advantage plan so requires). The additional benefits often duplicate what would otherwise be available through a private Medigap policy. See Q 1139 through Q 1149 for more information on Medigap insurance.

### 1130. What are the special rules regarding Medigap protections under the Medicare Advantage program?

If an individual described below seeks to enroll in a Medigap policy within sixty-three days of the events described next, the issuer may not (1) deny or condition the issuance of a Medigap policy that is offered or available, (2) discriminate in the pricing of a policy because of health status, claims experience, receipt of health care, or medical condition, and (3) impose a preexisting condition exclusion. See Q 1139 through Q 1149 for more information about Medigap insurance.

There is guaranteed issuance of Medigap Plans A, B, C, F, K or L for:

(1) Individuals enrolled under an employee welfare benefit plan that provides benefits supplementing Medicare if the plan terminates or ceases to provide all benefits.

(2) Persons enrolled with a Medicare Advantage organization who discontinue under circumstances permitting disenrollment other than during an annual election period. These include (1) the termination of the entity's certification, (2) the individual moves outside the entity's service area, or (3) the individual elects termination due to cause.

(3) Persons enrolled with a risk or cost contract HMO, a similar organization operating under a demonstration project authority, a health care prepayment plan, or a Medicare SELECT policy, if enrollment ceases under the same circumstances that permit discontinuance of a Medicare Advantage election. In the case of a SELECT policy, there must also be no applicable provision in state law for continuation of the coverage.

(4) Individuals enrolled under a Medigap policy, if enrollment ceases because of the bankruptcy or insolvency of the issuer, or because of other involuntary termination of coverage (and there is no provision under applicable state law for the continuation of coverage), or the issuer violated or misrepresented a provision of the policy.

There is guaranteed issuance of Medigap Plans A, B, C, F, K, L, or the Medigap insurance policy that the individual most recently previously enrolled in, if the individual (1) was enrolled under a Medigap policy, (2) subsequently terminates enrollment and enrolls with a Medicare Advantage organization, a risk or cost contract HMO, a similar organization operating under a demonstration project authority or a Medicare SELECT policy, and (3) terminates the Medicare Advantage enrollment within twelve months, but only if the individual was never previously enrolled with a Medicare Advantage organization.

There is guaranteed issuance of *any* Medigap plan to an individual who, upon first becoming eligible for Medicare at age sixty-five, enrolled in a Medicare Advantage plan and disenrolled from the plan within twelve months of the effective date of enrollment.

## MEDICARE ADVANTAGE MARKETING RULES

### 1131. What are the rules about the marketing of Medicare Advantage plans?

Significant restrictions apply to marketing of Medicare Advantage plans to Medicare beneficiaries. These restrictions include:

- Prohibiting "cold calls" and other unsolicited contact. This prohibition includes door-to-door sales and unsolicited telephone calls. The rules do not prohibit plan mailings, but the final regulations prohibit calling to confirm that the beneficiary received the mailing. Agents may call in response to specific requests by beneficiaries to be contacted.

- Prohibiting sales activities at educational events. Events designed to provide the public with objective information about Medicare must be free of any marketing materials or enrollment information for a specific plan or organization. Plans and agents may hold sales events that are clearly labeled as such, but they may not be disguised as educational events.

- Prohibiting plans and agents from providing meals at Medicare sales meetings. Light refreshments and "snacks" are permissible.

- Prohibiting sales activities in settings where individuals receive health care services. This rule permits marketing in common areas such as waiting rooms, but prohibits marketing in treatment rooms. Plans may arrange meetings with residents in long-term care facilities as with any other private residence.

- Prohibiting marketing any nonhealth insurance product (such as life insurance or annuities) during a Medicare marketing or sales meeting.

Agents are also required to document that, prior to making an appointment, beneficiaries agree to the scope of products to be discussed at the meeting. Appointments made in person require written documentation; appointments made over the phone require recorded documentation. At a meeting in an agent's office or on the phone, additional products may not be discussed unless the beneficiary requests the information. In a meeting at a beneficiary's home, an agent may not discuss any product not within the originally-identified scope of the meeting. They must schedule a separate appointment at least forty-eight hours later.

# PART D: PRESCRIPTION DRUG INSURANCE

## 1132. What is Medicare Part D?

Medicare Part D is the prescription drug insurance program added to Medicare by the Medicare Prescription Drug, Improvement, and Modernization Act of 2003 (MMA).

Part D is a voluntary program of health insurance that covers a portion of outpatient prescription drug costs not generally covered by other Medicare programs, especially traditional Medicare Part A (Hospital Insurance) and Part B (Medical Insurance). Part D prescription drug plans are offered only through private insurance companies. Medicare beneficiaries wishing to enroll in a Part D plan may stay with original Medicare Parts A and B and enroll in a stand-alone Part D prescription drug insurance plan, or they may choose a Medicare Advantage plan that includes Part D prescription drug benefits as part of the Medicare Advantage plan's comprehensive benefit package. Part D prescription drug insurance is partially financed through premiums paid by participants, whether for stand-alone Part D plans or as part of a Medicare Advantage plan.

## 1133. When did Medicare Part D become effective?

Medicare Part D (Prescription Drug Insurance) became effective January 1, 2006, with initial enrollment for the first year beginning November 15, 2005, and running for six months.

## 1134. Who is eligible for Medicare Part D?

Any Medicare beneficiary who is entitled to Medicare Part A or enrolled in Part B is eligible to participate in Part D (Prescription Drug Insurance).

## 1135. What does the Part D (Prescription Drug Insurance) cost?

Generally, Part D (Prescription Drug Insurance) plans require beneficiaries to pay monthly premiums, meet an annual deductible, and pay coinsurance. Because Part D plans are offered only through private insurance plans, the premiums, deductibles and coinsurance vary from plan to plan. Premiums may be paid separately for a stand-alone Part D plan or as part of the monthly premium for a comprehensive Medicare Advantage plan.

Beneficiaries who choose not to enroll in Part D during their initial enrollment period may face a late enrollment penalty if they later choose to enroll in a Part D plan. The late enrollment penalty is the greater of "an amount that [the CMS] determines is actuarially sound for each uncovered month" or "1 percent of the base beneficiary premium" (the national average premium for the year of late enrollment) per month. The late enrollment penalty is calculated by multiplying 1 percent of the "national base beneficiary premium" ($32.42 in 2014, and $33.13 in 2015) times the number of full, uncovered months you were eligible but didn't join a Medicare Prescription Drug Plan and went without other creditable prescription drug coverage. The final amount is rounded to the nearest ten cents and added to your monthly premium. For example, for a beneficiary enrolling late in 2015, the penalty was approximately thirty-three cents per full month in which the beneficiary was eligible to enroll in a Part D plan but failed to do so.

Beneficiaries who have other sources of prescription drug coverage (such as through a former employer) may be able to maintain that coverage and delay enrollment in a Part D plan without incurring a penalty in the future. As long as a beneficiary maintains coverage that qualifies as "creditable coverage" (meaning generally that the coverage is at least as valuable – at least actuarially equivalent – as the standard Part D prescription drug package specified by Medicare), the beneficiary will not be subject to late enrollment penalties if he later enrolls in a Part D plan. Failure to maintain creditable prescription drug coverage for a period of sixty-three days or longer may subject an individual to a late enrollment penalty.

Entities (such as a former employer) offering prescription drug coverage to Part D eligible individuals must disclose to those individuals whether the coverage they provide is creditable coverage as defined by CMS. These entities must also inform CMS of the status of this coverage. See Q 1138.

## 1136. What benefits does Part D (Prescription Drug Insurance) provide?

Medicare establishes a standard prescription drug benefit under Part D (Prescription Drug Insurance). Participants with incomes below 135 percent, and between 135 percent and 150 percent, of the federal poverty guidelines will have lower cost-sharing requirements than under the standard benefit.

The Part D standard drug benefit in 2015 is:

| Prescription Drug Expenses | Beneficiary Costs | Medicare Pays |
|---|---|---|
| First $320 | 100% (up to $320) | Nothing |
| $320-$2,960 | 25% (up to $660) | 75% (up to $1,980) |
| $2,960-$6,680 | 100% (up to $3,720) | Nothing |
| Above $6,680 | Up to 5% (based on income) | 95% or more |

In the "Coverage Gap" ($2,960-$6,680), a Medicare beneficiary may have to pay for 47.5 percent of brand name drugs or 72 percent of generic drugs. Once a Medicare beneficiary has paid $4,700 out-of-pocket, the beneficiary is out of the Coverage Gap.

Beneficiaries with incomes below 135 percent of the federal poverty guidelines have no cost-sharing obligation for prescription drug expenses above $6,560. Beneficiaries with incomes between 135 percent and 150 percent of the federal poverty guidelines have $2.65 and $6.60 co-pays for generic and name-brand prescriptions. Those with incomes above 150 percent of the federal poverty level have 5 percent co-pays.

For 2015, 135 percent of the federal poverty guidelines is $15,754.50 for a single person and $21,235.50 for a married couple; 150 percent of the federal poverty guidelines is $17,505 for a single person and $23,595 for a married couple. Part D plans are available only through private insurance companies. Those insurers may offer prescription drug plans that vary from the Part D standard benefit as long as the plans (1) provide coverage, the actuarial value of which is at least equal to the actuarial value of the standard prescription drug coverage, (2) offer access to negotiated prices, and (3) are approved by the CMS.

Part D plans may also provide supplemental prescription drug coverage that offers cost-sharing reductions and optional drugs. A plan may charge a supplemental premium for the supplemental coverage. However, insurers offering Part D plans with supplemental coverage in an area must also offer a prescription drug plan in the area that provides only basic coverage for no additional supplemental premium. Basic coverage is either the statutorily defined standard benefit or the actuarial equivalent of such standard benefit without any supplemental benefits.

The monthly Medicare Part D base premium is set to pay 25.5 percent of the cost of standard coverage, based on bids submitted annually by Part D plans. The CMS releases the Medicare Part D base premium in early August each year. Actual premiums are based on this set premium, but can vary greatly by plans and regions. Beneficiaries with higher incomes must pay a premium adjustment based on their income. This premium adjustment is called the Income-Related Monthly Adjustment Amount (IRMAA), and is automatically deducted from the Social Security benefit.

| **Beneficiaries who file individual tax returns with income that is:** | **Beneficiaries who file joint tax returns with income that is:** | **Medicare Part D Income Related Monthly Adjustment Amount** | | |
|---|---|---|---|---|
| | | **2015** | **2014** | **2013** |
| Less than or equal to $85,000 | Less than or equal to $170,000 | $0.00 | $0.00 | $0.00 |
| Greater than $85,000 and less than or equal to $107,000 | Greater than $170,000 and less than or equal to $214,000 | $12.30 | $12.10 | $11.60 |
| Greater than $107,000 and less than or equal to $160,000 | Greater than $214,000 and less than or equal to $320,000 | $31.80 | $31.10 | $29.90 |
| Greater than $160,000 and less than or equal to $214,000 | Greater than $320,000 and less than or equal to $428,000 | $51.30 | $50.20 | $48.30 |
| Greater than $214,000 | Greater than $428,000 | $70.80 | $69.30 | $66.60 |

The Patient Protection and Affordable Care Act (PPACA) includes benefits to make Medicare prescription drug coverage (Part D) more affordable for beneficiaries. This is done through providing coverage through a coverage gap (also called the "donut hole") in Medicare prescription drug coverage.

The PPACA coverage provides the following:

- A discount on covered brand-name drugs when a person buys the drug at a pharmacy or orders the drugs through the mail
- Some coverage for generic and brand-name drugs
- Additional savings on brand-name and generic drugs during the coverage gap over the next several years until it's closed in 2020
- The coverage gap closes by maintaining the 50 percent discount the manufacturers offer and increasing what Medicare drug plans cover

## 1137. What notice must an employer who maintains a prescription drug plan provide to Medicare-eligible individuals?

Employers and plan sponsors who offer prescription drug coverage to individuals eligible for Medicare Part D (Prescription Drug Insurance) must advise those individuals whether the offered coverage is "creditable." Eligible individuals who do not enroll in Part D when first available, but who enroll later, have to pay higher premiums permanently, unless they have creditable prescription drug coverage. See Q 1138.

To determine that coverage is creditable, a sponsor need only determine that total expected paid claims for Medicare beneficiaries under the sponsor's plan will be at least equal to the total expected paid claims for the same beneficiaries under the defined standard prescription drug coverage under Part D. The determination of creditable-coverage status for disclosure purposes does not require attestation by a qualified actuary (unless the employer or union is applying for the retiree drug subsidy available under the MMA).

To assist sponsors in making the determination that coverage is creditable, the Centers for Medicare & Medicaid Studies (CMS) issued guidance with example "safe harbor" benefit designs. A plan design will automatically be deemed creditable if it includes:

1. coverage for brand and generic prescriptions;
2. reasonable access to retail providers and, optionally, for mail order coverage;
3. benefits payments designed to pay on average at least 60 percent of participants' prescription drug expenses; and
4. at least one of the following:
    a. an annual prescription drug benefit maximum of at least $25,000;
    b. an actuarial expectation that the plan will pay benefits of at least $2,000 per Medicare-eligible individual; or
    c. for plans that cover both medical expenses and prescription drugs, an annual deductible of no more than $250, an annual benefit maximum of at least $25,000, and a lifetime maximum of at least $1,000,000.

Under the CMS guidance, once a sponsor determines whether coverage is creditable, the sponsor must provide notice to all Part D-eligible individuals covered by or applying for the plan, including Part D-eligible dependents. In lieu of determining who is Part D-eligible, an employer sponsor may provide notice to all active employees, along with an explanation of why the notice is being provided.

The required notice to beneficiaries must, at a minimum:

1. contain a statement that the employer has determined that the coverage is creditable (or not creditable);

2. explain the meaning of creditable coverage;

3. explain why creditable coverage is important, and caution that higher Part D premiums could result if there is a break in creditable coverage of sixty-three days or more before enrolling in a Part D plan; and

4. if coverage is not creditable, explain that an individual may generally enroll in Part D only from November 15 through December 31 of each year.

CMS recommends that sponsors also provide the following clarifications in their notices:

- An explanation of a beneficiary's rights to a notice, i.e., the times when a beneficiary can expect to receive a notice and the times that a beneficiary can request a copy of the notice.
- An explanation of the plan provisions that affect beneficiaries when they (or their dependents) are Medicare Part D-eligible. These options may include, for example:
    - that they can retain their existing coverage and choose not to enroll in a Part D plan; or
    - that they can enroll in a Part D plan as a supplement to, or in lieu of, the other coverage;
    - if their existing prescription drug coverage is under a Medigap policy, that they cannot have both their existing prescription drug coverage and Part D coverage and that, if they enroll in Part D coverage, they should inform their Medigap insurer of that fact and the Medigap insurer must remove the prescription drug coverage from the Medigap policy and adjust the premium, as of the date the Part D coverage starts.
- Whether the covered individuals and/or their covered dependents will still be eligible to receive all of their current health coverage if they or their dependents enroll in a Medicare Part D prescription drug plan.
- A clarification of the circumstances (if any) under which the individual could re-enroll in employment-based prescription drug coverage if the individual drops the current coverage and enrolls in Medicare prescription drug coverage. (For Medigap insurers, this would be a clarification that the individual cannot get his prescription drug coverage back under such circumstances).
- Information on how to get extra help paying for a Medicare prescription drug plan including the contact information for the Social Security Administration (SSA).

Sponsors must also disclose to CMS whether the coverage is creditable. The disclosure must be made to CMS on an annual basis, and upon any change that affects whether the coverage is creditable. CMS has posted guidance on the timing and format of the required disclosure and a model Disclosure to CMS form on the CMS website at www.cms.hhs.gov/creditablecoverage.

## PRESCRIPTION DRUG MARKETING RULES

### 1138. What are the rules about the marketing of Medicare Part D (Prescription Drug Insurance) plans?

There are significant restrictions regarding the marketing of Medicare Part D plans:

- The rules broadly prohibit "cold calls" and other unsolicited contact. This prohibition includes door-to-door sales and unsolicited telephone calls. The rules do not prohibit plan mailings, but the final regulations prohibit calling to confirm that the beneficiary received the mailing. Agents may call in response to specific requests by beneficiaries to be contacted.

- The rules prohibit sales activities at educational events. Events designed to provide the public with objective information about Medicare must be free of any marketing materials or enrollment information for a specific plan or organization. Plans and agents may hold sales events that are clearly labeled as such, but they may not be disguised as educational events.

- The rules prohibit plans and agents from providing meals at Medicare sales meetings. The Centers for Medicare & Medicaid Services (CMS) has not yet defined the terms, but light refreshments and "snacks" are permissible.

- The rules prohibit sales activities in settings where individuals receive healthcare services. This rule permits marketing in common areas such as waiting rooms, but prohibits marketing in treatment rooms. Plans may arrange meetings with residents in long-term care facilities as with any other private residence.

- The rules prohibit marketing any non-health insurance product (such as life insurance or annuities) during a Medicare marketing or sales meeting.

The rules also require agents to document that, prior to making an appointment, beneficiaries agree to the scope of products to be discussed at the meeting. Appointments made in person require written documentation; appointments made over the phone require recorded documentation. At a meeting in an agent's office or on the phone, additional products may not be discussed unless the beneficiary requests the information. In a meeting at a beneficiary's home, an agent may not discuss any product not within the originally-identified scope of the meeting. They must schedule a separate appointment at least forty-eight hours later.

The same marketing restrictions apply to both Medicare Advantage and Medicare Part D prescription drug plans.

# MEDIGAP INSURANCE

## 1139. What is Medigap Insurance?

Medicare provides basic protection against the cost of health care, but it does not pay all medical expenses. For this reason, many private insurance companies sell supplemental insurance policies known as "Medigap" policies. The federal government does not sell or service insurance, but regulates the coverage offered by Medigap insurance. Many Medicare beneficiaries enrolled in Part A (Hospital Insurance) and Part B (Medical Insurance) also maintain Medigap policies to cover costs not paid for by Parts A and B.

Medigap insurance is a private insurance policy designed to help pay deductibles and/or coinsurance incurred by beneficiaries who are enrolled in original Medicare Part A (Hospital Insurance) and Part B (Medical Insurance). A Medigap policy may also pay for certain items or services generally not covered by Medicare at all, such as medical expenses incurred during foreign travel. Medigap policies coordinate only with original Medicare Parts A and B, not with Medicare Advantage plans. By law, a Medicare beneficiary cannot be sold a Medigap plan that duplicates benefits otherwise available to that beneficiary under Medicare, including through a Medicare Advantage plan.

## 1140. Is there an open enrollment period for Medigap policies?

Yes, an open enrollment period for selecting Medigap policies guarantees that, for six months immediately following the effective date of enrolling in Medicare Part B (Medical Insurance), a person age sixty-five or older cannot be denied Medigap insurance or charged higher premiums because of health problems.

No matter how a person enrolls in Part B (Medical Insurance)—whether by automatic notification or through an initial, special or general enrollment period—a person is covered by the guarantees if both of the following are true:

- The person is age sixty-five or older and is enrolled in Medicare for the first time, based on age rather than disability
- The person applies for Medigap insurance within six months of enrollment in Part B (Medical Insurance)

In some cases, however, even when a person buys a Medigap policy during his open enrollment period, the policy may still exclude coverage for "preexisting conditions" during the first six months the policy is in effect. Preexisting conditions are conditions that were either diagnosed or treated during the six-month period immediately before the Medigap policy became effective. (See Q 1141 for exceptions to this rule.)

Once the Medigap open enrollment period ends, a person may not be able to buy the policy of his or her choice. He or she may have to accept whatever Medigap policy an insurance company is willing to sell him or her.

In the case of individuals enrolled in Medicare Part B prior to age sixty-five, Medigap insurers are required to offer coverage, regardless of medical history, for a six-month period when the individual reaches age sixty-five. Insurers are prohibited from discriminating in the price of policies for an individual based on that person's medical or health status.

Also, although Medigap policies are standardized, premiums can vary widely. Insurers can reject an applicant who applies for a Medigap policy after the open enrollment period.

Once issued, all Medigap polices are guaranteed renewable. This means that they continue in force as long as the premium is paid.

## 1141. Does a Medicaid recipient need Medigap insurance?

Low-income people who are eligible for Medicaid usually do not need additional insurance. Medicaid generally covers almost all the health care needs of a beneficiary that are not paid for by Medicare, in addition to covering long-term nursing home care. If a person purchases Medigap insurance and later becomes eligible for Medicaid, that individual may ask that Medigap insurance benefits and premiums be suspended for up to two years while the individual is covered by Medicaid. If the person becomes ineligible for Medicaid benefits during the two years, the Medigap policy is automatically reinstated as of the date of Medicaid termination and on terms at least as favorable as those in effect at the time of initial suspension, provided the person gives proper notice and begins paying premiums again.

## 1142. Are there federal standards for Medigap policies?

Yes, Congress established federal standards for Medigap policies in 1990 and again in 2010. Most states have adopted regulations limiting the sale of Medigap insurance to no more than ten standard policies. One of the ten is a basic policy offering a "core package" of benefits. These standardized plans are identified as follows: A, B, C, D, F, G, K, L, M, and N. (Plans E, H, I, and J have not been sold since June 1, 2010, although beneficiaries who had purchased such policies before that date are able to maintain their coverage. Plans M and N became available June 1, 2010.) Plan A is the core package. Plans B, C, D, F, G, M, and N each have a different combination of benefits, but they all include the core package. Plans K and L do not include the core benefit package; they instead offer catastrophic coverage. The basic Plan A policy, offering the core package of benefits, is available in all states. The availability of other plans varies from state to state.

The core package of benefits which all policies (except Plans K and L) must contain includes:

- Part A (Hospital Insurance) coinsurance for the sixty-first through ninetieth day of inpatient hospitalization in any Medicare benefit period;
- Part A (Hospital Insurance) coinsurance for the sixty lifetime reserve days that can be used for an inpatient hospitalization that lasts more than ninety days;
- Part A (Hospital Insurance) expenses for an extra 365 days in the hospital;
- Part A (Hospital Insurance) and Part B (Medical Insurance) deductible for the cost of the first three pints of blood;

- Part B (Medical Insurance) coinsurance (20 percent of allowable charges in most cases); and
- Part A (Hospital Insurance) hospice coinsurance, if any.

## 1143. What additional benefits can be offered in the standard Medigap plans?

The following additional benefits above the basic core benefits can be covered:

- The entire Part A (Hospital Insurance) deductible payable for each new spell of illness requiring inpatient hospitalization
- The Part A (Hospital Insurance) coinsurance for days 21-100 of skilled nursing home care
- The annual Part B (Medical Insurance) deductible
- 80 percent of the "balance billing" paid by Part B (Medical Insurance) beneficiaries whose doctors do not accept assignment; 100 percent of other Part B (Medical Insurance) excess charges billed to beneficiaries
- 80 percent of the Medicare-eligible costs of medically necessary emergency care when the insured is traveling outside the United States
- "Innovative benefits" that are appropriate, cost-effective, and consistent with the goal of simplifying Medigap insurance—with prior approval by the state insurance commissioner

Certain policies sold before 2006 also offered limited coverage of outpatient prescription drug costs. Beneficiaries who purchased those policies before implementation of the Part D (Prescription Drug Insurance) benefit could maintain the policies, but no new policies with such benefits have been allowed after the introduction of Part D. Part D coverage in general is more generous than that available through old Medigap policies.

## 1144. What benefits are provided in each of the standard Medigap policies and the high deductible Medigap policies?

The Medigap policies offer the following benefits:

- Policy A is the basic core benefit package (see Q 1142).
- Policy B includes: (1) the basic core benefit package; and (2) payment of the Part A (Hospital Insurance) deductible payable for each new benefit period.
- Policy C includes: (1) the basic core benefit package; (2) the Part A (Hospital Insurance) deductible; (3) the Part A coinsurance for care in a skilled nursing home (days 21-100); (4) the Part B (Medical Insurance) deductible; and (5) coverage of foreign travel emergencies.

- Policy D includes: (1) the basic core benefit package; (2) the Part A (Hospital Insurance) deductible; (3) the Part A coinsurance for care in a skilled nursing home (days 21-100); and (4) coverage of foreign travel emergencies.

- Policy F includes: (1) the basic core benefit package, (2) the Part A (Hospital Insurance) deductible), (3) the Part A coinsurance for care in a skilled nursing home (days 21-100), (4) the Part B (Medical Insurance) deductible, (5) coverage of foreign travel emergencies, and (6) 100 percent coverage of excess provider charges under Part B (Medical Insurance).

  In addition, there is a policy that is the same as Policy F but with a $2,180 deductible (in 2015). This high-deductible policy covers 100 percent of covered out-of-pocket expenses once the deductible has been satisfied in a year. It requires the beneficiary of the policy to pay annual out-of-pocket expenses (other than premiums) in the amount of $2,180 before the policy begins payment of benefits. The deductible increases by the percentage increase in the Consumer Price Index for all urban consumers for the twelve-month period ending with August of the preceding year.

- Policy G includes: (1) the basic core benefit package, (2) the Part A (Hospital Insurance) deductible, (3) the Part A coinsurance for care in a skilled nursing home (days 21-100), (4) coverage of foreign travel emergencies; and (5) 100 percent coverage of excess provider charges under Part B (Medical Insurance).

Beginning in 2006, two more standard plans became available. These two plans do not include the entire core benefit package:

- Plan K includes: (1) coverage of 50 percent of Part B coinsurance, blood costs under Parts A and B, Part A hospice coinsurance, and Part A skilled nursing facility coinsurance; (2) coverage of 100 percent of Part A hospital inpatient coinsurance and 365 extra lifetime days of coverage of inpatient hospital services; (3) 50 percent of the Part A deductible; and (4) a limit on annual out-of-pocket spending under Part A and Part B to $4,940 (in 2015).

- Plan L includes: (1) coverage of 75 percent the Part B coinsurance, blood costs under Parts A and B, Part A hospice coinsurance, and Part A skilled nursing facility coinsurance; (2) coverage of 100 percent of the Part A hospital inpatient coinsurance and 365 extra lifetime days of coverage of inpatient hospital services; (3) 75 percent of the Part A deductible, and (4) a limit on annual out-of-pocket spending under Part A and Part B to $2,470 (in 2015).

Effective June 1, 2010, two new plans became available (both of which include the basic core benefit package):

- New Plan M duplicates Plan D, but with 50 percent coinsurance on the Part A deductible

- New Plan N duplicates Plan D with the Part B coinsurance being paid at 100 percent, *minus* a $20 copayment per physician visit and a $50 copayment per emergency room visit (unless the beneficiary was admitted to the hospital)

*The following plans are no longer available for purchase effective June 1, 2010* (but if an individual already had or bought one of these plans before June 1, 2010, that individual may keep that plan):

- Policy E includes: (1) the basic core benefit package; (2) the Part A (Hospital Insurance) deductible; (3) the Part A coinsurance for care in a skilled nursing home (days 21-100); (4) coverage of foreign travel emergencies; and (5) coverage of preventive screening and care.

- Policy H includes: (1) the basic core benefit package; (2) the Part A (Hospital Insurance) deductible; (3) the Part A coinsurance for care in a skilled nursing home (days 21-100); (4) coverage of foreign travel emergencies; and (5) coverage of 50 percent of the cost of outpatient prescription drugs after payment of a $250 deductible, up to a maximum benefit of $1,250. (See the paragraph below regarding prescription drug coverage.)

- Policy I includes: (1) the basic core benefit package; (2) the Part A (Hospital Insurance) deductible; (3) the Part A coinsurance for care in a skilled nursing home (days 21-100); (4) coverage of foreign travel emergencies; (5) at-home recovery assistance; (6) 100 percent of excess charges under Part B (Medical Insurance); and (7) 50 percent of the cost of outpatient prescription drugs after payment of a $250 deductible, up to a maximum benefit of $1,250. (See the paragraph below regarding prescription drug coverage.)

- Policy J includes: (1) the basic core benefit package; (2) the Part A (Hospital Insurance) deductible; (3) the Part A coinsurance for care in a skilled nursing home (days 21-100); (4) the Part B (Medical Insurance) annual deductible; (5) coverage of foreign travel emergencies; (6) at-home recovery assistance; (7) 100 percent of excess charges under Part B; (8) preventive screening and care; and (9) 50 percent of the cost of outpatient prescription drugs after payment of a $250 deductible, up to a maximum benefit of $3,000. (See the paragraph below regarding prescription drug coverage.)

  There is also a policy that is the same as Policy J but with a $2,180 deductible. This high-deductible policy covers 100 percent of covered out-of-pocket expense (in 2015) once the deductible has been satisfied in a year. It requires the beneficiary of the policy to pay annual out-of-pocket expenses (other than premiums) in the amount of $2,180 before the policy begins payment of benefits.

As of January 1, 2006, beneficiaries who held standard policies H, I, or J could choose between enrolling in Part D or maintaining their prescription drug coverage under their Medigap policies. Beneficiaries who chose to enroll in Part D could keep their existing plan H, I, or J, minus the prescription drug benefit, or could purchase a new Medigap policy. As of January 1, 2006, plans H, I, and J could be sold, but without the prescription drug benefit.

Some plan choices may not be available in Massachusetts, Minnesota, and Wisconsin because these states already required standardized Medigap policies prior to 1992.

## 1145. What are Medicare SELECT policies?

The difference between Medicare SELECT and regular Medigap insurance is that a Medicare SELECT policy may (except in emergencies) limit Medigap benefits to items and services provided by certain selected health care providers (including hospitals) or may pay only partial benefits when a patient gets health care from other health care providers.

Insurers, including some HMOs, offer Medicare SELECT in the same way they offer standard Medigap insurance. The policies are required to meet certain federal standards and are regulated by the states in which they are approved. A person is able to choose from among the available Medigap policies in the state, but the premiums charged for Medicare SELECT policies are generally lower than premiums for comparable Medigap policies that do not have Medicare SELECT's managed care feature.

State insurance departments have information about Medicare SELECT policies that have been approved for sale in their states.

## 1146. Should a person purchase the most comprehensive Medigap policy if he can afford the premiums?

Not necessarily. A person must determine which benefits he is likely to need before purchasing a Medigap policy. Often, a person does not need the most comprehensive policy.

For example, Policy A is the least expensive policy and offers the basic core package of benefits. Policies F and G might be considered if a person uses nonparticipating doctors—those who charge more than the amount approved by Medicare; however, excess charges are limited to 115 percent of what Medicare pays (see Q 1070). If the doctors charge no more than the amount approved by Medicare, less expensive policies such as Policy C or Policy D may be appropriate. Policy D also includes important benefits not covered by Policy A, such as coverage of custodial care at home following an illness or injury and the cost of coinsurance for skilled nursing home care.

## 1147. What Medigap insurance protections are there for those enrolled in the Medicare Advantage program?

Medicare Advantage expands the types of health plans that can contract with Medicare to enroll beneficiaries.

A person who currently has a Medigap policy may enroll in a Medicare Advantage plan and can keep the Medigap policy after enrollment. Keeping the Medigap policy may give a person time to determine whether to stay in the Medicare Advantage plan or return to the original Medicare plan with Medigap insurance. However, expenses paid for by the Medicare Advantage plan will not be reimbursed by the Medigap insurer. Eventually the person should drop Medigap coverage if satisfied with the Medicare Advantage plan.

A person already enrolled in a Medicare Advantage plan cannot buy Medigap insurance but may have the right to purchase a Medigap policy by returning to the original fee-for-service Medicare program (Parts A and B). To be guaranteed the right to buy Medigap insurance, the person must have enrolled in the Medicare Advantage plan at age sixty-five, must terminate enrollment in the Medicare Advantage plan within twelve months of entry into that plan, and must not have had any previous enrollment in a Medicare managed care plan.

If a Medicare Advantage plan terminates coverage because it leaves the Medicare program, plan enrollees have certain rights to new coverage, but these are time-limited. The Medicare Advantage plan is required to provide information to assist making a decision about enrolling in another Medicare Advantage plan or switching to original Medicare Parts A and B with a Medigap policy to supplement the coverage. In general, most individuals with Medicare have the right to guaranteed issue of any Medigap policies designated A, B, C, or F that are offered to new enrollees by issuers in the state.

This right applies to individuals by virtue of the involuntary termination of their coverage. However, certain Medicare beneficiaries in terminating Medicare Advantage plans may have another basis for entitlement to guaranteed issue of a Medigap policy. If a person had been enrolled in the Medicare Advantage plan for fewer than twelve months, was never enrolled in any other Medicare HMO, and had a previous Medigap policy, that person may return to the former Medigap policy if the previous Medigap insurance company still sells the policy in the state.

If that coverage is not available under the previous Medigap policy, the individual may purchase Medigap polices A, B, C, or F from any insurer that sells these policies in the state.

The insurance company selling the policy may not (1) deny or condition the sale of the policy, (2) discriminate in the pricing of the policy because of health status, prior history of claims experience, receipt of health care for a medical condition, or (3) impose an exclusion for any pre-existing condition.

But the individual has only sixty-three days after coverage ends to select a Medigap insurer. Also, if the individual moves outside the Medicare Advantage plan's service area, that person has sixty-three days to select a Medigap insurer.

An individual is guaranteed issuance of *any* Medigap policy if (1) at least sixty-five years old, (2) eligible for Medicare, (3) enrolled in a Medicare Advantage plan, and (4) disenrolled from that plan within twelve months of the effective date of enrollment.

See Q 1109 through Q 1131 for a complete description of Medicare Advantage (Part C).

### 1148. Are there rules for selling Medigap insurance?

Yes, both state and federal laws govern sales of Medigap insurance. Companies or agents selling Medigap insurance must avoid certain illegal practices.

It is unlawful to sell or issue to an individual entitled to benefits under Part A (Hospital Insurance) or enrolled under Part B (Medical Insurance): (1) a health insurance policy with knowledge that the policy duplicates health benefits the individual is otherwise entitled to under Medicare or Medicaid; (2) a Medigap policy with knowledge that the individual is entitled to benefits under another Medigap policy; or (3) a health insurance policy, other than a Medigap policy, with knowledge that the policy duplicates health benefits to which the individual is otherwise entitled.

Penalties do not apply, however, to the sale or issuance of a policy or plan that duplicates health benefits to which the individual is otherwise entitled if, under the policy or plan, all benefits are fully payable directly to or on behalf of the individual without regard to other health benefit coverage of the individual. In addition, for the penalty to be waived in the case of the sale or issuance of a policy or plan that duplicates benefits under Medicare or Medicaid, the application for the policy must include a statement, prominently displayed, disclosing the extent to which benefits payable under the policy or plan duplicate Medicare benefits.

The National Association of Insurance Commissioners (NAIC) has identified ten separate types of health insurance policies that must provide an individualized statement of the extent to which the policy duplicates Medicare. These policies include the following:

- Policies that provide benefits for expenses incurred for an accidental injury only
- Policies that provide benefits for specified limited services
- Policies that reimburse expenses incurred for specified disease or other specific impairments (including cancer policies, specified disease policies, and other policies that limit reimbursement to named medical conditions)
- Policies that pay fixed dollar amounts for specified disease or other specified impairments (including cancer, specified disease policies, and other policies that pay a scheduled benefit or specified payment based on diagnosis of the conditions named in the policy)
- Indemnity policies and other policies that pay a fixed dollar amount per day, excluding long-term care policies
- Policies that provide benefits for both expenses incurred and fixed indemnity
- Long-term care policies providing both nursing home and noninstitutional coverage
- Long-term care policies primarily providing nursing home benefits only
- Home care policies
- Other health insurance policies not specifically identified above

Certain policies are *not* required to carry a disclosure statement: (1) policies that do not duplicate Medicare benefits, even incidentally, (2) life insurance policies that contain long-term care riders or accelerated death benefits, (3) disability insurance policies, (4) property and casualty policies, (5) employer and union group health plans, (6) managed-care organizations with Medicare contracts, and (7) Health Care Prepayment Plans (HCPPs) that provide some or all Medicare Part B benefits under an agreement with the Centers for Medicare & Medicaid Services.

Policies offering only long-term care nursing home care, home health care, or community-based care, or any combination of the three, are allowed to coordinate benefits with Medicare and are not considered duplicative, provided the coordination is disclosed.

An insurer is subject to civil money and criminal penalties for failing to provide the appropriate disclosure statement. Federal criminal and civil penalties (fines) may also be imposed against any insurance company or agent that knowingly:

- sells a health insurance policy that duplicates a person's Medicare or Medicaid coverage, or any private health insurance coverage the person may have;
- tells a person that they are employees or agents of the Medicare program or of any government agency;
- makes a false statement that a policy meets legal standards for certification when it does not;
- sells a person a Medigap policy that is not one of the ten approved standard policies (after the new standards have been put in place in the person's state);
- denies a person that individual's Medigap open enrollment period by refusing to issue the person a policy, placing conditions on the policy, or discriminating in the price of a policy because of the person's health status, claims experience, receipt of health care, or the person's medical condition; or
- uses the United States mail in a state for advertising or delivering health insurance policies to supplement Medicare if the policies have not been approved for sale in that state.

The sale of a Medigap policy to a Medicaid beneficiary generally is prohibited, but there is no prohibition on sale of policies to low-income Medicare beneficiaries for whom Medicaid pays only the Part B (Medical Insurance) premiums.

## 1149. What should a consumer be aware of when shopping for Medigap insurance?

The Centers for Medicare & Medicaid Services (CMS) offers the following suggestions when shopping for Medigap insurance:

(1) *Review the plans.* The benefits in each of the standardized Medigap policies are the same no matter which insurance company sells it. Review the plans and choose the benefits that you need most.

(2) *Shop carefully before purchasing*. Although each of the standardized Medigap policies is the same no matter which insurance company sells it, the costs may be very different. Companies use different ways to price Medigap policies. Companies also differ in customer service. Call different insurance companies and compare cost and service before purchasing.

(3) *Don't buy more than one Medigap policy at a time*. It is illegal for an insurance company to sell a person a second Medigap policy unless they are told in writing that first Medigap policy will be cancelled when the second Medigap policy goes into effect. Anyone who tries to sell a Medigap policy when a person already has one should be reported.

(4) *Check for pre-existing conditions exclusions*. Before purchasing a Medigap policy, a consumer should find out whether it has a waiting period before it fully covers any pre-existing conditions. If the person has a health problem that was diagnosed or treated during the six months immediately before the Medigap policy starts, the policy might not cover the costs right away for care related to that health problem. Medigap policies must cover pre-existing conditions after the policy has been in effect for six months. Some insurance companies may have shorter waiting periods before covering a pre-existing condition. Other insurance companies may not have any waiting period. If a policy is purchased during the Medigap open-enrollment period, the insurance company must shorten the waiting period for pre-existing conditions by the amount of previous health coverage.

(5) *Be careful of switching from one Medigap policy to another*. A consumer should only switch policies to get different benefits, better service, or a better price. However, a policy that does not meet the person's needs should not be kept simply because the person has had it for a long time. If deciding to buy a new Medigap policy, the company must count the time the person had the same benefits under the first policy towards the pre-existing conditions waiting period. However, a waiting period may be necessary for pre-existing conditions for new benefits that covered under the first policy. A statement must be signed that says that the first policy will be canceled. The first policy should not be canceled until the consumer is sure that he wants to keep the new policy. A person has thirty days to decide if he wants to keep the new policy. This is called the free-look period.

(6) *Make sure to get a policy within thirty days*. A consumer should get his policy within thirty days. If the person does not, he should call the company and ask them to put in writing why the policy was delayed. If sixty days go by without an answer, he should call his State Insurance Department.

(7) *Watch out for illegal marketing practices*. It is illegal for an insurance company or agent to pressure a person into buying a Medigap policy, or lie or mislead a person to get him to switch from one company or policy to another. False advertising is also illegal. Another type of illegal advertising involves mailing cards to people who may want to buy insurance. If a person fills out and returns the card enclosed

in the mailing, the card may be sold to an insurance agent who will try to sell him a policy.

(8) *Neither the state nor federal government sells or services Medigap policies*. State Insurance Departments approve Medigap policies sold by private insurance companies. This means that the company and Medigap policy meet requirements of state law. Do not believe statements that Medigap insurance is a government-sponsored program. It is illegal for anyone to tell a person that they are from the government and try to sell him a Medigap policy. If this happens, that person should be reported to their State Insurance Department. It is also illegal for a company or agent to claim that a Medigap policy has been approved for sale in any state in which it has not been.

(9) *Find out if the insurance company is licensed*. An insurance company must meet certain standards in order to sell policies in a state. A person should check with his State Insurance Department to make sure that the insurance company with whom he is doing business is licensed in his state. This is for the consumer's protection. Insurance agents must also be licensed by the state and the state may require them to carry proof that they are licensed. The proof will show their name and the name of the companies they represent. Do not buy a policy from any insurance agent that cannot prove that he is licensed. A business card is not a license.

(10) *Start looking early so as not to be rushed*. Do not be pressured into buying a Medigap policy. Good sales people will not rush a person. Keep in mind, that if a consumer is within his six-month Medigap open enrollment period or in a situation where he has a guaranteed right to buy a Medigap policy, there are time limits to follow. Buying the Medigap policy of choice may be harder after the Medigap open-enrollment or special-protection period ends. This will be especially true if a pre-existing health condition exists. If a consumer is not sure whether a Medigap policy is what is needed, the salesperson should be asked to explain it to him with a friend or family member present.

(11) *Keep agents' and/or companies' names, addresses, and telephone numbers*. Write down the agents' and/or companies' names, addresses, and telephone numbers, or ask for a business card with this information.

(12) *If deciding to buy, fill out the application carefully*. Do not believe an insurance agent who says that medical history on an application is not important. Some companies ask for detailed medical information. Consumers must answer the medical questions even if they are applying during a Medigap open-enrollment period or are in a situation where they have the right to buy a Medigap policy. During these two times, the company cannot use answers to turn consumers down or use this information to decide how much to charge for a Medigap policy. However, if a consumer leaves out any of the medical information they ask for, the company could refuse coverage for a period of time for any medical condition that was not reported. The company also could deny a claim or cancel

a Medigap policy if a consumer sends in a bill for care of a health problem that was not reported.

(13) *Beware of nonstandardized plans*. It is illegal for anyone to sell a policy and call it a Medigap policy if it does not match the standardized Medigap policies sold in that state. A doctor may offer a "retainer agreement" that says he can provide certain non-Medicare-covered services and not charge the Medicare coinsurance and deductible amounts. This type of agreement may be illegal. If a doctor refuses to see a person as a Medicare patient unless that person pays him a yearly fee and signs a "retainer agreement," the person should call 1-800-MEDICARE.

(14) *Look for an outline of coverage*. A clearly worded summary of a Medigap policy must be given to each consumer. Read it carefully.

(15) *Do not pay cash*. Pay by check, money order, or bank draft payable to the insurance company, not to the agent or anyone else. Get a receipt with the insurance company's name, address, and telephone number for records.

CMS publishes a consumer-directed manual called "Choosing a Medigap Policy: A Guide to Health Insurance for People with Medicare". The guide is updated annually and is available on the CMS website at www.medicare.gov.

# HOW TO SUBMIT CLAIMS AND APPEALS

## CLAIMS PROCEDURE

### 1150. How does Medicare pay for Part A (Hospital Insurance) services?

Part A (Hospital Insurance) helps pay for covered services received in a hospital or skilled nursing facility or from a home health agency or hospice program. Hospitals, skilled nursing facilities, home health agencies, and hospices are called "providers" under Part A. Providers submit their claims directly to Medicare. The patient cannot submit claims for services. The provider will charge the patient for any part of the Part A (Hospital Insurance) deductible he has not met and any coinsurance he owes. Providers cannot require the patient to make a deposit before being admitted for inpatient care that is or may be covered under Part A.

Intermediaries process claims submitted on the patient's behalf by hospitals, skilled nursing facilities, home health agencies, hospices and certain other providers of services. When the Medicare intermediary pays a claim, the patient gets a *Notice of Medicare Benefit*. This notice is not a bill.

### 1151. How does a person submit Part B (Medical Insurance) claims?

Doctors, suppliers, and other providers of Part B (Medical Insurance) services are in most cases required to submit Medicare claims for the patient even if they do not take assignment. They must submit the claims by December 31 of the following year for services furnished during the first nine months of the year. Claims must be submitted by December 31 of the second following year for services furnished during the last three months of the year. A patient should notify the Medicare Administrative Contractor (MAC) for their area if the doctor or supplier refuses to submit a Part B (Medical Insurance) claim and the patient believes the services may be covered by Medicare.

The doctor or supplier must submit a form, called a CMS-1500, requesting that a Part B (Medical Insurance) payment be made for the patient's covered services, whether or not assignment is taken. The doctor or supplier completes form CMS-1500. The patient must sign the form before the doctor or supplier sends it to the proper Medicare carrier. If a patient's claim is for the rental or purchase of durable medical equipment, a doctor's prescription or certificate of medical necessity must be included with the claim.

In general, if the patient is enrolled in a coordinated care plan (such as an HMO), a claim will seldom need to be submitted on the patient's behalf. Medicare pays the HMO a set amount and the HMO provides the patient's medical care. Physicians, suppliers, and other providers of Part B (Medical Insurance) services bill the HMO to receive payment for their services at a contractually-agreed rate.

After the doctor, provider, or supplier sends in a Part B claim, Medicare will send the patient a notice called *Explanation of Your Medicare Part B Benefits* to tell the patient the decision on the claim. The notice gives the address and toll-free number for contacting the MAC if needed.

Payment can be made directly to the doctor or supplier. This is the *assignment method*. The doctor or supplier is prohibited from charging the patient anything above the 20 percent coinsurance amount and the amount of the patient's deductible, if the deductible has not been paid. Medicare pays the doctor or supplier 80 percent of the approved charge. If a provider does not accept assignment, the MAC still pays 80 percent of the approved charge, but directly to the patient who then pays the provider. The MAC will withhold from the payment any amount of the deductible not yet paid.

## 1152. What must an itemized bill contain?

The itemized bill must show (1) the date the patient received the services, (2) the place where the patient received the services, (3) a description of the services, (4) the charge for each service, (5) the doctor or supplier who provided the services, and (6) the patient's name and health insurance claim number, including the letter at the end of the number.

If the bill does not contain all of this information, payment may be delayed. It is also helpful if the nature of the patient's illness (diagnosis) is shown on the bill.

A doctor or supplier submitting a claim for the rental or purchase of durable medical equipment should include the bill from the prescription. The prescription must show the equipment needed, the medical reason for the need, and estimate how long the equipment will be medically necessary.

Before Medicare pays any charge for Part B (Medical Insurance) services or supplies, a beneficiary's record must show that the individual has satisfied the applicable Part B deductible for that year. Once a beneficiary has satisfied the deductible, physicians, other health care professionals, or supplies should send in future bills for covered services as soon as possible so that Medicare payment can be made promptly. If all medical bills for the year amount to less than the deductible, Part B (Medical Insurance) cannot pay any part of a person's bills for the year.

## 1153. What happens if the patient dies and payments are due?

Part A (Hospital Insurance) payments due from Medicare will be paid directly to the hospital, skilled nursing facility, home health agency, or hospice that provided covered services.

Special rules apply for services covered under Part B (Medical Insurance). If a bill was paid by the patient or with funds from the patient's estate, payment will be made either to the estate representative or to a surviving member of the patient's immediate family. If someone other than the patient paid the bill, payment may be made to that person. If the bill has not been paid and the doctor or supplier does not accept assignment, Part B (Medical Insurance) payment can be made to the person who has a legal obligation to pay the bill for the deceased patient. This person can claim Part B (Medical Insurance) payment either before or after paying the bill.

## 1154. Is there a time limit for submitting a Medicare claim?

In general, providers must file claims within one calendar year from the date of the covered service. In extremely limited circumstances (such as the delay being due to an error by Medicare or a beneficiary's retroactive Medicare entitlement), the one-year time limit may be waived by Medicare.

## 1155. Where does a physician or supplier send Part B (Medical Insurance) claims?

See Appendix H for the names and addresses of the Medicare Administrative Contractors (MACs) selected to handle Part B (Medical Insurance) claims in each state.

## 1156. Must Medicare claims be paid in a prompt manner?

Medicare Administrative Contractors (MACs), previously known called "carriers" for Part B (Medical Insurance) and "intermediaries" for Part A (Hospital Insurance), must pay Medicare claims promptly. Not less than 95 percent of "clean claim" payments must be issued, mailed, or otherwise transmitted within specified time limits. A clean claim is a claim that has no defect or impropriety or particular circumstance requiring special treatment that prevents timely payment from being made. The deadline for payment of a clean claim is thirty calendar days.

If payment is not issued, mailed, or otherwise transmitted within thirty calendar days on a clean claim, interest must be paid for the period beginning on the day after the required payment date and ending on the date on which payment is made.

MACs are prohibited from issuing, mailing or otherwise transmitting payment for any electronic claims within thirteen days after claim receipt. This prohibition on paying claims is expanded to twenty-six days for claims not submitted electronically.

# APPEALS PROCEDURE

## 1157. Does a beneficiary have the right to appeal a decision made on a claim?

Yes, if a Medicare beneficiary disagrees with a decision on the amount Medicare will pay on a claim or whether services received are covered by Medicare, the person has the right to ask for a review of the decision. The notice from Medicare tells the patient the decision made on the claim and what steps to take to appeal the decision. If a person needs more information about the right to appeal, he or she should contact the local Social Security office, the Medicare Administrative Contractor (MAC) that processed the initial claim, or the Quality Improvement Organization (QIO) in the beneficiary's state.

## 1158. How does a person appeal a Part B (Medical Insurance) claim?

After the doctor or supplier or other provider submits the claim for payment to the appropriate Medicare Administrator Contractor (MAC), Medicare will send a notice of the decision made on the claim. If the patient disagrees with the decision, he or she can ask the MAC that handled the claim to review it. The patient has six months from the date of the decision to ask the MAC to review it. If the patient disagrees with the MAC's written explanation of its review decision and the amount remaining in question is $100 or more, the patient has six months from the date of the review decision to request a hearing before a hearing officer. The patient may combine claims that have been reviewed or reopened, so long as all claims combined are at the proper level of appeal and the appeal for each claim combined is filed on time.

If a person disagrees with the hearing officer's decision and the amount in question is $500 or more, the person has sixty days from the date he or she receives the decision to request a hearing before an Administrative Law Judge. Cases involving $1,000 or more can eventually be appealed to a federal court.

To determine whether an individual meets the minimum amount in controversy needed for a MAC hearing ($100) or administrative law judge hearing ($500), the following rules apply:

(1) The amount in controversy is computed as the actual amount charged the patient for the items and services in question, less any amount for which payment has been made by the MAC and less any deductible and coinsurance amounts applicable in the particular case.

(2) A single patient may aggregate claims from two or more physicians/suppliers to meet the $100 or $500 thresholds. A single physician/supplier may aggregate claims from two or more patients to meet the $100 or $500 threshold levels of appeal.

(3) Two or more claims may be aggregated by an individual patient to meet the amount in controversy for a MAC hearing, only if the claims have previously been reviewed and a request for hearing has been made within six months after the date of the review determination(s).

(4) Two or more claims may be aggregated by an individual patient for an administrative law judge hearing, only if the claims have previously been decided by a MAC hearing officer and a request for an administrative law judge hearing has been made within sixty days after receipt of the MAC hearing officer's decision(s).

(5) When requesting a carrier hearing or an administrative law judge hearing, the appellant must specify in the appeal request the specific claims to be aggregated.

Two or more patients may aggregate their claims together to meet the minimum amount in controversy needed for an administrative law judge hearing ($500).

The determination as to whether the amount in controversy is $100 or more is made by the MAC hearing officer. The determination as to whether the amount in controversy is $500 or more is made by the administrative law judge.

When a civil action is filed by either an individual patient or two or more patients, the Centers for Medicare & Medicaid Services may assert that the aggregation principles may be applied to determine the amount in controversy for judicial review ($1,000).

## 1159. How does a person request a review by the Medicare Administrative Contractor that handled the claim?

A reconsideration request must be made in writing and filed at a Social Security Administration or the Centers for Medicare & Medicaid Services office, or in the case of a qualified Railroad

Retirement beneficiary, filed at a Railroad Retirement Board office. The request must be filed within six months of receipt of the notice of the initial determination, unless an extension of time for filing the request is granted.

The parties to a reconsideration determination are entitled to written notice specifying the reasons for the decision and advising them of their right to a hearing if the amount in question is $100 or more.

### 1160. How does a person request a hearing with a Medicare Administrative Contractor hearing officer?

An individual who is dissatisfied with a reconsideration determination is entitled to a hearing if the amount in controversy is $100 or more. The request for a hearing must be made in writing and filed at a Social Security Administration or the Centers for Medicare & Medicaid Services office or, in the case of a qualified Railroad Retirement beneficiary, at a Railroad Retirement Board office. The hearing request must be filed within six months after the date of an individual's receipt of notice of the reconsidered determination, unless the deadline is extended.

### 1161. How does a person appeal a Part A (Hospital Insurance) decision made by a Quality Improvement Organization (QIO)?

Quality Improvement Organizations (QIOs) make decisions on the need for hospital care. Whenever a patient is admitted to a Medicare-participating hospital, the patient is given *An Important Message From Medicare*, which describes the individual's appeal rights as a hospital patient and supplies the name, address, and phone number of the QIO in his or her state. The hospital is also required to provide the patient with *How to Request a Review of the Notice of Noncoverage*, which includes a general statement about the posthospital services to which the patient is entitled.

To determine whether a patient meets the minimum amount in controversy needed for a hearing ($100), the following rules apply:

(1) The amount in controversy is computed as the actual amount charged the patient for the items and services in question, less any amount for which payment has been made by the intermediary and less any deductible and coinsurance amounts applicable in the particular case.

(2) A single patient may aggregate claims from two or more providers to meet the $100 hearing threshold and a single provider may aggregate claims for services provided to one or more patients to meet the $100 hearing threshold.

(3) Two or more claims may be aggregated by an individual patient only if the claims have previously been reconsidered and a request for hearing has been made within sixty days after receipt of the reconsideration determination.

(4) When requesting a hearing, the appellant must specify in the appeal request the specific claims to be aggregated.

Also, two or more patients may aggregate their claims together to meet the minimum amount in controversy needed for a hearing ($100).

The determination as to whether the amount in controversy is $100 or more is made by the administrative law judge.

If a hospital, without consulting the QIO, recommends against admission to the hospital, review of this decision by the QIO may be obtained by writing to the QIO and requesting a review. If the QIO participated in the preadmission denial, a reconsideration of the denial can be requested. If an expedited request for review is made within three working days of the denial, the QIO has three working days to respond.

The appeals process for determinations of noncoverage after a patient is admitted to the hospital is similar to the process for preadmission denials. The hospital cannot charge the patient for the cost of an additional stay unless (1) the hospital or its utilization review committee determines that hospital care is no longer necessary, or the QIO states in writing that hospital care is unnecessary, and (2) the patient receives written notice that charges will be made beginning the third day after receipt of the notice and the decision may be appealed by following procedures specified in the notice.

The hospital must have either the agreement of the physician or the QIO before giving a patient written notice of noncoverage. If the physician, but not the QIO, agrees with the hospital, the patient may make a telephone request to the QIO for review, with a simultaneous written confirmation to the QIO of the request for review. If the patient makes this request prior to noon of the day following receipt of notice of noncoverage, the patient cannot be liable for hospital charges until noon of the working day after receipt of the QIO's decision. The QIO must determine, within one full working day of the request (and receipt of pertinent information and/or records from the hospital), the appropriateness of the hospital's decision that the beneficiary no longer requires inpatient hospital care.

If the patient does not appeal, he or she will be liable for all hospital charges beginning the third day after receipt of the hospital's notice.

If the QIO, rather than the physician, agrees with the hospital's initial notice of noncoverage, the patient can request that the QIO reconsider its decision. If the QIO upholds its initial decision, the patient is liable for all charges beginning the third day after receipt of the hospital's notice of noncoverage.

The patient should request that the QIO review the hospital's notice of noncoverage as soon as possible. If the patient requests a review while in the hospital or within three days of notice of noncoverage, the QIO must render its decision within three working days.

The patient may request a review by the QIO at any time within sixty days after receipt of the hospital's noncoverage determination. The QIO will have thirty days to issue a decision (unless the request was made within three days of receipt of the noncoverage determination or while the patient was hospitalized).

If the HMO, rather than the hospital, makes the determination of noncoverage, the patient may request an immediate QIO review of the determination.

For the immediate QIO review process, the following rules apply: (1) the patient or authorized representative must submit the request for immediate review to the QIO that has an agreement with the hospital in writing or by telephone by noon of the first working day after receipt of the written notice of the determination that the hospital stay is no longer necessary, (2) on the date it receives the patient's request, the QIO must notify the HMO that a request for immediate review has been filed, (3) the HMO must supply any information that the QIO requires to conduct its review by the close of business of the first full working day immediately following the day the enrollee submits the request for review, (4) in response to a request from the HMO, the hospital must submit medical records to the QIO by close of business of the first full working day immediately following the day the HMO makes its request, (5) the QIO must solicit views of the patient who requested the immediate QIO review, and (6) the QIO must make a determination and notify the patient, the hospital, and the HMO by close of business of the first working day after it receives the information from the hospital, the HMO, or both.

The HMO continues to be financially responsible for the costs of the hospital stay until noon of the calendar day following the day the QIO notifies the patient of its review determination. But the hospital may not charge the HMO if it was the hospital (acting on behalf of the patient) that filed the request for an immediate QIO review, and the QIO upholds the noncoverage determination made by the HMO.

The patient may appeal a QIO reconsideration decision to an administrative law judge within sixty days, provided the amount of the controversy is at least $200. Cases involving $2,000 or more can eventually be appealed to a federal court.

## 1162. How does a person appeal all other Part A (Hospital Insurance) claims?

Appeals of decisions on all other services (generally, those not relating to inpatient hospitalization) covered under Part A (Hospital Insurance) (skilled nursing facility care, home health care, hospice services, and some inpatient hospital matters not handled by QIOs) are handled by the Medicare Administrative Contractors (MACs). If a patient disagrees with the MAC's initial decision, the patient may request reconsideration. The request may be submitted directly to the MAC or through a Social Security office. Any Social Security office will help the patient request reconsideration.

If a patient disagrees with the MAC's reconsideration decision and the amount in question is $100 or more, the patient has sixty days from the date he or she receives the reconsideration decision to request a hearing by an administrative law judge. Cases involving $1,000 or more can eventually be appealed to a federal court.

## 1163. How does a person appeal a decision made by a Health Maintenance Organization (HMO)?

If a person has Medicare coverage through an HMO, decisions about coverage and payment for services will usually be made by the HMO. When the HMO makes a decision to deny payment for Medicare-covered services or refuses to provide Medicare-covered supplies requested by the patient, the patient will be given a *Notice of Initial Determination*. The HMO is also required to provide a full, written explanation of the patient's appeal rights.

If a patient believes that the decision of the HMO was not correct, the patient has the right to ask for reconsideration. The patient must file a request for reconsideration within sixty days after the patient receives the *Notice of Initial Determination*. The request for reconsideration may be mailed or delivered to the HMO or to a Social Security office.

The HMO must reconsider its initial determination to deny payments or services. If the HMO does not rule fully in the patient's favor, the HMO must send the patient's reconsideration request and its reconsideration determination to the Centers for Medicare & Medicaid Services (CMS) for a review and determination.

A patient may not proceed to the next level of administrative review until the HMO issues its decision or refers the matter to CMS.

An HMO must act on the patient's reconsideration request within sixty calendar days from the date of receipt of the request. If the reconsideration determination made by the HMO is entirely favorable to the patient, the HMO must notify the patient within the sixty-calendar-day period. If the HMO cannot make a decision that is fully favorable to the patient, the organization must submit the case file to CMS within the sixty-calendar-day period.

For good cause, CMS may allow exceptions to the sixty-day limit. "Good cause" is defined as unusual circumstances (such as natural disasters) which make it difficult or impossible for the patient to provide necessary information in a timely way. Failure of the HMO to provide the patient with a reconsideration determination within the sixty-day limit or to obtain a good-cause extension constitutes an adverse determination.

If the patient disagrees with the decision of CMS and the amount in question is $100 or more, the patient has sixty days from receipt of the decision to request a hearing before an administrative law judge. The amount in question can include any combination of Part A (Hospital Insurance) and Part B (Medical Insurance) services. Cases involving $1,000 or more can eventually be appealed to a federal court.

The rules regarding an immediate QIO review of a determination of noncoverage of inpatient hospital care by an HMO or hospital are discussed at Q 1161.

## 1164. What happens if an organization providing items or services to a person under Medicare ceases to continue providing those items or services?

An organization must provide assurances to the Centers for Medicare & Medicaid Services (CMS) that, in the event it ceases to provide items or services, the organization will provide or arrange for supplemental coverage of benefits related to a pre-existing condition. This coverage must be provided to individuals enrolled with the organization who receive Medicare benefits and must continue for the lesser of six months or the duration of the contract period.

# MEDICAID

## OVERVIEW

### 1165. What is Medicaid?

Medicaid (Title XIX of the *Social Security Act*) is a federal-state matching entitlement program that pays for medical assistance for certain vulnerable and needy individuals and families with low incomes and resources. The program became law in 1965 as a jointly funded cooperative venture between the federal and state governments to assist states in supplying medical assistance to eligible needy persons. Medicaid is the largest program funding medical and health-related services for America's poorest people.

The Medicaid program is jointly financed by the federal and state governments and administered by the states. Within federal rules, each state chooses eligible groups, types and ranges of services, payment levels for most services, and administrative and operating procedures. The nature and scope of a state's Medicaid program is described in the state plan that the state submits to the Centers for Medicare & Medicaid Services (CMS) for approval. The plan is amended whenever necessary to reflect changes in federal or state law, changes in policy, or court decisions.

Federal responsibility for the Medicaid program lies with the CMS in the Department of Health and Human Services (HHS).

States are required to provide certain basic medical assistance services to eligible recipients. These mandatory Medicaid services include inpatient and outpatient hospital care, health screening, diagnosis and treatment to children, family planning, physician services and nursing facility services to individuals over age twenty-one. States may also elect to cover any of over thirty specified optional services, which include prescription drugs, clinic services, personal care services, and services provided in intermediate care facilities for the mentally retarded.

To qualify for Medicaid, applicants must have both incomes and assets below certain limits, which vary from state to state.

Within broad national guidelines established by federal statutes, regulations and policies, each of the states (1) establishes its own eligibility standards, (2) determines the type, amount, duration, and scope of services, (3) sets the rate of payment for services, and (4) administers its own program. Medicaid policies for eligibility and services are complex, and vary considerably even among similar-sized and/or adjacent states. Thus, a person who is eligible for Medicaid in one state might not be eligible in another state; and the services provided by one state may differ considerably in amount, duration, or scope from the services provided in a similar or neighboring state. In addition, Medicaid eligibility and/or services within a state can change during the year.

Medicaid serves as a supplement to health insurance coverage provided by Medicare. Medicaid pays for extended nursing home care for elderly people who cannot afford to pay for it themselves. For those who qualify, Medicaid pays Medicare premiums, as well as Medicare coinsurance and deductibles. It may even pay the full cost of some services not covered by Medicare.

## 1166. What portion of Medicaid expenses are paid by the federal government?

The federal government pays a portion of the medical assistance expenditures under each state's Medicaid program, known as the Federal Medical Assistance Percentage (FMAP). The FMAP is determined annually by a formula that compares the state's average per capita income level with the national income average. States with a higher per capita income level are reimbursed a smaller share of their costs. By law, the FMAP cannot be lower than 50 percent nor higher than 83 percent.

The federal government shares in each state's expenditures for the administration of the Medicaid program. Most administrative costs are matched at 50 percent for all states, with higher rates for certain activities (such as development of mechanized claims processing systems). The Medicaid statute does provide for higher matching rates for certain functions and activities.

Federal payments to states for medical assistance have no set limit (cap); rather, the federal government matches (at FMAP rates) state expenditures for the mandatory services plus the optional services that the individual state decides to cover for eligible recipients, and matches (at the appropriate administrative rate) necessary and proper administrative costs.

# MEDICAID ELIGIBILITY

## 1167. What major groups are states required to cover?

States have some discretion in determining who their Medicaid programs will cover and the financial criteria for Medicaid eligibility. To be eligible for federal funds, states are required to provide Medicaid coverage for most individuals who receive federally assisted income maintenance payments, as well as for related groups not receiving cash payments. As part of the Patient Protection and Affordable Care Act (PPACA), in 2014 Medicaid eligibility will expand to include more low-income adults. As previously stated, states do have some discretion in determining who their Medicaid programs cover, and as a result some states will not be expanding their Medicaid coverage to include the additional low-income adults who would otherwise be eligible under the PPACA (see Q 1170).

Examples of the mandatory Medicaid eligibility groups (called Mandatory Categorically Needy) include the following:[1]

- Individuals who meet the requirements of Aid to Families with Dependent Children (AFDC) that were in effect in their states on July 16, 1996.
- Supplemental Security Income (SSI) recipients (or in states using more restrictive criteria—aged, blind, disabled, and institutionalized individuals).

1. 42 U.S.C. §1396a.

- Infants born to Medicaid-eligible pregnant women. Medicaid eligibility must continue throughout the first year of life, so long as the infant remains in the mother's household and she remains eligible (or would be eligible if she were still pregnant).

- Children under age six and pregnant women who meet the state's AFDC financial requirements or whose family income is at or below 133 percent of the federal poverty level. (The minimum mandatory income level for pregnant women and infants in certain states may be higher than 133 percent, if as of certain dates the states had established a higher percentage for covering these groups.) States are required to extend Medicaid eligibility until age nineteen to all children in families with incomes at or below the federal poverty level. Once eligibility is established, pregnant women remain eligible for Medicaid through the end of the calendar month ending sixty days after the end of the pregnancy, regardless of any change in family income. States are not required to have a resource test for these poverty-level related groups. However, any resource test imposed can be no more restrictive than that of the AFDC program for infants and children and the SSI program for pregnant women.

- Recipients of adoption assistance, foster care, and guardianship care under the Social Security Act.

- Certain Medicare beneficiaries. (See Q 1176.)

- Special protected groups who lose cash assistance because of the cash programs' rules, but who may keep Medicaid for a period of time. Examples are: persons who lose AFDC or SSI payments due to earnings from work or increased Social Security benefits; and two-parent, unemployed families whose AFDC cash assistance time is limited by the state and who are provided a full twelve months of Medicaid coverage following termination of cash assistance.

Certain qualified aliens, including certain permanent residents, certain persons claiming asylum, certain refugees, certain aliens whose deportation has been withheld, and certain veterans and their spouses and dependents, are covered under Medicaid. (Persons claiming asylum, refugees, and deportees are only required to be covered by Medicaid for the first five years of their status in those categories.)

## 1168. What are Supplemental Security Income states ("SSI States")?

Generally, the Social Security Act requires states to provide Medicaid benefits automatically to those receiving categorical welfare assistance. However, the Section 209(b) provision allows states to provide Medicaid benefits only to those persons who would have qualified for Medicaid on January 1, 1972, without adjustment for medical inflation rates. In most states, the Medicaid program includes ALL SSI recipients. These states are called "SSI States". Other states, however, cover only those persons who are age sixty-five, disabled, or blind and meet the Section 209(b) means test, which is more restrictive than the SSI means test. These states are called "Section 209(b) states." Examples of Section 209(b) states include: Connecticut, Hawaii,

Illinois, Indiana, Minnesota, Missouri, New Hampshire, North Dakota, Ohio, Oklahoma, and Virginia. These eleven states have elected to define disability more narrowly than the federal definition for SSI entitlement.

## 1169. Do states have the option of providing additional Medicaid coverage?

Yes, states have the option of providing Medicaid coverage for "Optional Categorically Needy" groups (as opposed to the Mandatory Categorically Needy described in Q 1167). These optional groups share characteristics of the mandatory groups, but the eligibility criteria are somewhat more liberally defined. Examples of the optional groups that states may cover as Optional Categorically Needy (and for which they will receive federal matching funds) under the Medicaid program include the following:

- Infants up to age one and pregnant women not covered under the mandatory rules whose family income is below 185 percent of the federal poverty level (the percentage is set by each state).
- Certain aged, blind, or disabled adults who have incomes above those requiring mandatory coverage, but below the federal poverty level.
- Children under age twenty-one who meet what were the AFDC income and resource requirements in effect in their state on July 16, 1996 (even though they do not meet the mandatory eligibility requirements).
- Children under age nineteen, or a younger age specified by the state, in households with incomes at or below 100 percent of the federal poverty level. States may provide a full, continuous twelve months of eligibility for such children.
- Institutionalized individuals with incomes and resources below specified limits. The amount is set by each state—up to 300 percent of the SSI federal benefits rate.
- Persons who would be eligible if institutionalized, but are receiving care under home and community-based services waivers.
- Recipients of state supplementary income payments.
- TB-infected persons who would be financially eligible for Medicaid at the SSI income level (only for TB-related ambulatory services and TB drugs).
- Individuals in HMOs Guaranteed Eligibility.
- Individuals receiving Hospice Care.
- Certain women needing treatment for Breast or Cervical Cancer.
- Individuals age nineteen through sixty-four at or below 133 percent of the Federal Poverty Level.
- "Medically needy" persons (described below).

The option to have a "medically needy" program allows states to extend Medicaid eligibility to additional qualified persons who may have too much income to qualify under the Mandatory or Optional Categorically Needy groups. This option allows them to "spend down" to Medicaid eligibility by incurring medical and/or remedial care expenses to offset their excess income, thereby reducing it to a level below the maximum allowed by that state's Medicaid plan. States may also allow families to establish eligibility as medically needy by paying monthly premiums to the state in an amount equal to the difference between family income (reduced by unpaid expenses, if any, incurred for medical care in previous months) and the income eligibility standard.

Eligibility for the Medically Needy program does not need to be as extensive as the Categorically Needy programs. But states that elect to include the medically needy under their plans are required to include certain children under age eighteen and pregnant women who, except for income and resources, would be eligible as categorically needy. They may choose to provide coverage to other medically needy persons: aged, blind, and/or disabled persons; certain relatives of children deprived of parental support and care; and certain other financially eligible children up to age twenty-one.

States can expand Medicaid eligibility for children under the State Children's Health Insurance Program. In order to be eligible for federal funds, states must submit to, and obtain approval from, the Secretary for Health and Human Services for a State Child Health Plan. States that elect to use the child health assistance funds to expand Medicaid eligibility and meet conditions for participating in the program are eligible to receive an enhanced Medicaid match for "optional targeted low-income children." Coverage may start retroactive to any or all of the three months prior to application if the person would have been eligible during the retroactive period. Coverage generally stops at the end of the month in which a person's circumstances change. Most states have additional "states only" programs to provide medical assistance to specified poor persons who do not qualify for Medicaid. Federal funds are not provided for state-only programs.

Medicaid does not provide health care services for all poor persons. To be eligible for Medicaid, a person must belong to one of the designated groups listed above, as well as meet income and assets/resources tests. Even under the broadest provisions of federal law (except for a few emergency services for certain persons), the Medicaid program does not provide health care services, even for very poor persons, unless they are under age twenty-one, pregnant, aged, blind, disabled, or in certain AFDC-type families. The Patient Protection and Affordable Care Act (PPACA) did expand the eligibility for coverage under Medicaid; however there are still states that have chosen not to include those who would be covered under this expansion. For more complete coverage of the PPACA expansion see Q 1167 and Q 1170.

## 1170. What affect does the Patient Protection and Affordable Care Act (PPACA) have on Medicaid eligibility?

Under the PPACA, Medicaid is set to expand its eligibility for coverage to include persons with income levels at or below 133 percent of the federal poverty level. In 2015, a standard 5 percent income disregard will apply to most individuals, effectively increasing the eligibility level to 138 percent of the poverty level. For the first three years of Medicaid expansion, the federal government will pay for the additional cost.

The Supreme Court has ruled that states may "opt-out" of the Medicaid expansion. Currently, fifteen states have opted out of Medicaid expansion, including Alabama, Alaska, Georgia, Idaho, Kansas, Louisiana, Maine, Mississippi, Montana, Nebraska, North Carolina, South Carolina, Texas, Wisconsin, and Wyoming. Another seven states are leaning toward not participating in the expansion, but have not yet made a final decision. These states include Florida, Missouri, New Hampshire, South Dakota, Tennessee, Utah, and Virginia.

If all states were to participate in this expansion, it is estimated that it would add fifteen million people to the Medicaid program. This expansion would continue to increase Medicaid participation to twenty-six million by 2020.

## MEDICAID SERVICES

### 1171. What basic services must be offered by Medicaid?

The Social Security Act requires that a state Medicaid program must offer medical assistance for certain basic services to most categorically needy populations. These services generally include the following:[1]

- Inpatient hospital services
- Outpatient hospital services
- Prenatal care
- Vaccines for children
- Physician services
- Nursing facility services for persons aged twenty-one or older
- Family planning services and supplies
- Rural health clinic services
- Home health care for persons eligible for skilled nursing services
- Laboratory and x-ray services
- Pediatric and family nurse-practitioner services
- Nurse-midwife services
- Federally-Qualified Health-Center (FQHC) services, and ambulatory services of an FQHC that would be available in other settings

1. 42 U.S.C. §1396d.

- Early and Periodic Screening, Diagnostic, and Treatment (EPSDT) services for children under age twenty-one

If a state chooses to include the medically needy population, the state plan must provide, as a minimum, the following services:

- Prenatal care and delivery services for pregnant women
- Ambulatory services to individuals under age eighteen and individuals entitled to institutional services
- Home health services to individuals entitled to nursing facility services

States may also receive federal matching funds for providing certain optional services. The most common optional Medicaid services include:

- Home health care services (eligibility does not depend on a need or discharge from a skilled nursing facility)
- Diagnostic services
- Clinic services
- Intermediate-care facilities for the mentally retarded
- Prescribed drugs and prosthetic devices
- Optometrist services and eyeglasses
- Dental care
- Hearing aids
- Nursing facility services for children under age twenty-one
- Transportation services
- Rehabilitation and physical therapy services
- Home and community-based care to certain persons with chronic impairments (this one is an option with an approved waiver).

States can use waivers to test new or existing ways to deliver and pay for health care services in Medicaid and the Children's Health Insurance Program (CHIP). Some of the items in the previous list as optional services would be included via these waivers. There are four primary types of waivers:

- Waivers for program flexibility to test new or existing approaches to financing and delivering Medicaid and CHIP

- Waivers to provide services through managed care delivery systems or otherwise limit people's choice of providers
- Waivers to provide long-term care services in home and community settings rather than institutional settings
- Simultaneously implementing two types of waivers to provide a continuum of services to the elderly and people with disabilities, as long as all Federal requirements for both programs are met

### 1172. Is AIDS covered under Medicaid?

Medicaid is the largest single payer of direct medical services for persons with AIDS.

States must provide the full range of Medicaid services covered in the state plan to eligible persons with HIV disease. States may also provide optional services that are often appropriate for people with HIV/AIDS (such as targeted case management, preventive services, and hospice care). All states cover FDA-approved prescribed drugs.

While Medicaid provides a range of health care services to people with AIDS and HIV, one of the most important is prescription drugs, an optional Medicaid benefit that all states have chosen to provide to their Medicaid populations. Under the Patient Protection and Affordable Care Act (PPACA), Medicaid eligibility will expand in 2014 to include many people with HIV who are not currently covered by the program. However, this coverage is still dependent on the state approving the Medicaid expansion plan. Many states have chosen to opt out of the expansion, or have not yet made a final decision about the expansion (see Q 1170). Individuals should contact their state Medicaid agency for state-specific criteria.

### 1173. What optional services may a state elect to provide?

States may elect to provide a number of other services for which federal matching funds are available. Some of the most frequently covered optional services are: clinic services, medical transportation services, intermediate-care facility services for the mentally retarded, optometrist services and eyeglasses, prescribed drugs, case management services, prosthetic devices, dental services, dentures, podiatry services, physical therapy, occupational therapy, speech, hearing, and language disorder services, chiropractic care, hospice care, respiratory care services, private duty nursing services, services for individuals age sixty-five and older in an institution for mental disease, self-directed personal assistance services, TB related services, inpatient psychiatric services for individuals under age twenty-one, other diagnostic, screening, preventive and rehabilitative services, and home and community-based care for functionally disabled elderly persons.

## PAYMENT UNDER MEDICAID

### 1174. How are providers of health care services paid under Medicaid?

Medicaid operates as a vendor payment program, with states paying providers directly. Providers participating in Medicaid must accept Medicaid payment rates as payment in full. States may pay for Medicaid services through various prepayment arrangements, such as Health Maintenance Organizations (HMOs). Within federally-imposed upper limits and specific restrictions, each state generally has broad discretion in determining the payment methodology and payment rate for services. Generally, payment rates must be sufficient to enlist enough providers so that covered services are available, at least to the extent that comparable care and services are available to the general population within that geographic area. States must make additional payments to qualified hospitals that provide inpatient services to a disproportionate number of Medicaid recipients and/or to other low-income persons under what is known as the Disproportionate Share Hospital (DSH) adjustment. These payments are limited.

The federal government pays a portion of the medical assistance expenditures under each state's Medicaid program, known as the Federal Medical Assistance Percentage (FMAP). The FMAP is determined annually by a formula that compares the state's average per capita income level with the national income average. States with a higher per capita income level are reimbursed a smaller share of their costs. By law, the FMAP cannot be lower than 50 percent nor higher than 83 percent.

## 1175. What is the amount and duration of Medicaid services?

Within broad federal guidelines, states determine the duration and amount of services offered under their Medicaid programs. They may limit, for example, the number of days of hospital care or the number of physician visits covered. But some restrictions apply: Limits must result in a sufficient level of services to reasonably achieve the purpose of the benefits. Limits on required (nonoptional) benefits may not discriminate among beneficiaries based on medical diagnosis or condition.

In general, states are required to provide Medicaid coverage for comparable amounts, duration, and scope of services to all categorically-needy and categorically-related eligible persons. There are two important exceptions: (1) Medically necessary health care services identified under the Early and Periodic Screening, Diagnostic, and Treatment (EPSDT) program for eligible children that are within the scope of mandatory or optional services under federal law must be covered, even if those services are not included as part of the covered services in that state's plan (i.e., only these specific children might receive that specific service), and (2) States may require "waivers" to pay for otherwise-uncovered Home and Community-Based Services (HCBS) for Medicaid-eligible persons who might otherwise be institutionalized (i.e., only persons so designated might receive HCBS). States have few limitations on the services that may be covered under these waivers, as long as the services are cost-effective (except that, other than as a part of respite care, they may not provide room and board for recipients). With certain exceptions, a state's Medicaid plan must allow recipients to have freedom of choice among participating providers of health care.

## 1176. How does Medicaid help with Medicare coverage for the needy, elderly, and disabled?

Persons who are eligible for Medicare and whose income and assets fall below specified limits may also receive help from Medicaid. For persons who are eligible for full Medicaid coverage, the Medicare health care coverage is supplemented by services that are available under their state's Medicaid program. For example, depending on the state, supplies and services such as eyeglasses, hearing aids, and nursing facility care beyond the 100-day noncustodial-care limit covered by Medicare, may be provided by the Medicaid program. However, if a person is a Medicare beneficiary, payments for any services covered by Medicare are made by Medicare before any payments are made by the Medicaid program; Medicaid is always "payor of last resort." Individuals who are covered by Medicare and who also have full Medicaid coverage are often referred to as "dual eligibles".

In addition, there are three groups of Medicare beneficiaries who may not be fully eligible for Medicaid, but who do receive some help through their state Medicaid program. Most of the Medicare beneficiaries helped by Medicaid are those identified as (1) Qualified Medicare Beneficiaries (QMBs) or as (2) Specified Low-Income Medicare Beneficiaries (SLMBs). QMBs are those Medicare beneficiaries who have resources at or below twice the standard allowed under the SSI program, and incomes below 100 percent of the federal poverty level. This includes people who are also fully eligible for Medicaid. For QMBs, the state pays the individual's Part A (Hospital Insurance) and Part B (Medical Insurance) premiums, as applicable, and Medicare coinsurance and deductibles, subject to limits that states may impose on payment rates. SLMBs are Medicare beneficiaries with resources like the QMBs, but with higher incomes (up to 120 percent of the federal poverty level). For SLMBs, the Medicaid program pays only the Part B (Medical Insurance) premiums. Persons who previously qualified for Medicare because of disability, but who lost entitlement because of their return to work (despite the disability), may – in some cases – purchase Medicare Part A and Part B coverage. Medicaid may pay the Part A premium and in some cases all or part of the Part B premium for these individuals, known as Qualified Disabled and Working Individuals (QDWIs), if they have incomes below 200 percent of the federal poverty level but do not meet any other Medicaid assistance category.

Medicaid pays Medical Insurance premiums for SLMBs with incomes up to 135 percent of the federal poverty level. States must permit all who qualify to apply. However, states must limit the number selected in a calendar year, so that the aggregate cost for the number served is estimated to equal the state's allocation from the federal government in that year. Selection by states is on a first-come, first-served basis.

## LONG-TERM CARE

### 1177. Does Medicaid provide coverage for long-term care?

Yes. Medicaid provides long-term care coverage for eligible people age twenty-one and older in certain settings and as long as the individuals satisfy applicable resource and income limits. Long-term care coverage under Medicaid generally covers nursing home services for all eligible people and also covers home and community-based services for people who would need to be in a nursing home if they did not receive the home care services. Most long-term care services assist people with Activities of Daily Living, such as dressing, bathing, and using the bathroom. Long-term care can be provided at home, in the community, or in a facility. For purposes of

Medicaid eligibility and payment, long-term care services are those provided to an individual who requires a level of care equivalent to that received in a nursing facility

In most states, Medicaid will also cover services that will help a person remain in his home, such as personal care services, case management, and help with laundry and cleaning. Medicaid will not pay for rent, mortgage, utilities, or food.

Medicaid does not cover assisted living – in most states. This would be the in-between stage before a nursing home, but when an individual is past independent living. This stage can be quite expensive and can last for quite a long time, so preparing in advance is important.

As with all Medicaid programs, eligibility for long-term care services will vary from state to state. Long-term care services that may be available to a person in one state may not be available in another state. For example, some states cover assisted living services, while others do not. An individual should contact their state Medicaid office to find out specific eligibility for that state.

## EXEMPT INCOME AND RESOURCES

### 1178. Are certain income and resources exempt from the financial eligibility standards that govern Medicaid eligibility?

A single individual will not qualify for Medicaid in most states unless he has less than $2,000 in countable assets.

In determining whether applicants for Medicaid meet asset criteria, certain assets are considered "countable" and other assets are considered "exempt." Exempt assets include the following:

- The cash value of permanent life insurance policies up to $1,500 of face value, and all life insurance policies with no cash value (term insurance).
- Household furnishings (furniture, paintings, appliances, etc.), which are exempt only while used in the applicant's home.
- Burial funds up to $1,500 (reduced by the face value of any cash-value life insurance polices otherwise exempted and any amounts held in an irrevocable burial fund trust). There is no dollar limit if the burial plan is irrevocable.
- Property used in a trade or business.
- Burial space (grave site, crypt, mausoleum, urn, grave marker).
- One automobile of any value: (1) for a married couple where one spouse is institutionalized, (2) if equipped for a handicapped person, (3) if used to obtain medical treatment, or (4) if used for employment. This exemption is limited to $4,500 in all other cases.

- Up to $500,000 of equity in a home provided it is the person's principal place of residence. This includes the land on which the home sits and any adjoining property. States may choose to increase this amount up to $750,000.
- Property owned with one or more other individuals, if the other owners use the property as the principal place of residence and would be forced to move if the property were sold.
- Personal effects, including clothing, photographs, jewelry, etc.

The home is treated as a resource after the individual has been institutionalized for six months, unless the individual's spouse or minor, disabled or blind child continues to reside in the home, or it can be shown that the individual may be able to leave the institution and return home.

Exempt assets lose that status upon the death of the Medicaid recipient. Therefore, the state may claim reimbursement from the recipient's estate. Medicaid authorities are sometimes granted a lien against the home, collectible after the death of the recipient (or the death of certain relatives living in the home) to compensate for Medicaid benefits paid to the homeowner.

Medicaid applicants must also meet income tests that vary by state. It is important to note that rules do differ quite significantly from state-to-state. In some of the states, there is no upper income limit for persons in nursing homes. The remaining states have "income caps" in determining eligibility for nursing home coverage. If a person has income below the private cost of nursing home care in one of the states where there is no upper income limit, he meets Medicaid's income test. For example, if a person has monthly income of $2,500 and the private cost of nursing home care is $3,000 (and he has less than $2,000 in countable assets), he or she will qualify for Medicaid. He will be required to pay all of his income, except for a small "personal needs allowance," to the nursing home and Medicaid pays the balance of the bill.

Federal law requires states with "income caps" to set their "income caps" no higher than 300 percent of the Federal SSI benefit level ($733 in 2015). Thus, the "income cap" can be no greater than $2,199 in 2015. Not all of the states using "income caps" set their cap at the maximum allowable level (300 percent of the SSI benefit level). For example, if a person's monthly income is $1,550 in a state that sets its cap at $1,500, he does not qualify for Medicaid.

## SPOUSAL IMPOVERISHMENT

### 1179. Are there guidelines regarding the amount of income the community spouse of a nursing home resident can maintain?

The expense of nursing home care can rapidly deplete the lifetime savings of elderly couples. Because of this there are specially mandated Medicaid eligibility rules for couples when one member needs nursing home care. The rules protect income and resources for the other member of the couple. Under these rules a healthy spouse is not required to give up all of his income or property simply for the spouse in need of nursing care to be eligible through Medicaid. This set of rules, called "spousal protections" allow the spouse of a nursing home resident to keep enough income and assets to live a life outside the nursing home. As with all Medicaid programs, there is great variation among states' spousal protections rules, but the basic guidelines are the same in every state.

Under the rules certain income, assets, and the couple's home are generally protected. The following guidelines remain true for all states:

Protected Income – The income of the spouse of the long-term care patient is protected as well as some of the long-term care patients income if it is needed to financially support the spouse. The money that a spouse may keep and that is exempt from the Medicaid eligibility calculation is called the Minimum Monthly Maintenance Needs Allowance (MMMNA). The MMMNA varies from state to state, but the federal government sets a minimum and a maximum periodically that is tied to poverty guidelines. Until July 1, 2015, the minimum is $1,966.25 and the maximum is $2,980.50. This income is disregarded by the state Medicaid agency in evaluating whether the needy spouse is financially eligible for Medicaid.

Protected Assets – The spouse of the long-term care patient is allowed to keep one-half of the couple's combined marital assets subject to state set minimum and maximum allowable amounts (within federal guidelines). The state will measure the resources of the spouse applying for Medicaid on the date that the spouse began a hospital or nursing home stay that lasted at least thirty days. The amount of resources that the healthy spouse, called the "community spouse" is allowed to keep is called the Community Spouse Resource Allowance (CSRA). The CSRA varies by state (within a federally established minimum and maximum CSRA).

If a spouse living in the community needs more income than the MMMNA or more resources than the CSRA, the spouse can seek a court order allowing a variation from the state agency's standard.

Protection of Home – Federal Medicaid rules protect a Medicaid recipient's home and property, which is an important protection for the community spouse. If a Medicaid recipient expresses intent to return to the home, the first $536,000 in equity is excluded as a resource when calculating whether the needy spouse is eligible for Medicaid. Some states choose to raise the equity limit to $802,000. States do have discretion about when they will disregard the value of a home in calculating eligibility; many states require that the recipient must be actually likely to return to the home, not just that the recipient intends to return to the home.

## 1180. What are the resource eligibility requirements that apply to a community spouse?

The spousal impoverishment provisions apply where the member of the couple who is in a nursing facility or medical institution is expected to remain there for at least thirty days. When the couple applies for Medicaid, an assessment of their resources is conducted. The couple's resources are combined and exemptions for the home, household goods, an automobile, and burial funds are taken into account. (See Q 1178 and Q 1179.) The result is the spousal resource amount. The spousal resource amount is the state's minimum resource standard ($23,844 in 2015) or the spousal share, which is equal to one-half of the couple's combined resources (not to exceed the maximum permitted by the state ($119,220 in 2015)).

In order to determine whether the spouse residing in a medical facility is eligible for Medicaid, a determination of the couple's total countable resources must be made. All resources held by both spouses are considered to be available to the spouse in the medical facility, except for the Protected Resource Amount (PRA). This PRA is the greatest of:

- the spousal resource amount;
- the state spousal resource standard, which is the amount that the state has determined will be protected for the community spouse;
- an amount transferred to the community spouse for her/his support as directed by a court order;
- an amount designated by a state hearing officer to raise the community spouse's protected resources up to the minimum monthly maintenance needs standard (150 percent of the federal poverty level for a household of two).

The remainder becomes attributable to the spouse that is residing in a medical institution as countable resources. If the amount of resources is below the state's resource standard, the individual is eligible for Medicaid. Once resource eligibility is determined, resources of the community spouse are not attributed to the spouse in the medical facility.

## 1181. What are the income eligibility requirements for Community Spouses?

The community spouse's income is not considered available to the spouse who is in the medical facility, and the two individuals are not considered a couple for these purposes. The state must use the income eligibility standards for one person rather than two. Therefore, the standard income eligibility process for Medicaid is used. (See Q 1178 to Q 1180.)

## 1182. What is the process for the posteligibility treatment of income for Community Spouses?

This process is followed after an individual in a nursing facility/medical institution is determined to be eligible for Medicaid. The posteligibility process is used to determine how much the spouse in the medical facility must contribute toward the cost of nursing facility/institutional care. The process also determines how much of the income of the spouse who is in the medical facility is actually protected for use by the community spouse.

Deductions are made from the total income of the spouse who is residing in the medical facility in the following order:

- A personal needs allowance of at least thirty dollars
- The community spouse's monthly income allowance—between $1,966.25 and $2,980.50 (in 2015)—as long as the income is actually made available to the spouse

- A family monthly income allowance
- An amount for medical expenses incurred by the spouse who is in the medical facility

The sum of these deductions subtracted from the income of the individual who is in the medical facility will result in the amount the individual must contribute to the cost of care.

## 1183. What Medicaid planning strategies can spouses use to help with eligibility?

As explained in preceding questions Medicaid will pay for nursing home care only for those who are eligible. While some safe-guards and asset protections remain in place for the community spouse, many people feel that these do not do enough to protect their assets. Since Medicaid will pay for nursing home care only for those with limited assets and will penalize those who give away assets to qualify for Medicaid, people have long used other strategies in to circumvent the rules penalizing gifts of assets. Some of the more popular strategies used for making gifts while avoiding a transfer penalty are listed here. However, take note that new rules have made these strategies either completely ineffective or very difficult.

- "Half a Loaf" Strategy – At one time, this strategy was one of the most commonly used gifting strategies. A senior who anticipated needing long-term care would gift half of his assets to those of his choosing (preserving "half a loaf"), and use the rest to pay for Medicaid during the penalty period. Using the half a loaf strategy, people often made gifts to family members on a monthly or bimonthly basis, based on state law. Now that the transfer penalty does not begin to run until a person applies for Medicaid and all of the other qualifications are met for Medicaid, periodic gifting is no longer effective.
- Annuities – An annuity is when a person pays a lump sum of cash in exchange for a series of guaranteed future payments during that person's lifetime. The strategy of purchasing an annuity to qualify for Medicaid still works for married couples, but there has been refinement in the law causing most of the older methods to be ineffective. The key to using this strategy successfully is to convert an asset into a stream of monthly income for the spouse who does not need long-term care. This works because only the income of the applicant is considered toward eligibility; income of the community spouse is excluded. Purchasing an annuity turns an excess asset into income, so the asset is transparent for Medicaid purposes. The annuity payments must be completed before the end of the community spouse's life expectancy. This rule prevents the likelihood that there would be annuity payments left for the heirs after the community spouse's death.

## 1184. Can a spouse refuse to support a spouse who has entered a nursing home, causing Medicaid to pay for the nursing home?

Theoretically, husbands and wives have an equal duty to support one another. In many instances, the spouse with more income and assets gets sick and enters a nursing home first. However, it is perfectly possible that the sick spouse will have very limited personal income and resources. In that case, the question becomes, what is the obligation of the healthy, more affluent, community spouse?

Perhaps surprisingly, Federal Medicaid law generally takes a "just say no" position. State Medicaid agencies are not allowed to deny Medicaid benefits to patients on the grounds that their wealthier spouses refuse to support them or let any of their own income or resources be used. However, part of the Medicaid application process is an agreement to assign support rights to the Medicaid agency. The Medicaid agency then has a legal right to sue the community spouse for nonsupport. Whether this is a meaningful threat to individual community spouses depends on the local policy. Some Medicaid agencies are very active in this matter, but most bring few non-support suits.

Community spouses who want to preserve their own financial position, but who do not want to engage in outright "spousal refusal" can enter into an agreement with the state Medicaid agency. Usually, offering 25 percent of the difference between the community spouse's actual income and the monthly maintenance allowance will be acceptable. Note that Medicaid benefits can be denied to the spouse of a healthy person who refuses to provide information about his financial situation, so make sure that potential community spouses provide disclosure, even if they want to make a spousal refusal.

## 1185. Is divorce a viable planning strategy for Medicaid purposes?

Generally, no. Medicaid rules favor married couples. Medicaid-motivated divorce (as distinct from couples who are genuinely unhappy, or where one partner wants to remarry) is usually inadvisable.

When a couple divorces, either their property is community property, which is equally divided between them, or it is marital property which must be "equitably" divided. There are many factors in equitable distribution, but the needs of the parties are considered more important than who owned the property originally, or who contributed the funds used to purchase it. Therefore, it is possible that a large percentage of the couple's property will be distributed to the sick spouse, with resulting negative consequences for Medicaid planning.

Also, divorce courts have the power to order spousal support, depending on the relative needs of the spouses. A person who needs extensive long-term care is incapable of self-support, so it is possible that the divorce court will order the healthy, and wealthier, spouse to provide income to the sick spouse.

Capacity is also a problem. Legal capacity is required to sue or be sued, and a person suffering from Alzheimer's disease or some other type of dementia may lack such capacity. If a guardian has already been appointed, the guardian may be able to handle the divorce. On the other hand, some states have taken the position that divorce litigation is so inherently personal that a guardian cannot take part in it. In those states, a demented person's marriage is effectively permanent, because there's no way to dissolve it by divorce.

# MEDICAID TRANSFER RULES

## 1186. Can a person transfer property in order to meet the eligibility requirements for Medicaid?

Transfers of property for less than fair market value prior to applying for Medicaid benefits can result in a denial of benefits. States' rules will vary significantly from state to state, however, states may delay eligibility for Medicaid benefits for a period of time whenever it is determined that a person institutionalized in a medical institution or nursing facility has disposed of resources for less than fair market value within sixty months before application for Medicaid benefits. A transfer is an outright gift, or an exchange for something worth less than the full value of the transferred property.

Certain transfers can be made within sixty months of the application without loss of Medicaid eligibility. The family home may be transferred to: (1) the community spouse (non-institutionalized spouse); (2) a child who is under age twenty-one, blind, or permanently and totally disabled; (3) an adult son or daughter residing in the home and providing care that delayed the person's need for care in a medical institution or nursing facility for at least two years; (4) a trust created solely for the benefit of disabled children of the applicant; (5) certain trusts created for a disabled child or grandchild under age sixty-five; and (6) a brother or sister who has an ownership interest in the house and who has been living in the home for at least one year immediately before the person's admission for care.

Also, eligibility is unaffected if the transferor can prove that the intent of the transfer was to dispose of the resources either at fair market value or for other valuable consideration, or the exclusive purpose of the transfer was not to qualify for Medicaid. States can also grant eligibility where denial would amount to undue hardship.

All transfers of jointly-owned property to others are deemed to the Medicaid applicant. This penalty applies when the action taken by a co-owner reduces or eliminates the Medicaid applicant's ownership or control of the asset.

Two ways to transfer assets to family members without disqualifying for Medicaid benefits are (1) by transferring the assets to family members more than sixty months before the person applies for Medicaid benefits, and (2) if the applicant is already in a nursing home or about to go into one, by retaining enough assets to pay for sixty months of care, transferring the balance, and not applying for Medicaid until sixty months after the date on which the last asset transfer is completed.

Any planning for Medicaid eligibility should be done with a clear understanding of all the present rules on the federal level and for the state in which the person(s) reside. These rules vary significantly from state to state, and change frequently. Additionally, it should be noted that there is the threat of criminal penalty for any lawyer or adviser assisting clients with Medicaid planning.

## 1187. How is the penalty period determined after an improper transfer of assets?

The penalty period of ineligibility for an improper transfer—see Q 1186—begins on the later of the first day of the month of the transfer or "the date on which the individual is eligible for medical assistance under the State plan…based on an approved application for such care but for the application of the penalty period." The penalty lasts for the number of months equal to the total value of transferred property divided by the average cost of nursing home care to a private patient in the state or community of the applicant (the average private-pay rate). All transfers made in the sixty months prior to the application date are aggregated in determining the length of the penalty period. There is no limit to the length of the penalty period.

For example, a Medicaid applicant who improperly transfers a house worth $350,000 in a state with an average cost of nursing home care of $3,500 a month will be penalized with 100 months of ineligibility for Medicaid ($350,000 ÷ $3,500 = 100). But if a person gives away a house worth $350,000 and then waits more than sixty months to apply for Medicaid, he or she does not have to report the transfer and will not incur the period of ineligibility.

The rules have been made more restrictive in recent years and mean that common gifting strategies involving "half a loaf" or consecutive monthly transfers no longer work. (See Q 1183.)

If both spouses enter a nursing home at or near the same time, states are required to apportion the penalty between the spouses so that only one penalty applies. For example, an improper transfer of $70,000 in a state with a nursing home cost of $3,500 will cause each spouse to be ineligible for ten months ($70,000 ÷ $3,500 = 20 ÷ 2 = 10).

A Medicaid applicant cannot have a portion of the transferred property returned to eliminate the transfer penalty. All assets transferred for less than fair market value must be returned in order to eliminate some or all of the penalty period.

Each state has procedures for waiver of the transfer penalty when the transfer penalty results in undue hardship.

## 1188. What are the rules under Medicaid regarding the purchase of annuities?

Under the *Deficit Reduction Act of 2005* (DRA), purchasing an annuity by or on behalf of an applicant is considered an improper transfer of assets (see Q 1183, Q 1186, and Q 1187) unless the annuity meets certain requirements.

The purchase of an annuity will not be treated as an improper transfer of assets if the:

1. state is named as the primary remainder beneficiary for at least the total amount of medical assistance paid by Medicaid on behalf of the applicant;

2. state is named as the secondary beneficiary after the community spouse or minor or disabled child;

3. annuity is purchased inside, or with proceeds from, a retirement account (IRA, Roth IRA, SEP-IRA, etc.)

Any annuity purchased on behalf of a Medicaid applicant must be irrevocable, nonassignable, actuarially sound, and provide for payments in equal amounts during the term of the annuity, with no deferral and no balloon payments.

Annuities purchased prior to February 8, 2006 (the effective date of the DRA) are governed by state-specific provisions. At a minimum, pre-DRA annuities must be actuarially sound (meaning they do not pay out over a time period exceeding the life expectancy of the Medicaid applicant).

## TRUSTS

### 1189. Can a trust be used to shelter a Medicaid applicant's assets?

There are considerable limits on the use of trusts to shelter a Medicaid applicant's assets. Trust assets created or funded by a Medicaid applicant or by his spouse are considered available to the applicant to the extent the applicant derives any benefit from the trust.

If an institutionalized person or spouse (or, at the option of a state, a noninstitutionalized person or spouse) disposes of trust assets for less than fair market value on or after the look-back date for trusts, the person is ineligible for Medicaid for the following time period:

- For an institutionalized person, the number of months of ineligibility is equal to the total of all assets transferred on or after the look-back date divided by the average monthly cost to a private patient of nursing facility services in the state at the time of application. Ineligibility begins on the first day of the first month during or after which assets have been transferred for less than fair market value.

- For a noninstitutionalized person, the number of months of ineligibility may not be greater than a number equal to the total value of all assets transferred on or after the look-back date, divided by the average monthly cost to a private patient of nursing facility services in the state at the time of application. Ineligibility begins on the first day of the first month during or after which assets have been transferred for less than fair market value.

The look-back period in the case of payments from a trust or portions of a trust that are treated as assets disposed of is sixty months before (1) the first date on which an institutionalized person is both institutionalized and has applied for Medicaid, or (2) the first date on which a non-institutionalized person applies for Medicaid or, if later, the date on which the individual disposes of assets for less than fair market value.

An individual is considered to have established a trust if assets of the individual were used to form all or part of the corpus of the trust and any of the following individuals established the trust other than by will:

- The individual

- The individual's spouse

- A person, including a court or administrative body, with legal authority to act in place of or on behalf of the individual or the individual's spouse
- A person, including any court or administrative body, acting at the direction or upon the request of the individual or the individual's spouse

In the case of a revocable trust, (1) the corpus of the trust is considered a resource available to the individual, (2) payments from the trust to or for the benefit of the individual are considered income of the individual, and (3) any other payments from the trust are considered assets disposed of by the individual.

Assets are defined as all income and resources of the individual and the individual's spouse, including any income or resources which the individual or the individual's spouse is entitled to but does not receive because of action: (1) by the individual or the individual's spouse; (2) by a person, including a court or administrative body, with legal authority to act in place of or on behalf of the individual or the individual's spouse; or (3) by any person, including any court or administrative body, acting at the direction or upon the request of the individual or the individual's spouse.

In the case of an irrevocable trust:

- If there are any circumstances under which payment from the trust could be made to or for the benefit of the individual, the portion of the corpus from which, or the income on the corpus from which, payment to the individual could be made is considered resources available to the individual, and payments from that portion of the corpus or income: (1) to or from the benefit of the individual, is considered income of the individual, and (2) for any other purpose, is considered a transfer of assets by the individual. (See preceding definition of "asset".)
- Any portion of the trust from which, or any income on the corpus from which, no payment could under any circumstances be made to the individual, is considered, as of the date of establishment of the trust (or, if later, the date on which payment to the individual was foreclosed), to be assets disposed of by the individual and the value of the trust is determined by including the amount of any payments made from such portion of the trust after that date.

A trust includes any legal instrument or device that is similar to a trust but includes an annuity only to such extent and in such manner as the Department of Health and Human Services specifies.

## 1190. Are there exceptions to the trust rules under Medicaid?

Yes. There are three exceptions. The following trusts are exempt from the Medicaid trust rules:

1. A trust established by a parent, grandparent, guardian, or court for the benefit of an individual who is disabled and under age sixty-five, using the individual's own funds.

2. A trust composed only of pension, Social Security, and other income of the individual, in states which make individuals eligible for institutional care under a special-income level, but do not cover institutional care for the medically needy.

3. A trust established by a disabled individual, parent, grandparent, guardian, or court for the disabled individual, using the individual's own funds, where the trust is made up of pooled funds and managed by a nonprofit organization for the sole benefit of each individual included in the trust.

In all of the above instances, the trust must provide that the state receives any funds, up to the amount of Medicaid benefits paid on behalf of the individual, remaining in the trust when the individual dies.

A trust will not be counted as available to an individual where the state determines that counting the trust would work an undue hardship.

## 1191. What is a Special Needs Trust (SNT)?

A Special Needs Trust (SNT) is a specialized legal document designed to benefit an individual who is disabled. A SNT is most often a stand-alone document, but it can also be created as part of someone's (such as the disabled person's parent) will. SNTs have been in use for many years, and were given an "official" legal status by Congress in 1993.

An SNT enables a disabled person, or an individual with a chronic or acquired illness, to have held in trust, for his or her benefit, an unlimited amount of assets. In a properly-drafted SNT, those assets are not considered countable assets for purposes of qualification for certain governmental benefits.

These benefits may include Supplemental Security Income (SSI), Medicaid, vocational rehabilitation, subsidized housing, and other benefits based upon need. For purposes of a SNT, an individual is considered impoverished if his or her personal assets are less than $2,000.

An SNT provides for supplemental and extra care over and above that which the government provides.

An SNT must be irrevocable. A properly-drafted SNT will include provisions for trust termination or dissolution under certain circumstances, and will include explicit directions for amendment when necessary.

An SNT can be used for supplemental and extra care over and above what the government provides. A properly-drafted SNT will work on a sliding scale; in the event that the government provides for 100 percent of the disabled beneficiary's needs the trust will provide nothing. If there are no governmental benefits available, the trust can provide 100 percent of what is needed.

A properly-drafted trust will address the issue concerning paybacks to Medicaid or other government sources. The law requires that repayment language must be included in all SNTs, whether repayment is required or not.

A SNT that is funded by parents or other third-party sources will not be required to pay back Medicaid. An SNT that is funded by a personal injury settlement that is properly court-ordered into the SNT will not be required to pay back Medicaid. The only assets within an SNT that are subject to the repayment obligation are those assets which originally belonged to the disabled individual that are transferred into the trust.

Examples of assets which would belong to the disabled individual in the first place include earnings from a job, savings, certain Social Security back payments, and personal injury recoveries which are not court-ordered into the SNT.

## 1192. What are the three different types of Special Needs Trusts (SNT)?

There are three types of Special NeedsTrusts (SNT). They are (1) a family-type trust, (2) a pooled trust, and (3) a court-ordered trust. These trusts are described in the subsequent questions.

## 1193. What is a family-type Special Needs Trust (SNT)?

The most commonly used SNT is a family-type trust, which is set up by the parents. The parents provide the money for the trust, often by will, and sometimes by purchasing life insurance payable to the trust.

In most cases, the parents write a will giving money or a house to the disabled son or daughter. After the beneficiary has died, anything left over goes to other family members. The left-over is called the "remainder."

Some parents place their property in a "living" or "inter vivos" trust, and provide in the trust that the disabled son or daughter is the beneficiary. With that type of trust, there is no need to wait for the parents to die. The trust becomes effective immediately. This is a good idea for families where aunts, uncles, and grandparents might want to leave money for the trust. Anyone can give money to the trust, either by writing a check or writing a will.

The key to a family-type SNT is that the money cannot be used for housing, food, or clothing. Those are considered basic needs under the Medicaid laws. If the disabled person is receiving free housing, food, or clothing from someone else, including a family member or a trust, then the government benefits will be reduced or eliminated.

The trust can be used to purchase a home, and perhaps rent it to the disabled person. The trust can pay for repairs, utilities and taxes for a home; it can purchase furnishings for the home. It can pay for vacations, summer camp, or trips. It can buy bowling shoes or other sporting equipment. It can pay for medical costs not otherwise covered by Medicaid, such as vitamins. It can pay for funeral and burial costs. It can pay for a lot of things, but it does not have to pay for anything unless the trustee thinks it is a good idea.

The parents generally serve as trustee as long as they are alive. When they die, a successor trustee must be ready to take over. Some parents choose a bank to serve as trustee, but banks are expensive and do not keep track of the disabled person's individual needs. A responsible family member is usually a better choice, if one can be found.

## 1194. What is a pooled Special Needs Trust (SNT)?

Anyone can put money into a pooled trust, including parents, grandparents, or even the individual with a disability.

The trust must be established through a non-profit association. The nonprofit agency that administers the trust takes care of all the tax preparation, investment decisions, and also serves as trustee. The cash is kept in a bank, but the nonprofit owns all the deeds to houses and other real estate, as trustee. Banks do not want to own real estate in trust because they are afraid of environmental problems.

Any money left in the trust after the beneficiary dies stays in the trust to help other persons with disabilities. The money does not go to the state.

A pooled trust can purchase a home for the beneficiary and rent it to him. Before the pooled trust is set up, the parents and other family members explain what they want the trust to pay for, and who should be consulted about these matters.

## 1195. What is a court-ordered Special Needs Trust (SNT)?

A court-ordered trust, also called a Type "A" special needs trust, is used only for special circumstances, such as where the person with a disability has inherited money, or received a court settlement.

Because the disabled person actually owns the money, the funds cannot be put into the usual SNT such as parents usually set up.

The "A" comes from the last letter of the federal statute, 42 U.S.C. §1396p(d)(4)(A).

Only certain people are allowed to set up this type of trust:

- The disabled person's parent
- The disabled person's grandparent
- The legal guardian
- A court

To qualify, the disabled person must be under sixty-five years old and meet the disability standards of Social Security. Someone who is not disabled enough to qualify for Social Security cannot have this type of trust.

The trust must specify that after the disabled person has died, anything left over will pay back the state for whatever medical assistance the government provided to the individual after the trust was set up. As a practical matter, that means that any unspent money will go to the government. It is unlikely that after Medicaid is paid back, anything will be left over.

## 1196. Should a Special Needs Trust (SNT) be set up during the grantor's life or as part of the grantor's will?

Generally, it is better to set up a Special Needs Trust (SNT) during the lifetime of the grantor. The advantage is that if other family members or friends of the disabled beneficiary wish to provide for the disabled beneficiary they may contribute to the already existing SNT. Another advantage is that if a person is chosen to be a successor trustee this person can gain experience as a trustee by acting as a cotrustee. Also, a trust created during the grantor's lifetime can be a "standby" trust that remains unfunded until the death of the grantor. Then the will or another trust of the grantor can simply add funds to the SNT at the grantor's death.

Another reason to create an SNT during the grantor's lifetime is that life insurance policies and retirement accounts can name the SNT as beneficiary of these policies or accounts more easily.

## 1197. What is the future of Special Needs Trusts (SNT)?

A number of states are imposing restrictions on distributions from SNTs. Most of these restrictions have been on self-settled trusts. But some states are also restricting third-party trust distributions.

There have been numerous court cases challenging these state-imposed restrictions. Decisions have been made which have both upheld the restrictions and struck them down. Because of these different results, it is very important for individuals to seek legal advice when setting up SNTs.

# ESTATE RECOVERIES

## 1198. Can a state recover nursing home and long-term care Medicaid expenses from the estate of a deceased Medicaid recipient?

States are required to recover the costs of nursing facility and other long-term care services furnished to a Medicaid beneficiary from the estate of the beneficiary unless undue hardship would result. The estate may include any real or personal property or other assets in which the beneficiary had any legal title or interest at the time of death, including the home. Different estate recovery provisions apply to individuals who purchase specified long-term care insurance policies in designated states.

According to the Centers for Medicare & Medicaid Services (CMS), "undue hardship" might exist when the estate subject to recovery is the sole income-producing asset of the survivors and the income is limited or is a homestead of modest value.

It is possible that a state may conclude that an undue hardship does not exist if the individual created the hardship by resorting to estate planning methods under which the individual divested assets in order to avoid estate recovery. A state may adopt a rebuttable presumption that, if the individual obtained estate planning advice from legal counsel and followed this advice, the resulting financial situation would not qualify for an undue-hardship waiver.

The estate-recovery rules apply only to the estates of Medicaid beneficiaries dying on or after October 1, 1993, only to benefits paid on or after that date, and only for costs for a

Medicaid recipient who was age fifty-five or older at the time the costs were incurred. Recovery of Medicaid costs cannot take place while the surviving spouse lives.

## DISCRIMINATION

### 1199. Does federal law require that Medicaid patients be admitted to any (and all) nursing homes?

There is no requirement that nursing homes participate in Medicaid. Nursing homes receive reimbursement for Medicaid patients but it is usually much lower than the rates nursing homes charge private-pay patients (those who use their own funds, insurance benefits, or a combination of the two). Most nursing homes participate in Medicaid, but the level of participation can vary. A nursing home can make all of its beds Medicaid beds, or it can have some Medicaid beds and some private-pay beds.

If a patient in a nursing home starts out paying privately, uses up all excess resources, and becomes eligible for Medicaid, the nursing home is prohibited by federal law from evicting the patient because the method of payment has changed from private payment to Medicaid. The patient can be evicted if he cannot pay the nursing home and is also ineligible for Medicaid.

The nursing home contract defines the rights and responsibilities of the nursing home and patient. There are limitations on certain contract provisions that affect Medicaid patients:

(1) A nursing home contract may not force the patient to give up the right to receive Medicare or Medicaid. A nursing home must counsel patients about the availability of these benefits.

(2) A nursing home contract may not force a relative or friend of the patient to guarantee payments in order to get the patient into the nursing home. A nursing home can require a person in charge of a potential resident's funds to commit those funds to the payment of nursing home bills.

(3) A nursing home cannot require a person or a person's family to pay more than the Medicaid rate in order to have a Medicaid-eligible person admitted to the nursing home.

## MANAGED CARE

### 1200. How has managed care changed the original Medicaid program?

A significant change to the original Medicaid program is the managed-care concept. Under managed-care systems, Health Maintenance Organizations (HMOs), Prepaid Health Plans (PHPs), or comparable entities agree to provide a specific set of services to Medicaid enrollees in return for fixed periodic payments for each enrollee. Managed-care programs seek to enhance access to quality care in a cost-effective manner. However, there are complexities in this, and waivers of certain parts of the Social Security Act are required. These waivers provide states with greater flexibility in the design and implementation of their Medicaid programs.

Section 1915(b) of the Social Security Act allows states to develop innovative health care delivery or reimbursement systems. Section 1115 of the Social Security Act allows statewide health care reform demonstrations for testing various methods of covering uninsured populations, and testing new delivery systems, without increasing costs.

Medicaid managed-care programs are growing rapidly and several states have converted their entire Medicaid programs into managed care. Over 16 million Medicaid recipients are enrolled in Medicaid managed-care programs—which is more than 50 percent of all Medicaid enrollees.

States can restrict choice by offering a choice between at least two managed-care organizations or Primary Care Case Managers (PCCMs), or at least one plan and one PCCM. States must permit individuals to change their enrollment for cause at any time, without cause within ninety days of notification of enrollment, and without cause at least every twelve months thereafter.

States may provide up to six months minimum enrollment that covers all managed-care entities.

There are protection for Medicaid beneficiaries in managed care, including (1) assuring coverage of emergency services, (2) protection of enrollee-provider communications, (3) grievance procedures, (4) demonstration of adequate capacity and services, (5) protecting enrollees against liability for payment, and (6) antidiscrimination.

## STATE LTC PARTNERSHIP PROGRAM

### 1201. What is a "qualified state long-term care insurance partnership?"

A qualified state long-term care insurance partnership is a state Medicaid plan amendment that provides for the disregard of assets or resources in an amount equal to the insurance benefit payments made to or on behalf of an individual who is a beneficiary under a qualifying Long-Term Care (LTC) insurance policy.

A qualifying LTC partnership policy must meet the following requirements:

1. The policy covers an insured who was a resident of the state when coverage first became effective under the policy.
2. The policy is a tax-qualified LTC insurance policy issued not earlier than the effective date of the state LTC partnership program.
3. The policy must meet the standards contained in the 2000 NAIC Model LTC Policy Act and Regulations.
4. The policy must contain the following inflation protection provisions:
    a. Buyers younger than age sixty-one—compound annual inflation protection
    b. Buyers ages sixty-one to seventy-five—some level of inflation protection
    c. Buyers age seventy-six or older—no inflation protection required

5. Agents selling the policy must receive appropriate training and demonstrate understanding of the policy.

6. The issuer of the policy must provide regular reports with information on policy benefits, claims, underwriting, terminations, and other information deemed appropriate.

7. The policy must not be subject to any state insurance mandates not applicable to all LTC insurance policies sold in the state.

Standards do exist (under the Deficit Reduction Act of 2005 9DRA)) for the uniform reciprocal recognition of LTC partnership policies, under which benefits paid by such policies will be treated the same by all states with qualified state LTC insurance partnerships. A state with a LTC insurance partnership is subject to the standards unless the state formally elects to be exempt from such standards.

# APPENDICES

# APPENDIX A
# SOCIAL SECURITY TABLES

## TABLE 1 — BENEFITS AS PERCENTAGE OF PIA

|  |  |
|---|---|
| **RETIREMENT BENEFIT** | |
| Starting at normal retirement age (NRA) (gradually rising from 65 to 67) | PIA |
| Starting age 62 or above (but below NRA) | PIA reduced |
| **DISABILITY BENEFIT** | PIA |
| **SPOUSE'S BENEFIT (husband or wife of retired or disabled worker)** | |
| Caring for child (under 16 or disabled) | 50% of PIA |
| Starting at NRA (gradually rising from 65 to 67) | 50% of PIA |
| Starting age 62 or above (but below NRA) | 50% of PIA reduced |
| **CHILD'S BENEFIT** | |
| Child of retired or disabled worker | 50% of PIA |
| Child of deceased worker | 75% of PIA |
| **MOTHER'S OR FATHER'S BENEFIT (widow(er) caring for child under 16 or disabled)** | 75% of PIA |
| **WIDOW(ER)'S BENEFIT (widow(er) not caring for child)** | |
| Starting at NRA (gradually rising from 65 to 67) | 100% of PIA |
| Starting age 60 or above (but below NRA) | 100% of PIA reduced |
| **DISABLED WIDOW(ER)'S BENEFIT** | |
| Starting age 50-60 | 71½% of PIA |
| **PARENT'S BENEFIT (dependent parent of deceased worker)** | |
| One dependent parent | 82½% of PIA |
| Two dependent parents | 75% of PIA (each) |

| TABLE 2<br>QUARTERS OF COVERAGE REQUIRED TO BE FULLY INSURED FOR RETIREMENT BENEFITS | | |
|---|---|---|
| Birth Year | Men | Women |
| 1892 or earlier | 6 | 6 |
| 1893 | 7 | 6 |
| 1894 | 8 | 6 |
| 1895 | 9 | 6 |
| 1896 | 10 | 7 |
| 1897 | 11 | 8 |
| 1898 | 12 | 9 |
| 1899 | 13 | 10 |
| 1900 | 14 | 11 |
| 1901 | 15 | 12 |
| 1902 | 16 | 13 |
| 1903 | 17 | 14 |
| 1904 | 18 | 15 |
| 1905 | 19 | 16 |
| 1906 | 20 | 17 |
| 1907 | 21 | 18 |
| 1908 | 22 | 19 |
| 1909 | 23 | 20 |
| 1910 | 24 | 21 |
| 1911 | 24 | 22 |
| 1912 | 24 | 23 |
| 1913 | 24 | 24 |
| 1914 | 25 | 25 |
| 1915 | 26 | 26 |
| 1916 | 27 | 27 |
| 1917 | 28 | 28 |
| 1918 | 29 | 29 |
| 1919 | 30 | 30 |
| 1920 | 31 | 31 |
| 1921 | 32 | 32 |
| 1922 | 33 | 33 |
| 1923 | 34 | 34 |
| 1924 | 35 | 35 |
| 1925 | 36 | 36 |
| 1926 | 37 | 37 |
| 1927 | 38 | 38 |
| 1928 | 39 | 39 |
| 1929 or after | 40 | 40 |

| TABLE 3<br>MINIMUM NUMBER OF QUARTERS OF COVERAGE NEEDED TO BE FULLY INSURED AT DEATH | | |
|---|---|---|
| Birth Year | 2014 | 2015 |
| 1952 or before | 40 | 40 |
| 1953 | 39 | 40 |
| 1954 | 38 | 39 |
| 1955 | 37 | 38 |
| 1956 | 36 | 37 |
| 1957 | 35 | 36 |
| 1958 | 34 | 35 |
| 1959 | 33 | 34 |
| 1960 | 32 | 33 |
| 1961 | 31 | 32 |
| 1962 | 30 | 31 |
| 1963 | 29 | 30 |
| 1964 | 28 | 29 |
| 1965 | 27 | 28 |
| 1966 | 26 | 27 |
| 1967 | 25 | 26 |
| 1968 | 24 | 25 |
| 1969 | 23 | 24 |
| 1970 | 22 | 23 |
| 1971 | 21 | 22 |
| 1972 | 20 | 21 |
| 1973 | 19 | 20 |
| 1974 | 18 | 19 |
| 1975 | 17 | 18 |
| 1976 | 16 | 17 |
| 1977 | 15 | 16 |
| 1978 | 14 | 15 |
| 1979 | 13 | 14 |

| TABLE 4<br>YEARS IN WHICH PERSON REACHES AGE 21 | |
|---|---|
| Birth Year | Year Person Reaches Age 21 |
| 1938 | 1959 |
| 1939 | 1960 |
| 1940 | 1961 |
| 1941 | 1962 |
| 1942 | 1963 |
| 1943 | 1964 |
| 1944 | 1965 |
| 1945 | 1966 |
| 1946 | 1967 |
| 1947 | 1968 |
| 1948 | 1969 |
| 1949 | 1970 |
| 1950 | 1971 |
| 1951 | 1972 |
| 1952 | 1973 |
| 1953 | 1974 |
| 1954 | 1975 |
| 1955 | 1976 |
| 1956 | 1977 |
| 1957 | 1978 |
| 1958 | 1979 |
| 1959 | 1980 |
| 1960 | 1981 |
| 1961 | 1982 |
| 1962 | 1983 |
| 1963 | 1984 |
| 1964 | 1985 |
| 1965 | 1986 |
| 1966 | 1987 |
| 1967 | 1988 |
| 1968 | 1989 |
| 1969 | 1990 |
| 1970 | 1991 |
| 1971 | 1992 |
| 1972 | 1993 |
| 1973 | 1994 |
| 1974 | 1995 |
| 1975 | 1996 |
| 1976 | 1997 |
| 1977 | 1998 |
| 1978 | 1999 |
| 1979 | 2000 |
| 1980 | 2001 |
| 1981 | 2002 |
| 1982 | 2003 |
| 1983 | 2004 |
| 1984 | 2005 |
| 1985 | 2006 |
| 1986 | 2007 |
| 1987 | 2008 |
| 1988 | 2009 |
| 1989 | 2010 |
| 1990 | 2011 |
| 1991 | 2012 |
| 1992 | 2013 |
| 1993 | 2014 |
| 1994 | 2015 |
| 1995 | 2016 |

| TABLE 5<br>NUMBER OF YEARS EARNINGS THAT MUST BE USED IN COMPUTING RETIREMENT BENEFITS<br>(less if person had an established period of disability) | | | | |
|---|---|---|---|---|
| Birth Year | Computation Age | Year of Computation | No. of Years | No. of Divisor Months |
| 1915 | 62 | 1977 | 21 | 252 |
| 1916 | 62 | 1978 | 22 | 264 |
| 1917 | 62 | 1979 | 23 | 276 |
| 1918 | 62 | 1980 | 24 | 288 |
| 1919 | 62 | 1981 | 25 | 300 |
| 1920 | 62 | 1982 | 26 | 312 |
| 1921 | 62 | 1983 | 27 | 324 |
| 1922 | 62 | 1984 | 28 | 336 |
| 1923 | 62 | 1985 | 29 | 348 |
| 1924 | 62 | 1986 | 30 | 360 |
| 1925 | 62 | 1987 | 31 | 372 |
| 1926 | 62 | 1988 | 32 | 384 |
| 1927 | 62 | 1989 | 33 | 396 |
| 1928 | 62 | 1990 | 34 | 408 |
| 1929 | 62 | 1991 | 35 | 420 |
| 1930 or later | 62 | 1992 or later | 35 | 420 |

## TABLE 6 — INSURED STATUS NEEDED FOR SOCIAL SECURITY BENEFITS

The worker must be FULLY insured to provide monthly benefits for:

... Retired worker (at age 62 or over)
... Spouse of retired worker (at age 62 or over)
... Spouse of retired worker (at any age if caring for a child)
... Child of retired worker
... Widow(er) of worker (at age 60 or over)
... Disabled widow(er) of worker (at age 50 or over)
... Dependent parent of deceased worker

The worker may be either FULLY or CURRENTLY insured to provide monthly benefits for:

... Child of deceased worker
... Widow(er) of worker (at any age if caring for child)

A disabled worker must be FULLY insured and (a) if disability began at or after age 31, must have worked in covered employment 5 out of the last 10 years, or (b) if disability began before age 31, must have worked in covered employment ½ of the quarters between age 21 and onset of disability (but not less than 6), to provide benefits for:

... Disabled worker (at any age)
... Child of disabled worker
... Spouse of disabled worker (at age 62 or over)
... Spouse of disabled worker (at any age if caring for a child)

A worker who is either FULLY or CURRENTLY insured qualified for the lump-sum death benefit if he is survived by (1) a spouse who was living with him at the time of his death, or (2) a dependent child or spouse eligible to receive social security benefits based on his earnings record.

## TABLE 7 — MAXIMUM AIME FOR RETIREMENT, SURVIVOR, AND DISABILITY BENEFITS*

(for workers earning $118,500 or more in 2015)

| Year of Birth | Normal Retirement Age | Death in 2015 | Disability in 2015 |
|---|---|---|---|
| 1953 | 9,031 | 8,739 | 8,640 |
| 1954 | 9,095 | 8,815 | 8,712 |
| 1955 | 9,151 | 8,892 | 8,788 |
| 1956 | 9,196 | 8,972 | 8,866 |
| 1957 | 9,233 | 9,020 | 8,950 |
| 1958 | 9,261 | 9,063 | 8,998 |
| 1959 | 9,287 | 9,097 | 9,041 |
| 1960 | 9,311 | 9,124 | 9,075 |
| 1961 | 9,337 | 9,139 | 9,103 |
| 1962 | 9,360 | 9,154 | 9,119 |
| 1963 | 9,405 | 9,168 | 9,134 |
| 1964 | 9,426 | 9,184 | 9,147 |
| 1965 | 9,447 | 9,197 | 9,162 |
| 1966 | 9,469 | 9,211 | 9,175 |
| 1967 | 9,488 | 9,227 | 9,190 |
| 1968 | 9,504 | 9,241 | 9,190 |
| 1969 | 9,523 | 9,259 | 9,205 |
| 1970 | 9,539 | 9,269 | 9,210 |

| Year of Birth | Normal Retirement Age | Death in 2015 | Disability in 2015 |
|---|---|---|---|
| 1971 | 9,556 | 9,289 | 9,228 |
| 1972 | 9,570 | 9,304 | 9,244 |
| 1973 | 9,586 | 9,322 | 9,244 |
| 1974 | 9,602 | 9,334 | 9,252 |
| 1975 | 9,615 | 9,347 | 9,257 |
| 1976 | 9,629 | 9,371 | 9,271 |
| 1977 | 9,638 | 9,376 | 9,268 |
| 1978 | 9,641 | 9,357 | 9,219 |
| 1979 | 9,654 | 9,368 | 9,214 |
| 1980 | 9,665 | 9,399 | 9,229 |
| 1981 | 9,668 | 9,437 | 9,259 |
| 1982 | 9,671 | 9,489 | 9,297 |
| 1983 | 9,671 | 9,539 | 9,297 |
| 1984 | 9,671 | 9,615 | 9,330 |
| 1985 | 9,671 | 9,634 | 9,356 |
| 1986 | 9,671 | 9,671 | 9,324 |
| 1987 | 9,671 | 9,671 | 9,276 |
| 1988 | 9,671 | 9,671 | 9,236 |
| 1989 | 9,671 | 9,671 | 9,267 |
| 1990 | 9,671 | 9,671 | 9,315 |

* Normal Retirement Age for unreduced benefits (PIA) increases by two months a year for workers reaching age 62 in 2000-2005; maintains age 66 for workers reaching age 62 in 2006-2016; increases by two months a year for workers reaching age 62 in 2017-2022; and maintains age 67 for workers reaching age 62 after 2022.

* AIME calculations assume that the worker earned the Social Security maximum earnings base in all years up to an including, respectively, the year before normal retirement ($118,500 is used for 2015 and later years), the year of death, the year before disability.

## TABLE 8 — AIME FOR WORKERS EARNING $7,000-$62,200 IN 2015*

| Year Born | AIME | Current Annual Earnings $7,000–16,200 | $16,200–25,400 | $25,400–34,600 | $34,600–43,800 | $43,800–53,000 | $53,000–62,200 |
|---|---|---|---|---|---|---|---|
| 1953 | Retirement | 661 | 1,180 | 1,698 | 2,217 | 2,738 | 3,256 |
| | Death | 630 | 1,123 | 1,617 | 2,112 | 2,607 | 3,100 |
| | Disability | 618 | 1,105 | 1,591 | 2,076 | 2,562 | 3,046 |
| 1954–1958 | Retirement | 689 | 1,229 | 1,769 | 2,309 | 2,850 | 3,390 |
| | Death | 634 | 1,133 | 1,630 | 2,128 | 2,627 | 3,124 |
| | Disability | 623 | 1,111 | 1,601 | 2,087 | 2,578 | 3,067 |
| 1959–1963 | Retirement | 736 | 1,315 | 1,892 | 2,470 | 3,047 | 3,626 |
| | Death | 647 | 1,158 | 1,666 | 2,175 | 2,684 | 3,192 |
| | Disability | 634 | 1,133 | 1,630 | 2,128 | 2,627 | 3,124 |
| 1964–1968 | Retirement | 796 | 1,419 | 2,045 | 2,669 | 3,294 | 3,918 |
| | Death | 676 | 1,205 | 1,736 | 2,265 | 2,795 | 3,324 |
| | Disability | 658 | 1,176 | 1,692 | 2,210 | 2,725 | 3,244 |
| 1969–1973 | Retirement | 835 | 1,491 | 2,146 | 2,801 | 3,457 | 4,112 |
| | Death | 708 | 1,264 | 1,821 | 2,377 | 2,933 | 3,490 |
| | Disability | 683 | 1,220 | 1,758 | 2,294 | 2,831 | 3,367 |
| 1974–1978 | Retirement | 869 | 1,551 | 2,233 | 2,916 | 3,598 | 4,280 |
| | Death | 742 | 1,325 | 1,907 | 2,489 | 3,073 | 3,653 |
| | Disability | 708 | 1,264 | 1,820 | 2,376 | 2,931 | 3,487 |
| 1979–1983 | Retirement | 889 | 1,590 | 2,288 | 2,987 | 3,686 | 4,384 |
| | Death | 791 | 1,413 | 2,034 | 2,656 | 3,276 | 3,898 |
| | Disability | 737 | 1,317 | 1,895 | 2,473 | 3,052 | 3,632 |
| 1984–1988 | Retirement | 895 | 1,597 | 2,299 | 3,002 | 3,705 | 4,407 |
| | Death | 869 | 1,552 | 2,234 | 2,916 | 3,599 | 4,281 |
| | Disability | 775 | 1,382 | 1,989 | 2,597 | 3,205 | 3,813 |

* AIMEs are approximate and based on the assumption that the worker has had 6% pay raises each year through 2015. AIME calculations for retirement assume that the worker's current earnings stay the same until Normal Retirement Age. Match AIMEs with AIMEs closest to them in Tables 10, 11, and 12 to determine benefits.

## TABLE 9 — AIME FOR WORKERS EARNING $62,200-$118,500 IN 2015*

| Year Born | AIME | Current Annual Earnings | | | | | |
|---|---|---|---|---|---|---|---|
| | | $62,200–71,400 | $71,400–80,600 | $80,600–89,800 | $89,800–99,000 | $99,000–108,200 | $108,200–118,500 |
| 1953 | Retirement | 3,775 | 4,292 | 4,810 | 5,303 | 5,809 | 6,313 |
| | Death | 3,594 | 4,089 | 4,581 | 5,046 | 5,519 | 5,994 |
| | Disability | 3,534 | 4,018 | 4,502 | 4,958 | 5,419 | 5,887 |
| 1954–1958 | Retirement | 3,930 | 4,470 | 5,011 | 5,551 | 6,088 | 6,621 |
| | Death | 3,623 | 4,120 | 4,617 | 5,117 | 5,613 | 6,097 |
| | Disability | 3,555 | 4,043 | 4,532 | 5,020 | 5,509 | 5,982 |
| 1959–1963 | Retirement | 4,204 | 4,781 | 5,360 | 5,936 | 6,515 | 7,094 |
| | Death | 3,704 | 4,212 | 4,721 | 5,230 | 5,738 | 6,247 |
| | Disability | 3,622 | 4,120 | 4,617 | 5,116 | 5,615 | 6,112 |
| 1964–1968 | Retirement | 4,543 | 5,166 | 5,792 | 6,418 | 7,040 | 7,667 |
| | Death | 3,854 | 4,384 | 4,915 | 5,445 | 5,974 | 6,503 |
| | Disability | 3,760 | 4,277 | 4,793 | 5,311 | 5,828 | 6,345 |
| 1969–1973 | Retirement | 4,769 | 5,423 | 6,079 | 6,733 | 7,390 | 8,045 |
| | Death | 4,045 | 4,602 | 5,157 | 5,714 | 6,268 | 6,826 |
| | Disability | 3,905 | 4,442 | 4,978 | 5,516 | 6,051 | 6,588 |
| 1974–1978 | Retirement | 4,962 | 5,645 | 6,327 | 7,007 | 7,690 | 8,374 |
| | Death | 4,238 | 4,821 | 5,404 | 5,986 | 6,568 | 7,150 |
| | Disability | 4,042 | 4,598 | 5,154 | 5,710 | 6,265 | 6,820 |
| 1979–1983 | Retirement | 5,084 | 5,783 | 6,482 | 7,181 | 7,879 | 8,579 |
| | Death | 4,518 | 5,142 | 5,761 | 6,384 | 7,004 | 7,625 |
| | Disability | 4,210 | 4,788 | 5,367 | 5,946 | 6,524 | 7,103 |
| 1984–1988 | Retirement | 5,109 | 5,811 | 6,513 | 7,216 | 7,918 | 8,620 |
| | Death | 4,964 | 5,647 | 6,329 | 7,010 | 7,692 | 8,375 |
| | Disability | 4,421 | 5,027 | 5,636 | 6,245 | 6,851 | 7,459 |

* AIMEs are approximate and based on the assumption that the worker has had 6% pay raises each year through 2015. AIME calculations for retirement assume that the worker's current earnings stay the same until Normal Retirement Age. Match AIMEs with AIMEs closest to them in Tables 10, 11, and 12 to determine benefits.

## TABLE 10—WORKER'S AND SPOUSE'S RETIREMENT BENEFITS*

| Average Indexed Monthly Earnings | Worker FRA (PIA) | Spouse FRA | Total FRA Benefit | Worker FRA - 3** | Spouse FRA - 3 | Total FRA - 3 Benefit | Worker FRA and Spouse FRA - 3 |
|---|---|---|---|---|---|---|---|
| 9,700 | 2,780 | 1,390 | 4,170 | 2,224 | 1,043 | 3,267 | 3,823 |
| 9,675 | 2,776 | 1,388 | 4,164 | 2,221 | 1,041 | 3,262 | 3,817 |
| 9,650 | 2,773 | 1,387 | 4,160 | 2,218 | 1,040 | 3,258 | 3,813 |
| 9,625 | 2,769 | 1,385 | 4,154 | 2,215 | 1,038 | 3,254 | 3,807 |
| 9,600 | 2,765 | 1,383 | 4,148 | 2,212 | 1,037 | 3,249 | 3,802 |
| 9,575 | 2,761 | 1,381 | 4,142 | 2,209 | 1,035 | 3,244 | 3,796 |
| 9,550 | 2,758 | 1,379 | 4,137 | 2,206 | 1,034 | 3,241 | 3,792 |
| 9,525 | 2,754 | 1,377 | 4,131 | 2,203 | 1,033 | 3,236 | 3,787 |
| 9,500 | 2,750 | 1,375 | 4,125 | 2,200 | 1,031 | 3,231 | 3,781 |
| 9,475 | 2,746 | 1,373 | 4,119 | 2,197 | 1,030 | 3,227 | 3,776 |
| 9,450 | 2,743 | 1,372 | 4,115 | 2,194 | 1,029 | 3,223 | 3,772 |
| 9,425 | 2,739 | 1,370 | 4,109 | 2,191 | 1,027 | 3,218 | 3,766 |
| 9,400 | 2,735 | 1,368 | 4,103 | 2,188 | 1,026 | 3,214 | 3,761 |
| 9,375 | 2,731 | 1,366 | 4,097 | 2,185 | 1,024 | 3,209 | 3,755 |
| 9,350 | 2,728 | 1,364 | 4,092 | 2,182 | 1,023 | 3,205 | 3,751 |
| 9,325 | 2,724 | 1,362 | 4,086 | 2,179 | 1,022 | 3,201 | 3,746 |
| 9,300 | 2,720 | 1,360 | 4,080 | 2,176 | 1,020 | 3,196 | 3,740 |
| 9,275 | 2,716 | 1,358 | 4,074 | 2,173 | 1,019 | 3,191 | 3,735 |
| 9,250 | 2,713 | 1,357 | 4,070 | 2,170 | 1,017 | 3,188 | 3,730 |
| 9,225 | 2,709 | 1,355 | 4,064 | 2,167 | 1,016 | 3,183 | 3,725 |
| 9,200 | 2,705 | 1,353 | 4,058 | 2,164 | 1,014 | 3,178 | 3,719 |
| 9,175 | 2,701 | 1,351 | 4,052 | 2,161 | 1,013 | 3,174 | 3,714 |
| 9,150 | 2,698 | 1,349 | 4,047 | 2,158 | 1,012 | 3,170 | 3,710 |
| 9,125 | 2,694 | 1,347 | 4,041 | 2,155 | 1,010 | 3,165 | 3,704 |
| 9,100 | 2,690 | 1,345 | 4,035 | 2,152 | 1,009 | 3,161 | 3,699 |
| 9,075 | 2,686 | 1,343 | 4,029 | 2,149 | 1,007 | 3,156 | 3,693 |
| 9,050 | 2,683 | 1,342 | 4,025 | 2,146 | 1,006 | 3,153 | 3,689 |
| 9,025 | 2,679 | 1,340 | 4,019 | 2,143 | 1,005 | 3,148 | 3,684 |
| 9,000 | 2,675 | 1,338 | 4,013 | 2,140 | 1,003 | 3,143 | 3,678 |
| 8,975 | 2,671 | 1,336 | 4,007 | 2,137 | 1,002 | 3,138 | 3,673 |
| 8,950 | 2,668 | 1,334 | 4,002 | 2,134 | 1,001 | 3,135 | 3,669 |
| 8,925 | 2,664 | 1,332 | 3,996 | 2,131 | 999 | 3,130 | 3,663 |
| 8,900 | 2,660 | 1,330 | 3,990 | 2,128 | 998 | 3,126 | 3,658 |
| 8,875 | 2,656 | 1,328 | 3,984 | 2,125 | 996 | 3,121 | 3,652 |
| 8,850 | 2,653 | 1,327 | 3,980 | 2,122 | 995 | 3,117 | 3,648 |
| 8,825 | 2,649 | 1,325 | 3,974 | 2,119 | 993 | 3,113 | 3,642 |
| 8,800 | 2,645 | 1,323 | 3,968 | 2,116 | 992 | 3,108 | 3,637 |
| 8,775 | 2,641 | 1,321 | 3,962 | 2,113 | 990 | 3,103 | 3,631 |
| 8,750 | 2,638 | 1,319 | 3,957 | 2,110 | 989 | 3,100 | 3,627 |
| 8,725 | 2,634 | 1,317 | 3,951 | 2,107 | 988 | 3,095 | 3,622 |
| 8,700 | 2,630 | 1,315 | 3,945 | 2,104 | 986 | 3,090 | 3,616 |
| 8,675 | 2,626 | 1,313 | 3,939 | 2,101 | 985 | 3,086 | 3,611 |
| 8,650 | 2,623 | 1,312 | 3,935 | 2,098 | 984 | 3,082 | 3,607 |
| 8,625 | 2,619 | 1,310 | 3,929 | 2,095 | 982 | 3,077 | 3,601 |
| 8,600 | 2,615 | 1,308 | 3,923 | 2,092 | 981 | 3,073 | 3,596 |
| 8,575 | 2,611 | 1,306 | 3,917 | 2,089 | 979 | 3,068 | 3,590 |
| 8,550 | 2,608 | 1,304 | 3,912 | 2,086 | 978 | 3,064 | 3,586 |
| 8,525 | 2,604 | 1,302 | 3,906 | 2,083 | 977 | 3,060 | 3,581 |
| 8,500 | 2,600 | 1,300 | 3,900 | 2,080 | 975 | 3,055 | 3,575 |
| 8,475 | 2,596 | 1,298 | 3,894 | 2,077 | 974 | 3,050 | 3,570 |
| 8,450 | 2,593 | 1,297 | 3,890 | 2,074 | 972 | 3,047 | 3,565 |
| 8,425 | 2,589 | 1,295 | 3,884 | 2,071 | 971 | 3,042 | 3,560 |

## TABLE 10—WORKER'S AND SPOUSE'S RETIREMENT BENEFITS* (cont'd)

| Average Indexed Monthly Earnings | Worker FRA (PIA) | Spouse FRA | Total FRA Benefit | Worker FRA - 3** | Spouse FRA - 3 | Total FRA - 3 Benefit | Worker FRA and Spouse FRA - 3 |
|---|---|---|---|---|---|---|---|
| 8,400 | 2,585 | 1,293 | 3,878 | 2,068 | 969 | 3,037 | 3,554 |
| 8,375 | 2,581 | 1,291 | 3,872 | 2,065 | 968 | 3,033 | 3,549 |
| 8,350 | 2,578 | 1,289 | 3,867 | 2,062 | 967 | 3,029 | 3,545 |
| 8,325 | 2,574 | 1,287 | 3,861 | 2,059 | 965 | 3,024 | 3,539 |
| 8,300 | 2,570 | 1,285 | 3,855 | 2,056 | 964 | 3,020 | 3,534 |
| 8,275 | 2,566 | 1,283 | 3,849 | 2,053 | 962 | 3,015 | 3,528 |
| 8,250 | 2,563 | 1,282 | 3,845 | 2,050 | 961 | 3,012 | 3,524 |
| 8,225 | 2,559 | 1,280 | 3,839 | 2,047 | 960 | 3,007 | 3,519 |
| 8,200 | 2,555 | 1,278 | 3,833 | 2,044 | 958 | 3,002 | 3,513 |
| 8,175 | 2,551 | 1,276 | 3,827 | 2,041 | 957 | 2,997 | 3,508 |
| 8,150 | 2,548 | 1,274 | 3,822 | 2,038 | 956 | 2,994 | 3,504 |
| 8,125 | 2,544 | 1,272 | 3,816 | 2,035 | 954 | 2,989 | 3,498 |
| 8,100 | 2,540 | 1,270 | 3,810 | 2,032 | 953 | 2,985 | 3,493 |
| 8,075 | 2,536 | 1,268 | 3,804 | 2,029 | 951 | 2,980 | 3,487 |
| 8,050 | 2,533 | 1,267 | 3,800 | 2,026 | 950 | 2,976 | 3,483 |
| 8,025 | 2,529 | 1,265 | 3,794 | 2,023 | 948 | 2,972 | 3,477 |
| 8,000 | 2,525 | 1,263 | 3,788 | 2,020 | 947 | 2,967 | 3,472 |
| 7,975 | 2,521 | 1,261 | 3,782 | 2,017 | 945 | 2,962 | 3,466 |
| 7,950 | 2,518 | 1,259 | 3,777 | 2,014 | 944 | 2,959 | 3,462 |
| 7,925 | 2,514 | 1,257 | 3,771 | 2,011 | 943 | 2,954 | 3,457 |
| 7,900 | 2,510 | 1,255 | 3,765 | 2,008 | 941 | 2,949 | 3,451 |
| 7,875 | 2,506 | 1,253 | 3,759 | 2,005 | 940 | 2,945 | 3,446 |
| 7,850 | 2,503 | 1,252 | 3,755 | 2,002 | 939 | 2,941 | 3,442 |
| 7,825 | 2,499 | 1,250 | 3,749 | 1,999 | 937 | 2,936 | 3,436 |
| 7,800 | 2,495 | 1,248 | 3,743 | 1,996 | 936 | 2,932 | 3,431 |
| 7,775 | 2,491 | 1,246 | 3,737 | 1,993 | 934 | 2,927 | 3,425 |
| 7,750 | 2,488 | 1,244 | 3,732 | 1,990 | 933 | 2,923 | 3,421 |
| 7,725 | 2,484 | 1,242 | 3,726 | 1,987 | 932 | 2,919 | 3,416 |
| 7,700 | 2,480 | 1,240 | 3,720 | 1,984 | 930 | 2,914 | 3,410 |
| 7,675 | 2,476 | 1,238 | 3,714 | 1,981 | 929 | 2,909 | 3,405 |
| 7,650 | 2,473 | 1,237 | 3,710 | 1,978 | 927 | 2,906 | 3,400 |
| 7,625 | 2,469 | 1,235 | 3,704 | 1,975 | 926 | 2,901 | 3,395 |
| 7,600 | 2,465 | 1,233 | 3,698 | 1,972 | 924 | 2,896 | 3,389 |
| 7,575 | 2,461 | 1,231 | 3,692 | 1,969 | 923 | 2,892 | 3,384 |
| 7,550 | 2,458 | 1,229 | 3,687 | 1,966 | 922 | 2,888 | 3,380 |
| 7,525 | 2,454 | 1,227 | 3,681 | 1,963 | 920 | 2,883 | 3,374 |
| 7,500 | 2,450 | 1,225 | 3,675 | 1,960 | 919 | 2,879 | 3,369 |
| 7,475 | 2,446 | 1,223 | 3,669 | 1,957 | 917 | 2,874 | 3,363 |
| 7,450 | 2,443 | 1,222 | 3,665 | 1,954 | 916 | 2,871 | 3,359 |
| 7,425 | 2,439 | 1,220 | 3,659 | 1,951 | 915 | 2,866 | 3,354 |
| 7,400 | 2,435 | 1,218 | 3,653 | 1,948 | 913 | 2,861 | 3,348 |
| 7,375 | 2,431 | 1,216 | 3,647 | 1,945 | 912 | 2,856 | 3,343 |
| 7,350 | 2,428 | 1,214 | 3,642 | 1,942 | 911 | 2,853 | 3,339 |
| 7,325 | 2,424 | 1,212 | 3,636 | 1,939 | 909 | 2,848 | 3,333 |
| 7,300 | 2,420 | 1,210 | 3,630 | 1,936 | 908 | 2,844 | 3,328 |
| 7,275 | 2,416 | 1,208 | 3,624 | 1,933 | 906 | 2,839 | 3,322 |
| 7,250 | 2,413 | 1,207 | 3,620 | 1,930 | 905 | 2,835 | 3,318 |
| 7,225 | 2,409 | 1,205 | 3,614 | 1,927 | 903 | 2,831 | 3,312 |
| 7,200 | 2,405 | 1,203 | 3,608 | 1,924 | 902 | 2,826 | 3,307 |
| 7,175 | 2,401 | 1,201 | 3,602 | 1,921 | 900 | 2,821 | 3,301 |
| 7,150 | 2,398 | 1,199 | 3,597 | 1,918 | 899 | 2,818 | 3,297 |
| 7,125 | 2,394 | 1,197 | 3,591 | 1,915 | 898 | 2,813 | 3,292 |

### TABLE 10—WORKER'S AND SPOUSE'S RETIREMENT BENEFITS* (cont'd)

| Average Indexed Monthly Earnings | Worker FRA (PIA) | Spouse FRA | Total FRA Benefit | Worker FRA - 3** | Spouse FRA - 3 | Total FRA - 3 Benefit | Worker FRA and Spouse FRA - 3 |
|---|---|---|---|---|---|---|---|
| 7,100 | 2,390 | 1,195 | 3,585 | 1,912 | 896 | 2,808 | 3,286 |
| 7,075 | 2,386 | 1,193 | 3,579 | 1,909 | 895 | 2,804 | 3,281 |
| 7,050 | 2,383 | 1,192 | 3,575 | 1,906 | 894 | 2,800 | 3,277 |
| 7,025 | 2,379 | 1,190 | 3,569 | 1,903 | 892 | 2,795 | 3,271 |
| 7,000 | 2,375 | 1,188 | 3,563 | 1,900 | 891 | 2,791 | 3,266 |
| 6,975 | 2,371 | 1,186 | 3,557 | 1,897 | 889 | 2,786 | 3,260 |
| 6,950 | 2,368 | 1,184 | 3,552 | 1,894 | 888 | 2,782 | 3,256 |
| 6,925 | 2,364 | 1,182 | 3,546 | 1,891 | 887 | 2,778 | 3,251 |
| 6,900 | 2,360 | 1,180 | 3,540 | 1,888 | 885 | 2,773 | 3,245 |
| 6,875 | 2,356 | 1,178 | 3,534 | 1,885 | 884 | 2,768 | 3,240 |
| 6,850 | 2,353 | 1,177 | 3,530 | 1,882 | 882 | 2,765 | 3,235 |
| 6,825 | 2,349 | 1,175 | 3,524 | 1,879 | 881 | 2,760 | 3,230 |
| 6,800 | 2,345 | 1,173 | 3,518 | 1,876 | 879 | 2,755 | 3,224 |
| 6,775 | 2,341 | 1,171 | 3,512 | 1,873 | 878 | 2,751 | 3,219 |
| 6,750 | 2,338 | 1,169 | 3,507 | 1,870 | 877 | 2,747 | 3,215 |
| 6,725 | 2,334 | 1,167 | 3,501 | 1,867 | 875 | 2,742 | 3,209 |
| 6,700 | 2,330 | 1,165 | 3,495 | 1,864 | 874 | 2,738 | 3,204 |
| 6,675 | 2,326 | 1,163 | 3,489 | 1,861 | 872 | 2,733 | 3,198 |
| 6,650 | 2,323 | 1,162 | 3,485 | 1,858 | 871 | 2,730 | 3,194 |
| 6,625 | 2,319 | 1,160 | 3,479 | 1,855 | 870 | 2,725 | 3,189 |
| 6,600 | 2,315 | 1,158 | 3,473 | 1,852 | 868 | 2,720 | 3,183 |
| 6,575 | 2,311 | 1,156 | 3,467 | 1,849 | 867 | 2,715 | 3,178 |
| 6,550 | 2,308 | 1,154 | 3,462 | 1,846 | 866 | 2,712 | 3,174 |
| 6,525 | 2,304 | 1,152 | 3,456 | 1,843 | 864 | 2,707 | 3,168 |
| 6,500 | 2,300 | 1,150 | 3,450 | 1,840 | 863 | 2,703 | 3,163 |
| 6,475 | 2,296 | 1,148 | 3,444 | 1,837 | 861 | 2,698 | 3,157 |
| 6,450 | 2,293 | 1,147 | 3,440 | 1,834 | 860 | 2,694 | 3,153 |
| 6,425 | 2,289 | 1,145 | 3,434 | 1,831 | 858 | 2,690 | 3,147 |
| 6,400 | 2,285 | 1,143 | 3,428 | 1,828 | 857 | 2,685 | 3,142 |
| 6,375 | 2,281 | 1,141 | 3,422 | 1,825 | 855 | 2,680 | 3,136 |
| 6,350 | 2,278 | 1,139 | 3,417 | 1,822 | 854 | 2,677 | 3,132 |
| 6,325 | 2,274 | 1,137 | 3,411 | 1,819 | 853 | 2,672 | 3,127 |
| 6,300 | 2,270 | 1,135 | 3,405 | 1,816 | 851 | 2,667 | 3,121 |
| 6,275 | 2,266 | 1,133 | 3,399 | 1,813 | 850 | 2,663 | 3,116 |
| 6,250 | 2,263 | 1,132 | 3,395 | 1,810 | 849 | 2,659 | 3,112 |
| 6,225 | 2,259 | 1,130 | 3,389 | 1,807 | 847 | 2,654 | 3,106 |
| 6,200 | 2,255 | 1,128 | 3,383 | 1,804 | 846 | 2,650 | 3,101 |
| 6,175 | 2,251 | 1,126 | 3,377 | 1,801 | 844 | 2,645 | 3,095 |
| 6,150 | 2,248 | 1,124 | 3,372 | 1,798 | 843 | 2,641 | 3,091 |
| 6,125 | 2,244 | 1,122 | 3,366 | 1,795 | 842 | 2,637 | 3,086 |
| 6,100 | 2,240 | 1,120 | 3,360 | 1,792 | 840 | 2,632 | 3,080 |
| 6,075 | 2,236 | 1,118 | 3,354 | 1,789 | 839 | 2,627 | 3,075 |
| 6,050 | 2,233 | 1,117 | 3,350 | 1,786 | 837 | 2,624 | 3,070 |
| 6,025 | 2,229 | 1,115 | 3,344 | 1,783 | 836 | 2,619 | 3,065 |
| 6,000 | 2,225 | 1,113 | 3,338 | 1,780 | 834 | 2,614 | 3,059 |
| 5,975 | 2,221 | 1,111 | 3,332 | 1,777 | 833 | 2,610 | 3,054 |
| 5,950 | 2,218 | 1,109 | 3,327 | 1,774 | 832 | 2,606 | 3,050 |
| 5,925 | 2,214 | 1,107 | 3,321 | 1,771 | 830 | 2,601 | 3,044 |
| 5,900 | 2,210 | 1,105 | 3,315 | 1,768 | 829 | 2,597 | 3,039 |
| 5,875 | 2,206 | 1,103 | 3,309 | 1,765 | 827 | 2,592 | 3,033 |
| 5,850 | 2,203 | 1,102 | 3,305 | 1,762 | 826 | 2,589 | 3,029 |
| 5,825 | 2,199 | 1,100 | 3,299 | 1,759 | 825 | 2,584 | 3,024 |

## TABLE 10—WORKER'S AND SPOUSE'S RETIREMENT BENEFITS* (cont'd)

| Average Indexed Monthly Earnings | Worker FRA (PIA) | Spouse FRA | Total FRA Benefit | Worker FRA - 3** | Spouse FRA - 3 | Total FRA - 3 Benefit | Worker FRA and Spouse FRA - 3 |
|---|---|---|---|---|---|---|---|
| 5,800 | 2,195 | 1,098 | 3,293 | 1,756 | 823 | 2,579 | 3,018 |
| 5,775 | 2,191 | 1,096 | 3,287 | 1,753 | 822 | 2,574 | 3,013 |
| 5,750 | 2,188 | 1,094 | 3,282 | 1,750 | 821 | 2,571 | 3,009 |
| 5,725 | 2,184 | 1,092 | 3,276 | 1,747 | 819 | 2,566 | 3,003 |
| 5,700 | 2,180 | 1,090 | 3,270 | 1,744 | 818 | 2,562 | 2,998 |
| 5,675 | 2,176 | 1,088 | 3,264 | 1,741 | 816 | 2,557 | 2,992 |
| 5,650 | 2,173 | 1,087 | 3,260 | 1,738 | 815 | 2,553 | 2,988 |
| 5,625 | 2,169 | 1,085 | 3,254 | 1,735 | 813 | 2,549 | 2,982 |
| 5,600 | 2,165 | 1,083 | 3,248 | 1,732 | 812 | 2,544 | 2,977 |
| 5,575 | 2,161 | 1,081 | 3,242 | 1,729 | 810 | 2,539 | 2,971 |
| 5,550 | 2,158 | 1,079 | 3,237 | 1,726 | 809 | 2,536 | 2,967 |
| 5,525 | 2,154 | 1,077 | 3,231 | 1,723 | 808 | 2,531 | 2,962 |
| 5,500 | 2,150 | 1,075 | 3,225 | 1,720 | 806 | 2,526 | 2,956 |
| 5,475 | 2,146 | 1,073 | 3,219 | 1,717 | 805 | 2,522 | 2,951 |
| 5,450 | 2,143 | 1,072 | 3,215 | 1,714 | 804 | 2,518 | 2,947 |
| 5,425 | 2,139 | 1,070 | 3,209 | 1,711 | 802 | 2,513 | 2,941 |
| 5,400 | 2,135 | 1,068 | 3,203 | 1,708 | 801 | 2,509 | 2,936 |
| 5,375 | 2,131 | 1,066 | 3,197 | 1,705 | 799 | 2,504 | 2,930 |
| 5,350 | 2,128 | 1,064 | 3,192 | 1,702 | 798 | 2,500 | 2,926 |
| 5,325 | 2,124 | 1,062 | 3,186 | 1,699 | 797 | 2,496 | 2,921 |
| 5,300 | 2,120 | 1,060 | 3,180 | 1,696 | 795 | 2,491 | 2,915 |
| 5,275 | 2,116 | 1,058 | 3,174 | 1,693 | 794 | 2,486 | 2,910 |
| 5,250 | 2,113 | 1,057 | 3,170 | 1,690 | 792 | 2,483 | 2,905 |
| 5,225 | 2,109 | 1,055 | 3,164 | 1,687 | 791 | 2,478 | 2,900 |
| 5,200 | 2,105 | 1,053 | 3,158 | 1,684 | 789 | 2,473 | 2,894 |
| 5,175 | 2,101 | 1,051 | 3,152 | 1,681 | 788 | 2,469 | 2,889 |
| 5,150 | 2,098 | 1,049 | 3,147 | 1,678 | 787 | 2,465 | 2,885 |
| 5,125 | 2,094 | 1,047 | 3,141 | 1,675 | 785 | 2,460 | 2,879 |
| 5,100 | 2,090 | 1,045 | 3,135 | 1,672 | 784 | 2,456 | 2,874 |
| 5,075 | 2,086 | 1,043 | 3,129 | 1,669 | 782 | 2,451 | 2,868 |
| 5,050 | 2,083 | 1,042 | 3,125 | 1,666 | 781 | 2,448 | 2,864 |
| 5,025 | 2,079 | 1,040 | 3,119 | 1,663 | 780 | 2,443 | 2,859 |
| 5,000 | 2,075 | 1,038 | 3,113 | 1,660 | 778 | 2,438 | 2,853 |
| 4,975 | 2,071 | 1,036 | 3,107 | 1,657 | 777 | 2,433 | 2,848 |
| 4,950 | 2,063 | 1,032 | 3,095 | 1,650 | 774 | 2,424 | 2,837 |
| 4,925 | 2,055 | 1,028 | 3,083 | 1,644 | 771 | 2,415 | 2,826 |
| 4,900 | 2,047 | 1,024 | 3,071 | 1,638 | 768 | 2,405 | 2,815 |
| 4,875 | 2,039 | 1,020 | 3,059 | 1,631 | 765 | 2,396 | 2,804 |
| 4,850 | 2,031 | 1,016 | 3,047 | 1,625 | 762 | 2,386 | 2,793 |
| 4,825 | 2,023 | 1,012 | 3,035 | 1,618 | 759 | 2,377 | 2,782 |
| 4,800 | 2,015 | 1,008 | 3,023 | 1,612 | 756 | 2,368 | 2,771 |
| 4,775 | 2,007 | 1,004 | 3,011 | 1,606 | 753 | 2,358 | 2,760 |
| 4,750 | 1,999 | 1,000 | 2,999 | 1,599 | 750 | 2,349 | 2,749 |
| 4,725 | 1,991 | 996 | 2,987 | 1,593 | 747 | 2,339 | 2,738 |
| 4,700 | 1,983 | 992 | 2,975 | 1,586 | 744 | 2,330 | 2,727 |
| 4,675 | 1,975 | 988 | 2,963 | 1,580 | 741 | 2,321 | 2,716 |
| 4,650 | 1,967 | 984 | 2,951 | 1,574 | 738 | 2,311 | 2,705 |
| 4,625 | 1,959 | 980 | 2,939 | 1,567 | 735 | 2,302 | 2,694 |
| 4,600 | 1,951 | 976 | 2,927 | 1,561 | 732 | 2,292 | 2,683 |
| 4,575 | 1,943 | 972 | 2,915 | 1,554 | 729 | 2,283 | 2,672 |
| 4,550 | 1,935 | 968 | 2,903 | 1,548 | 726 | 2,274 | 2,661 |
| 4,525 | 1,927 | 964 | 2,891 | 1,542 | 723 | 2,264 | 2,650 |

## TABLE 10—WORKER'S AND SPOUSE'S RETIREMENT BENEFITS* (cont'd)

| Average Indexed Monthly Earnings | Worker FRA (PIA) | Spouse FRA | Total FRA Benefit | Worker FRA - 3** | Spouse FRA - 3 | Total FRA - 3 Benefit | Worker FRA and Spouse FRA - 3 |
|---|---|---|---|---|---|---|---|
| 4,500 | 1,919 | 960 | 2,879 | 1,535 | 720 | 2,255 | 2,639 |
| 4,475 | 1,911 | 956 | 2,867 | 1,529 | 717 | 2,245 | 2,628 |
| 4,450 | 1,903 | 952 | 2,855 | 1,522 | 714 | 2,236 | 2,617 |
| 4,425 | 1,895 | 948 | 2,843 | 1,516 | 711 | 2,227 | 2,606 |
| 4,400 | 1,887 | 944 | 2,831 | 1,510 | 708 | 2,217 | 2,595 |
| 4,375 | 1,879 | 940 | 2,819 | 1,503 | 705 | 2,208 | 2,584 |
| 4,350 | 1,871 | 936 | 2,807 | 1,497 | 702 | 2,198 | 2,573 |
| 4,325 | 1,863 | 932 | 2,795 | 1,490 | 699 | 2,189 | 2,562 |
| 4,300 | 1,855 | 928 | 2,783 | 1,484 | 696 | 2,180 | 2,551 |
| 4,275 | 1,847 | 924 | 2,771 | 1,478 | 693 | 2,170 | 2,540 |
| 4,250 | 1,839 | 920 | 2,759 | 1,471 | 690 | 2,161 | 2,529 |
| 4,225 | 1,831 | 916 | 2,747 | 1,465 | 687 | 2,151 | 2,518 |
| 4,200 | 1,823 | 912 | 2,735 | 1,458 | 684 | 2,142 | 2,507 |
| 4,175 | 1,815 | 908 | 2,723 | 1,452 | 681 | 2,133 | 2,496 |
| 4,150 | 1,807 | 904 | 2,711 | 1,446 | 678 | 2,123 | 2,485 |
| 4,125 | 1,799 | 900 | 2,699 | 1,439 | 675 | 2,114 | 2,474 |
| 4,100 | 1,791 | 896 | 2,687 | 1,433 | 672 | 2,104 | 2,463 |
| 4,075 | 1,783 | 892 | 2,675 | 1,426 | 669 | 2,095 | 2,452 |
| 4,050 | 1,775 | 888 | 2,663 | 1,420 | 666 | 2,086 | 2,441 |
| 4,025 | 1,767 | 884 | 2,651 | 1,414 | 663 | 2,076 | 2,430 |
| 4,000 | 1,759 | 880 | 2,639 | 1,407 | 660 | 2,067 | 2,419 |
| 3,975 | 1,751 | 876 | 2,627 | 1,401 | 657 | 2,057 | 2,408 |
| 3,950 | 1,743 | 872 | 2,615 | 1,394 | 654 | 2,048 | 2,397 |
| 3,925 | 1,735 | 868 | 2,603 | 1,388 | 651 | 2,039 | 2,386 |
| 3,900 | 1,727 | 864 | 2,591 | 1,382 | 648 | 2,029 | 2,375 |
| 3,875 | 1,719 | 860 | 2,579 | 1,375 | 645 | 2,020 | 2,364 |
| 3,850 | 1,711 | 856 | 2,567 | 1,369 | 642 | 2,010 | 2,353 |
| 3,825 | 1,703 | 852 | 2,555 | 1,362 | 639 | 2,001 | 2,342 |
| 3,800 | 1,695 | 848 | 2,543 | 1,356 | 636 | 1,992 | 2,331 |
| 3,775 | 1,687 | 844 | 2,531 | 1,350 | 633 | 1,982 | 2,320 |
| 3,750 | 1,679 | 840 | 2,519 | 1,343 | 630 | 1,973 | 2,309 |
| 3,725 | 1,671 | 836 | 2,507 | 1,337 | 627 | 1,963 | 2,298 |
| 3,700 | 1,663 | 832 | 2,495 | 1,330 | 624 | 1,954 | 2,287 |
| 3,675 | 1,655 | 828 | 2,483 | 1,324 | 621 | 1,945 | 2,276 |
| 3,650 | 1,647 | 824 | 2,471 | 1,318 | 618 | 1,935 | 2,265 |
| 3,625 | 1,639 | 820 | 2,459 | 1,311 | 615 | 1,926 | 2,254 |
| 3,600 | 1,631 | 816 | 2,447 | 1,305 | 612 | 1,916 | 2,243 |
| 3,575 | 1,623 | 812 | 2,435 | 1,298 | 609 | 1,907 | 2,232 |
| 3,550 | 1,615 | 808 | 2,423 | 1,292 | 606 | 1,898 | 2,221 |
| 3,525 | 1,607 | 804 | 2,411 | 1,286 | 603 | 1,888 | 2,210 |
| 3,500 | 1,599 | 800 | 2,399 | 1,279 | 600 | 1,879 | 2,199 |
| 3,475 | 1,591 | 796 | 2,387 | 1,273 | 597 | 1,869 | 2,188 |
| 3,450 | 1,583 | 792 | 2,375 | 1,266 | 594 | 1,860 | 2,177 |
| 3,425 | 1,575 | 788 | 2,363 | 1,260 | 591 | 1,851 | 2,166 |
| 3,400 | 1,567 | 784 | 2,351 | 1,254 | 588 | 1,841 | 2,155 |
| 3,375 | 1,559 | 780 | 2,339 | 1,247 | 585 | 1,832 | 2,144 |
| 3,350 | 1,551 | 776 | 2,327 | 1,241 | 582 | 1,822 | 2,133 |
| 3,325 | 1,543 | 772 | 2,315 | 1,234 | 579 | 1,813 | 2,122 |
| 3,300 | 1,535 | 768 | 2,303 | 1,228 | 576 | 1,804 | 2,111 |
| 3,275 | 1,527 | 764 | 2,291 | 1,222 | 573 | 1,794 | 2,100 |
| 3,250 | 1,519 | 760 | 2,279 | 1,215 | 570 | 1,785 | 2,089 |
| 3,225 | 1,511 | 756 | 2,267 | 1,209 | 567 | 1,775 | 2,078 |

## TABLE 10—WORKER'S AND SPOUSE'S RETIREMENT BENEFITS* (cont'd)

| Average Indexed Monthly Earnings | Worker FRA (PIA) | Spouse FRA | Total FRA Benefit | Worker FRA - 3** | Spouse FRA - 3 | Total FRA - 3 Benefit | Worker FRA and Spouse FRA - 3 |
|---|---|---|---|---|---|---|---|
| 3,200 | 1,503 | 752 | 2,255 | 1,202 | 564 | 1,766 | 2,067 |
| 3,175 | 1,495 | 748 | 2,243 | 1,196 | 561 | 1,757 | 2,056 |
| 3,150 | 1,487 | 744 | 2,231 | 1,190 | 558 | 1,747 | 2,045 |
| 3,125 | 1,479 | 740 | 2,219 | 1,183 | 555 | 1,738 | 2,034 |
| 3,100 | 1,471 | 736 | 2,207 | 1,177 | 552 | 1,728 | 2,023 |
| 3,075 | 1,463 | 732 | 2,195 | 1,170 | 549 | 1,719 | 2,012 |
| 3,050 | 1,455 | 728 | 2,183 | 1,164 | 546 | 1,710 | 2,001 |
| 3,025 | 1,447 | 724 | 2,171 | 1,158 | 543 | 1,700 | 1,990 |
| 3,000 | 1,439 | 720 | 2,159 | 1,151 | 540 | 1,691 | 1,979 |
| 2,975 | 1,431 | 716 | 2,147 | 1,145 | 537 | 1,681 | 1,968 |
| 2,950 | 1,423 | 712 | 2,135 | 1,138 | 534 | 1,672 | 1,957 |
| 2,925 | 1,415 | 708 | 2,123 | 1,132 | 531 | 1,663 | 1,946 |
| 2,900 | 1,407 | 704 | 2,111 | 1,126 | 528 | 1,653 | 1,935 |
| 2,875 | 1,399 | 700 | 2,099 | 1,119 | 525 | 1,644 | 1,924 |
| 2,850 | 1,391 | 696 | 2,087 | 1,113 | 522 | 1,634 | 1,913 |
| 2,825 | 1,383 | 692 | 2,075 | 1,106 | 519 | 1,625 | 1,902 |
| 2,800 | 1,375 | 688 | 2,063 | 1,100 | 516 | 1,616 | 1,891 |
| 2,775 | 1,367 | 684 | 2,051 | 1,094 | 513 | 1,606 | 1,880 |
| 2,750 | 1,359 | 680 | 2,039 | 1,087 | 510 | 1,597 | 1,869 |
| 2,725 | 1,351 | 676 | 2,027 | 1,081 | 507 | 1,587 | 1,858 |
| 2,700 | 1,343 | 672 | 2,015 | 1,074 | 504 | 1,578 | 1,847 |
| 2,675 | 1,335 | 668 | 2,003 | 1,068 | 501 | 1,569 | 1,836 |
| 2,650 | 1,327 | 664 | 1,991 | 1,062 | 498 | 1,559 | 1,825 |
| 2,625 | 1,319 | 660 | 1,979 | 1,055 | 495 | 1,550 | 1,814 |
| 2,600 | 1,311 | 656 | 1,967 | 1,049 | 492 | 1,540 | 1,803 |
| 2,575 | 1,303 | 652 | 1,955 | 1,042 | 489 | 1,531 | 1,792 |
| 2,550 | 1,295 | 648 | 1,943 | 1,036 | 486 | 1,522 | 1,781 |
| 2,525 | 1,287 | 644 | 1,931 | 1,030 | 483 | 1,512 | 1,770 |
| 2,500 | 1,279 | 640 | 1,919 | 1,023 | 480 | 1,503 | 1,759 |
| 2,475 | 1,271 | 636 | 1,907 | 1,017 | 477 | 1,493 | 1,748 |
| 2,450 | 1,263 | 632 | 1,895 | 1,010 | 474 | 1,484 | 1,737 |
| 2,425 | 1,255 | 628 | 1,883 | 1,004 | 471 | 1,475 | 1,726 |
| 2,400 | 1,247 | 624 | 1,871 | 998 | 468 | 1,465 | 1,715 |
| 2,375 | 1,239 | 620 | 1,859 | 991 | 465 | 1,456 | 1,704 |
| 2,350 | 1,231 | 616 | 1,847 | 985 | 462 | 1,446 | 1,693 |
| 2,325 | 1,223 | 612 | 1,835 | 978 | 459 | 1,437 | 1,682 |
| 2,300 | 1,215 | 608 | 1,823 | 972 | 456 | 1,428 | 1,671 |
| 2,275 | 1,207 | 604 | 1,811 | 966 | 453 | 1,418 | 1,660 |
| 2,250 | 1,199 | 600 | 1,799 | 959 | 450 | 1,409 | 1,649 |
| 2,225 | 1,191 | 596 | 1,787 | 953 | 447 | 1,399 | 1,638 |
| 2,200 | 1,183 | 592 | 1,775 | 946 | 444 | 1,390 | 1,627 |
| 2,175 | 1,175 | 588 | 1,763 | 940 | 441 | 1,381 | 1,616 |
| 2,150 | 1,167 | 584 | 1,751 | 934 | 438 | 1,371 | 1,605 |
| 2,125 | 1,159 | 580 | 1,739 | 927 | 435 | 1,362 | 1,594 |
| 2,100 | 1,151 | 576 | 1,727 | 921 | 432 | 1,352 | 1,583 |
| 2,075 | 1,143 | 572 | 1,715 | 914 | 429 | 1,343 | 1,572 |
| 2,050 | 1,135 | 568 | 1,703 | 908 | 426 | 1,334 | 1,561 |
| 2,025 | 1,127 | 564 | 1,691 | 902 | 423 | 1,324 | 1,550 |
| 2,000 | 1,119 | 560 | 1,679 | 895 | 420 | 1,315 | 1,539 |
| 1,975 | 1,111 | 556 | 1,667 | 889 | 417 | 1,305 | 1,528 |
| 1,950 | 1,103 | 552 | 1,655 | 882 | 414 | 1,296 | 1,517 |
| 1,925 | 1,095 | 548 | 1,643 | 876 | 411 | 1,287 | 1,506 |
| 1,900 | 1,087 | 544 | 1,631 | 870 | 408 | 1,277 | 1,495 |

## TABLE 10—WORKER'S AND SPOUSE'S RETIREMENT BENEFITS* (cont'd)

| Average Indexed Monthly Earnings | Worker FRA (PIA) | Spouse FRA | Total FRA Benefit | Worker FRA - 3** | Spouse FRA - 3 | Total FRA - 3 Benefit | Worker FRA and Spouse FRA - 3 |
|---|---|---|---|---|---|---|---|
| 1,875 | 1,079 | 540 | 1,619 | 863 | 405 | 1,268 | 1,484 |
| 1,850 | 1,071 | 536 | 1,607 | 857 | 402 | 1,258 | 1,473 |
| 1,825 | 1,063 | 532 | 1,595 | 850 | 399 | 1,249 | 1,462 |
| 1,800 | 1,055 | 528 | 1,583 | 844 | 396 | 1,240 | 1,451 |
| 1,775 | 1,047 | 524 | 1,571 | 838 | 393 | 1,230 | 1,440 |
| 1,750 | 1,039 | 520 | 1,559 | 831 | 390 | 1,221 | 1,429 |
| 1,725 | 1,031 | 516 | 1,547 | 825 | 387 | 1,211 | 1,418 |
| 1,700 | 1,023 | 512 | 1,535 | 818 | 384 | 1,202 | 1,407 |
| 1,675 | 1,015 | 508 | 1,523 | 812 | 381 | 1,193 | 1,396 |
| 1,650 | 1,007 | 504 | 1,511 | 806 | 378 | 1,183 | 1,385 |
| 1,625 | 999 | 500 | 1,499 | 799 | 375 | 1,174 | 1,374 |
| 1,600 | 991 | 496 | 1,487 | 793 | 372 | 1,164 | 1,363 |
| 1,575 | 983 | 492 | 1,475 | 786 | 369 | 1,155 | 1,352 |
| 1,550 | 975 | 488 | 1,463 | 780 | 366 | 1,146 | 1,341 |
| 1,525 | 967 | 484 | 1,451 | 774 | 363 | 1,136 | 1,330 |
| 1,500 | 959 | 480 | 1,439 | 767 | 360 | 1,127 | 1,319 |
| 1,475 | 951 | 476 | 1,427 | 761 | 357 | 1,117 | 1,308 |
| 1,450 | 943 | 472 | 1,415 | 754 | 354 | 1,108 | 1,297 |
| 1,425 | 935 | 468 | 1,403 | 748 | 351 | 1,099 | 1,286 |
| 1,400 | 927 | 464 | 1,391 | 742 | 348 | 1,089 | 1,275 |
| 1,375 | 919 | 460 | 1,379 | 735 | 345 | 1,080 | 1,264 |
| 1,350 | 911 | 456 | 1,367 | 729 | 342 | 1,070 | 1,253 |
| 1,325 | 903 | 452 | 1,355 | 722 | 339 | 1,061 | 1,242 |
| 1,300 | 895 | 448 | 1,343 | 716 | 336 | 1,052 | 1,231 |
| 1,275 | 887 | 444 | 1,331 | 710 | 333 | 1,042 | 1,220 |
| 1,250 | 879 | 440 | 1,319 | 703 | 330 | 1,033 | 1,209 |
| 1,225 | 871 | 436 | 1,307 | 697 | 327 | 1,023 | 1,198 |
| 1,200 | 863 | 432 | 1,295 | 690 | 324 | 1,014 | 1,187 |
| 1,175 | 855 | 428 | 1,283 | 684 | 321 | 1,005 | 1,176 |
| 1,150 | 847 | 424 | 1,271 | 678 | 318 | 995 | 1,165 |
| 1,125 | 839 | 420 | 1,259 | 671 | 315 | 986 | 1,154 |
| 1,100 | 831 | 416 | 1,247 | 665 | 312 | 976 | 1,143 |
| 1,075 | 823 | 412 | 1,235 | 658 | 309 | 967 | 1,132 |
| 1,050 | 815 | 408 | 1,223 | 652 | 306 | 958 | 1,121 |
| 1,025 | 807 | 404 | 1,211 | 646 | 303 | 948 | 1,110 |
| 1,000 | 799 | 400 | 1,199 | 639 | 300 | 939 | 1,099 |
| 975 | 791 | 396 | 1,187 | 633 | 297 | 929 | 1,088 |
| 950 | 783 | 392 | 1,175 | 626 | 294 | 920 | 1,077 |
| 925 | 775 | 388 | 1,163 | 620 | 291 | 911 | 1,066 |
| 900 | 767 | 384 | 1,151 | 614 | 288 | 901 | 1,055 |
| 875 | 759 | 380 | 1,139 | 607 | 285 | 892 | 1,044 |
| 850 | 751 | 376 | 1,127 | 601 | 282 | 882 | 1,033 |
| 825 | 742 | 371 | 1,113 | 594 | 278 | 872 | 1,020 |
| 800 | 720 | 360 | 1,080 | 576 | 270 | 846 | 990 |

* The retirement age when unreduced benefits are available will be increased to age 67 in gradual steps starting in the year 2000. If you were born in 1943-1954, your retirement age for full benefits is 66. If you were born in 1955-1959, your retirement age for full benefits is your 66th birthday plus two months for every year you were born after 1954. If you were born in 1960 and after, your retirement age for full benefits is 67.

** Benefits listed are 80% of the corresponding PIA, but age 62 benefits are reduced further if worker is born in 1938 or after. Ex: Benefits is 75% of PIA for workers born in 1943-1954 and 70% of PIA for workers born in 1960 and after.

## TABLE 11—SURVIVOR'S BENEFITS

| Average Indexed Monthly Earnings | Worker's PIA | Surviving Spouse & 1 Child; or 2 Children | Surviving Spouse & 2 Children; or 3 Children | One Child (No Mother) | Widow or Widower Age 60 | Widow or Widower FRA | Each of Two Parents | Sole Parent | Maximum Family Benefits |
|---|---|---|---|---|---|---|---|---|---|
| $9,700 | $2,780 | $4,170 | $4,865 | $2,085 | $1,988 | $2,780 | $2,780 | $2,294 | $4,865 |
| $9,675 | $2,776 | $4,164 | $4,858 | $2,082 | $1,985 | $2,776 | $2,776 | $2,290 | $4,858 |
| $9,650 | $2,773 | $4,160 | $4,852 | $2,080 | $1,983 | $2,773 | $2,773 | $2,288 | $4,852 |
| $9,625 | $2,769 | $4,154 | $4,845 | $2,077 | $1,980 | $2,769 | $2,769 | $2,284 | $4,845 |
| $9,600 | $2,765 | $4,148 | $4,838 | $2,074 | $1,977 | $2,765 | $2,765 | $2,281 | $4,838 |
| $9,575 | $2,761 | $4,142 | $4,831 | $2,071 | $1,974 | $2,761 | $2,761 | $2,278 | $4,831 |
| $9,550 | $2,758 | $4,137 | $4,826 | $2,069 | $1,972 | $2,758 | $2,758 | $2,275 | $4,826 |
| $9,525 | $2,754 | $4,131 | $4,819 | $2,066 | $1,969 | $2,754 | $2,754 | $2,272 | $4,819 |
| $9,500 | $2,750 | $4,125 | $4,812 | $2,063 | $1,966 | $2,750 | $2,750 | $2,269 | $4,812 |
| $9,475 | $2,746 | $4,119 | $4,805 | $2,060 | $1,963 | $2,746 | $2,746 | $2,265 | $4,805 |
| $9,450 | $2,743 | $4,115 | $4,800 | $2,057 | $1,961 | $2,743 | $2,743 | $2,263 | $4,800 |
| $9,425 | $2,739 | $4,109 | $4,793 | $2,054 | $1,958 | $2,739 | $2,739 | $2,260 | $4,793 |
| $9,400 | $2,735 | $4,103 | $4,786 | $2,051 | $1,956 | $2,735 | $2,735 | $2,256 | $4,786 |
| $9,375 | $2,731 | $4,097 | $4,779 | $2,048 | $1,953 | $2,731 | $2,731 | $2,253 | $4,779 |
| $9,350 | $2,728 | $4,092 | $4,774 | $2,046 | $1,951 | $2,728 | $2,728 | $2,251 | $4,774 |
| $9,325 | $2,724 | $4,086 | $4,767 | $2,043 | $1,948 | $2,724 | $2,724 | $2,247 | $4,767 |
| $9,300 | $2,720 | $4,080 | $4,760 | $2,040 | $1,945 | $2,720 | $2,720 | $2,244 | $4,760 |
| $9,275 | $2,716 | $4,074 | $4,753 | $2,037 | $1,942 | $2,716 | $2,716 | $2,241 | $4,753 |
| $9,250 | $2,713 | $4,070 | $4,747 | $2,035 | $1,940 | $2,713 | $2,713 | $2,238 | $4,747 |
| $9,225 | $2,709 | $4,064 | $4,740 | $2,032 | $1,937 | $2,709 | $2,709 | $2,235 | $4,740 |
| $9,200 | $2,705 | $4,058 | $4,733 | $2,029 | $1,934 | $2,705 | $2,705 | $2,232 | $4,733 |
| $9,175 | $2,701 | $4,052 | $4,726 | $2,026 | $1,931 | $2,701 | $2,701 | $2,228 | $4,726 |
| $9,150 | $2,698 | $4,047 | $4,721 | $2,024 | $1,929 | $2,698 | $2,698 | $2,226 | $4,721 |
| $9,125 | $2,694 | $4,041 | $4,714 | $2,021 | $1,926 | $2,694 | $2,694 | $2,223 | $4,714 |
| $9,100 | $2,690 | $4,035 | $4,707 | $2,018 | $1,923 | $2,690 | $2,690 | $2,219 | $4,707 |
| $9,075 | $2,686 | $4,029 | $4,700 | $2,015 | $1,920 | $2,686 | $2,686 | $2,216 | $4,700 |
| $9,050 | $2,683 | $4,025 | $4,695 | $2,012 | $1,918 | $2,683 | $2,683 | $2,213 | $4,695 |
| $9,025 | $2,679 | $4,019 | $4,688 | $2,009 | $1,915 | $2,679 | $2,679 | $2,210 | $4,688 |
| $9,000 | $2,675 | $4,013 | $4,681 | $2,006 | $1,913 | $2,675 | $2,675 | $2,207 | $4,681 |
| $8,975 | $2,671 | $4,007 | $4,674 | $2,003 | $1,910 | $2,671 | $2,671 | $2,204 | $4,674 |
| $8,950 | $2,668 | $4,002 | $4,669 | $2,001 | $1,908 | $2,668 | $2,668 | $2,201 | $4,669 |
| $8,925 | $2,664 | $3,996 | $4,662 | $1,998 | $1,905 | $2,664 | $2,664 | $2,198 | $4,662 |
| $8,900 | $2,660 | $3,990 | $4,655 | $1,995 | $1,902 | $2,660 | $2,660 | $2,195 | $4,655 |
| $8,875 | $2,656 | $3,984 | $4,648 | $1,992 | $1,899 | $2,656 | $2,656 | $2,191 | $4,648 |
| $8,850 | $2,653 | $3,980 | $4,642 | $1,990 | $1,897 | $2,653 | $2,653 | $2,189 | $4,642 |
| $8,825 | $2,649 | $3,974 | $4,635 | $1,987 | $1,894 | $2,649 | $2,649 | $2,185 | $4,635 |
| $8,800 | $2,645 | $3,968 | $4,628 | $1,984 | $1,891 | $2,645 | $2,645 | $2,182 | $4,628 |
| $8,775 | $2,641 | $3,962 | $4,621 | $1,981 | $1,888 | $2,641 | $2,641 | $2,179 | $4,621 |
| $8,750 | $2,638 | $3,957 | $4,616 | $1,979 | $1,886 | $2,638 | $2,638 | $2,176 | $4,616 |
| $8,725 | $2,634 | $3,951 | $4,609 | $1,976 | $1,883 | $2,634 | $2,634 | $2,173 | $4,609 |
| $8,700 | $2,630 | $3,945 | $4,602 | $1,973 | $1,880 | $2,630 | $2,630 | $2,170 | $4,602 |
| $8,675 | $2,626 | $3,939 | $4,595 | $1,970 | $1,878 | $2,626 | $2,626 | $2,166 | $4,595 |
| $8,650 | $2,623 | $3,935 | $4,590 | $1,967 | $1,875 | $2,623 | $2,623 | $2,164 | $4,590 |
| $8,625 | $2,619 | $3,929 | $4,583 | $1,964 | $1,873 | $2,619 | $2,619 | $2,161 | $4,583 |
| $8,600 | $2,615 | $3,923 | $4,576 | $1,961 | $1,870 | $2,615 | $2,615 | $2,157 | $4,576 |
| $8,575 | $2,611 | $3,917 | $4,569 | $1,958 | $1,867 | $2,611 | $2,611 | $2,154 | $4,569 |
| $8,550 | $2,608 | $3,912 | $4,564 | $1,956 | $1,865 | $2,608 | $2,608 | $2,152 | $4,564 |
| $8,525 | $2,604 | $3,906 | $4,557 | $1,953 | $1,862 | $2,604 | $2,604 | $2,148 | $4,557 |
| $8,500 | $2,600 | $3,900 | $4,550 | $1,950 | $1,859 | $2,600 | $2,600 | $2,145 | $4,550 |
| $8,475 | $2,596 | $3,894 | $4,543 | $1,947 | $1,856 | $2,596 | $2,596 | $2,142 | $4,543 |
| $8,450 | $2,593 | $3,890 | $4,537 | $1,945 | $1,854 | $2,593 | $2,593 | $2,139 | $4,537 |
| $8,425 | $2,589 | $3,884 | $4,530 | $1,942 | $1,851 | $2,589 | $2,589 | $2,136 | $4,530 |

## TABLE 11—SURVIVOR'S BENEFITS (cont'd)

| Average Indexed Monthly Earnings | Worker's PIA | Surviving Spouse & 1 Child; or 2 Children | Surviving Spouse & 2 Children; or 3 Children | One Child (No Mother) | Widow or Widower Age 60 | Widow or Widower FRA | Each of Two Parents | Sole Parent | Maximum Family Benefits |
|---|---|---|---|---|---|---|---|---|---|
| $8,400 | $2,585 | $3,878 | $4,523 | $1,939 | $1,848 | $2,585 | $2,585 | $2,133 | $4,523 |
| $8,375 | $2,581 | $3,872 | $4,516 | $1,936 | $1,845 | $2,581 | $2,581 | $2,129 | $4,516 |
| $8,350 | $2,578 | $3,867 | $4,511 | $1,934 | $1,843 | $2,578 | $2,578 | $2,127 | $4,511 |
| $8,325 | $2,574 | $3,861 | $4,504 | $1,931 | $1,840 | $2,574 | $2,574 | $2,124 | $4,504 |
| $8,300 | $2,570 | $3,855 | $4,497 | $1,928 | $1,838 | $2,570 | $2,570 | $2,120 | $4,497 |
| $8,275 | $2,566 | $3,849 | $4,490 | $1,925 | $1,835 | $2,566 | $2,566 | $2,117 | $4,490 |
| $8,250 | $2,563 | $3,845 | $4,485 | $1,922 | $1,833 | $2,563 | $2,563 | $2,114 | $4,485 |
| $8,225 | $2,559 | $3,839 | $4,478 | $1,919 | $1,830 | $2,559 | $2,559 | $2,111 | $4,478 |
| $8,200 | $2,555 | $3,833 | $4,471 | $1,916 | $1,827 | $2,555 | $2,555 | $2,108 | $4,471 |
| $8,175 | $2,551 | $3,827 | $4,464 | $1,913 | $1,824 | $2,551 | $2,551 | $2,105 | $4,464 |
| $8,150 | $2,548 | $3,822 | $4,459 | $1,911 | $1,822 | $2,548 | $2,548 | $2,102 | $4,459 |
| $8,125 | $2,544 | $3,816 | $4,452 | $1,908 | $1,819 | $2,544 | $2,544 | $2,099 | $4,452 |
| $8,100 | $2,540 | $3,810 | $4,445 | $1,905 | $1,816 | $2,540 | $2,540 | $2,096 | $4,445 |
| $8,075 | $2,536 | $3,804 | $4,438 | $1,902 | $1,813 | $2,536 | $2,536 | $2,092 | $4,438 |
| $8,050 | $2,533 | $3,800 | $4,432 | $1,900 | $1,811 | $2,533 | $2,533 | $2,090 | $4,432 |
| $8,025 | $2,529 | $3,794 | $4,425 | $1,897 | $1,808 | $2,529 | $2,529 | $2,086 | $4,425 |
| $8,000 | $2,525 | $3,788 | $4,418 | $1,894 | $1,805 | $2,525 | $2,525 | $2,083 | $4,418 |
| $7,975 | $2,521 | $3,782 | $4,411 | $1,891 | $1,803 | $2,521 | $2,521 | $2,080 | $4,411 |
| $7,950 | $2,518 | $3,777 | $4,406 | $1,889 | $1,800 | $2,518 | $2,518 | $2,077 | $4,406 |
| $7,925 | $2,514 | $3,771 | $4,399 | $1,886 | $1,798 | $2,514 | $2,514 | $2,074 | $4,399 |
| $7,900 | $2,510 | $3,765 | $4,392 | $1,883 | $1,795 | $2,510 | $2,510 | $2,071 | $4,392 |
| $7,875 | $2,506 | $3,759 | $4,385 | $1,880 | $1,792 | $2,506 | $2,506 | $2,067 | $4,385 |
| $7,850 | $2,503 | $3,755 | $4,380 | $1,877 | $1,790 | $2,503 | $2,503 | $2,065 | $4,380 |
| $7,825 | $2,499 | $3,749 | $4,373 | $1,874 | $1,787 | $2,499 | $2,499 | $2,062 | $4,373 |
| $7,800 | $2,495 | $3,743 | $4,366 | $1,871 | $1,784 | $2,495 | $2,495 | $2,058 | $4,366 |
| $7,775 | $2,491 | $3,737 | $4,359 | $1,868 | $1,781 | $2,491 | $2,491 | $2,055 | $4,359 |
| $7,750 | $2,488 | $3,732 | $4,354 | $1,866 | $1,779 | $2,488 | $2,488 | $2,053 | $4,354 |
| $7,725 | $2,484 | $3,726 | $4,347 | $1,863 | $1,776 | $2,484 | $2,484 | $2,049 | $4,347 |
| $7,700 | $2,480 | $3,720 | $4,340 | $1,860 | $1,773 | $2,480 | $2,480 | $2,046 | $4,340 |
| $7,675 | $2,476 | $3,714 | $4,333 | $1,857 | $1,770 | $2,476 | $2,476 | $2,043 | $4,333 |
| $7,650 | $2,473 | $3,710 | $4,327 | $1,855 | $1,768 | $2,473 | $2,473 | $2,040 | $4,327 |
| $7,625 | $2,469 | $3,704 | $4,320 | $1,852 | $1,765 | $2,469 | $2,469 | $2,037 | $4,320 |
| $7,600 | $2,465 | $3,698 | $4,313 | $1,849 | $1,762 | $2,465 | $2,465 | $2,034 | $4,313 |
| $7,575 | $2,461 | $3,692 | $4,306 | $1,846 | $1,760 | $2,461 | $2,461 | $2,030 | $4,306 |
| $7,550 | $2,458 | $3,687 | $4,301 | $1,844 | $1,757 | $2,458 | $2,458 | $2,028 | $4,301 |
| $7,525 | $2,454 | $3,681 | $4,294 | $1,841 | $1,755 | $2,454 | $2,454 | $2,025 | $4,294 |
| $7,500 | $2,450 | $3,675 | $4,287 | $1,838 | $1,752 | $2,450 | $2,450 | $2,021 | $4,287 |
| $7,475 | $2,446 | $3,669 | $4,280 | $1,835 | $1,749 | $2,446 | $2,446 | $2,018 | $4,280 |
| $7,450 | $2,443 | $3,665 | $4,275 | $1,832 | $1,747 | $2,443 | $2,443 | $2,015 | $4,275 |
| $7,425 | $2,439 | $3,659 | $4,268 | $1,829 | $1,744 | $2,439 | $2,439 | $2,012 | $4,268 |
| $7,400 | $2,435 | $3,653 | $4,261 | $1,826 | $1,741 | $2,435 | $2,435 | $2,009 | $4,261 |
| $7,375 | $2,431 | $3,647 | $4,254 | $1,823 | $1,738 | $2,431 | $2,431 | $2,006 | $4,254 |
| $7,350 | $2,428 | $3,642 | $4,249 | $1,821 | $1,736 | $2,428 | $2,428 | $2,003 | $4,249 |
| $7,325 | $2,424 | $3,636 | $4,242 | $1,818 | $1,733 | $2,424 | $2,424 | $2,000 | $4,242 |
| $7,300 | $2,420 | $3,630 | $4,235 | $1,815 | $1,730 | $2,420 | $2,420 | $1,997 | $4,235 |
| $7,275 | $2,416 | $3,624 | $4,228 | $1,812 | $1,727 | $2,416 | $2,416 | $1,993 | $4,228 |
| $7,250 | $2,413 | $3,620 | $4,222 | $1,810 | $1,725 | $2,413 | $2,413 | $1,991 | $4,222 |
| $7,225 | $2,409 | $3,614 | $4,215 | $1,807 | $1,722 | $2,409 | $2,409 | $1,987 | $4,215 |
| $7,200 | $2,405 | $3,608 | $4,208 | $1,804 | $1,720 | $2,405 | $2,405 | $1,984 | $4,208 |
| $7,175 | $2,401 | $3,602 | $4,201 | $1,801 | $1,717 | $2,401 | $2,401 | $1,981 | $4,201 |
| $7,150 | $2,398 | $3,597 | $4,196 | $1,799 | $1,715 | $2,398 | $2,398 | $1,978 | $4,196 |
| $7,125 | $2,394 | $3,591 | $4,189 | $1,796 | $1,712 | $2,394 | $2,394 | $1,975 | $4,189 |

## TABLE 11—SURVIVOR'S BENEFITS (cont'd)

| Average Indexed Monthly Earnings | Worker's PIA | Surviving Spouse & 1 Child; or 2 Children | Surviving Spouse & 2 Children; or 3 Children | One Child (No Mother) | Widow or Widower Age 60 | Widow or Widower FRA | Each of Two Parents | Sole Parent | Maximum Family Benefits |
|---|---|---|---|---|---|---|---|---|---|
| $7,100 | $2,390 | $3,585 | $4,182 | $1,793 | $1,709 | $2,390 | $2,390 | $1,972 | $4,182 |
| $7,075 | $2,386 | $3,579 | $4,175 | $1,790 | $1,706 | $2,386 | $2,386 | $1,968 | $4,175 |
| $7,050 | $2,383 | $3,575 | $4,170 | $1,787 | $1,704 | $2,383 | $2,383 | $1,966 | $4,170 |
| $7,025 | $2,379 | $3,569 | $4,163 | $1,784 | $1,701 | $2,379 | $2,379 | $1,963 | $4,163 |
| $7,000 | $2,375 | $3,563 | $4,156 | $1,781 | $1,698 | $2,375 | $2,375 | $1,959 | $4,156 |
| $6,975 | $2,371 | $3,557 | $4,149 | $1,778 | $1,695 | $2,371 | $2,371 | $1,956 | $4,149 |
| $6,950 | $2,368 | $3,552 | $4,144 | $1,776 | $1,693 | $2,368 | $2,368 | $1,954 | $4,144 |
| $6,925 | $2,364 | $3,546 | $4,137 | $1,773 | $1,690 | $2,364 | $2,364 | $1,950 | $4,137 |
| $6,900 | $2,360 | $3,540 | $4,130 | $1,770 | $1,687 | $2,360 | $2,360 | $1,947 | $4,130 |
| $6,875 | $2,356 | $3,534 | $4,123 | $1,767 | $1,685 | $2,356 | $2,356 | $1,944 | $4,123 |
| $6,850 | $2,353 | $3,530 | $4,117 | $1,765 | $1,682 | $2,353 | $2,353 | $1,941 | $4,117 |
| $6,825 | $2,349 | $3,524 | $4,110 | $1,762 | $1,680 | $2,349 | $2,349 | $1,938 | $4,110 |
| $6,800 | $2,345 | $3,518 | $4,103 | $1,759 | $1,677 | $2,345 | $2,345 | $1,935 | $4,103 |
| $6,775 | $2,341 | $3,512 | $4,096 | $1,756 | $1,674 | $2,341 | $2,341 | $1,931 | $4,096 |
| $6,750 | $2,338 | $3,507 | $4,091 | $1,754 | $1,672 | $2,338 | $2,338 | $1,929 | $4,091 |
| $6,725 | $2,334 | $3,501 | $4,084 | $1,751 | $1,669 | $2,334 | $2,334 | $1,926 | $4,084 |
| $6,700 | $2,330 | $3,495 | $4,077 | $1,748 | $1,666 | $2,330 | $2,330 | $1,922 | $4,077 |
| $6,675 | $2,326 | $3,489 | $4,070 | $1,745 | $1,663 | $2,326 | $2,326 | $1,919 | $4,070 |
| $6,650 | $2,323 | $3,485 | $4,065 | $1,742 | $1,661 | $2,323 | $2,323 | $1,916 | $4,065 |
| $6,625 | $2,319 | $3,479 | $4,058 | $1,739 | $1,658 | $2,319 | $2,319 | $1,913 | $4,058 |
| $6,600 | $2,315 | $3,473 | $4,051 | $1,736 | $1,655 | $2,315 | $2,315 | $1,910 | $4,051 |
| $6,575 | $2,311 | $3,467 | $4,044 | $1,733 | $1,652 | $2,311 | $2,311 | $1,907 | $4,044 |
| $6,550 | $2,308 | $3,462 | $4,039 | $1,731 | $1,650 | $2,308 | $2,308 | $1,904 | $4,039 |
| $6,525 | $2,304 | $3,456 | $4,032 | $1,728 | $1,647 | $2,304 | $2,304 | $1,901 | $4,032 |
| $6,500 | $2,300 | $3,450 | $4,025 | $1,725 | $1,645 | $2,300 | $2,300 | $1,898 | $4,025 |
| $6,475 | $2,296 | $3,444 | $4,018 | $1,722 | $1,642 | $2,296 | $2,296 | $1,894 | $4,018 |
| $6,450 | $2,293 | $3,440 | $4,012 | $1,720 | $1,639 | $2,293 | $2,293 | $1,892 | $4,012 |
| $6,425 | $2,289 | $3,434 | $4,005 | $1,717 | $1,637 | $2,289 | $2,289 | $1,888 | $4,005 |
| $6,400 | $2,285 | $3,428 | $3,998 | $1,714 | $1,634 | $2,285 | $2,285 | $1,885 | $3,998 |
| $6,375 | $2,281 | $3,422 | $3,991 | $1,711 | $1,631 | $2,281 | $2,281 | $1,882 | $3,991 |
| $6,350 | $2,278 | $3,417 | $3,986 | $1,709 | $1,629 | $2,278 | $2,278 | $1,879 | $3,986 |
| $6,325 | $2,274 | $3,411 | $3,979 | $1,706 | $1,626 | $2,274 | $2,274 | $1,876 | $3,979 |
| $6,300 | $2,270 | $3,405 | $3,972 | $1,703 | $1,623 | $2,270 | $2,270 | $1,873 | $3,972 |
| $6,275 | $2,266 | $3,399 | $3,965 | $1,700 | $1,620 | $2,266 | $2,266 | $1,869 | $3,965 |
| $6,250 | $2,263 | $3,395 | $3,960 | $1,697 | $1,618 | $2,263 | $2,263 | $1,867 | $3,960 |
| $6,225 | $2,259 | $3,389 | $3,953 | $1,694 | $1,615 | $2,259 | $2,259 | $1,864 | $3,953 |
| $6,200 | $2,255 | $3,383 | $3,946 | $1,691 | $1,612 | $2,255 | $2,255 | $1,860 | $3,946 |
| $6,175 | $2,251 | $3,377 | $3,939 | $1,688 | $1,609 | $2,251 | $2,251 | $1,857 | $3,939 |
| $6,150 | $2,248 | $3,372 | $3,934 | $1,686 | $1,607 | $2,248 | $2,248 | $1,855 | $3,934 |
| $6,125 | $2,244 | $3,366 | $3,927 | $1,683 | $1,604 | $2,244 | $2,244 | $1,851 | $3,927 |
| $6,100 | $2,240 | $3,360 | $3,920 | $1,680 | $1,602 | $2,240 | $2,240 | $1,848 | $3,920 |
| $6,075 | $2,236 | $3,354 | $3,913 | $1,677 | $1,599 | $2,236 | $2,236 | $1,845 | $3,913 |
| $6,050 | $2,233 | $3,350 | $3,907 | $1,675 | $1,597 | $2,233 | $2,233 | $1,842 | $3,907 |
| $6,025 | $2,229 | $3,344 | $3,900 | $1,672 | $1,594 | $2,229 | $2,229 | $1,839 | $3,900 |
| $6,000 | $2,225 | $3,338 | $3,893 | $1,669 | $1,591 | $2,225 | $2,225 | $1,836 | $3,893 |
| $5,975 | $2,221 | $3,332 | $3,886 | $1,666 | $1,588 | $2,221 | $2,221 | $1,832 | $3,886 |
| $5,950 | $2,218 | $3,327 | $3,881 | $1,664 | $1,586 | $2,218 | $2,218 | $1,830 | $3,881 |
| $5,925 | $2,214 | $3,321 | $3,874 | $1,661 | $1,583 | $2,214 | $2,214 | $1,827 | $3,874 |
| $5,900 | $2,210 | $3,315 | $3,867 | $1,658 | $1,580 | $2,210 | $2,210 | $1,823 | $3,867 |
| $5,875 | $2,206 | $3,309 | $3,860 | $1,655 | $1,577 | $2,206 | $2,206 | $1,820 | $3,860 |
| $5,850 | $2,203 | $3,305 | $3,855 | $1,652 | $1,575 | $2,203 | $2,203 | $1,817 | $3,855 |
| $5,825 | $2,199 | $3,299 | $3,848 | $1,649 | $1,572 | $2,199 | $2,199 | $1,814 | $3,848 |

## TABLE 11—SURVIVOR'S BENEFITS (cont'd)

| Average Indexed Monthly Earnings | Worker's PIA | Surviving Spouse & 1 Child; or 2 Children | Surviving Spouse & 2 Children; or 3 Children | One Child (No Mother) | Widow or Widower Age 60 | Widow or Widower FRA | Each of Two Parents | Sole Parent | Maximum Family Benefits |
|---|---|---|---|---|---|---|---|---|---|
| $5,800 | $2,195 | $3,293 | $3,841 | $1,646 | $1,569 | $2,195 | $2,195 | $1,811 | $3,841 |
| $5,775 | $2,191 | $3,287 | $3,834 | $1,643 | $1,567 | $2,191 | $2,191 | $1,808 | $3,834 |
| $5,750 | $2,188 | $3,282 | $3,829 | $1,641 | $1,564 | $2,188 | $2,188 | $1,805 | $3,829 |
| $5,725 | $2,184 | $3,276 | $3,822 | $1,638 | $1,562 | $2,184 | $2,184 | $1,802 | $3,822 |
| $5,700 | $2,180 | $3,270 | $3,815 | $1,635 | $1,559 | $2,180 | $2,180 | $1,799 | $3,815 |
| $5,675 | $2,176 | $3,264 | $3,808 | $1,632 | $1,556 | $2,176 | $2,176 | $1,795 | $3,808 |
| $5,650 | $2,173 | $3,260 | $3,802 | $1,630 | $1,554 | $2,173 | $2,173 | $1,793 | $3,802 |
| $5,625 | $2,169 | $3,254 | $3,795 | $1,627 | $1,551 | $2,169 | $2,169 | $1,789 | $3,795 |
| $5,600 | $2,165 | $3,248 | $3,788 | $1,624 | $1,548 | $2,165 | $2,165 | $1,786 | $3,788 |
| $5,575 | $2,161 | $3,242 | $3,781 | $1,621 | $1,545 | $2,161 | $2,161 | $1,783 | $3,781 |
| $5,550 | $2,158 | $3,237 | $3,776 | $1,619 | $1,543 | $2,158 | $2,158 | $1,780 | $3,776 |
| $5,525 | $2,154 | $3,231 | $3,769 | $1,616 | $1,540 | $2,154 | $2,154 | $1,777 | $3,769 |
| $5,500 | $2,150 | $3,225 | $3,762 | $1,613 | $1,537 | $2,150 | $2,150 | $1,774 | $3,762 |
| $5,475 | $2,146 | $3,219 | $3,755 | $1,610 | $1,534 | $2,146 | $2,146 | $1,770 | $3,755 |
| $5,450 | $2,143 | $3,215 | $3,750 | $1,607 | $1,532 | $2,143 | $2,143 | $1,768 | $3,750 |
| $5,425 | $2,139 | $3,209 | $3,743 | $1,604 | $1,529 | $2,139 | $2,139 | $1,765 | $3,743 |
| $5,400 | $2,135 | $3,203 | $3,736 | $1,601 | $1,527 | $2,135 | $2,135 | $1,761 | $3,736 |
| $5,375 | $2,131 | $3,197 | $3,729 | $1,598 | $1,524 | $2,131 | $2,131 | $1,758 | $3,729 |
| $5,350 | $2,128 | $3,192 | $3,724 | $1,596 | $1,522 | $2,128 | $2,128 | $1,756 | $3,724 |
| $5,325 | $2,124 | $3,186 | $3,717 | $1,593 | $1,519 | $2,124 | $2,124 | $1,752 | $3,717 |
| $5,300 | $2,120 | $3,180 | $3,710 | $1,590 | $1,516 | $2,120 | $2,120 | $1,749 | $3,710 |
| $5,275 | $2,116 | $3,174 | $3,703 | $1,587 | $1,513 | $2,116 | $2,116 | $1,746 | $3,703 |
| $5,250 | $2,113 | $3,170 | $3,697 | $1,585 | $1,511 | $2,113 | $2,113 | $1,743 | $3,697 |
| $5,225 | $2,109 | $3,164 | $3,690 | $1,582 | $1,508 | $2,109 | $2,109 | $1,740 | $3,690 |
| $5,200 | $2,105 | $3,158 | $3,683 | $1,579 | $1,505 | $2,105 | $2,105 | $1,737 | $3,683 |
| $5,175 | $2,101 | $3,152 | $3,676 | $1,576 | $1,502 | $2,101 | $2,101 | $1,733 | $3,676 |
| $5,150 | $2,098 | $3,147 | $3,671 | $1,574 | $1,500 | $2,098 | $2,098 | $1,731 | $3,671 |
| $5,125 | $2,094 | $3,141 | $3,664 | $1,571 | $1,497 | $2,094 | $2,094 | $1,728 | $3,664 |
| $5,100 | $2,090 | $3,135 | $3,657 | $1,568 | $1,494 | $2,090 | $2,090 | $1,724 | $3,657 |
| $5,075 | $2,086 | $3,129 | $3,650 | $1,565 | $1,491 | $2,086 | $2,086 | $1,721 | $3,650 |
| $5,050 | $2,083 | $3,125 | $3,645 | $1,562 | $1,489 | $2,083 | $2,083 | $1,718 | $3,645 |
| $5,025 | $2,079 | $3,119 | $3,638 | $1,559 | $1,486 | $2,079 | $2,079 | $1,715 | $3,638 |
| $5,000 | $2,075 | $3,113 | $3,631 | $1,556 | $1,484 | $2,075 | $2,075 | $1,712 | $3,631 |
| $4,975 | $2,071 | $3,107 | $3,624 | $1,553 | $1,481 | $2,071 | $2,071 | $1,709 | $3,624 |
| $4,950 | $2,063 | $3,095 | $3,610 | $1,547 | $1,475 | $2,063 | $2,063 | $1,702 | $3,610 |
| $4,925 | $2,055 | $3,083 | $3,596 | $1,541 | $1,469 | $2,055 | $2,055 | $1,695 | $3,596 |
| $4,900 | $2,047 | $3,071 | $3,582 | $1,535 | $1,464 | $2,047 | $2,047 | $1,689 | $3,582 |
| $4,875 | $2,039 | $3,059 | $3,568 | $1,529 | $1,458 | $2,039 | $2,039 | $1,682 | $3,568 |
| $4,850 | $2,031 | $3,047 | $3,554 | $1,523 | $1,452 | $2,031 | $2,031 | $1,676 | $3,554 |
| $4,825 | $2,023 | $3,035 | $3,540 | $1,517 | $1,446 | $2,023 | $2,023 | $1,669 | $3,540 |
| $4,800 | $2,015 | $3,023 | $3,526 | $1,511 | $1,441 | $2,015 | $2,015 | $1,662 | $3,526 |
| $4,775 | $2,007 | $3,011 | $3,512 | $1,505 | $1,435 | $2,007 | $2,007 | $1,656 | $3,512 |
| $4,750 | $1,999 | $2,999 | $3,498 | $1,499 | $1,429 | $1,999 | $1,999 | $1,649 | $3,498 |
| $4,725 | $1,991 | $2,987 | $3,484 | $1,493 | $1,424 | $1,991 | $1,991 | $1,643 | $3,484 |
| $4,700 | $1,983 | $2,975 | $3,470 | $1,487 | $1,418 | $1,983 | $1,983 | $1,636 | $3,472 |
| $4,675 | $1,975 | $2,963 | $3,456 | $1,481 | $1,412 | $1,975 | $1,975 | $1,629 | $3,461 |
| $4,650 | $1,967 | $2,951 | $3,442 | $1,475 | $1,406 | $1,967 | $1,967 | $1,623 | $3,450 |
| $4,625 | $1,959 | $2,939 | $3,428 | $1,469 | $1,401 | $1,959 | $1,959 | $1,616 | $3,439 |
| $4,600 | $1,951 | $2,927 | $3,414 | $1,463 | $1,395 | $1,951 | $1,951 | $1,610 | $3,429 |
| $4,575 | $1,943 | $2,915 | $3,400 | $1,457 | $1,389 | $1,943 | $1,943 | $1,603 | $3,418 |
| $4,550 | $1,935 | $2,903 | $3,386 | $1,451 | $1,384 | $1,935 | $1,935 | $1,596 | $3,407 |
| $4,525 | $1,927 | $2,891 | $3,372 | $1,445 | $1,378 | $1,927 | $1,927 | $1,590 | $3,396 |

## TABLE 11—SURVIVOR'S BENEFITS (cont'd)

| Average Indexed Monthly Earnings | Worker's PIA | Surviving Spouse & 1 Child; or 2 Children | Surviving Spouse & 2 Children; or 3 Children | One Child (No Mother) | Widow or Widower Age 60 | Widow or Widower FRA | Each of Two Parents | Sole Parent | Maximum Family Benefits |
|---|---|---|---|---|---|---|---|---|---|
| $4,500 | $1,919 | $2,879 | $3,358 | $1,439 | $1,372 | $1,919 | $1,919 | $1,583 | $3,386 |
| $4,475 | $1,911 | $2,867 | $3,344 | $1,433 | $1,366 | $1,911 | $1,911 | $1,577 | $3,375 |
| $4,450 | $1,903 | $2,855 | $3,330 | $1,427 | $1,361 | $1,903 | $1,903 | $1,570 | $3,364 |
| $4,425 | $1,895 | $2,843 | $3,316 | $1,421 | $1,355 | $1,895 | $1,895 | $1,563 | $3,354 |
| $4,400 | $1,887 | $2,831 | $3,302 | $1,415 | $1,349 | $1,887 | $1,887 | $1,557 | $3,343 |
| $4,375 | $1,879 | $2,819 | $3,288 | $1,409 | $1,343 | $1,879 | $1,879 | $1,550 | $3,332 |
| $4,350 | $1,871 | $2,807 | $3,274 | $1,403 | $1,338 | $1,871 | $1,871 | $1,544 | $3,321 |
| $4,325 | $1,863 | $2,795 | $3,260 | $1,397 | $1,332 | $1,863 | $1,863 | $1,537 | $3,311 |
| $4,300 | $1,855 | $2,783 | $3,246 | $1,391 | $1,326 | $1,855 | $1,855 | $1,530 | $3,300 |
| $4,275 | $1,847 | $2,771 | $3,232 | $1,385 | $1,321 | $1,847 | $1,847 | $1,524 | $3,289 |
| $4,250 | $1,839 | $2,759 | $3,218 | $1,379 | $1,315 | $1,839 | $1,839 | $1,517 | $3,279 |
| $4,225 | $1,831 | $2,747 | $3,204 | $1,373 | $1,309 | $1,831 | $1,831 | $1,511 | $3,268 |
| $4,200 | $1,823 | $2,735 | $3,190 | $1,367 | $1,303 | $1,823 | $1,823 | $1,504 | $3,257 |
| $4,175 | $1,815 | $2,723 | $3,176 | $1,361 | $1,298 | $1,815 | $1,815 | $1,497 | $3,246 |
| $4,150 | $1,807 | $2,711 | $3,162 | $1,355 | $1,292 | $1,807 | $1,807 | $1,491 | $3,236 |
| $4,125 | $1,799 | $2,699 | $3,148 | $1,349 | $1,286 | $1,799 | $1,799 | $1,484 | $3,225 |
| $4,100 | $1,791 | $2,687 | $3,134 | $1,343 | $1,281 | $1,791 | $1,791 | $1,478 | $3,214 |
| $4,075 | $1,783 | $2,675 | $3,120 | $1,337 | $1,275 | $1,783 | $1,783 | $1,471 | $3,204 |
| $4,050 | $1,775 | $2,663 | $3,106 | $1,331 | $1,269 | $1,775 | $1,775 | $1,464 | $3,193 |
| $4,025 | $1,767 | $2,651 | $3,092 | $1,325 | $1,263 | $1,767 | $1,767 | $1,458 | $3,182 |
| $4,000 | $1,759 | $2,639 | $3,078 | $1,319 | $1,258 | $1,759 | $1,759 | $1,451 | $3,171 |
| $3,975 | $1,751 | $2,627 | $3,064 | $1,313 | $1,252 | $1,751 | $1,751 | $1,445 | $3,161 |
| $3,950 | $1,743 | $2,615 | $3,050 | $1,307 | $1,246 | $1,743 | $1,743 | $1,438 | $3,150 |
| $3,925 | $1,735 | $2,603 | $3,036 | $1,301 | $1,241 | $1,735 | $1,735 | $1,431 | $3,139 |
| $3,900 | $1,727 | $2,591 | $3,022 | $1,295 | $1,235 | $1,727 | $1,727 | $1,425 | $3,128 |
| $3,875 | $1,719 | $2,579 | $3,008 | $1,289 | $1,229 | $1,719 | $1,719 | $1,418 | $3,118 |
| $3,850 | $1,711 | $2,567 | $2,994 | $1,283 | $1,223 | $1,711 | $1,711 | $1,412 | $3,107 |
| $3,825 | $1,703 | $2,555 | $2,980 | $1,277 | $1,218 | $1,703 | $1,703 | $1,405 | $3,096 |
| $3,800 | $1,695 | $2,543 | $2,966 | $1,271 | $1,212 | $1,695 | $1,695 | $1,398 | $3,086 |
| $3,775 | $1,687 | $2,531 | $2,952 | $1,265 | $1,206 | $1,687 | $1,687 | $1,392 | $3,075 |
| $3,750 | $1,679 | $2,519 | $2,938 | $1,259 | $1,200 | $1,679 | $1,679 | $1,385 | $3,064 |
| $3,725 | $1,671 | $2,507 | $2,924 | $1,253 | $1,195 | $1,671 | $1,671 | $1,379 | $3,053 |
| $3,700 | $1,663 | $2,495 | $2,910 | $1,247 | $1,189 | $1,663 | $1,663 | $1,372 | $3,043 |
| $3,675 | $1,655 | $2,483 | $2,896 | $1,241 | $1,183 | $1,655 | $1,655 | $1,365 | $3,032 |
| $3,650 | $1,647 | $2,471 | $2,882 | $1,235 | $1,178 | $1,647 | $1,647 | $1,359 | $3,021 |
| $3,625 | $1,639 | $2,459 | $2,868 | $1,229 | $1,172 | $1,639 | $1,639 | $1,352 | $3,011 |
| $3,600 | $1,631 | $2,447 | $2,854 | $1,223 | $1,166 | $1,631 | $1,631 | $1,346 | $3,000 |
| $3,575 | $1,623 | $2,435 | $2,840 | $1,217 | $1,160 | $1,623 | $1,623 | $1,339 | $2,989 |
| $3,550 | $1,615 | $2,423 | $2,826 | $1,211 | $1,155 | $1,615 | $1,615 | $1,332 | $2,978 |
| $3,525 | $1,607 | $2,411 | $2,812 | $1,205 | $1,149 | $1,607 | $1,607 | $1,326 | $2,968 |
| $3,500 | $1,599 | $2,399 | $2,798 | $1,199 | $1,143 | $1,599 | $1,599 | $1,319 | $2,957 |
| $3,475 | $1,591 | $2,387 | $2,784 | $1,193 | $1,138 | $1,591 | $1,591 | $1,313 | $2,946 |
| $3,450 | $1,583 | $2,375 | $2,770 | $1,187 | $1,132 | $1,583 | $1,583 | $1,306 | $2,936 |
| $3,425 | $1,575 | $2,363 | $2,756 | $1,181 | $1,126 | $1,575 | $1,575 | $1,299 | $2,925 |
| $3,400 | $1,567 | $2,351 | $2,742 | $1,175 | $1,120 | $1,567 | $1,567 | $1,293 | $2,914 |
| $3,375 | $1,559 | $2,339 | $2,728 | $1,169 | $1,115 | $1,559 | $1,559 | $1,286 | $2,903 |
| $3,350 | $1,551 | $2,327 | $2,714 | $1,163 | $1,109 | $1,551 | $1,551 | $1,280 | $2,893 |
| $3,325 | $1,543 | $2,315 | $2,700 | $1,157 | $1,103 | $1,543 | $1,543 | $1,273 | $2,882 |
| $3,300 | $1,535 | $2,303 | $2,686 | $1,151 | $1,098 | $1,535 | $1,535 | $1,266 | $2,871 |
| $3,275 | $1,527 | $2,291 | $2,672 | $1,145 | $1,092 | $1,527 | $1,527 | $1,260 | $2,860 |
| $3,250 | $1,519 | $2,279 | $2,658 | $1,139 | $1,086 | $1,519 | $1,519 | $1,253 | $2,843 |
| $3,225 | $1,511 | $2,267 | $2,644 | $1,133 | $1,080 | $1,511 | $1,511 | $1,247 | $2,821 |

## TABLE 11—SURVIVOR'S BENEFITS (cont'd)

| Average Indexed Monthly Earnings | Worker's PIA | Surviving Spouse & 1 Child; or 2 Children | Surviving Spouse & 2 Children; or 3 Children | One Child (No Mother) | Widow or Widower Age 60 | Widow or Widower FRA | Each of Two Parents | Sole Parent | Maximum Family Benefits |
|---|---|---|---|---|---|---|---|---|---|
| $3,200 | $1,503 | $2,255 | $2,630 | $1,127 | $1,075 | $1,503 | $1,503 | $1,240 | $2,799 |
| $3,175 | $1,495 | $2,243 | $2,616 | $1,121 | $1,069 | $1,495 | $1,495 | $1,233 | $2,778 |
| $3,150 | $1,487 | $2,231 | $2,602 | $1,115 | $1,063 | $1,487 | $1,487 | $1,227 | $2,756 |
| $3,125 | $1,479 | $2,219 | $2,588 | $1,109 | $1,057 | $1,479 | $1,479 | $1,220 | $2,734 |
| $3,100 | $1,471 | $2,207 | $2,574 | $1,103 | $1,052 | $1,471 | $1,471 | $1,214 | $2,712 |
| $3,075 | $1,463 | $2,195 | $2,560 | $1,097 | $1,046 | $1,463 | $1,463 | $1,207 | $2,691 |
| $3,050 | $1,455 | $2,183 | $2,546 | $1,091 | $1,040 | $1,455 | $1,455 | $1,200 | $2,669 |
| $3,025 | $1,447 | $2,171 | $2,532 | $1,085 | $1,035 | $1,447 | $1,447 | $1,194 | $2,647 |
| $3,000 | $1,439 | $2,159 | $2,518 | $1,079 | $1,029 | $1,439 | $1,439 | $1,187 | $2,625 |
| $2,975 | $1,431 | $2,147 | $2,504 | $1,073 | $1,023 | $1,431 | $1,431 | $1,181 | $2,604 |
| $2,950 | $1,423 | $2,135 | $2,490 | $1,067 | $1,017 | $1,423 | $1,423 | $1,174 | $2,582 |
| $2,925 | $1,415 | $2,123 | $2,476 | $1,061 | $1,012 | $1,415 | $1,415 | $1,167 | $2,560 |
| $2,900 | $1,407 | $2,111 | $2,462 | $1,055 | $1,006 | $1,407 | $1,407 | $1,161 | $2,538 |
| $2,875 | $1,399 | $2,099 | $2,448 | $1,049 | $1,000 | $1,399 | $1,399 | $1,154 | $2,516 |
| $2,850 | $1,391 | $2,087 | $2,434 | $1,043 | $995 | $1,391 | $1,391 | $1,148 | $2,495 |
| $2,825 | $1,383 | $2,075 | $2,420 | $1,037 | $989 | $1,383 | $1,383 | $1,141 | $2,473 |
| $2,800 | $1,375 | $2,063 | $2,406 | $1,031 | $983 | $1,375 | $1,375 | $1,134 | $2,451 |
| $2,775 | $1,367 | $2,051 | $2,392 | $1,025 | $977 | $1,367 | $1,367 | $1,128 | $2,429 |
| $2,750 | $1,359 | $2,039 | $2,378 | $1,019 | $972 | $1,359 | $1,359 | $1,121 | $2,408 |
| $2,725 | $1,351 | $2,027 | $2,364 | $1,013 | $966 | $1,351 | $1,351 | $1,115 | $2,386 |
| $2,700 | $1,343 | $2,015 | $2,350 | $1,007 | $960 | $1,343 | $1,343 | $1,108 | $2,364 |
| $2,675 | $1,335 | $2,003 | $2,336 | $1,001 | $955 | $1,335 | $1,335 | $1,101 | $2,342 |
| $2,650 | $1,327 | $1,991 | $2,321 | $995 | $949 | $1,327 | $1,327 | $1,095 | $2,321 |
| $2,625 | $1,319 | $1,979 | $2,299 | $989 | $943 | $1,319 | $1,319 | $1,088 | $2,299 |
| $2,600 | $1,311 | $1,967 | $2,277 | $983 | $937 | $1,311 | $1,311 | $1,082 | $2,277 |
| $2,575 | $1,303 | $1,955 | $2,255 | $977 | $932 | $1,303 | $1,303 | $1,075 | $2,255 |
| $2,550 | $1,295 | $1,943 | $2,234 | $971 | $926 | $1,295 | $1,295 | $1,068 | $2,234 |
| $2,525 | $1,287 | $1,931 | $2,212 | $965 | $920 | $1,287 | $1,287 | $1,062 | $2,212 |
| $2,500 | $1,279 | $1,919 | $2,190 | $959 | $914 | $1,279 | $1,279 | $1,055 | $2,190 |
| $2,475 | $1,271 | $1,907 | $2,168 | $953 | $909 | $1,271 | $1,271 | $1,049 | $2,168 |
| $2,450 | $1,263 | $1,895 | $2,147 | $947 | $903 | $1,263 | $1,263 | $1,042 | $2,147 |
| $2,425 | $1,255 | $1,883 | $2,125 | $941 | $897 | $1,255 | $1,255 | $1,035 | $2,125 |
| $2,400 | $1,247 | $1,871 | $2,103 | $935 | $892 | $1,247 | $1,247 | $1,029 | $2,103 |
| $2,375 | $1,239 | $1,859 | $2,081 | $929 | $886 | $1,239 | $1,239 | $1,022 | $2,081 |
| $2,350 | $1,231 | $1,847 | $2,060 | $923 | $880 | $1,231 | $1,231 | $1,016 | $2,060 |
| $2,325 | $1,223 | $1,835 | $2,038 | $917 | $874 | $1,223 | $1,223 | $1,009 | $2,038 |
| $2,300 | $1,215 | $1,823 | $2,016 | $911 | $869 | $1,215 | $1,215 | $1,002 | $2,016 |
| $2,275 | $1,207 | $1,811 | $1,994 | $905 | $863 | $1,207 | $1,207 | $996 | $1,994 |
| $2,250 | $1,199 | $1,799 | $1,972 | $899 | $857 | $1,199 | $1,199 | $989 | $1,972 |
| $2,225 | $1,191 | $1,787 | $1,951 | $893 | $852 | $1,191 | $1,191 | $983 | $1,951 |
| $2,200 | $1,183 | $1,775 | $1,929 | $887 | $846 | $1,183 | $1,183 | $976 | $1,929 |
| $2,175 | $1,175 | $1,763 | $1,907 | $881 | $840 | $1,175 | $1,175 | $969 | $1,907 |
| $2,150 | $1,167 | $1,751 | $1,885 | $875 | $834 | $1,167 | $1,167 | $963 | $1,885 |
| $2,125 | $1,159 | $1,739 | $1,864 | $869 | $829 | $1,159 | $1,159 | $956 | $1,864 |
| $2,100 | $1,151 | $1,727 | $1,842 | $863 | $823 | $1,151 | $1,151 | $950 | $1,842 |
| $2,075 | $1,143 | $1,715 | $1,820 | $857 | $817 | $1,143 | $1,143 | $943 | $1,820 |
| $2,050 | $1,135 | $1,703 | $1,798 | $851 | $812 | $1,135 | $1,135 | $936 | $1,798 |
| $2,025 | $1,127 | $1,691 | $1,777 | $845 | $806 | $1,127 | $1,127 | $930 | $1,777 |
| $2,000 | $1,119 | $1,679 | $1,755 | $839 | $800 | $1,119 | $1,119 | $923 | $1,755 |
| $1,975 | $1,111 | $1,667 | $1,733 | $833 | $794 | $1,111 | $1,111 | $917 | $1,733 |
| $1,950 | $1,103 | $1,655 | $1,711 | $827 | $789 | $1,103 | $1,103 | $910 | $1,711 |
| $1,925 | $1,095 | $1,643 | $1,690 | $821 | $783 | $1,095 | $1,095 | $903 | $1,690 |

## TABLE 11—SURVIVOR'S BENEFITS (cont'd)

| Average Indexed Monthly Earnings | Worker's PIA | Surviving Spouse & 1 Child; or 2 Children | Surviving Spouse & 2 Children; or 3 Children | One Child (No Mother) | Widow or Widower Age 60 | Widow or Widower FRA | Each of Two Parents | Sole Parent | Maximum Family Benefits |
|---|---|---|---|---|---|---|---|---|---|
| $1,900 | $1,087 | $1,631 | $1,668 | $815 | $777 | $1,087 | $1,087 | $897 | $1,668 |
| $1,875 | $1,079 | $1,619 | $1,646 | $809 | $771 | $1,079 | $1,079 | $890 | $1,646 |
| $1,850 | $1,071 | $1,607 | $1,624 | $803 | $766 | $1,071 | $1,071 | $884 | $1,624 |
| $1,825 | $1,063 | $1,595 | $1,603 | $797 | $760 | $1,063 | $1,063 | $877 | $1,603 |
| $1,800 | $1,055 | $1,583 | $1,582 | $791 | $754 | $1,055 | $1,055 | $870 | $1,582 |
| $1,775 | $1,047 | $1,571 | $1,570 | $785 | $749 | $1,047 | $1,047 | $864 | $1,570 |
| $1,750 | $1,039 | $1,559 | $1,558 | $779 | $743 | $1,039 | $1,039 | $857 | $1,558 |
| $1,725 | $1,031 | $1,547 | $1,546 | $773 | $737 | $1,031 | $1,031 | $851 | $1,546 |
| $1,700 | $1,023 | $1,535 | $1,534 | $767 | $731 | $1,023 | $1,023 | $844 | $1,534 |
| $1,675 | $1,015 | $1,523 | $1,522 | $761 | $726 | $1,015 | $1,015 | $837 | $1,522 |
| $1,650 | $1,007 | $1,511 | $1,510 | $755 | $720 | $1,007 | $1,007 | $831 | $1,510 |
| $1,625 | $999 | $1,499 | $1,498 | $749 | $714 | $999 | $999 | $824 | $1,498 |
| $1,600 | $991 | $1,487 | $1,486 | $743 | $709 | $991 | $991 | $818 | $1,486 |
| $1,575 | $983 | $1,475 | $1,474 | $737 | $703 | $983 | $983 | $811 | $1,474 |
| $1,550 | $975 | $1,463 | $1,462 | $731 | $697 | $975 | $975 | $804 | $1,462 |
| $1,525 | $967 | $1,451 | $1,450 | $725 | $691 | $967 | $967 | $798 | $1,450 |
| $1,500 | $959 | $1,439 | $1,438 | $719 | $686 | $959 | $959 | $791 | $1,438 |
| $1,475 | $951 | $1,427 | $1,426 | $713 | $680 | $951 | $951 | $785 | $1,426 |
| $1,450 | $943 | $1,415 | $1,414 | $707 | $674 | $943 | $943 | $778 | $1,414 |
| $1,425 | $935 | $1,403 | $1,402 | $701 | $669 | $935 | $935 | $771 | $1,402 |
| $1,400 | $927 | $1,391 | $1,390 | $695 | $663 | $927 | $927 | $765 | $1,390 |
| $1,375 | $919 | $1,379 | $1,378 | $689 | $657 | $919 | $919 | $758 | $1,378 |
| $1,350 | $911 | $1,367 | $1,366 | $683 | $651 | $911 | $911 | $752 | $1,366 |
| $1,325 | $903 | $1,355 | $1,354 | $677 | $646 | $903 | $903 | $745 | $1,354 |
| $1,300 | $895 | $1,343 | $1,342 | $671 | $640 | $895 | $895 | $738 | $1,342 |
| $1,275 | $887 | $1,331 | $1,330 | $665 | $634 | $887 | $887 | $732 | $1,330 |
| $1,250 | $879 | $1,319 | $1,318 | $659 | $628 | $879 | $879 | $725 | $1,318 |
| $1,225 | $871 | $1,307 | $1,306 | $653 | $623 | $871 | $871 | $719 | $1,306 |
| $1,200 | $863 | $1,295 | $1,294 | $647 | $617 | $863 | $863 | $712 | $1,294 |
| $1,175 | $855 | $1,283 | $1,282 | $641 | $611 | $855 | $855 | $705 | $1,282 |
| $1,150 | $847 | $1,271 | $1,270 | $635 | $606 | $847 | $847 | $699 | $1,270 |
| $1,125 | $839 | $1,259 | $1,258 | $629 | $600 | $839 | $839 | $692 | $1,258 |
| $1,100 | $831 | $1,247 | $1,246 | $623 | $594 | $831 | $831 | $686 | $1,246 |
| $1,075 | $823 | $1,235 | $1,234 | $617 | $588 | $823 | $823 | $679 | $1,234 |
| $1,050 | $815 | $1,223 | $1,222 | $611 | $583 | $815 | $815 | $672 | $1,222 |
| $1,025 | $807 | $1,211 | $1,210 | $605 | $577 | $807 | $807 | $666 | $1,210 |
| $1,000 | $799 | $1,199 | $1,198 | $599 | $571 | $799 | $799 | $659 | $1,198 |
| $975 | $791 | $1,187 | $1,186 | $593 | $566 | $791 | $791 | $653 | $1,186 |
| $950 | $783 | $1,175 | $1,174 | $587 | $560 | $783 | $783 | $646 | $1,174 |
| $925 | $775 | $1,163 | $1,162 | $581 | $554 | $775 | $775 | $639 | $1,162 |
| $900 | $767 | $1,151 | $1,150 | $575 | $548 | $767 | $767 | $633 | $1,150 |
| $875 | $759 | $1,139 | $1,138 | $569 | $543 | $759 | $759 | $626 | $1,138 |
| $850 | $751 | $1,127 | $1,126 | $563 | $537 | $751 | $751 | $620 | $1,126 |
| $825 | $742 | $1,113 | $1,113 | $557 | $531 | $742 | $742 | $612 | $1,113 |
| $800 | $720 | $1,080 | $1,080 | $540 | $515 | $720 | $720 | $594 | $1,080 |

## TABLE 12—DISABILITY BENEFITS

| Average Indexed Monthly Earnings | Disabled Worker | Disabled Worker Spouse and Children | One Child (No Spouse) | Spouse FRA-3 |
|---|---|---|---|---|
| 9,700 | 2,780 | 4,170 | 1,390 | 1,043 |
| 9,675 | 2,776 | 4,164 | 1,388 | 1,041 |
| 9,650 | 2,773 | 4,160 | 1,387 | 1,040 |
| 9,625 | 2,769 | 4,154 | 1,385 | 1,038 |
| 9,600 | 2,765 | 4,148 | 1,383 | 1,037 |
| 9,575 | 2,761 | 4,142 | 1,381 | 1,035 |
| 9,550 | 2,758 | 4,137 | 1,379 | 1,034 |
| 9,525 | 2,754 | 4,131 | 1,377 | 1,033 |
| 9,500 | 2,750 | 4,125 | 1,375 | 1,031 |
| 9,475 | 2,746 | 4,119 | 1,373 | 1,030 |
| 9,450 | 2,743 | 4,115 | 1,372 | 1,029 |
| 9,425 | 2,739 | 4,109 | 1,370 | 1,027 |
| 9,400 | 2,735 | 4,103 | 1,368 | 1,026 |
| 9,375 | 2,731 | 4,097 | 1,366 | 1,024 |
| 9,350 | 2,728 | 4,092 | 1,364 | 1,023 |
| 9,325 | 2,724 | 4,086 | 1,362 | 1,022 |
| 9,300 | 2,720 | 4,080 | 1,360 | 1,020 |
| 9,275 | 2,716 | 4,074 | 1,358 | 1,019 |
| 9,250 | 2,713 | 4,070 | 1,357 | 1,017 |
| 9,225 | 2,709 | 4,064 | 1,355 | 1,016 |
| 9,200 | 2,705 | 4,058 | 1,353 | 1,014 |
| 9,175 | 2,701 | 4,052 | 1,351 | 1,013 |
| 9,150 | 2,698 | 4,047 | 1,349 | 1,012 |
| 9,125 | 2,694 | 4,041 | 1,347 | 1,010 |
| 9,100 | 2,690 | 4,035 | 1,345 | 1,009 |
| 9,075 | 2,686 | 4,029 | 1,343 | 1,007 |
| 9,050 | 2,683 | 4,025 | 1,342 | 1,006 |
| 9,025 | 2,679 | 4,019 | 1,340 | 1,005 |
| 9,000 | 2,675 | 4,013 | 1,338 | 1,003 |
| 8,975 | 2,671 | 4,007 | 1,336 | 1,002 |
| 8,950 | 2,668 | 4,002 | 1,334 | 1,001 |
| 8,925 | 2,664 | 3,996 | 1,332 | 999 |
| 8,900 | 2,660 | 3,990 | 1,330 | 998 |
| 8,875 | 2,656 | 3,984 | 1,328 | 996 |
| 8,850 | 2,653 | 3,980 | 1,327 | 995 |
| 8,825 | 2,649 | 3,974 | 1,325 | 993 |
| 8,800 | 2,645 | 3,968 | 1,323 | 992 |
| 8,775 | 2,641 | 3,962 | 1,321 | 990 |
| 8,750 | 2,638 | 3,957 | 1,319 | 989 |
| 8,725 | 2,634 | 3,951 | 1,317 | 988 |
| 8,700 | 2,630 | 3,945 | 1,315 | 986 |
| 8,675 | 2,626 | 3,939 | 1,313 | 985 |
| 8,650 | 2,623 | 3,935 | 1,312 | 984 |
| 8,625 | 2,619 | 3,929 | 1,310 | 982 |
| 8,600 | 2,615 | 3,923 | 1,308 | 981 |
| 8,575 | 2,611 | 3,917 | 1,306 | 979 |
| 8,550 | 2,608 | 3,912 | 1,304 | 978 |
| 8,525 | 2,604 | 3,906 | 1,302 | 977 |
| 8,500 | 2,600 | 3,900 | 1,300 | 975 |
| 8,475 | 2,596 | 3,894 | 1,298 | 974 |
| 8,450 | 2,593 | 3,890 | 1,297 | 972 |

## TABLE 12—DISABILITY BENEFITS (cont'd)

| Average Indexed Monthly Earnings | Disabled Worker | Disabled Worker Spouse and Children | One Child (No Spouse) | Spouse FRA-3 |
|---|---|---|---|---|
| 8,425 | 2,589 | 3,884 | 1,295 | 971 |
| 8,400 | 2,585 | 3,878 | 1,293 | 969 |
| 8,375 | 2,581 | 3,872 | 1,291 | 968 |
| 8,350 | 2,578 | 3,867 | 1,289 | 967 |
| 8,325 | 2,574 | 3,861 | 1,287 | 965 |
| 8,300 | 2,570 | 3,855 | 1,285 | 964 |
| 8,275 | 2,566 | 3,849 | 1,283 | 962 |
| 8,250 | 2,563 | 3,845 | 1,282 | 961 |
| 8,225 | 2,559 | 3,839 | 1,280 | 960 |
| 8,200 | 2,555 | 3,833 | 1,278 | 958 |
| 8,175 | 2,551 | 3,827 | 1,276 | 957 |
| 8,150 | 2,548 | 3,822 | 1,274 | 956 |
| 8,125 | 2,544 | 3,816 | 1,272 | 954 |
| 8,100 | 2,540 | 3,810 | 1,270 | 953 |
| 8,075 | 2,536 | 3,804 | 1,268 | 951 |
| 8,050 | 2,533 | 3,800 | 1,267 | 950 |
| 8,025 | 2,529 | 3,794 | 1,265 | 948 |
| 8,000 | 2,525 | 3,788 | 1,263 | 947 |
| 7,975 | 2,521 | 3,782 | 1,261 | 945 |
| 7,950 | 2,518 | 3,777 | 1,259 | 944 |
| 7,925 | 2,514 | 3,771 | 1,257 | 943 |
| 7,900 | 2,510 | 3,765 | 1,255 | 941 |
| 7,875 | 2,506 | 3,759 | 1,253 | 940 |
| 7,850 | 2,503 | 3,755 | 1,252 | 939 |
| 7,825 | 2,499 | 3,749 | 1,250 | 937 |
| 7,800 | 2,495 | 3,743 | 1,248 | 936 |
| 7,775 | 2,491 | 3,737 | 1,246 | 934 |
| 7,750 | 2,488 | 3,732 | 1,244 | 933 |
| 7,725 | 2,484 | 3,726 | 1,242 | 932 |
| 7,700 | 2,480 | 3,720 | 1,240 | 930 |
| 7,675 | 2,476 | 3,714 | 1,238 | 929 |
| 7,650 | 2,473 | 3,710 | 1,237 | 927 |
| 7,625 | 2,469 | 3,704 | 1,235 | 926 |
| 7,600 | 2,465 | 3,698 | 1,233 | 924 |
| 7,575 | 2,461 | 3,692 | 1,231 | 923 |
| 7,550 | 2,458 | 3,687 | 1,229 | 922 |
| 7,525 | 2,454 | 3,681 | 1,227 | 920 |
| 7,500 | 2,450 | 3,675 | 1,225 | 919 |
| 7,475 | 2,446 | 3,669 | 1,223 | 917 |
| 7,450 | 2,443 | 3,665 | 1,222 | 916 |
| 7,425 | 2,439 | 3,659 | 1,220 | 915 |
| 7,400 | 2,435 | 3,653 | 1,218 | 913 |
| 7,375 | 2,431 | 3,647 | 1,216 | 912 |
| 7,350 | 2,428 | 3,642 | 1,214 | 911 |
| 7,325 | 2,424 | 3,636 | 1,212 | 909 |
| 7,300 | 2,420 | 3,630 | 1,210 | 908 |
| 7,275 | 2,416 | 3,624 | 1,208 | 906 |
| 7,250 | 2,413 | 3,620 | 1,207 | 905 |
| 7,225 | 2,409 | 3,614 | 1,205 | 903 |
| 7,200 | 2,405 | 3,608 | 1,203 | 902 |
| 7,175 | 2,401 | 3,602 | 1,201 | 900 |

## TABLE 12—DISABILITY BENEFITS (cont'd)

| Average Indexed Monthly Earnings | Disabled Worker | Disabled Worker Spouse and Children | One Child (No Spouse) | Spouse FRA-3 |
|---|---|---|---|---|
| 7,150 | 2,398 | 3,597 | 1,199 | 899 |
| 7,125 | 2,394 | 3,591 | 1,197 | 898 |
| 7,100 | 2,390 | 3,585 | 1,195 | 896 |
| 7,075 | 2,386 | 3,579 | 1,193 | 895 |
| 7,050 | 2,383 | 3,575 | 1,192 | 894 |
| 7,025 | 2,379 | 3,569 | 1,190 | 892 |
| 7,000 | 2,375 | 3,563 | 1,188 | 891 |
| 6,975 | 2,371 | 3,557 | 1,186 | 889 |
| 6,950 | 2,368 | 3,552 | 1,184 | 888 |
| 6,925 | 2,364 | 3,546 | 1,182 | 887 |
| 6,900 | 2,360 | 3,540 | 1,180 | 885 |
| 6,875 | 2,356 | 3,534 | 1,178 | 884 |
| 6,850 | 2,353 | 3,530 | 1,177 | 882 |
| 6,825 | 2,349 | 3,524 | 1,175 | 881 |
| 6,800 | 2,345 | 3,518 | 1,173 | 879 |
| 6,775 | 2,341 | 3,512 | 1,171 | 878 |
| 6,750 | 2,338 | 3,507 | 1,169 | 877 |
| 6,725 | 2,334 | 3,501 | 1,167 | 875 |
| 6,700 | 2,330 | 3,495 | 1,165 | 874 |
| 6,675 | 2,326 | 3,489 | 1,163 | 872 |
| 6,650 | 2,323 | 3,485 | 1,162 | 871 |
| 6,625 | 2,319 | 3,479 | 1,160 | 870 |
| 6,600 | 2,315 | 3,473 | 1,158 | 868 |
| 6,575 | 2,311 | 3,467 | 1,156 | 867 |
| 6,550 | 2,308 | 3,462 | 1,154 | 866 |
| 6,525 | 2,304 | 3,456 | 1,152 | 864 |
| 6,500 | 2,300 | 3,450 | 1,150 | 863 |
| 6,475 | 2,296 | 3,444 | 1,148 | 861 |
| 6,450 | 2,293 | 3,440 | 1,147 | 860 |
| 6,425 | 2,289 | 3,434 | 1,145 | 858 |
| 6,400 | 2,285 | 3,428 | 1,143 | 857 |
| 6,375 | 2,281 | 3,422 | 1,141 | 855 |
| 6,350 | 2,278 | 3,417 | 1,139 | 854 |
| 6,325 | 2,274 | 3,411 | 1,137 | 853 |
| 6,300 | 2,270 | 3,405 | 1,135 | 851 |
| 6,275 | 2,266 | 3,399 | 1,133 | 850 |
| 6,250 | 2,263 | 3,395 | 1,132 | 849 |
| 6,225 | 2,259 | 3,389 | 1,130 | 847 |
| 6,200 | 2,255 | 3,383 | 1,128 | 846 |
| 6,175 | 2,251 | 3,377 | 1,126 | 844 |
| 6,150 | 2,248 | 3,372 | 1,124 | 843 |
| 6,125 | 2,244 | 3,366 | 1,122 | 842 |
| 6,100 | 2,240 | 3,360 | 1,120 | 840 |
| 6,075 | 2,236 | 3,354 | 1,118 | 839 |
| 6,050 | 2,233 | 3,350 | 1,117 | 837 |
| 6,025 | 2,229 | 3,344 | 1,115 | 836 |
| 6,000 | 2,225 | 3,338 | 1,113 | 834 |
| 5,975 | 2,221 | 3,332 | 1,111 | 833 |
| 5,950 | 2,218 | 3,327 | 1,109 | 832 |
| 5,925 | 2,214 | 3,321 | 1,107 | 830 |
| 5,900 | 2,210 | 3,315 | 1,105 | 829 |

## TABLE 12—DISABILITY BENEFITS (cont'd)

| Average Indexed Monthly Earnings | Disabled Worker | Disabled Worker Spouse and Children | One Child (No Spouse) | Spouse FRA-3 |
|---|---|---|---|---|
| 5,875 | 2,206 | 3,309 | 1,103 | 827 |
| 5,850 | 2,203 | 3,305 | 1,102 | 826 |
| 5,825 | 2,199 | 3,299 | 1,100 | 825 |
| 5,800 | 2,195 | 3,293 | 1,098 | 823 |
| 5,775 | 2,191 | 3,287 | 1,096 | 822 |
| 5,750 | 2,188 | 3,282 | 1,094 | 821 |
| 5,725 | 2,184 | 3,276 | 1,092 | 819 |
| 5,700 | 2,180 | 3,270 | 1,090 | 818 |
| 5,675 | 2,176 | 3,264 | 1,088 | 816 |
| 5,650 | 2,173 | 3,260 | 1,087 | 815 |
| 5,625 | 2,169 | 3,254 | 1,085 | 813 |
| 5,600 | 2,165 | 3,248 | 1,083 | 812 |
| 5,575 | 2,161 | 3,242 | 1,081 | 810 |
| 5,550 | 2,158 | 3,237 | 1,079 | 809 |
| 5,525 | 2,154 | 3,231 | 1,077 | 808 |
| 5,500 | 2,150 | 3,225 | 1,075 | 806 |
| 5,475 | 2,146 | 3,219 | 1,073 | 805 |
| 5,450 | 2,143 | 3,215 | 1,072 | 804 |
| 5,425 | 2,139 | 3,209 | 1,070 | 802 |
| 5,400 | 2,135 | 3,203 | 1,068 | 801 |
| 5,375 | 2,131 | 3,197 | 1,066 | 799 |
| 5,350 | 2,128 | 3,192 | 1,064 | 798 |
| 5,325 | 2,124 | 3,186 | 1,062 | 797 |
| 5,300 | 2,120 | 3,180 | 1,060 | 795 |
| 5,275 | 2,116 | 3,174 | 1,058 | 794 |
| 5,250 | 2,113 | 3,170 | 1,057 | 792 |
| 5,225 | 2,109 | 3,164 | 1,055 | 791 |
| 5,200 | 2,105 | 3,158 | 1,053 | 789 |
| 5,175 | 2,101 | 3,152 | 1,051 | 788 |
| 5,150 | 2,098 | 3,147 | 1,049 | 787 |
| 5,125 | 2,094 | 3,141 | 1,047 | 785 |
| 5,100 | 2,090 | 3,135 | 1,045 | 784 |
| 5,075 | 2,086 | 3,129 | 1,043 | 782 |
| 5,050 | 2,083 | 3,125 | 1,042 | 781 |
| 5,025 | 2,079 | 3,119 | 1,040 | 780 |
| 5,000 | 2,075 | 3,113 | 1,038 | 778 |
| 4,975 | 2,071 | 3,107 | 1,036 | 777 |
| 4,950 | 2,063 | 3,095 | 1,032 | 774 |
| 4,925 | 2,055 | 3,083 | 1,028 | 771 |
| 4,900 | 2,047 | 3,071 | 1,024 | 768 |
| 4,875 | 2,039 | 3,059 | 1,020 | 765 |
| 4,850 | 2,031 | 3,047 | 1,016 | 762 |
| 4,825 | 2,023 | 3,035 | 1,012 | 759 |
| 4,800 | 2,015 | 3,023 | 1,008 | 756 |
| 4,775 | 2,007 | 3,011 | 1,004 | 753 |
| 4,750 | 1,999 | 2,999 | 1,000 | 750 |
| 4,725 | 1,991 | 2,987 | 996 | 747 |
| 4,700 | 1,983 | 2,975 | 992 | 744 |
| 4,675 | 1,975 | 2,963 | 988 | 741 |
| 4,650 | 1,967 | 2,951 | 984 | 738 |
| 4,625 | 1,959 | 2,939 | 980 | 735 |
| 4,600 | 1,951 | 2,927 | 976 | 732 |

## TABLE 12—DISABILITY BENEFITS (cont'd)

| Average Indexed Monthly Earnings | Disabled Worker | Disabled Worker Spouse and Children | One Child (No Spouse) | Spouse FRA-3 |
|---|---|---|---|---|
| 4,575 | 1,943 | 2,915 | 972 | 729 |
| 4,550 | 1,935 | 2,903 | 968 | 726 |
| 4,525 | 1,927 | 2,891 | 964 | 723 |
| 4,500 | 1,919 | 2,879 | 960 | 720 |
| 4,475 | 1,911 | 2,867 | 956 | 717 |
| 4,450 | 1,903 | 2,855 | 952 | 714 |
| 4,425 | 1,895 | 2,843 | 948 | 711 |
| 4,400 | 1,887 | 2,831 | 944 | 708 |
| 4,375 | 1,879 | 2,819 | 940 | 705 |
| 4,350 | 1,871 | 2,807 | 936 | 702 |
| 4,325 | 1,863 | 2,795 | 932 | 699 |
| 4,300 | 1,855 | 2,783 | 928 | 696 |
| 4,275 | 1,847 | 2,771 | 924 | 693 |
| 4,250 | 1,839 | 2,759 | 920 | 690 |
| 4,225 | 1,831 | 2,747 | 916 | 687 |
| 4,200 | 1,823 | 2,735 | 912 | 684 |
| 4,175 | 1,815 | 2,723 | 908 | 681 |
| 4,150 | 1,807 | 2,711 | 904 | 678 |
| 4,125 | 1,799 | 2,699 | 900 | 675 |
| 4,100 | 1,791 | 2,687 | 896 | 672 |
| 4,075 | 1,783 | 2,675 | 892 | 669 |
| 4,050 | 1,775 | 2,663 | 888 | 666 |
| 4,025 | 1,767 | 2,651 | 884 | 663 |
| 4,000 | 1,759 | 2,639 | 880 | 660 |
| 3,975 | 1,751 | 2,627 | 876 | 657 |
| 3,950 | 1,743 | 2,615 | 872 | 654 |
| 3,925 | 1,735 | 2,603 | 868 | 651 |
| 3,900 | 1,727 | 2,591 | 864 | 648 |
| 3,875 | 1,719 | 2,579 | 860 | 645 |
| 3,850 | 1,711 | 2,567 | 856 | 642 |
| 3,825 | 1,703 | 2,555 | 852 | 639 |
| 3,800 | 1,695 | 2,543 | 848 | 636 |
| 3,775 | 1,687 | 2,531 | 844 | 633 |
| 3,750 | 1,679 | 2,519 | 840 | 630 |
| 3,725 | 1,671 | 2,507 | 836 | 627 |
| 3,700 | 1,663 | 2,495 | 832 | 624 |
| 3,675 | 1,655 | 2,483 | 828 | 621 |
| 3,650 | 1,647 | 2,471 | 824 | 618 |
| 3,625 | 1,639 | 2,459 | 820 | 615 |
| 3,600 | 1,631 | 2,447 | 816 | 612 |
| 3,575 | 1,623 | 2,435 | 812 | 609 |
| 3,550 | 1,615 | 2,423 | 808 | 606 |
| 3,525 | 1,607 | 2,411 | 804 | 603 |
| 3,500 | 1,599 | 2,399 | 800 | 600 |
| 3,475 | 1,591 | 2,387 | 796 | 597 |
| 3,450 | 1,583 | 2,375 | 792 | 594 |
| 3,425 | 1,575 | 2,363 | 788 | 591 |
| 3,400 | 1,567 | 2,351 | 784 | 588 |
| 3,375 | 1,559 | 2,339 | 780 | 585 |
| 3,350 | 1,551 | 2,327 | 776 | 582 |
| 3,325 | 1,543 | 2,315 | 772 | 579 |

## TABLE 12—DISABILITY BENEFITS (cont'd)

| Average Indexed Monthly Earnings | Disabled Worker | Disabled Worker Spouse and Children | One Child (No Spouse) | Spouse FRA-3 |
|---|---|---|---|---|
| 3,300 | 1,535 | 2,303 | 768 | 576 |
| 3,275 | 1,527 | 2,291 | 764 | 573 |
| 3,250 | 1,519 | 2,279 | 760 | 570 |
| 3,225 | 1,511 | 2,267 | 756 | 567 |
| 3,200 | 1,503 | 2,255 | 752 | 564 |
| 3,175 | 1,495 | 2,243 | 748 | 561 |
| 3,150 | 1,487 | 2,231 | 744 | 558 |
| 3,125 | 1,479 | 2,219 | 740 | 555 |
| 3,100 | 1,471 | 2,207 | 736 | 552 |
| 3,075 | 1,463 | 2,195 | 732 | 549 |
| 3,050 | 1,455 | 2,183 | 728 | 546 |
| 3,025 | 1,447 | 2,171 | 724 | 543 |
| 3,000 | 1,439 | 2,159 | 720 | 540 |
| 2,975 | 1,431 | 2,147 | 716 | 537 |
| 2,950 | 1,423 | 2,135 | 712 | 534 |
| 2,925 | 1,415 | 2,123 | 708 | 531 |
| 2,900 | 1,407 | 2,111 | 704 | 528 |
| 2,875 | 1,399 | 2,099 | 700 | 525 |
| 2,850 | 1,391 | 2,087 | 696 | 522 |
| 2,825 | 1,383 | 2,075 | 692 | 519 |
| 2,800 | 1,375 | 2,063 | 688 | 516 |
| 2,775 | 1,367 | 2,051 | 684 | 513 |
| 2,750 | 1,359 | 2,039 | 680 | 510 |
| 2,725 | 1,351 | 2,027 | 676 | 507 |
| 2,700 | 1,343 | 2,015 | 672 | 504 |
| 2,675 | 1,335 | 2,003 | 668 | 501 |
| 2,650 | 1,327 | 1,991 | 664 | 498 |
| 2,625 | 1,319 | 1,979 | 660 | 495 |
| 2,600 | 1,311 | 1,967 | 656 | 492 |
| 2,575 | 1,303 | 1,955 | 652 | 489 |
| 2,550 | 1,295 | 1,943 | 648 | 486 |
| 2,525 | 1,287 | 1,931 | 644 | 483 |
| 2,500 | 1,279 | 1,919 | 640 | 480 |
| 2,475 | 1,271 | 1,907 | 636 | 477 |
| 2,450 | 1,263 | 1,895 | 632 | 474 |
| 2,425 | 1,255 | 1,883 | 628 | 471 |
| 2,400 | 1,247 | 1,871 | 624 | 468 |
| 2,375 | 1,239 | 1,859 | 620 | 465 |
| 2,350 | 1,231 | 1,847 | 616 | 462 |
| 2,325 | 1,223 | 1,835 | 612 | 459 |
| 2,300 | 1,215 | 1,823 | 608 | 456 |
| 2,275 | 1,207 | 1,811 | 604 | 453 |
| 2,250 | 1,199 | 1,799 | 600 | 450 |
| 2,225 | 1,191 | 1,787 | 596 | 447 |
| 2,200 | 1,183 | 1,775 | 592 | 444 |
| 2,175 | 1,175 | 1,763 | 588 | 441 |
| 2,150 | 1,167 | 1,751 | 584 | 438 |
| 2,125 | 1,159 | 1,739 | 580 | 435 |
| 2,100 | 1,151 | 1,727 | 576 | 432 |
| 2,075 | 1,143 | 1,715 | 572 | 429 |
| 2,050 | 1,135 | 1,703 | 568 | 426 |

## TABLE 12—DISABILITY BENEFITS (cont'd)

| Average Indexed Monthly Earnings | Disabled Worker | Disabled Worker Spouse and Children | One Child (No Spouse) | Spouse FRA-3 |
|---|---|---|---|---|
| 2,025 | 1,127 | 1,691 | 564 | 423 |
| 2,000 | 1,119 | 1,679 | 560 | 420 |
| 1,975 | 1,111 | 1,667 | 556 | 417 |
| 1,950 | 1,103 | 1,655 | 552 | 414 |
| 1,925 | 1,095 | 1,643 | 548 | 411 |
| 1,900 | 1,087 | 1,631 | 544 | 408 |
| 1,875 | 1,079 | 1,619 | 540 | 405 |
| 1,850 | 1,071 | 1,607 | 536 | 402 |
| 1,825 | 1,063 | 1,595 | 532 | 399 |
| 1,800 | 1,055 | 1,583 | 528 | 396 |
| 1,775 | 1,047 | 1,571 | 524 | 393 |
| 1,750 | 1,039 | 1,559 | 520 | 390 |
| 1,725 | 1,031 | 1,547 | 516 | 387 |
| 1,700 | 1,023 | 1,535 | 512 | 384 |
| 1,675 | 1,015 | 1,523 | 508 | 381 |
| 1,650 | 1,007 | 1,511 | 504 | 378 |
| 1,625 | 999 | 1,499 | 500 | 375 |
| 1,600 | 991 | 1,487 | 496 | 372 |
| 1,575 | 983 | 1,475 | 492 | 369 |
| 1,550 | 975 | 1,463 | 488 | 366 |
| 1,525 | 967 | 1,451 | 484 | 363 |
| 1,500 | 959 | 1,439 | 480 | 360 |
| 1,475 | 951 | 1,427 | 476 | 357 |
| 1,450 | 943 | 1,415 | 472 | 354 |
| 1,425 | 935 | 1,403 | 468 | 351 |
| 1,400 | 927 | 1,391 | 464 | 348 |
| 1,375 | 919 | 1,379 | 460 | 345 |
| 1,350 | 911 | 1,367 | 456 | 342 |
| 1,325 | 903 | 1,355 | 452 | 339 |
| 1,300 | 895 | 1,343 | 448 | 336 |
| 1,275 | 887 | 1,331 | 444 | 333 |
| 1,250 | 879 | 1,319 | 440 | 330 |
| 1,225 | 871 | 1,307 | 436 | 327 |
| 1,200 | 863 | 1,295 | 432 | 324 |
| 1,175 | 855 | 1,283 | 428 | 321 |
| 1,150 | 847 | 1,271 | 424 | 318 |
| 1,125 | 839 | 1,259 | 420 | 315 |
| 1,100 | 831 | 1,247 | 416 | 312 |
| 1,075 | 823 | 1,235 | 412 | 309 |
| 1,050 | 815 | 1,223 | 408 | 306 |
| 1,025 | 807 | 1,211 | 404 | 303 |
| 1,000 | 799 | 1,199 | 400 | 300 |
| 975 | 791 | 1,187 | 396 | 297 |
| 950 | 783 | 1,175 | 392 | 294 |
| 925 | 775 | 1,163 | 388 | 291 |
| 900 | 767 | 1,151 | 384 | 288 |
| 875 | 759 | 1,139 | 380 | 285 |
| 850 | 751 | 1,127 | 376 | 282 |
| 825 | 742 | 1,113 | 371 | 278 |
| 800 | 720 | 1,080 | 360 | 270 |

# APPENDIX B
# FEDERAL EMPLOYEE TABLES

## TABLE 1—GENERAL PAY SCHEDULE FOR FEDERAL GOVERNMENT WORKERS EFFECTIVE IN JANUARY 2014

**Note that 2015 numbers were not available as this 2015 edition went to press**

| Step | 1 | 2 | 3 | 4 | 5 | 6 | 7 | 8 | 9 | 10 |
|---|---|---|---|---|---|---|---|---|---|---|
| GS-1 | $17,981 | $18,582 | $19,180 | $19,775 | $20,373 | $20,724 | $21,315 | $21,911 | $21,934 | $22,494 |
| 2 | 20,217 | 20,698 | 21,367 | 21,934 | 22,179 | 22,831 | 23,483 | 24,135 | 24,787 | 25,439 |
| 3 | 22,058 | 22,793 | 23,528 | 24,263 | 24,998 | 25,733 | 26,468 | 27,203 | 27,938 | 28,673 |
| 4 | 24,763 | 25,588 | 26,413 | 27,238 | 28,063 | 28,888 | 29,713 | 30,538 | 31,363 | 32,188 |
| 5 | 27,705 | 28,629 | 29,553 | 30,477 | 31,401 | 32,325 | 33,249 | 34,173 | 35,097 | 36,021 |
| 6 | 30,883 | 31,912 | 32,941 | 33,970 | 34,999 | 36,028 | 37,057 | 38,086 | 39,115 | 40,144 |
| 7 | 34,319 | 35,463 | 36,607 | 37,751 | 38,895 | 40,039 | 41,183 | 42,327 | 43,471 | 44,615 |
| 8 | 38,007 | 39,274 | 40,541 | 41,808 | 43,075 | 44,342 | 45,609 | 46,876 | 48,143 | 49,410 |
| 9 | 41,979 | 43,378 | 44,777 | 46,176 | 47,575 | 48,974 | 50,373 | 51,772 | 53,171 | 54,570 |
| 10 | 46,229 | 47,770 | 49,311 | 50,852 | 52,393 | 53,934 | 55,475 | 57,016 | 58,557 | 60,098 |
| 11 | 50,790 | 52,483 | 54,176 | 55,869 | 57,562 | 59,255 | 60,948 | 62,641 | 64,334 | 66,027 |
| 12 | 60,877 | 62,906 | 64,935 | 66,964 | 68,993 | 71,022 | 73,051 | 75,080 | 77,109 | 79,138 |
| 13 | 72,391 | 74,804 | 77,217 | 79,630 | 82,043 | 84,456 | 86,869 | 89,282 | 91,695 | 94,108 |
| 14 | 85,544 | 88,395 | 91,246 | 94,097 | 96,948 | 99,799 | 102,650 | 105,501 | 108,352 | 111,203 |
| 15 | 100,624 | 103,978 | 107,332 | 110,686 | 114,040 | 117,394 | 120,748 | 124,102 | 127,456 | 130,810 |

## LOCALITY PAY ADJUSTMENTS

**Combined national and locality pay adjustments for 32 locations in 2014 are listed below.**

| Location | Adjustment | Location | Adjustment |
|---|---|---|---|
| Atlanta | 19.29% | Miami | 20.79% |
| Boston | 24.80% | Milwaukee | 18.10% |
| Buffalo | 16.98% | Minneapolis | 20.96% |
| Chicago | 25.10% | New York | 28.72% |
| Cincinnati | 18.55% | Philadelphia | 21.79% |
| Cleveland | 18.68% | Phoenix | 16.76% |
| Columbus | 17.16% | Pittsburgh | 16.37% |
| Dallas | 20.67% | Portland | 20.35% |
| Dayton | 16.24% | Raleigh-Durham | 17.64% |
| Denver | 22.52% | Richmond | 16.47% |
| Detroit | 24.09% | Sacramento | 22.20% |
| Hartford | 25.82% | San Diego | 24.19% |
| Houston | 28.71% | San Francisco | 35.15% |
| Huntsville | 16.02% | Seattle | 21.81% |
| Indianapolis | 14.68% | Washington | 24.22% |
| Los Angeles | 27.16% | Rest of U.S. | 14.16% |

## TABLE 2—BASIC MONTHLY RETIREMENT ANNUITY FOR CSRS EMPLOYEES

| High-3 Annual Salary | Years of Service | | | | | | | |
|---|---|---|---|---|---|---|---|---|
| | 5 | 10 | 15 | 20 | 25 | 30 | 35 | 40 |
| $15,000 | $ 94 | $ 203 | $ 328 | $ 453 | $ 578 | $ 703 | $ 828 | $ 953 |
| 16,000 | 100 | 217 | 350 | 483 | 617 | 750 | 883 | 1,017 |
| 17,000 | 106 | 230 | 372 | 514 | 655 | 797 | 939 | 1,080 |
| 18,000 | 113 | 244 | 394 | 544 | 694 | 844 | 994 | 1,144 |
| 19,000 | 119 | 257 | 415 | 574 | 732 | 891 | 1,049 | 1,207 |
| 20,000 | 125 | 270 | 438 | 604 | 771 | 938 | 1,104 | 1,271 |
| 21,000 | 131 | 284 | 459 | 634 | 809 | 984 | 1,159 | 1,334 |
| 22,000 | 138 | 298 | 481 | 665 | 848 | 1,031 | 1,215 | 1,398 |
| 23,000 | 144 | 311 | 503 | 695 | 886 | 1,078 | 1,270 | 1,461 |
| 24,000 | 150 | 325 | 525 | 725 | 925 | 1,125 | 1,325 | 1,525 |
| 25,000 | 156 | 339 | 547 | 755 | 964 | 1,172 | 1,380 | 1,589 |
| 26,000 | 163 | 352 | 574 | 785 | 1,002 | 1,219 | 1,435 | 1,652 |
| 27,000 | 169 | 366 | 591 | 816 | 1,041 | 1,266 | 1,491 | 1,716 |
| 28,000 | 175 | 379 | 613 | 846 | 1,079 | 1,313 | 1,546 | 1,779 |
| 29,000 | 181 | 393 | 634 | 876 | 1,118 | 1,359 | 1,601 | 1,843 |
| 30,000 | 188 | 406 | 656 | 906 | 1,156 | 1,406 | 1,656 | 1,906 |
| 31,000 | 194 | 420 | 678 | 936 | 1,195 | 1,453 | 1,711 | 1,970 |
| 32,000 | 200 | 433 | 700 | 967 | 1,233 | 1,500 | 1,767 | 2,033 |
| 33,000 | 206 | 447 | 722 | 997 | 1,272 | 1,547 | 1,822 | 2,097 |
| 34,000 | 213 | 460 | 744 | 1,027 | 1,310 | 1,594 | 1,877 | 2,160 |
| 35,000 | 219 | 474 | 766 | 1,057 | 1,349 | 1,641 | 1,932 | 2,224 |
| 36,000 | 225 | 488 | 788 | 1,088 | 1,388 | 1,688 | 1,988 | 2,288 |
| 37,000 | 231 | 501 | 809 | 1,118 | 1,426 | 1,734 | 2,043 | 2,351 |
| 38,000 | 238 | 515 | 831 | 1,148 | 1,465 | 1,781 | 2,098 | 2,415 |
| 39,000 | 244 | 528 | 853 | 1,178 | 1,503 | 1,828 | 2,153 | 2,478 |
| 40,000 | 250 | 542 | 875 | 1,208 | 1,542 | 1,875 | 2,208 | 2,542 |
| 41,000 | 256 | 555 | 897 | 1,239 | 1,580 | 1,922 | 2,264 | 2,605 |
| 42,000 | 263 | 569 | 919 | 1,269 | 1,619 | 1,969 | 2,319 | 2,669 |
| 43,000 | 269 | 582 | 941 | 1,299 | 1,657 | 2,016 | 2,374 | 2,732 |
| 44,000 | 275 | 596 | 963 | 1,329 | 1,699 | 2,063 | 2,429 | 2,796 |
| 45,000 | 281 | 609 | 984 | 1,359 | 1,734 | 2,109 | 2,484 | 2,859 |
| 46,000 | 288 | 623 | 1,006 | 1,390 | 1,773 | 2,156 | 2,540 | 2,923 |
| 47,000 | 294 | 636 | 1,028 | 1,420 | 1,811 | 2,203 | 2,595 | 2,986 |
| 48,000 | 300 | 650 | 1,050 | 1,450 | 1,850 | 2,250 | 2,650 | 3,050 |
| 49,000 | 306 | 663 | 1,071 | 1,479 | 1,888 | 2,296 | 2,704 | 3,113 |
| 50,000 | 312 | 676 | 1,092 | 1,509 | 1,926 | 2,342 | 2,759 | 3,163 |
| 51,000 | 318 | 689 | 1,114 | 1,539 | 1,964 | 2,389 | 2,814 | 3,239 |
| 52,000 | 325 | 704 | 1,137 | 1,570 | 2,004 | 2,437 | 2,870 | 3,304 |
| 53,000 | 331 | 717 | 1,158 | 1,600 | 2,042 | 2,483 | 2,925 | 3,367 |
| 54,000 | 337 | 730 | 1,180 | 1,630 | 2,080 | 2,530 | 2,980 | 3,430 |
| 55,000 | 343 | 744 | 1,202 | 1,660 | 2,119 | 2,577 | 3,035 | 3,494 |
| 56,000 | 350 | 758 | 1,224 | 1,691 | 2,158 | 2,624 | 3,091 | 3,558 |
| 57,000 | 356 | 771 | 1,246 | 1,721 | 2,196 | 2,671 | 3,146 | 3,621 |
| 58,000 | 362 | 784 | 1,267 | 1,750 | 2,234 | 2,717 | 3,200 | 3,684 |
| 59,000 | 368 | 798 | 1,289 | 1,781 | 2,273 | 2,764 | 3,256 | 3,748 |
| 60,000 | 375 | 812 | 1,312 | 1,812 | 2,312 | 2,812 | 3,312 | 3,812 |
| 61,000 | 381 | 825 | 1,333 | 1,841 | 2,350 | 2,858 | 3,366 | 3,875 |
| 62,000 | 387 | 839 | 1,355 | 1,872 | 2,389 | 2,905 | 3,422 | 3,939 |
| 63,000 | 393 | 852 | 1,377 | 1,902 | 2,427 | 2,952 | 3,477 | 4,002 |
| 64,000 | 400 | 866 | 1,399 | 1,932 | 2,441 | 2,999 | 3,532 | 4,066 |

## TABLE 2—BASIC MONTHLY RETIREMENT ANNUITY FOR CSRS EMPLOYEES (cont'd)

| High-3 Annual Salary | Years of Service | | | | | | | |
|---|---|---|---|---|---|---|---|---|
| | 5 | 10 | 15 | 20 | 25 | 30 | 35 | 40 |
| $65,000 | $406 | $880 | $1,422 | $1,964 | $2,505 | $3,047 | $3,589 | $4,130 |
| 66,000 | 413 | 894 | 1,444 | 1,994 | 2,544 | 3,094 | 3,644 | 4,194 |
| 68,000 | 425 | 921 | 1,488 | 2,054 | 2,621 | 3,188 | 3,754 | 4,321 |
| 70,000 | 438 | 948 | 1,531 | 2,115 | 2,698 | 3,281 | 3,865 | 4,448 |
| 72,000 | 450 | 975 | 1,575 | 2,175 | 2,775 | 3,375 | 3,975 | 4,575 |
| 74,000 | 463 | 1,002 | 1,619 | 2,235 | 2,852 | 3,469 | 4,085 | 4,702 |
| 76,000 | 475 | 1,029 | 1,663 | 2,296 | 2,929 | 3,563 | 4,196 | 4,829 |
| 80,000 | 500 | 1,083 | 1,750 | 2,417 | 3,083 | 3,750 | 4,417 | 5,083 |
| 83,000 | 519 | 1,124 | 1,816 | 2,507 | 3,199 | 3,891 | 4,582 | 5,274 |
| 86,000 | 538 | 1,165 | 1,881 | 2,598 | 3,315 | 4,031 | 4,748 | 5,465 |
| 90,000 | 563 | 1,219 | 1,969 | 2,719 | 3,469 | 4,219 | 4,969 | 5,719 |
| 93,000 | 581 | 1,259 | 2,034 | 2,809 | 3,584 | 4,359 | 5,134 | 5,909 |
| 96,000 | 600 | 1,300 | 2,100 | 2,900 | 3,700 | 4,500 | 5,300 | 6,100 |
| 100,000 | 625 | 1,354 | 2,188 | 3,021 | 3,854 | 4,688 | 5,521 | 6,354 |
| 110,000 | 688 | 1,490 | 2,406 | 3,323 | 4,240 | 5,156 | 6,073 | 6,990 |

## TABLE 3—BASIC MONTHLY RETIREMENT ANNUITY FOR FERS EMPLOYEES

| High-3 Annual Salary | Years of Service | | | | | | | |
|---|---|---|---|---|---|---|---|---|
| | 5 | 10 | 15 | 20 | 25 | 30 | 35 | 40 |
| $15,000 | $ 63 | $ 125 | $ 188 | $ 250 | $ 313 | $ 375 | $ 438 | $ 500 |
| 16,000 | 67 | 133 | 200 | 267 | 333 | 400 | 467 | 533 |
| 17,000 | 71 | 142 | 213 | 283 | 354 | 425 | 496 | 567 |
| 18,000 | 75 | 150 | 225 | 300 | 375 | 450 | 525 | 600 |
| 19,000 | 79 | 158 | 238 | 317 | 396 | 475 | 554 | 633 |
| 20,000 | 83 | 167 | 250 | 333 | 417 | 500 | 583 | 667 |
| 22,000 | 92 | 183 | 275 | 367 | 458 | 550 | 642 | 733 |
| 24,000 | 100 | 200 | 300 | 400 | 500 | 600 | 700 | 800 |
| 26,000 | 108 | 217 | 325 | 433 | 542 | 650 | 758 | 867 |
| 28,000 | 117 | 233 | 350 | 467 | 583 | 700 | 817 | 933 |
| 30,000 | 125 | 250 | 375 | 500 | 625 | 750 | 875 | 1,000 |
| 32,000 | 133 | 267 | 400 | 533 | 667 | 800 | 933 | 1,067 |
| 34,000 | 142 | 283 | 425 | 567 | 708 | 850 | 992 | 1,133 |
| 36,000 | 150 | 300 | 450 | 600 | 750 | 900 | 1,050 | 1,200 |
| 38,000 | 158 | 317 | 475 | 633 | 792 | 950 | 1,108 | 1,267 |
| 40,000 | 167 | 333 | 500 | 667 | 833 | 1,000 | 1,167 | 1,333 |
| 42,000 | 175 | 350 | 525 | 700 | 875 | 1,050 | 1,225 | 1,400 |
| 44,000 | 183 | 367 | 550 | 733 | 917 | 1,100 | 1,283 | 1,467 |
| 46,000 | 192 | 383 | 575 | 767 | 958 | 1,150 | 1,342 | 1,533 |
| 48,000 | 200 | 400 | 600 | 800 | 1,000 | 1,200 | 1,400 | 1,600 |
| 50,000 | 208 | 417 | 625 | 833 | 1,042 | 1,250 | 1,458 | 1,667 |
| 53,000 | 221 | 442 | 663 | 883 | 1,104 | 1,325 | 1,546 | 1,767 |
| 55,000 | 229 | 458 | 688 | 917 | 1,146 | 1,375 | 1,604 | 1,833 |
| 57,000 | 238 | 475 | 713 | 950 | 1,188 | 1,425 | 1,663 | 1,900 |
| 60,000 | 250 | 500 | 750 | 1,000 | 1,250 | 1,500 | 1,750 | 2,000 |
| 65,000 | 271 | 542 | 813 | 1,083 | 1,354 | 1,625 | 1,896 | 2,167 |
| 66,000 | 275 | 550 | 825 | 1,100 | 1,375 | 1,650 | 1,925 | 2,200 |
| 68,000 | 283 | 567 | 850 | 1,133 | 1,417 | 1,700 | 1,983 | 2,267 |
| 70,000 | 292 | 583 | 875 | 1,167 | 1,458 | 1,750 | 2,042 | 2,333 |
| 72,000 | 300 | 600 | 900 | 1,200 | 1,500 | 1,800 | 2,100 | 2,400 |
| 74,000 | 308 | 617 | 925 | 1,233 | 1,542 | 1,850 | 2,158 | 2,467 |
| 76,000 | 317 | 633 | 950 | 1,267 | 1,369 | 1,643 | 1,916 | 2,190 |
| 80,000 | 333 | 667 | 1,000 | 1,333 | 1,667 | 2,000 | 2,333 | 2,667 |
| 83,000 | 346 | 692 | 1,038 | 1,383 | 1,729 | 2,075 | 2,421 | 2,767 |
| 86,000 | 358 | 717 | 1,075 | 1,433 | 1,792 | 2,150 | 2,508 | 2,867 |
| 90,000 | 375 | 750 | 1,125 | 1,500 | 1,875 | 2,250 | 2,625 | 3,000 |
| 93,000 | 388 | 775 | 1,163 | 1,550 | 1,938 | 2,325 | 2,713 | 3,100 |
| 96,000 | 400 | 800 | 1,200 | 1,600 | 2,000 | 2,400 | 2,800 | 3,200 |
| 100,000 | 417 | 833 | 1,250 | 1,667 | 2,083 | 2,500 | 2,917 | 3,333 |
| 110,000 | 458 | 917 | 1,375 | 1,833 | 2,292 | 2,750 | 3,208 | 3,667 |

## TABLE 4
## AMOUNT OF INSURANCE PROTECTION UNDER THE FEDERAL EMPLOYEES GROUP LIFE INSURANCE ACT OF 1980 (P.L. 96-427) EFFECTIVE OCTOBER 1, 1981*

| Annual Pay | | | Amount of Group Life Insurance | | | | |
|---|---|---|---|---|---|---|---|
| Greater than - | But not greater than - | Basic Insurance Amount | Age 35 and Under | Age 36 (1.9) | Age 37 (1.8) | Age 38 (1.7) | Age 39 (1.6) |
| $ 0 | $ 8,000 | $10,000 | $20,000 | $19,000 | $ 18,000 | $17,000 | $16,000 |
| 8,000 | 9,000 | 11,000 | 22,000 | 20,900 | 19,800 | 18,700 | 17,600 |
| 9,000 | 10,000 | 12,000 | 24,000 | 22,800 | 21,600 | 20,400 | 19,200 |
| 10,000 | 11,000 | 13,000 | 26,000 | 24,700 | 23,400 | 22,100 | 20,800 |
| 11,000 | 12,000 | 14,000 | 28,000 | 26,600 | 25,200 | 23,800 | 22,400 |
| 12,000 | 13,000 | 15,000 | 30,000 | 28,500 | 27,000 | 25,500 | 24,000 |
| 13,000 | 14,000 | 16,000 | 32,000 | 30,400 | 28,800 | 27,200 | 25,600 |
| 14,000 | 15,000 | 17,000 | 34,000 | 32,300 | 30,600 | 28,900 | 27,200 |
| 15,000 | 16,000 | 18,000 | 36,000 | 34,200 | 32,400 | 30,600 | 28,800 |
| 16,000 | 17,000 | 19,000 | 38,000 | 36,100 | 34,200 | 32,300 | 30,400 |
| 17,000 | 18,000 | 20,000 | 40,000 | 38,000 | 36,000 | 34,000 | 32,000 |
| 18,000 | 19,000 | 21,000 | 42,000 | 39,900 | 37,800 | 35,700 | 33,600 |
| 19,000 | 20,000 | 22,000 | 44,000 | 41,800 | 39,600 | 37,400 | 35,200 |
| 20,000 | 21,000 | 23,000 | 46,000 | 43,700 | 41,400 | 39,100 | 36,800 |
| 21,000 | 22,000 | 24,000 | 48,000 | 45,600 | 43,200 | 40,800 | 38,400 |
| 22,000 | 23,000 | 25,000 | 50,000 | 47,500 | 45,000 | 42,500 | 40,000 |
| 23,000 | 24,000 | 26,000 | 52,000 | 49,400 | 46,800 | 44,200 | 41,600 |
| 24,000 | 25,000 | 27,000 | 54,000 | 51,300 | 48,600 | 45,900 | 43,200 |
| 25,000 | 26,000 | 28,000 | 56,000 | 53,200 | 50,400 | 47,600 | 44,800 |
| 26,000 | 27,000 | 29,000 | 58,000 | 55,100 | 52,200 | 49,300 | 46,400 |
| 27,000 | 28,000 | 30,000 | 60,000 | 57,000 | 54,000 | 51,000 | 48,000 |
| 28,000 | 29,000 | 31,000 | 62,000 | 58,900 | 55,800 | 52,700 | 49,600 |
| 29,000 | 30,000 | 32,000 | 64,000 | 60,800 | 57,600 | 54,400 | 51,200 |
| 30,000 | 31,000 | 33,000 | 66,000 | 62,700 | 59,400 | 56,100 | 52,800 |
| 31,000 | 32,000 | 34,000 | 68,000 | 64,600 | 61,200 | 57,800 | 54,400 |
| 32,000 | 33,000 | 35,000 | 70,000 | 66,500 | 63,000 | 59,500 | 56,000 |
| 33,000 | 34,000 | 36,000 | 72,000 | 68,400 | 64,800 | 61,200 | 57,600 |
| 34,000 | 35,000 | 37,000 | 74,000 | 70,300 | 66,600 | 62,900 | 59,200 |
| 35,000 | 36,000 | 38,000 | 76,000 | 72,200 | 68,400 | 64,600 | 60,800 |
| 36,000 | 37,000 | 39,000 | 78,000 | 74,100 | 70,200 | 63,300 | 62,400 |
| 37,000 | 38,000 | 40,000 | 80,000 | 76,000 | 72,000 | 68,000 | 64,000 |
| 38,000 | 39,000 | 41,000 | 82,000 | 77,900 | 73,800 | 69,700 | 65,600 |
| 39,000 | 40,000 | 42,000 | 84,000 | 79,800 | 75,600 | 71,400 | 67,200 |
| 40,000 | 41,000 | 43,000 | 86,000 | 81,700 | 77,400 | 73,100 | 68,800 |
| 41,000 | 42,000 | 44,000 | 88,000 | 83,600 | 79,200 | 74,800 | 70,400 |
| 42,000 | 43,000 | 45,000 | 90,000 | 85,500 | 81,000 | 76,500 | 72,000 |
| 43,000 | 44,000 | 46,000 | 92,000 | 87,400 | 82,800 | 78,200 | 73,600 |
| 44,000 | 45,000 | 47,000 | 94,000 | 89,300 | 84,600 | 79,900 | 75,200 |
| 45,000 | 46,000 | 48,000 | 96,000 | 91,200 | 86,400 | 81,600 | 76,800 |
| 46,000 | 47,000 | 49,000 | 98,000 | 93,100 | 88,200 | 83,300 | 78,400 |
| 47,000 | 48,000 | 50,000 | 100,000 | 95,000 | 90,000 | 85,000 | 80,000 |
| 48,000 | 49,000 | 51,000 | 102,000 | 96,900 | 91,800 | 86,700 | 81,600 |
| 49,000 | 50,000 | 52,000 | 104,000 | 98,800 | 93,600 | 88,400 | 83,200 |
| 50,000 | 51,000 | 53,000 | 106,000 | 100,700 | 95,400 | 90,100 | 84,800 |

## AMOUNT OF INSURANCE PROTECTION UNDER THE FEDERAL EMPLOYEES GROUP LIFE INSURANCE ACT OF 1980 (P.L. 96-427) EFFECTIVE OCTOBER 1, 1981*

| Amount of Group Life Insurance | | | | | | Amount of Group Accidental Death and Dismemberment Insurance |
|---|---|---|---|---|---|---|
| Age 40 (1.5) | Age 41 (1.4) | Age 42 (1.3) | Age 43 (1.2) | Age 44 (1.1) | 45 and Over (1.0) | |
| $15,000 | $14,000 | $13,000 | $12,000 | $11,000 | $10,000 | $10,000 |
| 16,500 | 15,400 | 14,300 | 13,200 | 12,100 | 11,000 | 11,000 |
| 18,000 | 16,800 | 15,600 | 14,400 | 13,200 | 12,000 | 12,000 |
| 19,500 | 18,200 | 16,900 | 15,600 | 14,300 | 13,000 | 13,000 |
| 21,000 | 19,600 | 18,200 | 16,800 | 15,400 | 14,000 | 14,000 |
| 22,500 | 21,000 | 19,500 | 18,000 | 16,500 | 15,000 | 15,000 |
| 24,000 | 22,400 | 20,800 | 19,200 | 17,600 | 16,000 | 16,000 |
| 25,500 | 23,800 | 22,100 | 20,400 | 18,700 | 17,000 | 17,000 |
| 27,000 | 25,200 | 23,400 | 21,600 | 19,800 | 18,000 | 18,000 |
| 28,500 | 26,600 | 24,700 | 22,800 | 20,900 | 19,000 | 19,000 |
| 30,000 | 28,000 | 26,000 | 24,000 | 22,000 | 20,000 | 20,000 |
| 31,500 | 29,400 | 27,300 | 25,200 | 23,100 | 21,000 | 21,000 |
| 33,000 | 30,800 | 28,600 | 26,400 | 24,200 | 22,000 | 22,000 |
| 34,500 | 32,200 | 29,900 | 27,600 | 25,300 | 23,000 | 23,000 |
| 36,000 | 33,600 | 31,200 | 28,800 | 26,400 | 24,000 | 24,000 |
| 37,500 | 35,000 | 32,500 | 30,000 | 27,500 | 25,000 | 25,000 |
| 39,000 | 36,400 | 33,800 | 31,200 | 28,600 | 26,000 | 26,000 |
| 40,500 | 37,800 | 35,100 | 32,400 | 29,700 | 27,000 | 27,000 |
| 42,000 | 39,200 | 36,400 | 33,600 | 30,800 | 28,000 | 28,000 |
| 43,500 | 40,600 | 37,700 | 34,800 | 31,900 | 29,000 | 29,000 |
| 45,000 | 42,000 | 39,000 | 36,000 | 33,000 | 30,000 | 30,000 |
| 46,500 | 43,400 | 40,300 | 37,200 | 34,100 | 31,000 | 31,000 |
| 48,000 | 44,800 | 41,600 | 38,400 | 35,200 | 32,000 | 32,000 |
| 49,500 | 46,200 | 42,900 | 39,600 | 36,300 | 33,000 | 33,000 |
| 51,000 | 47,600 | 44,200 | 40,800 | 37,400 | 34,000 | 34,000 |
| 52,500 | 49,000 | 45,500 | 42,000 | 38,500 | 35,000 | 35,000 |
| 54,000 | 50,400 | 46,800 | 43,200 | 39,600 | 36,000 | 36,000 |
| 55,500 | 51,800 | 48,100 | 44,400 | 40,700 | 37,000 | 37,000 |
| 57,000 | 53,200 | 49,400 | 45,600 | 41,800 | 38,000 | 38,000 |
| 58,500 | 54,600 | 50,700 | 46,800 | 42,900 | 39,000 | 39,000 |
| 60,000 | 56,000 | 52,000 | 48,000 | 44,000 | 40,000 | 40,000 |
| 61,500 | 57,400 | 53,300 | 49,200 | 45,100 | 41,000 | 41,000 |
| 63,000 | 58,800 | 54,600 | 50,400 | 46,200 | 42,000 | 42,000 |
| 64,500 | 60,200 | 55,900 | 51,600 | 47,300 | 43,000 | 43,000 |
| 66,000 | 61,600 | 57,200 | 52,800 | 48,400 | 44,000 | 44,000 |
| 67,500 | 63,000 | 58,500 | 54,000 | 49,500 | 45,000 | 45,000 |
| 69,000 | 64,400 | 59,800 | 55,200 | 50,600 | 46,000 | 46,000 |
| 70,500 | 65,800 | 61,100 | 56,400 | 51,700 | 47,000 | 47,000 |
| 72,000 | 67,200 | 62,400 | 57,600 | 52,800 | 48,000 | 48,000 |
| 73,500 | 68,600 | 63,700 | 58,800 | 53,900 | 49,000 | 49,000 |
| 75,000 | 70,000 | 65,000 | 60,000 | 55,000 | 50,000 | 50,000 |
| 76,500 | 71,400 | 66,300 | 61,200 | 56,100 | 51,000 | 51,000 |
| 78,000 | 72,800 | 67,600 | 62,400 | 57,200 | 52,000 | 52,000 |
| 79,500 | 74,200 | 68,900 | 63,600 | 58,300 | 53,000 | 53,000 |

## AMOUNT OF INSURANCE PROTECTION UNDER THE FEDERAL EMPLOYEES GROUP LIFE INSURANCE ACT OF 1980 (P.L. 96-427) EFFECTIVE OCTOBER 1, 1981*

| Annual Pay | | | Amount of Group Life Insurance | | | | |
|---|---|---|---|---|---|---|---|
| Greater than - | But not greater than - | Basic Insurance Amount | Age 35 and Under | Age 36 (1.9) | Age 37 (1.8) | Age 38 (1.7) | Age 39 (1.6) |
| 51,000 | 52,000 | 54,000 | 108,000 | 102,600 | 97,200 | 91,800 | 86,400 |
| 52,000 | 53,000 | 55,000 | 110,000 | 104,500 | 99,000 | 93,500 | 88,000 |
| 53,000 | 54,000 | 56,000 | 112,000 | 106,400 | 100,800 | 95,200 | 89,600 |
| 54,000 | 55,000 | 57,000 | 114,000 | 108,300 | 102,600 | 96,900 | 91,200 |
| 55,000 | 56,000 | 58,000 | 116,000 | 110,200 | 104,400 | 98,600 | 92,800 |
| 56,000 | 57,000 | 59,000 | 118,000 | 112,100 | 106,200 | 100,300 | 94,400 |
| 57,000 | 58,000 | 60,000 | 120,000 | 114,000 | 108,000 | 102,000 | 96,000 |
| 58,000 | 59,000 | 61,000 | 122,000 | 115,900 | 109,800 | 103,700 | 97,600 |
| 59,000 | 60,000 | 62,000 | 124,000 | 117,800 | 111,600 | 105,400 | 99,200 |
| 60,000 | 61,000 | 63,000 | 126,000 | 119,700 | 113,400 | 107,100 | 100,800 |
| 61,000 | 62,000 | 64,000 | 128,000 | 121,600 | 115,200 | 108,800 | 102,400 |
| 62,000 | 63,000 | 65,000 | 130,000 | 123,500 | 117,000 | 110,500 | 104,000 |
| 63,000 | 64,000 | 66,000 | 132,000 | 125,400 | 118,800 | 112,200 | 105,600 |
| 64,000 | 65,000 | 67,000 | 134,000 | 127,300 | 120,600 | 113,900 | 107,200 |
| 65,000 | 66,000 | 68,000 | 136,000 | 129,200 | 122,400 | 115,600 | 108,800 |
| 66,000 | 67,000 | 69,000 | 138,000 | 131,100 | 124,200 | 117,300 | 110,400 |
| 67,000 | 68,000 | 70,000 | 140,000 | 133,000 | 126,000 | 119,000 | 112,000 |
| 68,000 | 69,000 | 71,000 | 142,000 | 134,900 | 127,800 | 120,700 | 113,600 |
| 69,000 | 70,000 | 72,000 | 144,000 | 136,800 | 129,600 | 122,400 | 115,200 |
| 70,000 | 71,000 | 73,000 | 146,000 | 138,700 | 131,400 | 124,100 | 116,800 |
| 71,000 | 72,000 | 74,000 | 148,000 | 140,600 | 133,200 | 125,800 | 118,400 |
| 72,000 | 73,000 | 75,000 | 150,000 | 142,500 | 135,000 | 127,500 | 120,000 |
| 73,000 | 74,000 | 76,000 | 152,000 | 144,400 | 136,800 | 129,200 | 121,600 |
| 74,000 | 75,000 | 77,000 | 154,000 | 146,300 | 138,600 | 130,900 | 123,200 |
| 75,000 | 76,000 | 78,000 | 156,000 | 148,200 | 140,400 | 132,600 | 124,800 |
| 76,000 | 77,000 | 79,000 | 158,000 | 150,100 | 142,200 | 134,300 | 126,400 |
| 77,000 | 78,000 | 80,000 | 160,000 | 152,000 | 144,000 | 136,000 | 128,000 |
| 78,000 | 79,000 | 81,000 | 162,000 | 153,900 | 145,800 | 137,700 | 129,600 |
| 79,000 | 80,000 | 82,000 | 164,000 | 155,800 | 147,600 | 139,400 | 131,200 |
| 80,000 | 81,000 | 83,000 | 166,000 | 157,700 | 149,400 | 141,100 | 132,800 |
| 81,000 | 82,000 | 84,000 | 168,000 | 159,600 | 151,200 | 142,800 | 134,400 |
| 82,000 | 83,000 | 85,000 | 170,000 | 161,500 | 153,000 | 144,500 | 136,000 |
| 83,000 | 84,000 | 86,000 | 172,000 | 163,400 | 154,800 | 146,200 | 137,600 |
| 84,000 | 85,000 | 87,000 | 174,000 | 165,300 | 156,600 | 147,900 | 139,200 |
| 85,000 | 86,000 | 88,000 | 176,000 | 167,200 | 158,400 | 149,600 | 140,800 |
| 86,000 | 87,000 | 89,000 | 178,000 | 169,100 | 160,200 | 151,300 | 142,400 |
| 87,000 | 88,000 | 90,000 | 180,000 | 171,000 | 162,000 | 153,000 | 144,000 |
| 88,000 | 89,000 | 91,000 | 182,000 | 172,900 | 163,800 | 154,700 | 145,600 |
| 89,000 | 90,000 | 92,000 | 184,000 | 174,800 | 165,600 | 156,400 | 147,200 |
| 90,000 | 91,000 | 93,000 | 186,000 | 176,700 | 167,400 | 158,100 | 148,800 |

## AMOUNT OF INSURANCE PROTECTION UNDER THE FEDERAL EMPLOYEES GROUP LIFE INSURANCE ACT OF 1980 (P.L. 96-427) EFFECTIVE OCTOBER 1, 1981*

| Amount of Group Life Insurance | | | | | | Amount of Group Accidental Death and Dismemberment Insurance |
|---|---|---|---|---|---|---|
| Age 40 (1.5) | Age 41 (1.4) | Age 42 (1.3) | Age 43 (1.2) | Age 44 (1.1) | 45 and Over (1.0) | |
| 81,000 | 75,600 | 70,200 | 64,800 | 59,400 | 54,000 | 54,000 |
| 82,500 | 77,000 | 71,500 | 66,000 | 60,500 | 55,000 | 55,000 |
| 84,000 | 78,400 | 72,800 | 67,200 | 61,600 | 56,000 | 56,000 |
| 85,500 | 79,800 | 74,100 | 68,400 | 62,700 | 57,000 | 57,000 |
| 87,000 | 81,200 | 75,400 | 69,600 | 63,800 | 58,000 | 58,000 |
| 88,500 | 82,600 | 76,700 | 70,800 | 64,900 | 59,000 | 59,000 |
| 90,000 | 84,000 | 78,000 | 72,000 | 66,000 | 60,000 | 60,000 |
| 91,500 | 85,400 | 79,300 | 73,200 | 67,100 | 61,000 | 61,000 |
| 93,000 | 86,800 | 80,600 | 74,400 | 68,200 | 62,000 | 62,000 |
| 94,500 | 88,200 | 81,900 | 75,600 | 69,300 | 63,000 | 63,000 |
| 96,000 | 89,600 | 83,200 | 76,800 | 70,400 | 64,000 | 64,000 |
| 97,500 | 91,000 | 84,500 | 78,000 | 71,500 | 65,000 | 65,000 |
| 99,000 | 92,400 | 85,800 | 79,200 | 72,600 | 66,000 | 66,000 |
| 100,500 | 93,800 | 87,100 | 80,400 | 73,700 | 67,000 | 67,000 |
| 102,000 | 95,200 | 88,400 | 81,600 | 74,800 | 68,000 | 68,000 |
| 103,500 | 96,600 | 89,700 | 82,800 | 75,900 | 69,000 | 69,000 |
| 105,000 | 98,000 | 91,000 | 84,000 | 77,000 | 70,000 | 70,000 |
| 106,500 | 99,400 | 92,300 | 85,200 | 78,100 | 71,000 | 71,000 |
| 108,000 | 100,800 | 93,600 | 86,400 | 79,200 | 72,000 | 72,000 |
| 109,500 | 102,200 | 94,900 | 87,600 | 80,300 | 73,000 | 73,000 |
| 111,000 | 103,600 | 96,200 | 88,800 | 81,400 | 74,000 | 74,000 |
| 112,500 | 105,000 | 97,500 | 90,000 | 82,500 | 75,000 | 75,000 |
| 114,000 | 106400 | 98,800 | 91,200 | 83,600 | 76,000 | 76,000 |
| 115,500 | 107,800 | 100,100 | 92,400 | 84,700 | 77,000 | 77,000 |
| 117,000 | 109,200 | 101,400 | 93,600 | 85,800 | 78,000 | 78,000 |
| 118,500 | 110,600 | 102,700 | 94,800 | 86,900 | 79,000 | 79,000 |
| 120,000 | 112,000 | 104,000 | 96,000 | 88,000 | 80,000 | 80,000 |
| 121,500 | 113,400 | 105,300 | 97,200 | 89,100 | 81,000 | 81,000 |
| 123,000 | 114,800 | 106,600 | 98,400 | 90,200 | 82,000 | 82,000 |
| 124,500 | 116,200 | 107,900 | 99,600 | 91,300 | 83,000 | 83,000 |
| 126,000 | 117,600 | 109,200 | 100,800 | 92,400 | 84,000 | 84,000 |
| 127,500 | 119,000 | 110,500 | 102,000 | 93,500 | 85,000 | 85,000 |
| 129,000 | 120,400 | 111,800 | 103,200 | 94,600 | 86,000 | 86,000 |
| 130,500 | 121,800 | 113,100 | 104,400 | 95,700 | 87,000 | 87,000 |
| 132,000 | 123,200 | 114,400 | 105,600 | 96,800 | 88,000 | 88,000 |
| 133,500 | 124,600 | 115,700 | 106,800 | 97,900 | 89,000 | 89,000 |
| 135,000 | 126,000 | 117,000 | 108,000 | 99,000 | 90,000 | 90,000 |
| 136,500 | 127,400 | 118,300 | 109,200 | 100,100 | 91,000 | 91,000 |
| 138,000 | 128,800 | 119,600 | 110,400 | 101,200 | 92,000 | 92,000 |
| 139,500 | 130,200 | 120,900 | 111,600 | 102,300 | 93,000 | 93,000 |

## AMOUNT OF INSURANCE PROTECTION UNDER THE FEDERAL EMPLOYEES GROUP LIFE INSURANCE ACT OF 1980 (P.L. 96-427) EFFECTIVE OCTOBER 1, 1981*

| Annual Pay | | | Amount of Group Life Insurance | | | | |
|---|---|---|---|---|---|---|---|
| Greater than - | But not greater than - | Basic Insurance Amount | Age 35 and Under | Age 36 (1.9) | Age 37 (1.8) | Age 38 (1.7) | Age 39 (1.6) |
| 91,000 | 92,000 | 94,000 | 188,000 | 178,600 | 169,200 | 159,800 | 150,400 |
| 92,000 | 93,000 | 95,000 | 190,000 | 180,500 | 171,000 | 161,500 | 152,000 |
| 93,000 | 94,000 | 96,000 | 192,000 | 182,400 | 172,800 | 163,200 | 153,600 |
| 94,000 | 95,000 | 97,000 | 194,000 | 184,300 | 174,600 | 164,900 | 155,200 |
| 95,000 | 96,000 | 98,000 | 196,000 | 186,200 | 176,400 | 166,600 | 156,800 |
| 96,000 | 97,000 | 99,000 | 198,000 | 188,100 | 178,200 | 168,300 | 158,400 |
| 97,000 | 98,000 | 100,000 | 200,000 | 190,000 | 180,000 | 170,000 | 160,000 |
| 98,000 | 99,000 | 101,000 | 202,000 | 191,900 | 181,800 | 171,700 | 161,600 |
| 99,000 | 100,000 | 102,000 | 204,000 | 193,800 | 183,600 | 173,400 | 163,200 |
| 100,000 | 101,000 | 103,000 | 206,000 | 195,700 | 185,400 | 175,100 | 164,800 |
| 101,000 | 102,000 | 104,000 | 208,000 | 197,600 | 187,200 | 176,800 | 166,400 |
| 102,000 | 103,000 | 105,000 | 210,000 | 199,500 | 189,000 | 178,500 | 168,000 |
| 103,000 | 104,000 | 106,000 | 212,000 | 201,400 | 190,800 | 180,200 | 169,600 |
| 104,000 | 105,000 | 107,000 | 214,000 | 203,300 | 192,600 | 181,900 | 171,200 |
| 105,000 | 106,000 | 108,000 | 216,000 | 205,200 | 194,400 | 183,600 | 172,800 |
| 106,000 | 107,000 | 109,000 | 218,000 | 207,100 | 196,200 | 185,300 | 174,400 |
| 107,000 | 108,000 | 110,000 | 220,000 | 209,000 | 198,000 | 187,000 | 176,000 |
| 108,000 | 109,000 | 111,000 | 222,000 | 210,900 | 199,800 | 188,700 | 177,600 |
| 109,000 | 110,000 | 112,000 | 224,000 | 212,800 | 201,600 | 190,400 | 179,200 |
| 110,000 | 111,000 | 113,000 | 226,000 | 214,700 | 203,400 | 192,100 | 180,800 |
| 111,000 | 112,000 | 114,000 | 228,000 | 216,600 | 205,200 | 193,800 | 182,400 |
| 112,000 | 113,000 | 115,000 | 230,000 | 218,500 | 207,000 | 195,500 | 184,000 |
| 113,000 | 114,000 | 116,000 | 232,000 | 220,400 | 208,800 | 197,200 | 185,600 |
| 114,000 | 115,000 | 117,000 | 234,000 | 222,300 | 210,600 | 198,900 | 187,200 |
| 115,000 | 116,000 | 118,000 | 236,000 | 224,200 | 212,400 | 200,600 | 188,800 |
| 116,000 | 117,000 | 119,000 | 238,000 | 226,100 | 214,200 | 202,300 | 190,400 |
| 117,000 | 118,000 | 120,000 | 240,000 | 228,000 | 216,000 | 204,000 | 192,000 |
| 118,000 | 119,000 | 121,000 | 242,000 | 229,900 | 217,800 | 205,700 | 193,600 |
| 119,000 | 120,000 | 122,000 | 244,000 | 231,800 | 219,600 | 207,400 | 195,200 |
| 120,000 | 121,000 | 123,000 | 246,000 | 233,700 | 221,400 | 209,100 | 196,800 |
| 121,000 | 122,000 | 124,000 | 248,000 | 235,600 | 223,200 | 210,800 | 198,400 |
| 122,000 | 123,000 | 125,000 | 250,000 | 237,500 | 225,000 | 212,500 | 200,000 |
| 123,000 | 124,000 | 126,000 | 252,000 | 239,400 | 226,800 | 214,200 | 201,600 |
| 124,000 | 125,000 | 127,000 | 254,000 | 241,300 | 228,600 | 215,900 | 203,200 |
| 125,000 | 126,000 | 128,000 | 256,000 | 243,200 | 230,400 | 217,600 | 204,800 |
| 126,000 | 127,000 | 129,000 | 258,000 | 245,100 | 232,200 | 219,300 | 206,400 |
| 127,000 | 128,000 | 130,000 | 260,000 | 247,000 | 234,000 | 221,000 | 208,000 |
| 128,000 | 129,000 | 131,000 | 262,000 | 248,900 | 235,800 | 222,700 | 209,600 |
| 129,000 | 130,000 | 132,000 | 264,000 | 250,800 | 237,600 | 224,400 | 211,200 |
| 130,000 | 131,000 | 133,000 | 266,000 | 252,700 | 239,400 | 226,100 | 212,800 |
| 131,000 | 132,000 | 134,000 | 268,000 | 254,600 | 241,200 | 227,800 | 214,400 |
| 132,000 | 133,000 | 135,000 | 270,000 | 256,500 | 243,000 | 229,500 | 216,000 |
| 133,000 | 134,000 | 136,000 | 272,000 | 258,400 | 244,800 | 231,200 | 217,600 |
| 134,000 | 135,000 | 137,000 | 274,000 | 260,300 | 246,600 | 232,900 | 219,200 |
| 135,000 | 136,000 | 138,000 | 276,000 | 262,200 | 248,400 | 234,600 | 220,800 |
| 136,000 | 137,000 | 139,000 | 278,000 | 264,100 | 250,200 | 236,300 | 222,400 |
| 137,000 | 138,000 | 140,000 | 280,000 | 266,000 | 252,000 | 238,000 | 224,000 |
| 138,000 | 139,000 | 141,000 | 282,000 | 267,900 | 253,800 | 239,700 | 225,600 |
| 139,000 | 140,000 | 142,000 | 284,000 | 269,800 | 255,600 | 241,400 | 227,200 |
| 140,000 | 141,000 | 143,000 | 286,000 | 271,700 | 257,400 | 243,100 | 228,800 |

## AMOUNT OF INSURANCE PROTECTION UNDER THE FEDERAL EMPLOYEES GROUP LIFE INSURANCE ACT OF 1980 (P.L. 96-427) EFFECTIVE OCTOBER 1, 1981*

| Amount of Group Life Insurance | | | | | | Amount of Group Accidental Death and Dismemberment Insurance |
|---|---|---|---|---|---|---|
| Age 40 (1.5) | Age 41 (1.4) | Age 42 (1.3) | Age 43 (1.2) | Age 44 (1.1) | 45 and Over (1.0) | |
| 141,000 | 131,600 | 122,200 | 112,800 | 103,400 | 94,000 | 94,000 |
| 142,500 | 133,000 | 123,500 | 114,000 | 104,500 | 95,000 | 95,000 |
| 144,000 | 134,400 | 124,800 | 115,200 | 105,600 | 96,000 | 96,000 |
| 145,500 | 135,800 | 126,100 | 116,400 | 106,700 | 97,000 | 97,000 |
| 147,000 | 137,200 | 127,400 | 117,600 | 107,800 | 98,000 | 98,000 |
| 148,500 | 138,600 | 128,700 | 118,800 | 108,900 | 99,000 | 99,000 |
| 150,000 | 140,000 | 130,000 | 120,000 | 110,000 | 100,000 | 100,000 |
| 151,500 | 141,400 | 131,300 | 121,200 | 111,100 | 101,000 | 101,000 |
| 153,000 | 142,800 | 132,600 | 122,400 | 112,200 | 102,000 | 102,000 |
| 154,500 | 144,200 | 133,900 | 123,600 | 113,300 | 103,000 | 103,000 |
| 156,000 | 145,600 | 135,200 | 124,800 | 114,400 | 104,000 | 104,000 |
| 157,500 | 147,000 | 136,500 | 126,000 | 115,500 | 105,000 | 105,000 |
| 159,000 | 148,400 | 137,800 | 127,200 | 116,600 | 106,000 | 106,000 |
| 160,500 | 149,800 | 139,100 | 128,400 | 117,700 | 107,000 | 107,000 |
| 162,000 | 151,200 | 140,400 | 129,600 | 118,800 | 108,000 | 108,000 |
| 163,500 | 152,600 | 141,700 | 130,800 | 119,900 | 109,000 | 109,000 |
| 165,000 | 154,000 | 143,000 | 132,000 | 121,000 | 110,000 | 110,000 |
| 166,500 | 155,400 | 144,300 | 133,200 | 122,100 | 111,000 | 111,000 |
| 168,000 | 156,800 | 145,600 | 134,400 | 123,200 | 112,000 | 112,000 |
| 169,500 | 158,200 | 146,900 | 135,600 | 124,300 | 113,000 | 113,000 |
| 171,000 | 159,600 | 148,200 | 136,800 | 125,400 | 114,000 | 114,000 |
| 172,500 | 161,000 | 149,500 | 138,000 | 126,500 | 115,000 | 115,000 |
| 174,000 | 162,400 | 150,800 | 139,200 | 127,600 | 116,000 | 116,000 |
| 175,500 | 163,800 | 152,100 | 140,400 | 128,700 | 117,000 | 117,000 |
| 177,000 | 165,200 | 153,400 | 141,600 | 129,800 | 118,000 | 118,000 |
| 178,500 | 166,600 | 154,700 | 142,800 | 130,900 | 119,000 | 119,000 |
| 180,000 | 168,000 | 156,000 | 144,000 | 132,000 | 120,000 | 120,000 |
| 181,500 | 169,400 | 157,300 | 145,200 | 133,100 | 121,000 | 121,000 |
| 183,000 | 170,800 | 158,600 | 146,400 | 134,200 | 122,000 | 122,000 |
| 184,500 | 172,200 | 159,900 | 147,600 | 135,300 | 123,000 | 123,000 |
| 186,000 | 173,600 | 161,200 | 148,800 | 136,400 | 124,000 | 124,000 |
| 187,500 | 175,000 | 162,500 | 150,000 | 137,500 | 125,000 | 125,000 |
| 189,000 | 176,400 | 163,800 | 151,200 | 138,600 | 126,000 | 126,000 |
| 190,500 | 177,800 | 165,100 | 152,400 | 139,700 | 127,000 | 127,000 |
| 192,000 | 179,200 | 166,400 | 153,600 | 140,800 | 128,000 | 128,000 |
| 193,500 | 180,600 | 167,700 | 154,800 | 141,900 | 129,000 | 129,000 |
| 195,000 | 182,000 | 169,000 | 156,000 | 143,000 | 130,000 | 130,000 |
| 196,500 | 183,400 | 170,300 | 157,200 | 144,100 | 131,000 | 131,000 |
| 198,000 | 184,800 | 171,600 | 158,400 | 145,200 | 132,000 | 132,000 |
| 199,500 | 186,200 | 172,900 | 159,600 | 146,300 | 133,000 | 133,000 |
| 201,000 | 187,600 | 174,200 | 160,800 | 147,400 | 134,000 | 134,000 |
| 202,500 | 189,000 | 175,500 | 162,000 | 148,500 | 135,000 | 135,000 |
| 204,000 | 190,400 | 176,800 | 163,200 | 149,600 | 136,000 | 136,000 |
| 205,500 | 191,800 | 178,100 | 164,400 | 150,700 | 137,000 | 137,000 |
| 207,000 | 193,200 | 179,400 | 165,600 | 151,800 | 138,000 | 138,000 |
| 208,500 | 194,600 | 180,700 | 166,800 | 152,900 | 139,000 | 139,000 |
| 210,000 | 196,000 | 182,000 | 168,000 | 154,000 | 140,000 | 140,000 |
| 211,500 | 197,400 | 183,300 | 169,200 | 155,100 | 141,000 | 141,000 |
| 213,000 | 198,800 | 184,600 | 170,400 | 156,200 | 142,000 | 142,000 |
| 214,500 | 200,200 | 185,900 | 171,600 | 157,300 | 143,000 | 143,000 |

* P.L. 96-427 revised the group term life insurance coverage available to civil service employees. The amounts of group term life shown in this table became effective October 1, 1981.

# APPENDIX C
# SERVICE MEMBERS AND VETERANS TABLES

## TABLE 1—COMPARATIVE RANKS

### *Comparative Officer Ranks*

| GRADE | ARMY | AIR FORCE | MARINE CORPS | NAVY |
|---|---|---|---|---|
| **COMMISSIONED OFFICERS** | | | | |
| O-10 | General | General | General | Admiral |
| O-9 | Lieutenant General | Lieutenant General | Lieutenant General | Vice Admiral |
| O-8 | Major General | Major General | Major General | Rear Admiral (Upper Half) |
| O-7 | Brigadier General | Brigadier General | Brigadier General | Rear Admiral (Lower Half) |
| O-6 | Colonel | Colonel | Colonel | Captain |
| O-5 | Lieutenant Colonel | Lieutenant Colonel | Lieutenant Colonel | Commander |
| O-4 | Major | Major | Major | Lieutenant Commander |
| O-3 | Captain | Captain | Captain | Lieutenant |
| O-2 | First Lieutenant | First Lieutenant | First Lieutenant | Lieutenant Junior Grade |
| O-1 | Second Lieutenant | Second Lieutenant | Second Lieutenant | Ensign |
| **WARRANT OFFICERS** | | | | |
| W-5 | Chief Warrant Officer | None | Chief Warrant Officer 5 | USN Chief Warrant Officer |
| W-4 | Chief Warrant Officer 4 | None | Chief Warrant Officer 4 | USN Chief Warrant Officer 4 |
| W-3 | Chief Warrant Officer 3 | None | Chief Warrant Officer 3 | USN Chief Warrant Officer 3 |
| W-2 | Chief Warrant Officer 2 | None | Chief Warrant Officer 2 | USN Chief Warrant Officer 2 |
| W-1 | Warrant Officer 1 | None | Warrant Officer 1 | USN Warrant Officer 1 |

### *Comparative Ranks—Enlisted Personnel*

| GRADE | ARMY | AIR FORCE | MARINE CORPS | NAVY |
|---|---|---|---|---|
| E-9 | Sergeant Major | Chief Master Sergeant | Sgt. Major & M/Gy. Sgt. | Master Chief Petty Officer |
| E-8 | 1st Sgt. & Master Sgt. | Senior Master Sergeant | 1st Sgt. & Master Sgt. | Senior Chief Petty Officer |
| E-7 | Sergeant First Class | Master Sgt. & 1st Sgt. | Gunnery Sergeant | Chief Petty Officer |
| E-6 | Staff Sergeant | Technical Sergeant | Staff Sergeant | Petty Officer, First Class |
| E-5 | Sergeant | Staff Sergeant | Sergeant | Petty Officer, Second Class |
| E-4 | Corporal | Senior Airman | Corporal | Petty Officer, Third Class |
| E-3 | Private First Class | Airman, First Class | Lance Corporal | Seaman |
| E-2 | Private | Airman | Private, First Class | Seaman Apprentice |
| E-1 | Private | Airman, Basic | Private | Seaman Recruit |

## TABLE 2—BASIC MONTHLY PAY RATES†
### Effective January 1, 2014
### Note that 2015 numbers were not available as this 2015 edition went to press
### 2 or Less Years through Over 10 Years

| Pay Grade | 2 or less | Over 2 | Over 3 | Over 4 | Over 6 | Over 8 | Over 10 |
|---|---|---|---|---|---|---|---|
| **COMMISSIONED OFFICERS** | | | | | | | |
| O-10 | - | - | - | - | - | - | - |
| O-9 | - | - | - | - | - | - | - |
| O-8 | 9,946.20 | 10,272.00 | 10,488.30 | 10,548.60 | 10,818.60 | 11,269.20 | 11,373.90 |
| O-7 | 8,264.40 | 8,648.40 | 8,826.00 | 8,967.30 | 9,222.90 | 9,475.80 | 9,767.70 |
| O-6 | 6,125.40 | 6,729.60 | 7,171.20 | 7,171.20 | 7,198.50 | 7,507.20 | 7,547.70 |
| O-5 | 5,106.60 | 5,752.50 | 6,150.60 | 6,225.60 | 6,474.30 | 6,622.80 | 6,949.50 |
| O-4 | 4,405.80 | 5,100.30 | 5,440.80 | 5,516.40 | 5,832.30 | 6,171.00 | 6,593.10 |
| O-3 | 3,873.90 | 4,391.40 | 4,739.70 | 5,167.80 | 5,415.30 | 5,687.10 | 5,862.60 |
| O-2 | 3,347.10 | 3,812.10 | 4,390.50 | 4,538.70 | 4,632.30 | 4,632.30 | 4,632.30 |
| O-1 | 2,905.20 | 3,024.00 | 3,655.50 | 3,655.50 | 3,655.50 | 3,655.50 | 3,655.50 |
| **COMMISSIONED OFFICERS (with over 4 years active duty service as an enlisted member or warrant officer)** | | | | | | | |
| O-3E | - | - | - | 5,167.80 | 5,415.30 | 5,687.10 | 5,862.60 |
| O-2E | - | - | - | 4,538.70 | 4,632.30 | 4,779.90 | 5,028.60 |
| O-1E | - | - | - | 3,655.50 | 3,903.30 | 4,047.90 | 4,195.20 |
| **WARRANT OFFICERS** | | | | | | | |
| W-5 | - | - | - | - | - | - | - |
| W-4 | 4,003.50 | 4,306.50 | 4,429.80 | 4,551.60 | 4,761.00 | 4,968.30 | 5,178.00 |
| W-3 | 3,655.80 | 3,808.20 | 3,964.50 | 4,015.80 | 4,179.60 | 4,501.80 | 4,837.20 |
| W-2 | 3,234.90 | 3,540.90 | 3,635.40 | 3,699.90 | 3,909.90 | 4,236.00 | 4,397.40 |
| W-1 | 2,839.80 | 3,145.20 | 3,227.40 | 3,401.10 | 3,606.60 | 3,909.30 | 4,050.60 |
| **ENLISTED MEMBERS** | | | | | | | |
| E-9 | - | - | - | - | - | - | 4,836.90 |
| E-8 | - | - | - | - | - | 3,959.40 | 4,134.30 |
| E-7 | 2,752.50 | 3,004.20 | 3,119.10 | 3,271.50 | 3,390.60 | 3,594.90 | 3,709.80 |
| E-6 | 2,380.80 | 2,619.60 | 2,735.10 | 2,847.60 | 2,964.90 | 3,228.60 | 3,331.50 |
| E-5 | 2,181.00 | 2,327.40 | 2,440.20 | 2,555.10 | 2,734.50 | 2,922.30 | 3,076.20 |
| E-4 | 1,999.50 | 2,101.80 | 2,215.80 | 2,328.00 | 2,427.30 | 2,427.30 | 2,427.30 |
| E-3 | 1,805.40 | 1,918.80 | 2,034.90 | 2,034.90 | 2,034.90 | 2,034.90 | 2,034.90 |
| E-2 | 1,716.90 | 1,716.90 | 1,716.90 | 1,716.90 | 1,716.90 | 1,716.90 | 1,716.90 |
| E-1* | 1,531.50 | - | - | - | - | - | - |

## TABLE 2—BASIC MONTHLY PAY RATES† (cont'd)
### Effective January 1, 2014
### Note that 2015 numbers were not available as this 2015 edition went to press
### Over 12 Years through Over 26 Years

| Pay Grade | Over 12 | Over 14 | Over 16 | Over 18 | Over 20 | Over 22 | Over 24 | Over 26 |
|---|---|---|---|---|---|---|---|---|
| **COMMISSIONED OFFICERS** | | | | | | | | |
| O-10 | - | - | - | - | 16,072.20 | 16,150.50 | 16,486.80 | 17,071.50 |
| O-9 | - | - | - | - | 14,056.80 | 14,259.90 | 14,552.10 | 15,062.40 |
| O-8 | 11,802.00 | 11,924.70 | 12,293.40 | 12,827.10 | 13,319.10 | 13,647.30 | 13,647.30 | 13,647.30 |
| O-7 | 10,059.00 | 10,351.20 | 11,269.20 | 12,043.80 | 12,043.80 | 12,043.80 | 12,043.80 | 12,105.60 |
| O-6 | 7,547.70 | 7,976.70 | 8,735.10 | 9,180.30 | 9,625.20 | 9,878.40 | 10,134.60 | 10,632.00 |
| O-5 | 7,189.50 | 7,499.70 | 7,974.00 | 8,199.30 | 8,422.20 | 8,675.70 | 8,675.70 | 8,675.70 |
| O-4 | 6,921.30 | 7,149.60 | 7,280.70 | 7,356.60 | 7,356.60 | 7,356.60 | 7,356.60 | 7,356.60 |
| O-3 | 6,151.50 | 6,302.40 | 6,302.40 | 6,302.40 | 6,302.40 | 6,302.40 | 6,302.40 | 6,302.40 |
| O-2 | 4,632.30 | 4,632.30 | 4,632.30 | 4,632.30 | 4,632.30 | 4,632.30 | 4,632.30 | 4,632.30 |
| O-1 | 3,655.50 | 3,655.50 | 3,655.50 | 3,655.50 | 3,655.50 | 3,655.50 | 3,655.50 | 3,655.50 |
| **COMMISSIONED OFFICERS (with over 4 years active duty service as an enlisted member or warrant officer)** | | | | | | | | |
| O-3E | 6,151.50 | 6,395.40 | 6,535.50 | 6,726.00 | 6,726.00 | 6,726.00 | 6,726.00 | 6,726.00 |
| O-2E | 5,220.90 | 5,364.30 | 5,364.30 | 5,364.30 | 5,364.30 | 5,364.30 | 5,364.30 | 5,364.30 |
| O-1E | 4,340.10 | 4,538.70 | 4,538.70 | 4,538.70 | 4,538.70 | 4,538.70 | 4,538.70 | 4,538.70 |
| **WARRANT OFFICERS** | | | | | | | | |
| W-5 | - | - | - | - | 7,118.40 | 7,479.60 | 7,748.40 | 8,046.30 |
| W-4 | 5,493.90 | 5,770.50 | 6,033.90 | 6,249.30 | 6,459.30 | 6,768.00 | 7,021.80 | 7,311.00 |
| W-3 | 4,995.00 | 5,177.70 | 5,366.10 | 5,704.50 | 5,933.10 | 6,069.90 | 6,215.40 | 6,413.10 |
| W-2 | 4,556.40 | 4,751.10 | 4,902.90 | 5,040.60 | 5,205.30 | 5,313.60 | 5,399.70 | 5,399.70 |
| W-1 | 4,247.70 | 4,442.40 | 4,595.40 | 4,735.80 | 4,906.80 | 4,906.80 | 4,906.80 | 4,906.80 |
| **ENLISTED MEMBERS** | | | | | | | | |
| E-9 | 4,946.40 | 5,084.70 | 5,246.70 | 5,411.10 | 5,673.60 | 5,895.60 | 6,129.30 | 6,486.90 |
| E-8 | 4,242.90 | 4,372.80 | 4,513.80 | 4,767.60 | 4,896.30 | 5,115.30 | 5,236.80 | 5,535.90 |
| E-7 | 3,914.40 | 4,084.20 | 4,200.30 | 4,323.90 | 4,371.60 | 4,532.40 | 4,618.50 | 4,946.70 |
| E-6 | 3,530.40 | 3,591.30 | 3,635.70 | 3,687.30 | 3,687.30 | 3,687.30 | 3,687.30 | 3,687.30 |
| E-5 | 3,094.80 | 3,094.80 | 3,094.80 | 3,094.80 | 3,094.80 | 3,094.80 | 3,094.80 | 3,094.80 |
| E-4 | 2,427.30 | 2,427.30 | 2,427.30 | 2,427.30 | 2,427.30 | 2,427.30 | 2,427.30 | 2,427.30 |
| E-3 | 2,034.90 | 2,034.90 | 2,034.90 | 2,034.90 | 2,034.90 | 2,034.90 | 2,034.90 | 2,034.90 |
| E-2 | 1,716.90 | 1,716.90 | 1,716.90 | 1,716.90 | 1,716.90 | 1,716.90 | 1,716.90 | 1,716.90 |
| E-1* | - | - | - | - | - | - | - | - |

† See Table 1 for rank corresponding with pay rate. Rates are rounded to nearest dollar.

* Applies to personnel who have served less than 4 months on active duty.

## TABLE 3—CSRS MILITARY MONTHLY RETIREMENT PAY
## Effective January 1, 2014

**Note that 2015 numbers were not available as this 2015 edition went to press**

### RETIREES WHO ENTERED SERVICE BEFORE SEPTEMBER 8, 1980

| Pay Grade* Over | 50.00% 20 Yrs | 52.50% 21 Yrs | 55.00% 22 Yrs | 57.50% 23 Yrs | 60.00% 24 Yrs | 62.50% 25 Yrs | 65.00% 26 Yrs | 67.50% 27 Yrs | 70.00% 28 Yrs | 72.50% 29 Yrs | 75.00% 30 Yrs |
|---|---|---|---|---|---|---|---|---|---|---|---|
| O-10 | $8,036 | $8,438 | $8,883 | $9,287 | $9,892 | $10,304 | $11,096 | $11,523 | $11,950 | $12,377 | $12,804 |
| O-9 | $7,028 | $7,380 | $7,843 | $8,199 | $8,731 | $9,095 | $9,791 | $10,167 | $10,544 | $10,920 | $11,297 |
| O-8 | $6,660 | $6,993 | $7,506 | $7,847 | $8,188 | $8,530 | $8,871 | $9,212 | $9,553 | $9,894 | $10,235 |
| O-7 | $6,022 | $6,323 | $6,624 | $6,925 | $7,226 | $7,527 | $7,869 | $8,171 | $8,474 | $8,777 | $9,079 |
| O-6 | $4,813 | $5,053 | $5,433 | $5,680 | $6,081 | $6,334 | $6,911 | $7,177 | $7,442 | $7,708 | $7,974 |
| O-5 | $4,211 | $4,422 | $4,772 | $4,989 | $5,205 | $5,422 | $5,639 | $5,856 | $6,073 | $6,290 | $6,507 |
| O-4 | $3,678 | $3,862 | $4,046 | $4,230 | $4,414 | $4,598 | $4,782 | $4,966 | $5,150 | $5,334 | $5,517 |
| O-3 | $3,151 | $3,309 | $3,466 | $3,624 | $3,781 | $3,939 | $4,097 | $4,254 | $4,412 | $4,569 | $4,727 |
| O-2 | $2,316 | $2,432 | $2,548 | $2,664 | $2,779 | $2,895 | $3,011 | $3,127 | $3,243 | $3,358 | $3,474 |
| O-1 | $1,828 | $1,919 | $2,011 | $2,102 | $2,193 | $2,285 | $2,376 | $2,467 | $2,559 | $2,650 | $2,742 |
| W-5 | $3,559 | $3,737 | $4,114 | $4,301 | $4,649 | $4,843 | $5,230 | $5,431 | $5,632 | $5,834 | $6,035 |
| W-4 | $3,230 | $3,391 | $3,722 | $3,892 | $4,213 | $4,389 | $4,752 | $4,935 | $5,118 | $5,300 | $5,483 |
| W-3 | $2,967 | $3,115 | $3,338 | $3,490 | $3,729 | $3,885 | $4,169 | $4,329 | $4,489 | $4,649 | $4,810 |
| W-2 | $2,603 | $2,733 | $2,922 | $3,055 | $3,240 | $3,375 | $3,510 | $3,645 | $3,780 | $3,915 | $4,050 |
| W-1 | $2,453 | $2,576 | $2,699 | $2,821 | $2,944 | $3,067 | $3,189 | $3,312 | $3,435 | $3,557 | $3,680 |
| E-9 | $2,837 | $2,979 | $3,243 | $3,390 | $3,678 | $3,831 | $4,216 | $4,379 | $4,541 | $4,703 | $4,865 |
| E-8 | $2,448 | $2,571 | $2,813 | $2,941 | $3,142 | $3,273 | $3,598 | $3,737 | $3,875 | $4,014 | $4,152 |
| E-7 | $2,186 | $2,295 | $2,493 | $2,606 | $2,771 | $2,887 | $3,215 | $3,339 | $3,463 | $3,586 | $3,710 |
| E-6 | $1,844 | $1,936 | $2,028 | $2,120 | $2,212 | $2,305 | $2,397 | $2,489 | $2,581 | $2,673 | $2,765 |
| E-5 | $1,547 | $1,625 | $1,702 | $1,780 | $1,857 | $1,934 | $2,012 | $2,089 | $2,166 | $2,244 | $2,321 |

* See Table 1, for rank corresponding to pay grade.

## TABLE 4—RATES OF DEPENDENCY AND INDEMNITY COMPENSATION— SURVIVING SPOUSE AND CHILDREN OF VETERAN WHO DIED BEFORE JANUARY 1, 1993* 38 USC §1311 Effective December 1, 2013

**Note that 2015 numbers were not available as this 2015 edition went to press**

| Pay Grade* | Surviving Spouse** Only | Surviving Spouse** and 1 Child | Surviving Spouse** and 2 Children | Extra Per Child |
|---|---|---|---|---|
| **COMMISSIONED OFFICERS** | | | | |
| O-10 | $2,633*** | $2,939 | $3,245 | $306 |
| O-9 | $2,400 | $2,706 | $3,012 | $306 |
| O-8 | $2,244 | $2,550 | $2,856 | $306 |
| O-7 | $2,043 | $2,349 | $2,655 | $306 |
| O-6 | $1,893 | $2,199 | $2,505 | $306 |
| O-5 | $1,679 | $1,985 | $2,291 | $306 |
| O-4 | $1,526 | $1,832 | $2,138 | $306 |
| O-3 | $1,439 | $1,745 | $2,051 | $306 |
| O-2 | $1,347 | $1,653 | $1,959 | $306 |
| O-1 | $1,302 | $1,608 | $1,914 | $306 |
| **WARRANT OFFICERS** | | | | |
| W-4 | $1,475 | $1,781 | $2,087 | $306 |
| W-3 | $1,394 | $1,700 | $2,006 | $306 |
| W-2 | $1,354 | $1,660 | $1,966 | $306 |
| W-1 | $1,302 | $1,608 | $1,914 | $306 |
| **ENLISTED PERSONNEL** | | | | |
| E-9 | $1,404**** | $1,710 | $2,016 | $306 |
| E-8 | $1,347 | $1,653 | $1,959 | $306 |
| E-7 | $1,276 | $1,582 | $1,888 | $306 |

* See Table 1, for rank corresponding to pay grade. Surviving spouses of veterans who die after January 1, 1994, receive a basic monthly DIC rate of $1,233 in 2014. Each child is entitled to $306 a month in 2014. Surviving spouses of veterans who die before January 1, 1993, are entitled to the benefits listed above or the new formula, whichever provides the greater benefits.

** Monthly rate for the surviving spouse is increased by $306 if he or she is a patient in a nursing home or is virtually helpless or blind.

*** If the veteran served as Chairman of the Joint Chiefs of Staff or Chief of Staff to one of the services, the surviving spouse's rate shall be $2,826.

**** The payment to a surviving spouse alone if the veteran was Sergeant Major of the Army, Senior Enlisted Advisor of the Navy, Chief Master Sergeant of the Air Force, or Sergeant Major of the Marine Corps, or Master Chief Petty Officer of the Coast Guard is $1,516.

## TABLE 5—RATES OF DEPENDENCY AND INDEMNITY COMPENSATION—PARENTS
### Effective December 1, 2013

**Note that 2015 numbers were not available as this 2015 edition went to press**

| Annual Income Amount | 1 Parent Only (1) | Each of 2 Parents Not Living Together (1) | Each of 2 Parents Living Together or Remarried Parent Living with Spouse (2) |
|---|---|---|---|
| $800 | $611 | $442 | $415 |
| 900 | 603 | 436 | $415 |
| 1,000 | 595 | 429 | $415 |
| 1,100 | 587 | 422 | 412 |
| 1,200 | 579 | 414 | 409 |
| 1,300 | 571 | 406 | 406 |
| 1,400 | 563 | 398 | 403 |
| 1,500 | 555 | 390 | 400 |
| 1,600 | 547 | 382 | 396 |
| 1,700 | 539 | 374 | 392 |
| 1,800 | 531 | 366 | 388 |
| 1,900 | 523 | 358 | 384 |
| 2,000 | 515 | 350 | 379 |
| 2,100 | 507 | 342 | 374 |
| 2,200 | 499 | 334 | 369 |
| 2,300 | 491 | 326 | 363 |
| 2,400 | 483 | 318 | 359 |
| 2,500 | 475 | 310 | 353 |
| 2,600 | 467 | 302 | 347 |
| 2,700 | 459 | 294 | 341 |
| 2,800 | 451 | 286 | 335 |
| 2,900 | 443 | 278 | 329 |
| 3,000 | 435 | 270 | 322 |
| 3,100 | 427 | 262 | 315 |
| 3,200 | 419 | 254 | 308 |
| 3,300 | 411 | 246 | 300 |
| 3,400 | 403 | 238 | 292 |
| 3,500 | 395 | 230 | 284 |
| 3,600 | 387 | 222 | 276 |
| 3,700 | 379 | 214 | 268 |
| 3,800 | 371 | 206 | 260 |
| 3,900 | 363 | 198 | 252 |
| 4,000 | 355 | 190 | 244 |
| 4,100 | 347 | 182 | 236 |
| 4,200 | 339 | 174 | 228 |
| 4,300 | 331 | 166 | 220 |
| 4,400 | 323 | 158 | 212 |
| 4,500 | 315 | 150 | 204 |
| 4,600 | 307 | 142 | 196 |
| 4,700 | 299 | 134 | 188 |
| 4,800 | 291 | 126 | 180 |

## TABLE 5—RATES OF DEPENDENCY AND INDEMNITY COMPENSATION—PARENTS (cont'd)

**Effective December 1, 2013**

**Note that 2015 numbers were not available as this 2015 edition went to press**

| Annual Income Amount | 1 Parent Only (1) | Each of 2 Parents Not Living Together (1) | Each of 2 Parents Living Together or Remarried Parent Living with Spouse (2) |
|---|---|---|---|
| 4,900 | 283 | 118 | 172 |
| 5,000 | 275 | 110 | 164 |
| 5,100 | 267 | 102 | 156 |
| 5,200 | 259 | 94 | 148 |
| 5,300 | 251 | 86 | 140 |
| 5,400 | 243 | 78 | 132 |
| 5,500 | 235 | 70 | 124 |
| 5,600 | 227 | 62 | 116 |
| 5,700 | 219 | 54 | 108 |
| 5,800 | 211 | 46 | 100 |
| 5,900 | 203 | 38 | 92 |
| 6,000 | 195 | 30 | 84 |
| 6,100 | 187 | 22 | 76 |
| 6,200 | 179 | 22 | 68 |
| 6,300 | 171 | 6 | 60 |
| 6,400 | 163 | 5 | 52 |
| 6,500 | 155 | 5 | 44 |
| 6,600 | 147 | 5 | 36 |
| 6,700 | 139 | 5 | 28 |
| 6,800 | 131 | 5 | 20 |
| 6,900 | 123 | 5 | 12 |
| 7,000 | 115 | 5 | 5 |
| 7,100 | 107 | 5 | 5 |
| 7,200 | 99 | 5 | 5 |
| 7,300 | 91 | 5 | 5 |
| 7,400 | 83 | 5 | 5 |
| 7,500 | 75 | 5 | 5 |
| 7,600 | 67 | 5 | 5 |
| 7,700 | 59 | 5 | 5 |
| 7,800 | 51 | 5 | 5 |
| 7,900 | 43 | 5 | 5 |
| 8,000 | 35 | 5 | 5 |
| 8,100 | 27 | 5 | 5 |
| 8,200 | 19 | 5 | 5 |
| 8,300 | 11 | 5 | 5 |
| 8,300-14,391 | 5 | 5 | 5 |
| 14,391-19,344 | 0 | 0 | 5 |
| over 19,344 | 0 | 0 | 0 |

(1) Payment based on total annual income

(2) Payment based on total combined annual income

# APPENDIX D
# MEDICARE TABLES

## TABLE OF HOSPITAL INSURANCE (PART A)
**Effective January 1, 2015**

| Service | Benefit | Medicare Pays | A Person Pays |
|---|---|---|---|
| **HOSPITALIZATION** Semiprivate room and board, general nursing, and other hospital services and supplies. | First 60 days | All but $1,260 | $1,260 |
| | 61st to 90th day | All but $315 a day | $315 a day |
| | 91st to 150th day[1] | All but $630 a day | $630 a day |
| | Beyond 150 days | Nothing | All costs |
| **SKILLED NURSING FACILITY CARE** Semiprivate room and board, skilled nursing and rehabilitative services and other services and supplies.[2] | First 20 days | 100% of approved Amount | Nothing |
| | Additional 80 days | All but $157.50 a day | $157.50 a day |
| | Beyond 100 days | Nothing | All costs |
| **POST-HOSPITAL HOME HEALTH CARE** Part-time or intermittent skilled care, home health aid services, durable medical equipment and supplies and other services. | First 100 days in spell of illness | 100% of approved amount; 80% of approved amount for durable medical equipment | Nothing for services; 20% of approved amount for durable medical equipment |
| **HOSPICE CARE** Pain relief, symptom management and support services for the terminally ill. | For as long as the doctor certifies need | All but limited costs for outpatient drugs and inpatient respite care | Limited costs for outpatient drugs and inpatient respite care |
| **BLOOD** When furnished by a hospital or skilled nursing facility during covered stay. | Unlimited if medically necessary | All but first 3 pints per calendar year | For first 3 pints[3] |

1. 60 Reserve days benefit may be used only once in a lifetime.
2. Neither Medicare nor private Medigap insurance will pay for most nursing home care.
3. Blood paid for or replaced under Part B of Medicare during the calendar year does not have to be paid for or replaced under Part A.

## TABLE OF MEDICAL INSURANCE (PART B) BENEFITS
### Effective January 1, 2015

| Service | Benefit | Medicare Pays | Patient Pays |
|---|---|---|---|
| **MEDICAL EXPENSE** Doctors' services, inpatient and outpatient medical and services surgical services and supplies, physical and speech therapy, diagnostic tests, durable medical equipment and other services. | Unlimited if medically necessary. | 80% of approved amount (after $147 deductible). Reduced to 50% for most outpatient mental health services. | $147 deductible,[1] plus 20% of approved amount and limited charges above approved amount.[2] |
| **CLINICAL LABORATORY SERVICES** Blood tests, urinalyses, and more. | Unlimited if medically necessary. | Generally 100% of approved amount. | Nothing for services. |
| **HOME HEALTH CARE** Part-time or intermittent skilled care, home health aide services, durable medical equipment and supplies and other services. | Unlimited but covers only home health care not covered by Hospital Insurance (Part A). | 100% of approved amount; 80% of approved amount for durable medical equipment. | Nothing for services; 20% of approved amount for durable medical equipment. |
| **OUTPATIENT HOSPITAL TREATMENT** Services for the diagnosis or treatment of illness or injury. | Unlimited if medically necessary. | Medicare payment to hospital based on hospital cost. | 20% of whatever the hospital charges (after $147 deductible).[1] |
| **BLOOD** | Unlimited if medically necessary. | 80% of approved amount (after $147 deductible and starting with 4th pint). | For first 3 pints plus 20% of approved amount for additional pints (after $147 deductible).[3] |
| **AMBULATORY SURGICAL SERVICES** | Unlimited if medically necessary. | 80% of predetermined amount (after $147 deductible). | $147 deductible, plus 20% of predetermined amount. |

1. Once a person has $147 of expense for covered services in 2015, the Part B deductible does not apply to any further covered services received for the rest of the year.
2. A person pays for charges higher than the amount approved by Medicare unless the doctor or supplier agrees to accept Medicare's approved amount as the total charge for services rendered.
3. Blood paid for or replaced under Part A of Medicare during the calendar year does not have to be paid for or replaced under Part B.

# APPENDIX E
# WHAT MEDICARE DOES NOT COVER

Some of these items can be covered by Medicare under certain conditions. See text for more detailed information on items covered under special conditions.

Acupuncture

Most chiropractic services

Cosmetic surgery (except after an accident)

Custodial care

Most dental care

Most prescription drugs and medicines taken at home (except through Medicare Part D)

Eyeglasses and eye examinations for prescribing, fitting, or changing eyeglasses

Foot care that is routine

Canadian or Mexican health care

Hearing aids and hearing examinations for prescribing, fitting, or changing hearing aids

Homemaker services

Meals delivered to the home

Naturopaths' services

Immunizations, except vaccinations against pneumococcal pneumonia, hepatitis B, or influenza virus; and immunizations required because of an injury or immediate risk of infection

Injections which can be self-administered

Nursing care on full-time basis in the home

Orthopedic shoes unless they are part of a leg brace and are included in the orthopedist's charge

Personal convenience items that the patient requests, such as a phone, radio, or television in the room at a hospital or skilled nursing facility

Physical examinations that are routine and tests directly related to such examinations

Private nurses

Private room

Services performed by immediate relatives or members of the patient's household

Services that are not reasonable and necessary

Services for which neither the patient nor another party on his behalf has a legal obligation to pay

Supportive devices for the feet

War claims occurring after the effective date of the patient's current Medicare coverage

Services payable by any of the following:

- Workers' Compensation (including black lung benefits)
- Liability or nofault insurance
- Employer group health plans for employees and their spouses
- Employer group health plans for people entitled to Medicare solely on the basis of end-stage renal disease
- Another government program

# APPENDIX F
# EXAMPLE OF MEDICARE BENEFITS

Mr. Smith is 69 years old, retired, and covered by Hospital Insurance (Part A), Medical Insurance (Part B), and Prescription Drug Insurance (Part D). After suffering a heart attack at his home in January 2015, he is taken to the hospital for surgery. Mr. Smith spends 15 days in the hospital and 7 days in a skilled nursing facility for therapy. When he returns home, he requires the services of a nurse and physical therapist for a short time to continue treatment.

| | Total cost: | Mr. Smith pays: | Medicare pays |
|---|---|---|---|
| **Hospital bill:**<br>*(Patient pays the deductible amount)* | \$3,500 | \$1,260 | \$2,240 |
| **Ambulance to hospital:**<br>*(Patient pays 20% plus amount higher than customary charge)* | \$70 | \$14 | \$56 |
| **Surgeon:**<br>*(Patient pays \$147 deductible and 20% of the remaining bill; Medicare pays 80% of the bill after the deductible)* | \$2,000 | \$517.60 | \$1,482.40 |
| **Anesthesiologist:**<br>*(Patient pays 20%; Medicare pays 80%)* | \$300 | \$60 | \$240 |
| **Skilled Nursing Facility:**<br>*(Patient pays nothing for first 20 days, then \$148 a day for 80 days)* | \$1,050 | \$0 | \$1,050 |
| **Home visits by nurse:**<br>*(Medicare pays for nurse required for medical reasons)* | \$90 | \$0 | \$90 |
| **Home visits by physical therapist:** | \$80 | \$0 | \$80 |
| **Equipment rental (wheelchair):**<br>*(Patient pays 20%; Medicare pays 80%)* | \$85 | \$17 | \$68 |
| **Prescription drugs at home:**<br>*(assuming standard \$325 deductible).* | \$200 | \$200 | \$0 |
| **Total Cost:** | \$7,375 | \$2,068.60 | \$5,306.40 |

# APPENDIX G
# FISCAL INTERMEDIARIES

Note: Fiscal intermediaries can answer questions about Hospital Insurance (Part A) bills and services, hospital care, skilled nursing care, and fraud. You may reach the fiscal intermediary for your state at 1-800-MEDICARE (1-800-633-4227).

| State | Carrier |
|---|---|
| **Alabama** | Blue Cross/Blue Shield of Alabama |
| **Alaska** | Noridian Administrative Services |
| **Arizona** | Noridian Administrative Services |
| **Arkansas** | Blue Cross Blue Shield of Arkansas |
| **California** | United Government Services |
| **Colorado** | TrailBlazer Health Enterprises, LLC |
| **Connecticut** | Empire Medicare Services |
| **Delaware** | Empire Medicare Services |
| **Florida** | First Coast Service Options, Inc. |
| **Georgia** | Blue Cross/Blue Shield of Georgia |
| **Hawaii** | United Government Services |
| **Idaho** | Noridian Administrative Services |
| **Illinois** | Adminastar Federal, Inc. |
| **Indiana** | Adminastar Federal, Inc. |
| **Iowa** | Noridian Administrative Services |
| **Kansas** | Blue Cross Blue Shield of Kansas |
| **Kentucky** | Adminastar Federal, Inc. |
| **Louisiana** | Trispan Health Services |
| **Maine** | Associated Hospital Services |
| **Maryland** | Highmark Medicare Services |
| **Massachusetts** | Associated Hospital Services |
| **Michigan** | United Government Services |
| **Minnesota** | Noridian Administrative Services |
| **Mississippi** | Trispan Health Services |
| **Missouri** | Mutual of Omaha Insurance Companies |
| **Montana** | Noridian Administrative Services |
| **Nebraska** | Blue Cross Blue Shield of Nebraska |
| **Nevada** | Mutual of Omaha Insurance Companies |
| **New Hampshire** | Anthem Health Plans of New Hampshire-Vermont |
| **New Jersey** | Blue Cross/Blue Shield of Tennessee |

# FISCAL INTERMEDIARIES (cont'd)

| State | Carrier |
|---|---|
| New Mexico | TrailBlazer Health Enterprises, LLC |
| New York | Empire Medicare Services |
| North Carolina | Palmetto Government Benefits Administrators (GBA) |
| North Dakota | Noridian Administrative Services |
| Ohio | Adminastar Federal, Inc. |
| Oklahoma | Chisholm Administrative Services |
| Oregon | Noridian Administrative Services |
| Pennsylvania | Highmark Medicare Services |
| Rhode Island | Arkansas Blue Cross and Blue Shield |
| South Carolina | Palmetto Government Benefits Administrators (GBA) |
| South Dakota | Noridian Administrative Services |
| Tennessee | Blue Cross/Blue Shield of Tennessee |
| Texas | TrailBlazer Health Enterprises, LLC |
| Utah | Noridian Administrative Services |
| Vermont | Anthem Health Plans of New Hampshire-Vermont |
| Virginia | United Government Services |
| Washington | Noridian Administrative Services |
| Washington D.C. | Highmark Medicare Services |
| West Virginia | United Government Services |
| Wisconsin | United Government Services |
| Wyoming | Noridian Administrative Services |
| American Samoa | United Government Services |
| Guam | United Government Services |
| Northern Mariana Islands | United Government Services |
| Puerto Rico | Cooperativa De Seguros De Vida (COSVI) |
| Virgin Islands | Cooperativa De Seguros De Vida (COSVI) |

# APPENDIX H
# MEDICARE CARRIERS

Note: Carriers can answer questions about Medical Insurance (Part B). To reach any of the carriers, call 1-800-MEDICARE (1-800-633-4227). If you are entitled to Medicare under the Railroad Retirement system, send your Medical Insurance claims to Palmetto GBA, 1-800-833-4455.

| State | Carrier |
|---|---|
| Alabama | Blue Cross/Blue Shield of Alabama |
| Alaska | Noridian Administrative Services |
| Arizona | Noridian Administrative Services |
| Arkansas | Blue Cross/Blue Shield of Arkansas |
| California | National Heritage Insurance Company |
| Colorado | Noridian Administrative Services |
| Connecticut | First Coast Service Options, Inc. |
| Delaware | Trailblazer Health Enterprises, LLC |
| District of Columbia | Trailblazer Health Enterprises, LLC |
| Florida | First Coast Service Options, Inc. |
| Georgia | Noridian Administrative Services |
| Hawaii | Noridian Administrative Services |
| Idaho | CIGNA (Connecticut General Life Ins. Co) |
| Illinois | Wisconsin Physicians Service |
| Indiana | AdminaStar Federal, Inc. |
| Iowa | Noridian Administrative Services |
| Kansas | Blue Cross/Blue Shield of Kansas |
| Kentucky | AdminaStar Federal, Inc. |
| Louisiana | Blue Cross/Blue Shield of Arkansas |
| Maine | National Heritage Insurance Company |
| Maryland | TrailBlazer Health Enterprises, LLC |
| Massachusetts | National Heritage Insurance Company |
| Michigan | Wisconsin Physician Services |
| Minnesota | Wisconsin Physician Services |
| Mississippi | Noridian Administrative Services |
| Missouri | Blue Cross/Blue Shield of Kansas (Western Missouri)<br>Medicare Services of Missouri (Eastern Missouri) |
| Montana | Noridian Administrative Services |
| Nebraska | Blue Cross/Blue Shield of Kansas |
| Nevada | Noridian Administrative Services |
| New Hampshire | National Heritage Insurance Company |

# MEDICARE CARRIERS (cont'd)

| State | Carrier |
|---|---|
| New Jersey | Empire Medicare Services |
| New Mexico | Blue Cross/Blue Shield of Arkansas |
| New York | HealthNow of Upstate New York (Upstate)<br>Empire Medicare Services (Downstate)<br>Group Health, Inc. (GHI Medicare) (Queens County) |
| North Carolina | CIGNA Medicare |
| North Dakota | Noridian Administrative Services |
| Ohio | Palmetto Government Benefits Administrators (GBA) |
| Oklahoma | Blue Cross/Blue Shield of Arkansas |
| Oregon | Noridian Administrative Services |
| Pennsylvania | Highmark Medicare Services |
| Rhode Island | Blue Cross/Blue Shield of Arkansas |
| South Carolina | Palmetto Government Benefits Administrators (GBA) |
| South Dakota | Noridian Administrative Services |
| Tennessee | CIGNA Medicare |
| Texas | TrailBlazer Health Enterprises, LLC |
| Utah | Noridian Administrative Services |
| Vermont | National Heritage Insurance Company |
| Virginia | TrailBlazer Health Enterprises, LLC |
| Washington | Noridian Administrative Services |
| West Virginia | Palmetto Government Benefits Administrators (GBA) |
| Wisconsin | Wisconsin Physician Service |
| Wyoming | Noridian Administrative Services |
| American Samoa | Noridian Administrative Services |
| Guam | Noridian Administrative Services |
| Northern Mariana Islands | Noridian Administrative Services |
| Puerto Rico | Triple-S, Inc. |
| Virgin Islands | Triple-S, Inc. |

# APPENDIX I
# MEDICARE QUALITY IMPROVEMENT ORGANIZATIONS (QIOS)

QIOs can answer questions about the quality of care and access to care in a Medicare-certified facility. QIOs cannot answer questions about a bill or about what Medicare covers. For Part A or Part B billing or coverage questions, call your Part B carrier or your Part A intermediary. See Appendix D. The toll-free or 800 numbers listed below, in many cases, can be used only in the state or service areas indicated.

| State | Quality Improvement Organizations (QIOs) | Phone |
|---|---|---|
| **Alabama** | Alabama Quality Assurance Foundation, Inc. | 1-205-970-1600 |
| **Alaska** | Mountain-Pacific Quality Health Foundation | 1-877-561-3202 |
| **Arizona** | Health Services Advisory Group Inc. | 1-602-264-6382 |
| **Arkansas** | Arkansas Foundation for Medical Care, Inc. | 1-501-649-8501 |
| **California** | Health Services Advisory Group | 1-818-409-9229 |
| **Colorado** | Colorado Foundation for Medical Care, Inc. | 1-303-695-3300 |
| **Connecticut** | Qualidigm | 1-860-632-2008 |
| **Delaware** | Quality Insights of Delaware | 1-302-478-3600 |
| **District of Columbia** | Delmarva Foundation | 1-202-293-9650 |
| **Florida** | Florida Medical Quality Assurance, Inc. | 1-813-354-9111 |
| **Georgia** | Georgia Medical Care Foundation | 1-404-982-0411 |
| **Hawaii** | Mountain-Pacific Quality Health Foundation | 1-808-545-2550 |
| **Idaho** | Qualis Health | 1-208-343-4617 |
| **Illinois** | Illinois Foundation for Quality Health Care | 1-800-386-6431 |
| **Indiana** | Health Care Excel | 1-317-347-4500 |
| **Iowa** | Iowa Foundation for Medical Care | 1-515-223-2900 |
| **Kansas** | Kansas Foundation for Medical Care | 1-785-273-2552 |
| **Kentucky** | Health Care Excel | 1-502-454-5112 |
| **Louisiana** | Louisiana Health Care Review, Inc. | 1-225-926-6353 |
| **Maine** | Northeast Health Care Quality Foundation | 1-603-749-1641 |
| **Maryland** | Delmarva Foundation | 1-410-822-0697 |
| **Massachusetts** | MassPro | 1-781-890-0011 |
| **Michigan** | Michigan Peer Review Organization | 1-248-465-7300 |
| **Minnesota** | Stratis Health | 1-952-854-3306 |

# MEDICARE QUALITY IMPROVEMENT ORGANIZATIONS (QIOS) (cont'd)

| State | Quality Improvement Organizations (QIOs) | Phone |
|---|---|---|
| **Mississippi** | Information and Quality Healthcare | 1-601-957-1575 |
| **Missouri** | Primaris | 1-573-817-8300 |
| **Montana** | Mountain-Pacific Quality Health Foundation | 1-406-443-4020 |
| **Nebraska** | Cimro of Nebraska | 1-402-476-1399 |
| **Nevada** | HealthInsight | 1-702-385-9933 |
| **New Hampshire** | Northeast Health Care Quality Foundation | 1-603-749-1641 |
| **New Jersey** | Healthcare Quality Strategies, Inc. | 1-732-238-5570 |
| **New Mexico** | New Mexico Medical Review Association | 1-505-998-9898 |
| **New York** | Island Peer Review Organization | 1-516-326-7767 |
| **North Carolina** | The Carolinas Center for Medical Excellence | 1-919-380-9860 |
| **North Dakota** | North Dakota Health Care Review, Inc. | 1-701-852-4231 |
| **Ohio** | Ohio KePRO | 1-216-447-9604 |
| **Oklahoma** | Oklahoma Foundation for Medical Quality | 1-405-840-2891 |
| **Oregon** | Acumentra Health | 1-503-279-0100 |
| **Pennsylvania** | Quality Insights of Pennsylvania | 1-717-671-5425 |
| **Rhode Island** | Rhode Island Quality Partners, Inc. | 1-401-528-3200 |
| **South Carolina** | The Carolinas Center for Medical Excellence | 1-803-251-2215 |
| **South Dakota** | South Dakota Foundation for Medical Care, Inc. | 1-605-336-3505 |
| **Tennessee** | QSource | 1-901-682-0381 |
| **Texas** | Texas Medical Foundation | 1-512-329-6610 |
| **Utah** | HealthInsight | 1-801-892-0155 |
| **Vermont** | Northeast Health Care Quality Foundation | 1-603-749-1641 |
| **Virginia** | Virginia Health Quality Center | 1-804-289-5320 |
| **Washington** | Qualis Health | 1-206-364-9700 |
| **West Virginia** | West Virginia Medical Institute, Inc. | 1-304-346-9864 |
| **Wisconsin** | MetaStar | 1-608-274-1940 |
| **Wyoming** | Mountain Pacific Quality Health Foundation | 1-307-637-8162 |
| **Puerto Rico** | Quality Improvement Professional Research Organization | 1-800-981-5062 |
| **Virgin Islands** | Virgin Islands Medical Institute | 1-340-712-2449 |

# APPENDIX J
# DURABLE MEDICAL EQUIPMENT REGIONAL CARRIERS

To reach any of the carriers listed below call 1-800-MEDICARE (1-800-633-4227).

| State | Regional Carrier |
|---|---|
| **Alabama** | CIGNA Medicare |
| **Alaska** | Noridian Administrative Services |
| **Arizona** | Noridian Administrative Services |
| **Arkansas** | CIGNA Medicare |
| **California** | Noridian Administrative Services |
| **Colorado** | Noridian Administrative Services |
| **Connecticut** | National Heritage Insurance Company |
| **Delaware** | National Heritage Insurance Company |
| **District of Columbia** | National Heritage Insurance Company |
| **Florida** | CIGNA Medicare |
| **Georgia** | CIGNA Medicare |
| **Hawaii** | Noridian Administrative Services |
| **Idaho** | Noridian Administrative Services |
| **Illinois** | AdminaStar Federal, Inc. |
| **Indiana** | AdminaStar Federal, Inc. |
| **Iowa** | Noridian Administrative Services |
| **Kansas** | Noridian Administrative Services |
| **Kentucky** | AdminaStar Federal, Inc. |
| **Louisiana** | CIGNA Medicare |
| **Maine** | National Heritage Insurance Company |
| **Maryland** | National Heritage Insurance Company |
| **Massachusetts** | National Heritage Insurance Company |
| **Michigan** | AdminaStar Federal, Inc. |
| **Minnesota** | AdminaStar Federal, Inc. |
| **Mississippi** | CIGNA Medicare |
| **Missouri** | CIGNA Medicare |
| **Montana** | Noridian Administrative Services |
| **Nebraska** | Noridian Administrative Services |
| **Nevada** | Noridian Administrative Services |
| **New Hampshire** | National Heritage Insurance Company |

# DURABLE MEDICAL EQUIPMENT REGIONAL CARRIERS (cont'd)

| State | Regional Carrier |
|---|---|
| New Jersey | National Heritage Insurance Company |
| New Mexico | CIGNA Medicare |
| New York | National Heritage Insurance Company |
| North Carolina | CIGNA Medicare |
| North Dakota | Noridian Administrative Services |
| Ohio | AdminaStar Federal, Inc. |
| Oklahoma | CIGNA Medicare |
| Oregon | Noridian Administrative Services |
| Pennsylvania | National Heritage Insurance Company |
| Rhode Island | National Heritage Insurance Company |
| South Carolina | CIGNA Medicare |
| South Dakota | Noridian Administrative Services |
| Tennessee | CIGNA Medicare |
| Texas | CIGNA Medicare |
| Utah | Noridian Administrative Services |
| Vermont | National Heritage Insurance Company |
| Virginia | CIGNA Medicare |
| Washington | Noridian Administrative Services |
| West Virginia | CIGNA Medicare |
| Wisconsin | AdminaStar Federal, Inc. |
| Wyoming | Noridian Administrative Services |
| American Samoa | Noridian Administrative Services |
| Guam | Noridian Administrative Services |
| Northern Mariana Islands | Noridian Administrative Services |
| Puerto Rico | CIGNA Medicare |
| Virgin Islands | CIGNA Medicare |

# APPENDIX K
# INSURANCE COUNSELING — GENERAL INFORMATION

In addition to insurance counseling, these state health insurance assistance program offices can answer questions about Medicare bills, Medigap policies, and Medicare plan choices.

| State | Phone |
|---|---|
| Alabama | 1-800-243-5463 |
| Alaska | 1-800-478-6065* |
| Arizona | 1-800-432-4040 |
| Arkansas | 1-800-224-6330 |
| California | 1-800-434-0222* |
| Colorado | 1-888-696-7213* |
| Connecticut | 1-800-994-9422* |
| Delaware | 1-800-336-9500* |
| District of Columbia | 1-202-739-0668 |
| Florida | 1-800-963-5337 |
| Georgia | 1-800-669-8387 |
| Hawaii | 1-888-875-9229 |
| Idaho | 1-800-247-4422* |
| Illinois | 1-800-548-9034* |
| Indiana | 1-800-452-4800 |
| Iowa | 1-800-351-4664 |
| Kansas | 1-800-860-5260 |
| Kentucky | 1-877-293-7447 |
| Louisiana | 1-800-259-5301* |
| Maine | 1-877-353-3771* |
| Maryland | 1-800-243-3425* |
| Massachusetts | 1-800-243-4636 |
| Michigan | 1-800-803-7174 |
| Minnesota | 1-800-333-2433 |
| Mississippi | 1-800-948-3090 |
| Missouri | 1-800-390-3330 |
| Montana | 1-800-551-3191* |
| Nebraska | 1-800-234-7119 |
| Nevada | 1-800-307-4444 |
| New Hampshire | 1-866-634-9412 |
| New Jersey | 1-800-792-8820* |
| New Mexico | 1-800-432-2080* |
| New York | 1-800-701-0501 |
| North Carolina | 1-800-443-9354* |
| North Dakota | 1-888-575-6611 |
| Ohio | 1-800-686-1578 |
| Oklahoma | 1-800-763-2828* |
| Oregon | 1-800-722-4134* |
| Pennsylvania | 1-800-783-7067 |
| Rhode Island | 1-401-462-4444 |
| South Carolina | 1-800-868-9095 |
| South Dakota | 1-800-536-8197 |
| Tennessee | 1-877-801-0044 |
| Texas | 1-800-252-9240 |
| Utah | 1-800-541-7735* |
| Vermont | 1-800-642-5119* |
| Virginia | 1-800-552-3402 |
| Washington | 1-800-562-6900 |
| West Virginia | 1-877-987-4463 |
| Wisconsin | 1-800-242-1060 |
| Wyoming | 1-800-856-4398 |
| American Samoa | 1-888-875-9229 |
| Guam | 1-888-875-9229 |
| Northern Mariana Islands | 1-888-875-9229 |
| Puerto Rico | 1-877-725-4300 |
| Virgin Islands | 1-340-772-7368 |

* In-State Calls Only

# APPENDIX L
# STATE AGENCIES ON AGING

Note: State agencies on aging can provide information and assistance on a variety of Medicare, insurance, and elder care issues.

**Alabama**
Department of Senior Services
RSA Plaza
770 Washington Avenue, Suite 470
Montgomery, AL 36130-1851
(800) 243-5463
(334) 242-5743

**Alaska**
Commission of Aging
Department of Health and Social Services
150 Third Street, No. 103
P.O. Box 110693
Juneau, AK 99811-0693
(907) 465-4879

**Arizona**
Department of Economic Security
Aging and Adult Administration
1789 West Jefferson Street, #950A
Phoenix, AZ 85007
(602) 542-4446

**Arkansas**
Division of Aging & Adult Services
P.O. Box 1437
700 Main Street, 5th Floor, S530
Little Rock, AR 72203-1437
(501) 682-2441

**California**
Department of Aging
1300 National Drive, #200
Sacramento, CA 95834
(916) 419-7500

**Colorado**
Division of Aging and Adult Services
Department of Human Services
1575 Sherman Street, 10th Floor
Denver, CO 80203-1714
(303) 866-2636

**Connecticut**
Bureau of Aging Community & Social Work Services
Department of Social Services
25 Sigourney Street
Hartford, CT 06106-5033
(860) 424-5277

**Delaware**
Services for Aging & Adults with Physical Disabilities
Dept. of Health & Social Services
1901 North DuPont Highway
New Castle, DE 19720
(800) 223-9074
(302) 255-9390

**District of Columbia**
Office on Aging
441 Fourth Street, NW, 9th Floor
Washington, DC 20001
(202) 724-5622

**Florida**
Department of Elder Affairs
4040 Esplanade Way, Suite 315
Tallahassee, FL 32399-7000
(800) 96ELDER
(850) 414-2000

**Georgia**
Division of Aging Services
Department of Human Resources
2 Peachtree Street N.W., 9th Floor
Atlanta, GA 30303-3142
(404) 657-5258

**Hawaii**
Executive Office on Aging
250 South Hotel Street, Suite 406
Honolulu, HI 96813-2831
(808) 586-0100

**Idaho**
Commission on Aging
3380 Americana Terrace, No. 120
P.O. Box 83720
Boise, ID 83720-0007
(208) 334-3833

**Illinois**
Department on Aging
421 E. Capitol Avenue, #100
Springfield, IL 62701-1789
(800) 252-8966
(217) 785-2870

**Indiana**
Division of Aging
402 W. Washington Street, #W454
P.O. Box 7083
Indianapolis, IN 46207-7083
(800) 545-7763
(317) 232-7123

**Iowa**
Department of Elder Affairs
Jessie Parker Building
510 East 12th St., Suite 2
Des Moines, IA 50319-9025
(515) 725-3301

**Kansas**
Department on Aging
New England Building
503 South Kansas Avenue
Topeka, KS 66603-3404
(785) 296-5222

**Kentucky**
Department for Aging & Independent Living
Cabinet for Health & Family Services
275 East Main Street, 3W-F
Frankfort, KY 40621
(502) 564-6930

**Louisiana**
Governor's Office of Elderly Affairs
P.O. Box 61 [ZIP 70821-0061]
412 N. 4th Street
Baton Rouge, LA 70802
(225) 342-7100

**Maine**
Office of Elder Services
Department of Health & Human Services
442 Civic Center Drive
11 State House Station
Augusta, ME 04333-0011
(207) 287-9200

**Maryland**
Department of Aging
301 West Preston Street, Suite 1007
Baltimore, MD 21201-2374
(410) 767-1100

**Massachusetts**
Executive Office of Elder Affairs
One Ashburton Place, 5th Floor
Boston, MA 02108
(800) 882-2003
(617) 222-7451

**Michigan**
Office of Services to the Aging
P.O. Box 30676
7109 West Saginaw, 1st Floor
Lansing, MI 48909-8176
(517) 373-8230

**Minnesota**
Board on Aging
Department of Human Services
P.O. Box 64976
St. Paul, MN 55164-0976
(800) 882-6262
(651) 431-2500

**Mississippi**
Council on Aging
Division of Aging & Adult Services
750 N. State Street
Jackson, MS 39202
(800) 948-3090
(601) 359-4925

**Missouri**
Division of Senior & Disability Services
Dept. of Health & Senior Sciences
P.O. Box 570
Jefferson City, MO 65102-0570
(800) 235-5503
(573) 526-3626

**Montana**
Office on Aging
Senior and Long-Term Care Division
Department of Public Health and Human Services
111 Sanders Street
P.O. Box 4210
Helena, MT 59604
(800) 551-3101
(406) 444-7788

**Nebraska**
State Unit on Aging
P.O. Box 95044
301 Centennial Mall - South
Lincoln, NE 68509-5044
(800) 942-7830
(402) 471-2307

**Nevada**
Division for Aging Services
Department of Health & Human Services
3416 Goni Road, Building D-132
Carson City, NV 89706
(775) 687-4210 x226

**New Hampshire**
Bureau of Elderly & Adult Services
Brown Building - 129 Pleasant Street
Concord, NH 03301-3857
(603) 271-4394

**New Jersey**
Division of Aging & Community Services
P.O. Box 807
240 W. State Street
Trenton, NJ 08625-0807
(800) 792-8820
(609) 292-4027

**New Mexico**
Aging and Long-Term Services Department
2550 Cerrillos Road
Santa Fe, NM 87505
(800) 432-2080
(505) 476-4755

**New York**
State Office for the Aging
Two Empire State Plaza
Albany, NY 12223-1251
(800) 342-9871
(518) 474-7012

**North Carolina**
Division of Aging & Adult Services
2101 Mail Service Center
693 Palmer Drive
Raleigh, NC 27699-2101
(919) 733-3983

**North Dakota**
Aging Services Division
Department of Human Services
600 East Boulevard Avenue
Department 325
Bismarck, ND 58505-0250
(800) 755-8521
(701) 328-4601

**Ohio**
Department of Aging
50 West Broad Street – 9th Floor
Columbus, OH 43215-5928
(800) 282-1206
(614) 466-7246

**Oklahoma**
Aging Services Division
Department of Human Services
2401 N.W. 23rd St., Suite 40
Oklahoma City, OK 73107-2442
(405) 521-2281

**Oregon**
Seniors & People with Disabilities
Department of Human Services
500 Summer Street, N.E., E02
Salem, OR 97301-1073
(800) 232-3020
(503) 945-6478

**Pennsylvania**
Department of Aging
Forum Place
555 Walnut Street, 5th Floor
Harrisburg, PA 17101-1919
(717) 783-1550

**Puerto Rico**
Governor's Office for Elderly Affairs
P.O. Box 191179
San Juan, PR 00919-1179
(787) 721-5710

**Rhode Island**
Department of Elderly Affairs
John O. Pastore Center
Benjamin Rush Building, No. 55
35 Howard Avenue
Cranston, RI 02920
(401) 462-0501

**South Carolina**
Lieutenant Governor's Office on Aging
Bureau of Senior Services
1301 Gervais Street
Suite 200
Columbia, SC 29201
(803) 734-9900

**South Dakota**
Office of Adult Services & Aging
Department of Social Services
700 Governor's Drive
Pierre, SD 57501-2291
(605) 773-3656

**Tennessee**
Commission on Aging & Disability
Andrew Jackson Building
500 Deaderick Street, No. 825
Nashville, TN 37243-0860
(615) 741-2056

**Texas**
Department of Aging & Disability Services
P.O. Box 149030 (W-619)
Austin, TX 78714-9030
(512) 438-3030

**Utah**
Division of Aging & Adult Services
Department of Human Services
120 North 200 West, Room 325
Salt Lake City, UT 84103
(801) 538-3910

**Vermont**
Dept of Disabilities, Aging & Independent Living
Weeks Building
103 South Main Street
Waterbury, VT 05676
(802) 241-2401

**Virginia**
Department for the Aging
1610 Forest Avenue, Suite 100
Richmond, VA 23229
(800) 552-3402
(804) 662-9333

**Washington**
Aging & Disability Services
Department of Social & Health Services
P.O. Box 45600
Olympia, WA 98504-5600 (mailing)
640 Woodland Square Loop SE
Lacey, WA 98503-1045 (physical)
(360) 725-2260

**West Virginia**
Bureau of Senior Services
1900 Kanawha Boulevard, East
3003 Town Center Mall
Charleston, WV 25305-0160
(304) 558-3317

**Wisconsin**
Bureau of Aging & Disability Resources
Department of Health & Family Services
One West Wilson Street, Room 450
P.O. Box 7851
Madison, WI 53707-7851
(800) 242-1060
(608) 266-3840

**Wyoming**
Division on Aging
Department of Health
6101 Yellowstone Road, Suite 259B
Cheyenne, WY 82002-0710
(800) 442-2766
(307) 777-7986

# APPENDIX M
# CENTERS FOR MEDICARE & MEDICAID SERVICES

| Regional Office | Customer Service | States Served |
|---|---|---|
| Region 1 - Boston | 617-565-1188 | CT, ME, MA, NH, RI, VT |
| Region 2 - New York | 212-616-2205 | NJ, NY, PR, VI |
| Region 3 - Philadelphia | 215-861-4140 | DE, DC, MD, PA, VA, WV |
| Region 4 - Atlanta | 404-562-7500 | AL, FL, GA, KY, MS, NC, SC, TN |
| Region 5 - Chicago | 312-886-6432 | IL, IN, MI, MN, OH, WI |
| Region 6 - Dallas | 214-767-6423 | AR, LA, NM, OK, TX |
| Region 7 - Kansas City | 816-426-5233 | IA, KS, MO, NE |
| Region 8 - Denver | 303-844-2111 | CO, MT, ND, SD, UT, WY |
| Region 9 - San Francisco | 415-744-3501 | AZ, AS, CA, GU, HI, MP, NV |
| Region 10 - Seattle | 206-615-2306 | AK, ID, OR, WA |

# INDEX

## (All references are to question numbers, unless otherwise noted.)

## A

## B



## C

## D

## G



## H

## I

## K



## L

## M

## N



## O



## P

# Q

## R

## W



## X